saur

Computers in the Humanities and the Social Sciences

Achievements of the 1980s
Prospects for the 1990s

Proceedings of the Cologne Computer Conference 1988
Uses of the Computer in the Humanities and Social Sciences
held at the University of Cologne
September 1988

Edited by

Heinrich Best
Informationszentrum Sozialwissenschaften, Bonn

Ekkehard Mochmann
Zentralarchiv für empirische Sozialforschung, Köln

Manfred Thaller
Max-Planck-Institut für Geschichte, Göttingen

K · G · Saur
München · London · New York · Paris 1991

CIP-Titelaufnahme der Deutschen Bibliothek

Computers in the humanities and the social sciences :
achievements of the 1980s – prospects for the 1990s ;
proceedings of the Cologne Computer Conference 1988 uses of
the computer in the humanities and social sciences held at the
University of Cologne, September 1988 / ed. by Heinrich Best
... - München ; London ; New York ; Paris : Saur, 1991
ISBN 3-598-11041-3
NE: Best, Heinrich [Hrsg.]; Computer Conference ‹1988, Köln›;
Universität ‹Köln›

Gedruckt auf säurefreiem Papier
Printed on acid-free paper

Printed in the Federal Republic of Germany

Druck / Printed by WS Druckerei, Bodenheim
Binden / Bound by Thomas Buchbinderei, Augsburg

ISBN 3-598-11041-3

TABLE OF CONTENTS

History

ACKNOWLEDGEMENTS

Cologne Computer Conference 1988:
Uses of the Computer in the Humanities and Social Sciences

Proceedings of the Cologne Computer Conference 1988:
Computers in the Humanities and the Social Sciences
Achievements of the 1980s - Prospects for the 1990s

Hosting and Conference Organisation:
Zentralarchiv für empirische Sozialforschung -
Zentrum für historische Sozialforschung.
Universität zu Köln

Financial Support:
Land Nordrhein-Westfalen,
Ministerium für Wissenschaft und Forschung.
Deutsche Forschungsgemeinschaft (DFG)

Financial Contribution and Equipment Support:
IBM Forschung und Lehre, (IBM Deutschland GmbH)
Peter von Dehn, Jens Kölle

Conference Preparation and Management:
Dagmar Klaff, Dagmar Otte-Wiese

Editorial Management, Text Processing and Design:
Angelika Ruf

Secretarial Support:
Marita Daniels, Doris Katzwinkel

Index:
Informationszentrum Sozialwissenschaften, Bonn

Further contributions to the Cologne Computer Conference 1988 were published in:

Computer Applications in the Historical Sciences.
Selected Contributions to the Cologne Computer Conference 1988.
- *Historische Sozialforschung/Historical Social Research (HSR)* 14(1989), 3;
- *Historische Sozialforschung/Historical Social Research (HSR)* 14(1989), 4;
- *Historische Sozialforschung/Historical Social Research (HSR)* 15(1990), 1;

HSR is published by Zentrum für Historische Sozialforschung (ZHSF)/Center for Historical Social Research. In case you are interested in the above mentioned volumes, please write to the managing editor of HSR:
Wilhelm H. Schröder, Zentralarchiv für Empirische Sozialforschung/ZHSF, Bachemerstr. 40, D - 5000 Köln 41.

Data Protection and Data Access.
Reports from Ten Countries on Data Protection and Data Access in Social Research, with an Annotated International Bibliography. Edited by Paul de Guchteneire and Ekkehard Mochmann. SWIDOC/IFDO, North-Holland, Amsterdam, 1990.

The Reports Cover: Canada, Denmark, Federal Republic of Germany, France, Great Britain, Hungary, The Netherlands, Norway, Sweden, United States of America.

Some extended and revised articles will be published in:

Neue Methoden der Analyse Historischer Daten.
Hrsg.: Heinrich Best und Helmut Thome. Historische Sozialforschung, Bd. 23, St. Katharinen, 1991

INTRODUCTION

The use of the computer in the humanities, which until recently was still a technique used only by a few specialists, has become a widespread practice today. The decoding of the symbolic language of medieval altar paintings, the determination of anonymous authors according to their special use of language, the improvement of the availability of extensive historical sources and of museum collections, the survey of the changes in the shape of families since the Middle Ages and the living conditions of working-class families in the 19th century, the reconstruction of the political careers of members of parliament, and the computer simulation modelling of historical events are only a few examples that can be cited of the now manifold usages of modern computer technologies in the Humanities.

Social research made intensive use of large computers already in the '60s and '70s. Now, the use of the computer in the social sciences is extending even further. Since approximately 90% of all households in western industrial societies have a telephone, it is possible to carry out surveys through computer-aided telephone interviews, the data being immediately recorded on screen. Electronic storage media allow one to work with a flood of data which would have been impossible a few years ago; the interconnection of computers in world wide networks opens new possibilities for scientists who can now communicate over thousands of kilometres from screen to screen. Modern computer technologies are becoming an aspect of everyday life. At the same time, teaching at universities and in schools has to match this challenge, particularly in the subjects which have traditionally been not so close to these technologies.

In addition, a rich fund of shared features provides a link between the humanities and the social sciences and enables a fruitful methodological debate beyond the limits of academic disciplines. Society, seen as a system of social relationships, and culture, seen as a system of symbols, produce fuzzy structures which can hardly be understood by an approach which only unsystematically uses information technologies and crude analytic tools. The variety and complexity of these structures is not the only problem. Another challenge lies in coming to terms with subtle "anthropolitical" ingredients such as choices, intentions and traditions. Here, there are no principal differences between the "harder" social sciences and the "soft" humanities, although it is often claimed that there are fundamental differences in their epistemology and source materials.

For instance, the sources being used by philologists are frequently supposed to be context-sensitive, in contrast to the data used by empirical sociologists. Context-sensitivity means that historical sources and literary texts reflect not only the facts with which they are officially concerned, but also the circumstances and intentions standing behind their compilation. There is certainly no doubt that historical sources and literary texts often show such ambiguities, but this is still not reason enough to draw a line between these disciplines. The answers given in a questionnaire will sometimes change quite dramatically if third parties are present during an interview, and the coding of open questions in an interview essentially throws up similar problems of ambiguity to be accepted when working with a historical text. Both cases call for a process of understanding.

Obviously, there is a convergence of the epistemology of the social sciences with the humanities which has eventually resulted in the development of a sociological "source criticism," analogous to the critical methods used by philologists evaluating their sources. Standardized study descriptions, for instance, serve this purpose in the secondary analysis of survey data.

The plea for cooperation can also be extended to the relationship between quantitative and qualitative approaches. Here, we also find that the actual closeness and convergence of methods and techniques has been obscured by the claim that they had to be fundamentally different. In general, empirical research is concerned with that which is observable, that which occurs with stochastic regularity and that which can be analyzed in logically consistent models. Today, the computer is used in all three domains. Methods of computer simulation display some possible order that will reveal a system of abstract rules; data banks are inventories of what has been empirically observed; and methods of statistical analysis determine the connection between facts and events occurring in reality. But these three ways of applying computers do not merely *co-exist*. The way in which they are *interrelated* opens the most fascinating possibilities modern computer technology has to offer. So, this way, we find that expert systems combine elements of simulation technology with the technology of data banks; methods of exploratory data analysis, like cluster analysis, provide immanent criteria for the organization of data bases; missing values techniques can be implemented in order to reconstruct lost or badly recorded evidence.

The contributions assembled in this volume were originally presented to the Cologne Computer Conference which took place from the 7th to the 10th of September 1988 in the lecture halls of the University of Cologne. It brought together approximately 500 delegates from 27 countries and offered about 200 lectures and demonstrations. It was the largest event of its kind in Europe and one of the largest in the world.

Our aim in organizing this conference was to overcome segmentation, which is the result of maintaining traditional boundaries between academic subcultures. Applying computer technologies should not cut short any reflections on the methodological consequences the computer approaches may cause. As we know from the history of technology, innovations have not only changed working processes, they also have changed the products themselves regardless of whether this was intended or not when these new technologies were introduced. Furthermore, the computer had an impact on working conditions in fields which had not been immediately expected, particularly with respect to the legal system under which the researcher is working. Therefore, a special section on data protection and data access provided a synopsis of the data protection legislation and its impact on research in ten countries.

For the first time, the Cologne Computer Conference combined three series of parallel conferences, which were all established during the past few years for the exchange of information on the use of computers in the humanities and social sciences. The series of conferences on data bases in the humanities and social sciences (ICDBHSS) had only taken place biannually in the USA up until today. Originally, it was the intention of the organizers of this well respected forum that it should alternate with a European series. This series, however, never materialized with the exceptions of a conference in Madrid and, now, with the Cologne conference.

At the same time, the Cologne Computer Conference continued the series of conferences of the International Federation of Data Organization for the social sciences, (IFDO). As an associate member of the International Social Science Council, this organization is a main coordinator for the further methodical development in the empirical social sciences and for international data transfer. As early as 1978, IFDO held the first international conference on the development of data protection in Cologne. And finally, the Cologne Computer Conference hosted the Association for History and Computing (AHC). Previously, this association has met annually in various European countries and was usually attended by between three and four hundred scholars.

Cologne was chosen as the site for the combined conference because the scholars at the University of Cologne have been pioneers in the use of computer technology. In the social sciences, the Zentralarchiv für empirische Sozialforschung, founded in 1960, was one of the first to play a leading role in the use of the computer. In 1977, the QUANTUM association, founded by Cologne sociologists and historians in cooperation with the American Social Science History Association, organized one of the first conferences on the use of data processing and quantitative methods in history, and thus marked a new era in the usage of computer techniques in the humanities. Since then, the Zentrum für historische Sozialforschung has been established as a department of the Zentralarchiv für empirische Sozialforschung on the basis of these early beginnings. It is one of the few research facilities which was founded in recent years working on the borderline between the humanities and social sciences.

Our efforts to promote the usage of computer technologies in the humanities and social sciences could not have been successful without the partnership of the Max-Planck-Institut für Geschichte in Göttingen.

Heinrich Best　　　　Ekkehard Mochmann　　　　Manfred Thaller

THE ELECTRONIC LIBRARY AND THE SCHOLARSHIP OF THE FUTURE

Joseph Raben
City University of New York
USA

The current situation of the electronic library exhibits some striking resemblances to the beginnings of the print library which has become the cornerstone of modern scholarship. Instead of multiple copies of a text being located in thousands of institutions around the world, as there are in print libraries, there tend to be unique electronic versions in specialized collections. German literature therefore exists primarily in Germany, Italian in Italy, French in France, and so on. Furthermore, these collections tend to specialize according to the perceived mission of the institutions that house them: historical research concentrates on historical materials, literary on literary materials, linguistic on linguistic materials, and so on. Thus do we recapitulate the origins of modern learning, and thus do we perpetuate the harmful compartmentalization that continues to fragment that world.

This condition results from the haphazard way in which the various components of the future electronic library were created. At the start, no one seems to have thought beyond the printed book that was a particular project's goal. Like the generals who are said always to be fighting the last war, the scholars who first took up the computer in the 1960s were locked into a print mentality. By concentrating, apparently, only on the concordance or verbal index that would eventuate, they usually treated the input medium, punched cards and computer tape, as if they were rough drafts of a written paper, fit only to be discarded once the central task was accomplished. We probably owe the great treasures of Nancy, Pisa and other major centers of computer-aided humanities research more to the long time required to complete their projects than to any prescient vision that the input they generated would prove perhaps more valuable than the immediate output.

There can be no blame attached to this response to the computer; if individual scholars compiling concordances and verbal indexes saw the machine merely as a means of producing printed books, they were only complying with the realities of academic advancement. These realities were both positive and negative. Not only were books the chief path to tenure and promotion, but the devotion to the computer itself as a tool for scholarly research and instruction was generally deemed a sign of unacceptable deviation from academic norms. More than one promising young academic career was threatened because administrators could not accept computer-related research as satisfying their concepts of scholarship. In responding to deans and chairs who constantly asked "Where is your book?" there was (and still is) little value in showing boxes of punched cards or reels of magnetic tape as evidence of scholarly achievement. It was best, therefore, to obliterate the damning evidence of academic heresy.

The evidence of any change in this situation is fragmentary and anecdotal. From time to time, news circulates of one more computer-related humanist who has been pulled, with some help from colleagues, through the knothole of tenure and promotion review. The notion of computer-assisted instruction based on electronic texts does not presently arouse the same violent negative reactions it formerly did. And the notion of the electronic library as a medium of both research and instruction is gaining wider acceptance.

Representative components of that twenty-first century library are evident in the program of this conference [i.e., the Internationa Conference on Data Bases in the Humanities and Social Sciences, Cologne FRG, 7-10 September 1988]. From every part of the world have come speakers to describe collections of texts, numerical data and visual images in a vast range of subjects. These cover archaeology, urban studies, history, demography, political science, epigraphy, economics, penology, historical jurisprudence, art history, museology, musicology, lexicology, literary studies and linguistics. They employ every currently available computer technology, including optical disks and hypercard, plus statistical analyses and computer-assisted instruction.

Many factors have contributed to this growth of machine-readable materials and programs for accessing and analyzing them. Among these is the growing awareness that the printed book is not the perfect medium for storing information. For one thing, it lacks permanence. From the days of clay tablets and papyrus, media for recording our knowledge have become increasing fragile. Today's paper - unless especially and expensively treated - contains high residues of the acids used to manufacture it. This "time bomb" is destroying books by the thousands every year. Those that do survive for a while are attacked by the heat and high humidity in most library stacks, and by users who underline, annotate, and even remove pages to suit their immediate needs. As a consequence, rare copies of valuable books must be deacidified by a costly and elaborate process and then stored in special collections where only reverent and certified scholars can read them. The remainder, the bulk of our print collections, crumble quietly but inexorably on millions of feet of library stacks.

Librarians, aware of these conditions, are becoming the most ardent advocates of the electronic library. Although they are limited in their capacity to bring it into being, they recognize its potential and long to see it realized. Frequent announcements in library journals and newsletters report with enthusiasm any and all progress toward optical storage of full text, as well as graphics. The dream they are following is a library as complete as today's, with full illustrations, all foreign types, and every other refinement evolved in the five hundred years that print has been our dominant mode of communication. The only difference is that it will be stored in an electronic medium which will permit instant retrieval and display, unlimited copying, and simple transmission anywhere. Their projection is that such a medium will have an essentially infinite life-span.

From the perspective of users rather than custodians of research materials, other deficiencies in the printed book include the difficulty of quickly locating specific information. When the quantity of material in print was relatively small, it was not beyond reason for a determined researcher to go through at least the most relevant documents and be reasonably sure that a satisfactory proportion of the pertinent information had been identified. At least this was the premise of graduate instruction in research methodology. Whether it was valid in the past is less certain than that it is totally invalid today. No matter how narrowly a research topic is conceptualized, the task of collecting the relevant data is beyond the capacity of any individual (or that of a team, assuming one can be organized for the task) to comb card catalogs and printed indexes. Researchers themselves must be added to the list of supporters for the concept of the electronic library as the only available means of continuing to add to the world's knowledge.

In addition to librarians and scholars, publishers likewise are beginning to appreciate the value of replacing or supplementing print journals with online versions. Since they recognize the economic risks in this type of venture, they are presently concentrating on scientific journals because those command much higher prices and because the demand for the latest information justifies electronic dissemination. But just as computers first served primarily the needs of the commercial and technological communities and only later became more generally available for humanistic and social science research and instruction, so it is almost inevitable that this new mode of publication, once it is established, will be used for increasingly varied types of material.

There already exist, in many parts of the world, the building materials of the future electronic library. Social scientists are making increased use of census tapes, the results of public opinion polls, and similar computer-analyzed materials which have been systematically collected by research institutes, usually associated with universities. Humanists have become awáre of the literary materials stored at the Institut National de la Langue francaise in Nancy, at the Istituto di Linguistica Computazionale in Pisa, at the Institut für Kommunkationsforschung und Phonetik in Bonn, and Norway's Research Center for the Humanities in Bergen. A promising sign of future extensions was the willingness of the French institute to release copies of all its tapes to the University of Chicago to facilitate studies of French literature in North America. A further sign of things to come is that this collection can be accessed through Bitnet.

In the process of change we are witnessing, new support is coming from the electronic information brokers. In the field of bibliography, the one most relevant to humanistic and social science interests, many commercial and not-for-profit organizations have caught up with the backload of data that needed conversion to electronic storage, and they do not have enough work for their staffs and computers. Faced with the choice of cutting back on operations or expanding into new endeavors, they are most likely to enter the market for dissemination of electronic texts. OCLC, the major distributor of cataloging data for U.S. and foreign libraries, is now debating just such an expansion program. A new company, the Electronic Text Corporation, has begun to distribute CD ROMs containing the complete texts of the Constitution papers, novels by such authors as Twain and Melville, and plays by Shakespeare.

How far and how rapidly this market develops will depend on the overall success of the CD ROM as a viable technology. After the failure of the videodisk, there is understandable caution about a deep commitment to this new storage and retrieval medium. As has been true of all computer-related innovations, this one must succeed first in the commercial and technological fields. But if it does, the benefits to humanists and social scientists are likely to be greater than any yet conferred by the computer revolution. The astounding capacity of the disk itself, plus its capacity for storing musical and visual information as well as text, make it the most suitable medium imaginable for the kind of rapid but precise intellectual exploration that will underlie the new computer-based scholarship.

Because all these potentials are becoming more evident all the time, the latest ally in the effort to develop electronic databases is the computer industry. As they compete for market share, humanists and social scientists now present opportunities that were not evident before microcomputers brought them in substantial numbers into the community of computer users. Various strategies are being employed, but chiefly large grants to major universities that encourage innovative applications. At Brown University in Rhode Island, for example, a hypertext approach to teaching literature draws on the availability of electronically stored information on the social, technological, biographical, literary and other associations with particular authors. A parallel effort at Stevens Institute of Technology in New Jersey encourages students in a liberal arts course on Galileo to analyze writings by and about him with an interactive concordance program. When fully developed, such systems can not only widen our sense of how electronic databases can be used in instruction but also instill in students an appreciation of how wide and interconnected are the elements of any intellectual study. That is a lesson that may well be learned by their instructors as well.

In this process, both students and instructors will be able to cross many boundaries that now segregate disciplines. The literary scholar or historian, long accustomed to working in a familiar corner of the library, will experience a new liberty to roam freely through many nooks in the almost infinite electronic library. Information from any number of adjacent fields - for example, art history, technology, religion, geography - can be drawn on to enrich and enlighten future studies. Aided by the new concepts of hypertext, which are beginning to find application in many domains, these new scholars will be developing skills and acquiring information in ways that will seem as different from traditional methods as working in a twentieth-century library differs from poring over parchment scrolls in the dimly lighted library in Alexandria.

To bring modern electronically based scholarship out of its medieval condition will require many steps that have been taken only falteringly or not at all. Scholars have, for example, traditionally devoted little attention to the needs or functions of librarians. As long as books and other materials were available in libraries, their users did not bother their heads about how they got there. That indifference can no longer be tolerated. If the various databases being laboriously created in all parts of the world are to become the genuine foundations of a new scholarship, they must be integrated into our established library system. They must be catalogued according to international conventions, and be made available to the widest possible community of scholars. Librarians are involving themselves increasingly in the development of textual databases. It behooves the scholarly community to reach out cooperatively from their side.

But because electronic databases presently resemble ancient manuscripts in that they generally exist in unique copies, there is another community with which electronic scholars can advantageously cooperate. The archivists have developed great expertise in cataloging and preserving records, and of late they have been charged with adding computer records to their holdings. The National Archives and Records Service of the United States, for example, has established an office to select and preserve machine-readable government records for the future study of American history. It is inconceivable that the same action has not been taken by the other national governments which similarly rely on computers to conduct their business. The community of archivists engaged in this work must also be involved in our task of building the electronic library of the future.

Another resource of great potential that has not yet been adequately recognized is the community of scholarly editors. Dozens of such individuals, usually working in small teams, are laboriously transcribing the letters, papers, diaries, manuscripts and other written legacies of famous and important writers. In this day of electronic typesetting, such work is always performed on word processors and so the texts are machine-readable. Since most of these materials are out of copyright, the machine-readable versions should be made widely available for the kinds of analysis that can be performed only by means of computers. The editors of these projects, who generally are still concerned only with the printed book versions that will crown their labors, must be educated to recognize that the machine-readable texts they are incidentally generating may well be of much greater scholarly use and importance than the pages that so faithfully reproduce the original manuscripts they are transcribing.

While there is steady growth in the number of individuals who are convinced that the combined availability of machine-readable text and software to analyze it must generate a new type of scholarship, it is worth while to recognize some of the hazards inherent in such a dramatic change in methodology. First is the danger of being lured into mere counting. Even before computers, there were scholars who argued, for example, that there were "key words" in the poetry of different centuries, like "honor" in the eighteenth and "nature" in the nineteenth. Although counts of words in samples of writing may have brought these words to the tops of frequency lists, one must immediately question the significance of such a figure. If poets wrote, for example, about honor, was it because this concept was a major concern of the age or because it was not? Is a poet's function to reflect the values of his age or to challenge them? Can all poets living in one century be lumped together as if they shared a single fixed vocabulary? Could the generalizations derived from studying poetic vocabulary be transferred to sociology textbooks?

We have as yet not nearly enough knowledge of how language behaves to generalize from the huge databases now becoming available to us. We have not yet enough experience with analyzing the vocabulary of individual artists to know what their norms are or how far they conform to or deviate from the norms of their societies. We do not know what an artist's "society" is - everyone living within one hundred miles, or only the individuals known to be close acquaintances, or perhaps the other authors (many of them dead for centuries) whose books were read most closely.

Underlying future computer-based studies must be a recognition that language is an ecological system, not unlike those of forests, oceans or deserts. Each element in such a system derives from predecessors and produces progenitors. In language, we trace etymologies, often into the dim recesses of hypothetical conjectures. We have become so good at this that we have formulated "laws" of linguistic behavior, not only rationalizing recorded evolutions but tentatively filling in gaps. But we must now extend our concepts of language to recognize the complex ways in which it functions in its social milieu. There is, for example, competition between words for acceptance and use, just as there is between seedlings on a forest floor for sunlight and water. Associations between words can parallel those between symbiotic species. Much larger laws describing the behavior of language still wait to be discovered, and the data that records them will be available in the electronic library.

There it will be possible to trace individual words and combinations of words across vaster ranges than we have ever before been able to contemplate. We will have the records of written language in a new format that will allow instant searches of incredible scope. At this time, no one is able to predict how such searches will increase our knowledge or reveal patterns that are presently obscured. It is the curse of all technologies that their true value becomes apparent long after they are developed. The steam engine, radio and television, atomic energy, the computer - all were intended originally for purposes quite different from those that have been found for them once they were accessible to large numbers of potential users.

Any predictions of where the computer and machine-readable data bases will lead scholarship are therefore restricted by the same type of limited vision. We are perpetually locked into the past, which is all we can even partially know. Let us then conjecture a merging of resources from two presently discrete disciplines: history and lexicography. Imagine, for example, matching a French dictionary against all the writings of the American Founding Fathers to determine where they relied on a foreign term for some concept they felt they could not express precisely in English. Imagine then going back a generation to learn whether the same terms had been common in an earlier time. Imagine going ahead the same distance to determine whether these terms were becoming a standard part of the political vocabulary. Imagine, finally, performing the reverse operation on comparable French documents with an English dictionary. Would data such as might be derived from such an experiment support any generalizations about the flow of ideas from one language area to the other? Efforts like this, which would be almost literally impossible today with most material available only in print, can rapidly and easily collect information of a sort and size that will surely force us to ask many new questions.

Defining those questions exactly is, of course, an impossible task. The example given is intended to suggest that scope of investigations that will be feasible in the new scholarly environment. The best lesson we are likely to learn from our analysis of these databases is that we are not getting answers to questions as much as we are generating new questions. And that is probably all to the good. If we are truly at the beginning of a new era in scholarship, then we can take warning from other beginnings. We can remember all the blind alleys that lured early investigators; our libraries are full of the records. We will do much better to maintain a tentative attitude, to remain healthfully skeptical, to place objectivity above the need for acclaim. We must accept the truth that we will never achieve final answers, for there are none, whether we use computers or not. Although it has not been heard for some time, there is still truth in the once-popular aphorism "Garbage in, garbage out." The electronic library will become a reality, if only because of the economic and other reasons given. Programs will be written (or existing ones will be applied) to analyze these new databases in new ways, imaginative or conventional. This work will be conducted in an atmosphere of informed cooperation or secretive individualism. But it will be done, one way or another, and the world in which we conduct our research and teaching will never be the same.

DATA VISUALISATION IN ARCHAEOLOGY

Paul Reilly, Andrew Walter
IBM UK Scientific Centre
United Kingdom

Introduction

To outsiders, archaeologists must appear to be a very odd breed of scientist. Not only does their garb tend to be outlandish, they have a very peculiar attitude to their data. Consider for a moment the process of archaeological excavation - probably the most well-known aspect of archaeological enquiry. Excavations are carried out to examine the residues of past human activities which manifest themselves as the stains left by former posts, or the foundations of ancient walls, for example. It is an unfortunate irony that in order to reveal what lies below, the archaeological excavator must remove, and thereby destroy, what lies above. The anthropologist Sir Edmund Leach has observed that in an anthropological context this would be rather like interviewing members from the society under study, asking them the questions you were currently interested in, and then shooting them!

Not surprisingly, archaeologists are very self-conscious about this ethical dilemma. On the one hand, if they do not excavate they will be deprived of much of the data required for the discipline to advance. On the other hand, they are exposed to the charge of vandalism. In order to come to terms with this problem archaeologists in different countries have developed their own codes of practice which try to ensure that each archaeological excavation has clearly defined research objectives, and that every archaeological formation uncovered is recorded in the finest detail. The net result, of course, is a large mass of descriptive and locational information. To deal with this ever-growing glut of data archaeologists have turned to machine-based data collection, storage and processing. In particular, advanced three-dimensional computer graphics are proving to be extremely powerful analytical and presentation tools.

Looking at Excavated Data

Paradoxically, although archaeological excavation can be characterised as an observational discipline the archaeologist never actually sees the whole formation under examination, but only a series of veneers arbitrarily produced as the excavation proceeds. At any given time part of the formation will have already been removed and part will remain out of view, buried beneath the exposed surface. It is necessary to integrate each of these separate perceptions of the formation in order to obtain a clearer idea of its totality. It is at this juncture that the computer provides a powerful analytical aid allowing a virtual reconstruction of the feature. Depending on the level of detail recorded, the computer can be used to reconstruct and analyse the shapes of the formations and the distributions of interesting categories of artefacts and ecofacts within them. The combination of a relational database management system linked to sophisticated graphics facilities provides an elegant analytical tool.

Different categories of artefact can be retrieved, either separately or in conjunction with other types, from a database and displayed three-dimensionally using computer graphics so that their spatial properties might be examined. The use of colour coding systems can be used to highlight certain features of the data. With the more advanced systems the graphical representations may be rotated, panned, zoomed and z-clipped dynamically. The ability to move around and through the representation in real-time enables the viewer to gain a much better impression of the shapes of the different components within the data. The model may be viewed from positions and perspectives that are impossible to obtain in the real world. Analysis of rubbish disposal processes in a pit from the mid-Saxon settlement of Hamwic has benefited from such graphics-database data exploration procedures (Colley et al 1988).

Other effects such as transparency or opaqueness may also be modelled to emphasis patterning within the data. Indeed, these properties have been invaluable in the analysis of a Bronze Age midden from Potterne in Wiltshire, England. Another approach which proved very effective in the midden project was the application of what might be termed an interactive animated sequence. A series of slices through the midden were isolated and changes in the degree of bone fragmentation down the profiles thus formed were computed and appropriate colour-codes were applied. It was hoped that trampled surfaces and rapidly built-up deposits would be revealed by this means. As each profile could be displayed or hidden on request, it proved possible to create a time-lapse-like animation by treating each profile as a separate frame within a movie and displaying them in a rapid sequence. However, since each frame was actually a separate vector image the viewer could continue to pan, zoom or rotate the animated sequence to quickly obtain optimum viewing aspects of specific features within the data (Reilly et al 1988). This fluid interaction between the researcher and the data means that data exploration can proceed in an iterative fashion with very fast cycle times between original hypothesis, data examination, modified theory, new hypothesis and so on.

Virtual Excavations for Training and Evaluation Studies

In certain cases, if the level of detail is sufficient, it becomes practicable to experiment with alternative excavation or survey strategies to determine whether it would be more efficient or cheaper to apply some other method. Put simply, it is possible to re-excavate or re-survey the virtual archaeological formation within the constraints of the recorded detail. Clearly, the ability to investigate the reliability of our own recording and data-processing procedures has major educational and training implications. In the case of the Saxon pit project mentioned above it was possible to simulate alternative excavation strategies. Thus, instead of excavating all of the pit and recording the precise three-dimensional position of each of more than 30 000 objects, different sized samples (e.g., half-sections, quadrants and columns) were re-excavated at this level of detail in order to determine whether similar information would be obtained by excavating only a proportion of the total pit. Similarly, the information yields one could expect from less precise recording procedures could be sought. For example, rather than record the exact three-dimensional position of each object, groups of objects could be aggregated on the basis of membership to a higher level entity. For instance, locations could be specified in terms of collection units. These may be natural contexts such as stratigraphic features (e.g., layers) or some arbitrarily imposed system for partitioning up space (e.g., spits or boxes). It is not hard to see the potential for using such systems in teaching. They are particularly attractive in that they pose no further threat to the archaeological record. Students need not go out and dig features to gain experience when more profound insights into how to cost and provide resources for excavations may be had by contrasting the various scenarios of excavating the same features using different techniques.

Looking at Survey Data

Modern-day archaeology is by no means confined to time-consuming and expensive excavations. It also includes field work involving aerial reconnaissance, geophysical prospecting and topographic surveys for example. These techniques also generate vast amounts of complex data.

Computer graphics are useful for enhancing very fine topographic details which are difficult or impossible to see on the ground. They also have an important role in the analysis of remotely-sensed data such as those derived from geophysical survey. It is fairly common these days to construct models of surfaces of earthworks for example on the basis of a collection of measured points. Once the computer generated surface has been produced it becomes possible to enhance details using a variety of techniques. The simplest is to exaggerate readings so that everything is bigger: that is, mounds are higher and ditches are deeper. However, one can then go further and create optimum lighting conditions for viewing the already enhanced features (Reilly 1988a: Chapter Nine; Spicer 1988). Archaeologists involved in aerial reconnaissance know that different lighting conditions and ground cover are particularly helpful for studying the form of certain sites of archaeological interest. Such conditions can be simulated on the computer model, and the archaeologist is freed to "fly" around the study area under ideal conditions. This method has the advantage of not being susceptible to the weather or seasonal vegetation growth!

The same techniques are equally applicable surveys that involve the measurement of properties which cannot be seen. For example, remotely sensed data, such as those collected during resistivity surveys, where probes are used to measure the resistance of buried soils, can be analysed in this way to reveal archaeological features. Going further, several types of data can be integrated. For instance, resistivity or surface collected data could be mapped onto a topographic or terrain model to help establish whether there is any relationship between the surface details and the buried information (e.g., Boismier & Reilly 1988). Terrain modelling (Harris 1988) and Geographic Information Systems (Kvamme 1986) have been identified as methods of great potential in archaeological landscape studies and in excavation analyses. The terrain-modelling approach is equally valid at the micro-topographical level and has proved useful in the examination and presentation of the three-dimensional soil silhouettes, known as the sand-people at the Royal Anglo-Saxon cemetery at Sutton Hoo, Suffolk (Reilly & Walter 1987; Reilly & Richards 1988).

Virtual Surveys for Training and Evaluation Studies

As in the case of excavation, simulation studies are allowing archaeologists to assess the reliability of their recording methodologies for field surveys. Mike Fletcher and Dick Spicer (forthcoming) have recently created an imaginary earthwork site, called

Clonehenge, comprising of a geometrically defined surface whose topography is known exactly. They have performed a number of simulated topographic surveys using different sampling procedures to obtain the measurements from which the terrain under study is to be recorded and re-modelled. Thus measurements have been collected on regular grids of points, at variable intervals along linear transects and from randomly distributed locations. By this means they hope to be able to determine which approach gives the best representation of the original surface being recorded.

A slightly different line of enquiry has been developed by Dr Irwin Scollar in relation to geophysical data. Scollar helped pioneer the technique of examining sites of archaeological interest by using computer-generated graphics to study remotely-sensed measurements of the magnetic and electrical properties of buried features (e.g., Scollar et al 1986). The method, however, is often plagued by considerable amounts of background noise which make it difficult to discern details in the data. This noise can be removed by using a number of different filtering techniques. Unfortunately, not all image-processing techniques are equally appropriate and frequently the order in which they are applied will crucially effect the quality of the results. In order to help him determine which techniques are most suitable for removing characteristic noise problems, Scollar synthesised an ideal set of geophysical reading from an imaginary Roman Fort. To these readings he added different types of noise and then proceeded to experiment with various filtering procedures to reveal the pure data (Scollar 1969). In the future we might expect artificial intelligence techniques to help less experienced practitioners choose the appropriate procedure to collect and process such survey data.

Reconstructing and Exhibiting Archaeological Material

In the area of reconstruction, graphics also have a role to play. It is not always feasible to generate the resources to build reconstructions on the scale of Knossos on Crete, or Jorvik in York. However, it is often important to build such reconstructions to appreciate how the original architects were manipulating space to create an impact with the buildings. Constructive Solid Geometry techniques were adopted by Dr John Woodwark in a reconstruction of the temple precinct of Roman Bath and the Roman Military Bath house at Caerleon (Smith 1985). The same sort of technology was employed in the construction of a model of the late Saxon minster of Winchester (Colley & Todd 1985). In this case an animated tour of the Saxon minster of Winchester was produced for the British Museum's Archaeology in Britain Exhibition, 1987, by generating a large sequence of views taken at increments along a route around and through the model.

In building such reconstructions it is necessary to explicitly define each element of the model. The process of defining the model is useful in that it forces attention back to the data. This may reveal problems or gaps which will cause the analyst to look out for, or record differently, certain types of evidence in a future investigation.

Solid-modelling may come to play an important role in the reconstruction of artefacts. The modelling of surface properties is an obvious application area. One may contrast aesthetics: for example, a decision to keep the patina on bronze objects in favour of exposing the bare metal. The pieces of a broken object can be joined together on a machine before attempting any restoration. Again the layout of showcases and exhibition lighting can be modelled before any work starts in the galleries. All these methods have the distinct advantage that the model produced can easily be repaired or modified if something is found wanting in the reconstruction.

It is not necessary to confine our attentions purely to form. Processes may also be modelled. It is possible to distort shapes. Given an object of known form one can simulate the types of distortions required to produce another shape, and thereby help us understand better what has happened to a particular object.

The Future: Hyperdocuments, Artificial Intelligence and Modelling

Undoubtedly, artificial intelligence will have a role to play in archaeological modelling and reconstruction. Our understanding of building techniques is just one application area. A pilot study, at IBM UK's Scientific Centre, is attempting to develop a rule-based system which will take a stock of 'stones' and decide where best to lay them in order to build a wall (Reilly 1988b: 37-8). With such detailed computer models we can hope to examine building techniques and, much more speculatively, help to restore ruined structures using the available debris. Others might wish to simulate the types of forces necessary to knock some buildings down. Such modelling would be particularly useful for testing hypotheses for explaining why certain structures collapsed. By making our assumptions explicit in the modelling systems we may also be in a better position to critically study our own reasoning processes and thereby isolate and make good any faults thus revealed.

Although computer-aided techniques of data visualisation and presentation are advancing rapidly, existing publishing practices severely hamper their wider application in information exchange. It is not too far-fetched to envisage archaeological accounts being published on mass-storage mediums such as videodisks. However, instead of referring to figure such and such, the commentator might employ sets of database operations and view parameters to demonstrate a particular phenomenon. This, of course, implies that the full data set should be made available together with a data management system, graphics facilities, and perhaps also a suitable statistical package, in a self-contained environment. Animated sequences, still photographs and audio material might also be integrated into the document. To make such a document readable would require a well thought-out and standardised system of cross referencing which would allow the user identify the various types of information associated with a particular fact, interpretation or statement.

We should look forward to the everyday use of hyperdocuments of the kind just outlined. In the meantime, computer database systems, high-level graphics systems, and artificial intelligence techniques are already beginning to allow archaeologist to ask new types of questions and to look at their data from positions which were previously impossible.

REFERENCES

BOISMIER, W.A. and REILLY, P. 1988. "Expanding the Role of Computer Graphics in the Analysis of Survey Data", in: Ruggles, C.N.L. & Rahtz, S.P.Q. (eds.). *Computing and Quantitative Methods in Archaeology 1987*. BAR International Series 393, Oxford, 221-225

COLLEY, S. and TODD, S. 1985. "Archaeological computing at the IBM UK Scientific Centre." *Archaeological Computing Newsletter* 4, 3-8

COLLEY, S.; TODD, S. and CAMPLING, N. 1988. "3-D Computer Graphics for Archaeological Data Exploration: An Example from Saxon Southampton." *Journal of Archaeological Science* 15, 99-106

FLETCHER, M. and SPICER, R.D. 1988 (forthcoming). "Clonehenge: an Experiment with Gridder Survey Data, to appear in Rahtz", S.P.Q. (ed.). *Computer and Quantitative Methods in Archaeology 1988. British Archaeological Reports*, International Series, Oxford

HARRIS, T. 1988. "Digital Terrain Modelling in Archaeology and Regional Planning", in: Ruggles, C.N.L. & Rahtz, S.P.Q. (eds.). *Computing and Quantitative Methods in Archaeology 1987*. BAR International Series 393, Oxford, 161-170

KVAMME, K. 1986. *An Overview of Geographic Information Systems for Archaeological Research*. Section 13 in Microcomputers in Archaeology, Workshop proceedings, April 23, 1986, Society of American Archaeology, New Orleans LA

REILLY, P. 1988a. *Computer Analysis of an Archaeological Landscape: Medieval Land Division in the Isle of Man.* British Archaeological Reports, British Series 190, Oxford

REILLY, P. 1988b. *Data Visualisation: Recent Advances in the Application of Graphic Systems to Archaeological Data.* IBM UK Scientific Centre Report 185, IBM UK, Winchester

REILLY, P.; LOCKER, A.M. and SHENNAN, S.J. 1988 (forthcoming). "Expanding the Role of Computer Graphics in the Analysis of Sub-Surface Data", to appear in Rahtz, S.P.Q. (ed.). *Computer and Quantitative Methods in Archaeology 1988.* British Archaeological Reports, International Series, Oxford

REILLY, P. and RICHARDS, J.D. 1988. "A New Perspective on Sutton Hoo: The Potential of 3-D Graphics", in: Ruggles, C.N.L. & Rahtz, S.P.Q. (eds.). *Computing and Quantitative Methods in Archaeology 1987*. BAR International Series 393, Oxford, 173-185

REILLY, P. and WALTER, A. 1987. "Three-Dimensional Recording in the Field: Preliminary Results." *Archaeological Computing Newsletter* 10, 7-12

RUGGLES, C.N.L. and RAHTZ, S.P.Q. (eds.). 1988. *Computing and Quantitative Methods in Archaeology 1987*. BAR International Series 393, Oxford

SCOLLAR, I. 1969. "A Program for the Simulation of Magnetic Anomalies of Archaeological Origin in a Computer." *Prospezioni Archeologische* 4, 59-83

SCOLLAR, I.; WEIDNER, B. and SEGETH, K. 1986. "Display of Archaeological Magnetic Data." *Geophysics* 51(3), 623-633

SMITH, I. 1985. "Sid and Dora's Bath Show Pulls in the Crowd." *Computing*, The Magazine, (27th June 1985), 7-8

SPICER, R.D. 1988. "Computer Graphics and the Perception of Archaeological Information: Lies, Damned Statistics and ... Graphics", in: Ruggles, C.N.L. & Rahtz, S.P.Q. (eds.). *Computing and Quantitative Methods in Archaeology 1987*. BAR International Series 393, Oxford, 187-200

AN ARCHAEOLOGICAL RESEARCH SUPPORT SYSTEM WITH DATABASES OF JAPANESE ANCIENT TOMBS AND GEOGRAPHICS

Kazumasa Ozawa
Department of Management Engineering
Osaka Electro-Communication University
Japan

1. Introduction

Many types of research support systems have so far been developed (Duong et al. 1978, Van Nuen et al. 1981, Matsuka et al. 1982). A common target, suggested in an overview of these existing systems, seems to be placed on building such systems as linked with special databases. This implies that a research support system should provide not only data processing tools but also stimulate information effective for problem solving. There would appear many problems in archaeology, in which such systems would act well as powerful research tools.

This paper describes a research support system for archaeological studies on a special type of Japanese ancient monuments: Between the 4th and 6th centuries AD, a large number of huge ancient tomb mounds, termed Keyhole (shaped) tombs, were built all over Japan (see Figure 1). Even today, more than three thousand of Keyhole tombs still remain in spite of excessive urbanization in modern Japan. Keyhole tombs have been playing the most important role in understanding of the so-called Ancient Tomb Period, in which the Japanese regime originally started. REDATO, short for our system, has been implemented to support archaeological studies on the Keyhole tombs by a variety of real-time processings including statistical analysis, pictorial and geographical processings and so on.

Figure 1: Contour Maps of the Keyhole Tomb Mounds

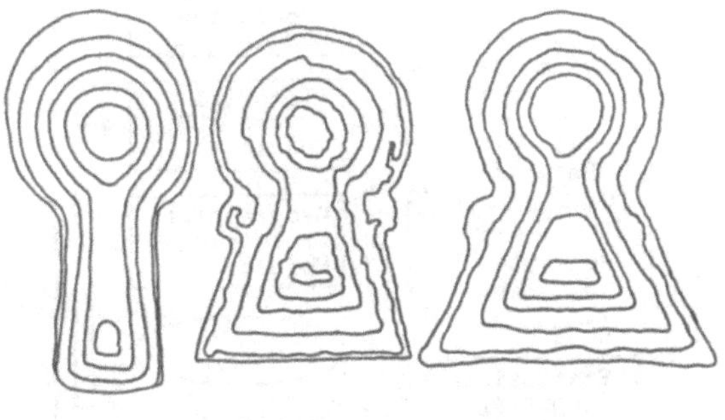

4c 5c 6c

2. Aims and Logical System Structure

A sort of cyclic process of thinking seems to underlie every study in archaeology: A unit cycle consists of modelling and its verification by fact. In most cases, imperfections may be detected in an assumed model. Then it is modified into a new model for verification in the next cycle. Usually, such verification is done by drawing distribution maps, statistical computing or other handling of actual data. REDATO mainly supports these verification tasks by its real-time processings.

A Keyhole tomb involves many kinds of archaeological aspects as well as other artifacts. Most aspects, which are classified into symbolical information can be described symbolically. On the other hand, non-symbolical aspects such as the shape of an artifact and the geographical position where it was found are also important in archaeology; these can be called pictorial and geographical information, respectively.

The following three types of databases play key roles in the sophisticated performance of our system, providing necessary information for real-time processings; Symbolical Database (SD), Pictorial Database (PD) and Geographical Database (GD). SD is relational in structure, storing 47 kinds of symbolically descriptive aspects. PD stores encoded strings of contours of the tomb mounds. GD has detailed line primitives to draw every part of the Japanese islands.

The system also includes a number of real-time processing modules to create or to recognize scientific information based on the three databases. Among them, the following four modules play leading parts in the performance of the system:

Symbolical Processing Module (SPM)
Pictorial Processing Module (PPM)
Geographical Processing Module (GPM)
Statistical Computing Module (SCM)

Figure 2: Logical Structure of REDATO

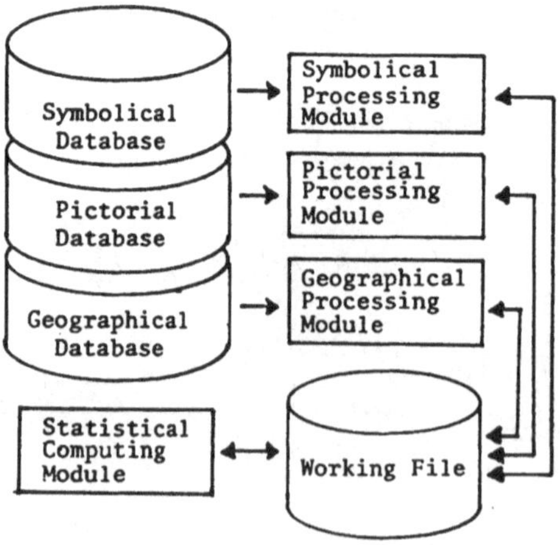

Figure 2 shows a rough sketch of the logical structure of our system REDATO. The first three modules SPM, PPM and GPM manage different types of data in SD, PD and GD, respectively. SCM handles numerical data sets. Inter-module communication is carried out through commonly accessible data sets defined in the working file.

3. Databases

As previously described, archaeological information of the Japanese ancient tombs has been classified into three types, i.e. symbolical, pictorial and geographical information, respectively. This classification appears to be effective to any other problem in archaeology: In most cases, archaeological report consists of text, sketches or plates of artifacts and distribution maps. This leads to the basic idea that makes our system linked with the following three databases:

Symbolical Database (SD)
The symbolical type of data include character strings such as name, address or type and numerical strings such as latitude, longitude, elevation or length. These items describing the Keyhole tombs have been called "attributes" in terms of database technology. In SD, 47 kinds of attributes have been defined. The conceptual schema to organize SD is based on the Codd's relational model (Codd 1970): SD is basically composed of eight tables each of which involves a group of attributes. All tables are hierarchically structured; one mother table and seven child tables. A number of attributes in the mother table are associated with PD and GD.

Pictorial Database (PD)
PD stores simply pictorial information of shapes of the tomb mounds (see Figure 1). The Freeman's chain coding (Fu 1976) has been introduced to describe contour lines of a Keyhole tomb mound. As shown in Figure 3, a given line can be coded by the method to a string of the octal primitives.

Figure 3: Freeman's Chain Code

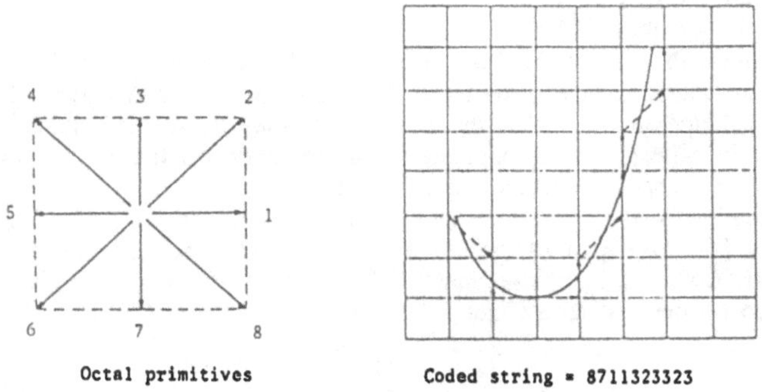

Geographical Database (GD)
In archaeology, distribution maps have been very important to illustrate geographical relations between sites or spots. Land maps are essential for drawing such distribution maps. Many computer techniques to store geographical maps have been presented (Olson 1983, Matsuyama et al. 1984). The data structure of GD has specially been designed, referring to these existing techniques: Partition of the Japanese islands can be described as hierarchy of three levels; region, prefecture and city level, respectively. A city, the smallest element of partition, can be drawn by a number of line elements. Since every prefecture is composed of a collection of cities, it can also be drawn by line elements; a region or the whole Japanese islands can be handled in the same way. GD stores all the line elements each of which is described as a series of points given in terms of latitude and longitude.

4. Data Processing Modules

REDATO include as main components the four data processing modules shown in Figure 2. These modules play their own parts in cooperative creation of stimulate information for the cyclic process of thinking. Inter-module communication is carried out through the commonly accessible data sets, termed C-set, defined in the working file. In our case, a C-set is such a set of the ancient tombs with a specified common property as defined by a module. A couple of existing C-sets can be reduced to a new C-set: this is nothing but set operation that belongs to SPM. Every module works in such closer cooperation with other modules, reorganizing actual data, stored in the databases, to qualify as useful for studies: Emphasis has also been placed on how to picturize the created products so as to recognize them quickly. In the following, the basic ideas to design the modules and their capabilities are presented:

Symbolical Processing Module (SPM)
This module is, basically, equivalent to the so-called database management system (DBMS) that is in charge of conventional retrieval from SD. One specific feature of SPM can be seen in its manner of query; every query should be given in a special graphical expression instead of an inquiry language such as INQL. A query is, in most cases, written by a logical expression which is composed of several conditions and logical operations AND and OR. For simplicity, suppose x and Y being such conditions as
x = "It is an Osaka Prefecture"
Y = "It is longer than 100m".
Figure 4 shows the SPM's graphical expressions for xANDy and xORy, respectively. A unit square island means a condition: Two unit islands x and y join a bigger island in the logical operator OR. On the other hand, they do not join in AND, standing independently. The graphical expression can be made on the display by specifying conditions and logical operators using a keyboard.

A collection of the items that agree with a query can be defined as a C-set in the working file. To a pair of the sets, one of the SPM's set operations, union (OR), intersection (AND), and substraction (SUB), can be applied. The newly compounded set can also be defined as a C-set.

Figure 4: Graphical Expressions of Queries

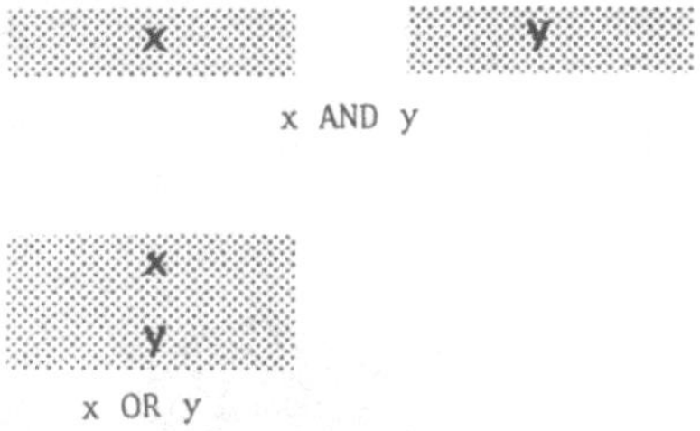

Pictorial Processing Module (PPM)
The main role of this module is to handle contour maps of Keyhole tomb mounds stored in PD. Basic functions of PPM include the drawing of the contour maps on the display, their logical zooming, and interactive measurement of dimensions of the mounds. These functions have been powerful for comparative studies on shapes of the mounds. PPM also provides the pictorial query processing as a high level of real-time processing.
Another powerful processing aims at automatic restoration of the tomb mound. Restoration of a broken artifact is a boring, but unavoidable task for every archaeologist. Such restoration has so far been carried out based on empirically acquired knowledge. The Keyhole tomb mound, especially its shape, chronologically changes so visibly as seen in Figure 1 that its quantitative analysis would be a matter of significance in Japanese archaeology. Since almost all the tomb mounds have never been so well-conserved as to serve such purposes, it has also been required to restore them. PPM rapidly depicts the restored shape of a Keyhole tomb mound on the display in terms of a contour map. This processing deeply depends on a collection of the rules, embedded in PPM, most of which have statistically been acquired: The collection is to be called a knowledge-base, which consists of rules related to the taxonomic studies. An example of such automatic restoration can be seen in Figure 5; the contour map in the left shows an actual mound and that in the right is its restored contours.

Geographical Processing Module (GPM)
A variety of distribution maps can quickly be obtained by GPM. The principle to draw a distribution map is very simple: It is completed by dotting a given set of items, according to their latitudes and longitudes on the land map concerned. Figure 6 shows an example of distribution map drawn by GPM. In general, a set of items to be dotted is given by the other modules in terms of C-set. The most specific processing of GPM is concerned with spatial clustering of spots. This processing aims at detecting a cluster of closely situated spots, termed a spatial cluster, on a distribution map. A sort of hunting procedure has been applied to this processing.

Figure 5: Automatic Restoration of a Keyhole Tomb Mound

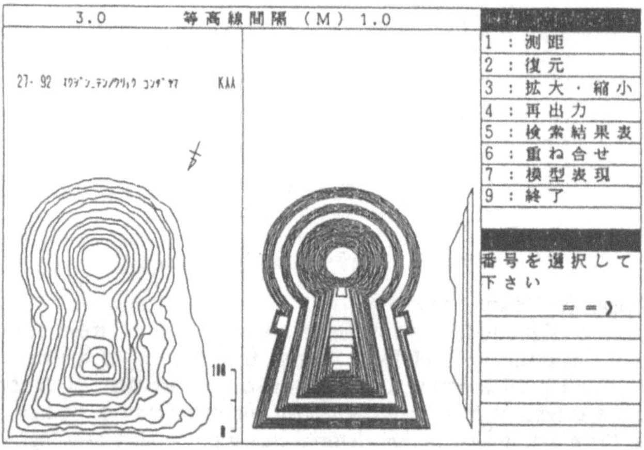

Figure 6: Distribution Map

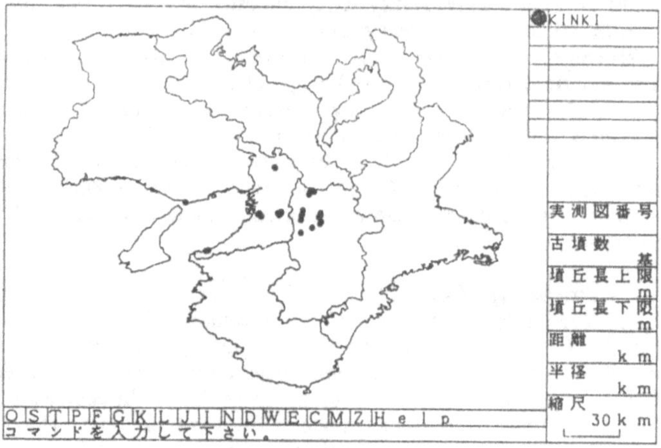

Statistical Computing Module (SCM)

This Module performs the linear regression analysis or conventional cluster analysis on numerical data given in terms of a C-set. SCM also provides a tool for the numerical transformation of a given set of data. The regression analysis of SCM consists of estimation of a linear regression equation and its graphical expression.

As is well-known, cluster analysis presents different results according to the definition of between-cluster distance (Ozawa 1985); single link, complete link or average link has frequently been used. SCM provides five options of between-cluster distances, including single link and others. Figure 7 shows a dendrogram of 33 Keyhole tombs selected by SPM, which is formed by the single link: Cutting a dendrogram with a horizontal line, corresponding to a threshold level, we can define a collection of clusters. Basically, the determination of the threshold level belongs to each archaeologist who is engaged in data handling. SCM supports the whole process of such clustering trials; when a computed result is dissatisfied, new trials can quickly be performed, for example, by changing the distance measure, the between-cluster distance or the threshold level.

Figure 7: Dendrogram

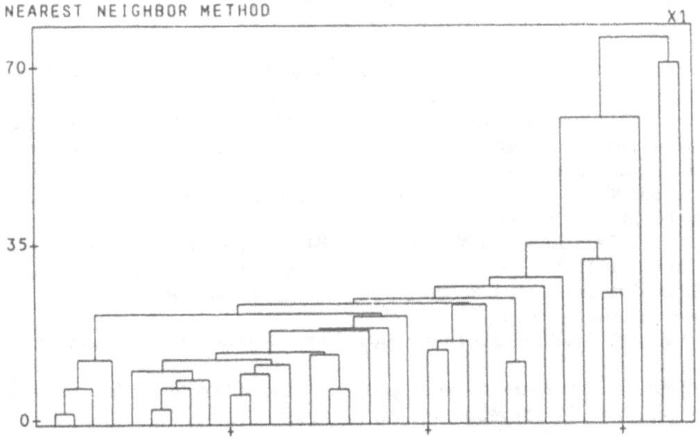

5. Conclusion

As far as the author's survey is concerned, no research support system just like REDATO has so far been implemented in archaeology. The author feels that other research support systems will also be feasible in such a way as REDATO. Before we think how to design a research support system, we have to think what it will be for: The subject in charge of research is not a computer, but an archaeologist. Every research work appears to involve a cyclic process of thinking done by an archaeologist. In principle, it may be most important how useful a research support system is for accelerating the process of thinking positively. It follows that the system should be specialized so as to fit the problem in which the archaeologist is engaged.

REDATO has been implemented on the FACOM M 360AP computer system of which specifications include 36 nano-seconds memory cycle time, 24MB CPU memory and 446MB by 12 disk memory devices. An end user of REDATO can manage all the modules through a colour graphic display unit of the computer system.

From the view-point of system design, there is a room to be improved in the present REDATO. One future task is to introduce an image database and its managing module to our system. Another task is to introduce artificial intelligence techniques more positively: Automatic inference linked with the knowledge-base appears to act well in support to chronological studies (Ozawa 1985) or taxonomic studies.

ACKNOWLEDGEMENT

The author thanks Professor Kenji Akiyama, without whose encouragement, REDATO would not have been implemented.

REFERENCES

CODD, E.F. 1970. "A Relational Model of Data for Large Shared Data Banks" *CACM*, vol. 13, 6, 377-387

DUONG, N.; LI, R.M. and SIMONS, D.B. 1978. *An Interactive Planning Model for River Basin Management*. Proc. of the 2nd Lawrence Symposium on Systems and Decision Sciences, 158-164

FU, K.S. 1976. *Digital Pattern Recognition*. Springer-Verlag, 105-106

MATSUKA, H. and SUGIMOTO, K. 1982. "Regional Planning Support System." *Journal of Inf. Proc. Soc. of Japan*, vol. 23, 9, 818-827

MATSUYAMA, T.; HAO, L. V. and NAGAO, M. 1984. *A File Organization for Graphic Information Systems Based on Spatial Proximity*. Comput. Vision, Graphics and Images Process.

OLSON, L. 1983. *Development of a Road Database from Map Overlays*. Proc. of the 3rd Scandinavian Conference on Image Analysis, 274-279

OZAWA, K. 1985. "A Stratificational Overlapping Cluster Scheme." *Pattern Recognition*, vol. 18, 3/4, 279-286

OZAWA, K. 1985. "A Rule-Based Archaeological Periodization System for Japanese Ancient Tombs." *Trans. of Inf. Prod. Soc. of Japan*, vol, 26, 2, 342-348

ON THE COMPUTER-AIDED CLASSIFICATION OF POTTERY SHAPES

L. Graca; K.-H. Laudan; P. Zamperoni
Institut für Nachrichtentechnik
Technische Universität Braunschweig
U. Kampffmeyer
L.A.S. - Laser Archive Service
Wachenheim
W.-R. Teegen
Seminar für Ur- und Frühgeschichte
Georg-August-Universität Göttingen
FRG

Ceramics have been selected as an example for demonstrating the analysis of shapes within the ARCOS-project (see Kampffmeyer 1986a-c, Lübbert & Kampffmeyer 1988), because they make up the most important and most numerous group of archaeological finds. This present study, however, which is concerned with the classification of shapes, takes into account solely the outline of the vessels. The shape of a vessel can be represented quite accurately by its profile. The ceramics which have been used in this study come very close to having a rotational symmetry or had respectively been meant by the potter to possess such a symmetry. For this reason, the left-hand outer contours of the vessels have been used for the classifications. The right-hand outer contours have been supplemented by reflection along the axis. The thickness of the sherd has been neglected at this stage of recording. Naturally, the shape is only one of a number of characteristics by which ceramics can be described. Wares, production techniques, function and ornaments - the latter most important in the context of chronological questions - are significant features in their own right.

This study was meant, therefore, above all as a check of classifications of shape, and of the automatic classification process. The results of such processes need to be useful for and compatable with conventional model building in archaeology. In addition, this study is meant to provide the methodological basis for the development of a classification module for the evaluation and data bank system ARCOS-2 (Kampffmeyer 1986a). It will not be fully automatic, but will rather function through interactive dialogue with the user ("interactive automatic classification"). The interactive automatical classification is the first step from a mere archaeological documentation system to an expert system (Kampffmeyer et al. 1988).

Material and Methods

In a first step 164 Neolithic vessels from Germany and Denmark were recorded and analysed (Kampffmeyer 1988). In that study the programs for image- and data-processing were developed and some cluster-analytical methods were tested (see Kampffmeyer et al. 1988, pp. 105ss.). In a second step 306 urns and grave vessels from the Villanovan necropolis at Veio-Quattro Fontanili (Italy) were studied using up-dated programs and further multivariate methods.

Methods of Recording

The outer contours of complete and reconstructable vessels types as taken from the find catalogues published so far have been drawn and have been given a uniform scale. The input for each profile consisted of a three-digit identification number, height and radius of the rim (in mm). The profiles were recorded with a video camera, the remaining data were input by keyboard. The DEC- PDP-15-computer of the Institute for Telecommunication, TU Braunschweig was at disposal for the analysis. The data recording can also be accomplished with the ARCOS-1-system as well. Profiles thus registered can be used directly for shape classifications, applying the methods presented here. In the future it is planned to record the shapes of ceramics with ARCOS-1 and to analyse them with the ARCOS-2.

The digitized profile drawings are simple grey scale ones (dark object, light background). For their analysis could we have applied methods of image processing. The contour can be described by chain-coding developed by H. Freeman (1965). The algorithm used was formulated by P. Zamperoni. With chain-coding, a check of plausabilities can be made and striking changes in the direction (such as rims, bottoms, sharp bends etc.) can be noted easily by the program. Given the scale which had been fed into the computer earlier, certain measures and characteristics were gained automatically from the contour-code during the investigation, which could the be used for further detailed analysis.

The method of chain-coding has rarely been used for the analysis of archaeological objects. A major advantage of this method is that a comparison of curves can be made fairly easy mathematically (by matrix operations) while the chains need little storage room inside the computer. This has a favourable effect on the working speed and on the number of sets of data which can be analyzed simultaneously. There is very little loss of information connected with the coding of contours as shown by our experiments (Kampffmeyer et al. 1988). It remains difficult to use transformations such as stretching or compressing on the chain-coded data. This is noticeable when two chains differing in length must be standardized in order to compare two objects with very differing heights.

In order to compare sherds with complete standard curves, important for the interactive automatic classification, it is necessary to extract certain defined sectors from these reference curves. The sherds are usually pieces from the rim or rim/neck or bottom of a vessel as the original position of a sherd from the side can rarely be ascertained. First extraction-programs have been written by K.-H. Laudan (cf. Zamperoni et al. 1988). First, empirically established archaeological definitions of the various sectors of a vessel were translated into programs and tested. The gradual alignment of the mathematical definitions is refined in such a manner that it results in a generally applicable definition for rim, neck, belly and bottom/base, independent of the size, structure and shape of the vessel. The entire method of segmentation is anchored on three clearly defineable points: base of rim, base of bottom and body sector of the vessel. All the information needed can independently be got out of the contour-code of the vessel profile by the program.

The variables which have been empirically established in this case can also be gained dynamically by a process controlled by the program itself. The same process can also be used for shapes other than the profiles of ceramics. If the system were to be refined and further distingiushing criteria were to be added, characteristic marks of vessels could be determined automatically. Such marks have been used in various studies in classification (cf. Kampffmeyer et al. 1988, chapter 2 with literature). In this manner, comparisons between differing analytical methods would become possible as well as a following-up of new questions.

Analytical Methods

Due to the limited storage capacity of the DEC-PDP-15 Computer it was possible to compare only up to 160 recorded profiles at one time. Therefore, the original Veio data-set had to be partitioned. This was done in various ways. In one partitioning, only large and structered vessels (mostly urns; data set nr 1) and smaller and less clearly structered vessels (data set nr 2) were grouped separately, with a few differing "control vessels" always included. In a second partitioning, the profiles 1-150 (data set nr 8; cf. fig. 1) and the profiles 151-306 (data set nr 9) respectively were compiled onto separate data files.

The entire contour was processed after obtaining the contour-code. Then some defined characteristics like height, bends, etc. were extracted for further analysis and sectors of the contour were segmented. The program is able to compare two sets of data at a time by calculating their distances. This can either be done for the entire contour, for two characteristics each, for two combinations of several characteristics or for the proportions. The distances are arranged in a similarity-matrix for each pair of profiles and then are evaluated by cluster-analysis. The program can then be used further to combine the distance-matrices of contours and other characteristics. These are distance calculations within a multi-dimensional space. They have been calculated with the "city-block" distance-function.

Procedures of Cluster-Analysis Applied

Cluster analysis of vessel profile data were conducted in order to ascertain "natural" groupings of the unpartitioned mass of data. Several methods of cluster-analysis have been used to this end. These are the single-linkage, complete-linkage, and centroid-cluster analysis methods. They have been used on the one hand to group the vessel profiles based solely on the outer contours, and on the other hand to group them by consulting other variously emphasized characetristics and/or combinations of characteristics. The grouping was based on the distance-matrices which had been obtained earlier. Checking the effectiveness of the three different types of cluster-analysis proved the complete-linkage cluster-analysis to show the best results. This method of automatic classification provided the structuring of the material closest to which the structure of the conventional archaeological classification. Dendrograms were chosen for the graphical representation of the results of the cluster analysis. When assessing them, however, it has to be noted that a change of succession is possible within the branches while the spacing remains the same (mobile-effect).

Results

Four selected sets of data made up of ca 150 vessels each were analysed, using the three methods of cluster-analysis (single-/complete-linkage, centroid) each. As the complete-linkage-method has shown the best results so far, only the structering of the material obtained by this method shall be discussed here. Certain characteristics and quotients have been weighted on the basis of empirically gained factors in order to produce more clear representations. The contour has been shown to contain all the essential information for the forming of groups. Nevertheless the result can be optimized by consulting further characteristics. The dendrogram (fig. 1; data set nr 8) shall be given as an example for this: The contour-code is combined with the Q1 quotient (rim diameter/height of vessel ratio). Here, the biconical urns form one large cluster "B" while the majority of additional grave-good vessels can be found in the clusters above. The cluster "A", however, is conspicuous. From a typological point of view it could have been expected in the "D" cluster. The urns form quite a homogeneous group in the "B" cluster, with the exception of one "runaway": this is the sperical vessel nr 58 which bears little similarity to its neighbours in one of the "Baa" subcluster. To sum up, one can say that the additional use of the quotient Q1 has been an improvement only for the structuring of the urns but not for any other vessel type. Variable results can be gained in the analysis of shapes of vessels if measures or quotients are added. In this manner it is possible to optimize the classification of certain shapes of vessels. More detailed studies should begin at this point.

It was the aim of K.-H. Laudan's work to group the above- mentioned segmented profile sectors and to compare them with the complete sectors (cf. Zamperoni et al. 1988). This was only partly successful. Structuring the segments by cluster analysis resulted in dendrograms which were conclusive in themselves. These dendrograms, however, are incomparable with those obtained from the complete profiles. When trying to allocate segments to the complete contours, it was very rarely possible to pick initial contours they had originated from. The process of segmentation can provide sensible sectors of the profile contour. No results can so far be obtained by comparing these separate sectors with one another or with complete contours. Further investigations are required here which will have to focus on the difficulties of "ranges of variation".

Conclusions

The application of mathematical analysis and representation methods has proved useful for the study of the ceramics in particular from the early Iron Age necropolis of Veio (Quattro Fontanili). The groupings obtained with the help of these methods are sensible from a functional-formal point of view (the sample has been divided into urns, simple shouldered vessels, etc.). In addition, these groupings offer starting-points for more detailed studies. It was shown that a weighting of the analysis with the help of additional factors and measures is effective.

The contour-coded profiles of vessels have been segmented successfully into the sectors rim, neck, body and bottom/base. A similarity comparision of the individual elements of the vessels is unsatisfactory so far and requires more work.

Both the methods already tested as well as these which have yet to be explored can be applied to standarized sets of ceramics from pottery findings such as ancient, medieval and post-medieval ceramic vessels or even the products of today's potters. These methods could help to answer specific questions, for example whether ancient metrical systems existed of if any workshop and/or potters can be identified, etc. The authors feel that a computer-aided classification of the shape of archaeological objects can be employed profitably in lots numerous branches of research.

Perspectives

Formally structuring pottery shapes is, of course, not an end in itself. Mere formal investigations disregarding technological and ornamental characteristics cannot be meaningful for addressing further questions, such as a critical analysis of style or chronological problems.
Future research should address the following questions:

1. Technical and methodological problems (standardization, application of further cluster-analytical and other multivariate methods, using entire profiles of vessels consisting of outer and inner contours should be analysed in order to be able to calculate things like the vessel's volume, the possible filling height of the vessel, etc.).
2. More important is the formulation of archaeological questions which can be answered by methods of automatic classification:
   * Detailed studies of wheel-made pottery from kiln-sites perhaps could help to identify the production of individual potters. This can be done with formal analyses in combination with other characteristics like fingerprints, potter's marks, technological and stylistic characteristics.
   * For economic questions its important to reconstruct the vessel function. Multivariate methods can help (cf. Stehli & Zimmermann 1980).
   * The vessel volume give important indications for the reconstruction of ancient metrological systems but also for ancient commerce, etc.

   The methods described above can also be used for the automatic classification of ancient metal (bronze) vessels having a rotational symmetry like calderons and situlae, etc. In combination with metal analyses a typology on the basis of technological and formal attributes could be pointed out.

NOTE

This paper will summarize the results of our work on computer-aided classification of the shape of ceramics (see Kampffmeyer et al. 1988, Zamperoni et al. 1988) and will give some new outlines for further research. Our studies are the outcome of a co-operation between the Technical University (TU) of Braunschweig (FRG) and the "Office for Archaeology and Informatics in Cultural Sciences" (BAIK) now at Wachenheim (FRG). These investigations formed a part of the *AR*chaeological *CO*mputer *S*ystem ARCOS which has been supported from 1982-1987 by the Volkswagen Foundation (see Kampffmeyer 1986a-c, Lübbert & Kampffmeyer 1988).

Figure 1: Dendrogram Representing the Results of a Complete-Linkage Cluster Analysis of Data Set 8, Using the Contour Code and the Unweighted Quotient Q1 (Rim Diameter/Vessel Height)

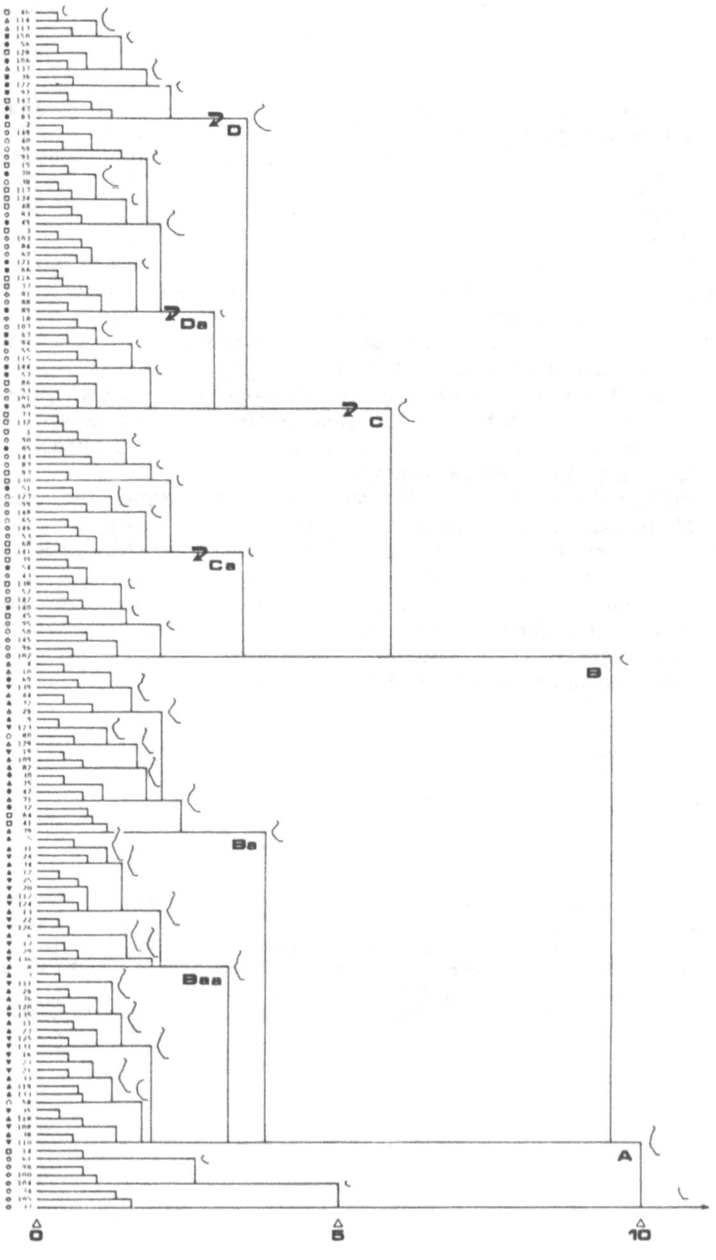

REFERENCES

D'ANDRIA, F. (ed.) 1987. "Informatica e archeologia classica. Atti del Convegno Internazionale promosso da Università di Lecce, Scuola Archeologica Italiana di Atene, Istituto per la Storia e per l'Archeologia della Magna Grecia. Lecce 12-13 Maggio 1986". *Archeologia e storia* 2. Galatina

FREEMAN, H. 1965. "A technique for the classification and recognition of geometric patterns". *Proceedings of the 3rd International Congress on Cybernetics*, Namur 1961, 348-369

LÜBBERT, U. und Kampffmeyer, U. 1988. "Forschungsprojekt 'ARCOS'. Ein Rechner- und Programmsystem für die Archäologie." *Archäologie in Deutschland* 1/1988, 36-40

KAMPFFMEYER, U. 1986a. *ARCOS-1. Eine Dokumentation zum 'Gerät zur automatischen bildhaften Erfassung der Form von Keramik'*. Karlsruhe 1986

KAMPFFMEYER, U. 1986b. "ARCOS - A video-computer-documentation system for the use in archaeology and historic sciences." *Computer Applications in Archaeology 1986*. Conference Proceedings. Birmingham, 91-147

KAMPFFMEYER, U. 1986c. "Dokumentations- und Datenbanksysteme in der Archäologie." Archäologie in Peru - Archäometrie. Ergebnisse des 1. Fachsysmposiums der Deutsch-Peruanischen Archäologischen Gesellschaft 1985 in München. *Archaeologia Peruana* 1, Stuttgart, 143-166

KAMPFFMEYER, U.; ZAMPERONI, P.; TEEGEN, W.-R. and GRACA, L. 1988. "Untersuchungen zur rechnergestützten Klassifikation der Form von Keramik." *Arbeiten zur Urgeschichte des Menschen* 11, Frankfurt

STECKNER, C. 1988. "Das SAMOS-Projekt" in: Steckner, C. (ed.). "Archäologie und neue Technologien." *Schriften des Deutschen Archäologen-Verbandes e.V.* 10. Freiburg 1988, 140-160

STEHLI, P. und ZIMMERMANN, A. 1980. "Zur Analyse neolithischer Gefäßformen". *Archaeo-Physika* 7, 147-177

ZAMPERONI, P.; TEEGEN, W.-R.; KAMPFFMEYER, U.; LAUDAN, K-H. 1988. "Nuove esperienze sulla classificazione computerizzata delle forme ceramiche, condotta sui materiali sepolcrali della necropoli di Veio, Quattro Fontanili." *Archeologia e informatica. Quaderni dei Dialoghi di Archeologia* 4, Roma, 157-170

DOCUMENTATION, AUTOMATIC MEASURING, OBJECT RETRIEVAL AND RECONSTRUCTION FOR ECONOMIC AND FUNCTIONAL RESEARCH IN ANCIENT COMMERCIAL POTTERY BY STATISTICAL ANALYSIS OF MATHEMATICAL OBJECT STRUCTURE (S A M O S)

Cornelius Steckner
Archäologisches Institut der Universität zu Köln
FRG

1. Summary

SAMOS is an empirical method of computer simulation and analysis of rotation symmetric form e.g. of pottery but also of glass, turned wood etc. The method is performed as a complete system for computer aided input, storage and graphics for research and publication. The system concerns SHAPE AS PRIMARY SOURCE OF INFORMATION AND RETRIEVAL.

The prototype is realized on a DEC VAX 750 mainframe, a portable version for mainframes, mini- and micro-computer is now written in D.A.S. ("*D*ata *A*nalysis *S*ystem" by gdp, Chilehaus, Hamburg (fig. 1)).

2. The Origin of the SAMOS System

SAMOS originates from field archaeology. It demonstrates how computer aided research can be employed in modern archaeology. On the other hand, it incorporates statistical methods frequently used in today's economic and social research. The material originally analyzed is late antique pottery from an excavation on Samos, Greece. The combined interests and experience of the authors Cornelius Steckner and Clemens Steckner (Gesellschaft für Datenanalyse und Programmierung, Hamburg) in archaeology and computer science made up the foundation of this new method. Lectures given by them at the Hamburg University on computers in historical research, emphasizing the use of image processing, encouraged them furthermore. Then, SAMOS was first presented at the 16th Meeting of the German Association of Archaeologists in May 1986 (C. Steckner and C. Steckner, SAMOS. Statistical Analysis of Mathematical Object Structure. A method for computer aided archaeological research, Bollettino d'informazioni 8 (1) 1987, p. 79-99).

3. Theoretical Background

Images, icons and other representations of objects usually are not used for retrieval. The computer only helps maintaining the archive index. Computerization thus results in nothing but an efficient electronic version of a simple card-filing cabinet. Increasing the number of elements used in the index and the degree of precision seems to increase the realism of description. With a classified description the computer has sufficient information for retrieval by comparing the descriptions. Objects are considered by this method as similar, if all their elements of description are similar.

Even the finest taxonomy will isolate the element from its context. Cutting form to smaller pieces only increases the resolution of the bit-map, not the realism. Any totality of form is different from any addition of its elements, either words or pixels. Using a computer for indexing results in sorting the substitute attributes and not the form itself. The system still is a catalogue and will not show any methodological progress.

To circumvent the theoretical and practical problems associated with using derived attributes and form measurements, the obvious solution is to process the shape of pottery directly. Thus, to work with image itself instead of coded substitutes promises progress in practice and theory. That is why our work is devoted to develop, with the totality of form at hand, a method. This method has all in sight from the same set of data: name, shape, form, type, metric value and other descriptive object information in a database.

Additionally, the mathematical description is given to the user by means of symbols, number or picture.

4. The Mathematical Description of Form

SAMOS is a method dealing with shaped form as basic information. But how can we get the mathematical description of the object? The three-dimensional pottery may be described as rotation of half the shape. The profile of pottery is equivalent to a kind of stencil or the way a vessel is shaped on the rotating potter's wheel. To get this information of form, a scale drawing of the profile is digitized. The information may be derived from the object itself or any equivalent e.g. the scientific drawing in a publication.

The information held by this two-dimensional line represents the basic information of the mathematical description of form. By this information a virtual vessel in real size is computed. This virtual body allows direct measuring and analysis of the vessel as well as its drawing printed in scale (fig. 2).

The computed body also is the basic information for classification, handling and manipulation (fig. 3). One of the most obvious advantages of SAMOS is its direct form finding and sorting facility. This module does a direct comparison of entire shape. Then, looking at a variety of shapes, it is evident that some specific forms are more or less identical. The program compares shapes just by mathematical comparison of the variety if individual shapes fit best.

By the same statistical methods fragments may be linked with complete objects for reconstruction. Also pottery may be grouped and transformed to type. By pattern recognition individual form can be compared with these types and vice versa. Equally, any metric value can be calculated for the individual as well as an average for the type. Vice versa, for study of ancient containers and economics also the volume of a filling may determine the size of the profile.

Figure 2:

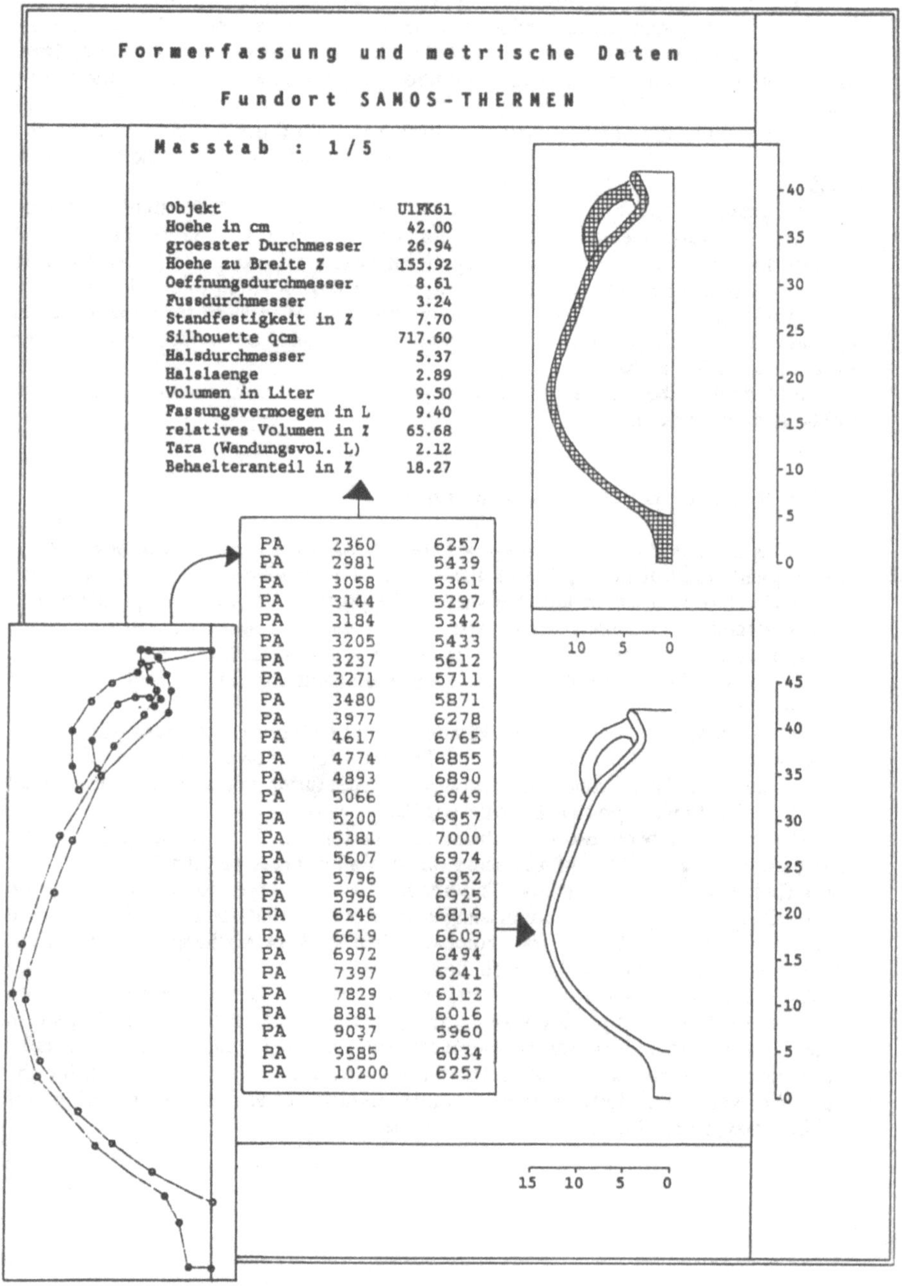
Formerfassung und metrische Daten
Fundort SAMOS-THERMEN
Masstab : 1/5
Objekt U1FK61
Hoehe in cm 42.00
groesster Durchmesser 26.94
Hoehe zu Breite % 155.92
Oeffnungsdurchmesser 8.61
Fussdurchmesser 3.24
Standfestigkeit in % 7.70
Silhouette qcm 717.60
Halsdurchmesser 5.37
Halslaenge 2.89
Volumen in Liter 9.50
Fassungsvermoegen in L 9.40
relatives Volumen in % 65.68
Tara (Wandungsvol. L) 2.12
Behaelteranteil in % 18.27
PA 2360 6257
PA 2981 5439
PA 3058 5361
PA 3144 5297
PA 3184 5342
PA 3205 5433
PA 3237 5612
PA 3271 5711
PA 3480 5871
PA 3977 6278
PA 4617 6765
PA 4774 6855
PA 4893 6890
PA 5066 6949
PA 5200 6957
PA 5381 7000
PA 5607 6974
PA 5796 6952
PA 5996 6925
PA 6246 6819
PA 6619 6609
PA 6972 6494
PA 7397 6241
PA 7829 6112
PA 8381 6016
PA 9037 5960
PA 9585 6034
PA 10200 6257
40
35
30
25
20
15
10
5
0
10 5 0
45
40
35
30
25
20
15
10
5
0
15 10 5 0

Figure 3:

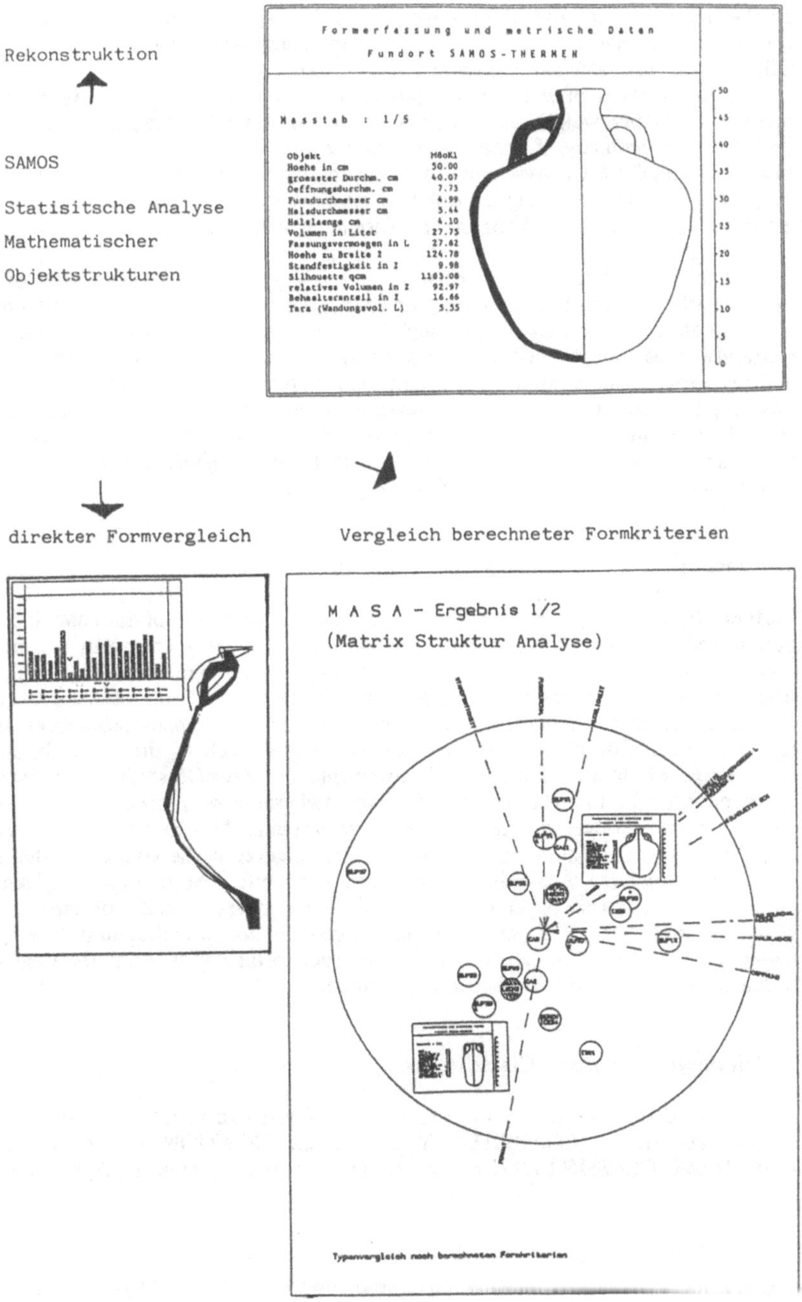
Rekonstruktion
SAMOS
Statisitsche Analyse
Mathematischer
Objektstrukturen
Formerfassung und metrische Daten
Fundort SAMOS-THERMEN
Masstab : 1/5
Objekt M8oK1
Hoehe in cm 50.00
groesster Durchm. cm 40.07
Oeffnungsdurchm. cm 7.73
Fussdurchmesser cm 4.99
Halsdurchmesser cm 5.44
Halslaenge cm 4.10
Volumen in Liter 27.75
Fassungsvermoegen in L 27.62
Hoehe zu Breite % 124.78
Standfestigkeit in % 9.98
Silhouette qcm 1163.08
relatives Volumen in % 92.97
Behaelteranteil in % 16.66
Tara (Wandungsvol. L) 5.55
50
45
40
35
30
25
20
15
10
5
0
direkter Formvergleich
Vergleich berechneter Formkriterien
M A S A - Ergebnis 1/2
(Matrix Struktur Analyse)
Typenvergleich nach berechneten Formkriterien

5. Economy

The profile of a vessel determines both, the quantity of material to form a vessel on the potter's wheel and its hollow space as a container. This way, the analysis of ancient commercial pottery is handled without the potter's wheel, without clay and kill, without steelyard, storehouse or cargo-vessel.

By the analysis of the physical properties of our virtual vessels we found the relation in empty weight and capacity of the examined containers. This relation evaluates the economy of cargo, if we assume that a light empty weight with large capacity related to a heavy container with relatively small hollow space reveals is purpose for expensive filling. In order to study this relation one normally needs an intact container to be filled for the measurement of capacity and also a steel-yard to find out gross-weight.

All this information now is computed in relation to the characteristics of form by the mathematical object structure. This way, the commercial purpose and value of a given container becomes visible - and in some respect the link of form and filling. Certainly, a ball-shaped container in general has the best relation in empty weight and net weight. But beyond the mathematical platitude of the surface of a ball now this may be studied for all shape in relation to any standard of weight and volume. As a first result the examination of ancient Roman "dipinti" has revealed that by using ancient commercial weight the capacity of a given container could be determined as well as the gross weight of a cargo.

6. Function and Classification Beyond Plain Words

Further study in shape has unveiled an interesting indicator of function linked to outline and plain words. The group 191 in Peter Mark Roget's Thesaurus of synonyms and antonyms combines the word of receptacles: amphora, ampulla, bottle, jar, decanter, ewer, cruse, carafe, crock, kit, canteen, flagon... . Some of these words do correspond to some fundamentals in shape which are ordered by proportion: bottle, jar, pot, bowl, dish, plate, tray. To a certain degree each of the words is used to name shape within a certain range of proportion. The SAMOS study of this indicator of shape brought to light that the fundamental value of proportion is based on another empiric value in shape: the relative volume. This indicator is exclusively calculated by the SAMOS-method, for it is the relation of the volume of the actual vessel to the volume of a ball with the same silhouette. The indicator is given as a percentage and unveils in combination with other measures some of the functions which link the shape of a pan to frying, the cooking-pot to boiling and cooking, the tea-pot to tea, the coffee-pot to coffee, the cruet to oil and vinegar, the flagon and bottle to wine and the scent-bottle to perfume.

7. Automatic Empirical Classification

All combined studies and statistical research in shape and measure are also devoted to the problem of CONSISTENCY IN CLASSIFICATION BY AUTOMATIC EMPIRICAL CLASSIFICATION. The study of rotation symmetric objects seems to be the best realistic field for empirical studies in the classification of three dimensional objects and database retrieval in general.

Figure 1: The *D*ata *A*nalysis *S*ystem (D.A.S.)

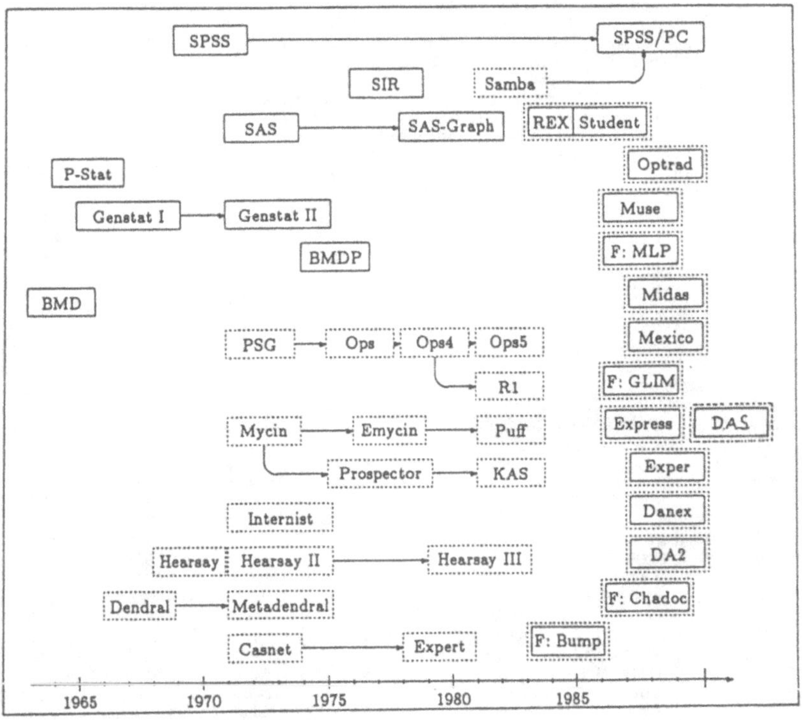

D.A.S. as *D*ata *A*nalysis *S*ystem is a relational database of the extense model introduced by E. F. Codd for large shared data banks - with a statistical programming language to select and to aggregate data. D.A.S. is like "Express" placed in the centre of the picture (a). This is to illustrate the rank of D.A.S. between statistical decision support at the top (boxes with line) and knowledge based decision suport (boxes with dotted line) at the foot. "F" stands for "foot end" as BUMP is a font end for MULTIVARIANCE. Therefore, boxes with line and dotted line and without the F mark integrated systems.

The illustration is following W. Gaul, Datenanalyse und Entscheidungsunterstützung, in: Rudolf Wille (Ed.), Klassifikation und Ordnung, Frankfurt 1989, p. 65.

Part b illustrates the D.A.S. - data analysis language for VMS, MS-DOS, OS/2 [an installation on UNIX and MVS/TSO also is available].

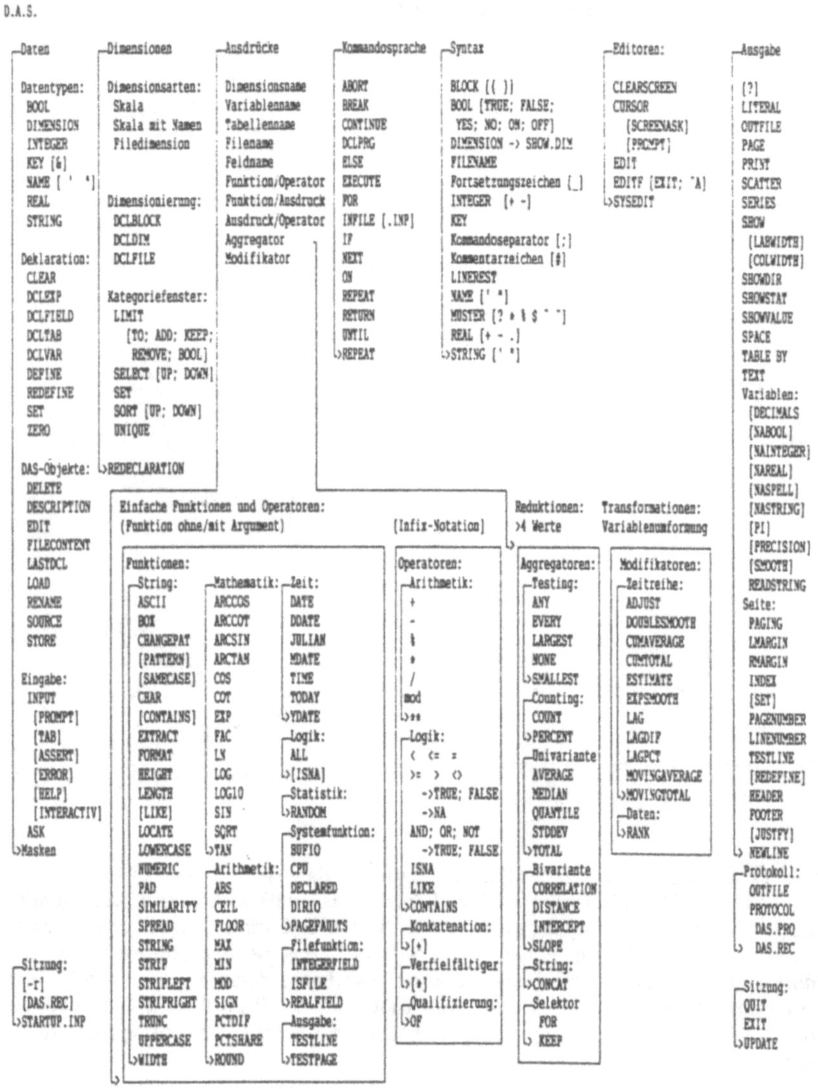

REFERENCES

KAMPFFMEYER, U.; ZAMPERONI, P.; TEEGEN, W.R. und GRACA, L. 1988. *Untersuchungen zur rechnergestützten Klassifikation der Form von Keramik*. Frankfurt, 69-72 (= Ziegert, Helmut (Hrsg.). Arbeiten zur Urgeschichte des Menschen 11)

MARTINI, W. und STECKNER, C. *Das Klostergut Samos-Stadt = SAMOS XVII* (in print)

SAMOS. Statistische Analyse Mathematischer Objekt-Strukturen. Zur computegestützten Analyse von Gebrauchskeramik der Thermengrabung Samos-Stadt, von Clemens Steckner und Cornelius Steckner vorgelegt zur 16. ordentlichen Mitgliederversammlung des Deutschen Archäologen-Verbandes in Mannheim 1986

Statistical Analysis of Mathematical Object-Structures, in: *SN/G: Report on Data Processing Projects in Art*. Pisa 1988, 389-391

STECKNER, C. 1985. Arabische Reformen und hansische Handelsnorm, in: *MISCELLANEA MEDIAEVALIA*, Vol. 17, 421-428

STECKNER, C. 1986. Die Weiterentwicklung sozial- und wirtschaftswissenschaftlicher Methoden für die computergestützte Sachkulturforschung. *dvg-Informationen* 4/95, 121-122

STECKNER, C. 1986. Rechner zeichnet und inventarisiert Keramik. *DArV Mitteilungen* 17.2, 45-47

STECKNER, C. 1986. *Klostergut und Villa Rustica. Ergebnisse der Thermengrabung Samos-Stadt*. Berichte des XI. Internationalen Kongresses für Christliche Archeologie. Lyon - Vienne - Grenoble - Genf - Aosta (in print)

STECKNER, Cl. und STECKNER, C. 1987. SAMOS: statistical analysis of mathematical object structure. A method for computer aided archaeological research. *Bollettino d'iformazioni* 8.1, 79-99

STECKNER, C. 1989. Les amphores LR 1 et LR 2 magasiné en contexte du pressoir du complexe ecclésial de Samos-Thermen, in: *Colloque sur la ceramique Byzantine. Ecole Française d'Archéologie Athen 1987*. Athens and Paris, 57-71

STECKNER, CL. und STECKNER, C. 1988. Begriffliche und empirische Objektordnung. Das SAMOS-Projekt, in: Steckner, Cornelius (Hrsg.). *Archäologie und neue Technologien*. Schriften des Deutschen Archäologen-Verbandes e.V., Freiburg, 110-139

STECKNER, C. 1988. Form and Filling, an Empirical Glance at Shape, in: *Proceedings of the 3rd symposium on ancient Greek and related pottery*. Copenhagen, 604-616

STECKNER, C. 1989. Das SAMOS-Projekt. Neue Wege der Informatikanwendung in der Archäologie. *Archäologie in Deutschland* 1, 16-21

STECKNER, C. 1989. Empirische Objektklassifikation. Begrifflich-empirische Ordnung am Beispiel rotationssymmetrischer Körper, in: Wille, Rudolf (Hrsg.). *Klassifikation und Ordnung*. Studien zur Klassifikation, Vol. 19, Frankfurt, 197-200

STECKNER, C. 1988. Empirische Objektklassifikation, Begriffsanalyse und Design, in: Lex, Wilfried (Hrsg.). *Begriffsanalyse und Künstliche Intelligenz*. Institut für Informatik, Clausthal-Zellerfeld (in print)

STECKNER, C. 1988. Suport a llarga distanzia sota Justina i Justi II., in: *Illa reunio d'arqueologia cristiana Hispanica* (in print)

STECKNER, C. 1988. SAMOS: *Dokumentation, Vermessung, Bestimmung und Rekonstruktion von Keramik. XIII.* Internationaler Kongreß für Klassische Archäologie Berlin (in print)

THE A R B O R INFORMATION SYSTEM FOR CLASSICAL ARCHAEOLOGY AND HISTORY OF ART (OR TREE STRUCTURES AS DOCUMENTS)

Michael Eisner
Gesellschaft für Mathematik und Datenverarbeitung, Darmstadt
FRG

Archaeological knowledge can be formally divided into object and method knowledge, whereby the former consists of the knowledge of the concrete nature of the individual research objects, such as buildings, sculptures or pictures (and is based on analysis), and the latter as the knowledge about how one evaluates the object knowledge with the help of interdisciplinary methods, e.g. chronology, typology, stylistics, hermeneutics, statistics or textual source critique (as in philology and history) (and leads to historical knowledge as the synthesis). Object knowledge is based on individual observation, and method knowledge on comparison. To the factual archaeological knowledge described in a paper, we have to add the reference knowledge that is the knowledge about the previous publications on the topic at hand and about the research history.

Archaeological knowledge is usually transferred over major spatial and temporal distances by means of printed publications consisting of text and illustrations. Usually a descriptive part, which is described as a "catalogue" if it covers several objects, serves for imparting (descriptive) object knowledge, while the (comparative) methodological knowledge is normally recorded in a "treatise". Mixed forms of these two also exist.

Viewed abstractly, method knowledge and the results thereof form the specific content of archaeology as a historical discipline, while object knowledge first of all presents quantitative and logistic problems. Not only that the number of objects which have been found and have more or less been well published is very large and is still increasing constantly, in addition, the acquisition of information about the objects is difficult, because the objects are scattered broardly and the publications not less so. If one tries to include the computer to archaeology as a scientific process, one will first of all assign to it the role of a carrier of object knowledge. This can only be coded textually at the beginning as it is difficult to process of pictorial (or even better spatial) object information to be based on the digitization of the nowadays conventional recording procedures which are two-dimensional in their results, such as photography and drawing, but should be based on three-dimensional techniques, such as e.g. stereophotogrammetry, holography and tomography. It is only when this stage has been reached that the computer is useful for enriching the archaeological method knowledge. The first steps in this direction are already taking place (Kampffmeyer 1986; Mazzola 1986; Kampffmeyer 1987, p. 79-104).

Normally, the textual description of an archaeological or art historical object uses a terminological inventory for differentiating the individual terminological recording levels of the objects. This terminological inventory is deduced in part from old text sources (historical authors, inscriptions), in part it has also established itself in the scientific world simply by means of long-lasting and uncontradicted use. Thus, communication can take place on its basis. It applies to a large number of objects, particularly in the archaeology of the Mediterranean region and in European art history that not only their

Figure 1: The Korallion Stele

morphological inventory - and thus the describing terminological inventory - is highly differentiated, but that they also often carry representations which, in their turn, are arranged in a more or less complex fashion. One only needs to think of medieval cathedral buildings as structures containing altars and other pictures and reliefs. In the textual description of such objects one uses a list of scientific terms which are in a hierarchical relation to one another - reflecting the division of the object into various parts. This is illustrated briefly in the Greek relief of the Korallion of the Kerameikos Cemetery in Athens (Fig. 1, acc. Conze 1922, Plate 98) which was made around or soon after the middle of the fourth century B.C. First, it has an architectonically formed frame, called a "naiskos", of lateral pilasters and a entablature with a pediment, with the entablature bearing the inscription. The relief area shows a woman sitting on a stool with her feet on a footstool. Behind her, half covered, another woman stands, further to the right two men. Behind the legs of the sitting woman one can see the head of a dog. The transformation of the pictorial representation into a division into various parts formulated in technical language yields, as one can only expect, a tree structure (Fig. 2) of the describing terms (Eisner 1984; Eisner 1985; Eisner 1988). In this context it appears most important to point out that the characteristic descriptive tree structure proves to be individually, i.e. dynamically, formed for each object. The same objects produce the same description trees, while more or less different ones produce trees which deviate from one another. As it is extremely rare for objects with complex structures to have precisely the same, the comparability plays a decisive role at the detail level in the science. It must also be maintained in the textual description of the object.

Figure 2: Tree Structure Describing the Korallion Stele

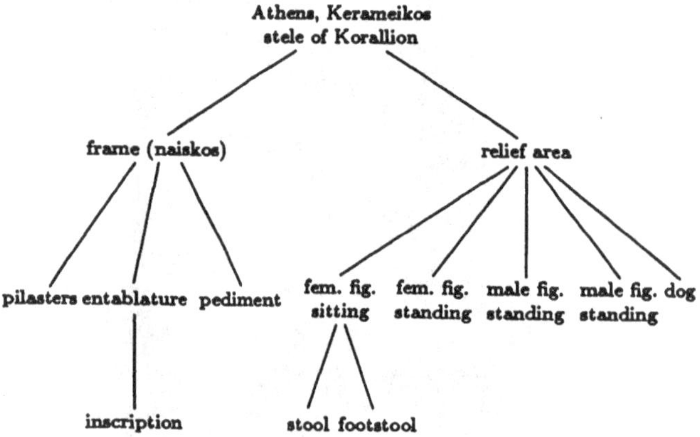

One hardly needs to mention that the classical data entry structures of computer science are invariantly depending on the relational or the hierarchical model (the later as a special case of the network model) according to the time of their definition and, therefore, cannot be used in such a manner. It is only a poor consolation in an age in which the archaeologist or art historian would like to buy a microcomputer and use it as an aid in his work - for instance for setting up a textual object knowledge bank - that by admitting pointer fields, finally everything becomes representable in every model. It is with some right that he can expect a user-friendly interface and not a solution (such as in the form of a quantity of data relations), which assumes a considerable analytical ability in computer science, which the person working primarily as a computer specialist has, but hardly the art scientist.

For the representation of hierarchically structured object descriptions, therefore, another way was selected than the conversion into firm data acquisition structures, namely a formal language appropriately called ARBOR. It consists of a text which differentiates between (later retrievable) descriptors and commentaries. The two language elements can be mixed as desired. A respective marking serves for recognizing the descriptors. An ARBOR text is divided into documents, with an individual document containing the description of a single research object. The extent of a document is unlimited and may contain as many descriptors as desired so that even complex objects can be described. If an object needs to be divided into various parts, document parts can be made accordingly. Data concerning the object as a whole, form the beginning so that this document part is described as the "header". Data on the individual parts of the object, each form a "subdocument", which is introduced by a "contextor" which expresses the degree of direct or indirect dependence from the header. The complexity of the parts is as unlimited as the document as a whole.

Figure 3: ARBOR Version of the Korallion Stele Description

*Athens, *necropolis of *Kerameikos, *stele of *Korallion, with *relief
- *frame (*naiskos)
-- one *pilaster at each side
-- *entablature
--- *inscription
-- *pediment
- relief *area
-- human *figure, *female, *sitting
--- *stool
--- *footstool
-- human *figure, *female, *standing on the left
-- human *figure, *male, *standing in the center
-- human *figure, * male, *standing on the right
-- *dog

A first test implementation requires an IBM PC or a compatible computer. Two programmes have been made. ASU (Arbor-Set-Up) and ART (Arbor-ReTrieval). ASU reads in an ASCII data file made by means of an editor with the ARBOR text which normally consists of a quantity of documents separated by empty lines. The character "*" (asterisk) presently serves as descriptor marking and the character "-" (hyphen) as contextor element (Fig. 3). If necessary, the header fills the whole length of the line, starting at the utmost left in column one. Single hyphens introduce subdocuments of the first order (that is those which depend directly on the header), two hyphens those of the second order (which do not depend directly on the header but on a subdocument of the first order) etc., while dependencies of the fourteenth order presently form the limit. ASU produces first a direct access data file of the ARBOR text which during retrieval is used for showing the documents found on the screen. In addition, a table of the individual descriptor and an internal representation of the contextor are set up (Fig. 4) which contains the serial numbers of the respective ARBOR document in the data file and a field of fourteen bytes with the description of the path of the description tree. Here, all successors dependent on the same predecessor in the tree structure or the root or document number are given a number from 1 to 255, while the field addresses "0" symbolize unoccupied or non-existent nodes. In this kind of path description, the contextor of a hierarchically subordinated descriptor can always be recognized by the fact that it contains the contextor of a hierarchically superordinate descriptor. Conversely, hierarchically superordinate contextors are contained in subordinated ones. Contextors of descriptors of the same hierarchical order are the same. The elements of the table, descriptor and contextor, are managed in the same ISAM data file.

Figure 4: Table of ARBOR Descriptors and Contextors

DESCRIPTOR	CONTEXTOR
Athens	135.0.0.0.0.0.0.0.0.0.0
necropolis	135.0.0.0.0.0.0.0.0.0.0
Kerameikos	135.0.0.0.0.0.0.0.0.0.0
stele	135.0.0.0.0.0.0.0.0.0.0
Korallion	135.0.0.0.0.0.0.0.0.0.0
relief	135.0.0.0.0.0.0.0.0.0.0
frame	135.1.0.0.0.0.0.0.0.0.0
naiskos	135.1.0.0.0.0.0.0.0.0.0
pilaster	135.1.1.0.0.0.0.0.0.0.0
entablature	135.1.2.0.0.0.0.0.0.0.0
inscription	135.1.2.1.0.0.0.0.0.0.0
pediment	135.1.3.0.0.0.0.0.0.0.0
area	135.2.0.0.0.0.0.0.0.0.0
figure	135.2.1.0.0.0.0.0.0.0.0
female	135.2.1.0.0.0.0.0.0.0.0
sitting	135.2.1.0.0.0.0.0.0.0.0
stool	135.2.1.1.0.0.0.0.0.0.0
footstool	135.2.1.2.0.0.0.0.0.0.0
figure	135.2.2.0.0.0.0.0.0.0.0
female	135.2.2.0.0.0.0.0.0.0.0
standing	135.2.2.0.0.0.0.0.0.0.0
figure	135.2.3.0.0.0.0.0.0.0.0
male	135.2.3.0.0.0.0.0.0.0.0
standing	135.2.3.0.0.0.0.0.0.0.0
figure	135.2.4.0.0.0.0.0.0.0.0
male	135.2.4.0.0.0.0.0.0.0.0
standing	135.2.4.0.0.0.0.0.0.0.0
dog	135.2.5.0.0.0.0.0.0.0.0

The retrieval programme ART permits in several steps the query for one or more (alternative) descriptors. Here, at first a primary hitlist comes into being giving the number of hits. This can then be restricted again according to eleven different search modes which permit the search - with differing weighting - in super- or subordinated contexts or in the same document part, in the header, in neighbouring contexts or possibly of their successors as well as, finally, completely independent of the hierarchical structure of the document. Documents with hits can be indicated or printed out at every retrieval stage.

Finally, I would like to point out the possibility of dealing with numerical ranges, i.e. with approximative numerical data, such as being used in measurements and very often in chronological statements in the applied disciplines mentioned at the beginning. We cannot go into this in any further detail here. The fact that archaeologists and art historians would be interested in an addition to a system which manages descriptive texts such as ARBOR for pictorial information is also only hinted at here.

REFERENCES

CONZE, A. 1922. *Die attischen Grabreliefs (1893-1922).*

EISNER, M. 1984. "Zur Rolle von Datenbanken als Instrument kunsthistorischen und archäologischen Fachwissens", in: Corti, L. (ed.). 1984. *Automatic Processing of Art History Data and Documents.* Pisa, Scuola Normale Superiore, September 24-27, 325-329

EISNER, M. 1985. "Zur Bedeutung der Datenverarbeitung als Hilfsmittel der Archäologie unter besonderer Berücksichtigung von Datenbanken." *Acta Praehistorica et Archäologica* 16/17 (1984/1985), 278-285

EISNER, M. 1988. *Zukunftsperspektiven archäologischer Wissensdarstellung auf dem Computer.* Bathron. Beiträge zur Architektur und verwandten Künsten. Für Heinrich Drerup zu seinem 80. Geburtstag, 115-120

KAMPFFMEYER, U.; RUPPRECHT, G. and WITTEYER, M. 1986. "ARCOS: Ein Computer zeichnet römische Keramik. Die Ergebnisse der Testuntersuchungen mit dem ARCOS 1 im Landesamt für Denkmalspflege, Abtg. Archäologische Denkmalspflege, in Mainz." *Mainzer Zeitschrift* 81, 191-200

KAMPFFMEYER, U. et al. 1987. *Untersuchungen zur rechnergestützten Klassifikation der Form von Keramik.*

MAZZOLA, G.; KRÖMKER, G. and HOFFMANN, R. 1986. *Rasterbild - Bildraster. Anwendungen der Graphischen Datenverarbeitung zur geometrischen Analyse eines Meisterwerkes der Renaissance: Raffaels "Schule von Athen".*

A DATA BASE ON POMPEII PAINTINGS AND FLOORS

Irene Bragantini
Istituto Universitario Orientale, Naples
Piergiorgio Gherardini
Consiglio Nazionale delle Ricerche, Rome
Franca Parise Badoni
Istituto Centrale per il Catalogo e la Documentazione, Rome
Italy

In recent years, the Istituto Centrale per il Catalogo e la Documentazione, the State Institute responsible for the cataloguing and documenting of all the documents of the Italian archaeological, historical and visual arts heritage, promoted in Pompeii a thorough photographic campaign: aim of the project was to produce an up-to-date record and detailed description of all the remains of paintings and floors preserved in situ, some of them severely threatened by two hundred years of exposure to every sort of damage.

During the years 1977-1980 approximately twenty thousand pictures were taken and catalogued: for the sake of completeness, photographs from other archives (Soprintendenza Archeologica, Napoli; Deutsches Archaeologisches Institut, Rome and Berlin, Fototeca Unione at the American Academy, Rome, Alinari and Anderson, Florence, Institut für Baugeschichte, Karlsruhe) were also included in the collection. Photographs from these archives are in fact of great historical value: most of them were executed at the time of the excavation and are invaluable if one considers the poor preservation state of a large portion of the material in situ.

With these additions, the archive amounts to about 24.000 pictures; the information and description relevant to each photograph have been recorded on a fiche covering the following entries:

1. code number (9 characters);
2. name of the house (45 characters);
3. object location, detailed to room, wall and wall-section (without space limitation);
4. material and technique (also without space limitation);
5. subject (without space limitation);
6. preservation status (45 characters, coded);
7. painting styles (16 characters, coded, according to the typology established by A. Mau, Geschichte der dekorativen Wandmalerei in Pompeji, Leipzig 1892);
8. structure of the wall partition (2 characters, coded, listing six) different schemes: antechamber/alcove; two-halved; concentric; continuous; symmetrical; paratactical);
9. medium (3 characters, coded, for floors, frescoes and stuccoes, plus 1 listing any ancient modification);
10. absolute chronology (45 characters; this entry has been used whenever possible and, mainly, when painting styles were not given);
11. bibliography (without space limitation);
12. negative number(s) (also without space limitation).

The complete set of fiches has already been published in three volumes (I. Bragantini, M. de Vos, F. Parise Badoni, V. Sampaolo, Pitture e pavimenti di Pompei, voll. I-III, Roma 1981, 1983, 1986), but of course the huge amount of data included in the volumes called for an automated treatment of these information and hence for the creation of a computerized data base. The description of the computer version is given later: we prefer to discuss first some problems and questions which can be conveniently posed with the help of a data base management system.

The urban division of Pompeii, as known in the scholarly literature, is expressed by a sequence of numbers indicating regions, insulae and house identification. This fact very conveniently provided us from the beginning with a sort of 'speaking code', to whom the room location was added. Two more numbers were included in order to uniquely identify the subject location; they refer to the position of the photographed subject in a physical and logical sequence within each room, from floor to ceiling, through N,E,S and W walls. Thus, 110040A02 means the second photograph of room (A) in house I 10, 4.

Being the subject description on a free text and the automation of the archive foreseen, a specialized dictionary was created for the sake of consistency, from the very beginning of the project. This dictionary was worked taking into account the evidence shown by ancient house decoration. It is perhaps worth noting here that the limited number of people involved in the project and its (relatively) fast accomplishment (four persons over a period of nine years, from the beginning to the publication of the last volume), should be considered as a positive factor whenever, as in our case, consistency and coherence are of greatest importance.

Also, it should be stressed that our data are concerned with an evidence limited in time and space. House decors were executed over a period spanning approximately from the II century BC to the final destruction of the town in 79 AD. Paintings and floors from Pompeii constitute therefore a kind of closed corpus and, as such, they have been divided in the past century in four styles or periods. They build up a chronological sequence in which each style covers a maximum period of three generations. To this, it must be added that domestic decor at the time was primarily a matter of craftsmanship: coherence and iteration can easily be inferred from the aforesaid, although each craftsman used every effort to avoid repetition and uniformity.

Moreover, questions regarding workshop organization as well as their relationship to the patrons are currently being raised in the scientific literature. Related to this is the problem of the possible existence of unified decorative schemes or programmatic painting in Antiquity; therefore, we felt that every way of helping these lines of inquiry by handling a huge quantity of information should be welcomed, the more so, being our evidence limited in time, space and nature of medium. Information regarding paintings and floors from an art historical as well as from a technical point of view have been stored. So, alongside with, e.g. the presence of certain figure-subjects in different periods or in different rooms, (e.g. Aphrodite and Ares on III style walls, end I c. B.C., beginning I c. A.D.):

CODICE	107190C02
UBICAZIONE	
PRECISAZ	tablino (c) parete N
MATER TEC	affresco
SOGGETTO	zoccolo nero: sfingi frontali in funzione di cariatide; zona mediana: edicola centrale con quadro (Aphrodite e Ares) in bordo nero, pannello laterale giallo con vignetta (amorino in volo) sormontato da fregio nero (natura morta con uccelli); zona superiore rossa: architetture
STATO	x
STILE	III IIB
STRUTTURA	SM
PASM	A
DATAZIONE	

BIBLIOGRAFIA	Maiuri NS 1929 pp. 362-366; Schefold W p. 36; Bastet 64

CODICE	111151402
UBICAZIONE	Casa del Primo Piano
PRECISAZ	cubicolo (14) parete E tyratto centrale
MATER TEC	affresco
SOGGETTO	zona mediana: quadro (toilette di Aphrodite alla presenza di Ares (foto prima del furto)
STATO	
STILE	III
STRUTTURA	
PASM	A
DATAZIONE	
BIBLIOGRAFIA	
NEGATIVI	AFSA8749 GFNE103041B

CODICE	5040A0701
UBICAZIONE	Casa di M. Lucretius Fronto
PRECISAZ	tablino (7) parete N
MATER TEC	affresco
SOGGETTO	zoccolo: hortus conclusus; predella: quadretti al centro, grottesche; zona mediana: edicola centrale con quadro (Aphrodite e Ares) e pannelli laterali con candelabro e quadro (paesaggio architettonico) appeso, separati da scorci architettonici con pluteo (a forma di edicola cieca); zona superiore: scenografia con quadro (natura morta con pesci) al centro, sovrastato da tripode delfico sotto compluvio, ai lati: balconi, porte con grifo acroteriale, cassette con maschere, tamburelli appesi, pergole con cratere a calice in funzione di fontana, porte semiaperte (da ricostruzione grafica)
STATO	
STILE	III IIB
STRUTTURA	SM
PASM	A
DATAZIONE	
BIBLIOGRAFIA	Curtius 1929 fig. 33; Allroggen 1974 p. 141 n. 47, 1 e; 47, 2

CODICE	702230F03
UBICAZIONE	Casa dell'Amore punito
PRECISAZ	tablino (f) parete S
MATER TEC	affresco
SOGGETTO	zona mediana: quadro centrale (tolto, Aphrodite e Ares), pannelli latyerali gialli (quello O avvampato)
STATO	n.c. +
STILE	III
STRUTTURA	
PASM	A
DATAZIONE	
BIBLIOGRAFIA	Mau W p. 430; pernice p. 413; Schefold W p. 172
NEGATIVI	79GFNN52451

CODICE	907160C08
UBICAZIONE	
PRECISAZ	cubicolo (c) parete O tratto centrale
MATER TEC	
SOGGETTO	zona mediana: quadro (+, figura maschile nuda seduta abbracciata da figura femminile, Aphrodite e Ares o Aineia e Dido ?)
STATO	n.c. +
STILE	III

STRUTTURA
PASM A
DATAZIONE
BIBLIOGRAFIA
NEGATIVI 79GFNN58730

CODICE 907160807
UBICAZIONE
PRECISAZ giardino (8) con nicchia absidale di fontana parete O, nicchia di fontana
MATER TEC mosaico, vetro
SOGGETTO mosaico policromo di vetro: fregio con Nereidi su delfini; catino con le Horai che assistono alla nascita di Aphrodite e Aphrodite in conchiglia tra Amorini; figure femminili in volo nei pennacchi; epistilio con amorini cacciatori; timpano con attributi di Aphrodite e Ares; visibili le semicolonne ornate da bende e collarini
STATO n.c. r
STILE III
STRUTTURA
PASM
DATAZIONE
BIBLIOGRAFIA Mau Bd.I 1883 pp. 150-154; IX 7, 4; Herrmann Bruckmann fig. 77; Briggs, Pompeian Decoration, London 1911;
Schefold W pp. 272, 273; Neuerburg pp. 132-133; Joly figg. 2, 27, 28, 32, I, n; Sear pp. 71-72

or the use of particular painting styles, the user will also find information on a variety of devices used by ancient craftsmen, such as 'line-slappings', i.e. impressions left by a colored rope in the damp plaster (line-slapping on I style walls, II c. B.C., beginning I c. B.C.):

CODICE 208050401
UBICAZIONE
PRECISAZ cubicolo (4), angolo SO
MATR TEC affresco
SOGGETTO zoccolo giallo; pianetto a finto marmo; zona mediana: due filari di bugne impresse con il cordoncino; pianetto, kyma reversa
STATO x
STILE I
STRUTTURA PT
PASM A
DATAZIONE
BIBLIOGRAFIA
NEGATIVI 78GFNN45685

guide-lines, preliminary sketches, compass-drawn grooves, pecked decorations or the extremely rare senopia.

Although paintings and floors constituted the principal aim of the project, other kinds of evidence have nonetheless been recorded while on the field. So, for example, the user will find information regarding the presence of various architectural elements (columns, capitals, impluvia, thresholds and so on) while, more generally, changing of plans, blocking of openings, ancient restorations and so on have also been listed and can easily be traced through the M (i.e. modifications) in entry no. 9.

As mentioned above, a computerized version of the data base has been created in 1987, in order to evaluate the huge quantity of information collected. As a result, indexes containing information of wide scholarly interest will be published soon.

Alongside with 'traditional' indexes, we felt that other fields of research, related to the history of Roman painting (and, more generally, to Roman 'Ausstattungsluxus'), could give rise to several other more specific computer based queries. To make it possible, such an activity, a user-friendly interface to the data base has been developed, so as to allow even "computer illiterates" to browse through the content of the archive, pursuing matters of their interest.

The set of procedures which make up this interface is a (single) computer program called POMPEII. We will next describe the essential features of this program, which has been made accessible for general use at the beginning of 1988 within the Archaeological Service of the ICCD in Rome.

The main purpose of a system allowing the automated treatment of the data collected in the three ICCD's volumes was, of course, to make possible a large number of comparisons, counts and context based information retrieval. A second, but not less important objective was that of data maintenance and updating.
This second aspect, though completely catered for by the system as realized, will not be covered here, being reserved to the data base administrator and hidden to the general public.

The information in the data base have been organized following in detail the fiche structure described above: this choice, though questionable from several points of view (e.g. redundancy, unstructured fields) was compelling, being the only way to completely avoid retyping of the data, which in that format were already available as a single text file on a magnetic tape (from the positive site, there is of course the one-to-one correspondence with the printed volumes).
The interface POMPEII basically allows three kinds of operations (besides the data base maintenance functions):

1. extraction of records (fiches) according to a variety of selection criteria. These criteria include search by code number fields content, list of terms collected into "glossaries", etc.;
2. compilation of "glossaries", i.e. alphabetically ordered lists including all the single words of any given field, along with their position in the data base;
3. several counts: of records belonging to selected subsets, of words used in any particular field.

The result of any function can be output either to the screen, or to the printer or a disc file for later use.

An essential feature of the program is its very easy interactive mode: all the functions are initiated through a menu-based dialog which, still leaving complete freedom, suggests answers and provides default values whenever appropriate. The system is a compiled program which runs under MS-DOS on any IBM PC compatible machine, provided, a suitable mass storage is available: to that respect, the minimum requirement is a 40 Megabytes hard disc.

It was clear from the beginning that any implementation, to be really useful to a broader scientific community, had to comply with (at least) two requirements: first, it needed a very simple and user-friendly front-end; secondly, it would have to run on hardware both, inexpensive and largely available. While the first requirement simply referred to the programming effort one was wanting, pursuing the second called for a definite environmental choice: the choice we made was the IBM PC (compatible) and MS-DOS combination, as far as the hardware was concerned and the dBASE III data base file format, as for the software. Having made that apparently too optimistic choice, the first problem to face, was the design of a suitable organization of the data, especially with respect to the dBASE III limitations in the field length and in the size of the (fixed length) records.

A preliminary statistical study of the data as published revealed that most records (and, among records, most fields) had rather small size, whereas only a minority of them was packed with a large amount of unstructured information. The above situation was, quite honestly, the less favorable to the adopted environmental constraints: just to give an idea of how bad things were, we note that had we fixed the record size to the maximum needed (i.e. that of the largest record), the total mass storage requirement, for the data base file only, would have been about 80 Megabytes. The obvious choice at this point was to split up each record in two sections, the first one large enough to hold all the information of the average size records, the second being provided for those records only whose size was above average. The problem of making the referencing mechanism, between the two sections of large records, completely unnoticed by the user was, of course, to be handled by the program.

The preliminary analysis of the fields' lengths suggested, for each field, what was to be considered a good (if not optimal) average size: in this way, it was possible to reduce the mass storage requirement to approximately 25 megabytes, a size manageable by computers of the chosen class.

Due to this accurate data organization and to a systematic recourse to auxiliary and indexing files, performances are very good, even on machines as slow as the first generation IBM ATs. Queries based on "glossaries" are given an immediate answer, while in the worst situations, i.e. in case of queries involving a complete arbitrary search on one or more unstructured fields, the waiting time can grow considerably (depending also on the hard disc accessing time). This fact, however, must not worry us, being only a minor drawback compared to other aspects, e.g. the large availability of MS-DOS based machines and the always decreasing cost of their fastest models.

MUSEUM DATABASES CONSTRUCTED USING STIPPLE

Peter Cannon-Brookes
Stipple Database Services Ltd., Culham
United Kingdom

The real world of museums is an untidy place. Not exactly chaotic, but richer perhaps in its variety than in its discipline. For the computer-illiterate museum curator venturing into the field of data management for the first time expectations are high and disappointment virtually inevitable, and much of the problem is due to the chronic inability of many computer-literates to communicate meaningfully with the outside world. Consequently, all too many of the technical requirements demanded by data processing departments and tacitly accepted in the museum environment today have been inspired by the perceived limitation of data management technology, not the intellectual requirements of the disciplines governing the collections, and remain unquestioned. Indeed, few seem to realise that most of these limitations and entrenched ways of thinking are laid down for the benefit of traditional computers, not the museums. Furthermore, the consequences of imposing retrospectively artificial uniformity can be highly undesirable. Museums are not in the business or re-writing history, or deliberately distorting data merely to adapt it to inadequate technology, but so long as the desired results are achieved, museum professionals, in company with historians and social scientists, are not particularly interested in the technology employed. Something of a crossroad has now been reached with regard to the utilisation of computerised techniques for the humanities, and whereas projects have previously tended to be technology-driven, they will in the future be increasingly application-driven.

A museum is an institution which collects on a systematic basis objects and knowledge about them, then conserves those objects and assembles that knowledge within a rational framework, and finally interprets both through publication in the widest sense. Thus, you cannot have a museum without both, objects and knowledge - the two are inseparable - and the assembly of the intellectual database of the institution is crucial to every aspect of its operations. In pursuing these objectives, the museums have in historic terms accumulated vast amounts of more or less well-organised objects and knowledge and, unless the whole raison d'être of museums is to be abandoned, they must continue to do so. It is the combination of large numbers of objects and massive resources of knowledge, interrelated on many levels, which is the identifying characteristic of the museum and the fundamental problem to be addressed when considering its automation. Computerisation is merely a means to this end.

Within the museum operation there is a wide variety of types of information required to perform a range of functions and, thus, the same pieces of information are often required, in different contexts, for the efficient discharge of those functions. The curator, the registrar, the conservator, the fund raiser and the tour organiser, all require information about people and a single person may be a donor to the curator, a collector to the registrar, a past employer of restorers to the conservator, a potential donor to the fund raiser and future traveller to the tour organiser. In order to carry out these different functions economically, without the actions of any one of the departmental specialists compromising those of the others, they all require an adequate overview of each of the relationships of that person to the institution of which they are members. In the small institution many different functions of this nature are carried out by a single official or a small group in constant oral communication, but in the larger institutions such networks of informal communications rapidly break down and have to be replaced by controlled access to the integrated information system of the institution or the institution ceases to operate effectively.

Similarly, within the curatorial operation a single person may be not only a donor of specimens and a source of information about their sources and past conservation history, but also the author of related books and articles and, for example, the pupil of certain significant scholars in the field and the teacher of others. Thus, the recognition of a relationship between two scholars may be as vital in coming to an understanding of a problem of taxonomy, as the recognition of relationship between a person and his tastes in foreign travel for the fund raiser. It is, however, self-evident that we cannot afford the manpower and other costs involved in trying to predict in advance all these information requirements and then writing programmes for each component and sub-component. Not even the proprietor of a relatively modest intellectual database or information system can afford the resources needed to write separate programmes for each object and function type. Consequently, the normal response is to limit by artificial means both, the data stored and the functions permitted so that the intellectual and other requirements of the institution are cut down to match the data management technology on offer and the budget available.

The alternative approach is to accept the multiple relationships demonstrated by the huge bodies of information which are characteristic of museums and evolve other data management strategies to meet those requirements. The natural structure of this information is that of a multi-dimensional network and the key lies in the recognition that although the network may in due course be immense, the building blocks are small and few in type. If the definitions or labelling of those entities, there is a relatively limited range of generic relationships between pairs of entities for which programmes require to be written. Stipple is a tool in which those programmes are embodied, and as such it can be applied to the organisation and utilisation of vast bodies of loosely related information. Very large networks of information can be rapidly constructed using the simple building blocks provided by the tool, with each entity and each relationship being defined, in data (cf. sticky label), as and when it is required. Stipple can handle all pieces of information with total consistency and the structure of the databases thereby created is the natural structure of the information itself and not an artificial structure dictated by the limitations of the technology being used.

Museum databases are by their very nature long-term operations and apart from entering data over a period of many years data itself have a built-in chronology. Thus, a computerised museum database is not limited to a single current set of pieces of information concerning the collections and the museum operation. Not only are there many variant pieces of information but different perceptions of whole areas of information. This means that a museum database has to be able to document the changing perceptions of its collections without prejudging qualitative issues and to maintain multiple taxonomic structures and other systems of classification for any corpus of objects. Indeed, museums are as much storehouses of knowledge as they are storehouses of objects, and local nomenclature, variant spellings, grammatical oddities and idiosyncrasies of syntax are all in their own right potentially valuable sources of information which should not be sacrificed for short term convenience.

The construction of large intellectual databases of this type, in which the subject disciplines and taxonomic structures form a key element, is only possible if the system can handle an almost infinite number of relationships between individual pieces of information and if semantic information is held in the same database as the material information. In the context of museum collections thesauri are valuable tools when sharply focused in a relatively narrow and clearly defined context, but they rapidly become unwieldy and intellectually constricting when an attempt is made to use them on a large scale. Furthermore, in the real world, no matter how consistently terms are to be used in the future, they were not in the past, and although the database of historical information constructed today may be new, its components and their contexts are not. The preservation of the integrity of data is crucial in the museum environment and although control of terminology is essential, its artificial limitation is unacceptable. Thus, a structured dictionary facility is to be preferred to an all-embracing standardised thesaurus and it is a key element in the data management strategy, lying at the core of an integrated museum database constructed using Stipple. However, implicit in such an approach is the ability to work in natural language, but this has the added advantages of both, reducing to a minimum the training required by operators to use Stipple fully and facilitating access to information stored in the museum database.

In broad terms, the museum operation can be broken down into three main functional sectors, the object-based components the prime concerns of the curatorial, conservation and collections management functions, the discipline-based or conceptual components - including semantic concerns such as standardised nomenclature and thesauri - concentrated in the library and archive as well as the curatorial departments, and finally the service components which include administration, resources management, membership development, security and interpretation. Nevertheless, all these functions draw, to differing extends, on data which appertains mainly to other functions and the practical problem for museum managers - particularly in the larger institutions - is the reconciling of the need for access to a wide range of information with its control and the often stringent requirements of data security. One cannot afford indefinitely the self-indulgence of numerous stand alone systems, each with its own operating and maintenance problems, if integrated systems with lower overall overheads and enhanced functions are available. All too often it is forgotten that the greatest cost today lies in neither hardware, nor software, but in the manpower required to operate a given system. Consequently all museum managers are their demand for greater productivity seeking to reduce their manpower requirements to a minimum. Office automation has to be a major element in the service component.

Today, museums are the threshold of a revolution, every bit as drastic as the impact of the New Technology on the production of newspapers. New systems of working are implicit in the adaption of the New Technology and the integration of an institution's data management. The luxury of fragmented approaches, with each department or unit 'doing its own thing', is over and apart from introducing comprehensive office automation at all levels and thereby hopefully achieving substantially higher efficiency in manpower utilisation, the same technology also provides the technical means by which very large scale intellectual databases can be assembled as the core of the museum's management and operating system. However, this solution can only be adopted if the security provided for information is no less rigorous than that which controls access to objects. Stipple addresses precisely these problems and of major importance to museum users is the facility that individual users and operators may add private data and relate it to records in the departmental or public domain so that, for instance, they can add to the database their own research material and other confidential information, without unauthorised users having access to that specified data. Control of access to data extends, if required, to the individual data element level, and users of the museum database can have individually tailored security profiles. Apart from encouraging curators and other specialists to use on a day-to-day basis the facilities provided and thereby, for example, preserve much knowledge which would otherwise tend to be lost, the overall scholarly productivity of the museum can be substantially improved.

Furthermore, the tailoring of security profiles allows controlled access to the museum database by researchers and the general public as well as a commensurate reduction in the manpower otherwise required by the museum to provide limited access to its information. In other words, terminals can be placed freely in the museum library and public areas, with the degree of access to information in the database depending upon the sign-on code employed. When preparing to open the museum to the public the general access sign-on code would be employed. However, this would not preclude a member of staff wishing to use that terminal subsequently signing on at it for a few minutes in order to obtain information not available to the general public, without having to return to his office, and on signing off that terminal would immediately revert to the general access standard.

Control of each and every operator's access to information in the database is only part of data security, and within the museum environment there has to be precise logging of all additions, deletions and other alterations to the database. All too often the importance of an effective audit trail and roll-back facilities have been neglected, and few micro computer/PC-based systems currently being used by museums for collections management provide effective audit facilities. In the real world mistakes are made, and from time to time dishonest persons are employed and thus, the wise museum manager needs to know not only what information is in his database but also who was responsible for entering it and when exactly that transaction took place. In an emergency that information has to be available immediately.

The compromised museum database has to incorporate security controls and internal checks and balances at least as effective as its paper-based equivalent. Many clever ideas and superficially attractive systems will remain prototypes or very limited in their application within the museum environment simply because the security of data has largely been ignored. On the other hand, rigorous control of data security down to data element level opens up the possibilities of sharing with totally disparate users the use of powerful machines which could not be justified, on economic grounds, for use by the museum alone, thereby encouraging existing commercial and industrial users of appropriate machines to provide at low cost to themselves sponsorship of local museums in the form of computer time/bureau services. Stipple runs on the IBM AS/400 (or System/48), without modification to its standard operating system, and exploits the range of features provided by this high security machine which was specifically designed for flexible but on-line operation.

Using Stipple in the museum's academic environment, complex catalogue entries etc. are readily created as well as departmental documents and letters. These can be cross-referenced to each other and to people, places, events, etc., stored in the database, and to words, phrases, concepts, etc., in the structured word list (containing some 140,000 words in the current development version) which is itself an integral part of the database. Thus, in a museum database created using Stipple, the contextual knowledge concerning the objects is accorded the same importance and facilities as the basic collections management information, whilst different perceptions of the truth are able to be stored and retrieved without distortion: the strategic aim being to control all terminology without limiting it and inhibiting access to the data. The scholar-curator is in his academic environment very familiar with variant information, and the intellectual history of the world is littered with examples of unfashionable or minority views which subsequently gain greater credence than those more favoured at the time. Conventional computerised systems are fundamentally unsuited to this world of uncertainty and changing value judgements, but the scholar-curator exploits positively the variations encountered as part of the real world of his subject discipline and all can convey valuable information. Indeed, for both, historians and students of literature, textual analysis would be a much less valuable tool if consistent spelling and syntax had always been used in the past. A museum database is thus as much concerned with words and their interrelationships as with objects per se, and by using Stipple its information system is driven by the museum's intellectual requirements rather than an adapted business or inventory control package.

A COLOR IMAGE DATABASE FOR AN ETHNOLOGY MUSEUM

A MULTI-WINDOW SYSTEM FOR ELECTRONIC CATALOGUING AND BROWSING OF ETHNOGRAPHIC SAMPLES ON THE PC

Jung-Kook Hong
IBM Research, Tokyo Research Laboratory, IBM Japan Ltd.
Sigeharu Sugita
National Museum of Ethnology, Osaka
Japan

Summary

We intended to provide facilities for storing and retrieving color and grey tone images and associated alphanumeric attribute data of ethnographic samples for the users of the National Museum of Ethnology. Our approach was as follows: 1. image retrieval by a combination of iterative relational query processing and a quick, sophisticated browsing of reduced-size-color image and attribute data in a multi-window frontend on the PC, 2. PC-to-main-frame link configuration, 3. multi-layered filing and display of compressed images, and 4. object-oriented visual man-database interface. We implemented an experimental system, incorporated these technologies, and it was judged to be convenient and powerful by the actual end-users.

1. Introduction

Requirements for image databases are found in many locations, such as offices, industries, hospitals and museums, where huge volumes of images have to be managed along with other types of data. Furthermore, image databases are used for domain-oriented applications by many types of users whose skills in computer operation and ways of use vary greatly. However, in spite of the efforts that have been put into research on the practical use of image databases (Gardrin 1984, Herot 1980, Wiederhold 1984, Young 1986), no generally accepted methods have yet been developed. In particular, computer experts have not developed a general approach to image databases for human sciences and museums, even though such an approach is expected to be very useful in promoting studies such as ethnology (Sugita 1987).

Definite solutions are needed for three research issues. The first concerns the efficient management of large-size individual image data and large-volume total image data with sufficient operational performance. The second concerns high-grade methods of image retrieval which are not found in traditional formatted database. The third is convenient and powerful man-database interaction.

In this paper we describe how we approached the three above-mentioned research issues in an application study for the National Museum of Ethnology for storing and retrieving images for the uses of the NME end-users who are researchers in the field of ethnology; furthermore, we aimed to study efficient approaches for other new applications requiring color image database. Here, we employed ideas and technology from the fields of image processing (Witten 1987, Young 1986), database systems (Gardrin 1984, Pictorial 1981, Wiederhold 1984) and programming languages (Copelan 1984, Goldberg 1981, Jarke 1985, Machintosh 1983).

2. Image Database Application and Requirements

Ethnology, or cultural anthropology, is the comparative study of the societies and cultures of the world's peoples, using ethnographic items such as masks, baskets and toys. Visual information is expected to be very useful in promoting ethnographic studies and the NME has been converting ethnographic items into 7-megabyte digitized image data files by using its own Image Input and Automatic Measuring System (Sugita 1987). The system gives color and grey-tone images from four different angles, and the actual dimensions and weight of each ethnographic item. Features of the items are described by researchers in several attributes for their research prospects. The variety and volume of the ethnographic items are increasing every year, and the volume of image data is now approaching one terabyte, which makes the retrieval difficult.

Our actual end-users are NME ethnological researchers, who use the data for their individual professional research purposes. In order to determine our technical approaches to an application-driven image database, we carefully studied and analyzed their requirements through interviews and inquiries, and built experimental systems at short intervals. The technical requirements which had to be solved for the NME's specific uses were as follows:

1. Efficient management of large-size and large-volume image data with associated alphanumeric attribute data. We had to discover not only how to store such large-scale multi-type data efficiently, but also how to access and transfer it rapidly so as to achieve a reasonable response time. A quick response is essential for any procedure involving image database manipulation.
2. Intelligent image retrieval. The user wants to retrieve images based on visually recognizable contents; sometimes the query contents are very numerous, and sometimes the user is unclear about what he or she is looking for. An unique image retrieval method should take account of three methods based on alphanumeric data, image display and real-time image understanding. "Intelligent" image retrieval and real-time image retrieval means that high grades of functionality, flexibility, professionality and responsibility are all realized during the image retrieval procedure for domain-oriented uses.
3. User friendly man-database interface for database manipulation. The user may have little computer experience, or a minimum of training, and yet may want to use the system for individual purposes in a sophisticated way. He or she always feels comfortable when personal computing environments are provided for all the procedures of image retrieval.

3. Overview of our Approach

To satisfy the above-mentioned requirements, we proposed the following technical approaches the functionality of which is embodied in an experimental system architecture (Fig. 1).

Figure 1: System Architecture

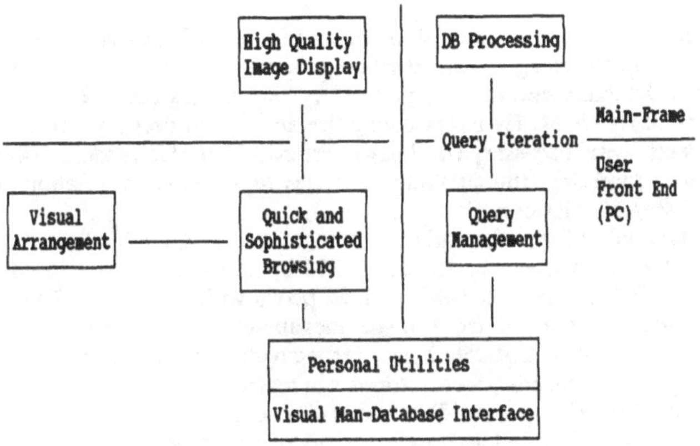

1. Image retrieval by a combination of ad hoc queries based on attribute data and quick, sophisticated color image browsing. Our image retrieval system is based on the flexible data-retrieval functions of a relational database, a sophisticated method of displaying images and a fast color-image compression/decompression method. Query conditions can be saved and revised to iterate the querying procedure. The user can filter a huge volume of image data by the initial queries based on attribute data, and can then visually select the precise images in which he or she is interested.

2. PC-main frame link system configuration. Large-scale database resources are managed for common uses under a main-frame computer, and PCs are employed as the user front-ends. Users are provided with a personal image retrieval environment while their queries and data are retrieved by interactive communication with the main-frame computer.

3. Multi-layered filing and displaying of compressed images. This technology aims to give rapid image access, transmittance and display by using conventional hardware and developing a fast image compression/decompression method. Compressed images of different sizes and color qualities are stored on writable optical disks used as archives and on magnetic disks used as fast image servers. They are displayed by a high-quality image display device for high-quality images, and by a PC, a low-end color image display device for color image browsing.

4. Object-oriented visual man-database interface. An unified user's view of the image database is provided by the "card-type mode" in which images, alphanumeric attribute data and query conditions are integrated. All the database resources are visualized in icons and manipulated with a mouse on a multi-window system.

4. System Implementation

4.1. Databases

For our experiments, we chose 2,725 ethnographic items such as masks, vessels, toys, and cutters for which image and attribute data were provided. This sample corresponds to a database size of 19 gigabytes for the images and 5.7 megabytes for the attributes of thirty items. By interviewing the actual end-users, we found that all the attribute items were necessary for image retrieval. For this reason, and because of flexible query processing, the attribute data was represented in relations on SQL DS (SQL/DS 1985), a relational database.

For multi-layered filing, the original images were quantized in color and compressed 128 by 128 pixels with 16 colors, 256 by 256 pixels with 156 colors, 512 by 512 pixels with 256 colors, and 1024 by 1024 pixels with 256 colors. The data size of the images was compressed from three megabytes for the original images to 2kbytes, 16kbytes, 64kbytes, and 250kbytes, respectively. The smallest images, which we call "Catalog Color Images", were stored on magnetic disk for quick, frequent, random access for browsing on the PC, and the others were stored on optical disk for high-quality display. Original grey-tone images of top, front, side and perspective views were also processed and compressed to 512 by 512 pixels with 16 grey levels, and stored on optical disk. Their data size was compressed from one megabyte for the original images to 32kbytes. The record numbers and data lengths of the smallest color images, and the disk numbers, sector addresses and data lengths of the others are managed, together with the attribute data, by the relational database.

4.2. System Configuration

Our experimental multi-user system configuration, which is implemented and running, is shown in Fig. 2. The hardware and software principally consist of general-purpose off-the-shelf products. The hardware consists of a main-frame computer, an IBM 5080 graphic display used as a high-quality image display device (with 256-color depth and 1024-by 1024 resolution), IBM-Japan PS/55 personal computers (with 16 color depth. and 1024-by-768 resolution) and two kinds of storage devices magnetic disks, and writable optical disks directly attached to an IBM S/370 block Multiplexer Channel.

The operating systems are VM/CMS on the main-frame computer, and PC/DOS on the PS/55 of IBM Japan PC. In the main-frame computer there are many independent VM users. The database manager communicates with the PC SQL/DS, SQL/DS manages and retrieve data while the 5080 driver and the optical disk driver access and display high-quality images stored on the optical disk. Requests to display high-quality images are sent from the PC to these drivers via database managers. Application programs on the PC provide the user with a visualized interface for the retrieval procedure. The query command manager on the PC manages all communications with the host computer.

4.3. Visual Man-Database Interface

We explored a multi-window system with icon and pop-up menus on the PC, which is uniquely designed for our actual end users. It is similar to the Macintosh window system (Macintosh 1983), and our original high-speed color image decoder is added for our unique application purpose. Multi-active overlapping window and the nesting window structure (Sakamura 1987) are also implemented to give a better human interface. Our original interface requests the users to directly react on the PC screen during the whole database retrieval procedure.

Figure 2: An Experimental System Configuration

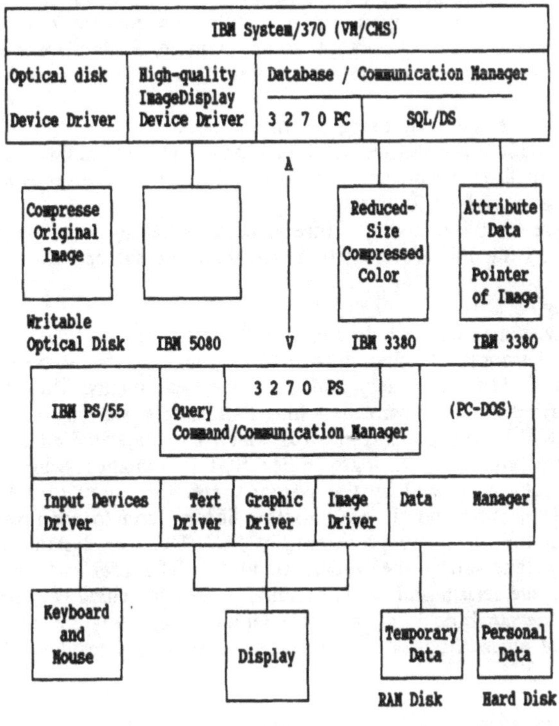

Icons are designed to be fitted with objects familiar to the actual end users in their daily work (Umesao 1969). These icons are displayed on the PC. The Icons of the "Library" and the "5080" show data retrieval processing on the attribute database, and the high-quality image display, respectively, which are managed under the main-frame computer for common uses. On the IBM5080, the user can display images in several ways. The "Set Operation" icon is a set operation function for generating a new data set from existing two data sets, called "Folder", on the PC. This function is performed within the PC environment, independently from DBMS on the host computer. The "Drawer" stores the folder which is the data set unit to be physically managed, and provides a unified user's view of the image database. "Information Card" and "Query Card" are included in each folder. On the information card, the catalog color image and attribute data are integrated to describe each object. To preserve the integrity of the original data, the user is given a field on this card for making his own note about the object. The query card contains twenty-three attribute items and fields for query input. These twenty-three attribute items were chosen on the basis of the data length which can be processed by SQL/DS for the LIKE predicate of SQL/DS.

4.4. Database Retrieval Procedure

The user starts and finishes the database retrieval procedure by choosing one of the commands contained in the pop-up menue of the drawer; these are 1. new folder generation, 2. folder erase, 3. folder copy, 4. folder naming, 5. data set browse, 6. query card open. A typical example of the database retrieval procedure is as follows:

(1) Formulate iterative query by using the query card.
(2) Browse the catalog color images, attribute data, and information cards.
(3) Display high-quality color and grey-tone images while browsing the information cards and attribute data.
(4) Select objective data sets and generate folders, either by visually arranging the data sets on the PC screen or by performing the set operations.

(1) Query Processing
To provide the user with a powerful data retrieval function, and to release the user from the difficulty and trouble of using; relational languages, a card-type facility is used instead of the SQL SELECT query and non-query statements. The conditions on character-type attributes are transformed into SQL query statements, with the predicate keyword LIKE, to retrieve any records which include specified characters. The query application program also loads other SQL commands, which are all implicitly and dynamically generated by the system. After the query card has been filled in, the folder is clicked and dragged to the library icon to send the query commands to the host for the query processing of SQL/DS. The system returns a count of all the rows that satisfy the query conditions. The user can iterate the querying step to revise the results and query conditions. The matching data set of the catalog color images, the attribute data, and the image data pointers are downloaded to the PC environment when the user is satisfied with the query results.

(2) Data Browsing
The query results downloaded from the host computer are stored in the folder on the PC, and the user then opens the folder to browse the data-set in the multi-window system of the PC. The data-sets are displayed very fast in the flexibly nested structure of our window system in order to permit the user to browse the data-sets by crossing between the three kinds of data-set. The units for browsing are each catalog color, image, each tupel of the attribute list, and each information card displayed on the current screen. Each unit is handled as an icon, to be accessed directly by a mouse and pop-up menu. Browsing the catalog color images gives the user a feeling like that he or she is turning pages of a printed commercial catalog file to find favorite goods.

The user can confirm the images in which he or she is interested looking at images with higher-quality color and resolution. The system requests the user simply to click the image and drag it to the 5080 icon on which a virtual screen of the high-quality image display is simulated. The display menu includes one color image

(1024X1024 pixels, 256 colors), four color images (512X512 pixels, 256 colors each), sixteen color images (512X512 pixels, 256 colors each), combination of a color image (512X512 pixels, 256 colors) and three grey-tone images with three different angles (512X512 pixels, 16 grey levels for each), and four grey-tone images with the same angle (512X512 pixels, 16 grey levels for each angle of top, front, and side). The user can browse on the PC the information cards and attribute data which correspond to the images displayed on the 5080.

(3) Visual Arrangement
To support the user's visual selection effectively and to supplement the power of relational languages, which is restricted to attribute-based query conditions, we provide a visual arrangement function. It is principally based on direct and interactive manipulations of icons on the current screen and movements of the data-sets in real time. Each catalog color image and each tupel of the attribute data list is handled as an icon on the current active screen and the user can change, erase and move display orders as if playing cards on a desk. He or she can separate some images from others by clicking the catalog color images displayed on the current screen and dragging them into a desired folder. At the same time, all the data on the information card is moved and stored as a new data-set. For example, a new folder with the theme "Baskets with a Tall Round Handle" can be generated using this function. The user can expect the same effects as with image retrieval based on image contents, which can never be expressed by using traditional relational languages.

5. Evaluation and Discussion

To evaluate the functions and user interface, we studied the responses from the actual end users who had used our experimental system. Their responses, and our subsequent discussions, were on the following lines:

1. The actual end users were aware of the capability and convenience of both, the experimental system and the image retrieval functions combining ad-hoc attribute query and quick browsing with visual interface.
2. They were satisfied with our system configuration of a PC-main frame link providing personal computing environment and shared large-scale database resources. The personalized utilities and data-saving functions were satisfactory for individual uses.
3. System response on the PC was satisfactory. Our experiments on the system response showed that 21% of the processing time was occupied by character-matching and creating a table; 44% by data transfer from the main-frame to the PC; 5% by display of the catalog color images on the PC; 1% by display of the attribute data on the PC; and 29% by display of high-quality images. The average display speeds were 0.3 seconds for a catalog color image, and 1.6 seconds for an information card, which were fast enough for practical use.
4. Further study is required on the following problems: (a) Improvement of the performance of PC-main frame communication. (b) Accustoming of query formulation on the PC. And (c) more intelligent image retrieval based on image contents and similarity.

ACKNOWLEDGEMENT

This paper describes some of the achievements of the joint project by the National Museum of Ethnology and IBM Japan, Ltd., entitled "Fundamental Studies of Computer Applications for Efficient Management and Use of Ethnological Information" (January 1986-March 1988). The authors are grateful to all their colleagues for their joint efforts.

REFERENCES

COPELAN, G. and MAIER, D. 1984. *Making Smalltalk a Database System.* Proc. ACM SIGMOD 316-325

GARDRIN, G. and GELENBE, E. (eds.). 1984. *New Applications of Databases.* Academic Press

GOLDBERG, A. 1981. "Introducing the Smalltalk 80 System." *Byte*, vol. 6, No. 8, 14-26

HEROT, C.F. 1980. "Spatial Management of Data." *ACM TODS*, vol. 5, No. 4, 493-513

JARKE, M. and VASSILIOU, Y. 1985. "A Framework for Choosing a Database Query Language." *ACM Computing Surveys*, vol. 17, Np. 3, 313-340

MACINTOSH, 1983. *Apple Computer, Inc.* Cupertino. CA.

MCKEOWN, D.M.Jr. 1983. *MAPS-The Organization of a Spatial Database System Using Imagery, Terrain, and Map Data.* CMU

Pictorial Information Systems. 1981. *IEFE Computer*, vol. 14, No. 11, 10-68

SAKAMURA, K. 1987. "The Design Approach of BTRON Human Interface." *The Tran. Inst. Electronics, Information and Communication Eng.*, vol. J70-D, No. 11, 2038-2046

SQL/DS System Concepts and Facilities. 1985. IBM Co., GH24-5013

SUGITA, S. and RABEN, J. (eds.). 1987. *Toward a Computer Ethnology.* Senri Ethnology Studies, National Museum of Ethnology, No. 20

UMESAO, T. 1969. *Chiteki-Seisan-no-Gijutsu.* Iwanami Co.

WIEDERHOLD, G. 1984. "Database." *IECF Computer*, vol. 17, No. 19, 247-323

WITTEN, I.H. et al. 1987. "Arithmetic Coding for Data Compression." *Communications of the ACM*, vol. 30, No. 6, 520-540

YOUNG T.Y. and FU, K.-S. (eds.). 1986. *Handbook of Pattern Recognition and Image Processing.* Academic Press

FINDING THE SIGNS: PICTURES OF MEDIEVAL LIFE

Gerhard Jaritz
Insitut für mittelalterliche Realienkunde Österreichs
Österreichische Akademie der Wissenschaften, Krems
Austria

I. Medieval Life

Studies into medieval life, particularly into the phenomena which we tend to call "daily life", have become popular on an international level during the last few years. Publishing results of research on daily life, quite a number of historians have been tempted to tell simply stories. Hard criticism against such "methods" has been expressed, particularly by German social historians (Kocka 1984; Kocka 1986). Certainly, every historian is a kind of storyteller. But if we reduce our efforts in finding, reconstructing or inventing stories of the past which often seem to be so similar to those of our present time or, on the contrary, so very much different, we might follow the wrong path.

Computer-aided historical research cannot prevent from storytelling. But it can certainly further or give new impulse to analytical and comparative studies. This is not only true for the history of periods offering serial mass-sources, but also for fields and times, for which we are more or less confronted with a rather irregular tradition of very different sources (Thaller 1987b).

The history of the daily life in the Middle Ages is no simple collection of pots, clothes or furniture. It is not only a description of work in the household or of the hardships of common people, adapted from some isolated sources. On the contrary, it is the comparative reconstruction of historical processes, of repetitive situations in the life of medieval people (Jaritz 1988a). Therefore, we cannot be satisfied with simply collecting and overtaking the message of the sources.

These sources for the history of medieval daily life are sometimes numerous and very different. They may be original objects, written documents or pictures (Kühnel 1982). They may show or contain facts (like, e.g., account-books, inventories or testaments; original objects), they may show personal opinions of certain social groups of society (like, e.g., chronicles, sermons or literary sources), they may mix fiction with reality (e.g. pictures or literary sources) (Jaritz 1984b). Their legitimate interpretation depends on their authors and recipients, on the situations and objects dealt with, etc. The "reality" of medieval daily life, therefore, can only be reconstructed by using comparative methods, by taking into account a large number of available sources and by being aware of their differences mentioned.

Successes in our efforts might be reached by the collection and interpretation of the highest possible number of sources. This certainly is a proud aim not to be realized by the next few generations of historians. Particularly concerning the history of daily life of the Middle Ages, we, though, had to start overcoming the isolated editions of sources. The necessity had been obvious to try hard to start a standardized and co-ordinated documentation, interpretation and analysis of them (Jaritz 1987; Jaritz 1988b). Moreover, the results of this work were to be easily available for every other historian. The realization of such efforts in the historical disciplines generally has certainly been started for quite a time by a number of institutions. Data collections of different kind and value were created. Some of them became useless after a short time because of various reasons. Others are used internationally by a number of historians. Some are in a status which gives rise to the hope that a broad accessibility will be guaranteed in the near future.

II. Pictures of Medieval Life

The pictorial source is an important medium for the research on the daily life of the past. Particularly for the period of the late Middle Ages, we have to emphasize that due to the "realism" of Gothic art, pictures contain much information on daily life and material culture (Vavra 1980; Vavra 1985). This statement certainly is nothing new. Numerous books on the Middle Ages, particularly those to be sold well, contain colorful illustrations trying to make the text more lively and to animate the reader in different ways. Medieval pictorial sources, though, must be more than media to illustrate the word of today's historian. They certainly also are more than an object, of which art history gets its legitimation. They are sources for the historian, opening a wide field of interpretation, of new aspects and of information beyond that contained in written sources.

Documentation and description of the contents of pictorial sources to be used by historians of daily life certainly is different from such done by curators of museums or by art historians (Corti 1984; Corti, Schmitt 1984). Certainly, all of them have to contain categories like artist, date, title, provenance, place where the object is kept, etc. The "iconographical" description, though, must be much more accurate, systematic and detailed for a field of research also being interested, to put it rather extremely, in the development and use of buttons or of bed-clothes.

Creating a data base containing information out of written sources is quite different from developing one being based on pictorial sources (Jaritz 1988b). Dealing with written sources, we more or less concentrate on the terminology of the source. We can decide if we want to do full-text analysis or if we use only certain information of the sources in a standardized way. This makes it at least feasible to keep the records as close to the primary source as possible or practicable. Using verbal descriptions of pictorial sources (or also of original objects), we never have the opportunity to deal with anything like original source-information or full-text. We are creating our own text. Nevertheless, we have to provide means to do the documentation and description as standardized as possible to guarantee another kind of closeness to the source. We have to use a terminology to be known and understood by other historians, we have to decide to what extent we will use today's language or a terminology derived from the language of medieval written sources. We have to be aware that our descriptions of the contents of the source will never be finished, but that we are working with a "living database" - to be altered, added to and extended, whenever new information is available.

At the "Institut für mittelalterliche Realienkunde Österreichs" (Institute of the History of the Medieval Material Culture of Austria) of the Austrian Academy of Arts and Sciences (Hundsbichler 1982), for about ten years now a computer-supported project has been on its way to collect and analyze medieval pictorial sources of mainly Austrian provenance with regard to their contents of information on daily life and material culture (Thaller 1980; Jaritz 1981; Vavra 1983; Jaritz 1984a). A continuously growing photo-archive of now about 20.000 b/w photos and color slides (including all detail photos) represents the basis for our investigations. In connection with other computer-supported projects, a standardized hierarchical scheme of categories was developed for the documentation and description of the pictures (see table). The descriptions are done in natural language using standardized terminology (see example).

Table: Hierarchical Description Scheme of Medieval Pictures

N (number)	N$archive nr./slide nr./negative nr.
G (object of art)	G$type/format/artist/title/provenance
D (documentation)	D$date post/date ante/place/prov./inst.
C (commentary)	C$measurement/pl.of origin/inv.nr./liter.
B (scene)	B$name/place
S (person)	S$sex/name/rank/gesture
T (part of S)	T$name/color/material/shape
A (attribute)	A$name/color/material/shape
T (part of A)	T$name/color/material/shape
U (part of T)	U$name/color/material/shape
K (dress)	K$name/color/material/shape
T (part of K)	T$name/color/material/shape
U (part of T)	U$name/color/material/shape
O (object)	O$name/color/material/shape
T (part of O)	T$name/color/material/shape
U (part of T)	U$name/color/material/shape

Possible additional categories in hierarchical relation to any A, K, O, T or U:

X (relation)	X$name/color/material/shape
Y (part of X)	Y$name/color/material/shape
Z (part of Y)	Z$name/color/material/shape

% ... = original text; # ... = verbal addition to any category.

Example of a description:

N$000448/7001249-7001252/3001534;3001537;3001538
G$PANEL PAINTING/PANEL OF THE ALBRECHTSALTAR/MASTER OF THE ALBRECHTSALTAR/BIRTH OF VIRGIN MARY/VIENNA
D$1438/1440/KLOSTERNEUBURG/LOWER AUSTRIA/STIFTSGALERIE
C$1260X1125/KLOSTERNEUBURG
B$BIRTH;BATH OF A CHILD/ROOM
S$W/MAIDSERVANT
K$VEIL/WHITE
K$GOWN/GREEN
K$BELT/BLACK
K$APRON/WHITE
S$W/ST.ANNE/WOMAN IN CHILDBED/LYING
K$VEIL/WHITE
K$SHIRT;NIGHTGOWN/WHITE
S$W;CH/VIRGIN MARY
K$NAPKIN/WHITE
O$BED
X$SHEET/WHITE
X$COUNTERPANE/RED;GOLD
Y$TEXTILE PATTERN

The data bank management system KLEIO (CLIO), developed by Manfred Thaller at the Max Planck-Institut für Geschichte in Göttingen (Thaller 1987a; Thaller 1988), became the framework in which these descriptions have been done and analyzed. Today, the data base, named REAL, is containing the documentation and the descriptions of about 5000 medieval pictorial sources (= about 200.000 lines of description), mainly of Austrian provenance. 4000 more are waiting to be described and analyzed within the next two years.

III. Signs and Patterns

Pictures contain persons, objects, situations and their connections. They have to be seen as media for the communication of humans being their producers, artists, patrons or the theological authority on one side, and their recipients of different rank, knowledge and needs on the other side. Pictures, therefore, contain signs to make this communication possible. They are based on patterns of intention (Kühnel 1980; Baxandall 1985). That way, interpretation of pictures is not only the description of their contents, but a description in connection with the mentioned communicative elements. A picture was aimed to motivate its spectators, above all the illiterates. It had to contain such signs and patterns which made this motivation possible. Particularly in religious Gothic art, these signs were elements taken out of everyday's knowledge of man, things which were very well known or even used by the recipients. They, though, did not stand for themselves, but being symbols, were to lead the spectator to the theological message. So, in theory every depicted object had its connection to the religious message. Today, we always must be conscious of that fact when investigating the picture's role as a source for the daily life of medieval society. Therefore, the main emphasis on using the REAL database is laid on finding the signs reconstructing their relevance, and interpreting the reality of those objects in daily life which were used as such signs in the pictures.

IV. Finding the Signs

Different possibilities of data retrieval are available. Finding the signs does not mean to get out certain persons, objects, situations and their connections through one single process, but to reach results through continuous communication between the historian and the contents of the data base. The starting point of most investigations is

1. the retrieval of certain described situations, persons, objects and/or their combinations. Based on such first results, one frequently will have to deal with certain groups of objects like e.g. dress, flowers or vessels. Therefore,
2. the use of already existing or newly created thesauri is adequate to answer questions concerning different groups and/or their connections. Moreover, for further interpretations,
3. the number of times in which objects or groups of them are occurring in the pictures may be relevant for investigating the importance of certain phenomena and their relation to each other. At last, only to mention one more of the main points of retrieval procedures, possibilities are available through KLEIO to
4. change the contents of the data base into codes being useable for statistical investigations, like, e.g., using SPSSx or another package for doing certain cross-tabulations, correlations, cluster-analysis, etc. (Thaller 1982).

Doing such research, we are able to find the occurrence of objects and their connections with persons, situations and other objects, their general or particular relevance, their development and change, etc. And that may become the basis for further questions in connection with original objects or the contents of written sources, with the phenomena in other regions or in other periods.

V. The Database REAL, its Usage and its Distribution

Being able to work with such a database in one institution, with the source material of this same institution, is very welcome by the people working for it. It also may be and actually is welcome to other historians working in specific fields of research, often far away from a history of daily life and material culture of the Middle Ages. Therefore, the "Institut für mittelalterliche Realienkunde Österreichs" became a kind of clearing-house for questions concerning history of daily life, particularly in connection with the interpretation of medieval pictorial sources. The database REAL is continuously updated and extended by new documents and descriptions. In the moment, it is available in a German version and in a smaller English test version.

The distribution of REAL to other historians and/or institutions is a question which must be the part of further communication and co-operation. Generally, the database has now reached a state, in which the "Institut für mittelalterliche Realienkunde Österreichs" is not only willing, but simply glad if REAL is used by many other members of the historians' community on an international level. The possibility for interested institutions to get a copy of REAL and the software necessary to use it is a step having been realized recently.

Indispensable part of REAL is the corpus of pictures stored in the photo-archive of the "Institut für mittelalterliche Realienkunde Österreichs". The distribution of them may in the moment lead to some serious problems, particularly concerning copying the whole amount of color slides - and for many interpretations one certainly needs the color slides and not only b/w photos. Only the co-operation of quite a number of institutions will make a solution possible.

VI. Aspects of Future Work

Many efforts regarding the further development of REAL will, therefore, depend on the realization of an intensified communication and co-operation with other more or less similar research-projects and interested institutions on an international level. The following main aspects and possibilities of developments in the near future may be mentioned:

1. An institutionalized exchange of "sources" with other institutions specialized on the documentation and interpretation of medieval pictures should be realized. Such an exchange of the Bildarchiv Marburg/Lahn and the "Institut für mittelalterliche Realienkunde Österreichs" is on the way to be realized.
2. Institutional agreements about the exchange and use of picture-databases and the effort to create more of them on an internationally standardized level should be reached.
3. The standardization of terminology of the descriptions should be discussed on an international level. In this field, certain efforts have been made during the last ten

years, just to mention the Getty Centre, the Dutch system Iconclass, the French "Thésaurus Iconographique", etc. (e.g., Couprie 1978; Garnier 1984).

4. The connection of picture-databases with others containing the material of written sources - particularly published ones made machine-readable through the use of the KDEM - does not seem to be unrealistic for the near future. The integration of large corpora of unpublished material like testaments, account-books, etc. is mainly hindered by the lack of personal being willing and able to put this material into the machine.
5. Internationally, quite a lot of discussions have taken place recently concerning the storage of pictorial sources on exchangeable media (optical discs, etc.). The problems with regard to analogous or digital picture storage should just be mentioned, but not further discussed here. The "Institut für mittelalterliche Realienkunde Österreichs" has decided to go the "digital way". In the next years the scanning of the pictures will be started, the necessary storage media provided and the connection between REAL and the stored pictures realized within KLEIO. Immediate image retrieval will then offer possibilities, which we today only can estimate vaguely, particularly with regard to the progress they may offer for further research, particularly with regard to pattern recognition. Similar efforts of other institutions will make this way easier for all sides concerned.
6. Plans for creating historical workstations have been discussed and presented just recently (Thaller 1987b, pp. 23-28), and also in other papers of this conference. A "History of Medieval Life" - Workstation may certainly be realized in the not too distant future. Again, international co-operative plans, designs and work will facilitate those efforts.

REFERENCES

BAXANDALL, M. 1985. *Patterns of Intention. On the Historical Explanation of Pictures.* New Haven, London, esp. 1-11

COUPRIE, L.D. 1978. "Constructing and Editing an Alphabetical Index to the Iconographic Classification with the Aid of Electronic Data - Processing." *First International Conference in Automatic Processing of Art History Data and Documents 2.* Pisa, 151-181

CORTI, L. (ed.). 1984. *Census. Computerization in the History of Arts 1.* Pisa, Los Angeles

CORTI, L. and SCHMITT, M. (eds.). 1984. *Automatic Processing of Art History Data and Documents.* papers, 2 vols., proceedings, 1. vol. Pisa, Los Angeles

GARNIER, F. 1984. *Thésaurus iconographique, système descriptif des representations.* Paris

HUNDSBICHLER, H. 1982. "Approaches to the Daily Life in the Middle Ages. Methods and Aims of the 'Institut für mittelalterliche Realienkunde Österreichs'." *Medium Aevum Quotidianum-Newsletter* 1, 19-25

JARITZ, G. 1981. "Daily Life in the Middle Ages, Iconography of Medieval Art and the Use of EDP." *Historical Social Research* 21, 43-55

JARITZ, G. 1984a. "EDV-Anwendung in der Ikonographie des Mittelalters." *Bericht über den fünfzehnten österreichischen Historikertag.* Wien, 373-384 (= Veröffentlichungen des Verbandes Österreichischer Geschichtsvereine 23)

JARITZ, G. 1984b. "Mittelalterliche Realienkunde: Quellenbefund und Quelleninterpretation." *Die Erforschung von Alltag und Sachkultur des Mittelalters. Methode - Ziel - Verwirklichung.* Wien, 33-44 (= Veröffentlichungen des Instituts für mittelalterliche Realienkunde Österreichs 6)

JARITZ, G. 1987. "Offenheit zur Öffnung? Das 'Kreuz' mit der Standardisierung", in: Hausmann, F. et al. (eds.). *Data Networks for the Historical Disciplines?* Graz, 129-134

JARITZ, G. 1988a. "Quantitative Methoden in der Alltagsgeschichte des Mittelalters", in: Botz, G. et al. (eds.). *Qualität und Quantität. Zur Praxis der Methoden der Historischen Sozialwissenschaft*. Frankfurt/Main, New York, in press (= Studien zur Historischen Sozialwissenschaft 10)

JARITZ, G. 1988b. "Towards Standards of Very Different Materials. Problems of Standardization in EDP-Supported Research on the Material Culture of the Middle Ages", in: Genet, J.-Ph. (ed.). *Standardisations et usages des bases des données historiques*. Paris, in press

KOCKA, J. 1984. "Zurück zur Erzählung? Plädoyer für historische Argumentation." *Geschichte und Gesellschaft* 10, 395-408

KOCKA, J. 1986. "Sozialgeschichte zwischen Strukturgeschichte und Erfahrungsgeschichte", in: Schieder, W.; Sellin, V. (eds.) *Sozialgeschichte in Deutschland 1*. Göttingen, 73-82

KÜHNEL, H. 1980. "Abbild und Sinnbild in der Malerei des Spätmittelalters." *Europäische Sachkultur des Mittelalter*. Wien, 83-100 (= Veröffentlichungen des Instituts für mittelalterliche Realienkunde Österreichs 4)

KÜHNEL, H. 1982. "Ziele der Erforschung der Sachkultur des Mittelalters." *Rotterdam Papers* IV, 119-130

THALLER, M. 1980. "Descriptor. Probleme der Entwicklung eines Programmsystems zur computerunterstützten Auswertung mittelalterlicher Bildquellen." *Europäische Sachkultur des Mittelalters*. Wien, 167-194 (= Veröffentlichungen des Instituts für mittelalterliche Realienkunde Österreichs 4)

THALLER, M. 1982. "Zur Formalisierbarkeit hermeneutischen Verstehens in der Historie", in: *Mentalitäten und Lebensverhältnisse. Rudolf Vierhaus zum 60. Geburtstag*. Göttingen, 441-453

THALLER, M. 1987a. "CLIO - Ein datenbankorientiertes System für die Historischen Wissenschaften: Fortschreibungsbericht." *Historical Social Research* 41, 88-92

THALLER, M. 1987b. "The Daily Life of the Middle Ages, Editions of Sources and Data Processing." *Medium Aevum Quotidianum-Newsletter* 10, 6-29

THALLER, M. 1988. *Kleio. Ein fachspezifisches Datenbanksystem für die Historischen Wissenschaften. Version 2.1.1.* Göttingen

VAVRA, E. 1980. "Kunstwerke als Quelle der Sachkulturforschung." *Europäische Sachkultur des Mittelalters*. Wien, 195-232 (= Veröffentlichungen des Instituts für mittelalterliche Realienkunde Österreichs 4)

VAVRA, E. 1983. "Möglichkeiten einer EDV-unterstützten Auswertung mittelalterlicher Bildquellen." *Beiträge zur Überlieferung und Beschreibung deutscher Texte des Mittelalters*. Göppingen, 43-55 (= Göppinger Arbeiten zur Germanistik 402)

VAVRA, E. 1985. "Mittelalterliche Kunstwerke - Illustration oder Quelle für die Sachkulturforschung." *Bericht über den sechzehnten österreichischen Historikertag in Krems/Donau*. Wien, 430-448 (= Veröffentlichungen des Verbandes Österreichischer Geschichtsvereine 25)

THE USE OF COMPUTER-AIDED DESIGN IN ART AND ARCHITECTURAL HISTORY

Ronald Stenvert
Rijksuniversiteit te Utrecht
Vakgroep Kunstgeschiedenis, Afdeling Bouwkunst
The Netherlands

The computer is one of the most overrated tools in scientific research, especially when working with non-textual data. Although it looks to be a very promising tool from the point of view of an art historian, the results are rather disappointing. At present, most of the scientific questions which arise in the field of art- and architectural history cannot yet be solved with the aid of the computer. And if so, there is a permanent danger of its creating more work than it solves.
In this paper, I would like to discuss why the marriage between art history and computer science is such an unhappy one, what its possibilities are and in which specific fields the first genuine results are to be expected.

First and foremost, we have to distinguish between two major ways of dealing with images and computers. The most widespread technique is that of translating the information from image into text, capturing the information into "ASCII-shackles", so to say. The other technique is that of trying to capture the information directly "into the computer": To everyone dealing with computer graphics, it is obvious that the latter technique is the most difficult.

The method of translating the information from the image into text is already used by several institutions to describe works of art. This is usually done on the basis of a relational database management system and sometimes extended to an information system, consisting of an user interface, several interlinked databases and a report facility. The results are not very encouraging.(1)

The reason for this lies in some fundamental art-historical problems. How do we describe a work of art? Every step in the process of describing means loss of information. The first step is our initial approach to the object. We seldom approach the object directly but use an image of it; we look at a photo of a painting or use a plan or elevation of a building. The next step involves even more loss of information: it is when we try to describe the image of the object in words and often, we come upon visual features for which no textual description yet exists. The amount of information lost can be illustrated with the saying: a picture says more than a thousand words. To prevent some of this loss, it is necessary to take some precautions.

On the other hand, scientific work consists of analyzing and classifying scientific data in order to reach a conclusion, and text is the vehicle to reach it. No object can exist without additional textual information. What is the use of analyzing objects when there are no textual data whatsoever about the maker, the representation or the origin? In order to prevent the loss of too much information and to structure the translation into text, thesauri are used. A thesaurus consists of a description control section, a classification structure and an alphabetical index.(2) At best, information systems and thesauri are connected interactively. By means of the thesaurus it is possible to control the consistency and structuring of the data more than before, but it takes a lot of effort to build an efficient one.

Using an information system, with or without a thesaurus, is one way to manage information on works of art. From a scientific point of view it is a crude one, sufficient to manage the most important information on a superficial level, but - used as a tool for in-depth analysis of visual information - it shows insuperable deficiencies. From this point of view, there are at least four major problems:

* building an information system without a clear idea of the possible retrieval structures of the entered data lacks all ground for real scientific results.
* information systems - but also thesauri - tend to create more work than they solve.
* the amount of data which is to be entered, is too demanding for an ordinary data typist, but insufficiently demanding for a scientist.
* the praised spin-off generally does not surpass simple educational purposes.

A somewhat negative conclusion from the above could be that presently, it is not possible to do the in-depth scientific research we would like to do in the field of art and architectural history with the aid of the computer. May be it is not all that bad but, due to the limitations of the present computers with respect to dealing with non-textual or graphical information, we are stuck with a mayor drawback.

Another approach is to try to delay the translation of information from the object into text as much as possible in order to prevent premature loss of information. That is where the capturing of the image "directly into the computer" comes in. Although, with this technique, there is also some loss of information, the assumption is that for specific fields of research, the use of graphical information of describing objects of art has more possibilities than we now realize.

The place of interactive video and optical disks in all this has been a very trivial one up to now. Most existing disks are controlled by the database with which they are connected. The search for an image stored on the optical disk is guided by the database. This means that every detail which could be searched for has to be translated into text, thereby reducing the use of the video disk to a set of illustrations. Without specific tools it is not yet possible to search directly the digitally stored image itself. But as a means of storage of large amounts of information, optical disks such as the WORM (Write Once Read Mostly) and the CD-ROM are the promise of the future.

There are two techniques for capturing the image "directly into" the computer; "bitmap"- and "vector"-storage. The bitmap approach consists of scanning the picture and storing it as a collection of pixels (short for picture-cells, the smallest particle of visual information). For comparison, every textual character on the computer screen normally consists of a block of 8 x 8 or 8 x 13 pixels. Scanning is also used in the "Fax-ing" of documents by telephone. This technique is also used in paint programs.

To represent an image, one uses simple geometrical figures like lines and arcs, instead of using a collection of pixels. To draw a line in this way, it is not necessary to have a string of pixels in bitmap fashion, but a starting point, an end point and a relation - line or arc - between. A digitizer is normally used to derive the essential information from the picture. Computer-Aided Design-programs (CAD) use this technique for data storage.

Without dwelling on technical details and restrictions, from an art-historical point of view, it is obvious that some works of art are better suited to one technique and some to the other. Paintings can best be approached with bit mapping techniques but drawings - and especially technical drawings - with vectorisation. For three-dimensional objects, like buildings and furniture, the technique to be used depends on the way the image is taken: photographs are better suited for bit mapping, drawings are better suited for vectorisation.

Capturing the image of an object "directly into" the computer is one thing, using the digital information thereby obtained for scientific research is another. To begin with bit mapping, it turns out that in the process of scanning we have more or less outwitted ourselves. By dividing the image into thousands of pixels, the coherence of the image is lost and it turns out to be difficult to construct algorithms. Analysis of the color and the quantity of the pixels does not pose any serious problems any more. Algorithms which can search and compare details within the picture though, are troublesome. In the fields of pattern recognition and image-processing much work has yet to be done. The growing knowledge in, for instance, medical science gave birth to some useful algorithms, like "boundary thickening" and "comparison with masks".(3)
These techniques are applied in a project for the National Museum of Ethnology in Japan.(4) For projects with less funding and smaller computers, like personal computers, there is yet a long way to go before it is possible to obtain all the appearances of Palladian windows in the work of Inigo Jones from a collection of digitized photos or all the mythological figures in the work of Rembrandt.
Although an image analysis program for paintings has been developed, the results are as yet poor.(5) A more "quick and dirty" approach is a tool for managing isolated parts of a bitmap and linking them with the accompanying textual data. Using a bitmap, it is possible to select specific parts of interest or significant details by drawing a window around them and only storing the coordinates of the window. This method, which we called "tagging and windowing", enables us to isolate as many details of a picture as needed, without copying the bitmap itself and, thus, without increasing the storage capacity significantly and connecting them with textual data. The major advantage is that we need not describe the image that extensively but can limit ourselves to a more global description. In a next step, the content of several windows of various pictures can be compared and analyzed on the level of the bitmap (fig. 1).

Figure 1: Possibilities and Problems Concerning the Use of Real Objects in Relation to the Computer

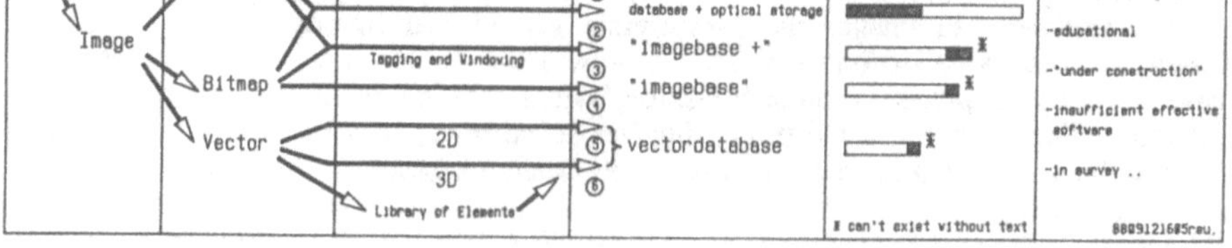

For specific scientific questions vectorisation looks to be a very useful aid, which could surpass the stage of only storage and retrieval of data and without the usual excessive amount of time needed to obtain the digital information. Although the computer cannot think, in some fields it can do things that could not be done before, because they were too timeconsuming or troublesome.

In the rest of this paper we will limit ourselves to the fields from which the above mentioned specific questions arise: architectural history and the kind of computer programs which manage vectors, Computer-Aided Design (CAD). In architectural history technical drawings are used to capture the relevant information of the object. Because of the three-dimensionality of the objects, there are specific agreements as how to represent this three-dimensional information as completely as possible into two-dimensional drawings; the orthonographic projection. From these drawings it is possible to make isometrical and axonometrical drawings(6), using not all, but a limited set of information to create a three-dimensional impression on the two-dimensional sheet of paper. Isometrical and axonometrical projections are in fact simplifications of the perspective projection with which artists have occupied themselves since the Renaissance. In architectural history, the use of perspective is often too laborious. CAD provides us with tools to work relatively easy with perspective views.(7)

But we need not go as far as that yet to see the advantages of CAD in managing architectural drawings in order to prepare them for analysis by the architectural historian. Although CAD started out to be a Computer-Aided DRAFTING program, with some adaptions it can be very useful for architectural historians. Because of its ability to use an unrestricted number of transparent layers combined with scaling facilities, it is simple to compare specific datable details with this tool, like mouldings of doors and windows. A step further is that of construction. On the basis of a plan it is sometimes possible to reconstruct the way the builders worked, or which proportional system they used. In most CAD-programs there is an option to define your own units of measurement, like for instance the historic Florentine Braccio. CAD can also facilitate the making and evaluation of alternative solutions for the reconstruction or completion of incomplete parts, without having to redraw them as often (fig. 2). The ability of CAD to use a standard parts library enables us to store much used historical details.
Although the just mentioned uses are only a little more than finger-exercises, it helps to reduce the vast amount of actual drawing needed to analyze architectural historical questions.

CAD can not only be used in two-dimensional drawings but also in the creation of three-dimensional drawings. And that is where the more interesting architectural questions come in.
The simplest way to use CAD in three-dimensions is to extrude parts of two-dimensional drawings and combine them in a three-dimensional model. A characteristic of CAD-systems is that they always use wire frame drawings to represent the three-dimensional model, which results in an image with the lines we usually see, but also with the lines which are usually hidden. To retain some speed in the complicated handling of three-dimensional images CAD systems have to use these wire-frames. It is possible to establish all kinds of views, perspective or isometrical on the three-dimensional model. A view can be taken from every angle. When the best views are established, a CAD algorithm can then hide the lines. This can be done by actual hiding the line or by filling the visual surfaces. These hidden lines and surface modelling algorithms require much arithmetic and cannot be done without a mathematical co-processor.(8) (fig. 3)
A more difficult approach is to combine two-dimensional information from a plan and

Figure 2: Reconstruction of a Pointed-Arch Window (Adamanshuis Zutphen, 1465)

Adamanshuis te Zutphen, rsu.

an elevation into one three-dimensional model. Extrusion alone is not sufficient, but it has to be combined with translation. With the aid of a strict working plan containing predefined sequences of steps, it is more efficiently possible to construct the required three-dimensional models.

The "quick and dirty" shortcut is to construct a three-dimensional image directly, consisting of simple geometrical forms like boxes, spheres, cylinders and cones on the basis of the measurements taken from the two-dimensional drawings. In this way, it is relatively easy to conduct studies of volume interacting with each other. Historical town planning can profit from this.

Volume studies - but better the combination of information from plans and elevations in a three-dimensional model - can help to reconstruct buildings from the past. With the aid of additional information obtained from research into the construction of a building itself, it is possible to reconstruct previous stages and visualize it in every way. The successive stages in the alterations of a building in past centuries can, thus, be represented. Needles to say that in this way alternatives can be evaluated and deficiencies in the actual data can be filled in.

Managing two- and three-dimensional information derived from drawings, without loosing the additional textual information in the process, can turn out to be a useful tool. More accurate analysis can be done without the burden of laborious drawing work. In the near future, it may even be possible to use the above described tool to tackle more fundamental art and architectural historical problems.
The problems of how the image we have of the past came into being, what paradigms scientists use to describe it and which historical constructions have been made, are genuine. May be CAD could lead the way to a better understanding of the historical process, with methodological notions like the evolution of shape and morphology, type and typology and even the intended meaning of the building, the iconology.(9) Famous theoreticians like Riegl, Wölfflin, Panofsky and Gombrich have tackled this problem, where for instance, "Zeitgeist" versus "Trail and Error" are evaluated.(10) Computer- and especially CAD-tools may be able to facilitate and refine the analysis of scientists.
At the University of Utrecht a survey is in progress for the Government Service for the Preservation of Monuments and Historic Buildings (Rijksdienst voor de Monumentenzorg) to investigate the use of CAD as a tool for capturing architectural history and reconstructing old buildings.

Figure 3: Perspective of a Roofconstruction, in VersaCAD, without Floors and Windbraces. ("De Drie Haringen", Brink 55 Deventer (1575))

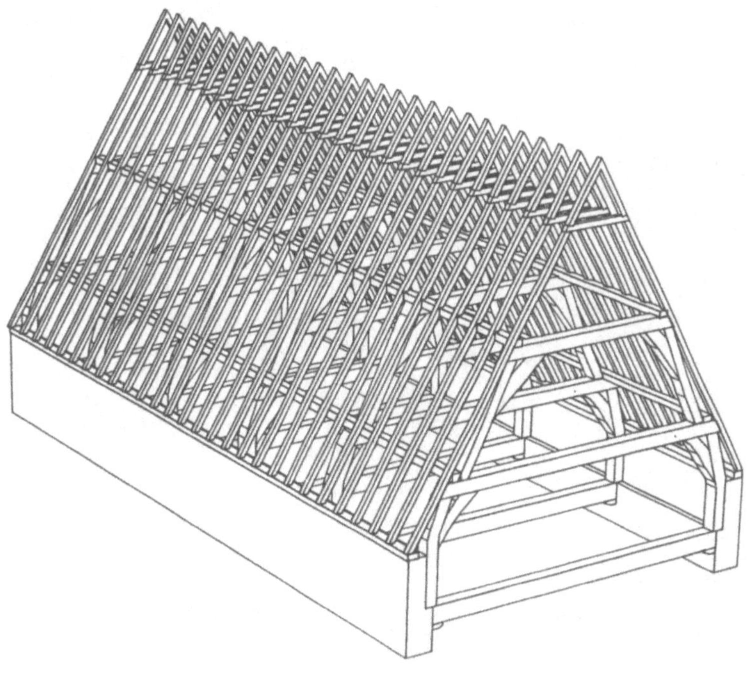

NOTES

1. SARASAN, Leonore. 1981. "Why Museum Computer Projects Fail". *Museum News*, 40-49
2. British Standards Institution, Guidelines for the establishment and development of monolingual thesauri, s.l. 1979.
3. Some techniques are described in: BACKER, E. et al. (eds.). 1986. First Quinquennial Review 1981-1986: Dutch Society for Pattern Recognition & Image Processing, Pijnacker. See also: PAVLIDIS, T. 1977. Structural Pattern Recognition. New York/Berlin
4. See elsewhere in these proceedings.
5. VAUGHAN, William. 1987. "The Automated Connoisseur: Image Analysis and Art History", in: Denley, Peter & Deian Hopkin (eds.). *History and Computing*. Manchester, 215-221
6. WRIGHT, Lawrence. 1983. Perspective in Perspective. London, e.a.
7. ROONEY, Joe; STEADMAN, Philip. 1987. *Principles of Computer-Aided Design*. London
   MITCHELL, William J.; LIGGETT, R.S. & KVAN, T. 1987. *The Art of Computer Graphics Programming: A Structured Introduction for Architects and Designers*. New York
8. The calculation of this image took a couple of hours on an AT-personal computer.
9. STEADMAN, Philip. 1979. *The Evolution of Designs*. Cambridge, e.a.
   STINY, G. & GIPS, J. 1978. "An Evaluation of Palladian Plans". *Environment and Planning* B, 5(1978), 199-206
10. BELTING, Hans et al. (eds.). 1988. *Kunstgeschichte: Eine Einführung*. Berlin
    RIEGL, Alois. 1923. *Stilfragen*. Berlin
    WÖLFFLIN, Heinrich. 1915. *Kunstgeschichtliche Grundbegriffe*. München
    PANOFSKY, Erwin. 1939. *Studies in Iconology*. Oxford
    GOMBRICH, E.H. 1960. *Art and Illusion*. London

COMPUTER AND MUSICOLOGY
AUTOMATIC TRANSCRIPTION OF 16TH CENTURY MUSIC: GERMAN LUTE TABLATURES

Hélène Charnassé
ERATTO/CNRS, Ivry-sur-Seine
France
Bernard Stepien
Computer Science Dpt., University of Ottawa
Canada

Editorial Problems for Ancient Music

The growing interest for ancient music and the increasing amount of pieces that have been brought to light in the last decades show the tremendous research work done by musicologists. But we often forget that ancient musical texts are not instantly accessible to the interprets, singers or instrumentalists.

Figure 1: German Organ Tablature. Sebastian Virdung, Musica getuscht, Bâle, 1511, f° Lv°

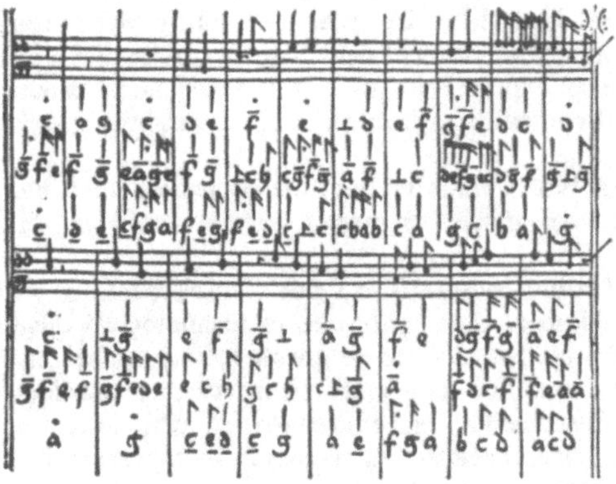

Musical notation has evolved from century to century to the convenient system we are familiar with that is very precise and very legible. Similarly, the presentation of musical pieces has also evolved due to an evolution in musical practices.

The ancient repertoire requires consequently a long and dedicated restitution work. The musicologist has to perform at least the following tasks:

1. Decode the original notation.
2. Determine for each element of this notation the corresponding modern notation.
3. Analyse the relationships between the original elements to find the musical structure of the notated piece.
4. Create a score notated on one or two staves. In accordance to modern standards, the obtained score should present a visual picture of the piece to perform.
5. Produce a camera-ready version for the printer.

There is no way to avoid the five above described steps in converting ancient music into modern notation. Currently, musicologists can only do this manually using pencils and erasers. A limited amount of pieces are published because the productivity of the manual system is extremely slow. The human and financial investment involved in this process is a major barrier to the knowledge of ancient music. Thousands of pieces are waiting for the researcher to take them out of the dark.

Towards an Automatic Transcription

Looking at the five accomplished tasks we discover that only the first one - the decoding of a given notation - requires actually (1988) the presence of a musicologist. The remaining ones: the correspondences with modern notation, the analysis of the musical text and the publishing of a score, can be automated.

Music has a natural advantage for automation. It is a language composed of sounds that are physical elements, measurable. A sound has two essential attributes: height and duration. Both can be represented numerically. The numbers representing notes can be used to compute relationships between them. The relationships are subjected to strict rules that are respected by authors. Those rules are well known by musicologists. They depend on the area, the country, the writing style, and more or less on the author. Those musical rules can be easily implemented in "rule based" artificial intelligence expert systems. For the last step, producing a camera-ready version, the actual computer assisted printing of music is a well developed aspect of micro computing.

As far back as 1965 I came up with the conclusion that due to the mathematical and logical nature of music, computer science could be of great help for the transcription.

At the time, I could consider two types of transcriptions. With vocal music, there was a serious problem of data entry due to technological developments. Each note has multiple attributes that have to be encoded, such as height, duration, orientation of stem, alteration, etc. The data entry effort was too considerable to benefit from any automation. Instrumental repertoire, written with letters and numbers was far more easy to capture, because each sound is represented by an alphanumeric character. This notation is called tablature.

A tablature is an instrumental oriented notation that indicates a finger position on the instrument itself. Since the middle ages, but essentially from the 15th to the 17th century, most of instrumental music was written in tablature. Hundreds of collections for organ, lute, guitar, harp, cithern are consequently inaccessible for modern performers. Computer science would be of great help.

Data Processing of German Lute Tablatures

The ERATTO team, founded in 1973, is devoting a part of its time to the development of a piece of software that would automate the transcription of tablatures. The first target was the transcription of German lute tablatures. It is a peculiar notation used in German countries from ca. 1475 to the end of the 16th century for printed books, and somewhat later for manuscripts. The musical text is presented using letters, numbers and essential signs of vocal music notation (duration, bar signs, etc.). Those characters represent finger positions on the neck of the lute, as illustrated in a picture at the beginning of the book. Each character corresponds to each string and fret intersection.

Figures 2 and 3: German Lute Tablature. Hans Gerle, Capitan, Tablatur auff die Laudten, Nuremberg, 1533, f° XXIIII v°. 2) Notation. 3) Set of Characters

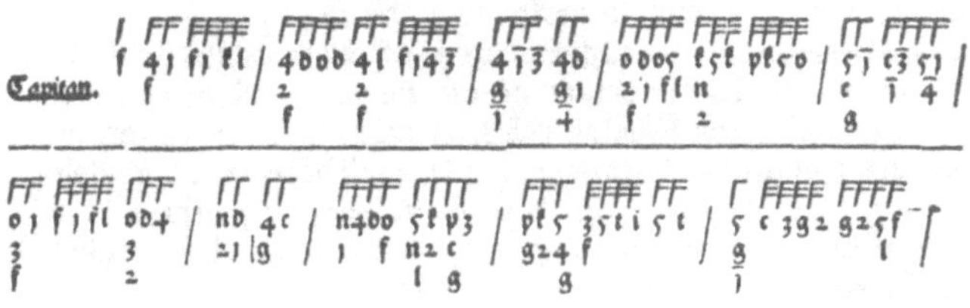

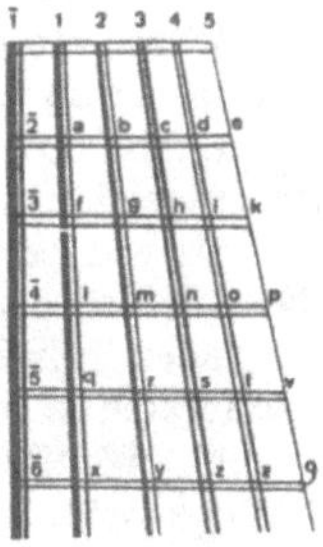

The surprising fact is that the layout of characters does not show the musical structure of the piece. With this notation, the musician presses the finger in the right places, and once hearing the sound it produces, he can figure out how the notes fit in the music he is interpreting.

Those are the two aspects of a transcription:

1. Translating a character into a note.
2. Integrate that note in its musical environment.

In a first step (1975-1979), we addressed only the two first topics:

* Decode the original notation.
* Determine for each element the corresponding modern notation

and we considered only the explicit elements of the tablature for which there was no doubt:

* Characters and musical signs.
* Height of a note corresponding to a character.
* Playing indications: characters placed on each other to indicate chords.
* Obvious rhythmic indications.

We then obtained a "raw" transcription that was incomplete, but that showed transcription could indeed be automated.

Figure 4: Hans Gerle, Capitan, Tablatur auff die Laudten, Nuremberg, 1533. Edition ERRATO/CNRS, Paris, 1975, II, p. 34. Computer Implementation: Henri Ducasse

Despite its imperfection, this transcription enabled us to grasp the underlying structure of the music that could not be seen in the tablature.

A ten years break in the work has enabled the musicologist to analyse the original notation to come up with algorithms to restructure the music.

In this second step, we addressed the third topic: analysis of relationships between the original elements to find the musical structure of the instrumental piece. This analysis was performed to establish reconstructing rules. A great help was given by the vocal models used by the authors of instrumental pieces. Those vocal models are generally well known today - as they were in those days. They are written in a counterpointic style and use mainly three or four superimposed melodic lines (called voices), all following strict musical stylistic rules.

The systematic comparison of the raw transcription with the vocal model enabled us to detect implicit elements in the tablature considered as constraining by the 16th century players. Most of the time, they are illogical ways of interpretation that are rejected by the lutenist, to leave only the logical solution as acceptable in accordance with the usage of the time or the knowledge of the vocal model. The internal logic of the notation has been progressively uncovered and also the oral transmission aspect of the playing has been confirmed.

Towards a Generic Tablature Software

The arrival of the micro-computer age and a cooperation with Bernard Stepien of the Computer Science Dpt. of the University of Ottawa enabled us to restart this project in 1986. Since then, we are developing a generic tablature processing software that is currently applied to German lute tablatures. The musicologist is now able to capture the tablature using a full screen method, exactly as with a word processor. It is a tablature processor. This software converts back and forth the external notation to a handy internal representation. This is used by the reconstructing module that produces a modern representation of the music that can be displayed and scanned on screen.

Presently, we are working on a rather complex tablature by Hans Newsidler. In this example, the author presents an instrumental version of a three voices song.

Figures 5 and 6: Hans Newsidler, Harraytre amours, Der ander Theil des Lautenbuchs, Nuremberg, 1536, f° Biij v°. 5) Tablature. 6) Melodic Lines

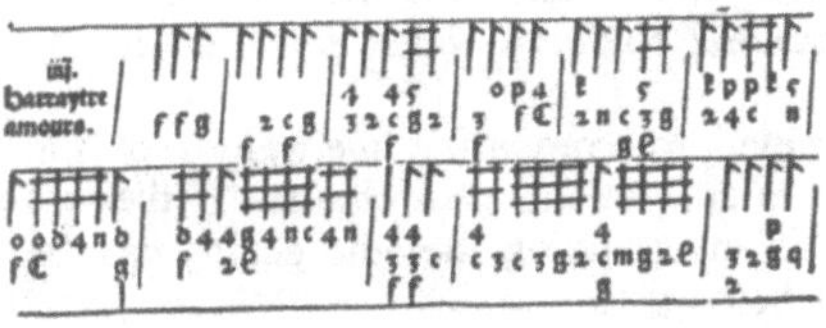

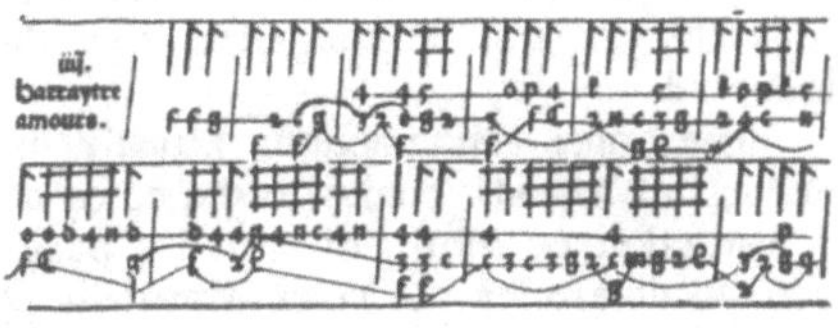

The tablature uses three virtual horizontal lines to show the three voices structure of the music. One line should correspond to one voice. However, when the space on the first or the second virtual line is free, the author frequently pushes up characters that normally belong to a lower line. As a result, characters belonging to different melodic lines are mixed up. Consequently, the player cannot directly discover the structure of the piece in the tablature.

The Restructuring Module: An Application of Artificial Intelligence

The musical structure has to be computed entirely. It is the most complex aspect of the transcription process. We have to find the three melodic lines and their correct position. This is a task perfectly fitted to the application of Artificial Intelligence. All the computations are performed on the internal representation that uses a continuous numeric system. This system is independent from the tablature notation, due to the lack of stability in that notation system.

Internal values of notes are compared and rules are applied to construct melodic lines using a chaining process. Each note is compared to the last note of a melodic chain to decide whether it belongs to that peculiar chain or not.

Figure 7: Construction of a Melodic Chain. Hans Newsidler, Ein seer guter organistischer Preambel, Der ander Theil des Lautenbuchs, Nuremberg, 1536, f° Aiijv°. Computer Implementation: Bernard Stepien

Various interesting tricks were empirically discovered. This includes the scanning direction and the relative importance of indicators. Testing on a corpus of one hundred and seventy pieces enabled us to calibrate the model allowing for a good degree of accuracy.

Once melodic chains are formed, we obtain "voices" and now the exact duration of each note can be computed from the minimal rhythmic value provided in the tablature.

The voice assignment is actually determined by comparing the values of the endings of melodic chains to the notes of saturated verticals (full chords). If there is a disruption of continuity, relative positions of overlapping melodic chains can be used to determine the voice a melodic chain belongs to.

Figure 8: Construction of Melodic Chains and Calcul of Durations. Hans Newsidler, Mater Patris, Der ander Theil des Lautenbuchs, Nuremberg, 1536, f° Biiij v°. Computer Implementation: Bernard Stepien

Results are constantly validated using the vocal models, and this comparison process is used to modify the computer rules we are implementing. To facilitate the exploration of the syntactic rules, we give the musicologist the choice of rules he wants to apply through a user friendly menu. He also can determine his own threshold values and one minute later he can see on the screen if he has made the right assumption.

Currently, the results obtained look quite good in the case of strict counterpointic style. The analysis of bad results shows that two distinctive types of algorithms have to be applied in a piece:

1. The counterpoint algorithm, based on continuities of melodic lines chains.
2. The "in imitatio" themes algorithm.

Themes are based on peculiar melodic lines that cross the natural boundaries of voices and that repeat the different voices. There is no continuity to be found here but similarities, because the melodic lines cross each other. This repetition factor is a key to the problem. One just has to detect repetition of melodic lines, separate them and assign them to voices.

We achieved the goal in two steps. Many pieces written during the 16th century start with a melodic theme that is imitated two, three or more times. For songs, this melodic theme was usually well known by all musicians, so by lutenists.

In a first step, we fed the model of the theme to the computer, and it would find the imitations and disentangle the phrases. However, themes appear also numerously elsewhere in a piece. Thus, finding the theme process was not possible and distracted from the original goal of total automation.

In June 1988 we completed an algorithm that detects automatically the presence of a repetitive theme. This process makes use of cognitive science and has been implemented in TURBO PROLOG. Presently, the themes have to be identical both in note and rhythm. More research is required to study variations and also integration of themes in a counterpointic environment.

Results and Perspectives

Our software is performing satisfactorily for strict counterpoint; current research is devoted to integrate the thematic sequences. More efforts will have to be devoted to the generalisation of applications to other musical or tablature styles, such as French and Italian tablatures that use more vertical writing style than German lute tablatures of the 16th century. This will require about two to three more years of work, considering my various tasks in the team of research and the very restricted availability of the computer scientist (few weeks in a year).

The musicologist will then be able to use an operational tool that will look like an enhanced word processor with intelligent capabilities. After computing the tablature on full screen he will be able to see the original tablature along with the transcription using the method of his choice and also the presentation of his choice. Flexibility due to the variety of tablature systems and modern notation presentation systems is the key preoccupation of our team.

All the intermediary steps required in a traditional edition will be unnecessary. The main benefits of this software are:

* Considerable time savings.
* Increase in scientific consistency.
* User friendliness of the process.

This achievement proves the benefits of computer science to musicology and paves the road to the development of new methods to uncover ancient musical texts, whether instrumental or vocal. This would revolutionize the methodology in musicology within the next ten years.

Figure 9: Results Obtained (1987)

REFERENCES

CHARNASSÉ, H. 1981. "La transcription automatique des tablatures, un aspect de la recherche méthodologique." *Report of the twelfth Congress of the International Musicological Society*. Kassel, 330-336

CHARNASSÉ, H. 1983. "Musicologie et informatique. L'analyse d'une notation instrumentale: la tablature de luth allemende." *Report of the Congrès international Informatique et Sciences Humaines*. LASLA. Liège, 177-194

CHARNASSÉ, H. 1988. "Informatique et Musique." *Report of the musicological round table. International Computer Music Conference*. IRCAM, 1984. Ivry-sur-Seine, ELMERATTO, 145 pp.

CHARNASSÉ, H. and DUBON, H. 1986. "L'emploi de l'informatique pour la transcription de l'édition des textes musicaux." *Report of congress Méthodes quantitatives et informatiques dans l'étude des textes*. Nice, 187-194

CHARNASSÉ, H. and DUCASSE, H. 1975-1978. "Hans Gerle, Tabulatur auff die Laudten, Nuremberg, 1533." *Automatic transcription by the ERATTO/CNRS team. Musicological studies by Hélène Charnassé and Raymond Meylan. Computer implementation: Henri Ducasse*. Paris, French Society of Musicology. I, Préludes, 47 pp. II, Pièces allemandes, 83 pp. III, Chansons francaises et trois, 47 pp. IV, Psaumes et motetes latins, 91 pp. V, Psaumes et motets latins, 39 pp.

CHARNASSÉ, H. and DUCASSE, H. 1978. "Hans Gerle, Musica und Tabulatur, Nuremberg, 1552." *Automatic transcription by ERATTO/CNRS team. Part 1: Musicologist: Hélène Charnassé and Raymond Meylan; part 2,3,4: Hélène Charnassé, Computer implementation: Henri Ducasse*. Irvy, ELMERATTO. 1, Préludes, 61 pp. 2, Préludes, 73 pp., Danses, 59 pp. 4, Danses, 57 pp.

CHARNASSÉ, H. and STEPIEN, B. 1986. "Automatic Transcription of Sixteenth Century Musical Notations." *Computers and the Humanities* 20, 179-190

STEPIEN, B. 1980. *Statistical software tools for computer-assisted analysis of Music.*

STEPIEN, B. 1989. "Automatic transcription of german lute tablatures. Part two: Computer implementations topics." *Computer Representations and Models in Music*. Lancaster

LOGRIPPO, L. and STEPIEN, B. 1984. "Cluster analysis for the Computer-assisted statistical analysis of melodies." *Computer Science*, TR-84-20. Ottawa University, 29 pp.

LOGRIPPO, L. and STEPIEN, B. 1988. "A software package for the classification of melodic lines." *Informatique et Musique. International Computer Music Conference*. IRCAM, 1984. Irvy-sur-Seine, ELMERATTO, 25-40

PELINSKY, R.; LOGRIPPO, L. and STEPIEN, B. 1981. "Typologies des contours mélodiques de chants personnels inuits réalisées à l'aide de l'ordinateur", in: Pelinksy, R. *La musique des inuits du caribou*. Montreal, 103-155

A DATABASE OF JUSTINIANEAN SOURCES

Giancarlo Taddei Elmi
Istituto per la documentazione giuridica CNR
Italy

1. The Research Project: A Database for the Interpretation of Roman Law Sources *

Romanists, up until World War II, have engaged in the research of a classical Roman law. Since the 1930's, the more concentrated utilization made of the historical and comparative methods has illustrated better the various periods in the Roman legal system. The research tools used by Romanists reflect the phases in the development of the discipline in this century.

The Interpolationum Index represents the first phase up until 1935. The bibliographical indices such as the Collectio illustrate the interdisciplinary nature of the second phase. We can see how the initial tool (the index of the interpolations) commenced with the ancient text whilst the latter (bibliographical) tools are divided into "mots clès", selected on the basis of modern interpretation. The experience gained in collecting the material for the creation of the Interpolationum Index, between 1935 and 1965, marks the passage between the two phases and can be used to indicate a way to improve them. The first step towards this improvement was suggested by Broggini, who suggested that the Interpolationum Index relating to the Codex Iustinianus presents "the study of the interpolationistic critique ... set out in a source index".

Similarly, the research began in 1965 by the editors of IURA, directed at "indexing the principal Roman legal texts which have been the subject of special critical or exegetic examination in monographs", tends to continue the tradition of the Index Interpolationum (see IURA 17, 1966, p. 805). The "electronic data base" proposed to the Italian National Research Council and in the course of construction under the direction of Professor Pierangelo Catalano of the 'La Sapienza' University of Rome, permits all the work to be carried out on a predetermined "documentary base", avoiding subjective selection by the researcher whose job it is to scan the documents (see P. Catalano, Archivio elettronico per l'interpretazione delle fonti giuridiche romane, SDHI 1985, pp. 453-457).

Furthermore, the database will give the user all the advantages of an information retrieval system and will permit him to overcome the limitations inherent in printed bibliographies and indices, including those drafted with the aid of the computer.
It must, however, be pointed out that the reordering of the enormous bibliography relating to the interpretation of Roman legal sources must begin with the ordering of these same sources.

The general objective of the research may be defined as the automated access to an ordered knowledge of the interpretation of Roman legal sources (from the ancient sacerdotal files up to modern classifications). For several reasons, this objective can only be reached in part. The first partial objective which can be practically reached is constituted by the "codified" sources of law or those enacted by Emperor Justinian I. The works of Justinian, seen as the meeting point between the East and West, are also the starting point of the so-called "Bizantine" and "European" traditions, which are both encompassed within the perspective of this research.

It would also be advisable, during the course of the research, to accumulate the bibliographical data relative to both, the Eastern and Western pre- and post-Justinian sources, with a view to widening this partial objective in the future.

The delimitation of the documentary base potentially made up of all the written interpretations of the sources is also difficult, because of the implications of scientific policy inherent in all the formal criteria used in setting these limits.

The documentary base must be limited according to formal temporal, spatial (geocultural), scientific and documentary criteria.

a) For the temporal limit, the starting date was fixed as the year in which the Interpolationum Index was completed, that is, 1965.
b) As far as the spatial limit is concerned, research began on the works edited in the European countries which belong today to the Romanist legal system (Romano-Germanic): Belgium, France, the Federal Republic of Germany, Italy, Holland, Spain, etc.
c) With regard to the scientific limit, research began on strictly Romanistic publications, or on the more generally legal-historical texts.
d) Regarding the documentary limit, both, articles published in journals and those appearing in volumes which are not journals but which are reviewed in journals must be taken into consideration.

2. The Database

The research began with articles published in 1983 and then went back as far as 1965. A group of researchers from the Faculty of Law at the University of Cagliari, under the direction of Professor Francesco Sitzia, scans the following journals: *"Anuario de historia del derecho Español"; "Bullettino dell'Istituto di diritto romano 'Vittorio Scialoja'"; "Iura. Rivista internazionale di diritto romano e antico"; "Index. Quaderni camerti di studi romanistici"; "Labeo. Rassegna di diritto romano"; "Revue historique de droit français et étranger"; "Revue internationale des droits de l'antiquité"; "Studia et documenta historiae et iuris"; "Tijdschrift voor Rechtsgeschiendenis"; "Zeitschrift der Savigny-Stiftung für Rechtsgeschichte. Rom. Abt."*

Currently, 1,500 articles have been analysed and the same number of documents has been produced, 500 of which have already been recorded on magnetic tape. The form outlining the structure of the documentary unit for retrieval, the software for generating the database with the Find retrieval system and the actual building of the experimental and provisional database storing 536 documents which can be searched by using all the Find functions, were created in collaboration with the technicians of the Computer Centre of the Italian Corte Suprema di Cassazione. This database is called FIURIS.

The documentary unit must be defined at the level of in-put, retrieval and out-put if an on-line database is to be created. Three kinds of relevant information are involved: relating to the sources, bibliographical and linguistic details. Researchers analysing the articles extract the information and write it out on forms divided into lines and columns. All the lines containing the same kind of information are called cards. The lines and, therefore, the cards can be of unlimited number whilst there are 80 columns. The information is subdivided by 'card' as follows:

card 01 data identifying the document and bibliographical details;
card 02 data relating to the author or editor;
card 03 title and/or equivalent information;
card 04 translated title (this has not as yet been used);
card 05 sources cited in full in the text and in full in the notes;
card 06 sources cited in the text;
card 07 sources cited in the notes.

Example of the structure of the document on in-put:

```
0101850047500089    000046000080    023602470000 04 005
010185004750restano+Riccardo,                               01
02018500475La 'cognitio extra ordinem': una chimera         01
05018500475I3.12.PR./I4.15.8.(P.238) D43.1./D50.13./D47.11. 01
05018500475(P.239) D50.13.(P.240)                           01
06018500475D19.1.52.2./D50.16.178.2./D3.5.46./D4.6.2.(P.239) 01
```

The documents on in-put are consecutively processed by programs which organize and transform them into a new 'defined' structure for 'retrieval'. The form of the document during 'retrieval' takes into account the fact that articulated retrieval through the parts of the document (channels) is provided for in the Italgiure/Find System. The subdivision into channels constitutes the logical structure of the document whilst the subdivision into 'cards' constitutes its physical structure.

Logical Structure		Physical Structure
Channel Name	Content	Card Type
CPER	journal code	01
AN	year of publication	01
TD	type of document	01
CL	language code	01
AUT	author's surname and Christian name	02
AUT1	surname and Christian name (sole datum)	02
PT	words in the title	03, 04
PNT	Latin or foreign words	03, 04
PK	key or conceptual words	03, 04
ED	editor (only for books)	04
F	quoted and cited source	05, 06, 07
FR	quoted sources	05
FCT	sources cited in the text	06
FCN	sources cited in the notes	07
FRCT	sources quoted and cited in the text	05, 06

The structure of the document shows that the information is mainly concerned with the sources. They are assigned the 'F' type retrieval channels (F, FR, FRCT, FCT, FCN). The other channels store linguistic-bibliographical information: the title of the document is assigned the PT, PK, PNT channels; the author, the AUT and AUT1 channels; the language, the CL channel; and the editor, the ED channel.

Example of the structure of the document on out-put:

REVUE HISTORIQUE DE DROIT FRANCAIS ET ETRANGER
00/03/1980
TD: articoli
BRISSET JACQUELINE
LE STOICISME ET LA VENGEANCE
D1.1.3. (P.59)

REVUE HISTORIQUE DE DROIT FRANCAIS ET ETRANGER
00/12/1981
TD: articoli
PIERI GEORGE
STATUT DES PERSONNES ET ORGANISATION POLITIQUE
AUX ORIGINES DE ROME
D50.16.105. (P.586) D49.15.7.1. (P.589)
D1.6.9. (P.592)

3. Searching the Database

The data base can be searched through the Italgiure/Find information retrieval system. Like all large retrieval systems, the fundamental principles of this system are based on the complete indexing of the document, the capacity to combine several data during the search logically and the morphological flexibility of the access keys.
The first principle means that the database can be accessed through any linguistic signs used in the text: the document is indexed under all the signs of which it is composed and, therefore, the indexing language corresponds exactly with the storage language.
Under the second principle, search strategies can be formulated by combining two or more signs through boolean-type logical operators (et=and, vel=or, non=not): these functions will be discussed in greater detail later in this paper in relation to retrieval at a logical level.

Flexibility of the access keys means the capacity to enter the system with linguistic forms of a fixed or variable length: this is so-called retrieval by truncated form or by roots which allows all the keys of a minimum length *n* and an unlimited maximum to be given as a response when starting off from a key made up of *n* characters.

The data in the FIURIS database can be placed in three homogeneous groups: the 'sources' to which the F, FR, FCT, FCN, FRCT channels are dedicated; language signs to which the PT, PK, PNT channels are dedicated and the bibliographical details to which CPER, AN, TD, CL, AUT, AUT1 are dedicated.

4. Retrieval by Sources

All the sources found in the original article are recorded in their complete form in the document and, for each source, the page of the text in which it is cited or printed.

In order to make retrieval of the 'sources' more flexible and efficacious, the important passages of the Corpus Juris have been subdivided according to their 'weight' into passages printed in full in the text or in a note passages cited in the text and passages cited in a note: each type of passage is recorded in a different section of the document as described above. This subdivision constitutes the physical structure of the document.

The computer allows a logical definition which is articulated in a different way and which increases retrieval capacity to be added to the physical definition of the document. Let us compare, in detail, the definition or logical structure relating to the 'sources' with their corresponding physical definition.

Logical Structure Physical Structure

F	FRCT	FR		05
		FCT		06
		FCN		07

Starting with three physical fields, five logical fields representing combinations of physical fields have been defined. Each logical field constitutes a retrieval channel which can be searched independently.

The division into logical fields facilitates the extremely flexible and articulated retrieval of the 'sources' and, in this respect, makes the FIURIS database original and unique among tools of this kind. Not only is it possible to find all the places (page number of the article) where a particular passage is discussed but it is also possible to calculate the weight of the passage (printed in the text or in a note, cited in the text, cited in a note) and, to some degree, the weight of the relative discussion.

All the 'sources', no matter how they are indicated in the articles (printed in the text or in a note, cited in the text, cited in a note), can be retrieved through the 'F' channel.

Only the 'sources printed in the text or in a note' and the 'sources cited in the text' can be jointly selected in the 'FRCT' channel; all and only the 'sources printed in the text and/or in a note' in the 'FR' channel; all and only the 'sources cited in the text' in the 'FCT' channel; and in the 'FCN' channel, all and only the 'sources cited in a note'.

Examples:
$F:D50.13.;
$FR:D43.1.;
$FCT:D50.16.178.2.;
$FCN:D4.6.2.;
$FRCT:D19.1.52.2.;
$F:D50.13.*D43.1.;
$FCT:D50.16.178.2.+FCN=D4.6.2.;

The system, as mentioned earlier, permits the access keys to be exploited in both, a rigid and flexible way by using the implicit or explicit trucation technique.
This provides greater articulation in retrieval by 'sources' in the sense that the 'source' 'd1.1', for example, can be considered in its entirety during a search and will give in out-put only the documents containing 'd1.1', or it can be considered as a minimum key resulting in the search being extended to all the 'sources' beginning with 'd1.1' and, therefore, to the whole 'title'.

Once the documents containing one or more 'sources' have been selected, the system is able to indicate the places (bibliographical details and page of the article) where the 'source' or 'sources' can be found.

A special procedure is at present being developed which will provide a print out of a document containing only the 'source' or 'sources' retrieved complete with the details about the journal or journals and the page or pages where the retrieved 'source' or 'sources' are to be located.

5. Bibliographical-linguistic Retrieval

Retrieval by 'sources', which is the main objective of the FIURIS data base, is enriched by the capacity to search the documents through bibliographical and linguistic keys.

The search can be made on a textual, morphological, semantic and logical level. The type of basic retrieval here is that which utilizes a fixed key and obtains in out-put all the documents where the exact linguistic sign used in the query appears. The language used in the query by the user is, in this case, exactly the same as the retrieval language and the language used in out-put; if the user uses the sign 'senatus', the system does not transform the sign, textual retrieval is carried out and only documents containing the sign 'senatus' without any conceptual expansion will be given in the out-put.

This type of retrieval is only possible in channels where the keys are not defined as 'truncated'; the PNT and AUT1 channels are of this kind. The PNT channel is used for retrieving Latin or foreign words as well as all the terms which cannot be found with the PT channel.

Examples:
$PNT:senatus;
$AUT1:Brisset;
$AUT1:Brisset Jacqueline;

The characteristic of working with complete or fixed forms (like those in so-called type 1 channels) is the impossibility of formulating truncated queries such as:

$PNT:senat;
$AUT1:Briss;

In these cases, it is necessary, as we shall see, to use a truncation symbol if the key of the type 1 channel is to be made flexible.

The PT command (channel) activates by definition an initial level of conceptual research, the expansion to declined or inflected forms; with the '$PT:senato' search, all the documents which have not only the lemma but also the feminine, plural and conjugated form can be retrieved.

Morphological retrieval is of a higher level. An attempt is made through it to go beyond the mere text in order to reach a conceptual expansion starting off from a common root: this is called retrieval by morphological expansion given that a common formal base is always required.

This type of retrieval is also called retrieval by truncated forms because an incomplete form is fed into the computer: the truncation function, in type 1 channels, is expressed with the dollar sign ($) placed at the end of the linguistic sign.

Example: $pt:senat$;

The query is automatically transformed from a monodatum to a multidatum as follows:

$pt:senato+senati+senatore+senatori+all the signs of any length whatsoever, but with the root or common minimum key 'senat'.

Some retrieval channels can be structured so that the signs contained in them are processed by definition as truncated forms or minimum keys (called type 2 channels). In this case, the retrieval as a rule is always by morphological expansion without being necessary to use the truncation symbol at the end of the sign.

All the channels relating to the 'sources' (F, FR, FCT, FCN, FRCT) have been defined in the FIURIS database as trucated type or type 2 channels; therefore, if the user formulates the search string '$F:d1.1' he receives in out-put all the documents containing the minimum key 'd1.1' as well as the documents containing longer keys, without limitation, such as 'd1.1.1.', 'd1.1.2.' but not 'd1.2.'.

The AUT channel processes the signs as truncated signs and considers 'Christian name and surname' to be separate keys.

Example: $AUT:Briss;
$AUT:Briss*Jacqueline;

The AUT1 channel, as mentioned earlier, is a type 1 channel which processes complete or fixed keys, but which, unlike AUT, considers 'Christian name and surname' to be only one key. This means that if truncation is required the $ sign must be used ('AUT1:Briss$,') and that the 'asterisk' operator should not be used if the 'Christian name and surname' is sought ($AUT1:Brisset Jacqueline;).

Anyone who wishes to 'block' the effect of the implicit expansion and formulate queries without truncated keys by definition must utilize the '/' command (stroke or slash) and repeat the key: for example, '$F:d1.1./d1.1.'. In this way, all and only the documents containing 'd1.1' are given in out-put.

Retrieval by semantic expansion, which allows to overcome the limitations arising out of synonymy and similarity in meaning, is important but not essential in information retrieval systems which index texts in full text in natural language (statutes, abstracts of court decisions, summaries or abstracts in natural language of articles from legal journals, etc.).

The accent of the 'document' in the FIURIS database is not placed as much on the language, which is limited to that of the title of the article, nor to the bibliographical details which are considered in relation to the 'sources', mainly on the 'sources' which, as has already been emphasised several times, are referred to in their entirety in the analysis of the articles.

The need for tools which contend with the ambiguity, variety and vagueness of natural language is barely felt in relation to this database.

It is, nevertheless, important to keep in mind that a search based on a given sign can be extended to signs within the semantic area centred on the initial sign with the PK command (channel).

There are two other help functions for conceptual retrieval: LINK and TEST. These permit chains of analogous terms (TEST) or chains of specific terms linked in the AND logical-semantic relation (LINK) to be activated with regard to a particular initial term.

The user, in practice, by using these functions, is provided with lists which aim at suggesting a range of possible terms for carrying out a specific search.

The FIURIS database, as described earlier, provides the possibility of using boolean-logical retrieval. The logical operations which can be used are co-presence or conjunction (AND), inclusive (OR) and exclusive disjunction (OR), and general (NOT) and specific exclusion (AND NOT).

The symbols for the operations are '*' for the AND-conjunction, '+' for the addition-inclusive disjunction, '(-)' for the general exclusion, '*(-)' for the specific exclusion; there is no direct operator for the exclusive disjunction operation in Find and if it is necessary to carry out a complex operation, more than one simple operator needs to be utilized. The hierarchy of the operations establishes that the AND and the exclusion operations are developed firstly and then the addition operations; if the user wishes to change the logical order of the operations he must utilize the brackets as in algebra. The first operation developed among the AND and the subtraction-exclusion operations is that found in the string from left to right.

Searches can also be formulated with *n* operators and *n* operands belonging to different retrieval channels: for example, words contained in the 'title' (PT) combined with data stored in type 'F' channels devoted to the 'sources' can be retrieved and the data in the various 'F' type channels can, in turn, be combined.

Examples:
$FR:D50.13.*D50.16.178.2.;
$FR:D50.13.*PT=cognitio*extra*ordinem;
$PT:senato+tribunato;
$PT:cognitio*extra*ordinem*AUT1=Orestano Riccardo;
$PT:(senato+tribunato)*AUT1=Arangio Ruiz Vincenzo;

NOTE

* See CATALANO, P. 1985. "Archivio elettronico per l'interpretazione delle fonti giuridiche romane", in: *Studia et Documenta Historiae et Iuris*, 453-457

THE MEDIEVAL AND EARLY MODERN DATA BANK IN EUROPE AND NORTH AMERICA

R. Bell, E. van Cauwenberghe
UFSAL, Brussels
Belgium

The Medieval and Early Modern Data Bank (MEMDB) provides scholars throughout Western Europe and North America with easy access to an electronic library of machine-readable information concerning Western history for the period circa AD 800-1800. MEMDB operates simultaneously at three distinct levels. First, it maintains a Master Data Set (MDS) that allows researchers to conduct interactive and integrates searches and retrievals of data stored online in a mainframe computer system operated by The Research Libraries Group, Inc. (RLG), in Stanford, California. This retrieval system is accessible from any telephone line in the world connected to a PC using DOS and a modem. Second, MEMDB archives at its Rutgers University office individual data sets that are of too specialized a nature to justify inclusion in the MDS and makes these archived data sets available on tape or floppy disk upon request. Third, MEMDB catalogues machine-readable data sets that are held by other archives and provides bibliographic information about these through RLG's Research Libraries Information Network (RLIN).

Through RLIN, its online information system, RLG links libraries, museums, record offices and research institutes in North America and Europe to give access to a present total of some 30 million bibliographic records. This is accomplished via terminals connected by telephone line to RLG's mainframe computer at Stanford. RLG, which already had more than a decade of experience in managing the standardization, acquisition, maintenance and distribution of bibliographic data, was interested in expanding its scope to include non-bibliographic information, arranged to cosponsor MEMDB.

The first major breakthrough came when Peter Spufford of the University of Cambridge agreed to convert his work-in-progress on currency exchange quotations into a machine-readable format and then to donate his results to MEMDB. In 1986, his *Handbook of Medieval Exchange* was published in London by the Royal Historical Society, and it is this fundamental work, listing over 13,000 exchanges dating from 1106 to 1500 and covering all of Europe, Byzantium, the Levant and North Africa that provided the first data set fully incorporated into MEMDB.

In December 1985, a group of medievalists from the United States, Canada and the Netherlands met with us and with RLG planners to help draft the outlines of MEMDB's proposed development. From this meeting there emerged a permanent Advisory Board, of which the current members are Willem P. Blockmans of the Rijksuniversiteit te Leiden, David Herlihy of Brown University, Harry A. Miskimin of Yale University, John Munro of the University of Toronto, Edward Peters of the University of Pennsylvania, Peter Spufford of the University of Cambridge, and Eddy Van Cauwenberghe of the Universitaire Faculteiten Sint-Aloysius, Brussels and the Katholieke Universiteit Leuven.

Our next major step involved the decision to develop a PC-based prototype of the MDS using Spufford's currency exchange quotations as the data base.

The prototype is available at a nominal charge (to cover the costs of commercial software packages included within it) by writing to any of the MEMDB offices listed at the conclusion of this essay.

The prototype embodies several central MEMDB principles concerning the ways in which machine-readable data sets should be made accessible. First, the system had to retain all the documentation conveyed with the data set, not just the tabular results and make this documentation easily and fully available. Scholars familiar with Spufford's book, or with others of its genre, already know that the documentation consists not only of source references, but also of explanatory texts that are essential if the data entries are to have full meaning. In the case of Spufford's *Handbook*, which includes a lengthy introduction that is necessary for the specialist and the neophyte alike, we concluded that a user of MEMDB who wished to retrieve simply a single currency exchange quotation nevertheless should be able easily to consult online all potentially useful explanatory material, starting with commentary relevant to the specific quotation, but including even the full introduction. This decision gave RLG specialists some interesting challenges, but they rose to the occasion. The prototype does and the full RLIN system will provide complete textual support for all its data sets with correct linkages provided for the user of specific text to specific tabular data.

Second, the system had to be extremely user-friendly, neither mystifying and frustrating to the novice who is unfamiliar with computers and may require frequent prompting or assistance, nor cumbersome and annoying to the experienced user who wants to be able to get results with as little interference as possible. The prototype uses only ten command verbs, eleven index nouns and a minimum of qualifiers (and, or, not) and punctuation ("",", -, /) to handle even the most complex searches of the Spufford data set. The structure or syntax of the command language also is easy to learn.

Third, the system had to be accessible at virtually all times, at a reasonable cost and without the need for sophisticated personal computers. The development of the PC-prototype convinced us that only a design involving both, PCs and a mainframe would work.

In 1989-90 MEMDB will migrate from its PC-prototype to the full RLIN environment. In North America, access to MEMDB through any of the more than 1500 existing RLIN terminals, or for that matter via any telephone line by dialling a local Telenet number, is not a problem. For Europe the situation is more complex, but now we are reaching a solution. By early 1989, the Centre National Universitaire Sud de Calcul (CNUSC) at Montpellier will have a high-speed direct link with Cornell University (U.S.A.). The Montpellier computer, in turn, provides a gateway to the TCP/IP Internet, a group of networks serving some 60,000 machines in Europe, among these the IBM 3090 at Leuven (to which we shall return shortly). At the other end of the line, Cornell's computer is linked via NSFNet to computers throughout North America, including the RLG/RLIN facilities at Stanford.

In 1988, MEMDB opened two European offices, one at Leiden under the direction of Willem Blockmans and the other at Brussels/Leuven under the direction of Eddy Van Cauwenberghe. These centers work in partnership with the Rutgers office and with RLG to implement the following goals:

1. identify data sets appropriate for acquisition by MEMDB and delivery through MEMDB,
2. establish standard conventions for coding and storing machine-readable data for use in historical research,

3. improve cooperation among international library systems in developing standardized bibliographic procedures for machine-readable data, in exchanging research materials and in sharing the costs of acquiring and preserving research materials.

The reader may ask just what will be available in MEMDB's Master Data Set and why the MDS concept is important. The MDS will include all works of a primarily tabular nature concerning the medieval and early modern history of the West that one would expect to find in the reference or consultation section of any good university library. It will also include bibliographic references to machine-readable data sets not incorporated in the MDS itself and, in the future, glossaries of weights and measures, gazetteers of Latin and vernacular place names and calendars of dates. Slated for inclusion in the MDS before it becomes available via RLIN late in 1989 are at least the following data sets: E. Van Cauwenberghe's and J.H. Munro's Low Countries mint data, Bell's transcription of the 1526/27 Rome household census, about 1,200 currency exchange quotations donated by Spufford that do not appear in his published *Handbook*, selected portions of N.W. Posthumus' *Nederlandse Prijsgeschiedenis*, and D. Ebeling and F. Irsigler's tape of grain prices and sales in Cologne, 1368-1797.

This is an eclectic list, the result of our decision to work out certain technical design questions before imposing a more traditional historical scheme upon which to base the expansion of the MDS. Nonetheless, it may give an idea of the range of information intended for the MDS and even from this short list we may perhaps draw an example to illustrate the advantages of a truly integrated master data set. A synthesis of Spufford's and Ebeling/Irsigler's data would be an arduous task using traditional printed sources and still very difficult treating them as two discrete machine-readable data sets, doing separate calculations of averages and trend lines for each set, adjusting for their differing variable structures and keeping track of cautionary notations, exceptions and qualifications. In contrast, once the two sets are in the MDS, the researcher has instant access to facilities for combining data entries from either set, or for separating them when necessary whether by date, by type of commodity, by author, by price range, etc. Add the Low Countries mint data and a silver basis may be constructed across different currencies; eventually, add a perpetual calendar and the user may quickly determine whether prices were higher just before Easter.

In a more imaginative vein, one may think of the master data set as placing the scholar in a room lined with the standard reference works, hundreds or even thousands of them. Via RLIN the user consulting MEMDB employs just a dozen or so commands to open instantly any or all volumes, to consult any or all of their tens of thousands of pages of information simultaneously, to view the full documentation for each individual data entry at a single keystroke and to construct and retrieve in electronic form for further analysis an essentially new data result set, culled from tens or even hundreds of different works. Yes, dozens of persons working for hundreds of hours could accomplish the same thing and the scholar's eye for what is crucial remains indispensable, but surely the technological time is right for using machines to expand vastly the researcher's vista. This is what the MDS accomplishes. Again, an analogy with more traditional library science considerations may be helpful. The most frequently consulted reference works in any library properly are placed on open shelves in a section where users may browse at will and do not need to fill out slips to call up a particular volume. It is this sort of work that belongs in the MDS.

The second level at which MEMDB operates, its offline data set archive, is of no less significance than the MDS. As with data sets in the MDS, holdings of the offline archive constitute published works made available to researchers in electronic form. So, also bibliographic references to the archived data sets are fully integrated within the RLIN master file and may be accessed via author, title, publisher and all the other categories used within RLIN.

To continue with the library analogy, other valuable, but more specialized and therefore less frequently consulted volumes in a traditional library are reached via a catalog reference and then a call slip. The offline archive operates in a similar fashion, with due allowance for the differences entailed in a heavily computer-based operation. The user starts with RLIN and the MDS and locates the reference to a data set held in the offline archive. Without leaving the RLIN environment, the user may request access to an offline data set; after specifying the mode in which the data are to be sent (tape, diskette, printout, etc.), the user's request is transmitted from RLIN to the offline archive where the request is translated by an MEMDB staff member into a batch-processed job and prepared for delivery, either by standard mail service, or electronically depending on the user's specifications.

In theory every data set could be part of the MDS, just as in theory a library could keep all its shelves open, but the negative aspects in both, traditional and electronic libraries outweigh the advantages of instant access to more specialized items. One of the major reasons for the MDS is its facility for integrating searches for related information across different data sets. Therefore, works that do not integrate well with the general character of MDS holdings, for example the individual baptismal records of a single parish or the shipments of a particular merchant, belong more properly in the offline archive. To include all data sets in the MDS, apart from the cost considerations involved, would result in overwhelming the user with data that in most cases would turn out to be an irrelevant distraction.

This constitutes a brief introduction to the Medieval and Early Modern Data Bank as it now exists and as it plans to grow in Europe and in North America. Further information about the current PC-prototype and about future developments, as well as queries and proposals for the addition of new data sets, may be addressed to any of the offices listed below.

The Medieval and Early Modern Data Bank
Department of History
Rutgers University
New Brunswick, New Jersey 08903
USA

The Medieval and Early Modern Data Bank
Rijksuniversiteit te Leiden
Vakgroep Geschiedenis
Leiden
The Netherlands

The Medieval and Early Modern Data Bank
Universitaire Faculteiten Sint-Aloysius
Vrijheidslaan, 17 1080-BRUSSEL
Afdeling Geschiedenis
Brussels
Belgium

NOTE

For information on RLG and its extensive information network, RLN, write to:

Corporate Affairs and Publications
The research Libraries Group, Inc.
Stanford, California 94305
USA

HOMO EX MACHINA
PROSOPOGRAPHY AND CHARTULARIES

Ingo H. Kropač
Forschungsinstitut für historische Grundwissenschaft
Karl Franzens Universität, Graz
Austria

At the Karl-Franzens-University of Graz, the *Forschungsinstitut für Historische Grundwissenschaften* is engaged, among others, in two large editing projects: The *Urkundenbuch der Steiermark und ihrer Regenten* (Hausmann 1988) and the *Urkundenbuch des Patriarchats Aquileia* (Härtel 1984; Härtel 1986). Aware of the long tradition of scholarly editing and the difficulties in critical revision of the documents, we created a concept of computer-supported edition which is based on a definition of editing, different from the common terminology: To edit a source means to make the contents and the structure of a source's information available as complete as possible in order to enable scientists to use the edition without the need to refer to the original. Computer-supported editing is mostly considered as a procedure that makes use of the computer to produce a classical printed edition by traditional methods (Ott 1973; Hockey 1980; Oakman 1980; Ott-Gabler-Sappler 1982; Gabler-Kreitmair 1986). But this is only one aspect of the various feasibilities of Historical Information Science. Our concept of computer-supported editing sees the *machine readable source* (Thaller 1986) and the *computer-supported knowledge* (Thaller 1987) about it as the general aim. A printed edition should be one result of editing as well as any other analysis that can be undertaken by the data. Of course, the concept of computer-supported editing has to pay attention to typographical needs and existing typesetting-software.

A critical edition always consists of the source's information, which can be represented on different levels and some auxiliary means, basing on the special knowledge of the editor, for example indices of persons or places or indications of the document's degree of authenticity. To ensure the correctness of dates and authenticity of persons mentioned in the documents according to the *discrimen veri ac falsi*, a computerized processing even of persons named in the documents seemed desirable. This was the point we decided to start a third project, the *Prosopographical Data Bank on the History of the South-East Territories of the Empire up to 1250* (PDB) (Kropac-Becker 1987; Kropac 1988). The linkage of textual and factual data bases and the including of representations of knowledge should enlarge the projects to an expert system in diplomatics for the afore mentioned territories.

1. The Textual Data Base UHSTXT1

The project *Urkundenbuch der Steiermark und ihrer Regenten* is a revised edition as well as a continuation of a chartulary (Zahn 1887 ff.) up to 1308, which became obsolete for the "state of the art" in diplomatics. About 200.000 different traditions out of archives from Austria, Yugoslavia, Italy, Liechtenstein, the Federal Republic of Germany and the CSSR wait for their critical revision. To ease the work and get a machine-readable basis to continue, we scanned the old chartulary using the Kurzweil Data Entry Machine at the Computing Center of Göttingen. After having collated the texts a data base was created, baptized UHSTXT1 (Urkundenbuch des Herzogthums Steiermark, Text, vol. 1). The contents of this data base is an exact copy of Zahn's chartulary; that means the acceptance of his texts, of his datings and of his decisions about authenticity. Although there are a lot of faults in Zahn's chartulary, it was a pioneer work for the late nineteenth century.

Regarding the tradition of the document in the duchy of Styria in the High Middle Ages, we get confronted with different levels in the development of charters (Fichtenau 1971; Mell 1911). Besides an early "chancellery" of the Traungauer (*marchioness* of Styria) (Wonisch 1926) most documents executed in Styria are transmitted as *notitiae traditionum* or *libri traditionum* of clerical institutions, especially of the monastery of Admont. Because of the unfortunate loss of four *Salbücher* at Admont the situation became more complicate (Fichtenau 1971, pp. 200-207; Zahn 1875, pp. XXXII-XXXIX). Most of the few sealed charters seem to be falsifications, most of the *notitiae traditionum* are not dated correctly; facts that emphasize the need for further diplomatic research (Fichtenau 1971, pp. 217-220).

Zahn's chartulary was not the first one in Styria. In the eighteenth century, the *Diplomataria sacra ducatus Styriae* were published, only dealing with the archives of clerical institutions. The foundation of the so-called *Joanneum* rendered collecting, central archiving and in this way a systematic editing of the sources possible. Zahn took notice only of the "Styrian soil" in the frontiers of the duchy in his time; he did not consider the territories in Upper and Lower Austria, which belonged to Styria before 1254, and the foreign real estate of the Styrian nobility. Zahn's emendations and corrections of the text should be handled with care, too, and the indices, more surveys than repertories (Zahn 1875, pp. XLVI-LII), are obsolete nowadays, some charters were considered to be falsification in the meantime. All these restrictions have to be regarded when working with the data base.

In the data base, every document of the chartulary is indicated by its reference as well as dating, place of issue, form of tradition and degree of authenticity evaluated by Zahn. Subordinate to this "headerline" follows the scanned text of the document. Special characters and diacritica are treated like the input for the typesetting system T_EX (Knuth 1986). In this way, we could transfer all characteristics of Zahn's version of the text into the data base.

The textual data base UHSTXT1 can be seen only as a working tool of the editing project, but it provides all information the traditional edition does. The computer enables the user of the data base to search his topics of interest much more faster than in the book. Especially for comparisons of dictations in the documents or research in semantics this "electronic weapon" (Genicot 1984) seems to be very useful. Of course, all features provided by the kleio-system, especially the menu-driven text retrieval mode, can be used for evaluations.

2. The "Prosopographical" Data Base UHS1

The factual data base UHS1 is considered as a module of the *Prosopographical Data Bank on the History of the South-East Territories of the Empire up to 1250* (PDB). This data base is an approach to an integrated prosopography of the southeast of the Empire. In order to realize this intention, two different steps in processing are provided: In a first phase, the occurrences of the persons mentioned in the documents are collected, without regard to a particular class or group. In a second phase, the individuals must be identified to link their namings and to get data bases which look like prosopographical catalogues. "Advanced" indices of medieval people like these should be seen as instruments for research in diplomatics as well as basic tools for the analyses of the medieval society.

To create a system as open as possible we defined five principles as prerequisites of the project:

1. The data bank has to be established according to the principles of source-oriented (as opposed to method-oriented) data processing (Thaller 1984; Thaller 1986a).
2. It must be guaranteed that information can be imported and exported. That means updating the data base as well as linking records to different structured "foreign" data bases, a procedure which is indispensable for computer supported editing and for the realization of the concept of machine readable *regesta*.
3. In the subject of data analyses and transformation, different processes of research have to be distinguished (Thaller 1982): an explorative phase of analysis, evaluation of inconsistencies of the source and the support of the techniques of Nominal Record Linkage (Wrigley 1973; Winchester 1985) as well as machine-supported coding.
4. Because of the complexity of these transformations, every user must be enabled to reconstruct every procedure step by step.
5. The PDB demands a high-flexible organization. It should be possible to use it even with small computers - i.e. PC's - as well as with minis and mainframes and accessed from Historical Workstations as background knowledge.

To implement a data bank according to the prerequisites mentioned above, we needed not only specific software, but also a carefully developed design. As software Manfred Thaller's kleio-package has been chosen (Thaller 1988), the design problem has lead to the concept of modular data bank organization. A step-by-step creation of the PDB can be provided by the distinction between *Primary Data Bases*, *Secondary Data Bases* and an additional *Toolbox*:

1. From every collection of documents, whether they are books or archives, a Primary Data Base is generated. It contains - as discussed later - the namings of persons as they appear in the source.
2. These modifications are reached through the generation of *Secondary Data Bases*, which can become completely different structures, depending on the precise purpose they are required for:
   - 2.1. The simplest of all Secondary Data Banks is a mere listing of Primary Data Bases. This *Cumulative Index of Entries* equals the informational contents with the sum of all linked Primary Data Bases and has the identical structure. Like the Primary Data Bases, these are indices of persons's names arranged according to the original documents.
   - 2.2. After persons are identified and the single namings are assigned to them, every Primary Data Base will be linked with itself to get an *Prosopographical Catalogue*. The identification and linkage is carried out through semi-automatic Record Linkage and - due to the small amount of information offered by the sources - this is the most difficult part of the entire analysis procedures. After the identification and linkage of individuals a new data structure will be generated.
   - 2.3. Through further linkage procedures which are simplified through the regulation

of name forms and verification of dates in step 2.2, *Cumulative Prosopographical Catalogues* can be established. Their contents depend on the linked catalogues; which of them are used for the cumulation process is optional to the user.

3. Furthermore, it is necessary to document all these steps as precisely as possible. All these documentations, command-procedures, tools and definitions of links are included in the *Toolbox*. So, all steps of identification and linkage can be tested intersubjectively and reconstructed in order to provide transparency to the users.

In the data base UHS1 all the namings of persons contained by the aforementioned *Urkundenbuch des Herzogthums Steiermark* are included. The single document is also the superordinate information unit which is described by reference, date and place of issue, and its type of tradition. Within the documents we are most of all interested in people mentioned, but also in the institutions that are related to them and in the date line of the document for purposes of control.

Each person can be found with the help of an identification code within the all-encompassing data bank as well as in the source from which it was taken. This code is also the passive part of the network expressing genealogical relationships. The names of the people have been left in original spelling, as has the description of persons such as surname, status, rank, profession etc. or predicates that express several of these simultaneously - this is why no "a priori" assignments can be made. The personal description is completed with information on the function in the document, the position in the series of persons holding the same function in the document, the status (alive, dead, notclear) and the genealogical relationships to other persons. The data entry is based on specific rules for each Elementary Information, which are documented and come with the data base.

3. A User-Defined Combination

We already stressed the term flexibility when discussing the design of our databases. Using one of the different feasibilities of combining information, related to the computer-supported edition, the two data bases were linked. This procedure is rather simple, because every single document is indicated by the same reference. The kleio-system offers file-merging-features to incorporate the entity *Text* of the textual data base into the structure of the factual one and generates a new data base:

Document: Reference/Dating/Place-of-Issue/Tradition

```
|
|------Text: Text
|
|------Person: Identification/(First)Name/Description/Function/
|              Number-of-Function/Status/Genealogical-Relationship
|
|-------I(nstitution): Function/Type/Name/Place
|
|-------Dating-Line: Text
|
```

Structure of the linked data base

In the data structure, the "headerline" of the single document is the same in each data base. On the first subordinate level in the model's hierarchy the entities of the former data bases are combined. As a result of this linkage kleio handles the full texts of the documents as efficient as the parts of the formalized semantic structure of the sources, in our example all occurrences of a person and their immediate semantic description. The new data base represents the text of the source as well as knowledge about the persons, their functions in the charters, their genealogical relationships etc. If the prosopographical catalogue will be released, a kind of expert system for the history of Styria in the High Middle Ages can be created.

This construction is a typical example for a user-oriented data base. We assume that user X is interested in formulas used in charters which have in common a special group of witnesses. This group shall consist of clergymen, appearing in the source in a specific order. So, user X is enabled to search for groups of persons which are specified by the function "witness", by the designation as clergymen imported from a thesaurus, in which the terminology of the field "description" has been classified, and by a similar, but not identical sequence of their appearance. After this rather complex search-process the user probably will create compendia of the vocabulary, occurring in the text of the documents found, in order to analyze semantic or syntactic properties of this set of documents. The texts can be examined in a user-friendly way: the menu-driven component of the kleio-system provides the definition and combination of various words and/or wordlists in different contexts to be viewed or printed (Thaller 1988, pp. 259-275). This process can be changed, of course. The analysed text may become the basis to further prosopographical research etc.

The short example should demonstrate, why the computer should not be used as a tool only for the creation of traditional printed editions. If a "source base" can be accessed in the environment of a *Historical Workstation* (Thaller 1987, pp. 22-29) as easily as a chartulary in the library, if the combination with other data bases in different ways is possible, we assume that our life as historian will become easier: we can concentrate in our topic of research without spending most of our time in looking up printed editions and getting annoyed by insufficient registers. Today's restrictions (as far as they really exist) should not divert us from the advantages of the future.

REFERENCES

FICHTENAU, H. 1971. "Das Urkundenwesen in Österreich vom 8. bis zum frühen 13. Jahrhundert." Wien-Köln-Graz (*Mitteilungen des Instituts für österreichische Geschichtsforschung*, Ergänzungsband 23)

GABLER, H.W. und KREITMAIR, W. 1986. "Der Computer als Arbeitshilfe für das wissenschaftliche Edieren", in: Gregor, B. und Krifka, M. (Hrsg.). *Computerfibel für die Geisteswissenschaften. Einsatzmöglichkeiten des Personal Computers und Beispiele aus der Praxis*. München, 203-211

GENICOT, L. 1984. "Some elementary remarks on the utility of computers in medieval history", in: Gilmour-Bryson, A. (ed.). *Computer applications to medieval studies*. Kalamazoo (Studies in medieval culture 17), 45-50

HÄRTEL, R. 1984. "Il progetto di ricerca e di edizione 'Urkundenbuch des Patriarchats Aquileia' (Codice diplomatico del patriarcato d'Aquileia)." *Memoriestoriche forogiuliesi* 64, 177-186

HÄRTEL, R. 1986. "Die älteren Urkunden des Klosters Moggio (bis 1250)". Wien (*Publikationen des Historischen Instituts beim österreichischen Kulturinstitut in Rom* II. Abt. Reihe 6 = Vorarbeiten zu einem Urkundenbuch des Patriarchats Aquileia 1)

HÄRTEL, R. und KROPAC, I.H. 1987. "Edition und Auswertung mittelalterlicher Urkunden: Probleme bei Standardisierung und Transfer fortlaufender Texte", in: Hausmann, F. et al. (eds.). *Data Networks for the Historical Disciplines? Problems and Feasibilities in Standardization and Transfer of Machine Readable Data*. Graz, 100-112

HAUSMANN, F. 1988. "Urkundenbuch der Steiermark und ihrer Regenten, Band I-II und V ff," in: Pickl, O. (ed.). *XXII. Bericht der Historischen Landeskommission für die Steiermark, 16. Geschäftsperiode (1982-1986)*. Graz

HOCKEY, S. 1980. *A Guide to Computer Applications in the Humanities*. London, 144-167

KNUTH, D.E. 1986. *The TeXbook*. Reading [etc.]

KROPAČ, I.H. 1988. *Informationssysteme in der Geschichtswissenschaft. Konzeption und Anwendung am Beispiel der Prosopographischen Datenbank zur Geschichte der südöstlichen Reichsgebiete bis 1250 (PDB)*. Graz (in print, will be published in spring 1989)

KROPAČ, I.H. und BECKER, P. 1987. "Die Prosopographische Datenbank zur Geschichte der südöstlichen Reichsgebiete bis 1250. Konzepte und Kurzdokumentation". *Medium Aevum Quotidianum* 10, 30-47

MELL, R. 1911. "Beiträge zur Geschichte der steirischen Privaturkunde." Graz-Wien (*Forschungen zur Verfassungs- und Verwaltungsgeschichte der Steiermark* 8/1)

OAKMAN, R.L. 1980. *Computer Methods for Literary Research*. Columbia, 113-138

OTT, W. 1973. "Computer applications in textual criticism", in: Aitken, A.J.; Bailey, R.W. and Hamilton-Smith, N. (eds.). *The Computer and Literary Studies*. Edinburgh, 199-206

OTT, W.; GABLER H.W. and SAPPLER, P. 1982. *EDV-Fibel für Editoren*. Stuttgart, 25-34

THALLER, M. 1982. "Zur Formalisierbarkeit hermeneutischen Verstehens in der Historie", in: *Mentalitäten und Lebensverhältnisse. Beispiele aus der Sozialgeschichte der Neuzeit. Rudolf Vierhaus zum 60. Geburtstag*. Göttingen, 439-454

THALLER, M. 1984. "Ungefähre Exaktheit. Theoretische Grundlagen und praktische Möglichkeiten einer Formulierung historischer Quellen als Produkte 'unscharfer Systeme'", in: Nagl-Docekal, H. und Wimmer, F. (Hrsg.). *Neue Ansätze in der Geschichtswissenschaft*. Vienna (Conceptus-Studien 1), 77-100

THALLER, M. 1986. "A Draft Proposal for a Standard for the Coding of Machine Readable Sources", *Historical Social Research* 40, 3-46

THALLER, M. 1986a. "Vorüberlegungen für einen internationale Workshop über die Schaffung, Verbindung und Nutzung großer interdisziplinärer Quellenbanken in den historischen Wissenschaften", in: M. Thaller (Hrsg.). *Datenbanken und Datenverwaltungssysteme als Werkzeuge historischer Forschung*. St. Katharinen (Historisch-Sozialwissenschaftliche Forschungen 20), 9-30

THALLER, M. 1987. "The Daily Life in the Middle Ages, Editions of Sources and Data Processing". *Medium Aevum Quotidianum Newsletter* 10, 6-28

THALLER, M. 1988. *Kleio. A Data Base System for Historical Research, Version 2.1.1*. Göttingen

WRIGLEY, E.A. 1973. *Identifying People in the Past*. London

WINCHESTER I. 1985. "Record Linkage in the Microcomputer Era: A Survey." Umea (*Demographic Data Base Newletter* 3)

WONISCH, O. 1926. "Über das Urkundenwesen der Traungauer." *Zeitschrift des Historischen Vereins für Steiermark* 22, 52-149

ZAHN, J.v. 1875 ff. *Urkundenbuch des Herzogthums Steiermark*. 3. vol., Graz 1875-1903

A DATA BASE FOR RESEARCH ON PERSONS AND GROUPS OF PERSONS IN THE MIDDLE AGES

Dieter Geuenich
FB1: Geschichte, University of Duisburg
FRG

A report about the *Duisburger Datenbank mittelalterlicher Personen und Personengruppen*, initiated by Karl Schmid, Freiburg, and Joachim Wollasch, Münster, now in cooperation with the Max Planck Institut für Geschichte, Göttingen.

As each medievalist knows, the prosopographical registration and exploration of persons of the early and high Middle Ages is hindered by several problems. The quality of the written sources of this period as well as the lack of adequate methods for their investigation are the reasons for these problems.

There is no lack of sources in which medieval persons are mentioned by their names. Hundreds of thousands of personal names are contained in charters and historiographical texts, in succession-lists and hagiographical works, but first of all in so called commemorative sources ("Memorialüberlieferung"), in particular the "libri vitae" or confraternity books (or "libri memoriales") and obituaries/necrologies. There are good reasons to assume that in these sources first of all the "Führungsschicht", the uppermost strata of the Frankish Empire were recorded; that is, not only the kings and emperors with their immediate relatives but also the so-called *imperial aristocracy* ("Reichsaristokratie"), the bishops and abbots of the realm, as well as the members of spiritual, esp. monastic communities. The last mentioned represented, as everybody knows, almost exclusively the cultural life of this time. Under this conditions it should be possible to register prosopographically all those persons, who actively participated in the policy of the Carolingian, Ottonian and Salian Empire, who played leading roles in the cultural life of this time, who worked as artists or poets. It should even be possible to reach those strata of society which lay below the "Führungsschicht" on top.

But the problems of medieval prosopography are first of all problems of the sources themselves and of their transmission. The already mentioned "commemorative sources" contain hundreds of thousands of names, but only names. These names can be dated and localized approximately in many cases; sometimes, they bear titles like *rex, episcopus, abbas, comes, presbiter, sanctimonialis* or *monachus*. But in most cases all this does not suffice to find the persons behind the names: that is, to register the mentioned persons prosopographically.

1. From Names to Persons

One more reason seriously worsens the situation: persons of the early Middle Ages bore only one name; surnames came up later. But how can hundreds of Adalberts,

Rudolfs or Konrads be distinguished from each other, if additional information is missing? Within the available space it is not possible to demonstrate adequately the problems of prosopographical research-methods here, leave alone to show possible solutions in detail. But the additional problem of the name-variance has to be mentioned.

There were, as everyone knows, no norms for medieval names. Their spelling varied and presumably also their pronunciation differed very much according to the region where a scribe lived. For historians without experience and knowledge of anthroponomy and phonology it may be difficult if not impossible to distinguish phonological variants of one personal name from those of an etymologically different name. For instance, *Hrothulf* and *Rusdolf* are derived of one name and could, therefore, belong to one person, whereas *Ruadolf* and *Ruadolt* would belong to different persons.

This problem of name-variance was obviously the decisive obstacle for the use of computers in medieval prosopography. On the other hand medieval prosopography needs this technical device in order to handle the enormous amounts of data, which have to be compared, item by item. Human memory cannot keep all available occurrences of one out of thousands of names in mind. The automatic lemmatization ("Lemmatisierung") with the help of a complex dictionary of all name-variants, suffixes and inflexions solves this problem, without forcing the researcher to normalize the important name-variants. Twenty years experience in this field are incorporated into the computer-dictionary WSF. This data base of name-elements, -suffixes, and -inflexions is structured according to the rules of Germanic name-composition and the grammar of the Germanic languages. It incorporates every derivation of a personal name which is stored in the main data base DMP, but every derivative is stored here only once (with indication of its frequency). This dictionary WSF has to be distinguished from the data base of names and persons, where the medieval source material is incorporated. This device, the possibility to index medieval personal names automatically under their Germanistic etyma, certainly is an important contribution to the field of medieval prosopography.

2. Name-Entries and Groups of Persons

Before describing the procedure for the automatic lemmatization of medieval personal names, another peculiarity of the way in which names have been transmitted to us, esp. in the libri memoriales, but also in lists of witnesses in charters etc., has to be mentioned; a peculiarity, which is another reason to make use of computer processing: usually, these names have no "context" in the sources. Therefore, the proximity to other names can be a decisive clue for identification of names with persons. In the witness lists of charters as well as in the commemorative name-entries of "libri memoriales", personal names often occur in only gradually varying surroundings. In other words: Many persons can only be identified, because they occur in several, more or less identical contexts.

Behind this stands the well-known fact that persons of the Middle Ages are represented in the written sources almost exclusively within their social surroundings. That is, they are mentioned as a member of a spiritual or monastic community, of a family or a "clan" ("Sippenverband"), as office-holder or representative of a social "order" ("ordo"), or in the context of a political group or alliance. The same or almost identical surroundings of personal names significant for a special group of persons, can often be the only indicator for identification of persons.

3. The Stored Material

The use of the data available have been demonstrated for the participants of the conference; for the readers of this volume, who are interested in our material, for whatever reasons, and who possibly want to use parts of it, I want to describe the data already processed. Four kinds of sources have been distinguished, because of the different kind of context information around the personal names:

1. Libri memoriales
2. Obituaries
3. Charters
4. Other historical material (historiography, letter, vitae etc.)

The large, completely stored sources are:

ad 1:
* The confraternity book of Reichenau abbey, ed. J. Autenrith, D. Geuenich, K. Schmid (= Monumenta Germaniae Historica, Libri Memoriales et Necrologia, Nova Series I); Hannover, 1978
* The confraternity books of St. Gall. Compare for the time being: Subsidia Sangallensia I. Materialien und Untersuchungen zu den Verbrüderungsbüchern und zu den älteren Urkunden des Stiftsarchivs St. Gallen, ed. M. Borgolte, D. Geuenich, K. Schmid (= St. Galler Kultur und Geschichte 16), St. Gallen, 1986, pp. 13-283
* Liber Viventium Fabariensis I: Faksimile-Edition, ed. A. Bruckner, H.R. Sennhauser, F. Perret, Basel, 1973. Cf. dazu D. Geuenich: Die ältere Geschichte von Pfäfers im Spiegel der Mönchslisten der Liber Viventium Fabariensis, in: Frühmittelalterliche Studien 9 (1975), pp. 226-252
* Liber memorialis von Remiremont, ed. E. Hlawitschka, K. Schmid, G. Tellenbach (= Monumenta Germaniae Historica, Libri memoriales 1), Dublin-Zürich, 1970
* Der Memorial- und Liturgiecodex von San Salvatore/Santa Giulia in Brescia, unter Mitwirkung von H. Becker, Maria Hasdenteufel-Röding hrsg. von A. Angenendt und Karl Schmid (=Monumenta Germaniae Historica, Libri Memoriales et Necrologia Nova Series IV), publ. 1989
* Das Verbrüderungsbuch von St. Peter in Salzburg. Vollständige Faksimile-Ausgabe im Originalformat der Handschrift A1 aus dem Archiv St. Peter in Salzburg, ed. K. Forstner (= Codices selecti 51), Graz, 1974
* Der Liber Vitae con Corvey. Einleitung, Register, Facsimile, ed. K. Schmid, J. Wollasch (= Veröffentlichungen der Historischen Kommission für Westfalen 40, Westfälische Gedenkbücher und Necrologien 2/1), Wiesbaden, 1983
* Liber Vitae Ecclesiae Dunelmensis, ed. J. Stevenson (= The publications of the Surtees Society 13), London, 1841, and J. Gerchow: Die Gedenküberlieferung der Angelsachsen. Mit einem Katalog der Libri Vitae und Necrologien (publ. 1988 in Arbeiten zur Frühmittelalterforschung)
* The commemorative sources of the monastry of Fulda: Die Klostergemeinschaft von Fulda im frühen Mittelalter, ed. K. Schmid (= Münstersche Mittelalter-Schriften 8, 1-3), München 1978

ad 2: * Synopse der cluneacensischen Necrologien, ed. J. Wollasch (= Münstersche Mittelalter-Schriften 39/1-2), München, 1983
* Die Totenbücher von Merseburg, Magdeburg und Lüneburg, ed. G. Althoff, J. Wollasch (= Monumenta Germaniae Historica, Libri Memoriales et Necrologia, Nova Series II), Hannover, 1983
* G. Althoff: Das Necrolog von Borghorst. Edition und Untersuchung (= Veröffentlichungen der Historischen Kommission für Westfalen 40, Westfälische Gedenkbücher und Necrologien 1), Münster 1978
* F. Neiske: Das ältere Necrolog von S. Savino in Piacenza. Edition und Untersuchung der Anlage (= Münstersche Mittelalter-Schriften 36), München 1979
* Das Martyrolog-Necrolog von St. Emmeram zu Regensburg, ed. E. Freise, D. Geuenich, J. Wollasch (= Monumenta Germaniae Historica, Libri Memoriales et Necrologia, Nova Series III), Hannover, 1986
* Das Martyrolog-Necrolog von Moissac/Duravel, ed. A. Müssigbrod, J. Wollasch (= Münstersche Mittelalter-Schriften 44), München, 1988. See A. Müssigbrod, Zur ältesten Schicht der Toteneinträge im Necrolog von Moissac, in: Frühmittelalterliche Studien 19 (1985), S. 350-378

ad 3: * Die älteren Urkunden [sc. of the "Stiftsarchiv St. Gallen"], in: Subsidia Sangallensia I (as ad I), S. 287-734
* The charters of Fulda: Die Klostergemeinschaft von Fulda (as ad 1)
* Traditiones Wizenburgenses. Die Urkunden des Klosters Weißenburg 661-864, ed. K. Glöckner, A. Doll (Arbeiten der Hessischen Kommission), Darmstadt, 1979
* Codex Laureshamensis 1-3, ed. K. Glöckner, Darmstadt, 1929-1936
* Recueil des chartes de l'abbaye de Cluny, ed. A. Bernard, A. Bruel, 6 vols., Paris 1897-1903

All together, in the meantime more than 400.000 personal name items have been stored in the data base DMP, derived mainly from obituaries (c. 180.000) and libri memoriales (c. 100.000). Esp. the material from charters (c. 120.000 name-items) needs to be supplemented further.

4. The Automatic Lemmatization

The personal names themselves have been incorporated into the data base without any changes or normalizations, as they are spelled in the manuscripts: because they are comparable by the automatic lemmatization. Even so, personal names can therefore be used as material for historical as well as philological research at the same time. Philologists can use the more or less dated and localized material in the original shape of the transmission. The correct lemmatization of the stored personal names is an indispensable precondition for all search runs of historians, which aim at finding persons and groups of persons. The quality of the results depends basically on this function. In other words: a wrong lemmatization makes qualified prosopographical results impossible. On the other hand, lemmatization of personal names must take into account historical/prosopographical as well as philological results and knowledge: about names and their bearers. Philological work has to be controlled by historians and vice versa.

5. The Structure of the Data

In the following tabulation of the fixed format for personal names, which is used in the data-base for storing and processing the name-items, the automatic-lemma-section is not incorporated. All data which are sent to us in this format can be lemmatized and compared with the complete material or parts of it in the data base. Of course, not all of the fields have to be used; but apart from the personal name itself, all information that can be extracted from the source should be communicated.

Communicated data do not necessarily have to come in this format, they have to follow conventions, however, which make the extraction of all necessary information possible for a conversion program.

from column	to	quantity	Nr.	contents
1	7	7	1	identification code of this occurrence of the personal name
28	28	1	3	kind of source ("+" = obituary,"#" = charter, "*" = confraternity book)
29	30	2	4	Source (e.g. "AF"" = confr. book of Reichenau)
34	37	4	6	provenance of namer entry (e.g. "AUGI" = Reichenau)
41	44	4	9	number of name within a list, charter, entry etc.
45	64	20	10	personal name (spelled as in manuscript!)
65	76	12	11-14	titles of office or social "order" (up to 4 titles)
81	84	4	19	provenance of person (e.g. "AUGI" = Reichenau)
86	86	1	21	entry related to a dead ("+") or living ("*") person
88	88	1	23	indication of relationship (father, son, mother etc.)
89	89	1	24	terminus ante/post of the entry (relating to field 25)
90	91	2	25	day (date of the entry of a person)
92	93	2	26	month (date of the entry of a person)
94	97	4	27	year (date of the entry of a person)
99	102	4	29	transmission (e.g. for charters)
103	103	1	30	function (e.g. in a charter: "E" = recipient, "I" = Intervenient)
118	119	2	37	writer (of a charter, entry etc.: figures)
123	123	1	41	uncertain reading of name ("?")

124	124	1	42	uncertain reading of title ("?")
125	125	1	43	uncertain reading of date ("?")
126	126	1	44	sex of the person ("M" male, "F" female)
128	131	4	46-49	annotations of textual critique to the readings (e.g. "R" = erased)
132	135	4	50	page/folio in manuscript
136	137	2	31	raster of the page (e.g. "A4")

PATTERNS OF SCIENTIFIC EVOLUTION: SHORT TERM CYCLES AND SECULAR WAVES

Suitbert Ertel
Institut für Psychologie
Universität Göttingen
FRG

Abstract

(1) A power spectrum of scientific discoveries and technical inventions (1700-1920) drawn from historical reference books displayed significant cyclic components with short-term period of 6-7 years. Cyclic changes of creativity should be interpretable, in principle, as resulting either from internal (cultural) or from external (environmental, physical) conditions. (2) A quantitative analysis of long-term discovery data revealed excursions from the historical baseline, notably an enormous production peak in the 17th century. These humps in the time-series of scientific breakthroughs reappeared with life data of discoverers/inventors taken from two biographical master indexes, they are thus regarded as method-independent. Certain difficulties connected with internal explanations of short- and/or long-term oscillations suggest to also consider external factors seriously, they might turn out to play a role analogous to Toynbee's "challenge and response". Results of follow-up studies devoted to external instigators of scientific creativity have already been obtained. An account of these, however, must be given elsewhere.

Creativity underlies all cultural evolution. Progress in the arts and science is said to be due to outstanding "acts of creation" (Arthur Koestler, 1964). Our understanding of such remarkable acts, however, is rather poor. Psychologists using tests and experiments to determine sources of creative behaviour notoriously report low correlations, (Taylor, I.A. & Getzels, J.W., 1975.). Nobel prize winners have been interviewed as to their introspections at moments of great discovery. They often give fuzzy answers resorting to metaphors like "inspiration" or "illumination". Neither on the individual level nor in historical perspective are we able to predict the occurrence of EUREKA breakthroughs.

Is cultural evolution a matter of chance comparable to Darwinian mutation and selection? In what follows, I give a preliminary sketch of results obtained in a series of unpublished studies devoted to the search for patterns of creation in cultural history (Ertel, 1983). This report centers on science, ignoring the arts and literature. Data are taken from historical records covering the 17th and 18th century, thus neglecting earlier periods. Both, creative events, i.e. scientific discoveries and technical inventions, and creative individuals, i.e. discoverers and inventors are units of observation. The report includes both approaches, the product as well as the producer. Yearly totals of observations were determined for the years 1600-1920. The primary mode of dealing statistically with data is time-series analysis. The results here are only on a descriptive level.

1. Creative Products: Discoveries and Inventions

Data were extracted from historical reference works (see figure 1). Wilhelm Conrad Röntgen's discovery of the X-rays is likely to be listed in any chronology of scientific discoveries. If an entry is found in any source of our sample, Röntgen's discovery contributes one count to the score of scientific creativity for 1895. Similarly, Wilhelm von Guericke's invention of the air pump, another likely entry in chronologies of scientific history, also contributes one count to the year of 1640.

By copying such entries from reference books into our database, we rely on previous selections of a number of science writers and/or editors. This is an advantage, on the one hand, since we exploit their expert knowledge. On the other hand, we are likely to take on, without correction, their selection biases. These, however, would very probably not be harmful. It suffices to be sure here that the present strategy excludes any possible selection bias of our own. In addition, since we have pooled data from different sources, as we did in the present study, biases and errors of editors may well cancewl each other, and, reliability of the data is thereby enhanced. No source that we found was excluded unless it presented the data in such a manner that they could not easily or objectively be excerpted.

Figure 1: Contributions of Creative Products to the Data Pool from 21 Reference Sources

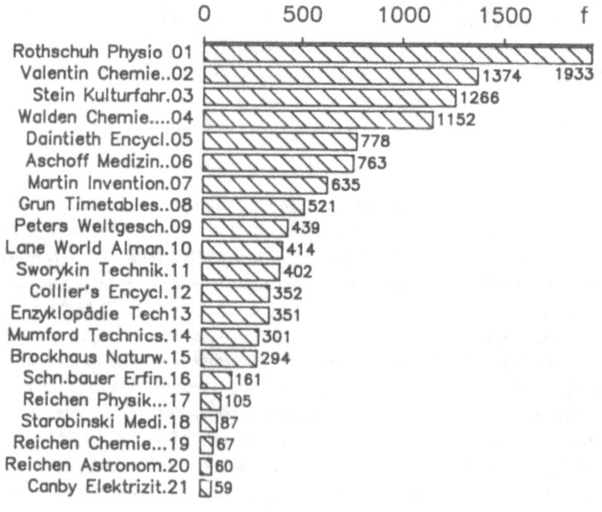

Figure 1 shows the yield of products from the 21 reference sources. The sample is comprehensive, but not exhaustive. Figure 2 shows contributions to our data from various fields of science. Apparently, the present sample is not quite balanced. Medicine, for example, seems to have many more entries than, e.g., physics. Since our goal is more general, it will, thus, not be impaired by this possible source of variance within the data pool.

Figure 2: Contributions of Creative Products to the Data Pool from 8 Fields of Science

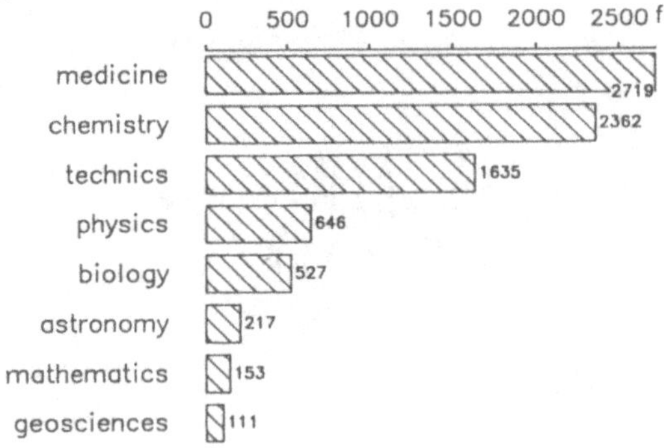

The data have been searched for patterns of relatively short duration as well as for patterns having possibly secular extension.

Short Term Variation

The first analysis was devoted to short-term cyclic variation. Figure 3 shows raw frequencies of scientific discoveries and technical inventions from 1700 - 1920. Visual inspection of this time series suggests some kind of regular oscillation.

Figure 3: Raw Frequencies of Creative Products by Year During the Period 1700-1920

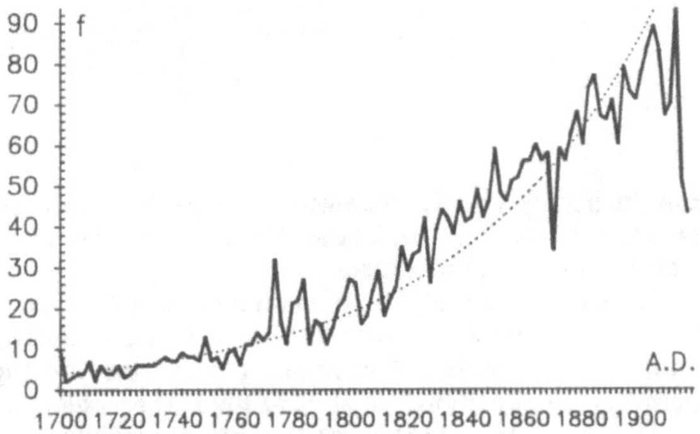

A delta-transformation was used to detrend the curve and to normalize its temporal variance. The cyclic variation became more pronounced, as can be seen in Figure 4.

Figure 4: Data of Figure 3, after Delta Transformation

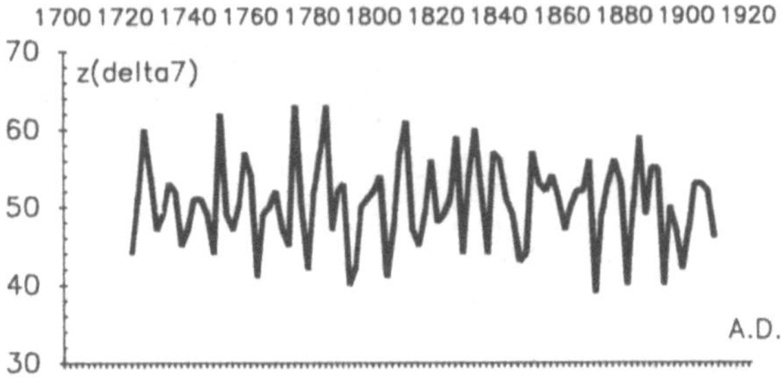

The results of the spectral analysis of the detrended time series (see figure 5) reaffirms what visual inspection of figures 3 and 4 are suggested. Two notable power devariations in the spectrum indicate significant cyclic oscillations of intellectual achievements with a period of 6-7 years.

Figure 5: Power Spectrum of the Time Series of Creative Products 1700-1920

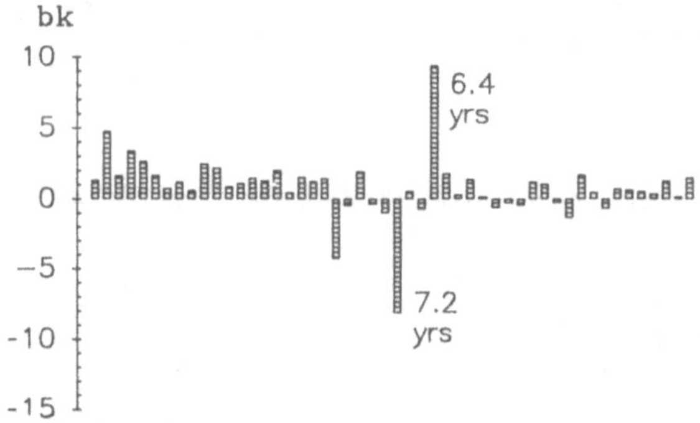

Intellectual achievements in history (results obtained in other cultural areas must be disregarded here) have regular temporal variation. Thus, it may be concluded that scientific creativity is not a matter of pure chance.

The next logical research step would be to determine whether the oscillations identified above are internally or externally caused. Cycles of cultural creativity may result from *internal* cultural change: Periods of increased general curiosity might emerge every now and then improving the conditions for striving towards revolutionary changes. Periods of excessive change may be followed by periods of orderly consummation (analogous to Kuhn's paradigm of "normal" science succeeding revolutionary change). Prolonged states of satiation may eventually give way to renewed general striving for innovation etc.

The causes of cyclic variation, however, might also be *external*. One is reminded here of Toynbee's reflections on historical evolution and his famous rule of "challenge and response". Toynbee included ecological (physical) factors as extraneous cultural instigators (Toynbee, 1934-1961). To apply his rule to the present case, we would have to try and find external factors capable of producing wavelike intellectual variation repeating itself every six to seven years. These factors must be expected to show the same pattern of oscillation. Results obtained by research devoted to external factors which might trigger short term cultural cycles will be reported elsewhere.

Long Term Changes

After having observed some short term lawfulness underlying scientific evolution it appeared promising to search the same data for long term variation. No detrending of time-series was now applied since this would have eliminated variation of any broader scope.

Figure 6 shows an unmodified time series of scientific discoveries from 1600 onwards consisting of five-year-units of observation (pentads). These pentad counts have been smoothed by using a three unit averaging window. Beginning in the 17th and accelerating in the 18th/19th centuries a long term upward trend is apparent. The general trend is consistent with everybody's expectation and need not interest us here.

However, the observation that the curve deviates twice from the historical baseline, is probably not expected. As can be seen in Figure 6, in the middle of the 17th century, frequencies of discoveries increased more rapidly than the general trend could have predicted. This exceptional flourish period was short (1650-1675), discoveries declined again and dropped to their long term level towards 1700. Another deviating peak of creativity, smaller than that of the 17th century, occurred late in the 18th (the latter will be disregarded in the discussion).

Figure 6: Scientific Discoveries 1600-1820, Drawn from 21 Sources with Three or More Citations (i.e. More Important Discoveries Selected). Maximum Frequency in the 17th Century = 100%

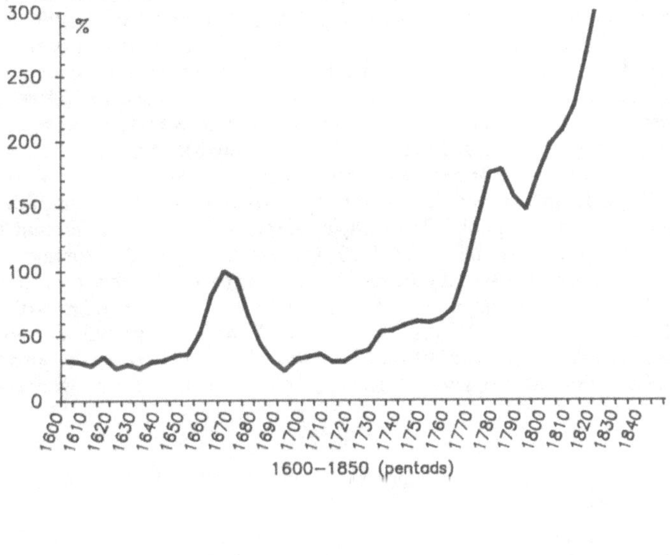

When I first saw the large 17th century hump in the curve some time ago I thought that it might have resulted from computational error or else from uneven sampling. But I did not find any such indication of an artefact: The present curve is indeed an exact replication of the earlier one based on a different and larger set of sources.

Could the editors of our reference sources share identical selection biases? Specifically, could historians of science have paid too much attention to what happened at the time when the first national academies of science were founded (in England 1662, in France 1666) emphasizing the pioneers too much compared to their followers whom they perhaps neglected?

I consider this as most unlikely. The academies promoted scientific progress continuously after their activities had started. It does not seem reasonable to assume that noteworthy scientific achievements were grossly overlooked towards the end of the 17th century if they had really occurred. Two to three decades after the founding of the academies their memberships were growing, outstanding discoveries were most probably subjected to scrutiny no less than before, and historians today would hardly have missed the topics of their discussions. In the next section independent empirical evidence for the reality of our observation will be added.

2. Producers: Discoverers and Inventors

As in an alternative approach, the number of productive years of inventors/discoverers were subjected to statistical analysis. We wanted to see whether the numbers of discoverers and inventors contributing to the advancement of science at a given historical moment would show long term variation similar in form to the variations observed for the quantity of productions. Ideally, we might find that the two time-series vary with each other.

The method to be applied now is similar to that applied before. A scientist who attained new insights during his professional life (by having made discoveries or inventions) is likely to be given an entry in biographical dictionaries. The more successful the scientist was - success being determined by expert consensus - the greater is the likelihood that his name will thus be present. Two comprehensive biographical indexes of scientists exist: Ireland and Pelletier. Norman Ireland's **Index to Scientists** (1962) lists about 7,800 names covering the world's history from ancient times to the present. The names have been extracted from 338 biographical publications up to 1961.

The second source, Pelletier's **Prominent Scientists** (1984) is an update of Ireland's index. Its entries resulted from screening biographical sources which appeared after Ireland's publication (1961-1983). Pelletier extracted 12,300 scientist names taken from 262 reference sources. The pages of these reference books were scanned by an electronic scanner and the data were transferred to machine readable storage.

All further statistics was based on producer scores, i.e. we decided that each scientist should contribute 15 productive years - the years from the 35th to the 50th birthday - to a common productivity pool. For example, a scientist born in 1600 contributed one productivity point each to the years 1635 through 1649 of the common data pool irrespective of whether he actually made his discoveries during this time span or not.

In both Ireland and Pelletier, the sources cited are indexed together with the names they cite. Ireland, e.g., found Isaac Newton cited in 62 biographical sources, while Pelletier found Newton indexed 40 times. James Gregory, a Scottish astronomer and contemporary of Newton (to give an example of a less important figure), is indexed only 5 times in Ireland and 7 times in Pelletier. Thus, an estimate of degrees of eminence was derivable from these counts of citation frequency. For the present purpose, the pool was divided in two, using the median number of citations as the dividing point: A sample of more eminent scientists was, thus, separated from a sample of less eminent ones.

Figure 7 summarizes the result: The two producer curves are shown above (Pelletier and Ireland, bold) together with the productions curve underneath which was taken from Figure 6. The upper curves have been raised to separate them from the curve beneath and from each other for the sake of better comparison.

Figure 7: Time Series of Producer Years for Sources Pelletier and Ireland (Bold), and of Discovery Events (Aggregate of 21 Sources, Thin). Above-Median Citation Frequencies Have Been Extracted. Below-Median Frequencies Are Represented for the Two Flourish-Curves as Thin Pointed Lines

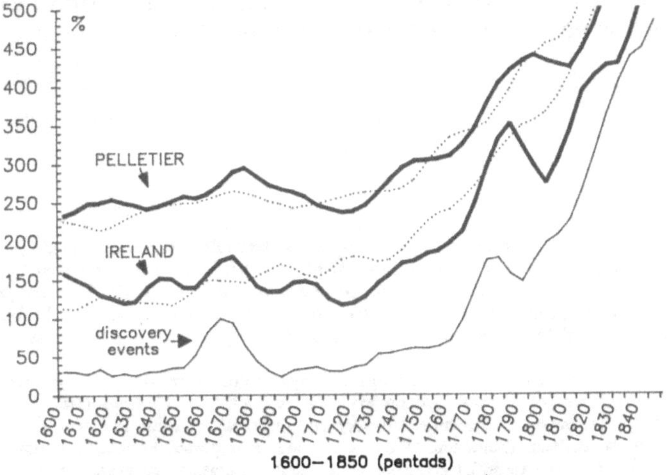

As can be seen, both Pelletier's and Ireland's time-series exhibit, with some 5-10 years delay(1), the expected increase from the baseline around 1670 which had been found in the product curve. The peak of the 1670s, therefore, may now be regarded as method-independent. It is concluded that scientific development in the 17th century in fact displayed the pattern of breakthroughs.

It may be noted in passing that the present result is valuable alone on methodological grounds: life data of creative personalities may apparently replace, to a certain degree, product data which are often more difficult to obtain, especially for earlier historical periods.

If the breakthroughs of the 1670s were due primarily to an increase in the quality of production - less due to an increase in number of producers, we should expect its effects to diminish or even disappear for scientists of lower productivity.

This has indeed been ascertained. For both sources, Pelletier (above) and Ireland (below) the breakthrough period is prominent only for the more eminent scientists (bold, solid curves) and not for the less eminent ones (dotted curves).

How can we explain this exceptional peak of intellectual accomplishment? Again we should consider both, internal and external causes. As an internal cause one might suspect that the desired peace after the turmoil of the Thirty Years War (1618-1648) may have relieved emotions and released more rational effort. If this premise holds, we should expect this hypothesized effect to vary between nations. National producer curves in Europe, however, do not differ much. In addition, there are empirical reasons to rule out the assumption that intellectual creativity was related to the political milieu of the time.(2)

We are, therefore, urged once again to also consider possible external causes. We would even not exclude, without investigation, some common external cause relating our second observation to the first: Short term cycles of intellectual accomplishment might be related to secular producer waves. Some further investigations have already been made, their results will be published elsewhere. The present report, which is the first on our project, is intended to display some of the challenging phenomena alone and tried to suggest that these phenomena truly exist, i.e. that they are objective and method-independent. The problem of explanation requires further study.

NOTES

1. This delay might easily be corrected by changing the pooling rule: The scientists might yield production counts for an earlier span of their age, say 30-44. Another correction is required for sources like Ireland which include too many birth years rounded to full or half centuries in earlier periods (1600, 1650) (a result of not having selected from the total pool more valuable sources). In Ireland, the two small humps around 1635-1650 and 1675-1700 are due to an accumulation of this lack of precision.

2. Simonton's historiometric studies which included hypotheses of relations between warfare or civil disturbance and creativity did not yield any evidence for positive effects either (Simonton, 1984, 164ff). In one study, he found that scientific discovery and technical invention had been adversely affected by international violence (Simonton, 1980), in another, he reported evidence for negative effects of political instability on (scientific) creativity of the next generation (20 years lag) (Simonton, 1975). Simonton would therefore have predicted, if anything, some dip in our time-series, either at the time of warfare itself or at postwar time, i.e. during the period at which time-series actually exhibit an opposite deflection.

REFERENCES

ERTEL, S. 1983. *Himmlische Inspirationen. Menschheit im Einflußbereich kosmischer Wetterlagen.* Unpublished manuscript. Göttingen: Institut für Psychologie

IRELAND, N.O. 1962. *Index to scientists of the world from ancient to modern times: Biographies and portraits.* Boston: Faxon

PELLETIER, P.A. 1985. *Prominent scientists. An index to collective biographies.* New York: Neal-Schuman (2nd ed.)

SIMONTON, D.K. 1975. "Sociocultural context of individual creativity: A transhistorical time-series analysis." *Journal of Personality and Social Psychology* 32, 1119-1133

SIMONTON, D.K. 1984. *Genius, creativity, and leadership. Historiometric inquiries*. Cambridge: Harvard University Press

SIMONTON, D.K. 1980. "Techno-scientific activity and war: A yearly time-series analysis, 1500-1903 A.D." *Scientometrics* 2, 251-255

TAYLOR, I.A. and GETZELS, J.W. 1975. *Perspectives in creativity*. Chicago: Aldine

TOYNBEE, A. 1934-1961. *A study of history*. 12. vol. Oxford: Oxford University Press

THE DATABASE *SAINT-LEGER*: COMPUTER AND HISTORY

José-Gentil Da Silva, Dominique Vignau
University of Nice
France

The database "SAINT-LEGER" was developed to retrieve knowledge from stored facts. These now include different kinds of material relating to modern times. Our aim is to extend it by extracting information from various historical sources about their places, events, people, decisions and choices. The name "SAINT-LEGER" is the one of the village in the County of Nice first studied with the help of the computer. This paper is a survey of our work on the richest annual population and cattle census series executed in the old regime County of Nice. The computer was used to build up a database for the study of these documents. Afterwards, we applied the data organization and its retrieval system to different material, the proceedings of some XVIIth century bankers meetings.

I. THE "SAINT-LEGER" FUND: AN EXCEPTIONAL MATERIAL FOR HISTORICAL RESEARCH

The main Record Office of Alpes-Maritimes (France) at Nice keeps the communal and parochial funds of many localities of the actual districts of the County of Nice.

In most cases, the registers of birth, marriage and death constitute predominantly the deposit set. Such "registres paroissiaux" ("Parochial Registers") represent a very important source of information on marriage, birth and death rates, but neither give information on migratory movements nor about actual family structures. This was not the purpose of these registers. Sometimes, a set of financial documents complementes these data. A proper demographic inquiry is rarely to be found.

Several localities have been able to transfer registers of population census and cattle called "consegne" (Italian term in the plural; sg.: "consegna"; in French: "consigne"). This word, both, means the annual counting operation and the file used to register the information. This process is to be inscribed within the framework of the centralizing policy of the House of Savoy to which Nice and his County have been submitted since September 1388, date of the feudal "deditio" towards the Duke. In fact, from the end of the Middle Ages, the population belonging to this dynasty was obliged to humour the ducal - and afterwards royal - Administration with regard to numerous laws stipulating the counting of persons and cattle. The fiscal scope of such an operation is well known but the aim is also one of cognizance. In this manner, individual countings were organized to value salt-tax, property-tax and poll-tax amounts; to know the possible number of men under arms, the one of unfortunate people to be exempted ("Roles des Miserables"), to set up the lists of defaulting and refractory persons ("Roles des Defaillants", "Roles des Recalcitrants") and even the parochial registers of souls statements ("Etats des Ames"). The Administration of the House of Savoy seems to have very soon realized the importance to succeed in centralizing the whole lot of these sparse information.

The little village called Saint-Leger, with several others, was given to the Sardinian States in September 5th, 1760, according to the Franco-Sardinian treaty signed on in Turin a few months before between Louis XV and Charles-Emmanuel III (March 24th, 1760). Thirteen years later, the community of Saint-Leger bears its first personal counting operation which will be strictly repeated till 1790. Afterwards, the French Revolution will integrate the whole region and interrupt this process. In fact, two periods are to be considered: 1773-1784 and 1785-1790. In any case, this does not spoil the set: the second period registers complete the first ones.

1. 1773-1784

From 1773 to 1784, the counting is made every year at the end of December and only deals with persons because the cattle is enumerated during the previous month of May. The first twelve "consegne" used to register the operation are all simply manuscript copybooks. The language then used is French. It is not to be wondered at: Italian and French have been enacted official languages in their respective application areas since the 1559 ducal edict delivered by Emmanuel-Philibert. This is another aspect of the perspicacity of the House of Savoy which always adapted the communal institutions to local particularities. Within these first registers, some manuscript columns are defined in which the writer registers the surname, the christian name, the age and the sex of each individual as well as his socio-professional quality, if possible. The census executed in Saint-Leger from 1773 on, takes into account two sub-totals for a family: the first one for "males" and the second one for "females". The total account of inhabitants per family is registered in a cumulative column whose account is carried forward. These first "consegne" are not very rich in information: even if they mention the spouses maiden names, they very rarely give information about the origins of people. Then, the temptation is great to consider all the inhabitants as native of Saint-Leger, excepted two servants and a farmer family attached to the priest. We shall later see how different reality is. The default of much fuller information concerning the individuals makes these first twelve "consegne" simple counting records. Fortunately, the following registers provide much more details about this population.

2. 1785-1790

On June 25th, 1785 the members of the community council are informed of the new census procedure. The Administration decides that time has come to put into operation the "Regolamento dei Pubblici" enacted on June 6th, 1775 which ordains, among other things, an annual census fixed on January. Henceforth, this operation becomes a real inquiry and nothing is neglected. First of all, the cattle is counted at the same time as persons and each householder is held responsible for his declaration. Then to do it, he is obliged to move to the "communal house" in a fixed and publicly notified date. Nobody can argue he did not know time and place, and failing persons are liable to a fine whose amount is quite exorbitant: five golden coins. Moreover, they would be condemned to pay a double property-tax. So, from 1785 on, in the case of annual census, the harsh regulations from the central Administration attest an extreme rationalization of the process.

This reinforcement of the administrative tutelage finds expression in the appearance of a printed, standardized census register. Henceforth, all the communities are asked to use the "consegna" imposed by Turin, and only this one. The register is bound, 30x45 cm and contains a sufficient number of pages to receive the entire information about people and cattle. Nothing is left to chance: everything to declare must be inscribed in the provided printed columns entitled in Italian. The meticulousness with which the Administration has thought to distinguish varieties within each animal species, attests the care for an exhaustive inquiry in the census process. Every question becomes more accurate and even carping. So, each householder must declare whether the cattle he possesses is his own and if so, whether it has been leased to him. For example, when Jean-Louis Belleoud declares to have some cattle leased to him by Mr Douhet, a citizen installed in Saint-Leger, this contract appears in both declarations. The householder must also give the most exact estimation of his real estate's cadastral value. The absent persons do not escape from it: their representative must specify where they are and for what personal reasons. Contrary to the first twelve registers, the ones of 1785-1790 are meticulously drawn up and the declarations are given with an extreme care. For instance, the 1790 register shows that Honoré Roux gives a real estate's estimation widely inferior to the one thousand pounds and seven beasts he declared the year before. The reason is inscribed: "... declares not possess any real estate, lives with half of the advantages of the property he has given on the occasion of the marriage of his daughter, does not declare any beast". The great lot of details appearing in these last registers makes them a real mine of information compared with the first twelve ones. Completing them, they have a retroactive effect which allows us to fill up former gaps. For example, we find here the origin of each inhabitant which was not mentioned in the first twelve registers and so we can see that about 30% of the spouses are not native of Saint-Leger but came from the surroundings. The migration is, henceforth, frequent and the obligation to give a real estate's estimation allows us to follow the evolution of the patrimonies, of their handing over mode (which is not necessarily the one of primogeniture) and of each householder's fortune. Moreover, by these documents, we get knowledge of different social groups existing within this population and an insight into the inhabitants' way of life.

The annual population and cattle census of Saint-Leger are constituting, for the County of Nice, the only uninterrupted series during the twenty years preceding the French Revolution. As a matter of fact, for the most part, the "consegne" of the other localities reached us with frequent ruptures, even in a sporadic way. Guillaumes, for instance, furnished only seven counting registers between 1780 and 1790, among which only the last four ones are identical and consecutive. Peone has given five, established from 1786 to 1790. This seems to be not a consequence of some hazardous documents conservation. We rather think that before 1785 in matter of census, law was not applied with the required rigour. By way of proof, we can establish the absence of continuous registers before 1785 and the appearance at this date of identical, standardized registers in many of these villages (see Figure 1). Finally, we can say that during the years before 1785 each community had to proceed to an annual counting of population and cattle according to the "Regolamento dei Pubblici" enacted ten years before and we can reasonably conclude they did not make it as formally as they were expected to do. It is possible that before 1785 some censuses of Saint-Leger's kind were processed hither and thither - the counting of the population of Nice is well known - but we think that the communities of this county have really neglected to do it during this period. It is the new administrative policy of the House of Savoy which makes things change in 1785.

Our study is based upon documents and they are available only from this date.

Figure 1:

Aspremont	1774		
Guillaumes		1780; 1783; 1784;	de 1787 à 1790
Peone			de 1786 à 1790
Saint-Etienne-de-Tineé			1786; 1787; 1789
Saint-Léger	de 1773 a 1784		de 1786 à 1790
Sainte Agnès	1774		
Tourrettes-Levens			1786

That is why Saint-Leger is really a model. Its series is continuous during eighteen years. This set is the only one for the region. However, before we made a thorough study these registers never formed the privileged subject of research; at the utmost, they are mentioned in regional-scope studies. We must say that Saint-Leger was and is still a thinly populated village and we must acknowledge that the demographic research feeds itself with more quantitative than qualitative data. This is a comprehensible way of study but it may lead to neglect for a long time some localities estimated as secondary, whose study nevertheless reveals very rich information about the communal institutions and daily life of the rural populations of the old regime County of Nice.

II. THE DATABASE "SAINT-LEGER": A TOOL FOR HISTORICAL STUDY

1. The Global Database

The database "SAINT-LEGER" has been conceived from all census registers in order to make the demographic study easier but also to allow the analysis of the evolution of this population. We have been able to follow the evolution of the family (composition, structure), the transmission of patrimonies, the transformation of the socio-professional qualities (are they necessarily cultivators from father to son?) and the evolution of behaviour (migration, marriage, etc.). In the database, the mode of data respects this progression. From left to right, the fields are the following: family number, name, christian name, sex, origin, socio-professional quality, familial status (i.e. the position of each member of the family). This information is followed by the eighteen continuous years for which we recorded the age of each individual and the main events which occurred during his life time (birth, marriage, death, migration, temporary absence, etc.). This constitutes the global database mainly destined to a longitudinal study of this population during almost twenty years. So, it has been possible to follow the individual, familial and communal evolutions with the help of a rather "economic" file taking only 200 Ko. It stands to reason that all sort, merge, extraction operations are feasible in this database, as well as the necessary calculations.

The family status (CHF for "Chef de famille" (householder), EPO for "Epouse" (spouse), D1.1 for the first descendant of the first generation (for example, the householder's son or daughter), COL for "Collateral" (brother, sister, cousin, etc...), designates each individual in regard to the householder registered in the 1773 "consegna", the first register of this series. As soon as a householder's change appears in a register (in most cases because of death, but not always as some householders transmit their patrimonies during their life time), all the family status change according to the new position of each member of the family. This new status is then to be considered until a contingent future householder's change, and so on... . By the way, the individual evolution and the family's one are easy to follow and to display.

2. The Yearly Databases

The global database "SAINT-LEGER" manages the demographic data concerning the whole population of the village from 1773 to 1790. This mass is not necessarily addressed completely. Thus, a transversal analysis of this or that year does not need data of the other ones. For example, a data processing relating to estimated patrimonies and cattle is only to be run with the 1785-1790 data, because this is the only period in which this information is available. It would be useless to address the global database in this case. It could even be pernicious in so far as the redundancies would slacken the processing. So, we divided the main database into eighteen yearly databases which do not affect its homogeneity but make the data processings easier and faster. The total or partial processing is chosen according to the aims. For both, the data extraction is the main tool used.

3. The Data Extraction

To extract some relational information to be used as elements of interpretation or explanation extraction, criteria are set into a zone which is the copy of the fields of the database headlines. These criteria can be very flexible: names, words of contemporary vocabulary, simple letters or numbers, signs and even arithmetical and logical operators. In fact, any character or group of characters existing in the database can be used as an extraction criterion. The operation can be simple with only one criterion, or multiple combining several ones. The data recording organization and the facility offered by the positioning of extraction criteria allow the user to ask everything he wants to obtain from the database. The results are depending on the questions. With the database "SAINT-LEGER" the demographic analysis is made much easier: every query about a phenomenon gives full information. For instance, let us consider the death rate of 1782 for persons enumerated in 1781. If we place the extraction's criterion "DC" under the field titled "en 1782", we get one householder, two spouses, one collateral and one infant. The sex, the age and the matrimonial situation also appear. It is reasonable that children born and dead after the 1781 census are ignored by this processing because they were not registered in 1781. Nevertheless, the database "SAINT-LEGER" principles can be extended to the study of the parochial registers. Another example will show the emigration during 1783. We place under the field "en 1783" the criterion ">" which indicates any leaving in the database. The result is four persons. Here, the advantages of our data management system become apparent: we are able to say immediately that 1) these moving persons are four spinsters; 2) two of them are sisters (seen thanks to the family number); 3) three of them are young and they definitely leave the village; 4) the last person moves to marry inside of the community (see Figure 2). A social study of the population can be supported by using the database "SAINT-LEGER" in this way. We place the criterion "CHF" (householder) under "en 1786" and we get the list of them. After a sorting of patrimony values in decreasing order, we can see the social composition of this population. Obviously, the greatest part of it is rural (only two householders registered as "bourgeois" with a very low number of beasts), but within this country people, the difference is great between the many "cultivateurs" and "journaliers" (cultivators and journeymen) and the rare "menagers" who live rather comfortably. The first four lines of this list show the category of the "piu apparenti" that is to say the better provided for who are the leading persons and the main members of the community council (see Figure 3). The extraction processed gives another information: The marriage rate for this year, concerning the householders. Simple arithmetic operations allow us to get the following results: in 1786, the community contains twenty-nine householders. Among them, we see eight widowed men and women (27,58%) and three bachelors (10,35%). This means that almost 38% of the householders live without any husband or wife. Moreover, the average of their ages is 52,3 years old. Are they living quite alone? This is a question the database "SAINT-LEGER" answers easily thanks to its organization which regroups under a specific number the members of a same family. So, we can see that several young couples are living with parents.

So, the very simple processings supported by the organization of the database "SAINT-LEGER" enable a first knowledge of a population, even before a detailed study is started.

The main interest of a tool is to be used more and more and for different purposes.

Figure 2:

FAM.	NOM	PRENOM	ORIGINE	QUALITE	H	F	en 1783	âge	M	C	V
9	COSTE	Marguerite	La Vignasse			X	D1.2 >>	23		X	
12	COSTE	Marie	Saint-Léger			X	D1.1 >>	18		X	
12	COSTE	Anne	Saint-Léger			X	D1.2 >>	16		X	
31	RIBOUET	Marianne	Saint-Léger			X	D1.1 -> MA	35	X		

III. AN APPLICATION TO ANOTHER HISTORICAL MATERIAL

We applied the principles of the database "SAINT-LEGER" to a different historical source, which is the corpus of the vocabulary appearing in the meetings of some bankers uring the XVIIth Century.

Figure 3:

FAM.	NOM	PRENOM	ORIGINE	QUALITE	H	F	en 1786	âge	m	c	v	Tot.Hab.	Tot.Bét.	Patrim.
7	BARET	Joseph	La Vignasse	Ménager	1		CHF	54	1			10	70	3500
21	DOUHET	Claude	Entrevaux	Bourgeois	1		CHF	66		1		2	9	3500
22	DOUHET	Jacques	Entrevaux	Bourgeois	1		CHF	46	1			8	3	3000
25	FOURNIER	Louis	Saint-Leger	Ménager	1		CHF	69	1			8	28	2000
18	COSTE	Joseph	Saint-Leger	Laboureur	1		CHF	57	1			4	13	1500
19	COSTE	Jean-Baptiste	Saint-Leger	Ménager	1		CHF	64			1	5	32	1500
27	JUSBERT	Esprit	Saint-Leger	Ménager	1		CHF n(D1)	48	1			5	9	1500
29	VERDOLIN	Marie	Annot	Ménager	1	1	CHF n(ALL)	43			1	4	14	1500
28	BONNET	Jean-Honore	Le Fugeret	Laboureur	1		CHF	69	1			5	4	1200
3	BARET	Esprit	La Vignasse	Ménager	1		CHF	25	1			6	33	1000
5	BELLEOUT	Joseph	Le Theron	Cultivateur	1		CHF	52	1			3	15	1000
16	COSTE	Honore	Saint-Leger	Ménager	1		CHF	51	1			4	11	1000
17	COSTE	Martin	Saint-Leger	Ménager	1		CHF	65	1			6	22	1000
26	JUSBERT	Augustin	La Vignasse	Ménager	1		CHF	46	1			6	42	1000
31	RIBOUET	Jean-Louis	Saint-Leger	Ménager	1		CHF	35	1			6	14	1000
9	COSTE	Joseph	La Vignasse	Journalier	1		CHF	43	1			5	18	600
12	COSTE	Marianne	Saint-Leger	Cultivateur		1	CHF	45			1	2	3	600
33	GILLOUX	Joseph	Entraunes	Prêtre	1		CHF	52		1		6	33	600
13	COSTE	Raphael	Saint-Leger	Journalier	1		CHF	75	1			2	0	500
30	ROUX	Honore	La Croix	Tisserand	1		CHF	75	1			4	6	400
2	BELLEOUD	Jean-Baptiste	Saint-Leger	Journalier	1		CHF	46		1		1	1	300
6	DOSOL	Joseph	Saint-Benoit	Cultivateur	1		CHF	51	1			3	13	300
11	DURAND	Catherine	Castillet	Journalier		1	CHF	51			1	3	10	300
23	RIBOUET	Marianne	Saint-Leger	Cultivateur		1	CHF	38			1	3	2	300
24	FOURNIER	Jean-Joseph	Saint-Leger	Ménager	1		CHF	77			1	9	49	300
15	COSTE	Joseph	Saint-Leger	Journalier	1		CHF	34	1			3	7	250
10	BOYER	Marie-Marguerite	Le Theron	Journalier		1	CHF	51			1	1	0	30
8	BELLEOUD	Jean-Louis	La Vignasse	Journalier	1		CHF	55			1	4	3	0
14	COSTE	Jean-Baptiste	Saint-Leger	Rentier	1		CHF	35	1			2	0	0

1. A Vocabulary Corpus of some XVIIth Century Bankers Meetings

The document upon which we worked is a set of twenty-four fair reports. This represents twenty-four groups of texts drawn up during every meeting without copying any previous one. In each act, we systematically find texts in a regular order relative to the appearance of the financial mechanisms which made the institution's efficacy. We called these necessary and successive actions "operations de base" ("basic operations"). The study of these homogeneous text series allowed us to discern the physiognomy of the meeting and what is today the subject of this paper, to draw the list of the indispensable vocabulary at "Bisenzone" between 1625 and 1635.

Figure 4:

	I			OPERATION II			III			IV			V			VI			VII		
VOCABLES	b	c	d	e	f	g	h	i	j	k	l	m	n	o	p	q	r	s	t	u	v
(Havere)	72	/	24	37	/	23							28	/	24	107	/	24	37	/	24
Cambio	28	/	22	40	/	24							56	/	24						
Cancelliere				34	/	24	24	/	24				23	/	23	27	/	23	22	/	21
Capitolo				24	/	24							22	/	22						
Cartella				24	/	24															
Consigliere				23	/	23															
Console				23	/	23															
Conto				25	/	23															
Decretare	22	/	22	21	/	21										21	/	21			
Descritto				24	/	21															
Distintamente				31	/	23															
Eccedere				24	/	24															
Entrare				22	/	22															
Essere				69	/	24										54	/	22	119	/	24
Fare	39	/	24	24	/	21															
Fiera	77	/	24	78	/	24	72	/	24				40	/	24	41	/	24	46	/	24
Metta				24	/	24															
Metter				24	/	21															
Nome				22	/	22															
Notare				35	/	24															
Ordine				21	/	21															
Pagamento				39	/	24	48	/	24												
Piazza				48	/	24							22	/	22				24	/	23
Presente	33	/	23	49	/	24	21	/	21				33	/	23						
Prezzo				72	/	24	24	/	24				26	/	24						
Restare				22	/	22															
Ritrovare				21	/	21															
Sedere				25	/	24													20	/	20
Seguire				22	/	22	24	/	24										24	/	24
Solito	23	/	20	25	/	22													20	/	20
Stabilire				46	/	24							24	/	24						
Successivamente	25	/	22	24	/	24	24	/	24												
Tempo				24	/	24	48	/	24												
Votatione	21	/	21	20	/	20													20	/	20
Voto				73	/	24															

2. The Data Extraction: Vocables Frequency and Moments

We must acknowledge that our whole approach lies upon the analysis of these words. Of course, it is not carried out for linguistic reasons; we consider what is said, when it is asserted, why and to which ends. Assertion is information. Our concern is the intervener, the writer translating his message and at what moment he does so (occasion, place). Time is interesting too: repetition is insistence; and also the time the intervener takes, that is to say duration.

The data were organized as follows: the first field receives the vocabulary. Giving a 80% efficacy to the indispensable words, we kept the ones which appear in the texts of at least twenty fairs out of twenty-four. Excluding names of persons and towns, we obtained a total of ninety-five vocables. This vocabulary is the main relation between

Figure 5:

	I			II			OPERATION III			IV			V			VI			VII		
VOCABLES	b	c	d	e	f	g	h	i	j	k	l	m	n	o	p	q	r	s	t	u	v
Bolognino				34	/	24	24	/	24							27	/	23	22	/	21
Cancelliere							24	/	24												
Capo							21	/	21												
Carantano							24	/	24												
Carlino							47	/	24												
Congregare	33	/	22				49	/	24												
Constante							23	/	23												
Corrente							23	/	23	31	/	24									
Ducato							104	/	24												
Effetto	25	/	22				24	/	23												
Fiera	77	/	24	78	/	24	72	/	24				40	/	24	41	/	24	46	/	24
Grosse							31	/	24												
Italia							24	/	24												
Maravedi							48	/	24												
Marche							50	/	24												
Mese							145	/	24												
Notifficare							23	/	23	30	/	23									
Oro							168	/	24												
Pagamento				39	/	24	48	/	24												
Paolo							24	/	24												
Presente	33	/	23	49	/	24	21	/	21				33	/	23						
Prezzo				72	/	24	24	/	24				26	/	24						
Prossimo							72	/	24										22	/	22
Publicare							48	/	24												
Scudo							383	/	24	293	/	22									
Seguire				22	/	2	24	/	24										24	/	24
Sole							24	/	24												
Stampa							24	/	24												
Successivamente	25	/	22	24	/	24	24	/	24												
Tempo				24	/	24	48	/	24												
Trattante	43	/	24				23	/	23										39	/	24

different preoccupations and corresponds to efficacious and convenient structures which determine the limits and warrant the discussion and decision rules.

Afterwards, from left to right, the following fields are filled with the frequencies of each vocable at each moment of the meeting. Seven fields were created corresponding to the seven "basic operations": Operation I: acceptance of the bills; Operation II: voting of the change; Operation III: proclamation of the exchange's rates and of the pay-day dates on the place; Operation IV: money registration; Operation V: bill-brokers' oath; Operation VI: balance's presentation; Operation VII: closure.

Figure 6:

	I			II			III			IV			V			VI			OPERATION VII		
VOCABLES	b	c	d	e	f	g	h	i	j	k	l	m	n	o	p	q	r	s	t	u	v
(H)avere	72	/	24	37	/	23							28	/	24	107	/	24	37	/	24
Bene																			21	/	21
Bilancio																25	/	24	45	/	24
Cancelliere				34	/	24	24	/	24				23	/	23	27	/	23	22	/	21
Condannare																			23	/	23
Consegnare																			24	/	24
Creditore																			41	/	24
Debitore																			24	/	23
Dichiarare																			28	/	24
Dover	36	/	22																31	/	23
Errore																			24	/	24
Essere				69	/	24										54	/	22	119	/	24
Fiera	77	/	24	78	/	24	72	/	24				40	/	24	41	/	24	46	/	24
Finire																			24	/	24
Interesse																			23	/	23
Piazza				48	/	24							22	/	22				24	/	23
Potere																			26	/	24
Pregiudicio																22	/	22	25	/	24
Prossimo							72	/	24										22	/	22
Sedere				25	/	24													20	/	20
Seguire				22	/	22	24	/	24										24	/	24
Solito	23	/	20	25	/	22													20	/	20
Terminare																			20	/	20
Trattante	43	/	24				23	/	23							51	/	24	39	/	24
Trovare																24	/	22	22	/	20
Votatione	21	/	21	20	/	20													20	/	20

As a word expresses a preoccupation, the data processing is very easy to run with the database "SAINT-LEGER" principles. The data extraction is applied to the frequency of words in each field that is to say at each moment of the meeting. As these moments are corresponding to the "basic operations", the data extraction gives the richest of them from the vocabulary point of view. So, we decided to place the criterion ">20" under each operation field, just on the left of the sign "/" which is a separator between the frequency and the number of texts. The results are the following: the most frequent operations are the second and the third ones (see Figures 4 and 5). It is not surprising in so far as they are the most numerous in discussion. Remember that Operation II deals with the voting of changes and Operation III is the place of proclamation of the rates of exchange and of the pay-day dates. In these occasions, some tensions may appear and the debates are certainly longer than on other occasions. Operation VII is interesting, too. The data extraction shows that it is the third one according to the numeric importance but also - and mainly - this processing makes appear another aspect which is the one of specific vocabulary. In this Operation VII vocables appear, whose constancy shows how they had to define once for all, at the leaving moment, the general situation or even how they express requirements and precautions. These are words like "condannare", "cancelliere", "errore", "essere", "finire", "pregiudicio", "terminare", "trattante", "trovare"... (see Figure 6).

So, we have been able to show that the main characteristic of a "basic operation" is its richness or insistence with regard to the indispensable vocabulary and we very easily displayed the more important of them from this point of view. We also pointed out a specific vocabulary appearing in specific contexts. This vocabulary is the one of particular meetings and it is used by men belonging to some "restricted groups".

3. Some "Restricted Groups" Meetings

In Plaisance (Italy), the Notary Giovanni Battista Aliprandi drew up the proceedings of the change fairs presided by Giulio Cesare Barelli, a business man of Milan, between 1625 and 1635. The men present at these meetings, the "feraldi", are thirty business men, bankers and merchant-bankers. They came with golden coins to fix the rules of two operations: change and return, two prices, the price of the present money and the one of the absent money. These meetings took place in "Bisenzone" which had been, for a while, Besancon (Franche-Comte), then Chambery (Savoy), then Plaisance, Novi and the surroundings of Genes. The main subjects of these meetings are the regulation of the use of money in business, the part taken by the draft and the bill of exchange and a care in harmonizing the business practice. During these meetings some tensions appear making some discussions longer. This produces a vocabulary corpus which allows us to know the involvement of the participants, of their groups and of the part taken by the general circumstances. It explains the implacable logic of all this according to the intended purposes which are pointed out by themselves. So, the frequency of words, the intensity with which they are asserted at a certain moment and their absence elsewhere indicate what these "restricted groups" are attending. Finally, all this expresses dated and located historic realities.

The interrogation of a database is always a matter of choices determined according to the aims to be reached. The data organization and the very flexible extraction criterions make the database "SAINT-LEGER" an easy to handle tool which allows a lot of investi-gations and fast calculations. It lets the user make choices and take up his own research in an imaginative way.

Nevertheless, such data processings do not give solutions to problems, they are only tools making work easier. The exploitation of the answers is the only way to bring research to a successful issue. History is the art of putting the "good" questions. We are trying to find them.

REFERENCES

DA SILVA, Jose-Gentil. 1970. *Lexique, Temps, Histoire*. 2 vols., Paris-Nanterre, 696 p.
VIGNAU, Dominique. 1988. *Histoire et Informatique*. Nice, 292 p.

ESTABLISHING A RECONSTRUCTIVE METASOURCE ON CENSORSHIP OF NOVELS IN THE EARLY FRENCH ENLIGHTENMENT

Hans-Christoph Hobohm
Institut für Angewandte Sozialforschung
University of Cologne
FRG

Not only on account of the famous article by Michel Foucault (1969) has it become a generally recognized fact that the social role of the writer as understood today has developed at the beginning of the 18th century. While for a long time artists and writers during the period of absolutism in the 17th century had strongly depended on patronage and protectionism, some writers started to break away from the traditional pattern of feudal production of culture well before the actual rise of the Enlightenment. It is true that in the beginning only a few writers were able to make a living out of writing but the fact that the first years of the 18th century had seen typically "modern" authors like René Lesage is clear evidence of the development of a literary market determined by laws different from those of noble and royal patronage. This tendency was, of course, enhanced by generally spreading alphabetization and the structural changes in society associated with it, which Habermas (1962) described as the structural change of the public.

Corresponding to the new readership, not only the profession of the author as such was born but along with it a fundamentally new product. It was no longer only panegyric in the broadest sense of the word but a saleable style of writing appropriate to the new activity of extensive reading, and to a growing literary market which guaranteed the writer a secure livelihood. While the period of courtly-aristocratic literature had been rather dominated by theatre and poetry, all over Europe one then found a new predilection for prose. Names such as Daniel Defoe and Jonathan Swift and their new novels - many times explicitly called bourgeois - are typical, often quoted examples. (cf. Jüttner 1987, Viala 1985).

Compared with England this development started slightly later in France. In many respects England was a precursor for modern developments, as, for instance, in the field of literature. Famous characters of the French "story" of the development of the literary market are Abbé Prévost with his novel "*Manon Lescaut*" (a novel still worth reading today), or Marivaux with "*Paysan Parvenu*". Both writers reformulate socio-psychological concepts such as the subject, the individual, sensitivity, or social achievement as such in the newly found communication medium "novel" (Sanders 1987). These two novels met with great public success which among other indications was reflected by a high number of pirated editions.

The reaction of Royal Censorship was appropriately in accordance with existing legislation (Hanley 1980). The censors could only punish some allegedly immoral tendencies in Manon, "the prostitute", whereas they had to leave relatively unmolested the peasant Jacob, "the parvenu", who, on principle, is more dangerous. However, when during the following years production figures of similar novels rose drastically, they were feeling more and more uncomfortable. After a period of indecision during the years

1735/36, Chancellor d'Aguesseau decided to prohibit the novel as a genre in early 1737, and ordered the reinforcement of post-censorship in order to counteract the flow of pirated editions from abroad. This proved to be the first attempt of royal censorship to adapt to the new reality of the literary market (Hobohm 1986). Authors and editors soon recognized in connection with the prohibition of the novel that the old guild-oriented "*Système de privilèges*" (i. e. the royal approval of book printing) was inadequate as far as the modern novel is concerned. Novel printing was now done illegally or transferred abroad which up until the Revolution helped to establish a very well functioning system of smuggling and a flourishing "Black Market" (cf. Darnton 1982).

Police authorities monitoring the book trade were well aware of the problem: despite the prohibition of the novel, production of novels and similarly 'disgraceful' literature had not decreased, and above all the number of "littérateurs" (as Diderot "immortalized" them with his "*Nephew of Rameau*") had constantly been rising. When the apparatus of preliminary censorship had not seemed to cope with this new phenomenon, the book supervising authority then paid particular attention to subsequent monitoring of the book trade. Because this also proved to be ineffective the authorities tried to get down to the roots of the trouble: editors and even the authors themselves were now submitted to preventive monitoring. Thus towards the end of the 1740s there would be the creation of what, according to my knowledge, can be called the first, formalized registration file of individuals in the western world.

The files saved from the archives of the Parisian Censorship Department are a complete and systematic documentation of this double process of the development of the literary market, and of the adaptation of the state-run supervising system to the new conditions of literary production. There are, for example, a great number of relatively complete, serial sources on the decisions of preliminary censorship as well as on seizures and confiscations of already printed books. François Furet and his "*Equipe*" which became famous under the name "*Livre et Société*" already used these sources in the mid 60s for intensive research on French book production during the Enlightenment. The research done in this context belongs to the most famous examples of "Annales"-historiography which has even today a fruitful tradition, not only in France.

The corpus of the sources in question is relatively indeterminable in dimension and it has, in fact, the most neglected disadvantage that it is unsystematically scattered over Parisian libraries and archives. Many historians are satisfied with the abundant material found in the manuscript section of the *Bibliothèque Nationale*. However, as far as some semi-serial sources such as "*ordonnances*" and "*Arrêts de Parlement*" are concerned one is, to a certain extent, dependent on the relatively unexplored archives of the *Bibliothèque Historique de la Ville de Paris* and the *Archives Nationales* which in connection with the collections of the *Bibliothèque Nationale* allow to paint a far more complete picture of book production than is generally thought of. The majority of transactions in the literary field - insomuch as they have been recorded in the files of the book trade guild or the police authorities - can be reconstructed down to the last detail. Undreamed-of treasures still wait here for systematical synthesis.

Normally source material is only consulted when looking at a definite research object, an author for instance. Just because it is so difficult to trace the information required in the vast amount of handwritten files one is often satisfied with individual data regarding specific questions although some files only become interesting in the synthesis, in connection with other documents. For dating purposes, for example, the so-called "*Registre des Permissions tacites*" is considered in research literature as relatively useless, as dates are not given. If, however, the whole process of censorship is reconstructed, we are able to reintegrate this dossier in its general context. Like fragments of a text, the puzzle of all individual data reveals the complex interplay of the book trade guild, the royal book police and the para-legal book market. In particular the less prominent events leave traces for the explanations of the change of the *epistemè*.

Apart from the purely serial sources of the actual censorship decisions (approbation lists, seizure and confiscation documents of the customs authorities), there is in my opinion one unique juridical source: namely, the above mentioned file of supervised persons established in the years between 1749 and 1753 by the police inspector Joseph d'Hémery (see Darnton 1984). According to a pre-printed pattern he tried - certainly not out of his passion as a private collector, as Robert Darnton suggests - to record all suspicious persons in the literary field and to observe them on a regular basis. By means of omnipresent police spies (the so-called flies: "*mouches*"), he obtained the following information on approximately 500 authors and just as many book traders and editors: the family and Christian name; the title; and the alias, where possible; the date of the investigations; the age of the person at this specific moment; their home province (that means at this time: their dialect); their physical appearance; their "profession" and their "story".

A particular characteristic of this file is the fact that it does not only include authors and book traders who had already become "liable to prosecution", but that it was an attempt to establish a documentation of virtually all persons involved in book production and living in Paris. Marivaux, for instance, is merely characterized as being "a member of the Académie Française who has written a lot of theatre plays and novels", whereas the comment on Diderot, who had already become dubious with his "*Bijoux indiscrets*", warns explicitly: "He is a clever boy but extremely dangerous". Thus, authors and book traders are not marked generally as "criminals"; the file is rather a preventive collection of information on two new social positions gaining gradually significance (and en passant one notes: there is the explicit mention of the "*auteur*" as a profession ("*métier*").

In my study I did not originally intend to focus so much on the philological-historical analysis of this specific source. And after all this file - neutral on its own - receives a far more important dimension when comparing it with other sources from the same context. In connection with the machine-readable recording of the sources concerning the literary field of the prohibited novel, this source was only one piece of a mosaic. A definite starting point of my data collection was the censorship lists of the years from 1730 to 1744 which can be considered one of the typical serial sources, as preferred in historical methodology of "*Annales*"- historiography. The records of all novels concerned, which constitute the basic corpus together with correct bibliographical information and a brief characterization of the content and form, were collected in order to assemble a first machine readable metasource. This information provides a basis for simple time diagrams of the development of novel censorship as well as for bivariate graphics on the characteristics of novel production in general. Information on the material aspect of the books in question and further, more detailed information on the story and the narration were gathered concerning the sample of novels appearing in the documents of 1737. This has allowed in-depth analysis of novel writing (Hobohm 1989).

Apart from these rather literary data, I incorporated in the database a series of standardized biographical data of (identifiable) living persons mentioned in the documents as authors or censors. In fact, because there is a great number of individuals about whom standard biographical dictionaries are not very instructive, much information of the biographical part of the database stems from the police file. As a result, the registered data on persons allows one to get an idea of their production of novels, and of their assessment by censorship authorities. What was originally intended to be used exclusively for statistical analysis of relevant sources became - practically as a by-product - a database for the entire production of novels in France during the period of the early Enlightenment. Besides simple retrievals on certain novels, on authors and/or censors, it always allows specific questions of a socio- and a literary-historical nature. For example: how do censorship authorities judge a certain genre of a novel? Or: what sort of novel is written by authors belonging to a certain social class? How are certain categories of persons judged by censorship authorities? Although still relatively restricted to the above mentioned period of time, the data collection is in its machine-readable form particularly useful as an element of a "historical workstation", as understood by Manfred Thaller (1988).

The project started by simply recording data of individual sources using dBASE and a small electronic typewriter. The sample of novels to be analysed more closely was then examined by means of a specially developed analysis pattern and described by uncontrolled keywords. The persons appearing in the registers as "author" or "censor" were partly identified on the basis of information derived from other archive sources and were - with the help of generally known biographical encyclopedias provided with a standardized biography referring to the period under investigation. Thus, eight different files were created which in relational as well as hierarchical manner describe 600 novels and more than 170 persons involved in the literary field of the prohibited novel in Paris round about 1737.

Let me now discuss some aspects of the analysis of the police file to demonstrate how one can make use of machine-readable registration of this kind of source. Calling Diderot, for example, a "*garçon*" (boy) leads to the hypothesis - an aspect also pursued by Robert Darnton - that the word has a negative connotation. A relatively quick inquiry into the machine-readable text of the file shows, however, that in reality the word is merely a clear indication of the person's age or his marital status. On the other hand one could also assume that the persons we would associate with libertinage have already been classified as such by d'Hémery. Yet again, a brief (machine-assisted) "look" at the texts reveals that d'Hémery uses this term rather as a definite designation of a genre or a style of writing and not of living. Names of libertines which would automatically come to our mind such as Crébillon fils are not categorized thereunder.

To take another example: one could assume that, when explicitly mentioning an author as having written a "novel", the author in question has somehow become involved in censorship. In fact, this does not seem to be consistent as, first, the word "novel" had actually been used in relatively few contexts. This is all the more surprising if one considers that the corpus discussed consists of novelists in the first place, and that the novel actually was the prohibited genre. Second, even when d'Hémery uses explicitly the word "*roman*", this does not concern authors particularly affected by censorship. More specific descriptions of persons, however, such as "un mauvais sujet" or "il a infiniment d'esprit" (i.e. the occurrence of the word "sujet" or "esprit") allow to a greater extent the conclusion that these persons were involved in the production of prohibited novels. Therefore it seems to be more likely that a distinctive and striking personality predetermines the writing of illicit literature as a style and a genre. Finally, it is the term "auteur" as such which reveals indeed a certain significance because Hémery applies it particularly often to authors who were writing novels prohibited by the censorship authorities. The sample of the prohibited novels of the Early French Enlightenment taken from the police file and submitted to discourse analysis is certainly not sufficient. Nevertheless it confirms, by arguing along this line, the relationship between the new position of the writer in society and the prohibited modern novel. This is clearly different from Robert Darnton's ethno-methodological text analysis by which d'Hémery's police reports are reduced to folkloristic imagery of the people (see also Chartier 1985).

Even more interesting are the analyses of the specific information fields of the investigation sheets. The only example which may be quoted here is the category "*signalement*" (appearance). Looking at the list of physiognomic descriptions of the authors in combination with their de-facto involvement in novel production and censorship decisions one reveals - although I would not argue for a causal relationship - some striking coincidences: a relatively great number of authors who are writing "bad" novels are not good-looking either. D'Hémery describes the "*littérateur*" and spy, Claude François Lambert, the author of the "*Nouveau Télémaque*" as being "small, of bad stature and spotty"; Jean-Baptiste Jourdan another unimportant scribe is described as "small, dirty-looking and repulsive". In contrast authors who had become well-reputed - although they could also produce illicit novels - are of a "beautiful physiognomy" as for example Crébillon fils.

This kind of questions seem always to be well treated by using such a sort of combined meta-source. Indeed, the texts of the police-reports on their own give information on the symbolic representations of the literary world in the mind of police inspector Joseph d'Hémery - however, one can say little about the social impact of a specific statement. Likewise the censorship lists and the decrees just by themselves would completely lack in liveliness, and their mere description would certainly not do justice to past representations. By means of machine-readable registration and by uniting such heterogeneous sources as those established by the book supervision authorities of the Ancien Régime we are offered - in terms of quality - other possibilities for describing past realities and social processes by extracting information from abundant serial sources. If one reads the sources in a meticulously hermeneutical way one would, indeed, be able to obtain comparable results, but if it is the question of so subtle a thing as the social position of the author, one is no doubt better off with the "archive on one's desk". To a certain extent, the analyses described should have shown the possibilities given by the immense archives of the Parisian book supervision authorities of the Enlightenment, and if it were feasible to continue their machine-readable registration, they could become an even more valuable instrument for research in the history of culture than they already are in their dusty paperform.

SOURCES

Bibliothèque Nationale: MS, N.A.F. 10781-10783 (author file); MS, FF 22106-22107 (booksellers file).

REFERENCES

CHARTIER, Roger. 1985. "Text, Symbols, and Frenchness". *Journal of Modern History* 57, 682-695

DARNTON, Robert. 1982. *The Literary Underground of the Old Regime*. Cambridge/Mass.: Harvard U.P.

DARNTON, Robert. 1984. "A Police Inspector Sorts his Files: the Anatomy of the Republic of Letters" in: *The Great Cat Massacre*. New York: Basic Books, 145-189 and 276-277

DARNTON, Robert. 1986. "The Symbolic Element in History". *Journal of Modern History* 58, 218-234

FOUCAULT, Michel. 1969. "Qu'est-ce qu'un auteur?" *Bulletin de la Société Française de Philosophie*, juillet-septembre ["What is an Author?" *Textual Strategies: Perspectives in Post- structuralist Criticism*, ed. by J. Harari, Ithaca, N.Y.]

GENET, Jean-Philippe. 1986. "Pour l'informatisation des dictionnaires biographiques". *Histoire et Mesure* 1:2, 99-110

HANLEY, William. 1980. "The Policing of Thought: Censorship in Eighteenth-Century France". *Studies on Voltaire and the Eighteenth Century 183*, 265-295

HABERMAS, Jürgen. 1962. *Strukturwandel der Öffentlichkeit*. Darmstadt: Luchterhand

HOBOHM, Hans-Christoph. 1986. "Der Diskurs der Zensur. Zum Wandel der literarischen Zensur zur Zeit der 'proscription des romans' (Paris, 1737)". *Romanistische Zeitschrift für Literaturgeschichte/Cahiers d'Histoire des Littératures Romanes* 10, 68-82

HOBOHM, Hans-Christoph. 1988a. "Jede Macht ist sich selbst die Nächste: zur personalen und sozialen Dimension von Zensur" in: H.G. Göpfert and E. Weyrauch (eds.). *'Unmoralisch an sich...': Zensur im 18. und 19. Jahrhundert*. Wiesbaden: Harrassowitz, 1988 (Wolfenbütteler Schriften zur Geschichte des Buchwesens; 13), 105-117

HOBOHM, Hans-Christoph. 1988b. "Using Databases for Everyday Work in Literary History. Exchange and Standardization Problems" in: J.P. Genet (ed.). *Standardization and Exchange of Machine Readable Data in the Historical Disciplines, III*. Paris, 289-294

HOBOHM, Hans-Christoph. 1989. "Le roman français à l'aube des Lumières. Analyse sociale de la production romanesque et de sa censure, 1730-1744". *Studies on Voltaire and the Eighteenth Century*. Oxford, forthcoming

JÜTTNER, Siegfried. 1987. "The Status of the Writer". *Seventh International Congress on the Enlightenment: introductory papers*. Oxford: Voltaire Fondation, 173-202

SANDERS, Hans. 1987. *Das Subjekt der Moderne. Mentalitätswandel und literarische Evolution zwischen Klassik und Aufklärung*. Tübingen: Niemeyer

THALLER, Manfred. 1988. "Data Bases v. Critical Editions". *Historical Social Research/Historische Sozialforschung*, 13:3, 129-139

VIALA, Alain. 1985. *Naissance de l'écrivain. Sociologie de la littérature à l'âge classique*. Paris: Minuit

AN ANALYSIS OF THE COMPONENTS OF ELITE MIGRATION: VIANO DO CASTELO, MINHO, 1826-1931

Arno Kitts
Skandia Actuarial Research Fellow
Department of Social Statistics
University of Southampton
United Kingdom

This paper presents methodological and substantive issues arising in an examination of the components of elite migration to and from the port-city of Viana do Castelo, and its hinterland (the northernmost district of Portugal) during the period from 1826-1931. To this end, it is divided into three main sections.

Firstly, the study of Portuguese emigration is discussed in general and the relevant literature is reviewed.

Secondly, the approach to the study of Portuguese migration adopted in this paper is introduced. In particular, the development of the Viana Database at the University of Southampton is described; aggregate data from the censuses of 1864, 1878, 1890 and 1900 are supplemented by individual-level data drawn from manuscript sources compiled in the port-city of Viana do Castelo: muster-rolls (1826-1833; 7,000 records), electoral registers (1834-1931; 40,000 records), passport books (1835-1896; 2,000 records), and cemetery lists (1855-1922; 11,000 records). Also, the reconstitution of Viana is briefly described.

Thirdly, the analyses performed to identify the components of elite migration to and from the port-city of Viana are described in detail. In order to provide some background to the components of elite migration presented in this paper, some previous research is described briefly. Two types of evidence of migration are examined in this paper. Indirect evidence of migration is available from passport book records; members of the elite who were issued with a passport were likely to have been emigrants, return migrants, or repeat migrants. Inferential evidence of migration is available from the electoral registers; members of the elite whose last appearance was on the electoral registers may have been out-migrants, who neither emigrated with a passport, nor were buried in Viana, but departed to other parts of Portugal. Inferential evidence of migration of the elite is examined using survival analysis techniques.

Portuguese Emigration

Over the last 500 years, emigration has played an integral part in the evolution of the demographic structure of Portugal. Initially, its purpose was the colonisation of Portugal's overseas territories. This was gradually overshadowed by its function as an opportunity for individuals to seek improved circumstances. During the last 100 years or so, emigration from Portugal reached levels surpassing those of most other European countries and the country registered a net population loss, second only to that of Ireland.

Also, as the nineteenth century progressed, return migration became an increasingly important phenomenon throughout Europe. In Portugal, this manifested itself in the myth of fortune and return. Remittances from emigrants had always had an influence on the economy, but in the late nineteenth century the economy of northern Portugal in particular was influenced by the *Brasileiros* - native born Portuguese who emigrated to Brazil to make their fortune and returned to Portugal to display their success.

The quantitative importance of Portuguese emigration has not been reflected in the literature. In comparison with the literature of European emigration, even the work of contemporary Portuguese scholars tends to be rather poor. Essentially this is because, hitherto, there has been a heavy reliance on anecdotal information, and a (closely associated) tendency to assume a historical-structural perspective of migration, thereby avoiding any detailed (quantitative) analysis. The detailed identification of the process of emigration has remained largely speculative because of the lack of systematically collected statistics. Nevertheless, two themes have remained central, the strong association of early emigration with commerce and that of the later exodus with the system of agriculture practised in the north-west of the country. These themes are corroborated by a vast amount of anecdotal information, and some quantitative evidence.

The knowledge that is available with respect to Portuguese emigration during the nineteenth and twentieth centuries can be summarised with reference to four main issues: clandestine emigration, return migration, emigrant remittances and emigrant characteristics. Clandestine emigration consisted of two streams: that of males aged 14-21, who were unable to obtain passports because of military conscription legislation and that consisting of people for whom the price of a passport was prohibitively high. However, very little quantitative evidence of clandestine emigration is available. The discussion of return migration is centred upon the myth of fortune and return, which still persists today; the *mineiro de torna viagem* (return migrant miners) of the eighteenth century became the *Brasileiro* (return migrant from Brazil) of the nineteenth, who, in turn, has become the *Francês* (return migrant from France) of the late twentieth century. With respect to remittances, although it is known that Portugal's fragile economy of the nineteenth century came to rely heavily on the income generated by the remittances and return of its emigrants, very little quantitative evidence is actually available. Finally, a broad comparison of the characteristics of Portuguese emigrants with those of other European countries illustrates that Portuguese emigration possessed some unique features. First, emigrants were predominately male until relatively recently. Second, in the nineteenth century, a large proportion of these male emigrants were young, often less than 14 years old. Third, the proportion of emigrants departing individually was decreasing in Portugal, while it was increasing throughout most of Europe. Finally, while the extent of return migration increased elsewhere, in Portugal it decreased.

The Viana Database

The paucity of aggregate demographic statistics for nineteenth century Portugal forces various sources of ancillary data to be exploited fully. An increasingly popular approach involves the reconstitution of one town or city using a database of several manuscript sources. This enables micro-level analyses to be performed, which enhance the understanding of the secular demographic trends that are derived from those aggregate statistics that are available.

The port-city of Viana do Castelo, situated on the northern bank of the mouth of the river Lima, provides an ideal opportunity for the investigation of these phenomena through the reconstitution of its population from the abundance of records generated by the Portuguese administrative system. With a population of just less than 10,000 during the nineteenth century, it is large enough to limit the effects of random variation, while not too large to preclude close examination of the individual-level data. In addition, its role as the administrative centre and principal port of the District of Viana offers the study of stage migration of the rural peasantry, and the migration of both, the urban poor and elite.

In order to identify important economic and demographic characteristics of the area under consideration, the agriculture, population and technological development of the District of Viana (the Alto Minho) are described. This description draws upon a recent study of the political, social and economic development of the Borough of Viana during the first three-quarters of the nineteenth century (Feijó 1983).

Next, the economic and demographic history of the port-city of Viana is described and local and national events in the nineteenth century are summarised in order to establish the circumstances under which the sources being used were created. In addition, census data are used to provide an initial picture of the population. This description draws upon a recent study of the demography of Portugal in general and of the port-city of Viana in particular during the second half of the nineteenth century (Reis 1987). The manuscript sources (muster-rolls, electoral registers, passport books, and cemetery lists) on which the reconstitution is currently based are then described in detail.

In order to enable records to be linked, both, within and between documents for subsequent analysis, several operations - the software requirements of record linkage - must be possible. One way to satisfy these requirements is to store the data in a powerful database. Reasons for choosing the Scientific Information Retrieval (SIR) Data Base Management System (DBMS) for the storage, standardisation and coding, linkage, and subsequent retrieval of the Viana Database are discussed and the actual software and techniques adopted are described briefly (see Doulton & Kitts 1988).

The Components of Elite Migration

In order to provide some background to the components of elite migration presented in this paper, some previous research is described briefly. First, changes in the level and structure of emigration from the District of Viana are identified by comparing emigrant characteristics (available from the passports issued in the three census years 1864, 1878, and 1890), with those of the population from which the emigrants were drawn (available from the censuses) using log-linear models of emigration rates. Second, a simple population model is developed which enables the extent of clandestine emigration from the District of Viana during the inter-censual periods 1864-1878, 1878-1890 and 1890-1900 to be investigated. Third, another simple population model is used to demonstrate that levels of female migration within Portugal may have been substantially higher than is suggested in the literature. The results of these analyses are described in greater detail elsewhere (Kitts 1988).

Turning to the port-city of Viana do Castelo, an analysis of the passport books provides a detailed picture of emigration during the nineteenth century. The analysis illustrates that the majority of emigrants were single males less than 21 years old, often being sent to Brazil to avoid military conscription. Also, a significant proportion of emigrants from Viana are shown to have been stage migrants, mainly from the immediate hinterland, but with some from further afield. To illustrate the typical migration patterns among the urban elite that are a focal point of this research, the life history of a particular merchant is presented.

The actual analyses of this paper examine evidence of migration among a sub-group of the electorate of Viana. This sub-group is defined as those individuals with recorded names consisting of three or more components who appear at least once on the electoral registers. The former part of this definition is necessary because the reconstitution of the population of Viana is currently restricted to males with recorded names consisting of three or more components. This sub-group of the electorate is referred to as the elite because there is known to have been an association between socioeconomic status and the number of components of Portuguese names. Of course, it is noted that for a definition of particular groups this approach is somewhat simplistic; for example, individuals with three or more component names who were recorded on electoral registers with just two or less component names are simply omitted.

In studying the migration of the urban elite, the time elapsing between the arrival of an individual, whether by birth or in-migration and their subsequent departure at some later date, whether by out-migration or death, is of interest. Survival analysis is a method by which the time elapsing between two such predefined events is studied. Some important issues in survival analysis are therefore reviewed with respect to the study of migration of the elite. Survival analysis is introduced in its earliest form - traditional life table analysis. The development and limitations of the proportional hazards model are discussed; approaches to the problem of unobserved heterogeneity are reviewed; mixture models are considered; and finally, alternative observational plans are described.

Trends in the size and characteristics of the electorate are described and log-linear models are used to compare the characteristics of the electorate in the census years of 1864 and 1878 with the population from which it was drawn. Also, a similar analysis is performed to identify the elite - the sample of the electorate with names consisting of three or more components. The elite is found to be a slightly biased sample of the electorate, weighted in favour of residents of the parish of Santa Maria Maior during the period from 1850-1878, who were unmarried and were engaged in commerce, the armed forces, public administration or the professions.

Migration of the elite is analysed through an examination of indirect and inferential evidence of temporary and permanent absence from Viana. Of course, the analysis is dependent on the record linkage of the muster-rolls, electoral registers, passport books and cemetery lists. References to possible inaccuracies of the record linkage are therefore discussed where appropriate. First, the retrieval of a statistical file of individual life histories from the Viana Database is described. Second, restriction of the dataset is considered in the context of the circumstances under which the original manuscript sources were created. Third, several exploratory analyses of the restricted elite are described; these provide some initial insight into the generation of individual life histories, while also serving to verify the quality of the data.

Next, indirect evidence of migration of the elite is examined. This evidence is available from passport book records; members of the elite who were issued with a passport were likely to have been emigrants, return migrants or repeat migrants. Estimates of emigration, stage migration, return migration and repeat migration are provided. The analyses suggest that the level of emigration exceeded 5%. Of these emigrants, a considerable proportion (25-49%) were stage migrants; return migration is estimated to have been of the order of 70-87%; and, of these return migrants, 25% later became repeat migrants.

Finally, inferential evidence of migration of the elite is examined. This evidence is available from the electoral registers; members of the elite whose last appearance was on the electoral registers may have been out-migrants who neither emigrated with a passport, nor were buried in Viana, but departed to other parts of Portugal. Inferential evidence of migration of the elite is examined using survival analysis techniques. In particular, hazards models of duration spent under observation in the elite (on the electoral registers) are estimated (see Figure 1). The analysis suggests that while out-migration (excluding emigration) was not significantly dependent on age or marital status, there were large occupational differentials and significant period effects.

Figure 1: Proportion Remaining on the Electoral Registers Since Year of First Entry, for Four Cohorts

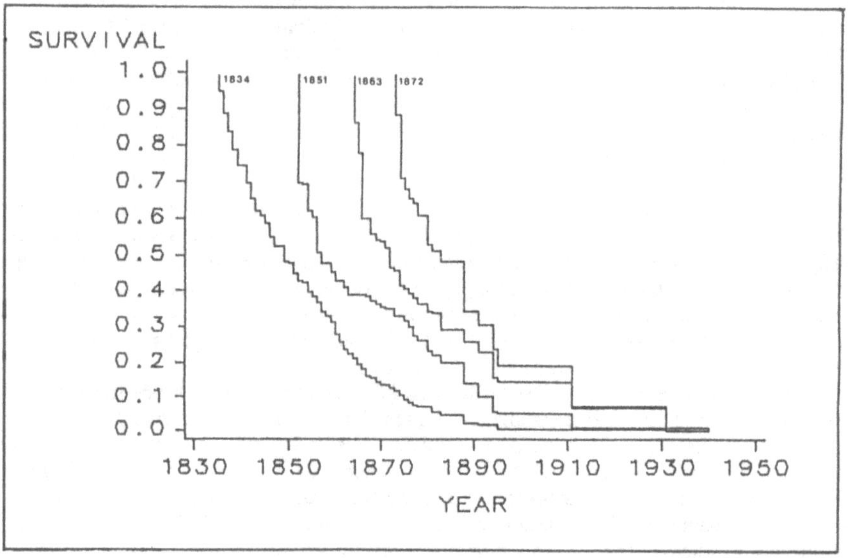

REFERENCES

DOULTON, David and KITTS, Arno. 1988. "The Storing and Processing of Historical Data," in Denley, Peter; Fogelvik, Stefan & Harvey, Charles (eds.). 1988. *History and Computing*, volume 2, Manchester University Press

FEIJÓ, Rui Graça de Castro. 1983. *Liberal Revolution, Social Change and Economic Development: the region of Viana (NW Portugal) in the first three quarters of the nineteenth century.* Unpublished Ph.D. thesis: Oxford University

KITTS, Arno. 1988. *An Analysis of the Components of Migration: Viana do Castelo, Minho, 1826-1931.* Unpublished Ph.D. thesis: University of Southampton

REIS, Elizabeth de Azevedo. 1987. *The Spatial Demography of Portugal in the Late Nineteenth Century: Evidences from the 1864 and 1878 Censuses.* Unpublished Ph.D. thesis: University of Southampton

THE FRENCH CRIMINAL JUSTICE SYSTEM BETWEEN 1831 AND 1981: A STATISTICAL DATA BASE

Bruno Aubusson de Cavarlay
Centre de Récherches Sociologiques sur le Droit
et les Institutions Pénales
UA313 CNRS, Paris
France

The data base we are building should give access to the French criminal statistics first published in the "Compte Général de la justice criminelle" that is the Criminal justice statistical report. This project is carried out within the CESDIP, Center of Sociological Research on Law and Penal Institutions, which is one of the two research centers of the French Department of Justice, associated with the CNRS. The project resources are a little less than two persons, computer time on the CIRCE's installations - that is the CNRS computer center - and microcomputers (OLIVETTI M24).

Our data source is made of one hundred and forty nine volumes of the Criminal Justice Statisical Reports and some Statistical Archives for the last years. Until the end of the nineteenth century, these reports were preceded by an official analysis giving retrospective tables. In this way, the volume for 1880 is the most complete. It gives, in five years means, the main series over fifty years. But from the early twentieth century, these analysis became very poor and since 1910 no retrospective has been published. Some historical works refer to these statistical publications (CHESNAIS 1976, LEVY 1987, ZEHR 1976). But they generally restrict their study to an aspect of penal repression, regardless of methodological or systemic considerations. So, until now, this data source has not been very much used and its access has become rather complex because of the total lack of explanations in the publication about statistical definitions. These reports now give some hundreds of thousands of figures without directions for use.

In 1972, the other research center of the French Justice Department, known at that time as Vaucresson Center, published a statistical retrospective work about juvenile deliquency (LEVADE 1972). As juvenile agencies and legislation really appear in French penal justice only after 1912 and become independant only after 1945, juvenile criminal statistics are very poor before this date. So, this publication gives only some age information about convicted people during the nineteenth century. We can only point that it did not use any computer. In the seventies, André DAVIDOVITCH and his Criminal Sociology Research unit gave the first start to a criminal statistical data base. But the computer data processing was stoped in 1973. Some of the series had already been used in sociological works (DAVIDOVITCH 1961, BOUDON & DAVIDOVITCH 1964) when A. DAVIDOVITCH then turned towards public prosecutor studies and restricted them to the present. We took the opposite direction. After some statistical and sociological investigation about the present criminal justice system (AUBUSSON 1985 & 1986), we decided that a historical statistical approach could be a good help to understand the actual shape of our penal system (LEVY & ROBERT 1984).

The statistical series are relevant for the whole national territory. Some of them are avalaible only at this level. Some others are also given by the reports at the local level for each jurisdiction. For the moment, we deal only with national series in a two steps process. At the first step, the data base includes only the series describing the criminal justice system in its general procedural aspect. Then, at the second step, we shall include series describing particular offenses.

As a matter of fact, our main difficulty in the beginning was the great volume of our statistical source. Even if we can imagine an automatic data acquisition (but we did not try it), it remains a great deal of work from the collection of figures to the completion of statistical series. And anyway, these data are useless without an interpretative frame giving a link between the figure production and the results. If all the criminal statistics were stored on line, they would still need guidelines to be accessible.

The statistical tables of the criminal justice reports are built according to the different stages of the French penal procedure: the public prosecutor activity with some data about police activity, the outcome of the judicial investigation and pretrial detention, court decisions. We have kept the main part of these tables or of their total sum by offenses or courts. Or rather, we choose to keep all the data we need to describe and understand the criminal justice system. But we did not make our choices at a single moment. We have rather proceeded by successive approaches, gathering more data as the analysis brought about new questions. As this process gets more complete, we can also give a more complete description of the data organisation.

The building of our data base is completing an operation started by A. DAVIDOVITCH's research unit a long time ago, we received from him when he took over a first version of the criminal statistics data base. But we soon discovered that the work had been drastically focused on an analysis of crime and deliquency. What was necessary to test hypotheses about delinquency levels and quality was not relevant to understand the criminal statistics organisation.

Criminal statistics are not a measure of crime, but they are quite relevant to give a quantitative picture of criminal justice (ROBERT 1985, AUBUSSON 1986). An offense does not produce by itself its statistical record. This record, starting with the victims reporting in some cases, or with a police or control agency intervention in some others, will appear only after an institutional process will have taken place. But nothing proves that this record gives us an unbiased, though indirect measurement of delinquency. On the contrary, it is well established that the trend of judicial reported cases is closely linked to victim behaviour and to the goals of police activity. On the other hand, judicial statistics are a fruitful approach to the actual running of the penal system: case selection and orientation, prosecution outcome, the extent of various penalties and the arrangements of different procedural channels (AUBUSSON 1986). So, I would just like to stress this point: since we must select from the available data, we are dependant on our theoretical orientations.

Besides the influence of the researcher's hypothesis upon data collection, we must also emphasize that the relationship between criminal data base building and research orientations has been transformed by hardware and software evolution. The most significant difference may be the end of labour division between computer activity and research. The social scientist can now make up his mind about theoretical choices as he is going on with micro-computer operations. Twenty years ago, the various computer steps had to be planned and it was nearly impossible to come more than one step back in the processing for cost and organisational reasons. So, initial choices were fundamental and they could differ according to one's goals: building a comprehensive data base or trying to implement a theoretical model about deliquency. This still remains important, but, in a natural micro-computer way, we are now able to manage data base building and data analysis in a complementary manner.

The "DAVIDO" data base - DAVIDO was the nickname given in a friendly way to DAVIDOVITCH by his fellow workers - is now made of about two hundred and thirty variables, from which only fourty are given for the whole period that is 1831-1981. Most of the others are available only until 1932. This important deficiency in statistical production was officially explained by economic reasons. But we already said that official interest in criminal statistics was decreasing before the first war, as we can measure it with the importance of preliminary reports of the "Compte General". And at that time, scientific interest was rather made of individual investigations about criminal personality. So, after skipping missing values, among which we have six missing years of war time, we get about twenty thousand figures.

We are now analysing these data at the national general level. The results will be published either in collective works dealing with specials topics or in a general report when we will be finished with offenses' processing. But that means about a hundred thousand more figures.

These numerical data are stored in a SAS data base (on host computer and on PC) and on floppies at the DBASE format. From these, we can process some intermediary tasks under FRAMEWORK software.

Figure 1:

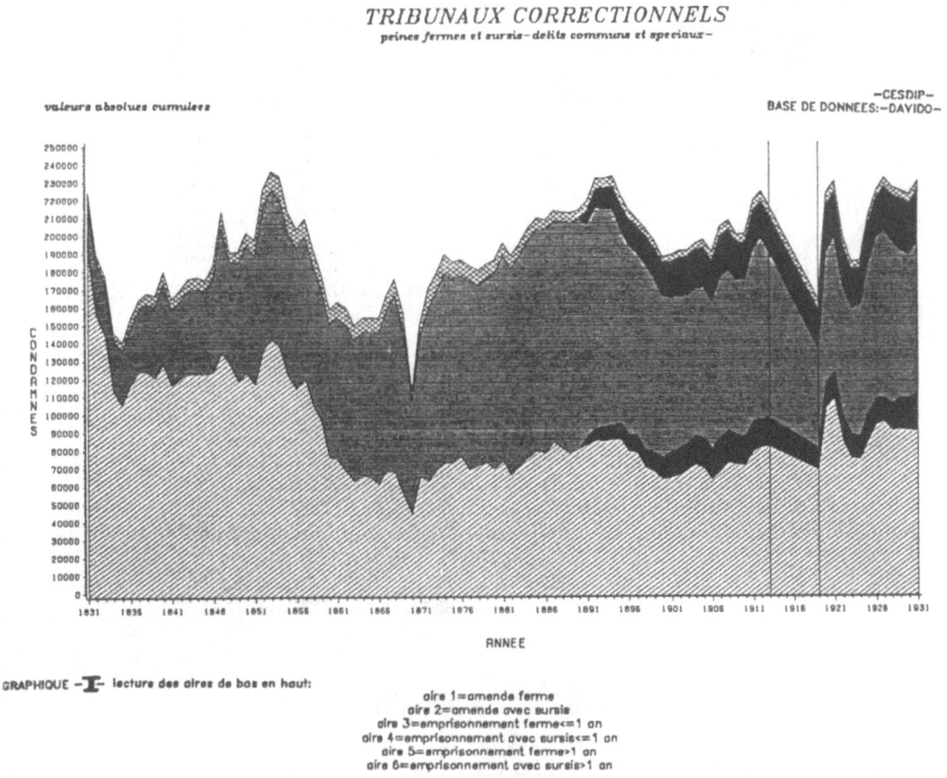

Table 1:

NOMBRE DE CONDAMNATIONS PRONONCEES
PAR LES TRIBUNAUX CORRECTIONNELS (1),
DISTINGUEES SELON LE TYPE DE PEINE

SOURCE : BASE DE DONNEES DAVIDO

PEINES PRONONCEES	EMPRISONNEMENT SUPERIEUR A UN AN	EMPRISONNEMENT INFERIEUR A UN AN	AMENDE	TOTAL DES CONDAMNATIONS
	NOMBRE	NOMBRE	NOMBRE	NOMBRE
ANNEE				
1831	5954	24288	193952	224194
1832	5742	27524	156791	190057
1833	5091	26787	144753	176631
1834	5177	26942	113545	145664
1835	5340	28902	105672	139914
1836	5993	31160	116619	153772
1837	6757	32861	124271	163889
1838	7179	35461	124850	167490
1839	6945	38344	120719	166008
1840	7498	43103	128797	179398
1841	6833	40717	116258	163808
1842	6866	41889	120462	169217
1843	7312	44768	123071	175151
1844	7478	45399	123097	175973
1845	6814	44779	122798	174391
1846	7154	51399	123990	182543
1847	8545	68130	134998	211673
1848	5417	55444	128808	189669
1849	6458	64477	118781	189716
1850	7261	69272	123608	200141
1851	8268	70261	116959	195488
1852	10214	78270	135424	223908
1853	10363	80749	142506	233618
1854	11260	80584	138223	230067
1855	11661	76765	122438	210864
1856	11063	76324	114281	201668
1857	11063	76202	120527	207792
1858	9797	75832	105421	191050
1859	9096	71217	97044	177357
1860	9150	71965	76030	157145
1861	9764	76244	75380	161388
1862	10044	79400	68550	157994
1863	9279	75941	62783	148003
1864	8989	77612	66104	152705
1865	9136	78596	64874	152606
1866	8456	82293	61220	151969
1867	8985	87574	68773	165332
1868	8797	96750	67995	173542
1869	8308	90688	55342	154338
1870	5356	61070	44685	111111

(CONTINUED)

(1). -DE 1955 A 1978, LES APPELS SONT INCLUS ET SEULS LES JUGEMENTS CONTRADICTOIRES ET PAR DEFAUT SONT COMPTES.

Table 1 (end):

NOMBRE DE CONDAMNATIONS PRONONCEES
PAR LES TRIBUNAUX CORRECTIONNELS (1).
DISTINGUEES SELON LE TYPE DE PEINE

SOURCE : BASE DE DONNEES DAVIDO

PEINES PRONONCEES	EMPRISONNEMENT SUPERIEUR A UN AN	EMPRISONNEMENT INFERIEUR A UN AN	AMENDE	TOTAL DES CONDAMNATIONS
	NOMBRE	NOMBRE	NOMBRE	NOMBRE
ANNEE				
1871	6595	77412	65043	149050
1872	9299	96026	62826	168151
1873	7494	99664	68476	175634
1874	8064	105552	72832	186448
1875	7322	102327	73006	182655
1876	6765	100990	76309	184064
1877	6683	105132	69101	180916
1878	6503	100441	71253	178197
1879	5963	102034	73299	181296
1880	5755	108717	69467	183939
1881	5578	113924	74084	193586
1882	5754	115149	65867	186770
1883	5576	116713	71507	193796
1884	5734	120713	75596	202043
1885	5442	123055	79564	208061
1886	4823	123746	78345	206914
1887	4288	122840	84439	211567
1888	3941	125725	81004	210670
1889	4008	128123	77988	210119
1890	3683	127256	80492	211431
1891	3978	125812	87118	216908
1892	4100	133919	92041	230060
1893	3707	133254	92871	235832
1894	4032	133751	93718	231501
1895	3795	122615	94824	221234
1896	3513	120641	88673	212827
1897	3149	116833	87944	207926
1898	2810	120486	79602	202898
1899	2972	114596	78604	196172
1900	2869	108572	75583	187024
1901	2738	106581	78683	188002
1902	2966	106817	80686	190469
1903	2616	104246	83559	190421
1904	2786	103986	87791	194563
1905	3380	106395	86571	196346
1906	3145	105516	80245	188906
1907	3116	112806	86650	202572
1908	3449	112268	90608	206325
1909	2799	107547	88491	198837
1910	3291	108635	87026	198952

(CONTINUED)

(1). -DE 1958 A 1978. LES APPELS SONT INCLUS ET SEULS LES JUGEMENTS CONTRADICTOIRES ET PAR DEFAUT SONT COMPTES.

The analysis implies synthethic variables and building of indicators which will be added to the data base. They will be mainly interpreted with graphics designed under SAS software. We use SAS as well for table printing since we appreciate the page setting performance of its TABULATE procedure. An example of these tables and graphics is given here with the correctional sentences. But this data processing is not enough to get an accurate historical understanding of penal justice. Here for instance, one should know and remember that the legislative modification about the prosecution of rural offenses during the 1850's led to a major decrease of fine sentences. Or that the emergence of a new rapid procedure in 1863 (the "flagrants delits") produced a strong increase in short prison sentences until the creation of suspended sentences in 1891. The effects of switching to correctional prosecution for criminal cases upon the longest prison sentences should not be forgotten anyway, to say nothing about the consequenses of pretrial detention... . So, the analysis of some series needs to take in account the whole system and to be aware of legislative and institutional modifications.

Beyond the statistical series, we have collected a great amount of information about statistical definitions, data production and breaking brought about by institutional changes. These materials are sorted in three parts.

First, we have associated to each series or subset coming from the same table, a text giving its source, its definition, its missing years, its consistency with other series and every consequent difficulty, including adjustements. All this is mainly an outcome of criminal statistics reports and archives. But it also includes the results of our methodological and quantitative analysis. Texts are stored in a FRAMEWORK outline according to the structure of tables. Their main goal is to give a technical description within the data publication. But they could also be a part of a documentary data base about criminal statistics.

More generally, the analysis prefacing each statistical report has been examined to pick up, beyond mere paraphrasing, any remark about statistics and their production. We use them as we are interpreting the evolution of the criminal justice system and sometimes, we find significative concordances or discordances between statistical evolution, legislative activity and official analysis. These manuscript reading notes can be used through a little DBASE file which gives for each one the matter and the series refered to the corresponding annotation.

Thirdly, we have gathered from different sources (statistical reports, statute books, specialized works) the various legislative and administrative texts which may have had some statistical consequences in the criminal justice activity. So we get about one hundred and sixty references, without the one hundred and fifty ministerial instructions about statistical data collection. These legislative references are also stored in a DBASE file, in association with the matters and the statistical series they may concern.

All these data - a FRAMEWORK outline and two DBASE files refering to the statistical reports and to the legislative corpus - are accessible with the same classification. This allows manual communications between them. But these three files are not yet integrated in a documentary data base associated with the numerical data base. Mixing numerical and textual data in the same base will need some software transformation since DBASE is not a good product for the last purpose.

We have some more work to do before giving public access to these data bases. Solutions depend on technical choices, legal protection and the number of users. A larger number of users could be interested in this database if it also contains prison data which are available in French statistical reports from the middle of the nineteenth century and some data about police activity for the present time.

REFERENCES

AUBUSSON de CAVARLAY, B. 1985. "Hommes, peines et infractions: la legalite de l'inegalite." *Année sociologique 35*, 275-309

AUBUSSON de CAVARLAY, B. 1987. *Les filières pénales*. Paris, CESDIP

CHESNAIS, J.C. 1976. *Les morts violentes en France depuis 1826, comparaisons internationales*. Paris, P.U.F.

DAVIDOVITCH, A. 1961. "Criminalite et repression en France depuis un siecle." *Révue francaise de sociologie II*, 30-49

DAVIDOVITCH, A. and BOUDON, R. 1964. "Les mecanismes sociaux des abandons de poursuite. Analyse experimentale par simulation." *Année sociologique, Troisième série 1964*, 111-244

LEVADE, M. 1972. *La délinquance des jeunes en France, 1825-1968*. Paris, Cujas

LEVY, R. 1986. "Un aspect de la mutation de l'economie repressive au XIXe siecle: la loi de 1863 sur le flagrant delit." *Révue Historique CCLXXIV/1*, 43-77

LEVY, R. and ROBERT, Ph. 1984. "Le sociologue et l'histoire penale." *Annales E.S.C. 39-2*, 400-422

ROBERT, Ph. 1985. *Les comptes du crime*. Paris, Le Sycomore

ZEHR, H. 1976. *Crime and the development of Modern Society*. London, Croom Helm

DATABASE APPLICATIONS IN ECONOMIC HISTORY: GERMAN TRANSPORT STATISTICS, 1835-1985

Andreas Kunz
Freie Universität Berlin
FRG

The Project

Reliable statistical information is indispensable to the economic historian. At the Section for Economic and Social History of the Free University of Berlin, a large-scale project on transport statistics has been conducted since 1986, in which time series on German transport in the 19th and 20th centuries are being compiled and edited on the basis of a thorough and critical examination of published and unpublished statistical sources.(1) The concept which governs this compilation effort stresses the role of transport as an economic sector whose productive capacity and actual production changed over time and can thus be measured and described in quantitative terms. Consequently, the overall objective is to collect, process and publish statistical (i.e. numeric) data on the performance of the major branches of transport - railways, inland and sea navigation, air, and road - over a time span of some 150 years. In terms of disaggregation of data, the results will offer statistical series broken down by regions and/or companies (e.g. railroad lines, steamship companies, etc.). With regard to the time span, the project covers the historically important first period of German industrialization (ca. 1850 to ca. 1880) as well as the so called "second wave of industrialization" around the turn of the century. Research results will be published initially in conventional book form as part of a new series on German historical statistics.(2) If possible, the full data set will be made available later on in a more complete fashion in form of a semi-public electronic database that would allow search requests on demand.

The Organization of Data Processing

Data processing in this project is done almost exclusively with the help of personal computers (PC) and standard commercial software. Only in one area - computer-based cartography - the Free University's mainframe has been employed. The early option for the PC, which in 1985 was still a venture of some sorts in view of the magnitude of the task ahead, has, on the whole, paid off. Not only does the PC provide a relative large degree of autarchy to the project group in terms of computer accessibility; the technological advances in both, hardware and software development in the past three years have, moreover, led to the happy fact of supply keeping pace with growing needs. With regard to software, care has been taken to keep the number of programs in use fairly small, not least in order to facilitate the training of student assistants employed in the project. Therefore, only three standard packages are currently being used:

1. The spreadsheet LOTUS 1-2-3 (together with several add-ons and add-ins) for the processing of strictly numeric data, i.e. such data where the source is already available in table format.

2. The database program dBASE III PLUS for the processing of mixed data, i.e. numeric data embodied in text, as well as structured textual data (e.g. bibliographical information).
3. The word processor MS-WORD for the processing of longer texts written for the project, e.g. introductions to the data handbooks.

Since conventional publication in bookform is one of the project's foremost aims, care has been taken to insure that the production of type-set materials via laser printer can be achieved with relative ease from within any of the programs in use.

BINWA - A Database on the Development of German Waterways Since 1850

BINWA (the name refers to the German term *BI*nnen*WA*sserstrassen) is one of several database applications conceived and realized within the project. Once completed, the database will contain useful information on the development of inland waterways in Germany since the mid-nineteenth century. While at this juncture BINWA has been conceived as a single-project database, chances for its later use as a semi-public database may be realized at some future point in time. If public access to the database should materialize - perhaps through a larger data archive on German historical statistics - BINWA will be combined with similar databases on related infrastructural developments in the transport sector, such as the growth of inland ports or the development of industrial settlements alongside inland waterways. The host to all databases will be a larger data bank preliminarily dubbed BINBASE.

a - The Structure of the Database

BINWA is a dBASE III database file which has been structured in a specific manner to accept numeric and alphanumeric data entries on items such as the length, depth and potential loading capacity of waterways, the latter measured in displacement of largest barges allowed on a specific river or canal. In addition, information is collected on such items as the number of locks, the number of ports and other loading facilities possessing direct links to railroad lines or on construction costs and financial profits derived from canal tolls and other fees. BINWA has been designed in such a way as to allow for the input of one "electronic reference card" per waterway and year, whereby relatively fixed data, i.e. data independent of the specific reference year, are connected with variable data, i.e. data dependent on a specific reference year. (For a screen image of an "electronic card", see Figure 1). The database is indexed in a way as to allow browsing through the records in chronological order within the various sets of data relating to a specific waterway. For example, once the user has successfully searched for an entry on the Elbe river pertaining to a specific year, he or she can then look at other entries for subsequent or previous years by merely hitting a single key for either forward or reverse scroll.

The field structure of the database file (cf. Figure 2) reflects its purpose as a means of storing qualitative and quantitative information (i.e. texts and numbers). There are character fields which accept both, textual and numeric data, although the latter cannot be used for quantitative purposes if entered in a character field. There are numeric fields, however, which will only accept numeric entries and are thus the basis for subsequent arithmetic or statistical calculations on the data compiled. All of the important quantitative information, e.g. length of waterways, number of ports, etc. is, therefore, entered in numeric fields. There are, furthermore, logical fields which enable the user to pinpoint subsets of data easily (e.g. metric scale Y/N to isolate data not entered in metric measurements). It goes without saying that several fields have been assigned to codes designed and implemented to enable the user to group data compiled in BINWA according to specific criteria. The most important one of these codes pertains to a classification system of so-called waterway regions. Since data evaluation performed later on can be based on these regions, quantification will lead to regionally-structured results, which in turn is an important contribution to future regionally oriented historical research. Altogether, nine waterway regions have been defined and encoded within the project: West- and East Prussian waterways, the Oder river, waterways of the Mark Brandenburg (incl. Berlin), the Elbe river, the Weser river, the river Ems and the north-west German canal system, the Rhine, the Danube and the Mittelland Canal (as of 1919). Quantitative information can thus be linked to a specific waterway region. To give but one example: with the help of the waterway-region code 3 the user can query the database for the total length of canals in the Brandenburg waterway area for a specific year, e.g. 1914; a numeric value will be returned in response to this and similar queries. In the final analysis, then, BINWA makes possible the controlled disaggregation of data according to a specific geographic category - the waterway region - which is a category pertinent to inland waterway transport.

Figure 1: Screen Image of BINWA Record

```
Wasserstraße          :  [Rhein                                          ]
Zweitname/Teilstrecke:  [Tl: Nied. Grenze bis Leopoldshafen             ]
-------------------------------------------------------------------------
I.FESTE ANGABEN: F_Nr.: [1    ] Typ: [f] WG: [7] RCode: [021 02k 05 03 ]

Häfen      : [Duisburg, Düsseldorf, Köln, Mainz, Mannheim u.a.         ]
ZP_STATBIN: [Emmerich, Duisburg, Düsseldorf, Köln, Mainz, Mannheim u.a]

Bauzeit: [                        ] Ursprüngliche Baukosten: [          ]
-------------------------------------------------------------------------
II.VARIABLE ANGABEN:     Bezugsjahr: [1893]   Angaben metrisch J/N?  [T]

Zahl d.Schleusen: [ 0]   Länge: [  623]       Tragfähigkeit:   [ 1400]
Kette/Seil J/N?  [F]     Tiefe: [    ][   ]   Schiffbarkeit:   [200-3]

Häfen mit EB-Anschluß      : [ 22]        Industrieanlagen: [    ]
Ladeplätze mit EB-Anschluß: [ 32]        Industriehäfen   : [    ]

Baukosten         : [          ]          Einnahmen         : [          ]
Laufende Kosten  : [          ]          Währungseinheit  : [          ]
-------------------------------------------------------------------------
Quelle(n):  [Führer 1893, Teil 1                  ] K_NR: [71T11893    ]

<W>eiter  <Z>urück  <E>ditieren  <B>emerkungen  <N>eue Abfrage  <M>enü
```

A number of other codes have been implemented for different purposes. They make possible, for example, a grouping of data according to the type of the waterway (river, canal, lake) or its geographic/administrative location (e.g.: Prussia, Kingdom of Saxony, etc.) However, statistical summaries cannot be performed on the basis of most of these codes, since numeric entries, such as the displacement of largest barges on waterways, are encoded according to waterway regions only.

Figure 2: Structure of Database File

```
Datenbankstruktur      : C:wstrasse.dbf
Anzahl der Datensätze :
Letztes Änderungsdatum:
Feld   Feldname     Typ          Länge    Dez
   1   WSTRASSE     Zeichen        45
   2   ZWEITNAME    Zeichen        45
   3   TSTRECKE     Zeichen         2
   4   WG           Zeichen         1
   5   TYP          Zeichen         1
   6   RCODE        Zeichen        14
   7   FNR          Zeichen         4
   8   BAUZEIT      Zeichen        20
   9   BAUKOSTEN    Zeichen        11
  10   HAEFEN       Zeichen        57
  11   ZP_STATBIN   Zeichen        57
  12   METRISCH     Logisch         1
  13   LÄNGE        Numerisch       5
  14   FW_TIEFE1    Numerisch       3       1
  15   FW_TIEFE2    Numerisch       3       1
  16   SCHLEUSEN    Numerisch       2
  17   TRAGFÄHIGK   Numerisch       5
  18   HÄFEN_EB     Numerisch       3
  19   I_HÄFEN      Numerisch       3
  20   LPLÄTZE_EB   Numerisch       3
  21   I_ANLAGEN    Numerisch       3
  22   KETTE_SEIL   Logisch         1
  23   SCHIFFBAR    Zeichen         5
  24   B_KOSTEN     Numerisch       8
  25   L_KOSTEN     Numerisch       8
  26   EINNAHMEN    Numerisch      10
  27   WÄHRUNG      Zeichen        10
  28   JAHR         Zeichen         4
  29   K_NR         Zeichen        11
  30   QUELLE       Zeichen        37
  31   BEMERKUNG    Zeichen       188
** Gesamt **                      571
```

b - The Sources

The main sources used for data collection and data entry in BINWA are navigational guides, maps and tables, and construction records. The most important single source, by far, is the official navigational guide to German waterways, published since 1893 by the Prussian ministry of public works, later by the Reich ministry of transport, which went through several editions right up to the 1940s.(3) A preliminary survey on inland waterways was published by the Prussian authorities in 1874, in this case, however, restricted to the Kingdom of Prussia and some of her adjacent territories.(4) For the years prior to 1874, the situation on reliable sources is, unfortunately, less satisfactory. There are scattered regional statistics, navigational maps as well as tables published in conjunction with them, which have to be located and scrutinized. Moreover, archival holdings (e.g. records on river improvements and canal construction) are being tapped.(5) Although the initial goal of the BINWA project is to collect data for specific reference years only - approximately one reference year per decade - locating sources for the entire period of about 150 years has not always been an easy task, especially for the early period of observation.

c - The Program

BINWA is not only a database but also a program. More specifically, it is a dBASE III application program written to facilitate the main chores of database operation such as data entry, the editing of data, data retrieval and the printing of data reports. The program is entirely menu-driven (cf. the printout of the main menu shown in Figure 3)

Figure 3: Main Menu of BINWA Program

```
==> B I N W A <==
■ Datenbank für Wasserstrassen ■
FU Berlin, ZI6, AWS, Version 2.0 (c) A.Kunz '87

* EINGANGSMENÜ *        [1]   Abfrage/Aufnahme

                        [2]   Stichwortsuche

                        [3]   Neuaufnahme ohne Abfrage

                        [4]   Editieren

                        [5]   Datenauswertung

                        [6]   Datei Service/Report

                        [7]   Zurück zu dBase

                        [0]   Betriebssystem

          Ihre Wahl?
```

in order to enable project members untrained in dBASE to use BINWA without any deeper knowledge of the database program itself. The menu structure also makes the program extremely user-friendly. As yet, the program exists in uncompiled form only, i.e. dBASE III (Plus) is necessary to run the program. While experienced dBASE users can leave BINWA at any time to work at the dBASE interactive command level, the operation from the menu level is preferred, not least because certain safety routines have been built in to avoid the deletion or duplication of data. On a PC-AT with a reasonably well-performing mass storage device (a 30 MB hard disk, preferably with low access time, suffices), data retrieval is generally fast enough for project purposes, particularly when searching with the name of the waterway in the indexed database (normal method of retrieval). Supplementary search routines enable the user to locate and organize data on the basis of, among other things, the name of ports and of statistical check points used within project, or by selection from a variety of regional codes.

d - Data Evaluation

The evaluation of data stored in BINWA can be done in several ways. Within the program itself, both, screen and printer oriented arithmetic and statistical routines to either count or summarize (numeric) data have been permanently installed and can thus be used by menu selection. For example, the combined length of waterways in a specific waterway region can be ascertained with the help of an option menu. When called upon, this option displays a classification scheme used within the project and allows the user to perform more complicated calculations on the length and loading capacity of waterways by merely hitting a few keys (see Figure 4 for an example of this routine). In a similar fashion, statistical reports can be compiled and printed with qualifiers for data selection being provided by a set of menu options (cf. Figure 5). Additional routines could be installed should it become necessary; alternatively, users with advanced knowledge in dBASE can run statistical queries at the dBASE command line. For more advanced statistical treatment, data can be transferred out of BINWA into a statistical package like SPSS or a spreadsheet like LOTUS 1-2-3. Data transfer is also the principle used in the cartographic presentation of data. With the aid of THEMAK2, a cartography program developed at the Free University, data originally compiled in BINWA are used in the construction of a series of thematic maps that may eventually lead to a computer atlas on German transport statistics.

Figure 4: BINWA Calculation Routine

```
STATBIN-Klassifizierungsschema für Wasserstrassen

 1.  Weniger als 50t (oder nicht schiffbar)
 2.  50t bis 100t ausschließlich
 3.  100t bis 200t ausschließlich
 4.  200t bis 400t ausschließlich
 5.  400t bis 600t ausschließlich
 6.  600t bis 1000t ausschließlich
 7  1000t bis 1350t ausschließlich
 8. 1350t bis 2000t ausschließlich
 9  2000t und mehr (größte Binnenschiffe)
[S] Seeschiffe von mehr als 3000t

                                                 Jahr:  [1874]
                                                   WG:  [7]
Wählen Sie eine Klassifizierung (1-9, S, Q=Quit) 4  Klasse:  [4]
     11 Sätze summiert
    länge
     668
Weitere Abfrage? (J/N)
```

Figure 5: BINWA Report

JAHR	WG	TYP	WASSERSTRASSE	TGFK	LÄNGE
** WASSERSTRASSENGEBIET 2					
1893	2	f	Oder	450	45
1893	2	f	Oder	465	116
1893	2	f	Oder	450	113
1893	2	f	Oder	500	205
1893	2	f	Oder	450	14
** Gruppensumme **					
					493
** WASSERSTRASSENGEBIET 3					
1893	3	k	Havel-Wasserstrasse	400	177
1893	3	k	Oder-Spree-Kanal	400	101
1893	3	k	Plauer Kanal, Alter	500	34
1893	3	k	Plauer Kanal, Neuer	450	30
1893	3	?	Rüdersdorfer Gewässer	400	9
1893	3	f	Spree	500	21
1893	3	f	Spree	400	24
1893	3	k	Spree	400	0
** Gruppensumme **					
					396
** WASSERSTRASSENGEBIET 4					
1893	4	f	Elbe	800	41
1893	4	f	Elbe	800	462
1893	4	f	Elbe	600	121
** Gruppensumme **					
					624
** WASSERSTRASSENGEBIET 7					
1893	7	f	Rhein	800	55
** Gruppensumme **					
					55
** WASSERSTRASSENGEBIET 8					
1893	8	f	Donau	800	154
** Gruppensumme **					
					154
*** Gesamt ***					
					1722

Note: A loading capacity of 400-800 tons and the year 1983 were given as search clues for the report.

NOTES

1. Quellen und Forschungen zur Historischen Statistik von Deutschland, ed. by W. Fischer, F. Irsigler, K.H. Kaufhold, H. Ott. St. Katharinen: Scripta Mercarurae, 1986 ff.
2. The project is run jointly by this author and Rainer Fremdling, University Groningen (Netherlands) and has been funded by the German Research Council.
3. Führer auf den deutschen Schiffahrtsstrassen, ed. by Königlich Preussisches Ministerium der öffentliche Arbeiten, Berlin 1894. Further editions: 1903, 1907, 1914, 1924-27, 1930s, 1940s.
4. Die Wasserstraßen in Preußen und in einigen angrenzenden Staaten, ed. by Ministerium für Handel, Gewerbe und Öffentliche Arbeiten, Berlin 1874.
5. For example, in the State Archives in Munich the first official geographical survey of the Bavarian Danube, undertaken in 1860, was found and evaluated. For the Rhine river, the annual statistical reports published by the Central Commission of the Navigation of the Rhine since 1835 contain useable data.

SYMBOLIC DIMENSIONS OF SERIAL SOURCES HERMENEUTICAL PROBLEMS OF RECONSTRUCTING POLITICAL BIOGRAPHIES BASED ON COMPUTERIZED RECORD LINKAGE

Carola Lipp
Ludwig-Uhland-Institut für empirische Kulturwissenschaft
Universität Tübingen
FRG

In the following, I will draw the outlines of a current research project on the revolution of 1848 that deals with the connection between political culture and everyday life (Kaschuba/Lipp 1984)(1). As it is based on computerized nominal record linkage I will conclude with some problems regarding the self-interpretative dimensions of sources and their implications for linkage procedures.

The object of this research project is the entire population of the city of Esslingen and their political activities leading up to and including the revolution of 1848. It is intended to reconstruct individual and collective political biographies in order to build the core of complex analyses of the political culture at that time. Of central interest are different styles of political behaviour and modes of articulation and action related to certain groups or individuals. Who took part in demonstrations and who preferred to announce his political values in the newspaper? When did certain people enter the political scene, join organizations, sign petitions or demonstrate publicly? How are their activities related to the group they join or live or work within? How does it fit into their personal life cycle? Are there processes of political adaptation, how and in which context do people learn certain styles of political behaviour etc.? These are some of the questions that are asked. The result will be a "thick description" (Medick 1984; Geertz 1983) of specific actions and groups, using descriptive and analytical statistical procedures as well as hermeneutical interpretation of the symbolic dimensions of political action.

One of the theses of the project is that the actual conditions of life experience and social relationship shape political behaviour that everyday life and its ingrown social structures are systematic prerequisites for political action. Political culture is understood as embedded in structures of life experience and habitus (Bourdieu 1977, p. 82f.). To reveal social and private networks underlying political activities is one of the major goals of this project. These networks include neighbourhood, which emerges as a force strong enough to transcend social stratum and workplace, both structures with a heavy impact on political behaviour. They also include family relations. The relationship between class formation processes, political organization and strategies of social reproduction or marriage will be one of the important fields of analyses. Scholars often repeat the phrase that organizations are marriage markets (Blackbourne 1980, p. 95), but no one could ever show it. By the use of demographic data, it is not only possible to link political behaviour to structures of individual life, but also to analyze demographic behaviour from a political point of view. The problem of generation, for example, is a central one in 1848, with regard to both intergenerational conflicts and persistence of traditional models of political behaviour.

Political attitude in this regard does not only mean public activity, but also behaviour in a domain which is still called the private sphere. One might ask, for instance, if self-identified democrats pursue marriage patterns consonant with their politics. This study reaches far beneath the level that studies of political culture studies usually get. If, for example, the liberal party tries to survive in the forties by organizing children's festivals and claiming to be the party of the future, the question might be asked if and how this idea shows up privately in certain family patterns and if there is a consistency between political and private goals.

Contrary to other studies, I do not concentrate on prominent groups or restrict my view to the social structures of certain politically dominant organizations, but I try to look at the whole system of organizations and cross-memberships, to determine how an activity is related to other forms of political participation, as signing petitions, voting, membership in cultural organizations, positions in the local executive and so on. Political attitude is thus explained in the context of an entire lifestyle, a whole construct of cultural activity. One part of the study thus deals with processes of political formation and organization. The other part concentrates on social substructures of political life.

Esslingen was a very busy place in 1848; there were many political declarations and active organizations. The sources are rich. Especially the voting lists of the city council give detailed information about the choice of every voter and allow for example to identify changing political factions and groups or to observe the coincidence of political pronouncements and actual behaviour.

What makes this study especially interesting is its focus on the city as a whole. One can thus not only identify the political activists, but also the non-participants. It is as well important to learn, among those permitted to vote for the National Assembly, who voted and who did not. Which are the structures that explain non-participation? Does the answer lie in socioeconomic constraints or, as it is in fact, in the neighbourhood and in the self-definition of certain professions like judges?

Methodologically, the concept is based on several steps of nominal record linkage which integrate data bases of different information levels and logical structures. The file management as well as the record linkage are done by Kleio, a data bank oriented system (Thaller 1988) which allows to handle dataformats quite flexibly and which provides differentiated procedures to merge files of different structure and, thus, combines the information of several sources. Till now, 9 files are linked. At the end nearly forty larger and smaller sized files will be matched. Naturally, the increase of information with each linkage quickens further identification routines.

Technically, the linkage procedure is done by computer, which means that the preparing of decisions and the comparing of nominal strings are done by system routines named *regula* and *connectio*. The identification, the linkage decision and the definition for the matching of two files are controlled manually. Though the computer supports identification, there are cases where known people are more easily identified and quicker linked by hand than by machine because of the simplicity of the selection process. Defining too many variables lames the computer; defining a broad frame produces too much paper and too many alternatives. The machine and Kleio's comparing functions are indispensable in complicated cases. Supported by Kleio and its integrated soundex algorithm, the problems of misspelling, spelling variations or homonyms can be solved far easier than by manual inspection of the file.

The complete data base includes three types of sources: a social data base, demographic data out of church records and political sources (see graphic). The latter enclose files of different types of information, among others a large series of petitions, information about positions in the city council and local organizations, membership rolls of associations, data from court records and the city council protocols, and detailed extracts from the very rich local newspaper, concerning single activities of individuals and groups. A data base in itself represents the local electoral lists, which deliver not only names and professions but the individual choice of each voter and this for a period from 1840 to 1848.

The centre and starting point is the social data base. It is founded on two inhabitant lists which provide basic information about the heads of more or less 2,250-2,500 households. Besides, last and first names, sex and living places, the population registers include information about the profession and sometimes even the place of work. Added to these files is an inhabitant-tax roll which catches hold of nonresident people, the mobile group of inhabitants, who are only staying for some months. Electoral lists for the national assembly and militia records with detailed information about the actual occupation and birth date and a list of house owners complete this complex, which consists of approximately 11,000 nominal entries, representing a population of 12,763 inhabitants; these data relate to approximately 3,600 grown up people, mostly male, because the female population is represented only by widows and self supporting working women. Referring to a period of 6 years from 1846 to 1852, the net of social data is thus tightly knit. All information, linked and not linked entries, out of the different files is integrated in one complex social data base, without changing the shape of the single file or discarding information.

In a second complex, the linkage of social data is controlled and deepened by church records. There are protestant, catholic and jewish family registers, which include three generations, the marrying couples and their parents as well as the kids and the future spouses of the second generation. As the church records cover a period from 1800 to 1870, these sources allow to reconstruct the intergenerational profile of the residential population. Both linkage processes, the family reconstitution as well as the social data base, are made parallelly and used as controlling instrument for the linkage process. After the completion of the internal linkage of the family records, this source will be embedded in the central data base. At the actual stage, the family reconstitution is still worked on, but the social data base is accomplished and partly linked with data out of membership rolls and petitions.

Besides the basic problem that record linkage always creates a social reality in itself and, therefore, represents a complex hermeneutical act, there emerge certain methodological problems with this approach. The technique of integrating a complex number of closely related data sets into one single file leads to multiple entries which are difficult to be used in statistical analysis. My social data base, for example, shows more than 6 profession entries from different periods. Thus, the question arises: Which one is to be used for statistical analyses, when I examine a linked source, which one originally does not contain information about the occupation? Ambiguous information, therefore, has to be structured along a longitudinal axis. Furthermore, the information of the entries usually differ quite remarkably. In a published official source like printed inhabitant registers, an artisan might be keen to show up in his learned profession, though the militia list reports that he works at that time in the factory. How is he to be treated?

Obviously, the register reflects a traditional status which could be the sign of his clinging to this social position. And this tendency might also be observed in a formal letter to the city council. On the other hand, it is important to file him as a factory worker, when he has signed a petition that runs through the staff of a certain factory.

To subsume such a person simply under the uniform category "actual profession", excludes an important social dimension. Obviously, he himself wants to be presented in a different way.

Methodologically, this problem could be solved by extrapolating certain career steps out of the material, by defining special thesauri for such groups of transitional professions and by separating analytical procedures. Therefore, I analyze each source at first in its own given social horizon and a second time with the aggregated career definition, which is developed out of the linked information and gets more specific with the accumulation of data. For the analysis of population structure or acting people, this means that sometimes a quite different social reality shows up. Besides the general danger that ambiguities might be the result of confusing people and false identifications and associations, my data base reveals certain characteristics of serial sources which are usually ignored or cannot be detected. As official sources printed inhabitant lists, at that time, tend to rise social status or to preserve a certain social profile. Factory working for example is noted as profession only in cases where factory working is regarded as something special.

Between 1847 and 1850, Esslingen, underwent a rapid social change caused by the founding of one of the most important machine factories in the south-west (Schomerus 1977). Population changed quickly at that time and so did the professional profile of the population. In the register of 1850, the skilled workers of the Esslinger Maschinenfabrik emphasize this fact in reporting their workplace, whereas workers in the textile factory use their learned profession and do not refer to their actual status. Though, there remains the question, whose value system is reflected by inhabitant registers? I tend towards the solution that there is a tendency to respectability which reflects the self reference of the documented people and which has its consequences not only in the representation of lower classes, but still more in the presentation of upper classes. Well-to-do owners of several houses or business places appear more than once in the registers without indication of their double identity. Cross checks with church records, therefore, show that the upper classes are usually overrepresented. I think, that this is a fact, which might be observed in other towns as well.

Therefore, the constituency of sources is very important. People, especially high ranking people, are playing a vast number of social and political roles, and this influences their representation in certain sources. I was confronted with this fact in linking my social data base with petitions. Usually, the petitions I am dealing with include only name and surname and, under certain conditions, they tell the profession. And here the problems of identification start. A petition addressed to the National Assembly in Frankfurt pleading for heavy duties on the import of wine was signed only by vintners and vineyard-owners. The linkage to the social data base revealed that the latter category contained a large number of different professions like coppersmiths, butchers or tanners, who referred to themselves as vineyard-owners, because this was reflecting their actual interest. One of these people, a confectioner, appeared in a different petition as merchant (Handlungsvorstand); and, indeed, he owned a little factory that produced vinegar, a fact that certainly gives bad reputation to his vineyard. That the same man also liked to use his titles of "Gemeinderat" or "commander of the civil army", is not astonishing. His self-referential notations changed, adapted to the situations and groups he was acting in.

Though there is a logical structure in this behaviour, these conditions complicate record linkage of process-produced sources enormously. On the other hand, it is this inherent social code which can sometimes lead to the identification of people. There exist certain rules of self-perception and contextual knowledge, which guide the modes of signing petitions. If the leader of a petition or the one who signs first on a page uses a professional connotation, the others will follow. Mostly petitions do not report professions because they are produced in a defined social group, which itself implies the social status of the petitioners. The existence of occupational categories in a petition, therefore, often indicates that there is a political but no obvious social or status relation between the acting people. If the signing people realize common patterns or structures, they are acting in, they tend not to give contextual information. When occupational connotations appear in these cases, they are meant to demonstrate social difference and, thus, break a logical sequence in the petition. In a list of 20 factory workers who do not sign with their profession, the trained baker might insist on his different background. When a petition passes a street, for example in a vintner's quarter, where closely interrelated people live, people who have the same family names and often the same profession, they usually try to identify themselves socially by writing the name of their father, or their surnames. Very often, the last one in the row does without these connotations because he may think that now when all the others have signed, he is socially defined and needs no further connotation. The same rule is followed by a council member, who came from a big vintner family and who never signed with his first name or his profession because he obviously expects to be known. And at last, after long puzzling, I can identify his rather prominent signature. When I am talking about symbolic dimensions of serial sources, I mean these forms of self presentation and self reference that should be reflected in record linkage processes.

Process produced data, which emerge out of context defined political situations like an association or neighbourhood, usually contain very little hints to identify persons. Therefore, a large social data base and a systematic testing of social networks is required, if those data should be linked. When this procedure is successful, record linkage is then able to reveal social structures that cannot be seen at the first sight. A last example: Petitions addressed to the National Assembly usually carry titles which are given to them by the registration bureau. An Esslinger petition pleading for protective duty was, thus, assigned to merchants and factory owners who headed the list. Closer inspection after record linkage, however, showed that more than 60% of the people who had signed were factory workers. A fact which enormously affects the interpretation of the material. Used in such a way, record linkage, for example, allows to follow the social route a petition takes. It can be shown in which groups, neighbourhoods or workshops the lists had circulated.

Complex record linkage, thus, reveals underlying social structure of political actions, and the integration in a central file allows, in a further step, to look at interrelated variables. The strength of this approach lies in its flexibility to focus on individuals and groups as well and to analyze common structures and rules of action. It is possible to examine the social context of a whole organization as well as to concentrate on certain prominent figures in the local elite. One can survey political activities and also the private lives of the actors. Multilevel analyses and testing makes it easy to look for dominant features of political behaviour. The capability of Kleio to manage complex file structures, the flexible and rich retrieval functions support not only record linkage processes, but make it possible to decode symbolic and self-referential dimensions of serial sources and, thus, enrich the interpretative possibilities. Canned routines which translate complex file structures into an arbitrary number of SPSS-matrices open the way to descriptive statistics as well as complex multivariate analyses.

Figure:

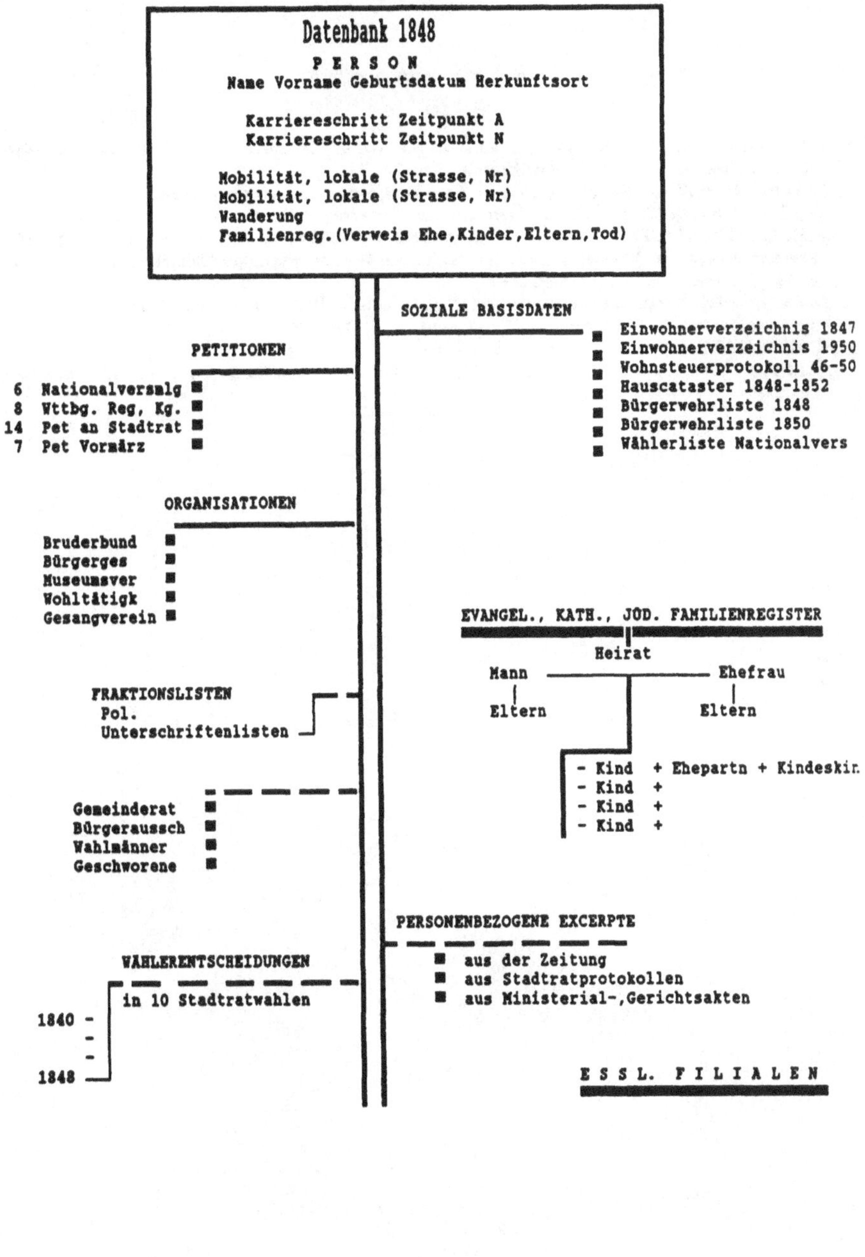
Datenbank 1848
PERSON
Name Vorname Geburtsdatum Herkunftsort
Karriereschritt Zeitpunkt A
Karriereschritt Zeitpunkt N
Mobilität, lokale (Strasse, Nr)
Mobilität, lokale (Strasse, Nr)
Wanderung
Familienreg. (Verweis Ehe, Kinder, Eltern, Tod)
SOZIALE BASISDATEN
Einwohnerverzeichnis 1847
Einwohnerverzeichnis 1950
Wohnsteuerprotokoll 46-50
Hauscataster 1848-1852
Bürgerwehrliste 1848
Bürgerwehrliste 1850
Wählerliste Nationalvers
PETITIONEN
6 Nationalversmlg
8 Wttbg. Reg, Kg.
14 Pet an Stadtrat
7 Pet Vormärz
ORGANISATIONEN
Bruderbund
Bürgerges
Museumsver
Wohltätigk
Gesangverein
EVANGEL., KATH., JÜD. FAMILIENREGISTER
Heirat
Mann
Ehefrau
Eltern
Eltern
- Kind + Ehepartn + Kindeskir
- Kind +
- Kind +
- Kind +
FRAKTIONSLISTEN
Pol.
Unterschriftenlisten
Gemeinderat
Bürgeraussch
Wahlmänner
Geschworene
PERSONENBEZOGENE EXCERPTE
aus der Zeitung
aus Stadtratprotokollen
aus Ministerial-, Gerichtsakten
WÄHLERENTSCHEIDUNGEN
in 10 Stadtratwahlen
1840 -
-
-
1848
ESSL. FILIALEN

NOTE

This project was supported by the "Deutsche Forschungsgemeinschaft".

REFERENCES

BLACKBOURNE, D. 1980. "Wie es eigentlich nicht gewesen ist", in: Blackbourne, D. and Eley, G. *Mythen der deutschen Geschichtsschreibung*. Frankfurt, Berlin, Wien

BOURDIEU, P. 1977. *Outline of a Theory of Practice*. Cambridge University Press

GEERTZ, C. 1983. *Dichte Beschreibung. Beiträge zum Verstehen kultureller Systeme*. Frankfurt

KASCHUBA, W. and LIPP, C. 1984. "Revolutionskultur 1848/1849", in: Reinalter, H. (Hrsg.). *Aufklärung Vormärz-Revolution*. Mitteilungen der internationalen Forschungsgruppe "Demokratische Bewegungen in Mitteleuropa". Bd. 4, Innsbruck, 20-24

MEDICK, H. 1984. "Missionare im Ruderboot?" Ethnologische Erkenntnisweisen als Herausforderung an die Sozialgeschichte. *Geschichte und Gesellschaft*, H. 3, 295-319

SCHOMERUS, H. 1977. *Die Arbeiter der Maschinenfabrik Esslingen*. Stuttgart

THALLER, M. 1988. *Kleio 2.1.1. Ein fachspezifisches Datenbanksystem für die Historischen Wissenschaften*. Göttingen

THE GERMAN PARLIAMENTARIAN DATA BASE: CATCHING THE COMPLEXITIES OF POLITICAL LIFE-HISTORIES

Heinrich Best, Ralph Ponemereo
Zentralarchiv für Empirische Sozialforschung, Cologne
FRG

I. From Social Background Analysis to Causal Analyses of Social Dynamics

Empirical studies of political elites for the most part were, and many of them still are static "social background analyses": a given configuration of "demographic" variables that is regional origin, denomination, education, main occupation and father's profession are considered as the "predisposing factor" causing the variations in the political attitudes of the elites or their relative success in obtaining power positions. The data used in "static" research designs of this kind are of a simple case by variable (NxV) structure and can be appropriately stored in a conventional flat-file format. However, information on sequences, timing of transitions and/or direct mutual relationship between members of the elites have to be neglected or they are only imperfectly represented in such a simple data base design. This turns out to be a major flaw, because research into political elites has demonstrated that the process of recruitment and socialization should be conceptualized as a sequence of roles, statuses, and experiences in the course of which people acquire leading positions and political attitudes. In such an approach the emphasis has shifted from the origins of elites or their demographical properties to the patterns of their life-histories and careers. At an other occasion, we introduced the term "political biography" to denote the sequential order of political experiences. Areas of political experiences include, apart from formal positions in the political system, a great variety of activities and roles by which political participation is realized, either indirectly or, sometimes, in an illegal way. If information on sequences and timing of transitions is provided, the process of "carriérisation" can be studied, i.e. the conditional interlocking of positions in a sequential order. It was claimed that the degree to which a formal career becomes a prerequisite to leading positions is a significant indicator for the differentiation of a political system. On the other hand, the contradictions and ambiguities of biographies become visible if sequences of positions are recorded.

Sequence makes a difference, but timing is of importance, too. The time interval between two events has an impact on the degree to which the first event has an effect on the second. On the other hand, in social processes there is forgetting, too. A person may have been persecuted for having violated certain political norms, but he may be admitted to offices later on if this is considered a youthful prank by gate-keeping agents. The intervals before benefits become available are socially selective mechanisms of a somewhat different kind. Such data may be used as indicators for the working of patronage or for the rigidity of persecution practices.

Extensive use of the potentials of life-history data was made in a research project on structure and change of German parliamentary leadership groups 1848-1933, run at the Institute for Applied Social Research at the University of Cologne and funded

by the German Science Foundation (DFG). Its main concern was the question in which ways and to which extent the shape of political biographies reflected the changing features of the German political system.
The patterns of political biographies were reconstructed in four steps:

* Firstly, we identified typical configurations of political experiences. Here, our essential interest was to explore whether the areas of political experiences were part of more comprehensive fields of political action whose composition reflected the structure of opportunity of political activities in Germany;
* then, we identified the sequences in which the entries into political areas of experiences were ordered. Here, we were specially interested in the question to which extent career patterns are detectable which are characteristic of a socially differentiated political system;
* further, we examined the timing of political experiences. Here, we were mainly concerned with the question whether there existed a contingency with transitions into other institutional areas of society as the professional and educational systems;
* finally, we outlined the distribution of political experiences in the course of historical time. In this context, we examined the question to which degree short and long term changes of the conditional framework for political actions intervened into the political biographies of the deputies.

II. The Formal Structure of Life-History Data

From a technical point of view, life-histories are configurations of variables (types of events), cases (persons) and units of time. They have a longitudinal structure, i.e., we have to reconstruct the succession of life-events - like, for instance the stages of a professional career - and to assign identifiers for each point of transition which locates them in historical time. By means of a simple conversion, using the year of birth as reference point, it is possible to represent the sequences in a life-historical succession. As a rule, the accuracy of measurement should be one year. For life-events, however, which are characterized by dense sequences, its precision should be increased to the exact day.

The complexities of event- or life-histories were first conceptualized by Raymond Catell in what he called the "Covariation Chart". Catell systematically set out the totality of relations open to observation within three cartesian coordinates. The (alpha) numerical entries made in the cells of the Covariation Chart are bound to the modes of biographical attributes. Thus, a_{ijk} is the state of person i to characteristic j at time k. The resulting data-matrix has the form of a three-dimensional "data-box". The classical cross-sectional research-design is represented by a "face" of this data-box (VxN), whereas for a longitudinal design a "slice" (VxNxT) is needed.

Theoretically, it would be possible to represent the "data-box" in a flat-file format by assigning time (or space) coordinates to each data point. But practically, the data-base would become unmanageable for many analytical purposes. Professional or political careers may consist of dozens of transitions. It is evident that any attempt to organize these complexities in a fixed format would soon exceed the limits of storage and core memory capacities. In the case of the 809 members of the National Frankfurt Assembly no less than about 40 000 observations, concerning sequencing and timing of occupational changes had to be processed. The application of more flexible DBMS-technologies, allowing for a "natural" representation of career patterns in the data soon turned out to be inevitable.

III. The Evaluation and Adaptation of an Appropriate Data Base System

To translate the complexities of the life histories of more than 5700 members of national parliaments between 1848 (Frankfurt National Assembly) and (March) 1933 turned out to be a major methodological challenge of the whole project. We started with the somewhat optimistic assumption that even the most complex data structure may be physically represented by a simple two-dimensional matrix often described as "flat file". But we had to experience soon that this flat file tended dramatically to expand comprising a reasonable amount of "non-information". Thus, the design of a data base firstly meant to define the rules of this complexity and then to store only the substantial data according to this rules. The most commonly used design models were provided by "old-fashioned" data base software using hierarchical and/or network models, i.e. the information was constructed as 1xN or NxM relationships. A significant disadvantage of this software was the prerequisite of defining all linkages between information elements before entering the data. If the chosen design did not fit the data as intended, or if new types of information with new linkages had to be incorporated - the entire data base had to be restructured physically by a complete unload-reload procedure for an internal redefinition following the new rules of the design. This was one of the major arguments against these data base management systems. Additionally, the manageability of these systems was poor because programming languages had to be mastered for performing retrievals and to implement interfaces.

A complete new data base philosophy was developed by Edgar F. Codd since the early 1970s at the IBM Research Lab directory in San Jose: the Relational Data Model. Based upon a mathematical model, it formalizes the data design so that all activities with the data will bring up predictable result if the design follows the rules of normalization, i.e. if the design is unambiguous, free of redundancies and contradictions. Logical links between information units should be derived from only one primary key. A second major idea was to establish a complete independence of physical data storage from logical data structure. The first item has to be completely covered by the kernel of the system: By the data base management system (DBMS) the user communicates on a logical level which is represented by relations and relational operations. Basically, these relations are 2-dimensional tables following strictly the rule that a single information element can be depicted by three meta informations: the table name, the primary key (represented by the rows) and the column. These relations may be retrieved by mathematical operators performing e.g. selections, projections, joins, etc., where the joining fields (columns) and operations (e.g. <,=,>) connecting the tables are freely definable, thus, enabling also hierarchical and/or network access. All information has to be accessible via a non-procedural data language which must be easy to learn and easy to use and be able to perform relational operations in the strict sense. This is SQL (Structured Query Language) which has been adopted by most RDBMS manufacturers and now follows a so-called ANSI-standard which means that a subset of commands looks alike in all RDBMS, but every manufacturer tries to develop more efficient and powerful commands. As a simple example a selection from a single table may be performed in the following way:

SELECT name, date_of_birth FROM biograf WHERE denomination = 'catholic'

But SQL is not only the user interface for retrieving, creating, deleting and updating tables. Modern RDBMS "speak" SQL which means even the software modules internally communicate via SQL downward to the real kernel of a system which has to work on the level of the operating system. As an example for the advantages of this design, the general user interface of INGRES (one of the major competitors in the RDMBS market besides ORACLE and DB2) may offer an example of these systems. Invoking INGRES means to activate the DBMS kernel "backend" and the menu driven user interface "frontend". This "frontend" shows several options like looking into the data dictionary for getting information about tables, options to manipulate and retrieve tables, designing menus and creating "joindefs" for fixed retrievals over more than one table, creating reports and applications or simply invoking SQL. "Frontend" and "backend" communicate via SQL and may reside neighbours in a PC core memory (struggling hard for every byte to operate!), but as an alternative, they also may reside on different machines in a local area network (LAN) or even a wide area network (WAN), where some end user in Germany can manipulate tables stored on a computer in America. Additionally, the newest versions allow for splitting tables among different machines looking like one continuous amount of information. Thus, modern RDBMS "after Codd" claim to offer flexible database design accompanied by a standardised data language to perform all needed activities manipulating the stored data, powerful instruments for creating applications supported by DBMS which guarantees the complete distinction between physical and logical operations in an environment of distributed data bases. So, the entire system shall cover all demands of all possible users: RDBMS are multi-purpose systems and may be engaged for a travel agencies booking system as well as to manage industrial production or public administration activities.

To cope with all these different demands, there exists a reasonable overhead of functions and modules to achieve the theoretically postulated functionality. First, RDBMS are strongly "transaction oriented". This means, they shall guarantee to access and/or to

1. manipulate information in a data base constantly and continuously
2. fulfil this central need a great variety of security tools have to be implemented to share access authorities between a large number of end users.
3. Not only data access security is essential but also data security with regard to data integrity in an environment of rapidly changing information like e.g. bank accounts. This is performed by very sophisticated logging and locking mechanisms to enable only single write permits while not preventing multiple read access to make sure that the end user permanently encounters a well defined status of the entire data bases as well as of a single information atom. This means a reasonable "slow-down" in access speed which can be avoided by specific data base tuning facilities. These specific supervision tasks can only be performed by a single user, the data base administrator (DBA), who will create and delete permits, perform tuning methods, control integrity and possible rollback after damage and is responsible for backups of the data base.
4. SQL serves as an easy-to-use tool for a data manipulation but tends to become

unhandy if several tables are involved in a retrieval. Additionally, a SQL user must know the structure of the data base in detail to compose the statements correctly. Not every employee can and shall know the data base entirely. So, modern RDBMS serve the end user with tools to create applications for special needs of departments in companies perfectly hiding the data base software and the design. These applications are generally composed of different menus, help texts and hidden SQL statements.

The creation of those applications itself is not a task for ad hoc usage because it needs a deep knowledge of the data base, the tuning options and - last but not least - the ability to write statements in (e.g. INGRES-) OSL, a 4GL-application language. Finally, since RDBMS are known as "slow", these systems offer a wide range of tuning tools by e.g. creating secondary indices using different storage methods to optimize each kind of access. Since each secondary index is physically stored as a table, a very sophisticatedly designed data base may comprise a very large amount of relations. The last two items show that RDBMS need not only a DBA but in addition (a team of) software engineers programming all these applications. So, as a conclusion, RDBMS may be described as optimized to perform as an "Information Management System" well applicable within an environment of rapid changing data. This leads to the main question evaluating these software for usage in the social sciences and humanities. Generally spoken, RDBMS are applicable because of their ability to manage complex data structures and retrieve information through very user friendly menu driven applications.

IV. The Use of SIR as DBMS for the German Parliamentarian Database

Reconsidering the central needs of a research project like the one on collective biographies of parliamentarians, the result of our evaluation was not to rely on RDBMS like INGRES or ORACLE but to use SIR (Scientific Information Retrieval), a system too often regarded as an "old fashioned" DBMS. The reasons for choosing SIR instead shall be discussed in the following:

* to start with the main distinction: RDBMS like INGRES are very useful to create an "information system", whereas SIR is designed to be used as an "analysis system" and data analysis is the main objective of a research project which makes use of the methodology of quantitative historical social research. Which are the main differences between these two kinds of data base application? Software manufacturers of modern RDBMS look on their products like priests of certain sects. Edgar F. Codd, its founder and chief-propagator confirmed his adherents to maintain the purity (and the superiority) of this relational model, always keeping in mind the "voice of the hill" which e.g. in the mid 70s published a warning cry under the title "Is your data base really relational?". Not unlike the ten commandments, Codd's twelve rules then had to be followed strictly by the manufacturers to be not kicked out of the church. Two of these rules shall be mentioned here to illustrate the disadvantages of "true" RDBMS for an analysis system. The first: every operation within a RDBMS manipulates relations via relational operators bringing up as a result again a relation - but what to do with this table regarding statistical analysis? It is only useful for performing a printout for visual interpretation. SIR also generates as a result of a query a 2-dimensional table called "summary buffer" as a binary file

ready for further use producing basic statistics, reports or tabulations. Of major importance is the ability to transfer this file directly into system files of the most commonly used statistical software packages like SPSSx, SAS, or BMDP. The second: RDBMS allow for so-called "null values" as a single exception of the relational model. This null value may be compared with the "system missing value" within standard statistical packages like SPSSx, but is not explicitly definable as an "ordinary" missing value. This is not acceptable for a researcher collecting data from historical sources. SIR is able to manage value types which may or may not be excluded from the analysis. But there are further distinctions between true RDBMS and SIR which had great influence on the decision to choose SIR:

* RDBMS store data "as is" that means numbers remain numbers and strings remain strings. SIR as a sort of "old-fashioned" software was designed looking at SPSS-users which suffered from the lack of statistical systems to manipulate complex data structures but wanted to work with a system that should be as familiar to them as old SPSS regarding the definition of data and manipulating them via a programming syntax. This is not only a question of attracting people via a known working environment but a totally different concept of data management. SIR also stores data "as is" if wanted but additionally is able to manage coded information interpreting a number as a code and, thus, handling a column of a table (record type) as a variable (and a row as a case). Then, the labelling and the status of the data is stored as system tables in the data dictionary so that a summary buffer file containing codes will be transferred into a procedure e.g. into a SPSSx system file accompanied by this meta information. Storing coded information also means to offer the option for efficient re-coding in a traditional manner social scientists are familiar with.
* RDBMS can handle complex data structures by using relational methods via free joining of fields. SIR was originally designed as a hierarchical and/or network data base system. Fortunately, the new version of this software system provides the user with a full relational data management tool so that using SIR means to have the option of switching between a relational environment and a hierarchical/network environment, even after a data base design following the latter principles by a simple command e.g. using the SQL interface and entering "set case off" with a subsequent possibility of free joining like in INGRES. SIR does not "speak" SQL but using it shows no difference comparing to "true" SQL systems. According to this two-way option, databases can be created without case (i.e. relational from the beginning) or case-oriented (i.e. with hierarchies and networks and a relational option). Hierarchy then means defining cases as basic nodes of information accompanied by 1*N information links in different tables (record types). These links are established by so-called "sort id's" which define the order and number of links to a node. Networks are established by a certain variable within a hierarchy pointing to a different type of case again accompanied by unrestricted deep nested hierarchies. A case then may be interpreted in two different ways: physically and logically. On the physical side, cases and their hierarchies of information are physical clusters on storage devices, accessed in an optimized way by the DMBS kernel looking along these sort "id's". This operation reduces disk operations and saves execution time comparing to RDBMS (but like these systems, SIR provides internal safety routines for access authorization and data integrity, too). On the logical side, cases are - to "speak INGRES" again -

natural joins between information elements. (A third interpretation refers explicitly to statistical analysis, where 2-dimensional data matrices composed of cases and variables are processed). The hierarchical operators (sort id's) themselves again may be interpreted in two ways: first, as a simple pointer between a case and a subsequent information group (variables) ranging from 1 to n. Secondly, they may be used to establish qualitative links not only counting sequences but mapping special occurrences of information groups like codes. So, this pre-defined links can be retrieved not only very fast but also very effective via control structures in retrieval operations looking for specific information within the hierarchy.

* As mentioned above, SIR does not "speak" SQL, it "speaks "PQL" that means even SQL statements are translated into the SIR specific retrieval (and programming) language PQL (Procedural Query Language). A procedural programming language allows to perform operations within (nested) loops combined with control structures like "if-then-else". This means, the end user has to learn how to use a correct syntax (again as close to SPSS as possible), he must know the data base structure very well, but he has the opportunity to perform very complex retrievals. RDBMS like INGRES do explicitly not serve users with procedural access methods, because they are a contradiction to the rules. If necessary, they only allow a so-called "embedded SQL" access to a data base, which means that SQL statements have to be realized in an ordinary programming language like FORTRAN, COBOL or PASCAL which performs the loops and control sequences and contains embedded SQL statements. This is a disadvantage insofar as the end user must have access to a compiler, he must know the syntax, and he does not have the opportunity - like in PQL - to incorporate all data base functions within his program. A PQL retrieval, then, consists of basic instructions which follow clearly the data base design, which is represented (in a case oriented design) by record-types nested in a hierarchical manner. If we take different types of cases (e.g. Members of Parliament and constituencies), the different hierarchies may be linked via pointers or pointer-record-types to establish a network of information. The syntax of a PQL-retrieval then is a simple looping through these record-types according to the structure of information and the needed data, accompanied by control structures very similar to SPSSx programming.

This syntax follows clearly the design of the database. It is not as easy-to-learn or easy-to-use as SQL, but within the typical situation of a research project, where a small staff is engaged in the design of the data base and after entering data is intended to perform analysis after retrieving the appropriate subset/aggregate of the data, the way of performing these retrievals is very closely connected to the aim of the analysis itself and cannot be completely transferred to a software engineer for creating applications (with a naturally limited "degree of freedom" regarding specific needs during the analysis process).

The creation of summary files for further statistical analysis using PQL offers a nearly unlimited flexibility retrieving data matrices of a case by variables format. The two major alternatives are an aggregation of hierarchical information or the organization of information on the level of events as e.g. a sequence of memberships in parliaments. Furthermore, for the analysis of transitions in the course of careers, a quasi time-series can be produced starting e.g. at the year of birth of the eldest member of parliament in a selected subset and ending with the demise of the youngest, collecting biographical information and displaying configurations of political or professional careers. The following example is a simple visualization of such a summary file using the SIR/graph package. It shows a time series of a 5 % sample of the members of the Frankfurt National Assembly 1848, where the virtual cases are the years beginning at 1795 and ending at 1900 to cover the complete span of the youngest and eldest M.P. The graph displays the membership in associations as one example for creating these kinds of result files for further statistical analysis of life cycles.

V. The Structure of the German Parliamentarian Database

The data base "Members of German National Parliaments 1848-1933" has been designed to perform these kinds of retrievals very easily. A second basic idea of the design was to facilitate the integration with comparable data bases in other European countries for cross-cultural research. It follows a three stage model:

* a hierarchical structure with M.P.'s as cases complemented by central biographical information like denomination, place of birth, etc. and subordinated sequences containing e.g. the professional career, membership in associations etc. with timing information
* a network structure with constituencies as cases directly linkable to persons
* a relational structure containing all non-coded information (e.g. all exact denotations of professions or associations).

The first two stages comprise only coded information or pointers to the relations. Later on, these relations can be joined freely to information elements of other data bases to define a link to persons then being collected in a retrieval.
As described above, the entire information is stored in record types connected to two different case types:

* Members of Parliament:
* record types comprising data about general biographical information like e.g. date and place of birth, denomination etc., specific record types on family titles, office titles, academic titles, subjects of studies, information about the mandates in state parliaments and national parliaments, political position, memberships in associations and societies, political protest and persecution, the professional career and roll call data.
* constituencies:
* record types comprising descriptions about constituencies, ecological data, and information on voters and votes for all ballots.

The design allows for hierarchical access e.g. combining the professional career with the political career of a person as well as network access, e.g. combining the votes cast for M.P.'s with his personal voting in the chamber. A relational access is intended to incorporate in the data base via specific information tables, e.g. for associations to serve the user with political and historical background information about a society as a value add-on to the facts about membership stored in one of the record types.

Figure:

THE DESIGN OF LIFE-HISTORY DATA

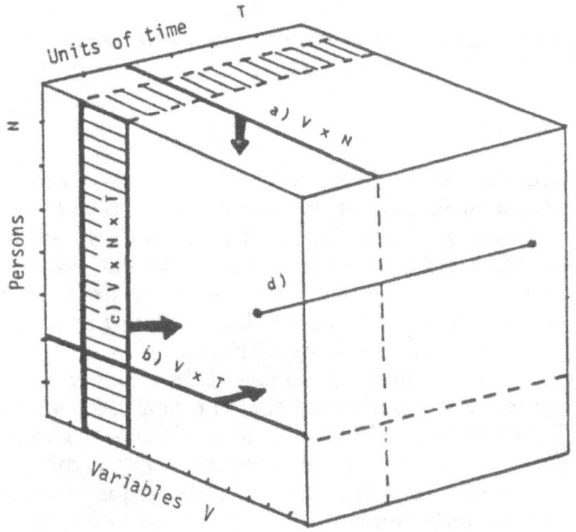

Source: Andreß (1985), p.13

REFERENCES

BEST, Heinrich. 1990. *Die Männer von Bildung und Besitz. Struktur und Handeln parlamentarischer Führungsgruppen in Deutschland und Frankreich 1948/49*. Bd. 90 der Schriften zur Geschichte des Parlamentarismus und der politischen Parteien. Düsseldorf

BEST, Heinrich. 1982. "Recruitment, Careers and Legislative Behaviour of German Parliamentarians 1848-1953." *Historical Social Research* 23, 20-54

BEST, Heinrich. 1985. "Biography and Political Behaviour: Determinants of Parliamentary Decision Making in Mid-Nineteenth Century Germany, France and Great Britain." *Historical Social Research* 33, 75-91

BEST, Heinrich. 1985. "Reconstructing Political Biographies of the Past: Configurations, Sequences, Timing, and the Impact of Historical Change", in: Millet, Hélène (ed.). *Informatique et Prosopographie*. Paris, 247-260

BEST, Heinrich. 1988. "A Comparative Analytical Data-Base for Research in Historical Parliamentary Leadership Groups", in: Genet, Jean-Philippe (ed.). *Standardisation et échange des bases de données historiques*. Paris, 255-263

BEST, Heinrich. 1989. "Computing the Unmeasurable: Estimating Missing Values in Legislative Roll-Call Analyses", in: Denley, Peter et al. (eds.). *History and Computing*. vol. 2, London, 104-116

PARTHIER, Ulrich. 1989. *INGRES: Datenbankmanagement der Zukunft*. Würzburg: Vogel. Chip Special.

TÜRK, Claudia. 1988. *SIR/LIGHT. Einführung in das relationale Datenbankmanagementsystem SIR/DBMS*. Hollen: IQBAL Verlag

THE MANY FACES OF A NATION IN ARMS: A DATA BASE ON BRITISH SOLDIERS OF THE FIRST WORLD WAR

Doron Lamm
University of London, Parkbedz College
United Kingdom

The British Empire entered the First World War with no system of conscription. The peacetime army was a small force of professional soldiers who volunteered for service mainly out of economic necessity. Recruitment to the pre-war army was adversely correlated with the demand for labour in economy. All this changed dramatically in the first months of the war. During September 1914, for example, a year's vintage of peacetime recruitment poured upon the helpless recruiting officers in a single day. 1.2 million new recruits joined the army by Christmas 1914, and the number rose to 6 million by the eve of the armistice in autumn 1918. There can be no doubt that this quantitative change was also a qualitative one. The small professional army of Victorian and Edwardian Britain turned - indeed overnight - into a Nation in Arms. In terms of the pre-war economy, six million men constituted almost a half of the occupied male labour force. These soldiers came from all walks of life, they represented all the sectors of the economy and all social strata.

On enlistment each of the candidates for recruiting had to submit certain particulars regarding his civilian life. For example, the attestation form of John William T. reveals that he was born in Aston, Birmingham. He was 21 years old when he joined the army on August 1914, i.e. he was born in 1893. Prior to his enlistment John W.T. was a carter living in Birmingham outside his father's household for at least three years. He was never an apprentice, nor was he married. The civil authorities had not imprisoned him and he did not have any previous military experience. From his signature we can judge that he was not illiterate, at least not in the sense that he could not sign his name. His Attestation Form also states his religious affiliation, the address of his next of kin and had he been married it would have also provided the place and date of marriage and dates of birth of children. On enlistment, John W.T. was also medically examined, his vision, teeth and physical development were assessed and his height and weight were recorded. By the end of the war a soldier's file also contained several other forms, most of which were concerned with his medical and military history. A detailed description of the available data is included in Lamm (1988). This unprecedented accumulation of official data on six million individuals is a major historical source on both, the wartime army and British society in the decades previous to the First World War.

It is worth while considering these documents also in a more general perspective. They all belong to a wider class of state documents known to the archivist as "Particular Instance Papers". These are usual official forms:

"the subject matter of which is the same though each relating to a different person"

and

> "while each individual document may be of little importance by itself, taken together these papers enable certain broad conclusions as to historical, economic and social trends to be drawn." (Great Britain, P.P. 1954)

For historians, such sources mean that individuals, who were for traditional historical scholarship undistinguishable members of a crowd, become now a viable subject for investigation. Incidently, as the age of paper-keeping by governments is drawing to its close due to technological change, more of them will be released and left to historians of modern societies for analysis.

However, Particular Instance Papers have also some notable disadvantages. The most obvious is their frightening volume. Therefore, they must be sampled. Sampling introduces the problem of representativeness, but even more so does the incidence of missing data. Out of the expected six million files of wartime soldiers only between two and three millions remained at our disposal. The process of selection was neither systematic nor documented. Most of the missing files were burnt during the blitz on London of the Second World War. An omission of such magnitude calls for a careful evaluation of the sample's representativeness. I shall do it by comparing sets of published official statistics with similar information extracted from the data base.

The best set of official statistics which was published by the British War Office on the wartime army, is a time series of the number of men who joined the army on each month of the war. This is a particularly important variable. The date of recruitment has been argued to be correlated with several other factors, ranging from degree of patriotism via social class and industrial affiliation to age, fitness and marital status (Dewey 1984). I extracted a similar time series of the monthly increase in recruitment and plotted the two cumulative curves in Figure 1.

Figure 1: Monthly Rates of Wartime Recruitment - Aug. 1914 to Nov. 1918 (Army Vs Sample)

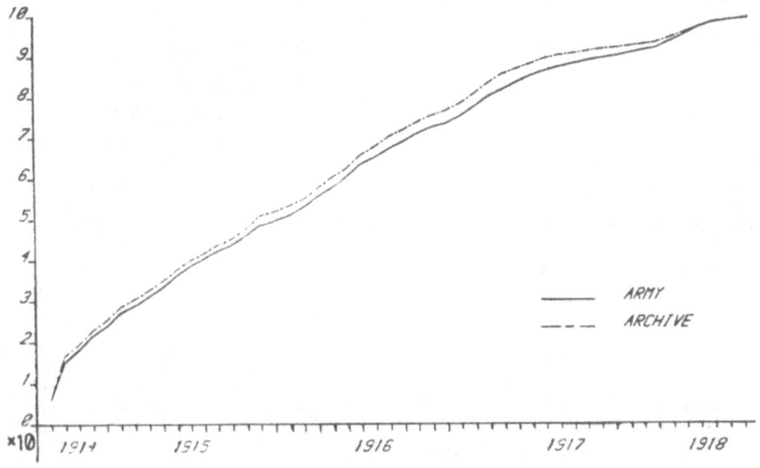

Both curves start in August 1914 and reach 100% at the armistice of November 1918. The goodness of fit between the two curves is quite clear. Indeed, in only five out of 52 months the curves actually move in an opposite direction. The small gap which opens already in September 1914 reached a cumulative maximum of only four percent in April 1917. That may suggest a slight over representation of pre-April 1917 recruits in the data base, particularly of the "great rush" of 1914. However, this variance is small in size and consequence.

The army never published a detailed geographical distribution of men in uniform so that the data base is the first to give the full spatial dimension of war-time recruiting. For comparative data I had to turn to the geographical distribution of the 1911 census of Great Britain. This cannot, of course, offer an ideal comparison. One cannot expect the soldiering males of 1914-1918 to have the same geographical distributionas of the whole of the British population some three to seven years earlier. But it would nevertheless provide us with a looser indicator for the geographical representation of the data.

Table 1: Spatial Spread of Civilians and Soldiers in Wage Regions

Wage Region	*Civilians (%)*	*Soldiers (%)*
London & Home Countries	21.80	23.12
The Southwest	6.67	5.20
The Rural Southeast	10.54	10.61
South Wales	4.32	3.32
Rural Wales & Hereford	1.88	1.19
Midlands	12.05	12.54
East & North Riding, Rutland, Lincolnshire	3.52	3.66
West Riding, Cheshire, Lancashire	21.68	25.28
Cumberland, Westmorland	0.81	0.85
Durham, Northumberland	5.06	4.85
South Scotland	0.64	0.65
Central Scotland	7.99	6.83
Northern Scotland	3.02	1.90
TOTAL	100.00	100.00

BRITAIN: WAGE REGIONS

The sample covers 83 out of 89 counties in Great Britain, which represent 99.65% of the 1911 population. None of the six counties which constitute the missing third of a percent, represents more than 0.1 of a percent of the population. Had the data base contained documents from an unrepresentative selection of regiments or record offices, such a widespread representation could not have been possible. When grouped into 13 wage regions, according to Hunt (1973), the geographical distribution of the data appears to be not only general but also proportional (see Table 1). Spearman's coefficient of rank correlation is a possible measure for this General agreement between the series. It takes the values between -1 for total disagreement and +1 where ranking is identical. In our case the coefficient is r=0.9890.

We can now leave the level of overall distributions and go one level deeper to focus on the database's ability to portray a sub-group, which in this case are the soldiers who got killed in action or died during the war. The army assessed the share of its casualties as ranging between 9.7% and 12.2% of the total establishment (Great Britain, P.P. 1921, pp. 62-72; P.P. 1922, pp. 28-29). The share of casualties in the database is 10.3%. Table 2 provides a breakdown of the dates of death into six periods. The two sets are almost identical, with a p value of 29.94 in a goodness off it test. Table 3 enables us to assess the accuracy of the age structure of the fatalities in the data base. Here, the figures for comparison are an adaptation of the Prudential Assurance Company's life tables for its British male clients, prepared with great effort and ingenuity by Dr. J. Winter (1986 p. 81). In effect, it is a comparison of two large surveys. Their similarity is, again, clear. The goodness of fit test for these two distributions resulted in a p value of 4.98. Further comparisons which confirm the data's representativeness and their ability to accurately portray sub-groups within the army are available in Lamm (1988).

Table 2: Yearly Rates of Wartime Casualties, August 1914 - September 1919

Died or Killed in Action

Between:	Sample	Army
4.08.1914 - 31.9.1914	1.0	1.0
1.10.1914 - 31.9.1915	14.2	13.9
1.10.1915 - 31.9.1916	22.6	21.8
1.10.1916 - 31.9.1917	25.2	28.4
1.10.1917 - 31.9.1918	27.6	27.6
1.10.1918 - 31.9.1919	9.4	7.3
total	100.0	100.0

No. of observations: 627

Table 3: Age Structure of Wartime Casualties

Age at Death	% of Sample's Casualties	% of Army's Casualties
16-19	8.91	11.76
20-24	35.61	37.15
25-29	25.28	22.31
30-34	16.85	15.17
35-39	10.32	9.18
40-44	2.23	3.07
45+	0.80	1.46
total	100.00	100.00

No. of observations: 629

The following are two examples of the data base's ability to be used for further research. Both refer to sub-groups. The first are, again, the fatalities. Although the "Lost Generation" of officers and men who died in the Great War was recently studied (Winter 1977, 1986), the major emphasis was put on the casualties of the social elite whose share in the total was unproportionately high. However, the overwhelming majority of the dead still came from the humbler background of the working classes and the lower middle class and due to lack of information, their characteristics remained unexplored.

It is customarily agreed that the earlier a soldier had joined, the higher were his chances of being killed due to longer exposure to risk. Table 4 confirms this assumption but for the interruption of the downward slope in 1916. However, exposure to risk was also influenced by physical fitness and the actual presence at the front during heavy fighting. 1916 had the highest record of men who served outside Great Britain and Ireland. It also had a lower rate of discharges from service on medical ground than any of the preceding years. 1915 experienced the waning of the voluntary spirit and a corresponding decline in the rate of enlistment. Many married men claimed to postpone their enlistment until a fairer system of recruitment, one that would exhaust the reservoir of young single men, would be implemented. By 1915, volunteers also learnt that army life was more secure and more bearable in the auxiliary forces, which enjoyed an increasing popularity. In contrast, 1916 saw both, the introduction of conscription and the killing grounds of the Somme. 42% of the 1916 conscripts were married - the highest rate since the start of the war. Unlike volunteers, conscripts had no control over their allocation within the army and the needs of the infantry proved to be paramount. Indeed, one in six men who died between June and October 1916 joined the army between January and April of the same year. This is a record achievement for death under such circumstances for the whole war.

Table 4: Variations in the Wartime Fatalities & Related Variables

Year of Recruitment	1914 (%)	1915 (%)	1916 (%)	1917 (%)	1918 (%)
Fatalities	12.6	9.7	11.5	7.0	1.9
Served Abroad	71.7	78.5	84.9	75.0	46.5
Medical Discharges	17.4	18.3	12.7	17.8	9.8
Married Soldiers	35.6	39.1	42.1	42.8	40.7

The fact that 1914 and 1916 proved deadlier years for healthy recruits is also reflected in the occupational distribution of mortality. Miners and Clerks suffered the highest rate of excess mortality. After manual labourers, miners had the fastest rate of recruitment during 1914. Almost 40% of all the miners who served were already soldiers by Christmas of that year. Clerks, who suffered the highest over-representation among the casualties did not hasten to enlist. Instead, they showed the highest increase during 1916. Another group which showed only a mild over-representation of casualties were manual labourers. A record of 45% of those who joined did so before the end of 1914. However, labourers enjoyed a high rate of rejection on medical grounds. Ill health might have wrecked their lives but during the war it kept some of them alive.

Turning to a different field of research interests, my other example concerns the Aliens - mainly Jewish immigrants from central and east Europe - who joined the British army. At the turn of the century, their living standards were the subject of a xenophobic debate on their impact on the degeneration of the British race. The data base enables us to depart from the terms of the contemporary debate and to compare the net nutritional status of these immigrants to that of other groups in the population. This is done by working out their average height which was substantially lower than that of the whole population, 64.70 and 66.11 inch respectively. It was then compared to the average height of another small religious group, the Baptists (66.50 inch), another national group, the Irish (66.06 inch) and to the average height of manual labourers (65.51 inch). In comparison to all three cases the Jews came out the shortest. No significant difference was detected between Jews who were born in the poverty of the East European "shtetls" (64.89 inch) and those who were born to the squalor of Britain's urban slums (64.91 inch). I then compared the height of the British Jews to information from another set of data on the Jews who were born in Ottoman Palestine and joined the British army in 1918. The average Palestinian Jew was found taller than either the British or the East European born jewish recruit (65.50 inch). These results are crude and should still be treated with caution, but they do systematically suggest the stake which aliens and first generation of British born had in the pre-war British society. They may also shed some light on the socio-economic background for the jewish demand for national self-determination which started at the turn of the century.

Despite a massive loss of documents, the data base on First World War soldiers proves a reliable historical source. It enables the user to examine data on the micro-level of the individual, to isolate variables hitherto unavailable for the study of the wartime army and to perform cross sectional analyses that were not possible with aggregate statistics.

REFERENCES

DEWEY, P.E. 1984. "Recruiting During the First World War." *The Historical Journal* 27, 2

Great Britain, Parliamentary Papers. 1921. Vol. 20. General Annual Report on the British Army 1914-1919 Cmd.1193

Great Britain, Parliamentary papers. 1922. Vol. 12. General Annual Report on the British Army 1918-1920 Cmd.1610

Great Britain, Parliamentary papers. 1954. Report of the (Grigg) Committee on Departmental Records Cmd.9163

HUNT, E.H. 1973. *Regional Wage Variations in Britain 1850-1914.*

LAMM, D. 1988. "British Soldiers of the First World War: Creation of a Representative sample." *Historical Social Research* 13, 4

WINTER, J. 1973. "Britain's 'Lost Generation' of the First World War." *Population Studies* 31, 3

WINTER, J. 1986. *The Great War and the British people.*

THE ESTABLISHMENT OF A UK HISTORICAL DATA ARCHIVE: PROBLEMS AND POSSIBILITIES

Kevin Schurer
Wolfson College, University of Cambridge
Cambridge Group for the History of Population and Social Structure
Marcia Freed Taylor
ESRC Data Archive, University of Essex
United Kingdom

BACKGROUND

The Association for History and Computing (AHC) was formed following the success of the conference of the same title, held at Westfield College, University of London, in April of 1986. The UK branch of the Association was constituted at a meeting held at the same venue a year later. Of its various commitments, the establishment of a UK archive to hold and disseminate historical data held in machine-readable form is a clear priority.

The ESRC Data Archive for the social sciences, located at the University of Essex has been in existence since 1969 and has since then developed a recognised expertise in the acquisition, handling, cataloguing, storage and dissemination of social science data. It now holds over 3000 data sets. Although the Archive holds some 40 to 50 data sets which might be classified as "historical", many of them major data sets, these are not separately catalogued or documented in a form that the special nature of historical data sources often require. The ESRC Data Archive has no specific policy of encouraging creators of historical machine-readable files to deposit their data. Because of its expertise in data handling and dissemination and its established reputation as a centre of information for social science researchers, the Essex Data Archive is nonetheless seen as the natural home of such an archive.

Following initial discussions between members of the Data Archive and the UK branch of the AHC, it was clear that, despite willingness on the part of the Data Archive, the special needs of an historical data archive could not be catered for within the current resources. It was agreed that the most suitable path to follow was to apply for additional funding in order to establish a separate archive for historical datasets, housed within the infrastructure of the Archive. Consequently, it was decided to apply to the ESRC for funds to carry out a feasibility study to evaluate the possibilities for forming such a history archive as well as the parameters of it.

PROPOSED FEASIBILITY STUDY

The project, if funding is found, will have five major aims:

* to undertake a survey of existing datafiles,
* to create a current awareness database in the area,
* to assess the service required of a history archive,

- to assess the relevance of the existing infrastructure of the Data Archive to the special needs of historical files and historians,
- to recommend future action.

Survey of Existing Stocks

The investigation of the current stock of historical data files in the United Kingdom, of those held and being created by researchers, would form the first stage of the feasibility study. The results would form the input into the current awareness database, an inventory of existing historical data sets and at the same time an indication of the potential holdings of the history archive. This database could be published separately as a 'state-of-the-art' report, or mounted on-line for searching by other researchers. This, in itself, would be a valuable outcome of the feasibility study.

It is proposed that this survey of current databases be carried out in close cooperation with a European-wide survey which will be mounted during the coming year. A project already underway in Holland (the subject of another paper in this session) will be joined by the Data Archive, the Zentrum für historischle Sozialforschung in Cologne, the Danish Data Archives and other researchers within the AHC network in surveying the historical research community throughout Western Europe. The resulting database could form an extremely valuable research resource in the future. Full UK participation will, of course, depend on the outcome of the funding application.

Investigation of Special Characteristics and Requirements

Historical datasets have special characteristics compared to the majority of contemporary social surveys. Their temporal and spatial characteristics, their often hierarchical non-rectangular structure will pose special problems. The project would therefore carry out a critical assessment of the ways in which historical data files differ from those already held by the Data Archive, covering the following aspects of preservation and dissemination:

1. *Acquisition and Publicity:*
   Acquisition procedures.
   Publicity and encouragement of secondary analysis.

2. *Processing and Preservation:*
   Data Processing requirements.
   Problems arising from the longitudinal (time series) character of much historical material.
   Problems arising from the spatially referenced aspect of many historical files.
   Particular problems of text files.
   Software requirements for processing.

3. *Documentation and Cataloguing:*
   Minimal documentation requirements.
   Standardisation of data collection and documentation methods.
   Standardised cataloguing and bibliographic referencing for historical files.

4. *Dissemination:*
   Methods of, and media for, dissemination required by historical researchers.
   Special dissemination-related procedures for historical files.

The specific problems posed by the documentation of historical data files have, over recent years, been the subject of much discussion. The need to implement standard methods for the description and documentation of machine-readable historical data files has been accepted, but as yet any wide-scale application of such techniques is still lacking. It is clear that much attention will need to be paid to this problem. Methods of cataloguing and integrating historical files within the existing cataloguing schemes of the European data archives are the subject of several other papers in this session. This too will form part of the work of the project team.

Beyond this, an investigation of the existing infrastructure of the Data Archive would be carried out, in an attempt to assess what alterations or additions would be needed to adequately deal with historical data. Hardware and software requirements and special facilities for the computerisation of non-machine-readable materials would be among the areas to which attention would be paid.

Quite clearly, special facilities and services might well be demanded by historical researchers which would differ from those of other social science researchers. Special educational activities, sub-setting procedures, re-formatting programs, documentation procedures might be among these. Their implications for the potential history archive would be investigated.

Although it is obvious that the acquisition, storage, documentation and cataloguing of data files is of central importance to the establishment of a potential historical data archive, such activities form only part of the role of the archive. An important part of the feasibility study will also be to evaluate the potential use of the archive to the academic community. In this respect, broader questions must also be asked concerning the secondary use of deposited datasets. To what extent can a data archive exist for the straight-forward deposit of historical material only? What will be the demand for such material by secondary users, and to what extent will the data meet researchers' requirements? Much of this is hypothetical since secondary use will ultimately depend on the nature of as yet undeposited material and the posing of as yet unframed research questions. Yet to a certain extent the utilisation of deposited machine-readable files will be reflected in the potential of such data to test conceptual problems posed by researchers other than the original principal investigator. In this respect it is seen that it is important not only to encourage researchers to deposit datasets, but also to stress the need for researchers to construct datasets in such a way that they maximise the potential for research. Again, it is clear that this is an area for decisive international co-operation and one which would certainly be an integral part of the remit of any historical archive established at the Data Archive.

DATA BASES IN SOCIAL SCIENCES INTEGRATION, NEEDS OF TODAY AND RESULTING CONCEPTS FOR THE FUTURE

Donald Bender, Walter Bien
Deutsches Jugendinstitut e.V., München
FRG

Today, the development of hardware and software tools is on a highly sophisticated level. Tools and technics of data handling are not perfect yet. Nevertheless, we believe the focus of development should change from specific instruments in data handling to concepts and tools of integration.

Using data bases in social sciences is normally related to the following user requests
* to know what data can be used
* to get the specific data the user is interested in
* to analyze these data with user specific instruments.

It is an illusion to believe that the solution for such needs can generally be found in one system. Data can be found on different sources (different media, different hardware components, differently written software components), retrieval as well as analysis can be done by different instruments. A user working on a specific problem is bound to a specific data set, most times on a specific computer configuration and often to a specific analysis algorithm. So, normally a user of a database has only few possibilities to decide what kind of hardware he could use. Often, the reach of software is also restricted. Therefore, a user needs a lot of help to match the data to the different elements of the analysis process. Maybe a solution could be an information system with a lot more features than a traditional database.

Such an information system should, therefore, consist at first of a defined set of interfaces or links:
* interfaces between different media such as paper, discs, tapes... (Input and Output)
* interfaces between different computer systems such as IBM, DEC, CDC, IBM - PC, ATARI...
* interfaces between different networks (Ethernet, V. 24, Tokenring,...)
* interfaces between different
  - computer operating systems (DOS, OS, VMS, UNIX)
  - data bank concepts (hierarchical, relational, network)
  - data bank languages (SQL, NATURAL)
  - data bank systems (ORACLE, INGRES, SIR, EDBMS)
* interfaces between different languages
  - computer languages (ALGOL, FORTRAN, LISP, PROLOG)
  - retrieval languages (GRIPS)
  - foreign languages (German, English, French)
  - theme or research specific languages (scientific, legal, administrative language)

* interfaces between different analysis systems (SAS, SPSS, BMDP, MAP, STATGRAF)
* interfaces between different data kinds
  - numerical data
  - alphanumerical data
  - documents
  - abstracts
  - pictures
  - tables

To get the topic of this paper, the aim of such an information system is not to speed up some retrieval procedures in the range of seconds, it is to speed up the transfer of data to the analysis instruments from months to weeks. Of course, in an information system there are not only links, there also some data. But data and interfaces are not enough to form an information system.

Marvellous data are data you will find, data you could not find are bad data. These data are marvellous or bad independent of their other qualities. So, a comfortable retrieval is a major need in an information system, but still not enough.

The description of the data should also be excellent, otherwise a user has no chance to find the information he is looking for. Often, the amount of information in describing a piece of data will be much more excessive than the amount of information themselves. Normally, this documentation of data exists in a handbook of the database, or worse, in a human expert. But in our opinion retrieval should also be possible in the description or documentation set. So, an information system should have a special database for this purpose. This lexicon should also describe all other components of the information system.

The DEUTSCHES JUGENDINSTITUT tries to build up a system guided by such ideas. Part of our paper will be a description of the planning and realization of our real system.

The information system is based on

* a *shell* of menus,
* a set of *tools* and
* several *SQL - databases.*

Databases are concerned with:

* lexicon (describing the following databases by documenting their tables and columns; documentations of tools constituting the information system)
* literature (youth, family, social support)
* statistics (population, family, youth, health)
  - Federal Republic of Germany (BRD)
  - states (Länder)
  - counties (Kreise)
* survey data

with links to foreign institutes and their databases such as

* DIMDI
* Central Archive for Empirical Social Research
* departments of statistics

and interfaces to analysis systems (e.g. SAS, SPSS, MAP,STATGRAF) realized on Hosts (μ-Vax) and PCs.

Figure 1 "DJI - Informationsystem" shows the logical structure of the system. The center is constituted by data organized in databases. The first shell is given by analysis instruments and interfaces. The second shell is the description of the whole information system, located in the lexicon. The last shell is the user interface which is realized as a system of menus. All shells are integrated in the ORACLE tools SQL-PLUS, SQL-FORMS and SQL-MENU.

The comfort of Software interfaces can be on different levels, beginning with data exchange with ASCII-files. These files contain only the raw data, without any information of the organization of this data in the source system, e.g. WRITE RECORDS in SIR. The next level contains interfaces that produce ASCII-files including information about the organization in the destination system. On the highest level, the interfaces produce destination system files with adequate organization informations and retrieval tools for the data, e.g. SASORACLE, SPSSORACLE.

Figure: DJI Information System

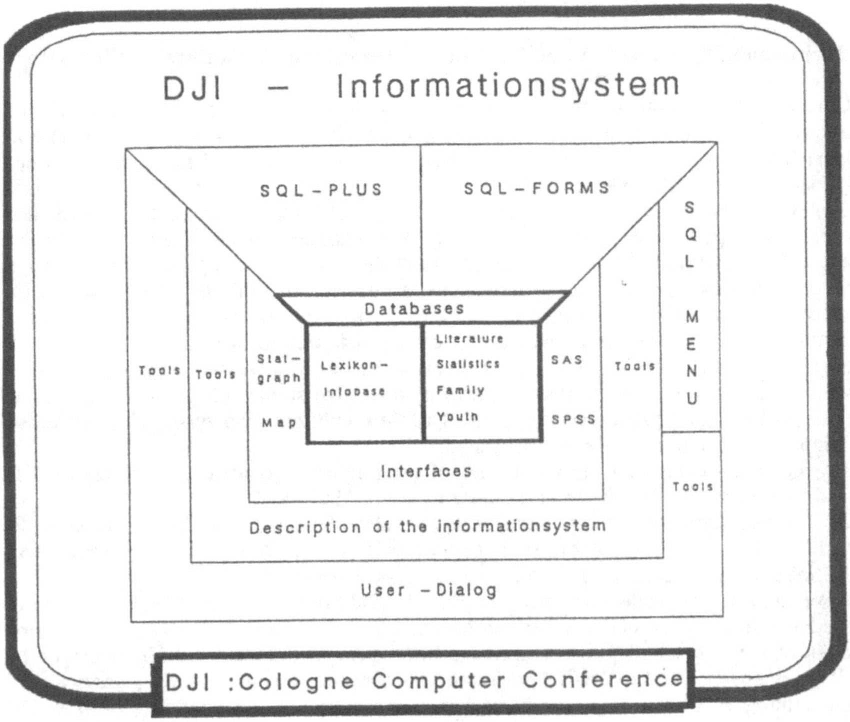

WORLD CULTURES: AN ELECTRONIC JOURNAL AND COMPARATIVE DATABASE

Sabine Schmidt, Thomas Schweizer(1)
University of Tübingen
FRG

This paper reviews current trends of comparative research in Cultural Anthropology, concentrating on the development of electronic databases and new lines of research. These current developments are tied to the increasing use of personal computers within the anthropological community and the growing emphasis on quantitative analysis. The databases being developed in Cultural Anthropology offer a wealth of information covering different aspects of community life and should thus be of interest for the wider social science community.

Background: Quantitative and Qualitative Approaches in Cultural Anthropology

Comparison of human cultures in space and time lies at the heart of the anthropological endeavour. Statistical comparative approaches reach back in time at least 100 years when Edward B. Tylor presented his cross-cultural study on avoidance between in-laws in 1889 [1966: 2]: "... the barbaric etiquette between husbands and their wives' relatives, and vice versa: They may not look at one another, much less speak, and they even avoid mentioning one another's names." Since the 1930s clustering techniques, factor analysis and multidimensional scaling have been applied to cross-cultural and regional comparisons to assess the similarity of cultures in Q-mode analysis (Driver 1970, Jorgensen 1974). In addition, causal connections between cultural variables have been established by way of contingency tables (as of Tylor), correlation and regression models. Up to now, the quantitative and statistical tradition within anthropology has its stronghold in comparative studies of extant ethnographic data. Besides the qualitative comparison of few cultures, two types of quantitative comparative studies can be distinguished:

1. regional studies of a larger number of geographically contiguous cultures (as has been done for North America, cf. Jorgensen 1980) and
2. cross-cultural studies of world-wide samples. Scholars like G.P. Murdock, R. Naroll as well as J.W.M. Whiting and H.E. Driver have brought comparative secondary analysis to a bloom in American Cultural Anthropology.

Nevertheless, the collection and analysis of qualitative data by a wide variety of methods still lies at the heart of anthropological fieldwork. To capture the actors' point of view by eliciting native texts has been a major preoccupation in ethnography (Werner and Schoepfle 1987). Today, the gap between the comparative statistical and the ethnographic tradition has narrowed. To ensure an understanding of how the ethnographer arrives at a description of the "observed", the interviews, as a primary source, are usually tape-recorded, transcribed and at a later stage processed by text analytic procedures. It is here that microcomputers are increasingly used, already in the field, for the collection, retrieval and preliminary analysis of these text-data bases.

In addition, they have facilitated the more and more common collection of specialized quantitative data and multivariate analysis, both now a part of modern fieldwork (Chibnik 1985, Bernard 1988). The microcomputer revolution had its impact on comparative anthropological inquiries as well, since the rather small cross-cultural datasets are still manageable. Thus, there is a considerable amount of responsiveness towards the application of microcomputers within the anthropological community.(2) Before introducing WORLD CULTURES, we will briefly summarize the development of comparative databases in Cultural Anthropology, which form the basis to statistical comparative studies.

The Creation of Comparative Databases

A review of past developments shows that cross-cultural secondary analysis not only profited from methodological innovation, the establishment of new theoretical paradigms and institutional efforts to further this research tradition, but gained momentum, whenever new databases with better retrieval of ethnographic data became available. This was the case in the 1940s when G.P. Murdock and others founded the Human Relations Area Files in New Haven, Conn. Basically, an archive of raw data from ethnographic reports filed according to content criteria, the HRAF aided the coding of data for exemplary cross-cultural research (Murdock 1949, Whiting and Child 1953). In the 1960s and 1970s G.P. Murdock and D.R. White (1969) set up a worldwide "Standard Cross-cultural Sample" (SCCS) and launched a series of cumulative cross-cultural codings for this sample at the University of Pittsburgh. A wealth of data on variables of anthropological, social behaviourial science interest and an increasing number of cross-cultural studies was the outcome of this major effort (Barry and Schlegel 1980, Paige and Paige 1981). In the 1980s the most important database development in cross-cultural research is the establishment of WORLD CULTURES, an electronic journal and comparative database, founded by D.R. White (now at the University of California at Irvine) in 1985. WORLD CULTURES is published four times a year on diskettes in either the IBM PC or the MACINTOSH format. It caters for anthropological and social/behaviourial science users equipped with micros, making available the whole range of the SCCS codes as well as other cross-cultural and regional datasets. WOLRD CULTURES includes

1. retrieval and data management facilities (the MAPTAP program) and it provides
2. a forum for methodological and substantive discussion of comparative method.

Now we will give you a short introduction to the contents and options of WORLD CULTURES.

WORLD CULTURES: Contents and Options

The Database

Central to the WORLD CULTURES database is the SCCS as most of the data relate to this sample. The SCCS is "a representative sample of the world's known and well described cultures, 186 in number, each 'pinpointed' to the smallest identifiable subgroup of the society in question at a specific point in time" (Murdock and White 1969: 329). This smallest subgroup usually is the local community, defined for coding purposes as a set of persons occupying a common territory and being connected by face-to-face relations. The time focus is set to the date of the earliest reliable ethnographic description. The pinpointing is useful to lend precision to coding of ethnographic materials. The cultures have been selected to achieve a reasonable distribution in space and time on the background of Murdock's historical and regional classification of the world's known cultures into nested clusters of similar cases. From each cluster one well-documented unit has been selected for the SCCS. To achieve temporal variation in the sample, some cases from ancient history, but of lesser data quality, have been included, too. Mean observation time in the SCCS is 1860, the median 1910. In essence, the SCCS is well-suited to test hypotheses which claim universal validity as the cultures chosen exhibit considerable variability in substantive variables as well as in their space and time foci.

Up to volume 3#1 (1987) 1118 variables coded for the SCCS have been documented in WORLD CULTURES. These variables comprise basic as well as more specialized codes different domains of human cultures. The data relate to economy, social organization (division of labor, kinship, social differentiation & hierarchy), politics, law, gender roles, socialization, and religion. The codes from the Pittsburgh coding project (Barry and Schlegel 1980) as well as more recent data from actual cross-cultural studies are incorporated into the WORLD CULTURES database. The electronic medium enables easy access to the data, quick correction of coder errors, and, moreover, it is an open system that can be expanded. New codes will be added as they become available. Some variables have only been coded for a fraction of the SCCS due to missing or insufficient data, leading possibly to a cumulation in multivariate analysis, but usually indicators will be available. In sum, the SCCS database contained in WORLD CULTURES is the most comprehensive dataset accessible for mainly non-industrialized human cultures available to date. So far 4 volumes have been published, with one diskette (vol 3#2) providing a self-guided tutorial to the facilities of WORLD CULTURES. In addition to cultural anthropological data, single issues include data from the fields of physical anthropology and primatology. In addition to being a database, WORLD CULTURES includes a program for the retrieval of specific data allowing a first inspection of data and application of simple statistical procedures.

The discussion section of WORLD CULTURES is devoted to issues of central concern for comparative research. There are codebooks and an extended ethnographic bibliography of the SCCS cases. Papers introduce new codes and present data quality considerations of extant variables. New methodological and technical developments in the field of comparative studies are discussed regularly. Thus, a forthcoming issue in 1988 will review cross-cultural sampling. A news section informs on current comparative research as well as on new hard- and software. Sometimes, programs on a shareware basis are distributed to WORLD CULTURES subscribers.

The MAPTAB Program

This data management and retrieval program built into WORLD CULTURES is called MAPTAB. The acronym indicates the mapping and tabulating facilities of MAPTAB. The program is menu-driven. MAPTAB can be used to view and save data matrices, to select cases and/or variables. It lists the codebook for the variables chosen and enables recoding of variables. For data analysis MAPTAB creates univariate frequency tables and contingency tables also allowing for control variables. MAPTAB files can also be imported into full-fledged statistics programs. Thus, MAPTAB saves datasets ready to use by the SYSTAT program. The mapping option displays values for one variable at a time for all the cases selected on a crude world map. This facilitates inspection of local or regional clusters in the distribution of variables. The incidence of diffusion or similarity due to common origin was of much concern in the methodology of cross-cultural studies. In a comment to Tylor's 1889 paper the statistician F. Galton (1889 [1966: 23]) embarked on the inflation of "duplicate copies of the same original" in the tables due to diffusion or historical connection which could lead to erroneous conclusions on the validity of hypotheses. Cross-culturalists up to the present try to measure the effect of diffusion or regional linkages on universal causal relationships among variables (cf. Schweizer 1987: ch. 4,5, Dow, Burton, White and Reitz 1984).

Comparative research in cultural anthropology of today makes use of multivariate models and tries to cross-fertilize method with substance (Burton and White 1987). It lends empirical precision to general theory; it specifies spatial and historical boundaries on supposedly universal relationships (White and Pesner 1983), thus, deepening our insight into the inner working of human culture. The WORLD CULTURES electronic journal and database is an important technical breakthrough as it facilitates easy access to and use of cross-cultural data.

NOTES

1. Sabine Schmidt is research associate, Thomas Schweizer Professor of Cultural Anthropology at the Völkerkundliches Institut, University of Tübingen, Schloß, D-7400 Tübingen, FRG.

2. The main split in the discipline is between explanatory and interpretive approaches. This distinction cross-cuts thematic content (e.g. materialist vs. mentalist research strategies) and it is not congruent to quantitative vs. qualitative analysis. The explanatory paradigms stress the quality of data collection, the control of ethnographic insights and the need to transcend mere description, whereas the interpretive paradigms are less inclined to these points. Cognitive anthropology in contrast to symbolic anthropology is for example a methodologically controlled explanatory paradigm employing a mentalist and qualitative research program. The recent trend to computer applications and statistics can be observed in the "American Anthropologist" as the leading journal of the explanatory paradigms. In 1988/89 a new "Journal of Quantitative Anthropology" has been founded. There are several newsletters on computer applications in anthropology. Subfields and specializations like demography, economic anthropology, network analysis and cognitive anthropology are particularly prone to these new trends (cf. Mitchell 1980, Chibnik 1985).

REFERENCES

BARRY, Herbert III; SCHLEGEL, Alice (eds.). 1980. *Cross-Cultural Samples and Codes*. Pittsburgh: Pittsburgh Univesity Press

BERNARD, H. Russell. 1988. *Research Methods in Cultural Anthropology*. Newbury Park: Sage

BURTON, Michael L. and WHITE, Douglas R. 1987. "Cross-Cultural Surveys Today." *Annual Review in Anthropology* 16, 135-157

DOW, Malcolm M.; Burton, Michael L.; WHITE, Douglas R. and REITZ, Karl P. 1984. "Galton's Problem at Network Autocorrelation." *American Ethnologist* 11, 754-770

DRIVER, Harold E. 1970. "Statistical Studies of Continuous Geographical Distributions", in: Naroll, Raoul and Cohen, Ronald. (eds.). *A Handbook of Method in Cultural Anthropology*. New York: Columbia University Press, 620-639

JORGENSEN, Joseph G. (ed.). 1974. *Comparative Studies by Harold E. Driver and Essays in his Honor*. New Haven: Human Relations Area Files Press

JORGENSEN, Joseph G. 1980. *Western Indians. Comparative Environments, Languages and Cultures of 172 Western American Indian Tribes*. San Francisco: W.H. Freeman

MITCHELL, J. Clyde (ed). 1980. *Numerical Techniques in Social Anthropology*. Philadelphia: Institute of the Study of Human Issues (ISHI)

MURDOCK, George Peter. 1949. *Social Structure*. New York: The Free Press

MURDOCK, George Peter and WHITE, Douglas R. 1969. "Standard Cross-Cultural Sample." *Ethnology* 8, 329-369

PAIGE, Karen Eriksen and PAIGE, Jeffery M. 1981. *The Politics of Reproductive Ritual*. Berkeley: University of California Press

SCHWEIZER, Thomas. 1987. *Methodological Problems of Cross-Cultural Comparison*. New Haven, Conn.: Human Relations Area Files Press

TYLOR, Edward B. 1966 [1889]. "On a Method of Investigating the Development of Institutions; Applied to Laws of Marriage and Descent", in: Moore, Frank W. (ed.). *Readings in Cross-Cultural Methodology*. New Haven: Human Relations Area Files Press, 1-22 [orig. *Journal of the Royal Anthropological Institute of Great Britain and Ireland* 18, 245-272]

WERNER, Oswald and SCHOEPFLE, G. Mark. 1987. *Systematic Fieldwork*. 2 volumes. Beverly Hills: Sage

WHITE, Douglas R. and PESNER, Robert. 1983. "Internal Replication, the System Concept, and Sources of Validity in Nonexperimental Research." *Behaviour Science Research* 18, 26-44

WHITING, John, W.M. and CHILD, Irvin L. 1953. *Child Training and Personality: A Cross-Cultural Study*. New Haven: Yale University Press

THE DATA BASE OF THE GERMAN "GENERAL SOCIAL SURVEY" (ALLBUS)

Michael Terwey
Zentralarchiv für Empirische Sozialforschung, Cologne
FRG

I. General Description of the ALLBUS-Survey

For a long time, the development of social sciences had been stalled by the lack of a regular basic data generation program. Official programs such as the census are often too limited in their scope to qualify for detailed sociological research. Other social surveys have often been shaped due to special research interests and have not been repeated regularly. Moreover, only a limited public might have access to these specialized social surveys. Sometimes, the data sets are interpreted exclusively by those researchers who initiated the research program. In other cases these data sets do become available to a broader public, but only after some primary evaluations through the initiators of the project.

To resolve this somewhat unsatisfactory situation the *"General Social Survey"* was established in 1972 as a national data program for the social sciences in the USA. Until 1987, this General Social Survey has been conducted fourteen times and it is a proven major data basis for the social sciences and the humanities in general. In the middle of the seventies, the idea of a nationwide general survey for social scientists was also taken up in Western Germany by *ZUMA* (Zentrum für *U*mfragen *M*ethoden und *A*nalysen, Mannheim) and by the *ZA* (*Zentralarchiv für empirische Sozialforschung*, Cologne) in close cooperation with some sociologists as principal investigators.(1) Thus, in 1980 the first *ALLBUS* (*All*gemeine *B*evölkerungs*u*mfrage der *S*ozialwissenschaften) was established as a German standard data generation program for social sciences. Since then, it has been running at intervals of two years, receiving ample acceptance in social science circles. Today ALLBUS-surveys are by far the most requested ones among the data sets distributed by the Central Archive for Empirical Social Research. We may conclude that ALLBUS fulfills its function as a general social survey for the scientific community in Germany.

Each ALLBUS consists of an independently drawn sample of about 3000 German respondents in the FRG and West Berlin, 18 years of age or over. The single surveys consist of about 400 - 500 variables. General descriptions of the studies, the various items and data are documented by four machine-readable codebooks obtainable at the Central Archive. These codebooks were generated in the Central Archive by using OSIRIS supplemented by some additional support-programs.

As far as the content of the surveys is concerned, a detailed *standard demography* is regularly repeated as part of the questionnaire containing diverse basic information about the respondents and their living conditions (e.g. respondent's age, sex, schooling, income, prestige, household). This is the fundamental instrument for the description of social structure and its changes.

Additional item groups of the studies tackle varying topics (e.g. cultural competence, social support networks, job situation, political and religious attitudes). Some emphasis is, of course, put on the approach to actual social problems (e.g. the role of the welfare state, environmental deterioration, aids), on the other hand, the replication of questions for the purpose of comparisons over periods of time and between different countries is stressed.

Parts of ALLBUS 1986 were integrated into the *International Social Survey Program* (ISSP), which is another important data program designed to compare countries with each other.(2) The main topic of the 1986 ISSP-part was the description of social networks. Future topics of ISSP-questionnaires coordinated with ALLBUS will be:

1988: Family and changing sex roles.

1990: Role of government (replication of the ISSP-study in 1985).

1992: Social Inequality (replication of the ISSP-study in 1987).

1994: Work orientations (replication of the ISSP-study in 1989).

II. Outline of the Cumulated ALLBUS-Surveys as an Easily Accessible Data Base

The cumulation of all individual ALLBUS-studies to a common data base is a big help in sociological research. This common base consists of data sets and a combined documentation of questionnaires. The cumulated file is presently composed of our four studies and currently includes 12045 respondents. This increase in the number of cases facilitates detailed investigation of minor subgroups as well as time trend studies.

A total of about 1000 distinct variables could be taken from the four ALLBUS-data sets.(3) Dealing with 1000 different variables and 12045 cases, which originated from four different studies, causes of course some technical problems. Furthermore, organization of the data should be such as to allow for further integration of future ALLBUS-surveys. Our present main criterion for the organisation of data is *easy accessibility* and *nearness to widespread statistical evaluation programs* as SPSS, OSIRIS, SAS or BMDP.

SPSS is the standard program package which is integrated into the data service of studies recently documented and distributed by the Central Archive. It is also the most often used evaluation possibility among our clients. Fortunately, the new versions of SPSS running as SPSS^x have taken on some special data management features.(4) Therefore, we have organized the cumulated ALLBUS-data in a SPSS^x-system file. This file is generated using the option of compression, which maximizes the number of variables stored in each computer word. Thus, the storage requirement is reduced for variables with small integer values and an optimal blocksize is automatically achieved. In a compressed system file the complete data of four cumulated surveys and integrated dictionary description require 14.4 megabyte storage.(5) This is even less than the size of the cumulated raw data set (18.8 megabyte), notwithstanding the descriptive dictionary information, which takes about .4 megabyte. Moreover, in a system file combined data and dictionary information are stored in binary format, which reduces the time required for reading and interpreting the data. Working with raw data, which are normally written in character format, would also increase processing time considerably.

Since the cumulated ALLBUS-file is now centrally stored and already available to all users at the Central Archive it is possible to have easy reading access. No other *retrieval procedure* is required for that purpose except some simple cards of SPSS^x. In addition, *immediate* entry into rather sophisticated statistical procedures is possible - unlike to some other data base management systems.

One could, of course, achieve this straightforward access to the data by simply *using the whole system file* and doing the special computations which are intended for analyses (e.g. frequencies, crosstabs, loglinear models). Although, on first sight this is the easiest way, it is certainly not the most efficient way as far as processing time and storage requirement for temporary scratch files are concerned. By including simple SELECT, DROP or KEEP statements into the SPSS-commands users can save much processing time. The first step in this direction would be to extract temporarily only those very variables which are required for a special analysis while basically still relying on the whole system file. A simple KEEP command is all that is required to achieve this. But if the user can anticipate that he will be repeatedly needing a special set of variables for various statistical evaluations, he may easily generate a small system file of his own including only this part of the whole data set. Table 1 (see page 195) illustrates what could happen if an assumed researcher having a research question requiring 50 variables neglects or uses some of these possibilities of saving processing time and storage requirements.

Although the above example of a data subset in Table 1 containing 50 variables is rather large for a special research problem, the various facilities of saving computer capacity perform quite well. The complete system file having already been stored on a central disk, a job specifying no file restriction at all (Filetype 1) requires no additional permanent space on the researcher's disk except for the output listing. What may be needed is only a larger amount of disk space for temporary scratch files. Without any data retrievals or exports it is immediately possible to get statistical results ranging from rather simple frequencies or crosstabs to rather complicated loglinear models. Differential cpu-times required under these conditions are shown in the first column of Table 1). But we might say, however, that our hypothetical researcher has been a bit lazy using no file restrictions at all for his computations and hence, he is unnecessarily prolonging his computer jobs.

In the second column of Table 1 a simple restriction is included as only 50 variables are temporarily kept for processing and evaluation. Besides the reduction of required disk space for temporary scratch files, we are already confronted with a notable reduction of computation time. For frequencies of all 50 variables (first row in column two) this abbreviation already is 59 seconds. Taking together both loglinear models done in one run (Job IIIa and Job IIIb) the abbreviation amounts to 299 seconds, meaning that the tasks can be performed five times faster after including a temporary selection of data to be used.

Although this is already progress to some extent, it is possible to save even more computer time if the data are to be evaluated repeatedly as, for instance, shown in our example. This requires some disk space on the side of the researcher for saving a smaller system file of his own. For our 50 variables this would amount to 1.14 megabyte if all ALLBUS-surveys are required for analyses. If only one ALLBUS (e.g. ALLBUS 1986) is needed this could be reduced to .3 megabyte. Generating these smaller system files would take 51 seconds or 45 seconds respectively and is easily executed by simple statements. Columns 3 and 4 again illustrate considerable further reductions of required computer time. These would be 100 seconds for frequencies (first row, comparing columns 1 and 3 of Table 1). For two loglinear models 336 seconds could be saved. This means that the task is performed in less than 1/18 of the time needed in the simplest type of file-specification.(6)

Table 1: Cumulated ALLBUS 1980-86: Cpu-Seconds Required on an IBM 4361 for Three Exemplary SPSS^x - Jobs Using Varying Types of Files and Data Selection

	Types of File Specification			
	Type I	Type II	Type III	Type IV
Job I	139 sec	80 sec	39 sec	15 sec
Job II	113 sec	46 sec	7 sec	2 sec
Job IIIa	252 sec	50 sec	13 sec	4 sec
Job IIIb	103 sec	6 sec	6 sec	3 sec

List of different file types and data selections involved:

Type I: Complete compressed systemfile ALLBUS 1980-86
(14795 blks, 12045 cases, 1015 variables)
used without any prior selection of variables for each run

Type II: Complete compressed systemfile ALLBUS 1980-86
(14795 blks, 12045 cases, 1015 variables)
used with temporary prior selection of 50 variables for each run

Type III: Compressed systemfile ALLBUS 1980-86
(1139 blks, 12045 cases, 50 variables)
time used for creating this file out of Type I: 52 seconds

Type IV: Compressed systemfile ALLBUS 1986
(309 blks, 3095 cases, 50 variables)
time used for creating this file out of Type I: 45 seconds

SPSS^x-Jobs specified for running different files:

Job I: Frequencies V1 to V50 including all statistics

Job II: Crosstabs V5 by V10 including all statistics

Job IIIa: Loglinear model (fitting model for 4 dichotomous variables)

Job IIIb: Second loglinear model, directly following the first in Job IIIa (fitting model for 4 dichotomous variables)

III. Concrete Examples of ALLBUS-Data

After discussing formal possibilities of saving computer time and disk space in a hypothetical research situation we will now present two short concrete examples of data in the cumulated file.

Chart 1: Duration of Past Unemployment Periode in the Last Ten Years

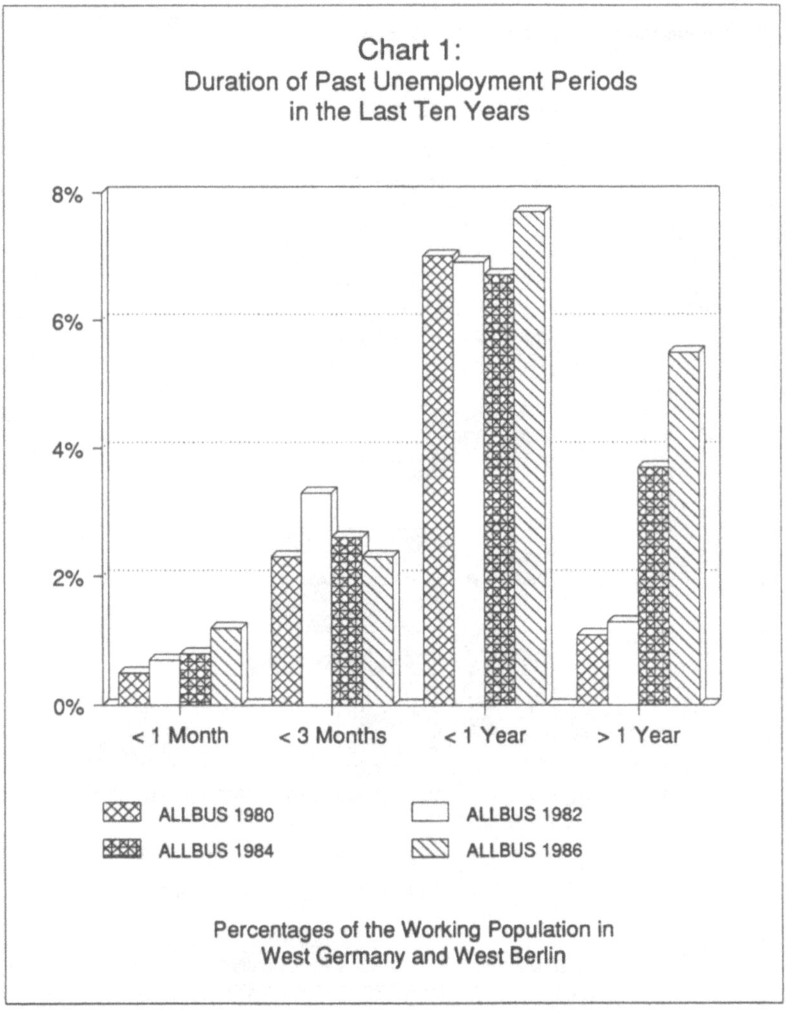

Chart 1 contains information about the duration of past unemployment for members of the German working population.(8) The results show a slight increase in the small percentages of persons who experienced short time unemployment (less than 1 month). On the other hand, a remarkable change occurs in the larger group of persons who were more than 1 year out of work. Long-term unemployment is a major social problem in Western Germany today. Of course, we do not need the ALLBUS-data in first place to point out this problem, since it can also be seen in official statistics; but we can now do detailed analyses concerning the differential background and attitudes of persons who have more or less experienced unemployment.

Chart 2: Frequencies of Church Attendance

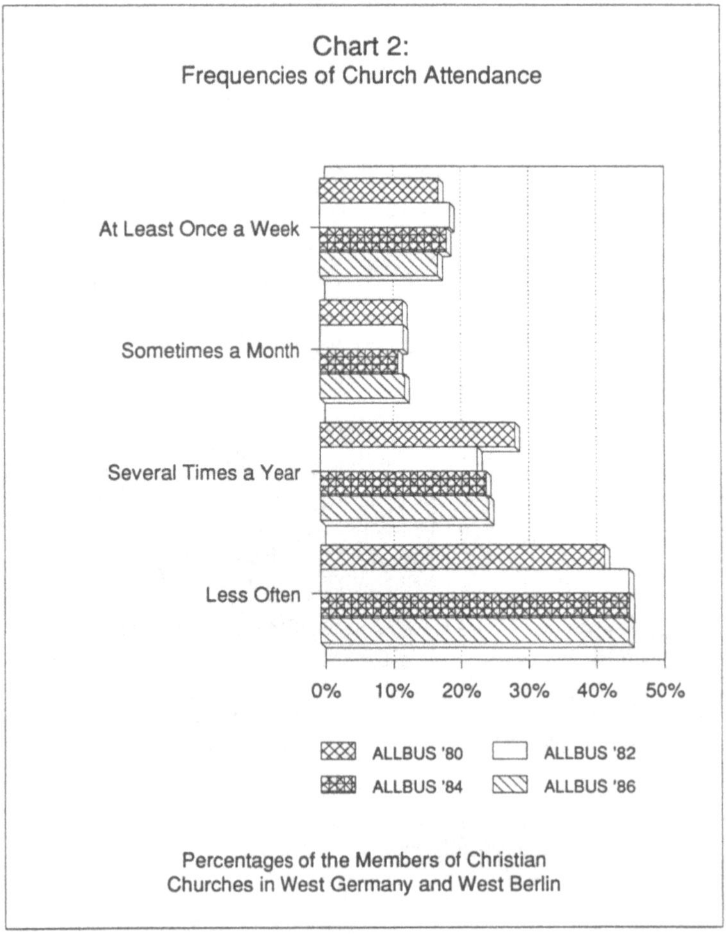

Our next example shown in Chart 2 is concerned with church attendance. Secularization is certainly one of the major social changes taking place in many present societies and the changes in the frequency of church attendance are an important indicator for secularization and growing distance towards traditional religious communities.(9) Earlier data for West Germany show that from the fifties up to the seventies a remarkable decline in church attendance had taken place. It might have been expected that this decline would have carried on during the eighties as a part of the general secularization process in modern society. On the contrary, our data show no apparent continuation of this tendency since 1980, but rather signs of stagnation. Affiliation to the church could temporarily have reached a rather low plafond and future development has to be looked out for. What could be said is that the number of persons without membership in a Christian church is still increasing, even though the large majority of the German population is at least formally belonging to a denomination, i.e. more than 90 %. Again we could take the chance of going into more detailed analysis. Moreover, survey data about the relative percentages of regular church attendants among nominal church members are a valuable supplement of official statistics as the validity of the latter on this subject is sometimes doubted even by experts.

IV. Perspective

The updated version of the cumulated ALLBUS 1980-86 will be soon distributed to our users at other research institutions. The forthcoming ALLBUS 1988 will be available in 1989. After its integration into the cumulated file a fundamental reorganization of data and documentation is planned. This will be established by gathering all variables over the years dealing with similar subjects into special moduls (e.g. a modul of variables describing job situations or a modul of items on political attitudes). Moreover, a small user's guide will be issued which contains informations on the data structure and suggestions for efficient handling and computation in SPSS^{x} or SPSS^{PC}.

Further considerations concern efficient procedures of text-inquiry for data selection, e.g. inquiry of codebook-texts leading to selective data retrievals. One possibility of inquiry is already established by the integration of ALLBUS-items into the Z.A.R.-system.(10) Notwithstanding, which types of data management will be established in the future, the standard outcome for a General Social Survey should be compatible with our users' basic statistical software and the handling of the data base should be easy for all users including those with basic knowledge about data processing techniques.

NOTES

1. The principal investigators who monitored the ALLBUS-program are:
   - ALLBUS 1980: M.R. Lepsius (Mannheim), E.K. Scheuch (Cologne), R. Ziegler (Munich).
   - ALLBUS 1982: M.R. Lepsius (Heidelberg), E.K. Scheuch (Cologne), R. Ziegler (Munich).
   - ALLBUS 1984: W. Müller (Mannheim), F.U. Pappi (Kiel), E.K. Scheuch (Cologne), R. Ziegler (Munich).
   - ALLBUS 1986 and ALLBUS 1988 (not available yet): K.U. Mayer (Berlin), W. Müller (Mannheim), F.U. Pappi (Kiel), E.K. Scheuch (Cologne), R. Ziegler (Munich).

The ALLBUS-program 1980-86 was funded by the DFG (Deutsche Forschungsgemeinschaft). Since 1988, it is financed regularly as a part of GESIS (Gesellschaft Sozialwissenschaftlicher Infrastruktureinrichtungen), which is a new institution for the support of social research financed by the Federal Government and the States. The data sets are documented and distributed by the Central Archive.

2. Participants of the ISSP in 1986 were: Austria, Australia, Federal Republic of Germany, Hungary, Italy, United Kingdom and United States of America. In 1988, the Netherlands are included and the inclusion of Ireland is planned. The ISSP-part of the questionnaire in Germany runs as an additional self-administered "drop off".

3. The *Zentralarchiv* at the University of Cologne serves as the ISSP archive (see Rolf Uher and Irene Müller, in: *ZA-Informationen* 23, 6-12). By July 1988, the following ISSP Data Sets were available at the *Zentralarchiv*:
   - ISSP 1985 module: "Role of Government"
   - ISSP 1986 module: "Social Networks"
   - ISSP 1987 module: "Social Inequality"

   Forthcoming is the
   - ISSP 1988 module: "Family and Sex Roles"

   Participants of the previous ISSP-surveys (up to August 1988):

Australia	(1985-1988)
Federal Republic of Germany	(1985-1988)
Great Britain	(1985-1988)
Ireland/Northern Ireland	(1986-1988)*
Italy	(1985-1988)
The Netherlands	(1987-1988)
Austria	(1985-1980)
Hungary	(1986-1988)
USA	(1985-1988)

   * The ISSP-surveys 1986 and 1987 were conducted later.

4. These 1000 distinct variables include all data of our four surveys. Colating this material has still to be finished in some details. The version of the cumulated ALLBUS 1980-86 which will be released for distribution to our users in 1989 will contain about 700 variables comprising all data out of the ALLBUS-surveys 1980-84 and those data out of the ALLBUS 1986 which are already replications of former ALLBUS-items. This reduction of the file will facilitate the handling of the cumulated data base. More information about future versions of the cumulated ALLBUS is available at the Central Archive for Empirical Social Research.

5. SPSS[x] also provides support for SAS- and OSIRIS-data sets. A passage to BMDP has been generated at the computation-center of the University of Cologne.

6. Dictionary-specifications include variable formats, variable labels, value labels and missing data definitions.

7. Note that our example is only concerned with cpu-seconds, i.e. time during which the computer is really active on our user's special jobs. Normally, users work under timesharing conditions and thus, a certain amount of time elapses during which the computer is busy for other users. Working with the complete system file could add for instance 898 seconds elapsed time for both loglinear models. This means that the whole job takes 1257 seconds. Doing the same task using a selected system file (Filetype III) under similar circumstances would yield a reduction of about 20 minutes.

8. Similar informations about unemployment periods of respondents who are not members of the German working population can be found in other ALLBUS-variables.

9. Cf. Michael Terwey. Traditionelle Religiosität und Säkularisierung in der Bundesrepublik Deutschland. Paper presented at the 13. annual meeting of the "Arbeitskreis religions- und kirchensoziologischer Forschungsinstitute (ArkiF)", 04/18-20/88, Cologne: Zentralarchiv für Empirische Sozialforschung.

10. See Mochmann, Ekkehard. 1974/75. "Information Access at the Data Item Level: Approaches to Indicator Retrieval from Survey Archive Data Bases", in: SICSOC Bulletin, vol. 6, nos. 2 & 3, 47-55.

FRAVIS - A PC BASED SYSTEM FOR DOCUMENTATION AND RETRIEVAL OF SURVEY QUESTIONS

Lorenz Gräf
Zentralarchiv für Empirische Sozialforschung, Cologne
FRG

1. Task

The database system FRAVIS - Fragenverwaltungs- und Informationssystem - (Questions Management- and Information- System) came into life as a byproduct of a research project. This project, an evaluation study of the 1987 German census, has a complex survey design. It includes a three wave panel and five further surveys. At the beginning of working on FRAVIS it was a simple DBASE-datafile and had been installed with the only scope to have an input validation of the variable names and variable labels in use in the various parts of our research project. Step by step in the continuation of the project, textmanagement functions were integrated, facilities to produce correspondence lists and continuity guides were added, frequencies output of SPSS was integrated, a thesaurus function was developed to reflect the topics of the indicators used and at last the report generator has been improved to produce codebooks quasi automatically. FRAVIS now is an integrated electronic codebook, a powerful instrument to manage the question base in research projects with complex designs.

What were the requirements FRAVIS had to meet to become a database system simplifying the management of the itempool in our multi wave study?

2. Requirements

In a research project with a complex survey design it is essential to manage the questions used in the different parts of the whole study efficiently. For continuity one needs a list of variable correspondence as well as a list of question correspondence. To avoid getting lost in the systemfiles it is necessary to identify each variable uniquely. In our research project the basic variable name uniquely identifies each variable. In the whole pool of variables there is no duplicate variable name. And at the same time each item or indicator has a unique identification number. Repeated questions have the same reference number.

Our rule to find variable names is the following: The first two digits are identical with the code for the part of the study (P1, P2, P3, Q1, Q2, Q3, Q4 or Q5), the next three digits contain the identification number of the item. In doing so the researcher is able to identify identical questions over multiwave files without being constrained to look into a variable correspondence list or a codebook. With that basic concept a question correspondence list is at the same time a variable correspondence list.

First requirement: Automatic generation of variable names
In order to establish automatic generation of variable names we had to ensure the uniqueness of the variable names. On the other hand those variables which contain

identical questions should be labelled with the same words. The database system, therefore, should be able to generate the new variable name and to allocate identical labels to identical questions automatically.

Second requirement: Support in producing SPSS-systemfiles
To minimize errors the system should store further characteristics of the items, like number of responses, value labels and missing data specifications. Report functions should be available to generate essential parts of an SPSS-Setup, like variable - and value labels statements, and other jobcards to manipulate existing systemfiles via - for example - KEEP or DROP statements.

Third requirement: Generating correspondence lists
Datacleaning, datamodification and transformation of variables will be easier if there is a continually updated question- and variable correspondence list.

Fourth requirement: Management of free text
To have a full documentation about the items used, it is indispensable to document the original notation of the questions and the original notation of all possible responses. Often unsuspected results will become easily evident observing the original question text. Furthermore, it is often useful to make further comments on the questions in use. If there are replications of items used in prior studies it is of an important help to have information about the original source of the question and the original marginal distribution of that item displayed on screen.

Fifth requirement: Management of results
For an general overview it is useful to have the results collected in the actual survey easily at hand. Therefore, the system should provide frequency tables for each variable.

Sixth requirement: Keyword index or thesaurus function
To ensure easy access the system has to offer a structured organisation of the items.

Seventh requirement: Codebook generation
Often an overview on screen cannot provide all information wanted. Options should be available to generate a complete, informative and thematically structured codebook.

3. The FRAVIS Solution

3.1 Software

As database language we selected DBASE IIIplus. This language is easy to use, widely spread and there are many add-on products to make programming more easy. As Compiler we have chosen CLIPPER because it offers a small wordstar-compatible editor which helped to install the management of text-information. The programm FRAVIS has been developed step by step accordingly to the needs of our research project.

3.2 The Logical Structure

The logical structure of the database is determined by the logical placement of the information. On the left side of the diagram below information associated with the items are located. These information contrast the information associated with each questionnaire, like frequencies, question numbers, survey number in the total research project. On the left side of the diagram we find the information related to the items: Question text, item label, reference number, thesaurus and response categories. Data are stored in six files, which are linked together in a specific way depending on the queries being made.

Figure 1: The Logical Structure

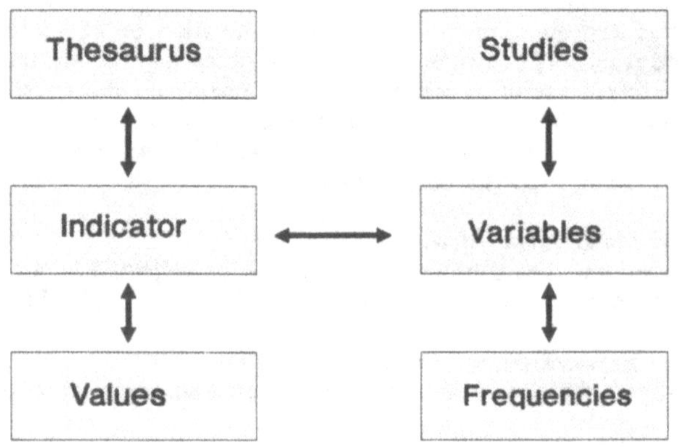

3.3 Integrated Electronic Codebook

In the actual version, FRAVIS provides functions to develop and print questionnaires out of the items stored in the system, to print correspondence lists and codebooks, to create setups for the SPSSX or SPSS/PC+ software and to make on-screen retrievals in a 'mini archive'. Supplied with these functions it is not only a product to manage the item base in research projects of every kind, single surveys as well as multi wave designs, but it is at the same time a powerful instrument to create some miniarchive. In general, FRAVIS is a useful tool if questions in different studies are to be linked. For a well specified set of studies connected, like the German General Social Survey (ALLBUS), the German election studies or the EUROBAROMETER Studies, it is suitable.

4. Working with FRAVIS

The database provided here as an example contains the International Social Survey Program ISSP of 1985. Six countries are involved and the questionnaires deal with the topic 'Role of Government'. The Database contains the English and the German question text, the English response categories and English variable labels.

4.1 The FRAVIS Standard Screen

After starting FRAVIS the system displays on screen the item having the lowest reference number in the itempool. This starting screen is shown in most of the functions. With few exceptions FRAVIS does not change screen-outlook. If this is necessary, FRAVIS opens windows on the main screen.

Figure 2: FRAVIS Standard Screen

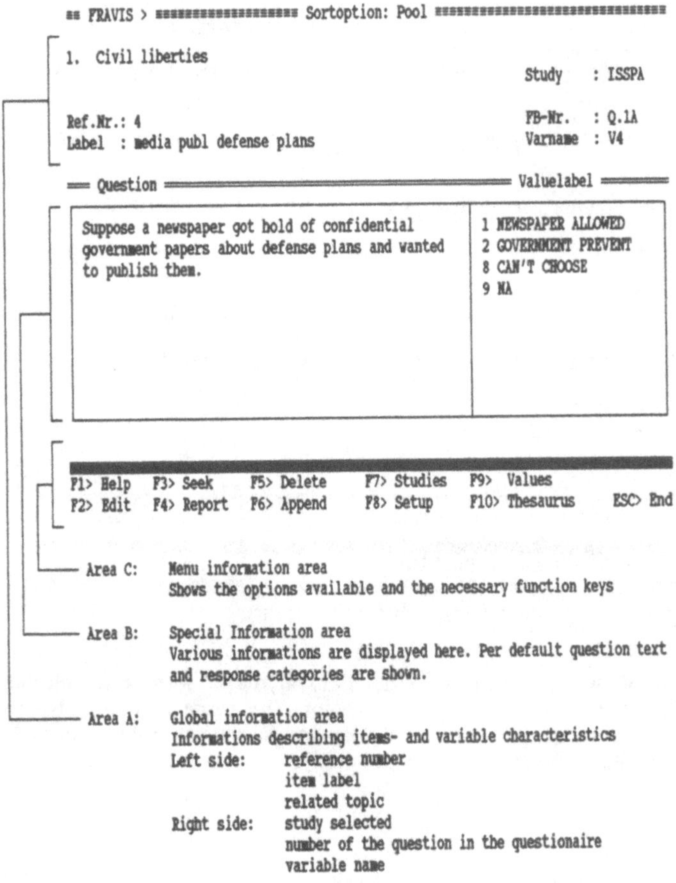

The screen of the standard display shows three distinct areas containing different types of information. In the bottom the menu keys are displayed. In the middle of the screen various information are presented. Normally, question texts and variable labels will be shown in that area. Information which describes the characteristics of the item is presented in the upper part of the screen. On the left side reference number, item label and correlated thesaurus topic are displayed. Information varying between questionnaires, e.g. the name of the questionnaire or study, the question number and the variable name is displayed at the right side.

4.2 Onscreen Overviews

In the middle of the screen the information displayed may vary. The marginals of the selected variable, a frequency table of all variables belonging to the focused item or the continuity guide of that item can take the place of the question text.

Figure 3: Frequency Table

== FRAVIS > ================== Sortoption: Pool ==============================

1. Civil liberties

Study : ISSPA

Ref.Nr.: 4 FB-Nr. : Q.1A

Label : media publ defense plans Varname : V4

Overview: Ref.nr. 4 — Frequencies

Value	Label	A	AUS	D	GB	I	USA
1	NEWSPAPER ALLOWED	211	233	229	360	317	97
2	GOVERNMENT PREVENT	513	1237	748	1067	1072	478
8	CAN'T CHOOSE	253	0	67	94	191	84
9	NA	10	58	4	9	0	18
Σ=		987	1528	1048	1530	1580	677

F1> Help F3> Seek F5> Delete F7> Studies F9> Values

F2> Edit F4> Report F6> Append F8> Setup F10> Thesaurus ESC> End

The display of the continuity guide functions at the same time as selection menu for choosing another study as leading view point. The name of the study chosen is then displayed in the right upper side of the screen. Frequency display, study footnote text will consequentially refer to that special study.

Figure 4: Continuity Guide of the Item

```
== FRAVIS > =================== Sortoption: Pool ================================

1.  Civil liberties
                                                              Study      : ISSPA

Ref.Nr.: 4                                                    FB-Nr.     : Q.1A
Label  : med   ═══ Continuity Guide ═══════                   Varname    : V4

== Fragetex  Studie    | Fb_nr   | Varname        ═══════ Valuelabel ═════

 Suppose a   ISSPA     Q.1A           V4               1 NEWSPAPER ALLOWED
 government  ISSPAUS   Q.1A           V4               2 GOVERNMENT PREVENT
 to publish  ISSPD     F.1            V4               8 CAN'T CHOOSE
             ISSPGB    Q.1A           V4               9 NA
             ISSPI     Q.1A           V4
             ISSPUSA   Q.1A           V4
             S1490     Q.1A           V4


F1> Help   F3> Seek     F5> Delete    F7> Studies    F9> Values
F2> Edit   F4> Report   F6> Append    F8> Setup      F10> Thesaurus       ESC> End
```

4.3 The FRAVIS Dialogue

The main functions are available by pressing the specific function key. Each function can be left by pressing the escape key. An interactive online help is available by pressing the function key one <F1>. In its actual concept FRAVIS is more an integrated electronic codebook than a sophisticated retrieval system. Moving through the database is possible by merely using the arrow keys. Browsing is possible in three different sort-options. Default sort-option is the reference number order. The second sort-option repeats the order of the questions in a questionnaire. Thirdly, it is possible to follow the thesaurus skipping through the database. The specific means of the arrow keys are described in mainfunction help menus. Reference number, question number, variable names and topics can be searched using the 'SEEK'-function.

4.4 Textmanagement

FRAVIS offers five freetext fields: The question text, the footnote which is related to the item, the footnote which is related to the variable (variable footnote), the documentation fields of the response categories and a textfield to store the study description. Text may be edited using wordstar like commands. The content of each textfield can be printed or stored in an ASCII file named "TEMP.TXT". It is also possible to retrieve an ASCII file which has also the name "TEMP.TXT". Therefore, it is possible to copy the text of one textfield into another textfield. The diagram below shows the content of the variable footnote textfield. In the case of the ISSP-itempool, variable footnotes contain question texts in the original language. Figure 5 shows the footnote related with V4 of the German part of the ISSP '85.

Figure 5: Footnote Textwindow

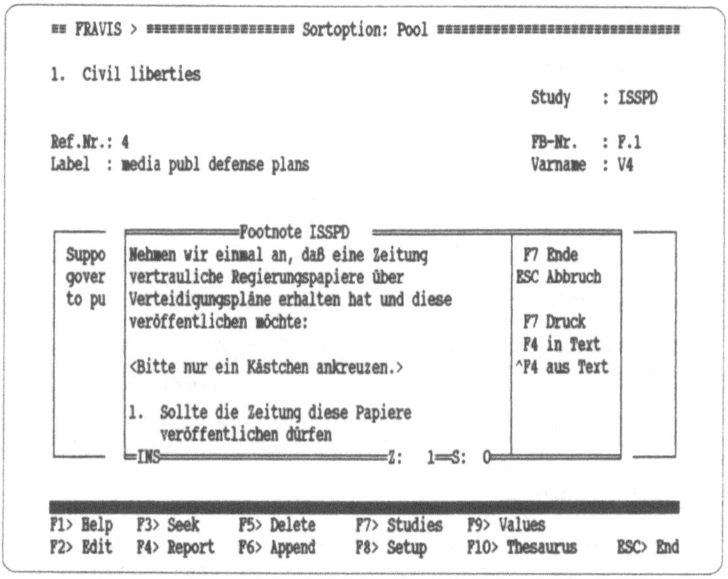

4.5 Study Selection

FRAVIS follows the concept of a miniarchive. The user can decide which studies out of the studypool he wants to observe. After choosing the 'Studies'-function <F7> FRAVIS displays the studies available in the pool. The number of studies included in the pool is limited only in terms of diskspace (and of speed). Information displayed in that screen are: status [AKTIV], study [Studie], code of the study [KUERZEL], and a 20 character description field for the study. Furthermore, by pressing the 'd'-key a free text field is available to store notes on that study.

Figure 6: Study Selection

```
== FRAVIS > =================== Study Selection ================================

            Aktiv  Studie    KUERZEL  NAME
--------------------------------------------------------------------------------
              +    ISSPA      A       Austria
              +    ISSPAUS    AUS     Australia
              +    ISSPD      D       Germany
              +    ISSPGB     GB      Great Britain
              +    ISSPI      I       Italy
              +    ISSPUSA    USA     United Staates
              -    S1490      ALL     ISSP 1985 cumulated

              4                            Studies available:        7

 Options:        <Ret.> Select/Unselect <D> Study-Deskription <F7> End
```

4.6 Thesaurus Maintenance

FRAVIS provides the researcher with a straightforward thesaurus function. The thesaurus has a maximal depth of four levels. The information forming the thesaurus is divided in two parts. The first part contains the information about the level and it is stored in the level number field [Absatz_nr]. The information describing the topic is stored in the field named 'ABS_TITEL'. The structure of the thesaurus depends only on the content of the level number field. Following the decimal classification the user himself structures the topics. The allocation of topics and items is made with the 'Edit'-function.

4.7 Import and Report Facilities

FRAVIS reads OSIRIS-cdbkdict files and SPSS-Setups, but normally expects a step by step entry of information. FRAVIS does not accept items which are not related to a specific questionnaire to ensure the integrity of the database. Information concerning the study or the questionnaire are expected first. In the 'Append'-function, the first information required is the number of the question in the questionnaire. If there are already other studies in the FRAVIS 'miniarchive', the database system asks if this question is a replication. If that item is replicated, FRAVIS automatically allocates item characteristics.

Figure 7: Edit Thesaurus

```
== FRAVIS > ==================== Edit Thesaurus ==================================

        ABSATZ_NR       ABS_TITEL
        1.              Civil liberties
        2.              Government and the familiy
        3.              Government and Social Inequality
        4.              Economic intervention
        8.              Demographic Informations
        9.              Sample Information

  Options:     <Ret.> Edit  <F4> Report  <F5> Delete  <F6> Append  <ESC> End
```

FRAVIS has an integrated report generator, which enables the user to produce formatted and unformatted output. It is possible to produce continuity guides, setups for statistical packages and codebooks. To create finished presentation outputs it is necessary to use the formatting power of wordprocessing software or of software for desktop publishing.

5. Conclusion

FRAVIS is still in the process of development. A first version of FRAVIS will be available in autumn 1989. Although working with FRAVIS is simple, difficulties may arise while transferring an existing database into FRAVIS. Producing codebooks with FRAVIS is possible only in combination with the Ventura Publisher. FRAVIS itself does not offer utilities to produce well formatted printable output. The finishing must be done with wordprocessing software.

Figure 8: Example of Codebook Production with FRAVIS

Anhang 2: *1.1.Einstellung zur VZ* *S.1*

1.VZ-Variablen

1.1. Einstellung zur VZ

009 EINSTELLUNG ZUR VZ

Panel 3.Welle: F06
Querschnitt 5: F04

In der Bundesrepublik Deutschland werden Volkszählungen, also Zählungen aller Bürger, in großen zeitlichen Abständen durchgeführt. Die letzte Volkszählung fand im Jahre 1970 statt, die nächste wird in diesem Jahr Ende Mai durchgeführt. Stehen Sie dieser kommenden Volkszählung im allgemeinen eher zustimmend oder eher ablehnend gegenüber?
Sagen Sie mir das bitte anhand dieser Skala. Der Wert 1 bedeutet, daß Sie der Volkszählung sehr ablehnend gegenüberstehen, der Wert 7 heißt, daß Sie der Volkszählung sehr zustimmend gegenüberstehen. Mit den Werten dazwischen können Sie Ihre Meinung abstufen.

		Panel 3.Welle			Querschnitt 5		
Wert	Etikett	N	Proz.	Adj. P.	N	Proz.	Adj. P.
1	Sehr ablehnend	74	5.8%	5.8%	67	6.8%	6.8%
2		96	7.5%	7.5%	55	5.6%	5.6%
3		114	8.9%	8.9%	79	8.0%	8.0%
4	Unentschieden	174	13.6%	13.6%	150	15.2%	15.2%
5		217	16.9%	17.0%	175	17.7%	17.7%
6		255	19.9%	19.9%	178	18.0%	18.1%
7	Sehr zustimmend	349	27.2%	27.3%	282	28.6%	28.6%
9	Keine Angabe	3	.2%		1	.1%	
		(1282)	(1282)	(1279)	(987)	(987)	(986)

EMPIRICAL RESEARCH ON THE PC: THE CASE OF OPEN ACCESS II

Werner J. Patzelt
Department of Political Science
University of Passau
FRG

Social scientists, involved in empirical research, need efficient devices of data storage, data processing, -analysis and -presentation. Consequently, they require efficient data base-, statistic-, graphic- and text processing programs. As a rule, they want two requirements to be met: these programs are supposed to run on a PC; and they should not only be compatible with each other, but, if possible, also integrated. In most cases, the second requirement is not yet met: the data base, statistical package, graphics and text system are located in separate programs. But having to import data base files into the statistical package or graphic system first without then being able to take over completed tables and diagrams into the text files of the text system, hampers the work process. Therefore, integrated program packages deserve the interest of the social scientist. No product on the market seems to fully satisfy all desires yet. But the integrated program package OPEN ACCESS II of Software Products International, Inc. comes close to accomplishing this task. In the first part of this paper, a short presentation of its most useful features will be given, and the second part will demonstrate the integration of OPEN ACCESS II into a typical research process.

I. OPEN ACCESS II and its Central Features

OPEN ACCESS II requires an IBM-compatible PC and MS-DOS 2.0 and higher. Although not obligatory, a hard disk facilitates the use of OPEN ACCESS II considerably. The integrated software package consists of different modules which may be acquired separately. The following ones are of special interest for the social scientist: data base; calculation program with a graphic system and a special statistical package; text system; and utilities. Designed for commercial, not scientific applications, OPEN ACCESS II does not meet all desires a sociologist or political scientist may have. However, the package can be improved according to these desires by additional tools constructed via the system's 'macro' function. On the whole, OPEN ACCESS II is rather easy to use, equipped with both a series of instructive handbooks and a detailed help file. The utility package supports highly personal system configurations and a great variety of printers and plotters. Given the necessary hardware equipment, OPEN ACCESS II can also be operated in a network system or allow communication and data exchange via telephone.

1. Data Base

The data base allows for 100 variables and a nearly unlimited number of cases per data base file. Furthermore, up to eight data base files can be linked by a common variable - e.g., the case number - to each other so that it is possible to work with data files combining 798 variables. Different sorts of data may be stored: numbers, texts (with a maximum length of 78 characters), logical values etc... . Data registration masks can be developed which actually can be adapted to all user's desires. It is very easy to delete or to change single entries or whole groups of cases or variables. A structured query language enables comfortable and accurate access to any given group of cases or variables. Crosstabulations as well as elementary monovariate statistics are offered. All information stored or produced by the data bank program can be printed either as a hardcopy or into an ASCII-file, which can be easily processed by any other program capable of reading ASCII. Especially via the DIF format, data can be exchanged very simply with other data base programs (for all questions concerning data exchange between OPEN ACCESS II and other programs see Helming 1988, 172-209). The possibility of developing optional macros facilitates the routine use of the data base enormously.

2. Calculation Program and Statistics

All data sets stored in the data base can be taken over selectively or entirely into the calculation program. The spreadsheet provides a maximum of 216 columns and 3000 rows and fulfils nearly every desire of mathematical or logical operations. Any part of the spreadsheet may be used for entries, formulas, diagrams and as special text or even data base area. Of course, any part of the spreadsheet can be printed as hardcopy or into an ASCII-file. The screen can be divided into a maximum of six windows, in which external calculation models can be shown and used. As in the data base, macros can be written using very simple commands so as to facilitate routine calculations.

The statistical package, completing the toolbox offered by OPEN ACCESS II, can analyze any data in the spreadsheet. Unfortunately, its primary contents are statistical models designed for the analysis of metric data (among others: metric correlation, different models of regression and ANOVA, parametric tests of significance), and therefore, it is rather disappointing for the social scientist (see Patzelt 1988). For the analysis of nominal and rank scaled data, it only provides a contingency table analysis with the chi2-test, the uncorrected contingency coefficient, ordinal ANOVA for independent and combined samples, the Mann-Whitney-U-test, and some other tests of significance. The whole field of rank correlation is non-existent. But thanks to the excellent calculation program this deficiency can be overcome simply by developing one's own calculation models and macros for efficient use. In this case, most of all current models of mono- and bivariate statistics can be utilized for non-metric data. However, such important areas of multivariate statistics as cluster-, factor- or discriminance analysis are still excluded. All results of statistical analysis can be printed on hardcopy or written either into a spreadsheet or into ASCII-files and, thus, be used both by the OPEN ACCESS II text system and any other text system capable of reading or converting ASCII-files. Furthermore, other useful ways of transferring data to or from other calculation programs are offered.

3. Graphics

The graphic module, integrated into the calculation module and easily operatable, provides simple and superimposed bar-, column- and line diagrams, circle- and spot diagrams, composed diagrams, and three dimensional figures. The diagrams can be printed both in black and white or colour, and both as highly accurate graphics and as text graphics (the latter with the exception of circle diagrams and 3-d-graphics). All completed diagrams can be incorporated in the text system integrated in OPEN ACCESS II; text graphics can be placed into calculation models as well. Since text graphics are stored as ASCII-files, they can be imported by all text systems capable of reading or converting ASCII-files. In the latter case, however, the resulting diagrams need a revision sometimes. If desired, exporting data stored and processed by OPEN ACCESS II to special graphic packages like MS-CHART is no real problem.

4. Text System

On the one hand, OPEN ACCESS II provides in the utility package a rather efficient text editor called 'memo pad' which creates ASCII-files. As it can be started from practically all sub-programs, it is excellently suited for the task of immediately registering all observations and ideas occurring during the examination of data, statistical results or diagrams. The files created with the 'memo pad' can be processed directly by the OPEN ACCESS II text system and utilized by any other text system capable of reading or converting ASCII-files. On the other hand, OPEN ACCESS II provides a special text system. However, this text system is unsuited for scientific editing, since it cannot produce footnotes so far. Nevertheless, this does not pose a great problem. Either you use the text system AccessScript instead, which is suited for integration with OPEN ACCESS II and practically meets all the researcher's desires. Or you use your traditional text system. If it is capable of reading or importing ASCII-files, all sorts of data can be exchanged with OPEN ACCESS II (only exception: highly accurate diagrams). Even more possibilities are available, if the text system can import or export DIF-files.

II. OPEN ACCESS II in the Research Process

Any researcher acquainted with PCs will, as a matter of fact, have all preparatory papers of a research project edited by a text system from the very beginning, e.g. using the text system of OPEN ACCESS II. A text system should be used especially for the preparation of data collections requiring questionnaires, coding sheets etc. so that these research tools can be improved and updated easily. In a postal survey, address management and mail merge functions, as offered by OPEN ACCESS II, will be valuable as well. During the preparation of research papers or articles for publication, the opportunities of graphic and text systems are more then welcome. Yet, all these possibilities are provided by special graphic and text systems as well. It is in the data recording and data analysis phase, where OPEN ACCESS II is of special value for a researcher who wants to become independent from the computer centre of his university or institute. Therefore, our discussion will concentrate on these two stages of the research process.

1. OPEN ACCESS II in the Data Recording Phase

As a rule, codes for data recording have to be fixed when preparing the questionnaire of a survey. Therefore, the data registration mask can already be built up and checked for practical use during the field work. The necessary procedure is quite simple. OPEN ACCESS II allows for a maximum of 15 pages per mask. Pages can be filled in according to individual desires, and any amount of explanatory text is possible, provided the maximum of 15 pages is not exceeded. The fields where data can be entered are simply marked by pressing a special key. Subsequently a menue is shown from which the characteristics of the expected data can be chosen. There are several ways to ascertain a recording process with a minimum of errors. When recording data, this mask is shown and the cursor automatically goes to each field where data are to be entered. After the record stage, control should take place. In OPEN ACCESS II both the structured query language and the short analysis function of the data base allow swift detection of data entries running out of reasonable numerical limits. Another function allows direct and simple control of each case's record as well as the necessary corrections. If necessary, even after completing the recording process, supplementary variables can be added to the data file, or single cases or variables can be dropped, or the characteristics of variables can be modified.

2. OPEN ACCESS II in the Data Analysis Phase

The precondition for data analysis is the ability to select exactly the desired variables and cases from the data base and to import them into a spreadsheet. In OPEN ACCESS II, this can be done in a very direct way. Subsequently, the selected data are checked according to the questions the researcher wants to answer. In our case quantitative data are analyzed. Normally, the process of quantitative data analysis runs as follows: frequency distributions, also broken down by additional variables, are tabulated, displayed and condensed into univariate statistics (measures of central tendency, form of distribution and spread); crosstabulations, also controlled by additional variables, are calculated, displayed and condensed into measures of association; bivariate tests of significance are used; and finally large groups of variables are analyzed employing multivariate models like cluster-, factor- or discriminance analysis. What can OPEN ACCESS II do for the social scientist in this stage of his research process?

Unfortunately, there are some serious gaps in the toolbox. Yet they can be filled by several macros written by the author and available from him. The logic of every macro is similar: an external calculation model is copied into the actual spreadsheet; the data are copied in this model; the calculation is done; and the results are formatted in a suitable way. Before discussing the use of OPEN ACCESS II for data analysis in some detail, we should consider the role which the graphic module and the 'memo pad' might play during this phase of the research process. Diagrams should be used not only for the purpose of data presentation, but also for the purpose of data examination, as visualized results frequently provide a more precise impression of what 'is going on in the data' than mere numbers and statistics do. As it is possible to store the format of different kinds of diagrams in special files and to assign them to any new data, 'standard diagrams' can be constructed very easily, especially when the editing process is routinized by a macro. But the most useful tool for imaginative and reflected data analysis is the memo pad. To be used whenever wanted without quitting the actual module, you can write down abstracted results, questions, commentaries, ideas and even short parts of research papers. To incorporate this possibility into one's own conduct of interactive research ascertains that no simple collecting of statistics takes place and that no valuable idea gets lost. It is obviously that the basis of research papers and articles meant for publication is laid very easily this way.

Now let us address the single steps of data analysis. No problems are encountered when analyzing ungrouped frequency distributions, as they are tabulated automatically when importing sorted data into the spreadsheet. A macro is required for grouped frequency distributions including percentages. The univariate statistics offered by OPEN ACCESS II operate exclusively with ungrouped frequency distributions and include, among others, mean, expected value, variance, standard deviation, sum, sum of squares, skewness and kurtosis. Obviously, statistics for nominal or ordinal data like the median, ranges or measures of entropy are missing and have, so far, to be supplemented by a personal toolbox of macros.

As for crosstabulations, OPEN ACCESS II offers two procedures, the one producing tables of ungrouped data, the other allowing for any grouping you might require. None of these procedures calculates percentages - another regrettable omission. A macro fills this gap and creates the wanted tables up to a 6 x 6 format. Another gap has to be filled by a macro, as soon as the information contained in a contingency table is to be condensed into a measure of association, because OPEN ACCESS II gives no ordinal measures and only a single (and misleading) nominal one. Yet, a macro written by the author calculates the measures most widely used (i.e. tau, gamma, d, d%, phi, C (corrected), V, Q and lambda). Supplemented by this macro, OPEN ACCESS II may pass as a convenient instrument for bivariate analysis. This holds true all the more, as the offered tests of significance for two dependent or independent samples are indeed satisfying.

The use of multivariate statistical models normally highlights the process of data analysis. OPEN ACCESS II offers multiple, stepwise and polynomial regression, and simple and randomized blocks ANOVA. Models of partial (rank-) correlation might be supplemented easily. As complex methods like cluster-, factor- or discriminance analysis can only be added by a professional statistician and programmer. Here the limits of OPEN ACCESS II, as it presents itself so far, are definitively reached.

Conclusion

It can be asserted that without the supplementary macros mentioned in the last section, the statistic module of OPEN ACCESS II is not too attractive for social scientists and that in this case an investment into OPEN ACCESS II will not pay. Having these additional tools at one's disposal, however, OPEN ACCESS II very well meets the requirements of a researcher not dealing with too great an amount of variables and wanting to do research on his own PC. Certainly, OPEN ACCESS II is far from being the 'ideal tool' for carrying out empirical research on a PC. For instance, it is rather awkward that every statistical calculation must be demanded anew for every variable or group of variables, because you cannot demand the same procedure for a whole list of variables. But with regard to the price of the system with its abilities, OPEN ACCESS II is no bad bargain. A student may purchase the whole package, including the statistic module, for a price of about 520.- DM, a researcher for about 830.-, whereas the 'normal' price is much higher: 2400.- DM! There cannot be any doubt that even 'normal' prices will go down as soon as the demand side of the market for scientific PC-software is better developed. Furthermore, it can be expected that program packages will become available that will fit the social scientist's desires even better, as soon as a considerable number of social scientists begin to articulate their wishes. Therefore, it seems certain that OPEN ACCESS II and its capabilities mark only the beginning, by no means the end of a development still going on.

After all, the central concern of this paper is not whether OPEN ACCESS II will become a widely used tool for empirical social research or not. The important point is that empirical research, which for so long has suffered from the deterring difficulties of 'handmade' statistical analysis and from the inconveniences of accessing great computing centres, now has got into the reach of virtually everybody. And this might make empirical research more popular than it still is and the social sciences more useful for practical purposes than they can be without more cumulative empirical knowledge. If it is true that the infrastructure of technical equipment has a serious impact on the suprastructure of consciousness and enacted norms, an upheaval of empirical research may be expected.

REFERENCES

HELMING, G. 1988. *Datenaustausch unter MS-DOS. Methoden und Techniken des Datentransfers zwischen Standardprogrammen, Individualprogrammen und Integrierten Paketen.* München, Wien

PATZELT, W.J. 1988. *Bemerkungen zum Statistik-Modul von OPEN ACCESS II.* Passau (mimeo)

Software Products International, Inc. 1986. *OPEN ACCESS II.* 7 volumes, München

PROFESSIONALIZATION IN A PARLIAMENTARY SYSTEM LENGTH OF MEMBERSHIP IN THE GERMAN REICHSTAG

An Application of Event-History Analysis to Historical Duration Data

Hans-Jürgen Andreß
University of Bielefeld
Faculty of Sociology
FRG

1. Introduction

1.1 Data and Research Objectives

The research reported herein is part of a larger study on professionalization in a parliamentary system. The project uses data about members of the German Reichstage (MRT for short) between 1867 and 1918 and has been initiated by Prof. H. Best (University of Cologne). The following analysis extends results obtained by Sombert (1988).

Among the various psychological, organisational and sociological theories of recruitment processes, the biographical approach by Herzog (1975, 1982) is attractive in several ways:

* Recruitment for a political career is viewed as a process of successive stages of selection, qualification, and mobility and not as a result of a single mobility step (e.g. social background) that places an individual on a specific career.
* The political system is modeled as a structure of opportunities yielding career patterns that are similar for certain groups of individuals.
* Entry into a political career may be determined by variables like social background and the proximity between main occupation and politics (termed "Abkömmlichkeit" by Weber). All following steps, however, depend on the positions achieved and the political experience gained during this process.
* A political career can be viewed as a self-enforcing process: On the one hand social distance to a private career will increase with the length of a political career. Thus, returning to a former job becomes increasingly difficult. On the other hand the benefits from a political job rise with every step in this career.

Therefore, a politician is interested in stabilizing his/her career to save the investments made in this job. This is done, for instance, by a vertical cumulation of political functions both on the local (where candidates are selected) and on the regional level (where political decisions are made).

Length of membership in a parliament is viewed as an important indicator of the degree of professionalization in a political career. It is the dependent variable of the following analysis and as indicated in section 1.2, the German Reichstag is an interesting example to study the changes of this variable in historical time. The following table lists all the other variables available from the Reichstag member data bank.

Explaining Variables

Variable	Category
Main occupation:	landowners capitalists, merchants craftsmen, shopkeepers civil service clergy liberal profession functionaries, journalists other
Party membership:	Conservatives Social Democrats Left Liberals Right Liberals Zentrum ("christian" party) other
Residence:	voting district elsewhere
Political function:	none only local only regional local and regional
Regional parliament:	no additional seat other state parliament Prussian parliament
Association:	no membership non-political association political association
Age:	years

To understand the role of these variables and the possible changes in Reichstag membership, it is necessary to give some information about the institutional framework of this German parliament.

1.2 The German Reichstag: Institutional Framework and Social Change

The German Reichstag was based on an universal, equal and secret selection. 382 members were elected directly using a majority vote system (+ 15 members for Elsaß-Lothringen since 1874). The election period lasted 3 years (5 years since 1888). The regional distribution of voting districts and the majority vote system favoured regional/conservative parties and handicapped Social Democrats.

Compared to other institutions of the German constitution (e.g. German Chancellor, Bundesrat), the political power of the Reichstag was low.(1) Besides that, the costs of attending Reichstag sessions were high for the individual politician.

Contrary to regulations in regional parliaments, now session allowance was paid until 1906. Only a minimal compensation for travelling expenses was given. Therefore, many MRT's were also members of regional parliaments (e.g. Prussia) or held functions in political parties and related organizations to gain a complementary income.(2) On the whole, a MRT career was not very attractive compared to careers in administration, armed forces or private economy, as can be seen by the fact that no MRT became chancellor or secretary of state or vice versa.

The institution Reichstag was introduced by Bismarck (German Chancellor) as an instrument of national unity against particularistic forces in single German states. During his reign, he played off all political parties against each other and used the Reichstag for his own objectives. After Bismarck's resignation (1890), the Reichstag gained more and more political power. In the years before World War I, de facto (not de jure) no chancellor could be nominated without confidence of the Reichstag majority. During all these years, the social composition of the Reichstag changed from a traditional association of notabilities to an association of members of well organized parties.

1.3 Hypotheses

Given these historical changes and the theoretical framework indicated in section 1.1, the following hypotheses were formulated:

1. Increasing professionalization of all MRT's from 1867 until 1918 will increase the length of Reichstag membership in general.
2. If a political career is viewed as a reinforcing process, it is expected to gain more and more stability with the length of membership.
3. However, length of membership is limited by age of the parliamentarian.
4. Given the costs of Reichstag membership, it is expected that regional distance of the member's residence has a negative impact on membership duration.
5. Membership in other parliaments and associations as well as political functions on the local or regional level reduce the costs of Reichstag membership and stabilize the member's political career. It is expected that they have a positive effect on membership duration.
6. Given the changing social and political composition of the Reichstag and its changing role in the German political system, it is expected that the influence of all variables changes in time. Namely
   a) the variables "political party" and "main occupation" reflect the changing composition and
   b) the variables "political function" and "membership in other parliaments and associations" will loose their importance.

2. Analysis

2.1 Statistical Problems of Event-History Analysis

A possible way of analyzing membership durations, is the computation of mean values for different groups of interest: e.g. MRT's from the early Reichstage versus MRT's from the late Reichstage. However, these statistics are biased by the fact that a completed membership duration cannot be observed for those MRT's that were members of the late Reichstage, since this observation period has been limited to the year of 1918. This bias is especially high, if the variable compared is time-dependent, as can be seen from the following table.

Mean and Median Membership Durations

Variable		All	Censored	%	Mean	Median
Beginning of membership:						
	1867-1873	775	0	,00%	6,15	3,97
	1874-1883	629	12	1,91%	7,31	4,67
	1884-1892	423	14	3,31%	7,87	6,08
	1893-1902	399	62	15,54%	9,21	7,61
	1903-1918	548	309	56,39%	6,37	9,59
Total		2774	397	14,31%	7,16	5,92

This table compares membership durations across historical time and as hypothesized durations increase until 1902. However, a considerable drop in mean duration is observed for the last cohort entering the Reichstag between 1903 and 1918. This is due to the fact that about 56% of this cohort (N=548) is still in office 1918, but their following careers have not been considered in the computations.(3)

more technically, these observations are censored by the end of the observation period and specialized methods, known as event-history or survival analysis, are needed to account for this arbitrary censoring scheme.(4) If, for instance, a medium membership duration is calculated, the upward trend of membership duration is clearly seen, even for the last cohort. This median is derived from an estimate of the probability of remaining in the Reichstag until a certain point in time (survivor function). This estimate considers events (completed memberships) as well as censored observations and, therefore, makes optimal use of all information available.(5)

2.2 Results

Using event-history analysis, it is possible to test multivariate models about membership durations investigating the effects of different explaining variables and the changes across historical time and across an individual's career. Instead of looking at durations, it is a common practice to analyze the rate at which certain events occur. Table 1 in the appendix shows the result of such a (log linear) rate model, assuming that the rate of leaving the Reichstag is constant across rime, but different across individuals with different characteristics. The explaining variables have been converted to 1/0-coded dummy variables measuring the effect of the corresponding category relative to the omitted category (reference group).

Since the original log-linear effects are hard to interpret, they have been converted to antilogarithms (exp) measuring relative change of the rate for the corresponding category compared to the reference group. In table 1, the estimated rate of the reference group equals 0,07 (log rate = -2,64) implying a mean membership duration of 14 years. Compared to this reference group, the rate of leaving Reichstag is 29% lower for those MRT's who report journalist or party functionary as the main occupation (mainly members of the Social Democratic party). In other words, Reichstag membership is lower for this group. On the other hand, craftsmen and shopkeepers have a shorter membership duration than the reference group (positive effect on rate). All other differences between occupational groups are not significant.

Social Democrats and members of the Zentrum party show a longer membership duration than the reference group while the membership of the Right Liberals is shorter. Contrary to our expectations, residence does dot have a significant effect, while political functions on the regional and /or local level, membership in other state parliaments as well as membership in political and non-political associations significantly prolongs Reichstag membership. All variables taken together significantly improve on a much simpler model that assumes a constant rate of leaving Reichstag across all individuals (see likelihood ratio test on the bottom of table 1).

Some interesting historical changes are summarized in tables 2-5. All these models include the variables of table 1 (estimates not shown) plus the effect of one particular variable across time:

1. Compared with the first period from 1867 to 1873, all following periods show an increasingly lower rate indicating an increasing membership duration across time (table 2).
2. The (prolonging) effect of memberships in other parliaments decreases until in the last period 1903-1918 this variable has no significant at all (table 3).
3. A similar change can be observed for membership in other associations, although the decrease is no so dramatic (table 5).
4. Finally differentiating the effect of political functions in historical time, it becomes obvious that this effect is only significant in one particular period from 1874 to 1883 (table 4).

Table 1: Determinants of Reichstag Membership

Variable	Estimate	S.E.	P exp	% change
Reference group:	-2,64	,13*	,07	
Main occupation:				
capitalists, merchants	,02	,08	1,02	2%
craftsmen, shopkeepers	,22	,10*	1,24	24%
civil service	,08	,06	1,09	9%
clergy	-,12	,11	,88	-12%
liberal profession	-,03	,09	,97	- 3%
functionaries, journalists	-,35	,10*	,71	-29%
other	,16	,10	1,18	18%
Party membership:				
Social Democrats	-,64	,13*	,53	-47%
Left Liberals	,11	,08	1,12	12%
Right Liberals	,20	,06*	1,22	22%
Zentrum ("christian party")	-,29	,07*	,75	-25%
other	,04	,07	1,04	4%

Residence:				
elsewhere	-,03	,05	,98	-2%
Political function:				
only local	-,27	,06*	,77	-23%
only regional	-,21	,06*	,81	-19%
local and regional	-,37	,08*	,69	-31%
Regional parliament:				
other state parliament	-,30	,05*	,74	-26%
Prussian parliament	-,45	,05*	,64	-36%
Association:				
non-political association	-,31	,05*	,74	-26%
political association	-,50	,08*	,61	-39%
Age:				
	,022	,002*	1,02	2%

Reference group: landowner, Conservatives, residence in voting district, no other political function, no member of regional parliament/association, age=0

Significance P<0.05: *

Model	This one	Constant	Likelihood-Ratio
Log-Likelihood	-7034,48	-7356,58	644,20
Degrees of freedom	2722	2743	21
Pseudo-R	4,38%	,00%	

Changing influence of selected variables 1867-1918

Table 2: Historical Changes of Membership Duration

Variable	1867	1874	1884	1893	1903
Period		-,17*	-,22*	-,39*	-,60*
		(,06)	(,07)	(,07)	(,07)

... all other variables controlled, estimates not shown

Log-Likelihood	-6993,37
Degrees of freedom	2718
Pseudo-R	4,94%

Reference group: landowners, Conservatives, residence in voting district, no other political function, no member of regional parliament/association, age=0, MRT since 1867-1873

Standard errors in brackets, significance P<0.05: *

Table 3: Membership in Regional Parliaments

Variable	1867	1874	1884	1893	1903
other state parlia.	-,70*	-,44*	-,36*	-,25*	,14
	(,11)	(,10)	(,12)	(,13)	(,12)
Prussian parliament	-,58*	-,58*	-,65*	-,35*	-,16
	(,11)	(,11)	(,12)	(,13)	(,12)

... all other variables controlled, estimates not shown

Log-Likelihood	-6976,58
Degrees of freedom	2710
Pseudo-R	5,17%

Reference group: see table 2

Standard errors in brackets, significance P<0.05: *

Table 4: Political Functions

Variable	1867	1874	1884	1893	1903
only local	-,26	-,26*	-,12	-,26	-,18
	(,13)	(,12)	(,13)	(,14)	(,13)
only regional	-,05	-,51*	-,01	-,05	-,19
	(,13)	(,14)	(,13)	(,14)	(,15)
local and regional	-,48	-,42*	-,23	-,26	-,11
	(,31)	(,18)	(,17)	(,16)	(,14)

... all other variables controlled, estimates not shown

Log-Likelihood	-6986,60
Degrees of freedom	2706
Pseudo-R	5,03%

Reference group: see table 2

Standard errors in brackets, significance P<0.05: *

Table 5: Membership in Political and Non-Political Associations

Variable	1867	1874	1884	1893	1903
non-political ass.	-,32*	-,42*	-,28*	-,18*	-,03
	(,10)	(,09)	(,10)	(,11)	(,11)
pol. association	-,51*	-,32*	-,87*	-,59*	-,03
	(,18)	(,18)	(,24)	(,19)	(,14)

```
... all other variables controlled, estimates not shown

Log-Likelihood            -6984,14
Degrees of freedom            2710
Pseudo-R                     5,06%

Reference group: see table 2

Standard errors in brackets, significance P<0.05: *
```

NOTES

1. The German Reichstag had the right of legislative approval and signed the budget.
2. This is especially true for Social democrats who were often employed by their party or by related organizations (e.g. labour unions, political newspapers).
3. 1918, the end of the German Empire and the beginning of the Weimar Republic, was chosen as the end of observation. However, the Reichstag was carried over to the new constitution (with a slightly different electoral system). Therefore, it was possible that a parliamentarian was reelected for the new Reichstag and "continued" the old "mandate".
4. See the textbooks cited in the references section.
5. Because of data problems, competing risks (e.g. death) have not been controlled. Also membership durations do not exclude possible interruptions of a MRT career. Both problems are referred to a more refined analysis in the near future.

REFERENCES

ANDREß, H.J. 1985. "Multivariate Analyse von Verlaufsdaten." *ZUMA-Methodentexte*. Bd.1, Mannheim

BLOSSFELD, H.P.; HAMERLE, A. und MAYER, K.U. 1986. *Ereignisanalyse.Statistische Theorie und Anwendung in den Wirtschafts- und Sozialwissenschaften*. Frankfurt

DIEKMANN, A. und MITTER, P. 1984. Methoden zur Analyse von *Zeitverläufen: Anwendung stochastischer Prozesse bei der Untersuchung von Ereignisdaten*. Stuttgart

HERZOG, D. 1975. *Politische Karrieren, Selektion und Professionalisierung politischer Führungsgruppen*. Opladen: Westdeutscher Verlag

HERZOG, D. 1982. *Politische Führungsgruppen*. Darmstadt: Luchterhand

KALBFLEISCH, J.D. and PRENTICE, R.L. 1980. *The statistical analysis of failure time data*. New York: Wiley

LAWLESS, J.F. 1982. *Statistical models and methods for lifetime data*. New York: Wiley

SOMBERT, K. 1988. *Politik als Beruf. Studien zur Professionalisierung politischer Rollen im Kaiserreich*. Unveröff. Diplomarbeit, Universität Köln

TUMA, N.B. and HANNAN, M.T. 1984. *Social dynamics: models and methods*. New York

APPLICATIONS OF CORRESPONDENCE ANALYSIS IN SOCIAL SCIENCE RESEARCH

Jörg Blasius
Zentralarchiv für Empirische Sozialforschung, Cologne
FRG

Introduction

Correspondence analysis was originally developed in France (Benzécri 1964, Escofier-Codier 1965) and can be traced back to Hirschfield (1935), who presented the first algebraic formulation of the "correlation" between rows and columns of a contingency table. Guttman and Hayashi adopted these ideas as an improvement of scaling techniques via principal component analysis and as a "quantification of qualitative data". Correspondence analysis can be seen as an analogy to these techniques, which is appropriate to discrete rather than to continuous variables.

The main characteristic of correspondence analysis is to display columns and rows of two-dimensional contingency tables simultaneously. Apart from the graphical display, all dimensions can be interpreted numerically. Similar to principal component analysis and multi-dimensional scaling, correspondence analysis makes use of the concept of a multi-dimensional space, the points of which are projected into a lower-dimensional sub-space. The plane of numerical presentation, marked by orthogonal vectors, is chosen to minimize the sum of the squared deviations. In effect, correspondence analysis is a powerful instrument for multiple explorative data analysis with nominal or higher order data.

First applications of correspondence analysis in the social science are traced back to the late 1970's in France. There, the method can be seen as a well known standard method with an own journal (Cahiers de l'Analyse des Donées), edited by the "father of correspondence analysis" Benzécri. One of the most famous applications in the social science is given by Bourdieu (1979) who used this method in his study "La Distinction". In the empirical part of this book, he describes fine differences within three classes, the upper classes, the middle classes, and the working classes.

A further application is given by Blasius (1987) who described first memberships in NS-organizations in the years between 1933 and 1942 by age, their fathers' home, country and status, sex, subject of study, and period of first loan. Dangschat and Blasius (1987) described socio-spatial disparities in Warsaw in 1978, indicated by a typology of planning districts, defined by characteristics of the planning districts' housing stock and socio-demographic characteristics. Thiessen and Rohlinger (1988) used the method for analysing panel data. In their study about job sharing of married couples, they showed changes in doing tasks (task of the man, task of the wife, task which they do together or alternate) like preparing meals, driving cars, repairing and ironing in the first four years (total three times of inquiry) after marrying. More applications and detailed descriptions of the method can be found in the books of Greenacre (1984) and Lebart et al. (1984).

Data

It can be shown that correspondence analysis is a very robust technique against missing data, additional variables, and curvilinear distributions. There are some important differences to other multivariate techniques like factor analysis, cluster analysis or discriminant analysis. As a more or less humoristic illustration we used data from a survey on various topics in empirical social research (ALLBUS) in Germany in 1986; focusing on a subset of questions concerning different aspects of activities in respect to a combined variable of sex and age (men up to 39 years, men between 40 and 59 years, men of 60 years and older, additionally women in the same categories). The respondents have been asked whether they were skilled, semi-skilled or unskilled in topics like dancing to pop music and waltz, playing chess and shortening (fitting) trousers. The focus of this article is on additional variables.

As a programme for analysing the data we used KORRES which is written in the matrix-oriented language SAS-PROC MATRIX by Blasius and Rohlinger (1988a,b). It is an easy to use programme. As an input the rows of different tables (in our example the different degrees of ability in the several topics) are simply concatenated by maintaining the given column structure, e.g. the six categories of our combined variable of sex and age.

Solutions

In a first step we only used two variables - fitting trousers and dancing to pop music - with three categories each. The input data is given in table 1, the graphical representation in figure 1.

Table 1: Input Data

A	YOUNGM	MIDAGEM	OLDM	YOUNGW	MIDAGEW	OLDW
TROUSYES	167.00	109.00	91.00	637.00	500.00	406.00
TROUSJAB	132.00	76.00	62.00	32.00	12.00	12.00
TROUSNO	308.00	291.00	165.00	23.00	10.00	11.00
POPDAYES	386.00	145.00	33.00	535.00	214.00	67.00
POPDAJAB	138.00	105.00	33.00	92.00	88.00	32.00
POPDANO	95.00	234.00	249.00	58.00	208.00	312.00

The first axis (horizontal line) determines 62.3 per cent of the total model. It appears to be dominated by the categories of female and male respondents. We call this axis "sex dimension". By matching the solutions of the columns (the six categories of the combined variable of sex and age) and the rows (the different cultural competencies) to the first axis, it can be seen that men have less ability for fitting trousers than women. Dancing to pop music, however, is not correlated with the sex categories, but the categories of this variable correlate highly with the second (the vertical) axis, which determines 36.2 per cent of the total model. By

Figure 1: First Correspondence Analysis

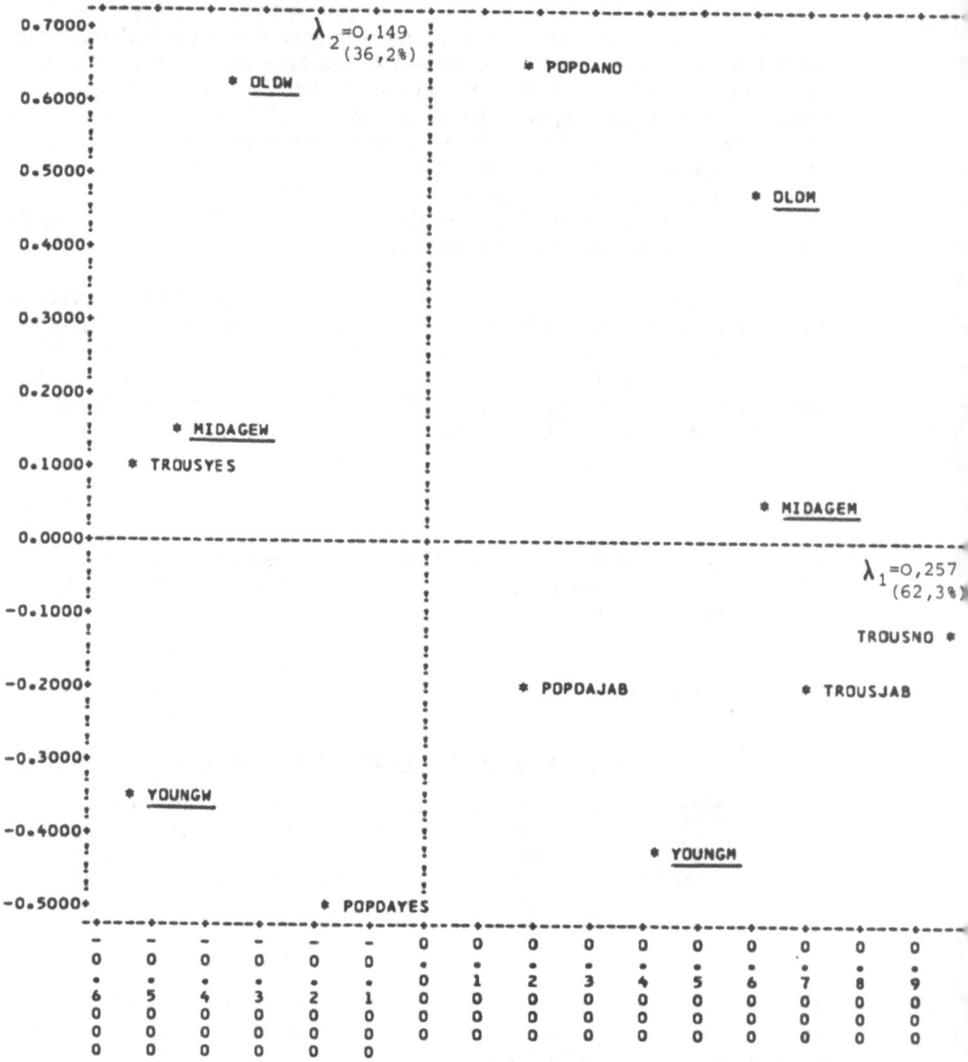

looking at the column variable it can be seen that old people (men and women) have rather little ability for dancing to pop music whereas the young people do have. We call this axis "age dimension".

The "sex" and "age" dimensions explain together 96.6 per cent of the total variation in the model. Only 3.4 per cent of the variation of the data can not be interpreted by the dimensions one and two.

A more detailed and precise interpretation is based on a numerical solution. It provides with scores for the correlations of columns and rows with the axes. This output is given in table 2.

Table 2: General Statistic

GENSTAT	MASS	SQCOR	INR	LOC1	QCOR1	INR1	LOC2	QCOR2	INR2
YOUNGM	0.202	0.993	0.183	0.429	0.492	0.144	-0.433	0.502	0.254
MIDAGEM	0.158	0.973	0.157	0.628	0.965	0.243	0.055	0.008	0.003
OLDM	0.104	0.979	0.155	0.608	0.604	0.150	0.479	0.375	0.160
YOUNGW	0.227	0.993	0.232	-0.535	0.680	0.253	-0.362	0.312	0.200
MIDAGEW	0.170	0.963	0.100	-0.460	0.874	0.140	0.146	0.088	0.024
OLDW	0.138	0.998	0.174	-0.360	0.251	0.070	0.622	0.748	0.359
TROUSYES	0.315	1.000	0.229	-0.539	0.968	0.355	0.098	0.032	0.020
TROUSJAB	0.054	0.936	0.073	0.696	0.863	0.101	-0.203	0.074	0.015
TROUSNO	0.133	0.997	0.305	0.963	0.981	0.480	-0.122	0.016	0.013
POPDAYES	0.227	0.993	0.156	-0.189	0.126	0.032	-0.495	0.867	0.374
POPDAJAB	0.080	0.663	0.022	0.178	0.284	0.010	-0.205	0.379	0.023
POPDANO	0.191	0.999	0.215	0.171	0.063	0.022	0.660	0.936	0.555

The first column (MASS) of table 2 lists the relative mass of each variable category, separately standardized for rows and columns. The second column (SQCOR) gives the variance explained by the first two axes. For example, 99.4 per cent of the variable "men up to 39 years" (YOUNGM), 100 per cent of the variable "ability for fitting trousers" (TROUSYES), but only 66.3 per cent of the variable "just a bit ability for dancing to pop music" (POPDAJAB) are explained by the first two axes.

The inertia (INR) measures the extent to which each variable determines the model. The values are calculated by multiplying the masses and the squared distances from the origin of the derived vector configuration - weighted by the relative part of each axis and standardized separately for row and column variables. It can be seen that the model receives its geometric orientation mainly from the inability for fitting trousers (INR=.305), the ability for fitting trousers (INR=.229), less from the inability and the ability for dancing to pop music and only to a negligible amount from the groups which have the named abilities just a bit. Column 6 and 9 can be interpreted similarly for each axis. It can be seen that the first axis (INR1) is determined to 83.5 per cent by the two categories "inability/ability for fitting trousers" (the two values in the column INR1 must be added), the second axis is determined to 92.9 per cent by the two extreme categories of the variable "ability for dancing to pop music".

All categories of the column variable (the combined variable of sex and age) are important for the determination of the geometric orientation of the total model (see INR) and the first axis (see INR1). Only very small influence on the geometric orientation of the second axis is given by the categories of "middle age women" (MIDAGEW) and "middle age men" (MIDAGEM) (see INR2).

Columns 4 and 7 give information on each variable's position of the first two axes, i.e. the coordinates of the vector endpoints location. Columns 5 and 8 contain the squared correlations with the axes. Their sum amounts to column 2, the total influence in the model. Column 2 can be interpreted similar to the communality in principal component analysis, columns 5 and 8 like squared factor loadings. The signs of the loadings are given by columns 4 and 7. The SQCOR and the two QCOR columns are most important for interpretation. Since the correlations indicate on which axes certain variables load jointly, they allow us to relate the combined variable of sex and age with the variables of cultural abilities.

The squared correlations of the variable categories define the positive or the negative section of an axis. In the given example the positive section of the first axis (the sex-dimension) is dominated by the three categories of men, the negative part by the three categories of women. Highly correlated with these categories are the different values of the "ability for fitting trousers". When comparing the signs in column 4, however, it can be seen that men are less skilled concerning this particular "cultural ability" than women.

The positive section of the second axis (the age-dimension) is defined by the old people (OLDW, OLDM), the negative part by the younger people (YOUNGM, YOUNGW). "Ability for dancing to pop music (POPDAYES)" stands on the same side as younger people, while "inability for dancing to pop music (POPDANO)" appears to be correlated with old age.

In the second part of this article, we will show that correspondence analysis produces very robust solutions. The addition of further variables to the model proofs to be the problen. Principal component analysis, for instance, is rather sensitive in this task. In our example, we added the following cultural abilities with three categories each: waltzing, playing chess, filling out tax formularies, adjusting a quartz watch, photographing and attaching a lamp. The column variable has not changed. The graphical solution of the extended model is given in figure 2.

When comparing the figures, we can see that the locations of the originally used categories have only slightly changed. The first axis in the second analysis (70.9 per cent explained variance) is determined by the sex categories, the second axis (23.5 per cent explained variance) is determined by the three categories of age. Analogously to the first analysis, we can use the same names for describing the axes. The difference between the two models of explained variance for the first axis (62.3 and 70.9) can be interpreted as an increase of the relative importance of this dimension.

The structure of the model has not changed. As in the first example, the ability (inability) for fitting trousers and the ability (inability) for dancing to pop music load on the same axes as before. The additional categories do not cause major distortion in the underlying correlations, i.e. the correlations of the categories (rows and columns) of model one remain to be the same as in model two. The numerical solution in table 3 provides with more details in this particular aspect.

Figure 2: Second Correspondence Analysis

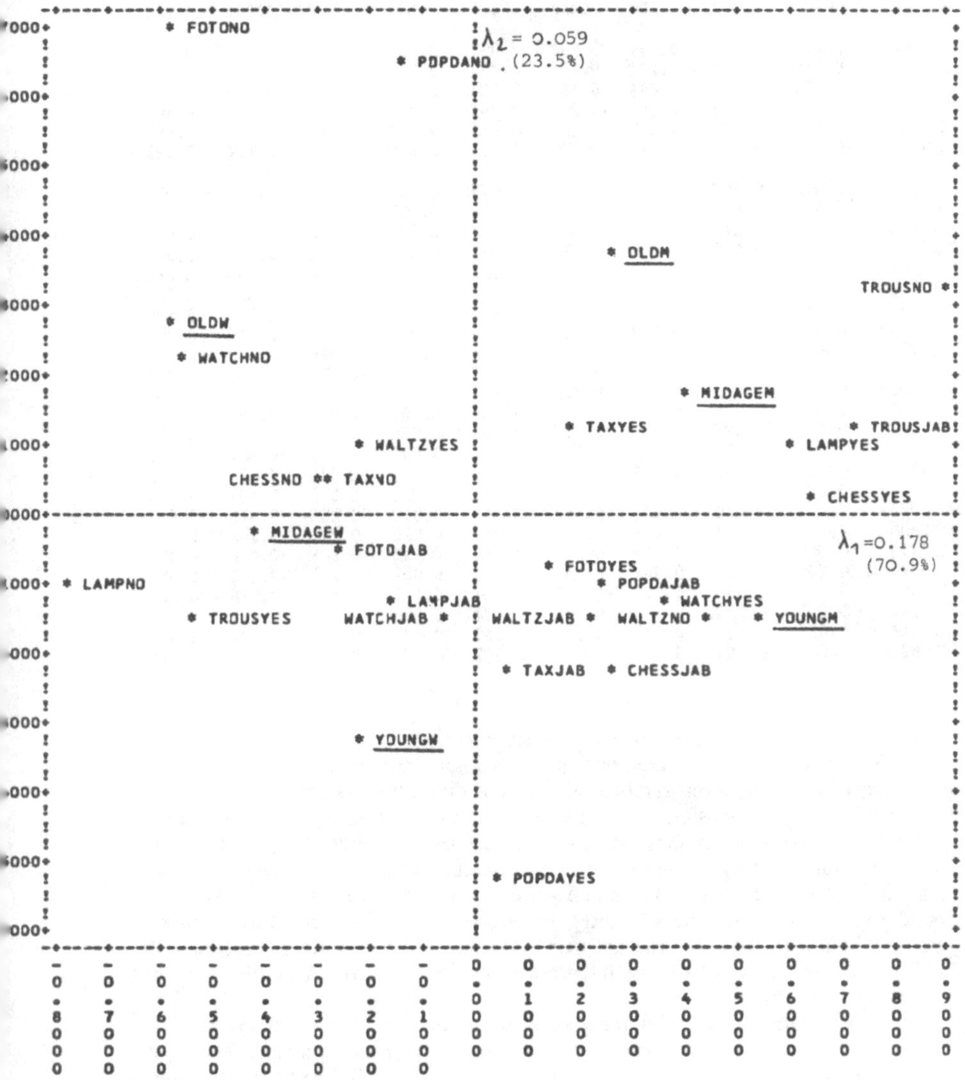

Table 3: General Statistic

GENSTAT	MASS	SQCOR	INR	LOC1	QCOR1	INR1	LOC2	QCOR2	INR2
YOUNGM	0.204	0.949	0.259	0.532	0.885	0.324	-0.144	0.065	0.071
MIDAGEM	0.159	0.911	0.132	0.403	0.777	0.145	0.167	0.134	0.075
OLDM	0.106	0.953	0.094	0.261	0.303	0.040	0.382	0.649	0.261
YOUNGW	0.225	0.976	0.142	-0.217	0.297	0.059	-0.328	0.679	0.409
MIDAGEW	0.169	0.920	0.126	-0.415	0.919	0.163	-0.015	0.001	0.001
OLDW	0.138	0.946	0.246	-0.589	0.772	0.268	0.280	0.174	0.183
WALTZYES	0.078	0.808	0.022	-0.218	0.679	0.021	0.095	0.130	0.012
WALTZJAB	0.026	0.924	0.008	0.226	0.651	0.007	-0.146	0.274	0.009
WALTZNO	0.023	0.673	0.030	0.447	0.602	0.026	-0.153	0.071	0.009
CHESSYES	0.029	0.932	0.050	0.637	0.931	0.066	0.023	0.001	0.000
CHESSJAB	0.019	0.944	0.009	0.267	0.561	0.007	-0.220	0.383	0.015
CHESSNO	0.079	0.939	0.031	-0.302	0.920	0.040	0.044	0.019	0.003
TROUSYES	0.079	0.999	0.096	-0.531	0.917	0.124	-0.159	0.083	0.034
TROUSJAB	0.013	0.954	0.029	0.713	0.924	0.038	0.128	0.030	0.004
TROUSNO	0.033	0.991	0.123	0.905	0.880	0.153	0.320	0.110	0.058
POPDAYES	0.057	0.996	0.065	0.048	0.008	0.001	-0.532	0.987	0.272
POPDAJAB	0.020	0.618	0.009	0.238	0.522	0.006	-0.103	0.097	0.004
POPDANO	0.048	0.996	0.087	-0.148	0.048	0.006	0.661	0.948	0.351
TAXYES	0.053	0.677	0.015	0.187	0.490	0.010	0.116	0.187	0.012
TAXJAB	0.030	0.939	0.007	0.057	0.058	0.001	-0.224	0.881	0.025
TAXNO	0.040	0.699	0.017	-0.272	0.685	0.017	0.039	0.014	0.001
WATCHYES	0.070	0.993	0.042	0.366	0.885	0.052	-0.127	0.107	0.019
WATCHJAB	0.012	0.470	0.003	-0.054	0.053	0.000	-0.153	0.418	0.005
WATCHNO	0.041	0.988	0.063	-0.569	0.842	0.075	0.237	0.146	0.039
LAMPYES	0.068	0.997	0.101	0.604	0.968	0.138	0.105	0.029	0.013
LAMPJAB	0.009	0.502	0.003	-0.158	0.299	0.001	-0.130	0.203	0.002
LAMPNO	0.049	0.998	0.123	-0.784	0.981	0.170	-0.105	0.018	0.009
FOTOYES	0.092	0.823	0.011	0.136	0.628	0.010	-0.076	0.196	0.009
FOTOJAB	0.023	0.887	0.007	-0.259	0.860	0.009	-0.046	0.027	0.001
FOTONO	0.011	0.764	0.049	-0.580	0.309	0.021	0.705	0.456	0.094

It can be seen that from the original columns only four categories remain to load on the first dimension, the other two are now highly connected with the second one. Nevertheless, the interpretation of the first dimension as sex-dimension and the second as age-dimension is the same as in the first analysis. In column 8 (QCOR2), it can be seen that additional to the two extreme categories of the ability for "dancing to pop music", only the middle category of "filling out a tax formulary" and - but less - the inability for "photographing" correlate with the second axis. Without the middle category of the ability for "adjusting a quartz watch" - which is loading on the third axis - all other categories are connected with the first one. In other words, the differentiations in these new variables are sex and not age specific.

Most important for receiving the geometric orientation of the first axis are the abilities and inabilities for "fitting trousers" and "attaching a lamp". The four categories of these two variables determine the first axis to 58.5 per cent (the four values in column 6 (INR1) must be added). The two extreme categories of the variable "dancing to pop music" determine the second axis to 62.3 per cent. Unimportant for a determination of this axis is the middle category, the ability for "filling out a tax formulary", although the category is highly correlated

(QCOR2=.881) with this axis. Nevertheless, this category can be interpreted as background variable - there is a high connection but no direct impact on this dimension. In the graphical display, it can be seen that this variable category is relatively near to the origin. Due to the fact that the squared distance from this point multiplied by the mass of the variable gives the inertia, the determination must be small.

In correspondence analysis the inclusion of additional variables has only a small influence on the geometric configuration of the start variables. Considering furthermore that there are no assumptions on the measurement level and on the distribution of the variables in correspondence analysis, it is recommended as a powerful instrument for explorative data analysis.

REFERENCES

BENZÉCRI, Jean-Paul. 1964. *Cours de Linguistique Mathématique*. Paris

BLASIUS, Jörg. 1987. "Korrespondenzanalyse - ein quantitatives Verfahren zur Analyse qualitativer Daten." *Historical Social Research - Historische Sozialforschung* 42/43, 172-189

BLASIUS, Jörg und ROHLINGER, Harald. 1988. "KORRES - Ein multivariates Programm zur Auswertung von zweidimensionalen Kontingenztabellen", in: Faulbaum, F. und Uehlinger, H.-M. (eds). *Fortschritte der Statistik-Software* 1, Stuttgart, 387-397

BLASIUS, Jörg und ROHLINGER, Harald. 1988. "KORRES - A Programme for Analysing Qualitative Data." *Psychometrika* 53, 425-426

BOURDIEU, Pierre. 1979. *La distinction. Critique social du jugement*. Paris

DANGSCHAT, Jens and BLASIUS, Jörg. 1987. "Social and Spatial Disparities in Warsaw in 1978: An Application of Correspondence Analysis to a 'Socialist' City." *Urban Studies* 24, 173-191

ESCOFIER-CODIER, Barbara. 1965. *L'Analyse des Correspondences*. Thèse du Doctorat, Rennes

GREENACRE, Michael. 1984. *Theory and Applications of Correspondence Analysis*. London

HIRSCHFIELD, H.O. 1935. "A Connection between Correlation and Contingency." *Proceedings of the Cambridge Philosophical Society* 31, 520-524

LEBART, Ludovic; MORINEAU, Alain and WARWICK, Kenneth M. 1984. *Multivariate Descriptive Statistical Analysis. Correspondence Analysis and Related Techniques for large Matrices*. New York

THIESSEN, Victor und ROHLINGER, Harald. 1988. "Die Verteilung von Aufgaben und Pflichten im ehelichen Haushalt." *Kölner Zeitschrift für Soziologie und Sozialpsychologie* 40, 640-658

COMPUTER-ASSISTED TELEPHONE INTERVIEWING (CATI) IN SOCIAL RESEARCH

Gerhard Christiansen
FORSA GmbH, Dortmund
FRG

The survey techniques of social research have been rapidly changing during the last twenty years. The classical face-to-face interview has been replaced more and more by the telephone interview: In the United States already 75 percent of survey research interviews are being conducted by telephone. In West Germany telephone interviewing has increased in numbers but it still amounts to only 14 percent.

Social research by telephone is not new. It has been applied for 50 years, mainly in industrial market research. The widespread distribution of telephones in the highly industrialized nations now makes it feasible to apply the telephone interview to surveys of the general population without getting severe biases with respect to most population parameters.

The major innovation is not the telephone interview as such, but the combination of telephone communication with the computer - the Computer-Assisted Telephone Interview (CATI).

CATI-systems use computer terminals operated by interviewers to display questions and accept responded answers in a telephone survey.

Since the early seventies, when the first CATI-systems were developed in the United States, many different types of CATI equipment have been constructed. The following overview of what CATI means and what it can do will be done by describing a specific system: The Research Machine, supplied by Pulse Train Technology Ltd (PTT), Guildford, UK, which is used by FORSA Gesellschaft für Sozialforschung und statistische Analysen mbH, a social research institute in Dortmund.

According to the purposes of a research institute serving the needs of many different clients - quick surveys for the actual identification of the opinion climate as well as complicated high-standard research for estimating specific population parameters to be used for prognosis and planning - and due to a heavy workload of interviews per day, FORSA uses a CATI system which offers all tasks of the social research process in an integrated and flexible way.

The Research Machine represents an integrated system of hardware and software, consisting of a number of application modules, the operating system, the computer - a DEC micro VAX-II - and the 45 terminals which serve the interviewers and the researchers who formulate the questionnaires, code answers from open-ended questions or analyse the data.

The cornerstone of the integrated research machine is a special programming language called QSL (Questionaire Specification Language). The QSL is a simple free format language without special control forms.

The language is used to write the questionnaire and to specify the question formats and data constraints. By writing a questionnaire, at the same time several other tasks of the research process are accomplished:

1. Presentation of the questionnaire on VDU-screens for CATI-interviewing.
2. Specification of the data-structure for key-entry, for checking and cleaning the data.
3. Production of a data base for data-analysis.
4. Specification of labels and text for the tables.

Without much programming the questionnaire is ready for interviewing as soon as it is typed into the machine. The interviewing module controls by pre-programmed and flexible masks the presentation of questions on the VDU-screen, by specifying the order of questions, branching instructions, response formats and checks. The interviewing module accepts and validates the data which are entered. Other features allow that series of questions are displayed in randomised order. Depending on the answers to previous questions the wording of questions can be changed: Some possible answers which do not apply to certain respondents are selectively removed. Scripts can be written to include the answers to previous questions.

Names can be displayed. Several answers can be combined, sums can be added up and the arithmetic results can be displayed embedded in the question text. Consistency checks over the course of an interview in order to detect discrepancies in respondent replies are readily applied.

CATI is not restricted to interviewing with standardized questionnaires. Answers to open-ended questions can be typed into the VDU and the open-ended coding module regulates the coding of the answers. That can be done immediately after finishing the interviews and while interviewing with other respondents is still going on.

Sampling has also been facilitated by CATI. The sampling units are selected automatically generating random numbers to be used as phone numbers. Integrating the computer with the telephone exchange system of the institute makes is possible that the dialling is done automatically and calls are directly transferred to the workstations of the interviewers. Hence, the interviewers only get households that are ready to talk.

The sample module distributes the sampling units to the interviewers. It takes a fresh sampling unit and assigns it to the first available interviewer working on the survey. The quota control module monitors completion of prescribed proportions (such as the regional distribution of the interviews) for stratified samples.

An appointments module helps scheduling the interviews. If a potential respondent is not able to be interviewed immediately, but agrees to an appointment at a later time, the interviewer calls up the appointment module and types the time of the call to be made into the machine. At the appointed time the machine will remember the appointment and assign the interview to the next available interviewer. It is further possible to programme a schedule for the repetitionof calls to engaged numbers and not answering ones based on a complicated system of priorities of calls and the likelihood of getting in touch with the respondents.

A major advantage of telephone interviewing is that it can be performed at a centralized location which in turn makes possible a close supervision of the work. The supervisors use a specific supervisor module of the Research Machine which shows the current state of all surveys for which interviewing is going on as well as productivity statistics of the whole work force or for individual interviewers. From her work station the supervisor can start and close surveys and assign and de-assign the interviewers to the surveys.

The immediate entry of CATI-data means that it is possible to run the data analysis as soon as the interview has been finished. A tabulation module provides the software for constructing tables with great flexibility of layout and text editing. Since SAS and SPSS statistical packages are available on the VAX/VMS computers they can also be used for data analysis.

The integration of several modules means that the Research Machine can be used not only for conducting computer assisted telephone surveys. It can be a very efficient tool for the analysis of historical documents, newspaper clips and other written material. Via the data entry module the texts can be stored by a data base module. The retrieval can be accomplished by a database searching module working from an interactive terminal where the text can also be analysed by calling up the on-line coding module and the various statistical packages.

Survey research has been substantially changed by CATI: The quality of measurement has improved because interviewing is a much more controlled activity.

1. The work load of the interviewers has been reduced enormously since all administrative tasks are left to the computer to do and the interviewers, therefore, can concentrate on the more important tasks of motivating the respondents and eliciting correct and relevant answers.
2. Interviewers do not need to remember anything said previously since the computer provides the necessary screening or sequencing.
3. The centralized location of interviewing makes it possible that the researcher is in much closer contact with the interviewing process. Researchers know what is going on and can immediately correct questions and interviewer behavior if something goes wrong.

CATI allows tailor-made research designs for all research questions which can be solved by surveys. It allows the construction of very complex questionnaires with intricate branching. Efficient and sophisticated sampling can be applied in extremely short time. Specific population segments, for which no sampling frames are available, can easily be interviewed by screening random digit dialling samples.

The whole research process is accelerated not only by the advantages of the telephone (that is sampling based on phone numbers and the omission of travel time) but also by the integration of several tasks of the research process, which now can be accomplished at the same time (questionnaire writing and data base construction or interviewing and data entry/coding).

The acceleration of the research process makes it possible to elicit information about social reality "just in time". Interviewing can take place when things happen. For instance, CATI-surveys can find out and report how people feel and react to political or media events immediately after they have occured.

FULL-QUASI-LIKELIHOOD ESTIMATION OF STRUCTURAL EQUATION MODELS WITH INCOMPLETE DATA

Steffen M. Kühnel
Zentralarchiv für Empirische Sozialforschung, Cologne
FRG

1. Introduction

In social sciences the analysis of structural equation models(1) has been established as a powerful approach to testing empirical hypotheses. Each analysis is based on two steps. In the first specification step the assumed relationships of a real world sector are transformed in a structural equation model. Usually, relationships between variables are represented by linear equations. In the second estimation step sampled data are used for estimating unknown model parameters as weights in these linear equations and for examining the correspondence of model and empirical data. If a model fits the data, the hypotheses implied by this model are confirmed. Otherwise they have probably to be modified.

For example, a social scientist may assume that an unobservable attitude influences the response behavior to the items in a questionnaire. In order to test this hypothesis he formulates a structural equation model in which the observed response variables are specified as linear functions of one unobserved latent attitude variable and uncorrelated residual variables. If this model is right the empirical covariances or correlations between the responses to the items in the questionnaire should show a specific pattern which will be proved by the estimation step.

The methods used for estimating the model parameters require a random sample without any missing data. But most often some data are missing. One source of missing data is, for example, panel mortality (attrition) in panel studies. The existence of missing data raises two questions:

a. How robust are our statistical methods under the condition of ignoring the missing data problem and analysing only those cases without missing data?
b. Are there any other techniques for investigating structural equation models with such incomplete data?

2. The Ignorability of Missingness

It can be shown (cf. Allison, 1987; Muthén et al., 1987) that the ignorability of missing data is dependent on the mechanism which generates missing data. RUBIN (1976) distinguishes three situations:

a. If the probability that some data are missing is not depending on the properties which are observed and is not depending on the unobserved properties, then these data are missing completely at random;

b. If the probability that some data are missing is not depending on the unobserved properties, but may depend on the properties that are observed, then these data are missing at random;
c. If the probability that some data are missing is not depending on the properties that are observed but depends on those properties that are not observed, then the data are observed at random;

If the data are missing completely at random, ignorating cases with missing data yields no problem. The usual statistical methods give correct results. But in all other situations the results may be biased. Therefore, wrong conclusions about the hypotheses under investigation can be drawn if only a subsample including cases without missing data is taken into consideration.

There is also an important difference between the two situations when the data are not completely random. If the data are observed at random, then a valid investigation of structural equation models needs the explicit specification of the missing data mechanism; that is, the process generating missing data itself must be taken into account as a part of the model. But if the data are missing at random it is only necessary to integrate appropriately all available information. The process which has generated missing data can be ignored. An adequate technique for this situation is the full-quasi-likelihood method.

3. Full-Quasi-Likelihood Estimation of Structural Equation Models

The full-quasi-likelihood (FQL) method is using the specification of structural equation models with latent variables and a simultaneous estimation for several data sets. If there are missing data in the sample the total sample is broken into subgroups without any missing data but with different numbers of observed variables. Imagine a scientist who wants to analyse responses to three items. Some respondents have answered to all of these three items but for some other respondents the answers to one or two items are missing. Now, it is possible to form one subgroup including the respondents without any missing data, a second subgroup including respondents for whom only the data of the first and the second item are valid, a third one, in which the data of the first and the third item are valid and so on.

For each of these subgroups a structural equation model is specified with identical structure and parameter values of the latent variables. Because not all items are observed in all subgroups, both, the theoretical constructs and the items are modelized as latent variables. Additionally, in each group auxiliary variables are specified representing the non-missing responses of an item. If responses to an item are observed, a link is made between the latent item variable and the corresponding auxiliary variable. Formally, the link is an identity equation which sets the auxiliary variable to be equal to the item variable. If an item is not observed in a group there is no link between the latent item variable and the respective auxiliary variable.

In the estimation step model parameters are estimated simultanously across all subgroups resulting in unique parameter estimations and fit measures. Judging a specific structure is done by comparing the fit of that model structure with the fit of an appropriate baseline model. In the baseline model only the means, variances and covariances of the items will be estimated as model parameters. Most often the fit of the baseline model is bad. Otherwise, a good fit of the baseline model can be interpreted as a hint that the data are missing completely at random.

4. An Example: The Reliability and Stability of the Attitude Towards the 1987 German Census

In this example the attitudes towards the 1987 German census are investigated. Figure 1 shows the design of an evaluation study on the 1987 German census.(2) In the first panel wave, 1941 respondents were interviewed in a representative sample of the German electorate before the census had started. Only 1097 respondents (56.5%) could be interviewed in the second panel wave shortly after the census. About half a year after the census, 952 respondents have been interviewed a third time. Additionally, the third wave includes 69 persons with missing second wave interview. Thus, the complete delitions of all cases with missing panel observations would reduce the sample to only 952 cases that is 49% of the first wave sample size. Using the FQL method the available data of all 1941 respondents will be incorporated in the analysis.

Figure 1:

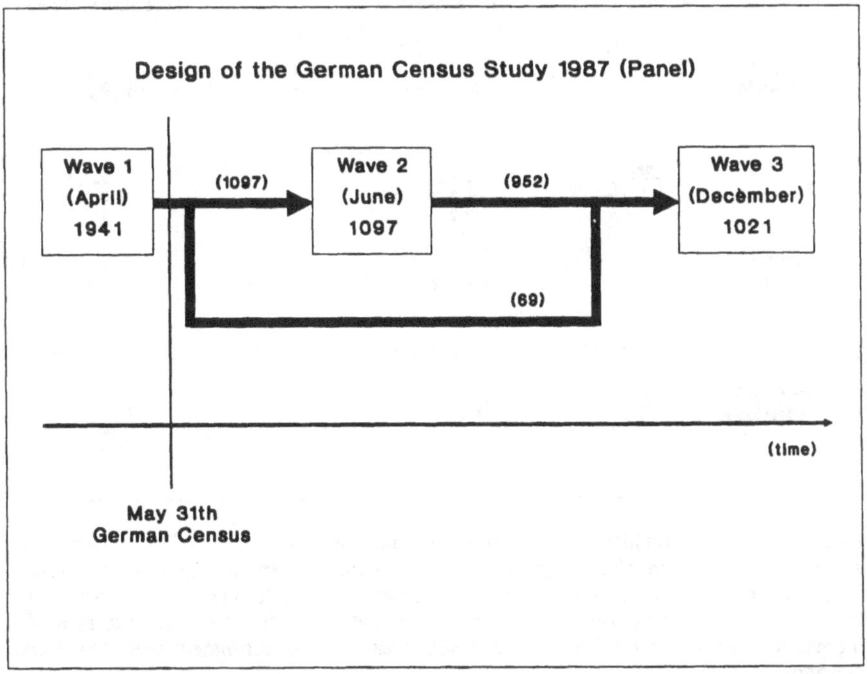

To do this, four subgroups are differentiated. The first group includes 952 respondents without any missing data; the second groups includes 69 respondents with first and third wave interviews only; the third group includes those 145 respondents with first and second wave interviews only; finally, the fourth group includes 775 respondents with first wave interviews only.

In all interviews the respondents were asked to give their general opinion on the 1987 German census on a seven point scale. The first category of this scale represents strong disagreement with the census, the seventh category represents strong agreement. The responses are interpreted as an indicator of the general attitude towards the census. To estimate the reliability and stability of this attitude a single indicator three-wave panel model is specified following the research tradition of Heise (1969) and Jagodzinski and Kühnel (1987).

Figure 2:

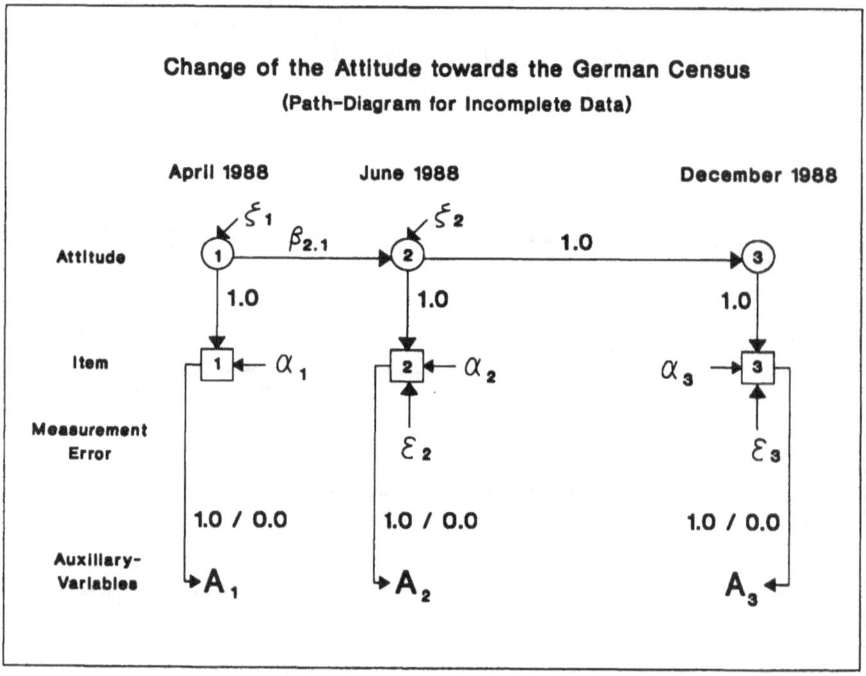

Figure 2 shows a graphical representation of the postulated model. Let us first look at the upper part of the diagram. The item variables are assumed to be linear functions of attitude variables and measurement errors. In the path diagram the influence of a variable on another one is indicated by an arrow. Greek symbols represent unknown model parameters which are to be estimated with the FQL method.

The main assumption of the model is the nominal parallelity of the second and third wave measurement. This means that in the second and third wave the reliabilties are equal and that there has been no attitude change in this time interval.(3) An attitude change is assumed only after the first wave. For technical reasons the first-wave measurement-error variance is set to zero.

Note two pecularities of the FQL method shown in figure 2. First, the method requires the specification of means in each structural equation model. In Figure 2 the means are symbolized as α-coefficients. Second, there are specified auxiliary variables in the model, symbolized by capital "A's". Whereas the upper part of the path diagram is identical in all four subgroups, the bottom part is varying. If the responses to an item are missing in any subgroup the corresponding auxiliary variable and the link between it and the item is omitted.(4)

Figure 3:

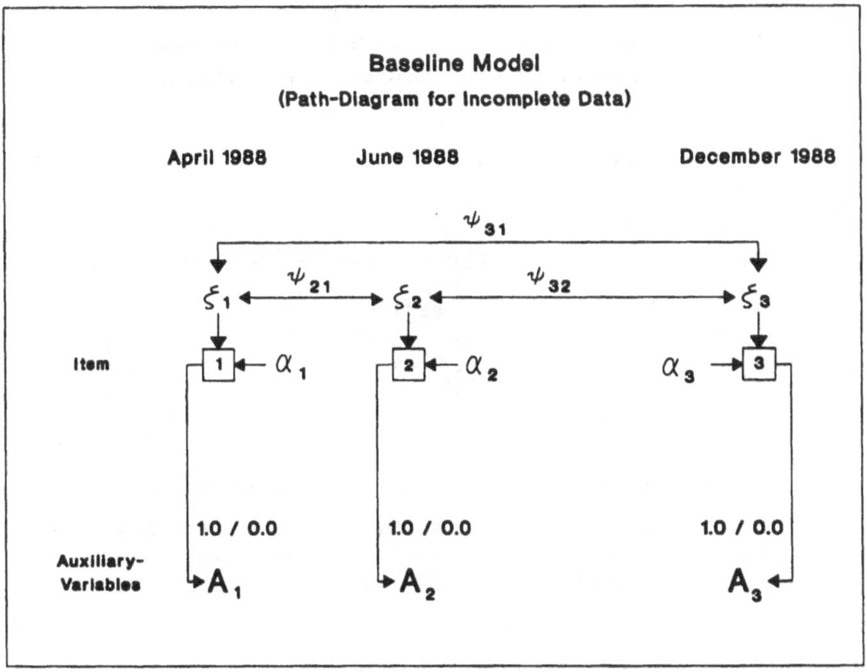

In the estimation step the model parameters and the goodness of fit are estimated simultaniously across the four subgroups. The fit of the model is necessaryly rather bad if missing data are not missing completely at random. Therefore, a judgement of the goodness of fit requires the comparison with a baseline model. The path diagram of an appropriate baseline model for the three-item data is shown in figure 3. In contrast to the model shown in figure 2 there is no restricted factor structure above the items in the baseline model.

The results of the final estimation step are given in figure 4. At first glance the fit of the attitude-change model looks very bad, but the comparison with the baseline models leads to the opposite conclusion. The fit of both models is nearly the same. The chisquare difference is only 0.04 with 2 degrees of freedom. This value corresponds to a probability level of 0.98, a nearly perfect fit.

The bad fit of the baseline models proves that the missingness is not completely at random. It is not possible to decide wether the data are missing at random or wether the data are observed at random. But there is some evidence that the data are indeed missing at random. Respondents who disagree with the census in the first interview have a higher probability for missingness in the following interviews. That is, the initially observed attitude towards the census correlates with the readiness for further interviews.

Figure 4:

Change of the Attitude towards the German Census

Standardized Solution (Auxiliary Variables Omitted)

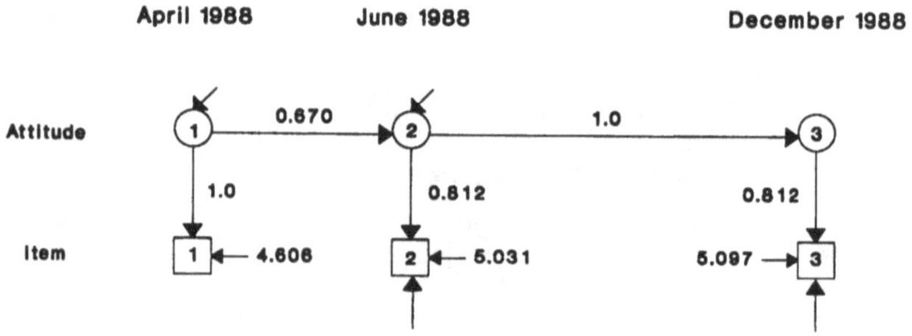

Attitude Change Model	Chisquare=34.23 df=14 Prob.<0.01
Baseline Model	Chisquare=34.19 df=12 Prob.<0.01
Modelfit	Chisquare= 0.04 df= 2 Prob.=0.98

The corrected fit of the attitude-change model is a confirmation of the assumption of nominally parallel measurements in the second and third interviews. Therefore, the parameter estimations can be interpreted. The standardized factor loadings of the items are the square roots of the reliability. The loading of 0.812 yields to satisfactory high reliability estimation of 0.66. The value of 1.0 in the first wave cannot be interpreted because it is a technical artifact. But one may assume that in the first interview the reliability is the same as in the following interviews.

The most interesting consequence of the model fit is that the assumption of perfect stability between second and third interviews is hold. After the census has started, there seems to be no further attitude change to it. This is also confirmed by almost identical means in the second and third wave.

On the other side, there are changes between first and second wave. The mean in the first wave is clearly lower than the means in the following interviews. Before the census, respondents had disagreed more often with the census than after the census. A further hint at attitude change is the correlation of only 0.67 between the attitudes in the first and second or third waves. But this value must be interpreted carefully. It is attenuated because there is no measurement error specified in the first wave. If one assumes a reliability of 0.66 in the first wave the correlation increases to a more realistic value of 0.825.

5. Conclusion

Missing data are a serious problem in the analysis of structural equation models. If data are not missing completely at random, the danger of wrong conclusions increases if one ignores cases with missing data. Fortunately, the FQL method warrants consistent model estimation if the data are missing at random. Using attrited panel data I have shown the proceeding of this new technique.

The FQL method may result in biased estimations if the data are observed at random. In such situations, only the explicit and correct specification of the process generating the missing data warrants unbiased estimations. But if the missing-data generating process is not correctly specified, the bias of miss-specification can be greater than the bias of FQL estimation. On the other side, the bias of the FQL method will be smaller if there are observed variables which correlate with the true missing-data generating process. Therefore, it seems nearly always the best to estimate structural equation models with the FQL method if there are a lot of missing data in a sample.

NOTES

1. For an introduction to this approach see Long (1983) or Saris and Stronkhorst (1984).
2. Figure 1 shows only the valid cases of the representative three wave panel part of our evaluation study. The full design of the study is more complex (cf. Scheuch et al., forthcoming). Moreover, only panel attrition is considered in this example. For reasons of simplicity, 11 respondents with other sources of missingness are excluded from the analysis.
3. Attitude change is measured here as a non perfect correlation.
4. This is true only in principle. The LISREL program (Jöreskog and Sörbom, 1988), used for computing the FQL solution, requires the same number of variables in each subgroup. Consequently, the program also needs as input data first and second moments for all auxiliary variables in each group. These moments are the empirical values if responses to an item are observed. But if the responses are missing in a subgroup, the variance of the corresponding auxiliary variable is set to the arbitrary value one. The mean and the covariances with the other auxiliary variables are to be set to zero.

   In the specification as a LISREL model, all auxiliary variables are formulated as observed Variables. If there are responses to an item, the loading of the auxiliary variable on this item is set to be one and the corresponding measurement error variance is set to be zero. If responses are missing the loading of the auxiliary variable, that item is set to be zero and the variance of the measurement errors of the auxiliary variable are estimated as an unknown parameter.

A further peculiarity of the LISREL program is the handling of means. If the responses of an item are observed, the mean of that item is restricted to be equal to the corresponding means in the other subgroups with non-missing data on this item. But if the responses are missing, the mean is estimaterd as an unknown parameter resulting in an estimate of zero as given as mean of the auxiliary variable in the data input.

REFERENCES

ALLISON, P.D. 1987. "Estimation of Linear Models with Incomplete data" in: Clogg, C.C. (ed.). *Sociological Methodology 1987*. Washington, DC: The American Sociological Association, 71-103

HEISE, D.R. 1969. "Seperating Reliability and Stability in Test-Retest-Correlation." *American Sociological Review* 34, 93-101

JAGODZISNKI, W. and KÜHNEL, S.M. 1987. "Estimation of Reliability and Stability in Single-Indicator Multiple-Wave Models." *Sociological Methods and Research* 15, 219-258

JÖRESKOG, K.G. and SÖRBOM, D. 1988. *LISREL 7. A Guide to the Program and Applications*. Chicago: SPSS Inc.

LONG, J.S. 1983. *Covariance Structure Models*. Beverly Hills: Sage

MUTHEN, B.; KAPLAN, D. and HOLLIS, M. 1987. "On Structural Equation Modeling with Data that are Not Missing Completely at Random." *Psychometrica* 52, 431-462

RUBIN, D.B. 1976. "Inference and Missing Data." *Biometrica* 63, 581-592

SARIS, W. and STRONKHORST, H. 1984. *Causal Modelling in Nonexperimental Research*. Amsterdam: Sociometric Research Foundation

SCHEUCH, E.K.; GRÄF, L. and KÜHNEL, S.M. Forthcoming. *Volkszählung und Volkszählungsprotest*. Statistisches Bundesamt (Hrsg.). Schriftenreihe Forum der Bundesstatistik. Stuttgart: Metzler-Poeschel

ANALYSIS OF NON-METRIC DEPENDENT VARIABLES

Ulrich Küsters
Bergische Universität Wuppertal
FRG

1. Introduction

This extended abstract presents several regression type models to analyze causal relationships of non-metric dependent variables with independent variables of arbitrary measurement level. A typical example of the application of a non-metric variable model is the analysis of the involvement of German teachers with national socialism dependent on the explanatory variables religion, sex, civil, birth control and size of residence. In this case, the dependent variable is not ordered categorically with several categories representing the membership in different NS organizations like NSDAP, SA, SS etc., where no natural ordering exists within the categories. Hence, the statistical variation of the dependent variables is restricted by the logical possibilities represented by the different categories. However, in metric regression models the variation of *all* variables is not restricted. Instead, all variables can vary over the entire length of the axis of real numbers. Due to this unlimited variation, the application of least squares may lead to the prediction of *negative probabilities* and *probabilities beyond* 1. Additionally, the least squares estimator is inefficient due to heteroscedasticity. Hence, special models must be used to analyze non-metric variables with a limited domain of values.

2. Construction Principles for Models to Analyze Unordered Categorical Variables

Conceptually, most regression type models to analyze unordered categorical variables may be explained by the random utility maximation principle. The key feature of a random utility maximation model is the assignment of a random utility U_{ti} to each category $i \in \{1, 2, ..., C\}$ of the dependent variable by a linear function disturbed by an error term:

$$U_{ti} = x_t \beta_i + \epsilon_{ti}, \qquad i = 1,..., C; \quad t = 1,..., n$$

The parameters β_i and the error terms ϵ_{ti} are specific to category i. The selection probability of category $y_t = i$ given by the values of the regressor x_t of case $t = 1,..., T$ is then specific by

$$P(y_t = i) = P(U_{ti} > U_{tj} \text{ for all } j = 1,..., C; j \neq i).$$

---

* Comments and suggestion on earlier drafts by Gerhard Arminger are gratefully acknowledged.

Note that the random utilities U_{ti} can vary over the entire real axis. Nevertheless, the selection probabilities are restricted between 0 and 1. Different error terms generate different model types. Two model types are common: This specification of the error term vector $\epsilon_t = (\epsilon_{t1},..., \epsilon_{tC})^T$ as a multivariate normal with expectation 0 and covariance matrix Σ yields the multinominal probit model (Daganz 1979). The multinominal logit model (Mc Fadden 1981, Bock 1975) emerges under the condition that the components $\{\epsilon_{tj}\}_{j=1,...,C}$ of the vector valued error term ϵ_t are independently distributed as type I extreme-value random variables with distribution function $F(z) = \exp\{-z-\exp(-z)\}$. The main advantage of the multinominal probit is its flexibility. Similarities among different categories can easily be taken into account using positive correlation terms in Σ. The main disadvantage, however, is that multinominal probits with more than 4 categories are computationally very difficult to estimate. While the multinominal logit cannot take similarities of categories into account it is usually preferred because of its straightforward estimation. This selection probabilities of the multinominal logit model can be expressed explicitly as

$$P(y_t = i \mid x_t) = \frac{\exp\{x_t ß_i\}}{1 + \Sigma^c_{j=2} \exp\{x_t ß_j\}}$$

where the standardization restriction $ß_1 = 0$ is used. The multinominal logit belongs to the class of exponentional models. Hence, the log-likelihood function is concave which simplifies estimation greatly. If all variables are unordered categorical the estimation of the parameters in a multinominal logit model may be performed by the estimation of an equivalent loglinear model (Jarausch, Arminger and Thaller 1986).

Noteworthy is the fact that the multinominal logit and the multinominal probit models specialize to the corresponding binomial models in the case of dichotomous dependent variables. Nevertheless, both models are rather different in the case of more than 2 categories because unobservable heterogeneity like similarities among the different categories cannot be handled within the multinominal logit framework. Due to the enormous difficulties of estimating multinominal probits, the multinominal logit was generalized to nested logits and tree-extreme value models by McFadden (1981) which allow the explicit modelling of some similarity structures.

3. Models to Analyze Ordered Categorical Variables

Models to explain the variation of unordered categorical variables using random utility maximization are based on the fact that the different alternatives of the dependent variable are distinct without any ordering among the alternatives. However, quite often a natural ordering among the alternatives occurs. A special class of models based on thresholds utilizes the additional information about relative ranks. The basic idea of threshold is the existence of an unobservable (latent) metric variable η which may vary over the whole real axis $\Re$. The latent variable is determined stochastically by the explanatory variables and may be interpreted as the propensity to fall into category i rather than into a reference category. Since the categories are ordered, only the first or the last category may be chosen as a reference category. Additionally, the real axis is partitioned by C - 1 ordered thresholds $\tau_1 < \tau_2 < ... < \tau_{C-1}$.

Whenever the latent variable $_t$ falls into the interval $(\tau_{i-1}, \tau_i]$, the dependent variable y_t lies in category $i \in \{1,..., C\}$. Given $x_t\beta$, the stochastic variation between the categories is caused by the stochastic behaviour of the disturbance term ϵ_t. Formally, threshold models may be constructed by the following equations

$$\eta_t = x_t\beta + \epsilon_t, \qquad t = 1,..., n,$$

$$y_t = i \Leftrightarrow \eta_t \; (\tau_{i-1}, \tau_i) \qquad i = 1, 2,..., C; \qquad t = 1,..., n$$

where it is assumed that the thresholds are ordered $-\infty = \tau_0 < \tau_1 < \tau_2 < ... < \tau_{C-1} < \tau_C = \infty$. Again, different models are generated by different error assumptions. The ordinal probit model emerges by setting ϵ_t to be standard normally distributed with distribution function $F(\epsilon) = (\sqrt{2\pi})^{-1} \int^{\epsilon}_{-\infty} \exp(-\frac{1}{2}z^2)dz$. If ϵ_t is distributed logistically with distribution function $F(\epsilon) = e^{\epsilon}/(1 + e^{\epsilon})$ the ordinal logit model (Bock 1975) is generated. Other models (Mc Cullagh 1980) can easily be constructed using an appropriate continuous distribution function for ϵ_t.

Note that a natural ordering of the dependent variable y_t does not suffice for choosing a threshold model. This is due to the fact that the effects attributed by the independent variables may be U-shaped in the sense that low and high values of the independent variables may yield high propensities toward high categories while only median-valued independent variables may lead to low propensities. In such a case two alternatives remain: In analogy to nonlinear metric regression a nonlinear predictor model in terms of β may be formulated. The second alternative consists in ignoring the natural ordering so that a model suitable for unordered variables is used. The stereotype model proposed by Anderson (1984) is a modification of the second alternative in using multinominal logits with special parametrizations incorporating certain ordering types.

A statistical treatment similar to the analysis of ordinal variables may be given to grouped metric dependent variables, where the exact value is not known but only the class membership within an interval. Ordinal models based on thresholds can be easily adapted by setting the thresholds to the fixed class bounds (Stewart 1983). Additionally the variance of ϵ_t must be freed.

Models to analyze censored variables may be easily incorporated within the framework of threshold models. A suitable solution of this problem is a mixture of the ordinary regression model with the binary probit model based on a censoring threshold. These approaches are described under the heading of Tobit-class models in Amemiya (1985).

4. Example

To demonstrate the analysis of nonmetric variables, a simple example applying a binary logit models to a 5-dimensional contingency table is given. The example and data set to be reanalysed is taken from Jarausch and Arminger (1988)(1) where a detailed analysis can be found. The focus of the study cited above is the analysis of the disposition of German teachers in the *Third Reich* towards membership in the "NSDAP" depending on factors like religion (REL), birth control (COH), size of residence (RES) and sex (SEX). The categories and coding of these variables are collected in the next table:

Symbol	Variable	Categories and Coding
REL	religion	1: Protestant, 2: Catholic, 3: None
COH	cohort	1: Empire, 2: late Empire, 3: early Weimar, 4: late Weimar, 5: Third Reich
RES	size of residence	1: rural, 2: urban
SEX	sex	1: male, 2: female

The size of residence, which was measured originally as a metric variable, was aggregated to a binary coded variable. Using this transformation, all variables can be considered to be unordered categorical. Such a model is most easily fitted by GLIM using the binary logit model formulation in connection with design matrices commonly used in the analysis of variance (Bock 1975). The estimation of a main effect model with the regressors REL, COH and SEX coded as cornered effects yields the following output:

```
[o]   terms =  1 + REL + COH + RES + SEX
[o]           estimate      s.e.      parameter
[o]      1     -0.8064    0.07698     1
[o]      2     -0.6503    0.05080     REL (2)
[o]      3      -1.293    0.06763     REL (3)
[o]      4      0.6514    0.08425     COH (2)
[o]      5      0.9343    0.08040     COH (3)
[o]      6       1.054    0.08329     COH (4)
[o]      7      0.5584    0.09897     COH (5)
[o]      8     -0.5912    0.04533     RES (2)
[o]      9      -1.370    0.05599     SEX (2)
```

The parameter estimates can be read as follows. Protestants were more often NSDAP-members then catholics, while persons without religious denomination were relatively rarely members of the NS-party. The effects of the birth cohort to membership was typically U-shaped. Persons who belong to the birth cohort of the early Weimar and the late Weimar were much more often involved in being members of the NSDAP than persons belonging to the birth cohorts of the Empire and the Third Reich. The reason of this U-effect may be attributed to two causes. The birth cohort of the Empire was mainly traditionally educated with strong emphasis on respect for the monarchy. The reason for the relative low frequency of NSDAP-members in the birth cohort of the Third Reich may be attributed to two causes. First, soldiers were not allowed to be members of the NSDAP. Second, within the war years the general propensity to become a member was much lowered. The effect of sex is obvious. The Nazi ideology emphasized that women should be mainly restricted to the private sphere in "producing" soldiers. Hence, their contribution to politics was not acknowledged. The second point and the higher interaction effects can easily be included by the addition of effects like +REL.SEX respectively +REL.SEX+REL.COH+SEX.COH+REL.COH.SEX which can be abbreviated in the case of third order effects to REL*COH*SEX.

5. Conclusions

Regression models to analyze non-metric dependent variables are readily used given the current state of statistical model theory. Nevertheless, many common software packages like GLIM (Payne 1985, McCullagh and Nelder 1983), LIMDEP (Greene 1986), SPSS, SAS and BMDP suffer either from the insufficient coverage of estimable models or from difficulty of use. While LIMDEP offers a broad range of estimators for nonmetric dependent variable models, the incorporation of qualitative regressors is unfeasible because the automatic generation of design matrices is not supported. If the analysis is restricted to dichotomous dependent variables or loglinear models GLIM is much easier to use, due to the automatic generation of designs using a simple fit directive. Because of the numerically difficult and demanding computation of multinominal probits no programming system provides its estimation. One alternative to the use of the statistical systems mentioned above is the use of the general matrix language GAUSS (Edlefsen and Jones 1986) which includes several application modules to estimate loglinear models, multinominal logit as well as ordinal and binary logit and probit models. Programming in GAUSS is described in Küsters and Arminger (1988). To increase the use of adequate models for data sets involving non-metric variables, statisticians working in the area of statistical computing are required to lower the amount of programming being done by non-specialists. Beyond the computational problems any user of non-metric variable models must direct his attention to the problem of structural and sampling zeros (Albert and Anderson 1984) and to the problem of model specification. Both issues are addressed in Armiger and Küsters (1986).

NOTE

The author is indebted to Gerhard Arminger for the permission to use this data set.

REFERNCES

ALBERT, A. and ANDERSON, J.A. 1984. "On the Existence of Maximum Likelihood Estimates in Logistic Regression Models." *Biometrika* 71, 1-10

AMEMIYA, T. 1985. *Advanced Economitrics*. Oxford

ANDERSON, J.A. 1984. "Regression and Ordered Categorical Variables (with discussion)." *Journal of the Royal Statistical Society* B, 1-30

ARMINGER, G. und KÜSTERS, U. 1986. "Statistische Verfahren zur Analyse qualitativer Variablen." *Forschungsberichte der Bundesanstalt für Straßenwesen 147*, Aachen

BOCK, R.D. 1975. *Multivariate Statistical Methods in Behaviourial Research*. New York

DAGANZO, C. 1979. *Multinominal Probit - The Theory and Its Application to Demand Forecasting*. New York

EDLEFSEN, L. and JONES, S. 1986. *GAUSS - Programming Language Manual*. Kent, Aptech System Inc.

GREENE, W. 1986. *LIMDEP - Reference - Manual*. New York University

JARAUSCH, K.H. and ARMINGER, G. 1988. "The German Teaching Profession and National Socialism: A Demographic Logit Model for Nazi Party Membership." Submitted to the *Journal of Interdisciplinary History*

JARAUSCH, K.H.; ARMINGER, G. und THALLER, M. 1985. *Quantitative Methoden in der Geschichtswissenschaft - Eine Einfürhung in die Forschung, Datenverarbeitung und Statistik*. Darmstadt

KÜSTERS, U. und ARMINGER, G. 1988. *Programmieren in GAUSS - Eine Einführung in das Programmieren statistischer und numerischer Algorithmen*. Stuttgart

MADDALA, G.S. 1983. *Limited-dependent and Qualitative Variables in Econometrics*. Cambridge

MCCULLAGH, P. 1980. "Regression models for ordinal data (with discussion)." *Journal of the Royal Statistical Society* B 20, 109-142

MCCULLAGH, P. and NELDER, J.A. 1983. *Generalized Linear Models*. London

MCFADDEN, D. 1981. "Econometric Models of Probabilistic Choice", in: Manski, C.F. and McFadden, D. (eds.). *Structural Analysis of Discrete Data with Econometric Applications*. Cambridge, Massachusetts, 198-272

PAYNE, C.D. 1985. (ed.). *The GLIM System Release 3.77*. Oxford, NAG - Royal Statistical Society

STEWART, M.B. 1983. "On the least squares estimation when the dependent variable is grouped." *Review of Economic Studies* L, 737-753

P A R A T
A PROGRAM FOR THE ESTIMATION OF PARAMETRIC TRANSITION RATE MODELS

Hilmar Schneider
University of Frankfurt, SFB 3
FRG

Introduction

The modelling of the change of observation units between discrete states over time is finding a growing interest in the social sciences. A fine example of an application to historical research can be found in the paper of Andreß in this volume. He analyses the duration of mandatories in the German Reichstag between 1848 and 1933. But there are many more fields of application waiting to be reaped. To mention some of them, possible questions could be the duration of wars, the time between the foundation and the disbanding of political parties, guilds or other organizations, or the change of human lifetime expectation during the centuries.

The given examples only distinguish between two different states of observation units over time: being a member of the Reichstag vs. not being a member,existence of a certain political party vs. non existence of this party, and so on. There is no original state and no destination state. Sometimes, it seems appropriate to use an extension to multiple destination states. In the case of formation of political parties, it might be of interest, to separate terminations in disbandment, merger with another party, and prohibition. This is referred to as the case of competing risks.

The transition rate may be understood as a measure of the instantaneous propensity of an observation unit to leave the presently occupied original state in favor of a new destination state. The unobservable transition rate is closely related to the observable duration between the time of entering the original state and the time of entering the destination state. Roughly speaking, the relationship is inverse: A high transition rate will produce a short duration, while a low transition rate leads to a long duration. Since the transition rate concept implies stochastic deviations of the observed durations, the given relationship does only hold true in terms of expectation, however. A single observation may therefore show a short duration, although the process generating transition is low itself. In this case, however, the mean of all observed durations will be high, of course.

There are several reasons, why one analyses unobservable transition rates instead of observable durations. The main reason is that not all of the observed durations are complete. This problem is called censoring, which means that either the time of leaving the original state is unknown (left-censoring), or the time of leaving the original state (right-censoring). Many historical data may be affected by this type of incompleteness. The date of foundation of organizations could be lost in the dark of history, while the time of their disbandment is known very well.The opposite case is as imaginable as well. When using observed duration as dependent variable, one would be forced to choose between two evils: either to set a censored duration equal to the true duration, which would always lead to underestimation, or to exclude to the true duration, which would always lead to underestimation, or to exclude censored observations, which would cause an unpredictable bias due to sample selection. Transition rate models, however, at least in the case of right censoring, allow for a very natural way of correct consideration within the estimation procedure. Another advantage of transition rate models over duration models consists in their possibility of considering time varying levels of the transition rates. The expected duration of a war, for example, could be crucially changed, when alliances burst in the course of a war. Such exogenous shifts of the transition rate may also be accompanied by endogenous variations of the transition rate. For example, the risk of death is high for new-born babies, decreases rapidly with growing age and will increase only as a certain threshold is passed.

Methodological Basics(1)

The individual transition rate $r_{iab}(t)$ is defined as the limit of the probability $q_{iab}(t,t^*)$ that observation unit i leaves original state *a* and enters destination state *b* between times t and t^*, provided that the original state *a* has been continuously occupied since $t=0$:

$$r_{iab}(t) = \lim_{(t^*-t) \to 0} \frac{q_{iab}(t,t^*)}{t^*-t}$$

t is denoting the time which has passed since i entered original state a. The above definition makes clear that the transition rate cannot be interpreted as a probability. As already mentioned, it is more appropriate to think of it as an instantaneous propensity to change states.

The sum over the transition rates to all possible destination states covers the instantaneous propensity to leave the original state *a*. It is called the hazard rate:

$$r_{ia}(t) = \sum_{j=1}^{J} r_{iaj}(t)$$

Here, J is denoting the number of competing risks.

The so-called survival function $G_{ia}(t)$ gives the probability that observation unit i is still in the original state *a* at time t. There is an important relationship between the hazard rate and the survival function:

$$G_{ia}(t) = \exp\left[- \int_0^t r_{ia}(\tau)\, d\tau \right]$$

The probability density function $f_{ia}(t)$ can be written as:

$$f_{ia}(t) = r_{ia}(t)\, G_{ia}(t)$$

The integral over $f_{ia}(t)$ between two subsequent times t and t^* contains the probability that an observation unit is entering one of the possible destination states between time t and time t^*. Figure 1 in the appendix gives a graphical illustration of the relationship between the three functions for a linearly increasing hazard rate. It should be noted that the density function can be solely expressed in terms of the hazard rate.

Standard Model Structure in PARAT

PARAT is one of the few available PC programs, which allow for the analysis of transition rate models.(2) It has been developed at the university of Frankfurt and is designed as a supplement module for GAUSS. The estimation of a transition rate model requires a decision about the model structure. Among the infinite number of possible model types, PARAT offers three models out of the widely used parametric proportional hazards class. This class is characterized in general by the following equation:

$$r_{iab}(t) = r_{0ab}(t)\ \exp(\underline{x}_{it}\underline{\beta}_{ab})$$

Here, the individual transition rate $r_{iab}(t)$ is depending on two multiplicatively connected components: the fist component is called the baseline transition rate $r_{0ab}(t)$ which is identical over all observations. The baseline transition rate catches endogenous time variation of the transition rate. The second component is a log-linear covariate function. $\underline{x}_{it}$ denotes the vector of covariate values of individual i at time t. Their effect is expressed by the parameter vector $\underline{\beta}_{ab}$, including a constant term β_{0ab}. Covariate differences are producing proportionally shifted levels of individual transition rate courses with regard to the baseline transition rate. It should be noted that under the given model structure covariate differences between observation units (interpersonal effects) have the same effect on the transition rate as changes of covariates over time (interpersonal effects).

The three different models presently implemented in PARAT are differing with respect to specification of the baseline transition rate. They can be listed as follows:

(1)	$r_{0ab}(t) = 1$	Exponential model
(2)	$r_{0ab}(t) = \exp(\alpha_{ab}t)$	Gompertz model
(3)	$r_{0ab}(t) = \exp(\alpha_{ab})\ t^{\exp(\alpha_{ab})-1}$	Weibull model

Within this context, α is denoting the functional parameter of the baseline transition rate. The Exponentional model assumes that variation of the transition rate over time is purely exogenous. The remaining two models are containing this as a special case (when α_{ab} equals 0), while their main purpose is to detect specific forms of endogenous time-dependency. Both of them allow for the discrimination of monotonously increasing from monotonously decreasing baseline transition rates. Figure 2 in the appendix gives a graphical comparison of the characteristic shapes of the given baseline functions.

Estimation of the Model Parameters

Estimation of the model parameters is accomplished via the maximum-likelihood method. The general log-likelihood function is given as:

$$L = \sum_{i=1}^{n} c_{iab} \ln(f_{ia}(t_i)) + (1-c_{iab}) \ln(G_{ia}(t_i))$$

$$= \sum_{i=1}^{n} c_{iab} \ln(r_{iab}(t_i)) - \int_0^{t_i} r_{ia}(\tau)\, d\tau$$

Here, c_{iab} is denoting a dummy variable indicating wether i entered destination state *b* at t_i ($c_{iab}=1$) or i being right-censored at t_i ($c_{iab}=0$). Complete observations contribute to the log-likelihood function with their value of the density function at t_i, while right-censored observations contribute with their value of the survival function at t_i. c_{iab} is controlling the selection between both. The consideration of left-censoring bears some awkward peculiarities and is currently not implemented in PARAT.(3) Maximization of the given function with respect to those parameters, which characterize the transition from original state *a* to a chosen destination state *b* is independent of the values of the parameters for other transition and thus the above equation becomes:

$$L = \sum_{i=1}^{n} c_{iab} \ln(r_{iab}(t_i)) - \int_0^{t_i} r_{iab}(\tau)\, d\tau$$

Note that the log-likelihood function solely depends on the model equation for the transition rate from original state *a* to destination state *b*. This fact is utilized in PARAT. The case of competing risks, however, is not implemented for being estimated simultaneously. It rather requires subsequent estimation of the present transitions, which is not a disadvantage with regard to estimation but with regard to performance. Optimization of the estimation function in PARAT is accomplished iteratively via the Newton-Raphson algorithm.

Data Representation of Time-Varying Covariates

In the case of time-constant covariates, it would be sufficient to generate a single row of data per observation unit containing the observed duration, the value of the censoring state (c_{iab}) and the values of the covariates. The case of time-varying covariates is somewhat more complicated, however, since it requires a set of data rows per observation unit. The number of rows depends on the number of different changing times of covariates. The consideration of time-varying covariates uses the following disintegration of the log-survival function:

$$\ln(G_{iab}(t) = - \int_0^{t_i} r_{iab}(\tau)\, d\tau = - \sum_{k=0}^{K} \int_{t_{ik}}^{t_{i(k+1)}} r_{iabk}(\tau)\, d\tau$$

with K denoting the number of changing times of covariates for observation unit i, $t_{i(K+1)}$ then equals the observed duration t_i. The given disintegration generates K+1 subspells per observation unit. The value of K is specific for each observation. Thus, the summing over observation units can be extended to a summing over subspells.

Note that the switch variable c_{iab} can only become one for the last subspell of an observation, provided that it ends with a transition to destination state *b*. Figure 3 in the appendix contains an example for the outcome of the described spell splitting procedure.

Incorporating Unobserved Heterogeneity

A more sophisticated model structure is available by introducing an error term ϵ into the covariate function. Then, the model equation becomes:

$$r_i(t) = r_o(t)\ \exp(\underline{x}_{it}\underline{\beta} + \varepsilon_i)$$

The purpose of this type of model is to control for unobserved heterogeneity, which leads to downward biased estimators of the baseline transition rate.(4) The problem can easily be described for the case of two unobserved homogenous subpopulations with different transition rate levels. As can be seen from figure 4 in the appendix, disregarding the existence of these two subgroups will result in a spurious negative time-dependency of the baseline transition rate. With time in progress, the subpopulation with the higher transition rate tends to die out more rapidly than the remaining subpopulation and, therefore, the latter is continuously increasing its relative weight for estimation. It should be clear that similar effects will result in any case, where mixing unobserved subpopulations are present.

Estimation of the extended model requires several assumptions about ϵ. PARAT uses the type of a finite mixture model. This means that ϵ takes on only a restricted number of M different levels Ω_m with probability P_m. Furthermore, it has to be assumed that the membership to one of the unobserved heterogeneity classes is uncorrelated with $\underline{x}$. Optimization of the corresponding likelihood function is done using an iterative alternating estimation of $\underline{P}$ on one hand and $\underline{\Omega}$ and $\underline{\beta}$ on the other.

Model Evaluation

PARAT produces a number of statistics which allow to analyse the model fit. These statistics are based on so-called deviance increments (Arminger 1986; 1987). A deviance increment measures the difference between the log-likelihood of a saturated model and its value actually obtained by a specified model. Deviance increments are computed per observation unit and thus may be used for outlier detection as well as for the calculation of a global measure of fit. Beyond this, they serve as weights in a Hausman test for asymptotic parameter consistency. This specification test uses the parameter differences between a weighted and an unweighed estimation to obtain a global test statistic.

Technical Remarks

For proper operation, PARAT requires the following hardware equipment: an IBM PC, AT or compatible computer and a mathematical co-processor. Software requirements are DOS 2.11 or later and GAUSS 1.49B or later. It should be noted that variates, however, may not exceed 90, although this will hardly become a problem in practice. Requests on PARAT should be addressed to the author.

Figure 1: The Relationship Between r(t), f(t) and G(t)

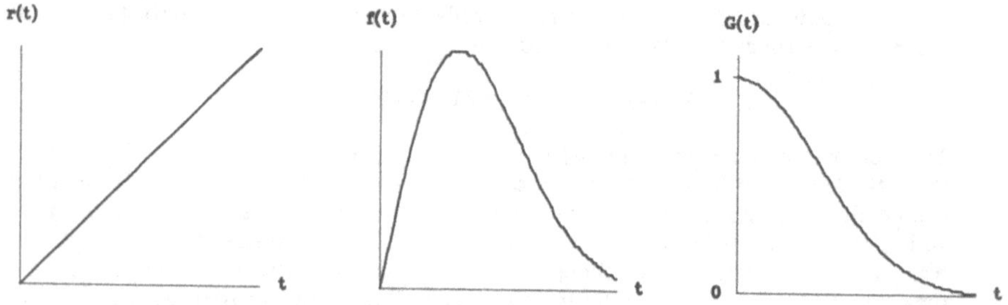

Figure 2: The Baseline Transition Rates in PARAT

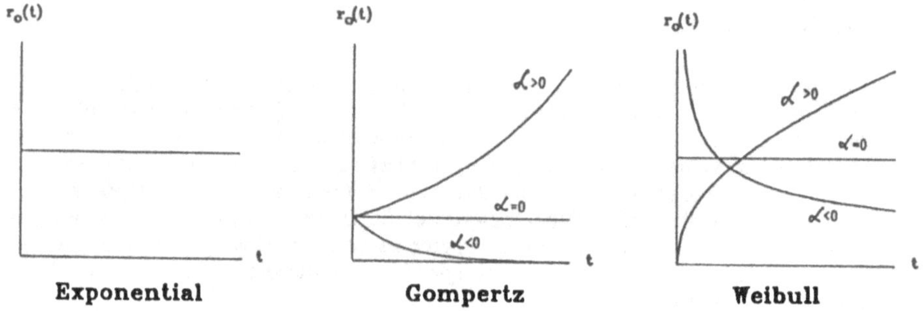

Figure 3: Example for Data Representation of Time-Varying Covariates in PARAT

The following example shows a spell of length 8. Column ITANF refers to t_{ik}, while ITEND refers to $t_{i(k+1)}$. IZS contains the values of the censoring state c_{iab} and X1 and X2 are denoting covariates. At time 2 X1 changes its value from 0 to 1, while X2 still remains constant. At time 4.5 X2 changes from 800 to 900, butnow X1 remains constant. At time 7.5 both variables change their values from 1 to 0 and from 900 to 950. the spell ends after 8 units of time with an observed transition from *a* to *b*.

ITANF	ITEND	IZS	X1	X2	
.	.	.	.	.	
.	.	.	.	.	
0	2	0	0	800	Spell is
2	4.5	0	1	800	Splitted at
4.5	7.5	0	1	900	Changes of
7.5	8	1	0	950	Covariates
.	.	.	.	.	
.	.	.	.	.	

Figure 4: The Effect of Mixing Unobserved Subpolations

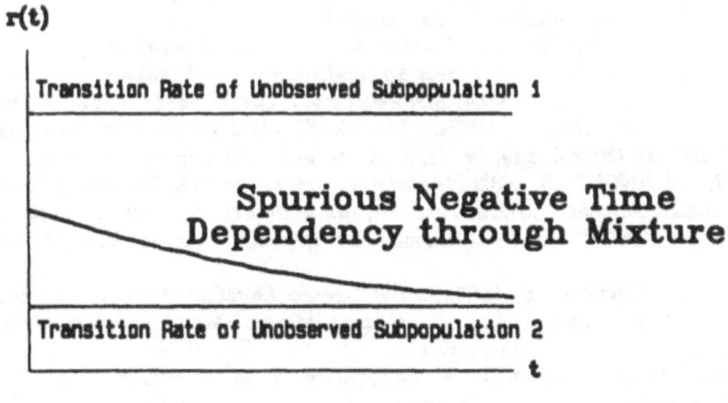

NOTES

1. The issues of this chapter are discussed in more detail by the textbooks of Andreß (1985), Blossfeld/Hamerle/Mayer (1986), Diekmann/Mitter (1984), Kalbfleisch/Prentice (1980), Lawless (1982) and Tuma/Hannan (1984).
2. An overview about available programs can be found in Andreß (1986), Hudec/Hitz/Müllner (1986), Kemeny (1986) and Mitter (1986).
3. For more details see Baydar (1987), Heckman/Singer (1985, pp. 74-88) and Tuma/Hannan (1984, pp. 128-132).
4. This problem has been extensively addressed in the work of Heckman and Singer (1982a; 1982b; 1984). See also Andreß (1988).

REFERENCES

ANDREß, H.-J. 1985. *Multivariate Analyse von Verlaufsdaten*. Mannheim

ANDREß, H.-J. 1986. "Software zur dynamischen Analyse diskreter abhängiger Variablen (Verlaufsdaten)", in: Lehmacher, W. und Hörmann, A. (eds.). *Statistik Software - 3. Konferenz über die wissenschaftliche Anwendung von Statistik-Software 1985*. Stuttgart, New York, 191-202

ANDREß, H.-J. 1988. "Spezifikationsfehler und unbeobachtete Heterogenität in Regressionsmodellen für Übergangsraten." *Kölner Zeitschrift für Soziologie und Sozialpsychologie* 40, 93-116

ARMINGER, G. 1986. *Deviance, Deviance Residuals and a Coefficient of Determination for Parametric Rate Models*. Paper presented at the Conference "Applications of Event History Analysis in Life Course Research". Berlin

ARMINGER, G. 1987. "Testing Against Misspecification in Parametric Rate Models", in: Mayer, K.U. and Tuma, N.B. (eds.). *Applications of Event History Analysis in Life Course Research*. Berlin, 679-699

BAYDAR, N. 1987. "What can Backward Recurrence Time Data Tell Us: An Application to Residental Mobility in the U.S.", in: Mayer, K.U. and Tuma, N.B. (eds.). *Applications of Event History Analysis in Life Course Research*. Berlin, 561-600

BLOSSFELD, H.-P.; HAMERLE, A. and MAYER, K.U. 1986. *Ereignisanalyse - Statistische Theorie und Anwendung in den Wirtschafts- und Sozialwissenschaften*. Frankfurt, New York

DIEKMANN, A. and MITTER, P. 1984. *Methoden zur Analyse von Zeitverläufen*. Stuttgart

HECKMAN, J.J. and SINGER, B. 1982a. "The Identification Problem in Econometric Models for Duration Data", in: Hildenbrand, W. (ed.). *Advances in Econometrics*. Cambridge, 39-77

HECKMAN, J.J. and SINGER, B. 1982b. "Population Heterogeneity in Demographic Models", in: Land, K.C. and Rogers, A. (eds.). *Multidimensional Mathematical Demography*. New York, 567-599

HECKMAN, J.J. and SINGER, B. 1984. "Econometric Duration Analysis." *Journal of Econometrics* 24, 63-132

HECKMAN, J.J. and SINGER, B. 1985. "Social Science Duration Analysis", in: Heckman, J.J. and Singer, B. (eds.). *Longitudinal Analysis of Labor Market Data*. Cambridge, London, New York, New Rochelle, Melbourne, Sydney, 39-110

HUDEC, M; HITZ, M and MÜLLNER, W. 1986. "Software für Survival Analysis - Ein vergleichender Überblick", in: Lehmacher, W. und Hörmann, A. (eds.). *Statistik Software - 3. Konferenz über die wissenschaftliche Anwendung von Statistik-Software 1985*. Stuttgart, New York, 203-213

KALBFLEISCH, J.D. and PRENTICE, R.L. 1980. *The Statistical Analysis of Failure Time Data*. New York, Chichester, Brisbane, Toronto

KEMENY,P. 1986. "Regressionsmodelle zur Analyse von Verwildauern", in: Lehmacher, W. und Hörmann, A. (eds.). *Statistik Software - 3. Konferenz über die wissenschaftliche Anwendung von Statistik-Software 1985*. Stuttgart, New York, 215-224

LAWLESS, J.F. 1982. *Statistical Models and Methods for Lifetime Data*. New York, Chichester, Brisbane, Toronto, Singapore

MITTER, P. 1986. "Statistische Analyse von Ereignisdaten. Methoden- und Software-Vergleich", in: Lehmacher, W. und Hörmann, A. (eds.). *Statistik Software - 3. Konferenz über die wissenschaftliche Anwendung von Statistik-Software 1985*. Stuttgart, New York, 225-235

SCHNEIDER, H. 1989. *PARAT - Benutzer-Handbuch - Version 1.02*. Sfb-3-Programmdokumentation. Frankfurt, Mannheim

TUMA, N.B. and Hannan, M.T. 1984. *Social Dynamics: Models and Methods*. Orlando, San Diego, San Francisco, New York, London, Toronto, Montreal, Sydney, Tokyo

REALIZATION OF MISSING DATA TECHNIQUES WITHIN STATISTICAL PROGRAM PACKAGES AND THEIR EMPIRICAL PERFORMANCE

Rainer Schnell
Institut für angewandte Sozialforschung, Köln
FRG

1. Introduction

Most datasets of empirical social research contain a certain amount of missing data (MD). The percentage of missing data varies with subject matter, population, data collection method, data editing etc. In most cases, the percentage lies within 1% and 10%. Despite this large amount, MD is ignored in most analyses. To attain unbiased estimates, the application of this procedure must assume that the data is missing at random (MAR). To test the MAR assumption, a lot of procedures are available (Frane 1978, Hill/Dixon 1981). Although these are in principle not able to test for every possible missing data generating process (Rubin 1976), in practice the simplest tests suffice to destroy any notion of randomness of the MD (Frane 1978: 27). It is remarkable that only a few methods exist, which are suitable for the analysis of data sets with systematically missing data (Little/Rubin 1987: 218-243). If MD problems are handled in practice at all, then only very simple estimation and substitution (imputation) methods are used.

2. Missing Data Techniques

Since it is hardly possible to give a complete survey of the mass of literature concerning MD techniques (Anderson/Basilevsky/Hum (1983), Schnell (1986: 83-137), only the most important methods will be mentioned here.

The generally best known methods are the different "missing data correlations", for example "pairwise", "listwise" or "allvalue". To the large group of parameter estimation methods belong two relatively new developments: the so called "EM algorithm" and a special class of econometric models, the "sample selection" or "Nelson-Heckman Models".

The sample selection models (Berk 1983, Little 1983) allow unbiased estimates of regression parameters to be obtained despite systematically missing values. These models are based on only one missing data generating process: the data are missing, if a latent variable exceeds an unobserved stochastic threshold. The main problem of these models is the specification of a theoretical model of the missing data generating process. Unfortunately, such theoretical substantive models rarely exist in the social sciences (outside of econometrics) so that applications can be found very seldom.

In the recent MD literature, the "EM algorithm" dominated as parameter estimation method. The "expectation maximization" (EM) algorithm is a general method for the computing of maximum likelihood estimates, which can (in principle) be utilized for any MD problem (Dempster/Laird/Rubin 1977). In this context the EM algorithm can be done by iterated separate multiple regressions for each pattern of missing data. Since this type of EM algorithm also estimates the missing values, it belongs to both groups of procedures. An implementation of this method can be found in BMDPAM as "ML" option with the ESTIMATE TYPE= command. Of course, it is possible to estimate the missing values directly by other methods. The process of estimating missing values is called "imputation". Imputation possesses two main advantages:

1. After the one-time imputation there is a complete "general purpose" dataset, which can be analyzed with traditional "complete data" methods and programs;
2. The imputation procedures probably reduce the bias due to systematically missing data, especially if the imputation is done by the producers of the dataset, which may have special information concerning the missing data generating process.

The simplest imputation method is pure guessing of a missing value, the next simplest imputation procedure is the replacement of the MD with the mean of the present data. In estimating correlations, this method is known as "Wilk's method". A slightly more complicated method is the "Cell Mean Substitution". Here, the MD are replaced by the mean of the subgroup, to which the case belongs. The problem of this and other subgroup-based techniques lies in determining of the subgroups, in this context called the "imputation classes".(1)

A somewhat more interesting set of techniques are the so-called "Hot-Deck" methods, which are mostly used in "official statistics", especially censuses. There is no universally agreed definition of Hot-Decks (Ford 1983:185-186), but all definitions mention the stochastic character of the imputation, using data from the incomplete dataset and a notion of "doubling" a complete case. This becomes more clear, if we differentiate between two classes of Hot-Deck procedures: sequential and simultaneous Hot-Decks. Sequential Hot-Decks begin by determining the imputation classes and initial values for the missing variable for each class. The incomplete dataset is processed sequentially. For each case of the incomplete dataset, the imputation class is determined. If the computer program encounters a valid value for the actual case, this value will be copied to the corresponding imputation cell (the case becomes a "donor"). If the computer program encounters a missing value, this missing value will be replaced by the current content of the imputation cell (the case becomes a "recipient"). This procedure is continued until the end of the file, then each case will have valid data for the imputed variable (Sande 1982, Ford 1983).

The more seldom used simultaneous Hot-Decks make use of matching variables (like the classifier variables for the imputation classes), but each incomplete case is imputed with the values of a complete case which has the smallest distance to the incomplete case on the matching variables. Very often the euclidean distance is used, sometimes the Mahalanobis distance. Procedures with such an imputation rule are sometimes called "nearest-neighbor" methods (Vacek/Ashikaga 1980).

Of course, a lot of multivariate methods for estimating missing values are available. One of the earliest methods (Dear 1959) computes the first principal component from the mean imputed correlation matrix. Obviously, it is possible to estimate missing values with regression procedures. This was suggested by Buck in 1960. Buck's method starts with a listwise correlation matrix. For each case i and every missing variable, the missing values are estimated by a multiple regression with all complete variables of case i as independent variables. Because each estimated value lies on the regression line, the resulting covariance matrix of the imputed dataset will be biased. Buck (1960:304) supposed a correction of the covariance matrix of the imputed dataset. This correction is not always mentioned in literature. Very often, every kind of regression procedure is named "Buck's method".

A lot of different regression-based procedures have been proposed (cf. Schnell 1986:117-119), but these are seldom used. Only iterated versions of a multiple regression procedure are common. An iterative multiple regression method to estimate missing values (without correction of the covariance matrix) was proposed by Federspiel, Monroe & Greenberg in 1959. Schmee/Hahn (1979) proposed such an "iterated least square" technique for the solution of censoring problems. Interestingly, as Beale/Little (1975:134-137) have shown, the iterated Buck-procedure (with correction) is identical to the above-mentioned EM algorithm.

3. Realization within Standard Packages

Only a few of the above-mentioned techniques are available as processing options within standard statistical packages like SPSS-X or SAS (in contrast to BMDP, which contains the program AM, permitting most MD-imputation techniques). Nevertheless, it is possible to realize these techniques with the data transformation and case selection capabilities of these programs. A few possibilities of imputing missing data in the datasets with a current simple statistical program package, SPSS-PC+, are illustrated. The examples include mean substitution, cell mean substitution, sequential Hot-Deck (casewise and variablewise replacement), Hot-Decks with "nearest-neighbor rule" (via QUICK CLUSTER), a principal component method very similar to the method proposed by DEAR (1959) and a multiple regression method. An iterated multiple regression imputation procedure, which would be identical to the EM algorithm for this task (with the exception of the necessary, but omitted correction of covariance matrix) is not possible within SPSS-PC+ without a lot of manual labor. This would require separate multiple regression equations for each set of observations with a different pattern of missing values.

4. Empirical Performance of the MD Techniques

The performance of the MD techniques is dependent on a long series of parameters, for example, missing data generating processes, amount of missing data, pattern of missing data, number of variables, number of cases, multicollinearity of the variables, shape of the distribution of the variables and last, but not least, on the criteria used to evaluate the procedures. Therefore, analytical results can be given only for very simple methods, special situations and only with the assumption of randomly missing data. As far as other missing data generating processes and the effect of imputation procedures on multivariate statistics are concerned, virtually no analytical results have been published.(2) The only way to evaluate a numerical procedure, when no analytical results can be obtained, is to use Monte Carlo simulation studies. The MD literature contains a great number of simulation studies, but only about ten of these are cited more than a few times.(3) Due to a lack of any standardization in this field, the simulations can not be compared directly, because the older studies seldom used an experimental design, so the results cannot be traced down to single factor combinations. Additionally, the studies used different estimation methods and performance criteria.(4) Despite this, there is a basic consensus concerning the performance of the techniques in the literature.(5) The simple imputation procedures (Mean, Cell and Hot-Decks) are not considered to be efficient in estimating covariances as the multivariate procedures. Dear's method seems to be efficient only, if there is a great amount of multicollinearity among the variables. Iterated multiple regression methods (especially the EM algorithm) seem to be the most efficient methods.

The most important limitation of the previous studies is the limitation to only one missing data generating process: with the exception of Van Guilder/Azen (1981) every simulation is based on the missing at random (MAR) assumption. In real-life applications, this assumption is almost always violated. If recommendations are developed, which method of MD imputation to choose in which situation, and the simulations are based on a MAR assumption, it must be assumed that there is no interaction effect between the estimation method and the missing data generating process with regard to the efficiency of the procedure. In other words: the procedure has to be equally efficient under every possible missing data generating process. To test this heroic assumption, a new simulation study was designed.

5. Design of the Simulation Study

The simulation was based on a full factorial design of four factors (sample size n: 100, 300, 500 cases; mean intercorrelation r=.2, .4, .6; percentage of incomplete data 1%, 5%, 10%; missing data generating process: Missing at Random=MAR, Missing at Random within Classes=MARC and a Hazard model: Missing above Threshold=MAT) with 3 levels for each factor, so that 3*3*3=81 different conditions were tested. For each condition 10 different datasets, each with 10 multivariate normal distributed variables of the given correlation structure, were generated.(6) Each of the resulting 810 different incomplete datasets was treated with 10 different MD techniques, giving a 3*3*3*3 full factorial design with repeated measures on the last factor. Ten different MD techniques were used: LISTWISE (complete cases), PAIRWISE (pairwise present data), MEAN (mean substitution), CELLMEAN (cell mean substitution), HOT-DECK (sequential variablewise case duplication), REGRESSION (simple regression), HAZARD (regression with MD indicator), DEAR (principal components), MULT (multiple regression), ILS (iterated multiple regression). Two aspects of the MD techniques should be explored: the bias in estimating correlation coefficients and the ability to estimate individual missing data.

6. Results

Under almost every tested condition, LISTWISE produces inferior results compared to PAIRWISE. In general, ILS is one of the best procedures under almost every experimental condition with regard to the estimation of correlations. But even the best procedures can lead to grossly misleading results under certain conditions. From a practical point of view, the percentage of correctly estimated missing values (HIT) is of primary importance. Despite the 7 categorized input values, for most MD-techniques the proportion of correctly estimated values lies between 0.25 and 0.40. HIT reaches maximum values of 45%, relatively independent of the number of missing values and given high intercorrelation and a large sample. But there are remarkable differences between the procedures. Especially the DEAR procedure is highly sensitive to the missing data generating process. The Hot-Deck is by far the worst procedure, while on the other hand, MULT and ILS are nearly undistinguishable in accuracy. Although the relative importance of experimental factors on the performance of the MD methods varies with both, method and missing data generating process (all MANOVA-interaction terms of the missing data generating process with the experimental variables are significant), a few trends are evident in the plots and the multiple regressions. Since the number of cases almost never has an effect, it seems safe to neglect this factor in future simulations. The relative importance of the amount of MD versus the mean intercorrelation depends on a lot of factors, but in general the intercorrelation is much more important for the multivariate procedures (DEAR, MULT, ILS) than for the other procedures. The more redundancy in the dataset, the better the estimates. As the MANOVAs illustrate, nearly every possible interaction between imputation method and experimental factors can be found, so, further generalizations are impossible. The results show a strong dependence of all procedures on the (in practice unknown) missing data generating process. The main conclusion of the simulation is, therefore, that a "best" procedure for estimating missing data does not exist. Even the "best" procedures in the simulation show a breakdown under certain conditions. Furthermore, the search for such a procedure seems to make no sense. Therefore, it seems to be necessary not simply to fill the gaps with an "automatic" procedure like BMDPAM, but to simulate different theoretical assumptions about the missing data generating process during the imputation. This "multiple imputation" (Rubin 1987) seems to be the only way to handle a data set with a not trivial amount of MD.

NOTES

1. For a critique of the theoretical assumptions of the concept of imputation classes, cf. Schnell (1986:104-106).
2. A few attempts have been made by Santos (1981) for regression parameters and by Brown (1983) for the estimation of factor loadings.
3. The most cited studies are Haitovsky (1968), Timm (1970), Gleason/Staelin (1975), Beale/Little (1975), Kim/Curry (1977) and Little (1979). The newer studies of Van Guilder/Azen (1981), Kaiser (1984) and Basilevsky/Sabourin/Hum/Anderson (1985) are much better designed as the old studies, but the results seldom changed (with the exception of the better performance of the pairwise method).
4. One interesting consequence of this situation was the rejection of the "pairwise"-correlation estimator, mainly due to the simulation results of Haitovsky in 1968. A lot of simulation studies excluded the pairwise estimator therefore in the design; the method was rejected on theoretical grounds by mathematical statisticians (Heiberger 1977). It is remarkable that in the last years the pairwise estimator has obtained much more theoretical support (Brown 1983) and even better simulation results (Finkbeiner 1979, Basilevsky et al. 1985, Schnell 1985) than before.
5. A modern, but incomplete review is given by Anderson/Basilevsky/Hum (1983). A very readable, but somewhat dated account can be found in Hamilton (1975). A critical review of most of the published simulation studies in given by Schnell (1986:138-157).
6. More details and a program listing (about 700 lines Fortran) can be found in Schnell (1986).

REFERENCES

ANDERSON, A.B.; BASILEVSKY, A. and HUM, D.J. 1983. "Missing Data: A Review of the Literature", in: Rossi, P.H.; Wright, J.D. and Anderson, A.B. (eds.). *Handbook of Survey Research*. New York, 415-493

BASILEVSKY, A.; SABOURIN, D.; HUM, D. and ANDERSON, A. 1985. "Missing Data Estimators in the General Linear Model: An Evaluation of Simulated Data as an Experimental Design." *Communications in Statistics, Simulation and Computation* 14, 2, 371-394

BEALE, E.M.L. and LITTLE, R.J.A. 1975. "Missing Values in Multivariate Analysis." *Journal of the Royal Statistical Society*, Series B, 37, 129-146

BERK, R.A. 1983. "An Introduction to Sample Selection Bias in Sociological Data." *American Sociological Review* 48, 386-398

BROWN, C.H. 1983. "Asymptotic Comparison of Missing Data Procedures for Estimating Factor Loadings." *Psychometrika* 48, 2, 269-291

BUCK, S.F. 1960. "A Method of Estimation of Missing Values of Multivariate Data Suitable for Use With an Electronic Computer." *Journal of the Royal Statistical Society*, Series B, 22, 302-307

DEAR, R.E. 1959. *A Principal Component Missing Data Method for Multiple Regression Models*. Technical Report SP-86, System Development Corporation, Santa Monica, Calif.

DEMPSTER, A.P.; LAIRD, N.M. and RUBIN, D.B. 1977. "Maximum Likelihood from Incomplete Data via the EM Algorithm." *Journal of the Royal Statistical Society*, Series B, 39, 1-22

FEDERSPIEL, C.F.; MONROE, R.J. and GREENBERG, B.G. 1959. *An Investigation of Some Multiple Regression Methods for Incomplete Samples*. University of North Carolina Institute of Statistics, Mimeo Series #236

FINKBEINER, C. 1979. "Estimation for the Multiple Factor Model when Data are Missing." *Psychometrika* 44, 409-420

FORD, B.L. 1983. "An Overview of Hot-Deck Procedures", in: Madow, W.G.; Olkin, I.; Rubin, D.B. (eds.). *Incomplete Data in Sample Surveys*. New York, vol. 2, 185-207

FRANE, J. 1978. "Missing Data and BMDP: Some Pragmatic Approaches", in: *ASA Proceedings of the Statistical Computing Section*, 27-33

GLEASON, T.C. and STAELIN, R. 1975. "A Proposal for Handling Missing Data." *Psychometrika* 40, 229-252

HAITOVSKY, Y. 1968. "Missing Data in Regression Analysis." *Journal of the Royal Statistical Society*, Series B, 63, 67-82

HAMILTON, M.A. 1975. *Regression Analysis When There are Missing Observations - A Survey and Bibliography. Technical Report 1-3-75*. Statistical Laboratory, Montana State University

HEIBERGER, R.M. 1977. "Regression with the Pairwise-Present Covariance Matrix: A Dangerous Practice", in: *ASA Proceedings of the Statistical Computing Section*, 38-47

HILL, M. and DIXON, W.J. 1981. "Missing Data: Search for Patterns", in: *ASA Proceedings of the Statistical Computing Section*, 57-60

KAISER, J. 1984. *The Estimation of Missing Values*. Ph.D. Thesis, University of Kansas

KIM, J.O. and CURRY, J. 1977. "The Treatment of Missing Data in Multivariate Analysis." *Sociological Methods and Research* 6, 2, 215-239

LITTLE, R.J.A. 1979. "Maximum Likelihood Inference for Multiple Regression with Missing Values: A Simulation Study." *Journal of the Royal Statistical Society*, Series B, 41, 1, 76-87

LITTLE, R.J.A. 1983. "The Nonignorable Case", in: Madow, W.G.; Olkin, I.; Rubin, D.B. (eds.). *Incomplete Data in Sample Surveys*. vol. 2, 383-413, New York

LITTLE, R.J.A. and RUBIN, D.B. 1987. *Statistical Analysis With Missing Data*. New York: Wiley

RUBIN, D.B. 1976. "Inference and Missing Data." *Biometrika* 63, 581-592

RUBIN, D.B. 1987. *Multiple Imputation for Nonresponse in Surveys*. New York: Wiley

SANDE, I.G. 1982. "Imputation in Surveys: Coping With Reality." *The American Statistician* 36, 3, 145-152

SANTOS, R.L. 1981. *Effects of Imputation on Complex Statistics*. Survey Research Center, Institute for Social Research, University of Michigan

SCHMEE, J. and HAHN, G.J. 1979. "A Simple Method for Regression Analysis with Censored Data." *Technometrics* 21, 4, 417-432

SCHNELL, R. 1985. "Zur Effizienz einiger Missing-Data-Techniken." *ZUMA Nachrichten* 17, 50-74

SCHNELL, R. 1986. *Missing-Data-Probleme in der empirischen Sozialforschung*. Dissertation, Bochum

TIMM, N.H. 1970. "The Estimation of Variance-Covariance and Correlation Matrices from Incomplete Data." *Psychometrika* 35, 417-437

VACEK, P.M. and ASHIKAGA, T. 1980. "An Examination of the Nearest Neighbor Rule for Imputing Missing Values", in: *ASA Proceedings of the Statistical Computing Section*, 326-331

VAN GUILDER, M. and AZEN, S. 1981. "Conclusions Regarding Algorithms for Handling Incomplete Data", in: *ASA Proceedings of the Statistical Computing Section*, 53-56

BASIC CONCEPTS AND NEW METHODS OF TIME SERIES ANALYSIS IN HISTORICAL SOCIAL RESEARCH

Winfried Stier
Mörschwil
Switzerland

PART ONE

Time Series Models

Hint: The main purpose of this lecture is the presentation of important concepts and tools of time series analysis in a non-technical way. Therefore, only elementary mathematical operations will be used. Proofs and a lot of details are omitted completely. In Part One fundamentals and modelling of time series are discussed. Part Two is dedicated to filter-problems in time series analysis. The two parts are independent of each other.

I. Fundamentals

1. Introduction

A time series is a set of time-ordered observations of a process. Each observation should be an internal level measurement of the process and the time separating successive observations should be constant.

2. Some Objectives of Time Series Analysis

The social scientist is interested in making inferences about the process underlying a given time series. This implies that we consider a given time series as a realization of an unknown process. If we succeed in identifying this unknown process, we can hope to "predict the future" of a social process. Furthermore, if we consider not only one time series but several series (a so-called "multivariate" instead of an "univariate" approach), we can hope to analyze dependencies between different social processes. This possibility seems to be especially promising for historical research.

Both, in the univariate and in the multivariate approach an identification of the unknown underlying process is only possible if we succeed in "modelling" properly a given time series. To achieve this, it is necessary to know some basic facts about stochastic processes which will be presented in the following.

II. Modelling of Time Series

1. Stochastic Processes

Simply spoken, a stochastic process is a sequence of random variables which are in general dependent (or correlated). In the special case where the random variables are uncorrelated, the process is called a "white-noise"-process. For such a process, the realization at a certain time point t_i bears no informations about the next realization in t_{i+1}. Such a process is unpredictable. In general, however, the correlation-structure of a stochastic process can be used for prediction.

Now, there are different types of stochastic processes. An important class of processes are the so-called "stationary" processes. They can be characterized by the fact that their mean and variance are constant for all time points. Besides that their correlation-structure is "homogeneous", which means that the correlation of two variables at different time-points does only depend on the length of the time-interval between the two time-points but not on the location of the two time-points on the time-scale. For "non-stationary"-processes one of these properties does not hold. There are certain "basic" stationary processes which prove to be very useful tools in building complex processes. These are the "autoregressive" - and the "moving-average"-processes. The simplest autoregressive process is given by the equation

$$X_t = \alpha X_{t-1} + u_t , \quad t = 1, 2, ...$$

where u_t denotes a white-noise-process. The simplest moving-average-process is defined by the equation

$$X_t = u_t + \beta u_{t-1} , \quad t = 1, 2, ...$$

This process is called a moving-average-process of order 1 (in short: MA (1)).

If we would try modelling a series by using either an AR- or a MA-process we frequently would see that the required order for a "good" model would be very high. This, however, would be an unsatisfactory state of affairs, since the precision of the estimation of the unknown parameters depends (given a limited set of data) on the number of parameters to be estimated. Therefore, we should look for models which contain as less parameters as possible. This is called the "principle of parsimony". Now, it can be shown that a good strategy to realize the principle consists in combining the two "pure" approaches which leads to the so-called ARIMA (p, q)-process:

$$X_t + \alpha_1 X_{t-1} + \alpha_2 X_{t-2} + ... + \alpha_p X_{t-p} = u_t + \beta_1 u_{t-1} + \beta_2 u_{t-2} + ... + \beta_q u_{t-q} .$$

2. ARIMA-Processes

Since practical time series frequently cannot be considered to be realizations of stationary processes, it seems to be a poor strategy to use stationary ARIMA (p, q)-processes as modelling tools. Fortunately, there exists a simple device which transforms non-stationary series to stationary - at least for most series encountering in practices. This transformation consists in differentiating a series.

If we are able to model a series after differentiating we call this an ARIMA (p, d, q)-process, where D = 1, 2, ... denotes the degree of differentiation.

Now, the modelling of a time series by an ARIMA (p, d, q)-process in general requires the following three steps:

1. *Identification* of the process-type (what are the proper values for p, d, q ?),
2. *Estimation* of the unknown parameters,
3. *Diagnostic checking* of the residuals.

PART TWO

Filtering of Time Series

1. Introduction

Filter-methods may be very important in investigating historical phenomena. For instance, the search for "long swings" is a famous and well-known subject which keeps busy historians and economists for more than fifty years and in which an extensive use of filters is made.

For the sake of clarity I shall firstly use a simulated time series. Let us suppose, we generate a time series in the following manner. The series is supposed to be additively composed of three components:

$$T_t = 0.001\ t^3 - 0.1\ t^2 + 0.5\ t + 100$$
$$C_t = 200\ .\ \sin 0.06\ \pi t$$
$$R_t \sim N\ (0,1)$$

that is

$$X_t = T_t + C_t + R_t\ ,\quad t = 1, \ldots, 200.$$

Now, let us forget that we know the components of the time series and let us consider X_t to be a real time series. If X_t is a real series, we might be interested in the following questions:

* Does X_t contain a cyclical component and if yes, how regularly does it involve in time?
* How does the trend develop in time?

Obviously, the first question seems to be the more difficult one: we have to extract a signal - namely the cyclical component C_t - which is contaminated by a second signal and by 'noise'. Of course, in our simple example, the trend is the more disturbing fact. This might be different in a different series. Now, how could we find out, if the series X_t contains a cyclical component at all?

2. Traditional Filter-Methods

What are the procedures usually and traditionally used in trend-eliminating?

Let us begin with the so-called 'method of least-squares'. The basic idea is the assumption that the trend follows a simple function of time whose coefficients are unknown. According to the 'least-squares'-principle, they are estimated in such a way that the differences between the values of the time series and the trend-values - squared and summed over all time-points - take a minimum.

The second approach used in time series analysis for estimating a trend are the so-called 'moving-averages'. A moving-average is defined by:

$$Y_t := \frac{1}{2q+1} \sum_{s=-q}^{+q} X_{t-s}, \quad t = q + 1, ..., N - q$$

where 2q + 1 denotes the length of the average and N the length of the time series.

Both approaches suffer from severe theoretical and practical drawbacks. Moving-averages as introduced above can be considered as special filters. A linear filter can simply be described as a transformation of a time series according to

$$Y_t := \sum_{s=-q}^{r} a_s X_{t-s}, \quad t = s + 1, ..., N - r$$

with

X_t : = filter-input (given time series)
Y_t : = filter output (given filtered series)
a_s : = filter weights.

3. Newer Filter Methods

The modern approaches to be discussed here are methods which are based on filter-theory. We have learned already that moving-averages can also be considered as filters, although more elementary ones. Modern filter-theory can be characterized by the fact that no ad-hoc-solutions (like simply moving averages) are accepted, but filters are designed in such a way that they accomplish pre-specified criteria. These criteria are chosen according to the problems to be solved or the aims of the analysis.

A characteristic feature of modern filter-theory is the fact that filter-design can be made in the **frequency-domain** and not only in the time domain. This possibility offers a lot of advantages which will become evident when we consider details and examples.

If we design a filter in the frequency domain, we have the possibility to eliminate or preserve frequencies according to the aims of our analysis. For instance, if a series is to be detrended, the filter has to eliminate the zero-frequency. All other frequencies have to be preserved. A filter of this kind is called a **high-pass** filter. If the trend is to be estimated, all low frequencies below the seasonal frequency should be left unaltered, whereas the high frequencies should be eliminated. Such a filter is called a **low-pass** filter.

The behaviour of a filter in the frequency-domain can be described completely by a function which is usually called: **'transfer function'**. This function gives us two informations: the first one shows us, if and how certain frequencies or frequency-bands are attenuated resp. eliminated or amplified. The second one shows, if there is a phase-shift between filter-input and filter-output. The transfer function of a filter is a complex function in general. Its absolute value gives us the first information. Therefore, this function is called the 'amplitude-function' of a filter.

Basically, there are two different approaches in modern filter theory. In the first one, the filtering is done in the time-domain. For certain types of filters like low-pass or band-pass filters (which are very important in practice), such a design may have the drawback of a remarkable phase-shift which may be disturbing in analyzing certain problems.

This phase-shift can be avoided if we use a different approach. Its essential feature is the fact that filtering is done in the frequency-domain and not in the time-domain as in the first approach. This can be achieved by a transformation of the data into the frequency-domain which can be done by using a so-called 'Discrete-Fourier-Transform' (DFT). I shall not discuss details here. Rather, let us finally consider an example. For illustration we use the series 'Turnover of Rye in Cologne 1531-1659'. For estimating the trend, a low-pass filter was chosen which preserves all oscillations with a period longer than 60 years. To estimate a trend-free series, a high-pass filter was used which is complementary to the low-pass. Finally, for analyzing any possible long cycles, a band-pass filter was taken which preserves all cycles between 20 and 60 years.

The series and the results of the filtering are shown in the following graph:

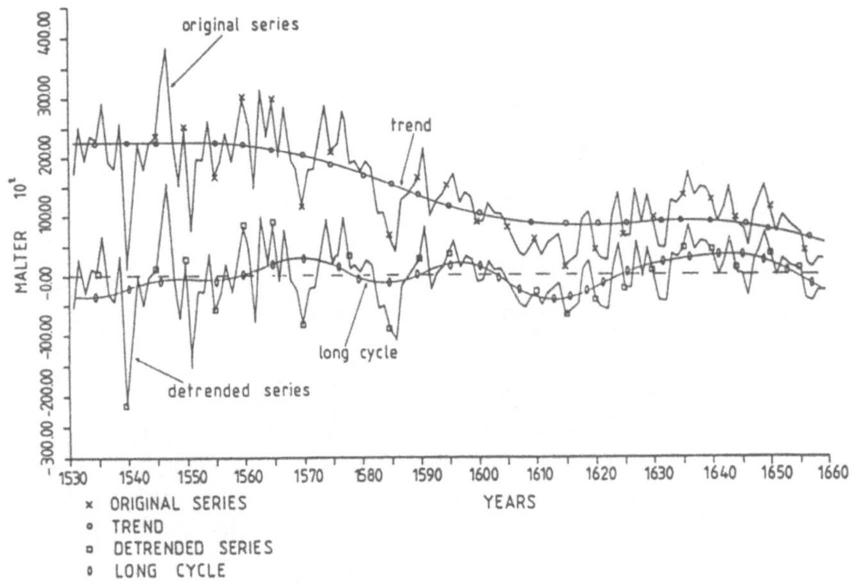

Turnover of Rye in Cologne 1531 - 1659

REFERENCES

SCHULTE, H. 1981. *Statistisch-methodische Untersuchungen zum Problem langer Wellen*. Königstein
STIER, W. 1978. *Konstruktion und Einsatz von Digitalfiltern zur Analyse und Prognose ökonomischer Zeitreihen*. Opladen
STIER, W. 1989. *Methoden der Zeitreihenanalyse*. Springer, forthcoming

SCALE-ANALYSIS ACCORDING TO R. J. MOKKEN - A PROBABILISTIC EXTENSION OF GUTTMAN SCALING

A Short Review of the Algorithm and a Comparison of MOKKEN-Scaling Results to Factor Analysis and MINISSA

E.J. Zimmermann
VGSPSmbH, Solingen-Bonn
FRG

Before discussing MOKKEN scaling in detail, we have to clarify the term "scale" itself: First of all, a scale is an instrument of measurement - that is, a scale is used for measuring the amount or level of a certain attribute in a set of objects. Measuring is done by assigning a scale value to each of the objects.

This is rather easily done in case of measuring size or weight. In social sciences, however, attributes usually are hypothetical constructs and the measuring instrument is a collection of recordings of reactions to a certain set of stimuli - as for instance a questionaire.

For simplicity purposes we will from now on talk about sets of items or item-sets, using these terms in their most general sense. Now, does every set of items automatically form a scale?

If we are satisfied with nominal scales, N items with I(n) categories each define

$$I(1) * I(2) * \ldots * I(N)$$

distinct classes all the objects can uniquely be assigned to (provided that they do not show undefined item-categories). Hence, nominal comparisons ("equal" or "not equal") can always be done because every given pair of objects does or does not belong to the same class.

Most hypotheses in social sciences, however, are formulated in terms of ordinal relations ("greater than", "less than") and, therefore, necessarily demand an ordinal instrument of measurement - an ordinal scale.

The simplest example for an ordinal scale is a single item with ordinally defined categories - but imagine the experimenter who wants to examine e.g. intelligence by a single item, such as:

"Please classify each object into one of these categories:

(1) very silly
(2) silly
(3) average
(4) intelligent
(5) highly intelligent

A rating like this would, of course, be regarded as rather subjective and wide-meshed.

It would surely be more reasonable to have each person try to solve a set of tasks and to calculate an intelligence score from the response-vector.

This procedure, however, implies that all the response-vectors at least can be ranked somehow (if ranking is possible, at least an ordinal scale is given. Whether or not this measures the attribute under study is yet another question).

In the most ideal case all types of (different) response-vectors found in a sample of respondents can be arranged in a pattern-matrix like the following by column-permutation only:

```
        Different response-vectors

Items   0 0 0 0 . . .                          (1: task solved
        1 0 0 0 . . .                           0: task not solved)
        1 1 0 0 . . .
        1 1 1 0 . . .
        1 1 1 1 . . .
        . . . .
        . . . .
        . . . .
```

If such a column-permutation can be found, the tasks form a perfect GUTTMAN-scale and the scale-value of a given object can simply be defined as the count of ones in its response-vector (GUTTMAN, 1950).

Usually, however, a perfect GUTTMAN scale cannot be found - that is: Even the best possible permutation results in a pattern-matrix that shows ones in the upper triangle and zeros in its lower one.
If we define

$$REP = 1 - E / NI$$

with: E: Number of errors (1 instead of 0, 0 instead of 1)
N: Number of respondents or different response-vectors
I: Number of items

we obtain a possible coefficient for the quality of a scale which - according to GUTTMAN - should not be less than 0.90.
GUTTMAN scalogram analysis now can be summarized as follows:

1. Permutate the columns of the response-matrix and choose the permutation with the maximum REP-coefficient.
2. Check, whether REP is above .90
   If so: Done.
   If not: Eliminate the item that causes most of the errors and loop back to step 1.

Since this procedure does not leave any room for random errors, it is called "deterministic".

MOKKEN scaling (MOKKEN, 1971) is usually regarded as a probabilistic extension of this procedure. Its algorithm can be outlined as follows:

1. Find the most "homogeneous" item-pair of the (remaining) item pool.
   1.1. Check whether these two are "homogeneous".
   If not: STOP - no (further) scale can be found.
   If yes: Regard these two as the start-set of a scale and proceed to step 2.

2. Try to extend the scale by one item:
   2a: Exclude all items definitely for this scale that show a negative "coefficient of homogeneity" with the current scale.
   2b: Check, whether there are any items left that are "homogeneous" to the current scale:
   If not: No further extension possible, scale completed. Proceed to step 4.
   If yes: Proceed to step 3.
3. Choose the item that yields the most "homogeneous" extended scale. Loop back to step 2.
4. Try to find another scale in the remaining set of scaled items. Therefore, loop back to step 1.

This algorithm is based upon the concept of "homogeneity". This is defined and measured by LOEVINGER's homogeneity coefficient H (LOEVINGER, 1947) which is defined as follows:

Given: 2 dichotomous items i and j, coded
1: item (task) solved
0: item (task) not solved.
and: Item i is more difficult (less often solved) than item j

This yields the following 2 by 2 - table of solving probabilities:

		Item j 0	Item j 1	
Item i	0	p (0,0)	p (0,1)	p (0,.)
	1	p (1,0)	p (1,1)	p (1,.)
		p (.,0)	p (.,1)	

with:
p (1,.) LE p (.,1)

H(i,j) then is defined as:

$$H(i,j) = 1 - \frac{p\,(1,0)}{p\,(1,.) \; * \; p\,(.,0)} \tag{1}$$

or - if we estimate the p(i,j) from the observed frequencies in a sample:

$$H(i,j) = 1 - \frac{n\,(1,0)}{(n(1,.) \; * \; n(.,0)) \; / \; N} \tag{1a}$$

This coefficient is equal to the DEL-coefficient of HILDEBRAND, LAING and ROSENTHAL (1977) with (1,0) as the error cell and it is equal to

$$\text{Phi(korr.)} = \text{Phi} \;/\; \text{Phi(max.)}$$

Regarding the cell (1,0) as the error cell for a homogeneous pair of dichotomous items, reflects the fact that this cell represents those objects that managed to solve the more difficult item i though they failed to solve the easier item j.

Looking at equation (1), it is obvious that the quotient part of it reflects the relation of the error-probability p(1,0) = E(i,j) and its 0-expectation (its expected value under the null-hypotheses) if it were predicted only from the (known) marginal distributions: p(1,.)*p(.,0) = E0(i,j). H(i,j) obviously becomes 0, if this quotient is 1 - that is if numerator and denominator are equal: E(i,j) = E0(i,j).
MOKKEN has shown that the statistic

$$\text{DELTA*} = \frac{(p(1,0) - p(1,.) * p(.,0)) - 0}{\text{Var}(p(1,0))} \qquad (2)$$

estimated as

$$\frac{n(1,0) - (n(1,.) * n(.,0)) \;/\; N}{\text{Var}(n(1,0))} \qquad (2a)$$

is sufficiently approximated by the normal distribution for larger N (30 and more) and, therefore, can easily be tested against zero. Thus, all necessary means to perform steps 1. and 1a. of the MOKKEN algorithm are available, since the most homogeneous item pair is the one with the highest H(i,j) (step 1.) which can be tested against zero (1a.). The other steps, however, require the definition of

* Homogeneity of a single item with a scale (H(i))
* Homogeneity of a scale (H)
* Testing these against zero.

H is defined as

$$H = 1 - \frac{E}{E0}$$

with: E: Sum of the p (0,1) corresponding to all H(i,j), i LT j, of all item pairs of the scale after reordering the items according to their difficulties.
E0: Sum of the corresponding 0-expectations

and H(i) is defined as

$$H(i) = 1 - \frac{E(i)}{E0(i)}$$

with: E(i): Sum of the p (0,1) of all H(i,j), i NE j
E0(i): Sum of the corresponding 0-expectation

For these coefficients MOKKEN showed that a statistic DELTA* similar to equation *(2a) can be defined, the distribution of which again is sufficiently well approximated by the normal distribution (for a detailed discussion the reader is referred to MOKKEN (1971)).

Talking about "significant differences from zero", it has to be stressed that this only means that there is NOT NO homogeneity. Whether or not a set of items makes up a reasonable scale has to be judged on other grounds. MOKKEN proposed to fix a minimum scalability-coefficient for a scale to be built and classified:

```
          H LT .30    "no scale"
   .30 LE H LT .40    "weak scale"
   .40 LE H LT .50    "medium scale"

(H=1.00: perfect GUTTMAN-Scale)
```

Yet - so far every scale regardless of its H-coefficient would be nothing more but a cluster of homogeneous items.

To get from this cluster to a scale the items have to be rank-ordered somehow - e.g. according to their (sample-)difficulties.
This implies the following 2 assumptions:

1: All the items of a cluster do measure the same attribute.
2: If the solving probabilities of the items of a cluster were plotted against the amount of the attribute, these items measure, these so called trace-lines would be monotonously increasing curves and they would not intersect. If the assumption is valid, an object's scale value can be defined as the rank of the most difficult item solved and the scale can be regarded as "ordinal".

To check the second assumption, MOKKEN proposed to visually inspect the so called p(++)- and p(--)-probabilities of all item pairs:

If the rows and columns of the matrices of those probabilities are ordered according to the item difficulties, the values in the rows as well as in the columns of the P(++)-matrix should be monotonously decreasing, whereas those of the P(--)-matrix should be monotonously increasing (trend-violations of about 0.03 or less MOKKEN regards as negligible).

HENNING & SIX (1980) proposed to check this assumption by applying KENDALL's W-coefficient to the P(++)- and P(--)-matrices.

A major disadvantage of the MOKKEN algorithm described so far is that it requires dichotomous data.
In 1982, however, MOLENAAR proposed an extension to polychotomous data. MOLENAAR assumes that each of the polychotomous items under study can be regarded as an ordinal "scale" consisting of M item steps (M item steps: M+1 item categories). Thus, for K item with M(k) item steps each there are

$$M(1)+ M(2)+...+M(k)$$

item steps to be arranged (interleaved) into a final scale.

Since each of the item-steps could be regarded as a dichotomous item, one could come to the - false - conclusion that scaling of polychotomous items could simply be done by recoding the data into as many dichotomous items as there are item-steps. The trouble with the steps of one item, however, is that they are not independent at all. If we e.g. look at steps i and i-1 of item k, it is obvious that due to the ordinal nature of the single items, it is logically impossible to find an object that solves step i though it did not solve step i-1 (hence, there is a logically impossible error cell). This means that the homogeneity of two items i and j has to be calculated directly from the corresponding (M(i)+1) * (M(j)+1) contingency table.
The way this is done shall now be illustrated by an example:

		Item i			
		0	1	2	Total
Item j	0	280	100	20	400
	1	10	80	10	100
	2	10	220	270	500
	Total	300	400	300	1000

(Tab.1)

Table 1 shows the contingency table of two items i and j. Now let us recall the definition of H(i,j) in the dichotomous case:

$$H(i,j) = 1 - E(i,j)/E0(i,j)$$

Since item i always was the easier one in terms of the sample solving probabilities, the (1,0)-cell automatically was the only error-cell and H(i,j) was pretty well defined.

In the polychotomous case, however, only the status of cell (0,0) is is predefined: It is NOT an error-cell. But which item step shall we take next? Is is easier to solve step 1 of item i or step 1 of item j?

To answer this question MOLENAAR (1982) introduces the term of "Cumulative Percentages Passed" (CPP), calculated from the marginal frequency of objects that have passed a given item step, starting at the most difficult step and cumulating to the easiest one. Table 2 gives the CPPs for our example.

		Item i			
		0	1	2	CPP
Item j	0	***	***		100
	1		***		60
	2		***	***	50
	CPP	100	70	30	0

(Tab.2)

For item j the CCP-column should be read as follows: 50% of the objects passed step 1 and 2, 60% passed step 1 and 100% did not pass any step (CPP-row for item i accordingly). Now, since 60% of the sample managed to solve step 1 of item j, whereas 70% of the sample passed step 1 of item j, the later seems to be easier. Thus, (0,1) should not be an error cell. The next two candidate non-error cells are (0,2) and (1,1). Since 60% is greater than 30%, we choose (1,1) and now have to proceed either with (2,1) or (1,2). Still CCP(j) is greater than CCP(i) (50 GT 30). So we choose (2,1) and - finally - (2,2) as non-error cells. Now, the error cells are pretty well defined as "the rest" and the sums of observed and expected frequencies in those error cells can be computed to determine the H(i,j)-coefficient.

Again, this H(i,j)-coefficient is a special case of the above mentioned DEL-coefficient and again a DELTA* statistic for tests against zero can be defined, the distribution of which is sufficiently well approximated by the normal distribution. Also, the coefficients H(i) and H can be generalized accordingly as well as the corresponding DELTA* statistics and, thus, the described scaling algorithm basically remains unchanged for polychotomous data.

Now, how does this algorithm do compared to factor analysis and MINISSA?

To answer this question, the three methods were applied to the same set of data: 98 divisions on various topics of 809 delegates of the Frankfurter Nationalversammlung (FNV).

The question studied was: Can those 98 bills be scaled somehow on basis of the votes (How many scales can be found, how can they be interpreted?)

Unfortunately, the data contained lots of missing values representing various reasons of non-votes (neutral, absent, etc.). So, a polychotomous analysis seemed to be inappropriate right from the start. Moreover, excluding all cases with missing values was impossible as well since nearly no cases would have been left.
Hence, two alternatives for dichotomous analyses remained:

A: "agree" vs. rest ("disagree"+others)
B: "disagree" vs. rest ("agree"+others)

The corresponding analyses yielded:

Analysis A: Three scales.

Scale A.1:	61 Items,	H = .52,	DELTA* = 511.62
Scale A.2:	31 Items,	H = .51,	DELTA* = 251.84
Scale A.3:	3 Items,	H = .44,	DELTA* = 18.73

Analysis B: Four scales

Scale B.1:	28 Items,	H = .51,	DELTA* = 218.53
Scale B.2:	56 Items,	H = .53,	DELTA* = 503.15
Scale B.3:	8 Items,	H = .44,	DELTA* = 44.35
Scale B.4:	2 Items,	H = .48,	DELTA* = 6.92

Since scales 3 and 4 in both analyses contain a very small number of items, we decided to keep only scales A.1, A.2 and B.1, B.2 respectively for comparison with other methods. Furthermore, looking at the overall statistics of the ?.1- and ?.2 - scales, it seemed that

A.1 = B.2 ; B.1 = A.2

So we cross-tabulated the scale-numbers:

		B-Scale	
		1	2
A-scale	1	1	56
	2	27	-

and found out that the B-scales were subsets of the A-scales. Thus, we kept only scales A.1 and A.2.

The next question necessarily was: What items do these scales consist of? Dealing with parliament-votes we assumed an association between the scale-numbers and the political wing that brought in the bill:

		Scale	
		1	2
Origin of bill	Left	60	3
	Right	1	28

Since MOKKEN-scaling can find unipolar scales only, we now assumed that the two scales represented the two branches of a bipolar "left-right"-scale. To check this, we inverted the coding of the "right"-items and re-ran the scaling procedure:

Analysis C: 6 scales.

Scale C.1:	10 Items,	H = .44,	DELTA* = 49.57
Scale C.2:	60 Items,	H = .56,	DELTA* = 418.25
Scale C.3:	6 Items,	H = .58,	DELTA* = 35.95
Scale C.4:	3 Items,	H = .74,	DELTA* = 26.34
Scale C.5:	5 Items,	H = .47,	DELTA* = 32.82
Scale C.6:	2 Items,	H = .47,	DELTA* = 5.08

Due to a small number of items or low H-coefficients, scales 4,5 and 6 were excluded and the C-scale numbers were cross-tabulated against the A-scale numbers:

		C-scale			
		1	2	3	
A-scale	1	5	40	2	47
	2	5	19	4	28
		10	59	6	75

Thus, 59 of 75 scalable items (78.6%) can be arranged on a "left-right"-scale, but it seems that there are 1 or 2 more dimensions consisting of bills that are judged not only on basis of their origin.

Similar results for the same data were obtained by BEST (1986) by means of factor analysis and MINISSA.

Now the question raised: Is there any "direct" relation between the MOKKEN scales and the above mentioned factor- and MDS-solutions?

To answer this, the means of the factor-loadings and the MINISSA dimension scores were calculated for the items of the scales A.1 and A.2:

	Means		
Scale	F.1	F.2	Dim.1
A.1	.67	.22	-.60
A.2	-.38	-.40	1.08

This led us to the following assumption:

Scale A.1 represents the "+++"-octant of the factor-space and the "-"-branch of the MINISSA-dimension.

Scale A.2 represents the "---"-octant of the factor-space and the "+"-branch of the MINISSA-dimension.

To check this, we dichotomized the essential factor loadings and dimension scores at pinewood 0 and, thus, obtained the following three 2 by 2 - tables:

	Factor 1	
	-	+
Scale A.1	2	59
A.2	28	3

	Factor 2 -	+
Scale A.1	3	58
A.2	28	3

	Factor 3 -	+
Scale A.1		10
A.2	6	

	Dimension 1 -	+
Scale A.1	27	4
A.2		17

Furthermore, we multiplied the H-coefficients of scale A.2 with -1 and correlated the H-coefficients of both scales together with the factor loadings and dimension scores:

	F.1	F.2	F.3	Dim.1
H(A.1), -H(A.2)	.90	.75	.98	-.93

Thus, we come to the final conclusion that the three methods basically had come to the same results with the only difference that MOKKEN-scaling is more reliable since it does not need the preassumptions of factor analysis nor can it be trapped in a local minimum of a stress-function like MINISSA.

REFERENCES

BEST, H. 1986. *Struktur und Handeln parlamentarischer Führungsgruppen in Deutschland und Frankreich 1848/49*. Habil.Schrift, Univ. Köln, Wirtschafts- und Sozialwissenschaftliche Fakultät, published under the title: *Die Männer von Bildung und Besitz*. Düsseldorf, 1990

COSTNER, H.L. 1965. "Criteria for measures of association". *American Sociological Review* 30

GUTTMAN, L. 1950. "The basis of scalogram analysis", in: Stouffer, S.A.; Guttman, L.; Suchman, E.A.; Lazarsfeld, P.F.; Star, S.A. & Clausen, J.A. (eds.). *Measurement and prediction*. Princeton: Univ. Press

HENNING, H.J. and SIX, B. 1980. "Konventionelle Merkmalserfassung vs. differentielle Skalierung. Teil 2: Differentielle Skalierung und ihre Anwendung auf die Erfassung altruistischer Einstellung". *Zeitschrift für differentielle und diagnostische Psychologie* 1

HILDEBRAND, D.K.; LAING, J.D. and ROSENTHAL, H. 1977. *Prediction analysis of cross-classifications*. New York: Wiley

LOEVINGER, J. 1947. "A systematic approach to the construction and evaluation of ability". *Psychological Monographs* 61(4)

MOKKEN, R.J. 1971. *A theory and procedure of scale analysis*. The Hague: Mouton

MOLENAAR, I.W. 1982. "Mokken scaling revisited". *Kwantitative Methoden* 3(8)

RUDINGER, G.; CHASELON, F.; ZIMMERMANN, E.J. and HENNING, H.J. 1985. *Qualitative Daten*. München: Urban & Schwarzenberg

INTERACTING WITH DIAGRAMS: USING A GRAPH BROWSER WITH A RESEARCH DATABASE

Janet Bagg, Nick Ryan
Computing Laboratory
University of Kent at Canterbury
United Kingdom

Introduction

The wide variety of subject areas encompassed by the social sciences and humanities show considerable diversity in their need for and use of diagrams both during the research process and in the final presentation of results. With the increasing availability of computer graphics much use is now made of presentation graphics software on both mainframes and microcomputers. Such software, whether in the form of separate programs or as an integrated part of database, spreadsheet or general purpose statistical packages, provides a range of techniques for summarising quantitative information. Other applications of computer graphics, particularly those not primarily intended to provide quantitative summaries, have been less common and often of specialised use only.

In the scientific and engineering communities where access to powerful workstations is now commonplace, highly interactive methods of using graphical images are frequently employed. Typically, the images are used not only to represent the results of queries on an underlying database, but also as a means of access to, and manipulation of the database. General purpose examples range from software development tools to CAD systems. Although many aspects of this style of computing, which usually employs a mouse or equivalent device in the selection of graphical objects, are now employed on some microcomputers there have been few attempts to develop appropriate tools and to assess their value to social science and humanities computing. One notable exception can be seen in the recent rapid growth in interest in geographical information systems which, as illustrated in papers by Barbara Morris and others at this conference, are beginning to find many uses beyond the parent discipline.

This paper is concerned with the interactive use of a different form of diagram which, although less widely applicable than those employed in presentation graphics or geographical information systems, has a number of uses across a range of disciplines. These diagrams often appear in highly specialised forms such as the anthropologist's kinship diagram or the archaeologist's stratigraphic sequence. Although there are many differences between the conventional forms of such diagrams, the common factor is that they may all be seen as elaborations of directed graphs. A graph consists simply of nodes (vertices) connected by lines (edges). A directed graph is one in which each edge has an assigned direction.

An Application-Configurable Graph Browser

Several programs, usually referred to as graph browsers that may be used to display and manipulate these structures have been described in the computing science literature in recent years (for example, Rowe et al 1987; Robins 1987). These are interactive programs that can lay out a graph from data specifying nodes and edges. A means of editing the diagram is normally also provided. These programs could be used for the types of applications discussed here but their generalised approach and use of simple abstract graphs would be certain to meet with considerable resistance from users with no direct interest in the underlying graph concept. Unlike computer scientists, anthropologists and archaeologists are often not, and indeed may have no reason to be, familiar with mathematical graph theory in order to construct and use their diagrams. Indeed, attempts to introduce mathematical ideas such as graph theory into these and other disciplines have in the past met with only limited success.

The *gnet* graph browser, which has been described in greater detail elsewhere (Ryan 1988), was designed to overcome these limitations. Experience with earlier software developed specifically for a genealogical application (Ryan 1985a) suggested that not only was a more generalised solution possible for this and similar applications, but also that such an approach could overcome many of the problems that can arise with too specialised a design of browser.

The basis of *gnet* is a general purpose graph browser acting as the front-end to a database controlled by the Ingres DBMS. The majority of its development has been done on a Sun workstation using the X window system. Diagrams can be created interactively or from data held in database tables. Nodes may be positioned manually or by the application of an automatic layout algorithm and the user may edit the diagram to provide a representation that adequately conveys the required information. Nodes and links may be moved, added or deleted as required simply by selecting the required menu function and diagram elements with the mouse. When nodes are moved or deleted the program ensures that the diagram remains consistent by moving or deleting associated links as necessary. Once a satisfactory configuration has been achieved the state of the diagram may be saved in the database for use in a later session, or written to a file in the form of, for example, PostScript instructions for a laser printer.

Gnet can be configured to produce diagrams in a form appropriate to the application. Thus, the archaeologist can be presented with a plausible representation of a sequence diagram with each context represented by a labelled box, whereas an anthropologist could see a conventional genealogical diagram with the nodes displayed as triangles or circles according to the sex of the represented individual. The two types of diagram also differ in the layout of the links representing relationships between nodes. The application-specific configuration is achieved by providing a number of rules describing the required form of the diagram and the logical meaning of known types of relationship.

The close integration between the graph browser and the database allows access to stored information about the nodes or objects through direct interaction with the diagram. The act of selecting a displayed node or link by a point-and-press mouse operation can be used to invoke any pre-defined query. A large number of options are available, most of which are equally applicable to all applications, and the program has been designed so that it is relatively easy for a competent programmer to add further options, should they be needed for a particular application. This approach to database queries can be further enhanced by the provision of a means to highlight those displayed nodes that represent the result of a conventional SQL query typed by the user. This latter facility is currently being refined, but was not present in the version discussed in the remainder of this paper.

Testing and evaluation form an essential part of the development of any computer software. Although much can be achieved through tests with both real and artificial data, the effective assessment of the value of a computer tool can only be achieved through its use in the context for which it is intended. *Gnet* is intended primarily as a research tool providing facilities for the exploration and manipulation of particular types of data.

A research project currently being undertaken by one of the authors (Janet Bagg) as part of an Economic and Social Research Council funded Doctoral Programme in Applied Computing in Social Anthropology has provided an ideal opportunity for such assessment. The project involves a computer aided study of social relations and life course in the Weald of Kent, England in the late 16th and 17th centuries.

The Application

A database has been built up of information relating to almost 7500 individuals based on the life-event registers of the parish of Biddenden by means of the researcher's own semi-automatic data entry and linkage program. This has been tied in with information from other records, notably wills, probate inventories and ecclesiastical court records.

One aspect of the research is to examine how kin relationships may have played a part in aspects of peoples lives, and the way in which such links might be used. It has been possible to reconstruct genealogies for many people using the parish registers and wills, but how to explore this type of data for such a purpose presents something of a problem. A possible solution might be to look at the information graphically, allowing other relevant information to be mapped onto a display of genealogical relationships.

Anthropologists generally display such information in a fairly standard graphical form. Some work had been done on building software for this type of application at UKC (Ryan 1985b; Davis 1985) using unilineal descent group kinship in North Africa. This, however, would not be suitable for the English data which requires bilateral representation and is not closely inter-connected. *Gnet* uses a more flexible approach and looked suitable for the English data.

The nature of the data itself presents some initial problems. Despite kinship being reckoned bilaterally in England, the parish registers and wills gave a mainly male oriented view, leading to the data being mostly organised patrilineally. Also a large number of marriages as well as descent chains created the potential for complex diagrams.

Using *gnet*

One facility offered by *gnet* is to display all related nodes starting from any single node. This seemed an obvious first exploratory step. From previous work in this area, I expected small discrete groups ranging from parents and children to a hundred persons or so. The actual result was one enormous, very complex diagram containing almost 3000 persons, nearly half of those in the database. Although the program was able to construct such a diagram, the result provided little to aid the human user. Even the ability to produce a skeleton diagram by removal of those who died in childhood, or even all those for whom no marriages or offspring are recorded, failed to reduce the result to a manageable diagram.

Obviously, this approach would not work in all cases. Another facility allows the 'growing' of a diagram from the core set of relationships - parents, spouses and children - of an individual (Figure 1). This can be an interesting way of browsing the database but lacks direction of itself. A further facility allows the paths between two nodes to be displayed. A combination of these two methods is being used to examine the genealogical relations of men holding the office of parish churchwarden (Figure 2). This was held by two men in each year, usually in two year overlapping stints. Genealogical relations are problematic in display terms as they are essentially multidimensional but must for the sake of clarity be represented in two-dimensional space. Hence the need to combine the simplicity of the 'path' method with the free-ranging complexity of the 'growing' method.

Figure 1: *gnet* Display Showing Expanded Relationships of John Fry (1560-16??)

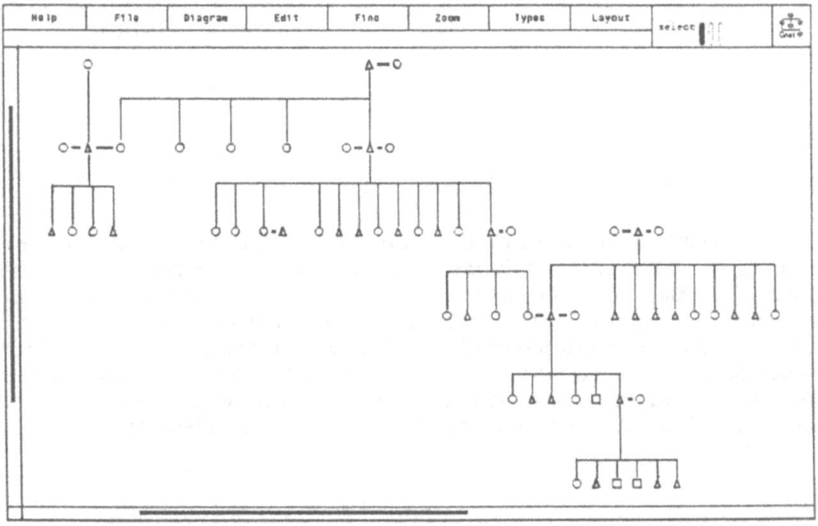

The problems encountered in using *gnet* have suggested ways in which the program might be improved as a research tool. Various modifications have been made as a result of experiences with this particular database. Amongst these, perhaps the most significant has been a change to the 'All Related' and 'Path' facilities to restrict searching to a user-specified depth. Thus, for example, it is now possible to display all relatives of a given individual who are within a chosen number of direct genealogical links.

The ability of the software to allow the user to explore the structure of her data has benefits and pitfalls. To an anthropologist, a constructed genealogy is a different thing from kinship, one cannot be read directly from the other. English kinship is ego-centered and selective. The diagrams attempt to draw together many such kin sets into a graph of people theoretically related, but this is only an artefact of the researcher and may

Figure 2: *gnet* Display Showing Relationships Between a Number of Men Who Held the Office of Churchwarden

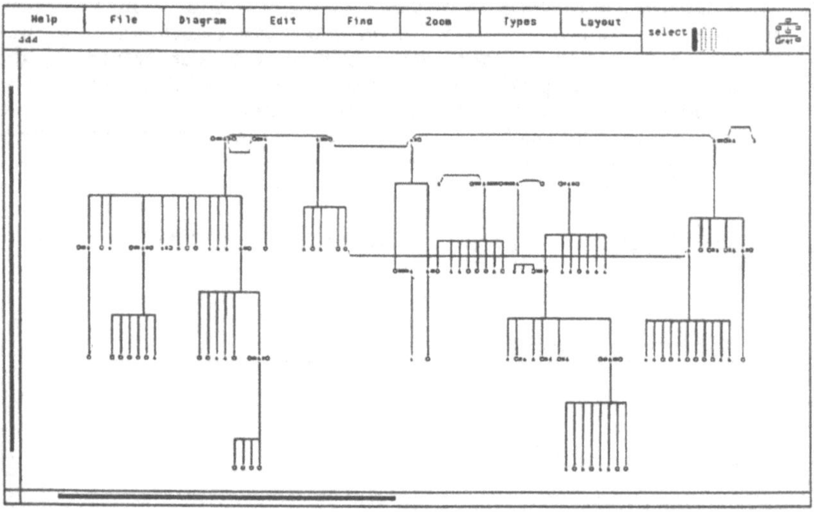

have little reality to the researched. Looking at a more generalised diagram of relationships may however permit the researcher to explore the selection and construction processes of kinship. It may also indicate where kin sets may overlap, one person being claimed as kin by two people who otherwise see themselves as unrelated, creating the potential for mediation. Other information, such as office holding, inheritance, and other forms of relationship can potentially be mapped onto such diagrams, allowing a different perspective. It must be remembered that *gnet* is a tool for data exploration and presentation. It is not and was never intended to be a quick problem solver.

REFERENCES

DAVIS, J.H.R. 1985. "A Background Note on Gtree." *Bulletin of Information on Computers in Anthropology* 3, 16-20, Centre for Social Anthropology and Computing, University of Kent

ROBINS, G. 1987. "The ISI Grapher: A Portable Tool for Displaying Graphs Pictorially." *Proceedings of Symboliikka '87, Helsinki, Finland*

ROWE, L.A.; DAVIS, M.; MESSINGER, E.; MEYER, C.; SPIRAKIS, C. and TUAN, A. 1987. "A Browser for Directed Graphs." *Software - Practice and Experience* 17, 1, 61-76

RYAN, N.S. 1985a. "Interactive Graphical Tools in the Social Sciences", in: Johnson, P. and Cook, S. (eds.). *People and Computers: Designing the Interface*. Cambridge University Press

RYAN, N.S. 1985b. "Gtree: A system for the interactive display and editing of kinship information." *Bulletin of Information on Computers in Anthropology* 3, 6-15, Centre for Social Anthropology and Computing, University of Kent

RYAN, N.S. 1988. "Browsing Through the Stratigraphic Record", in: Rahtz, S.P.Q. (ed.). *Computer and Quantitative Methods in Archaeology: CAA88*, 327-334, British Archaeological Reports, International Series no. 446

CARTO-NET: INTERNATIONAL ACCESS TO MAP AND ARCHIVE RECORDS

Barbara Morris
Geographical Information Systems Applications Institute (GISAI)
University of Edinburgh
United Kingdom

The CARTO-NET system for automated cataloguing offers the possibility for historians and social scientists to search, for the first time, for published maps, manuscript and archival material held in collections all over the world. CARTO-NET software is available from GIS Applications, Department of Geography, University of Edinburgh.

Up to now catalogue records of maps, manuscripts and archive material have been difficult to query in an integrated way because very few records of this kind have been automated and no system existed which was suitable to accommodate them all. CARTO-NET has been designed to overcome this problem. The development work has concentrated particularly on map collections but the closely related problems of automated cataloguing other non-book material such as manuscripts and archives have also been discussed with professionals working in these areas.

By conforming to previously agreed international standards for catalogue description and format, it has been possible for the CARTO-NET development team to build a system which could be used in a wide variety of libraries around the world. Cataloguing in CARTO-NET follows Anglo-American Cataloguing Rules [AACR2] (ed. Gorman and Winkler 1978, 1982) and the subsequent interpretation for cartographic materials (Stibbe 1982). On-line help is available on the cataloguing screen and more extensive on-line help can be called up on the HELP key for inexperienced cataloguers and searchers.

Catalogue records can be output in machine-readable format (MARC) for exchange with other institutions so that, in theory, no material need ever be catalogued more than once anywhere in the world. MARC was originally designed to allow catalogue records of books to be exchanged around the world. It was provided with an extension in 1983 to allow map records and other cartographic materials to be included. However, this extension has not proved to be sufficiently flexible for all map material. A full map catalogue record requires many more access points than those for a book because of the spatial dimension or geographical area covered.

Where machine-readable records for map and archive material already exist, these can be adapted and loaded into CARTO-NET. Work is currently going on in Edinburgh to load U.S. Library of Congress map catalogue records which are held in US MARC format into CARTO-NET. A test set of British Library UK MARC records of map and atlases from BLAISELINE is also being loaded into CARTO-NET. In both cases these records refer only to singly published maps, atlases or the First Level information about a map series. There has been no attempt in Britain or the United States to record, in a computerised form, information about map sheets which are part of a series. Since these comprise up to 90% of all published maps, this has been a severe loss. Only 10% were being adequately described in a MARC record, a very high proportion to be omitted from any automated system. The CARTO-NET system goes some way towards remedying this defect by recording information about individual copies of every map sheet and producing a cover diagram to complement these records. Complete bibliographical control of ALL maps can now be achieved. CARTO-NET uses the UK MARC format as a base and then allows each individual map sheet to be fully described to the level of recording which library holds individual copies. This feature allows union catalogues to be built in the future.

A particular feature of the CARTO-NET system is the automation of the graphic index or cover diagram. Graphic index diagrams showing map coverage have been one of the map librarian's traditional tools for map cataloguing and searching. Over a long period of use these can become almost illegible with manuscript additions. It is also difficult to find all maps of a particular area if they belong to many different series depicted on many different paper index diagrams. CARTO-NET allows the reader to use an on-screen cursor to identify his broad area of interest on a world map background. The continuous zoom facility enlarges a specific area, giving more background detail; this process can be continued until the search window is accurately defined. The geographical limits of the search area can then be combined with a search of the database record of the maps to retrieve the required material.

The digital background of the world which is currently used by CARTO-NET is World Databank II (WDB II), digitised in 1977 at a scale of approximately 1:3,000,000 for the United States Central Intelligence Agency. The tapes are available in the Public Domain. WDB II shows international boundaries and rivers. The density of detail can be controlled by the user from the on-screen menu according to the display scale on the computer screen and the amount of map sheet information which has been superimposed on it. More detailed digital backgrounds can be attached to CARTO-NET for the display of larger scale map cover. For the U.K. the Ordnance Survey 1:625,000 scale and Bartholomew 1:250,000 digital outlines are available. The Ordnance Survey cover includes the National Grid, three categories of roads, administrative boundaries, three categories of built-up area from cities down to villages and all the associated place-names. The Bartholomew cover has significantly more detail. As with WDB II, the user can control the level of background detail with a cursor or mouse from the on-screen menu. It will be possible to attach detailed digital background maps of other countries to CARTO-NET where these are available and required by individual libraries. It is particularly important to have detailed digital background maps on which to display large scale map coverage. The British Geological Survey is currently cataloguing all its mapping of the U.K. and Continental Shelf. The publishing progress and cover of individual map series can be searched and displayed on a graphics screen on the Ordnance Survey 1:625,000 scale digital background.

CARTO-NET can be linked with other geographically-referenced data sets such as reports, gazetteer entries, archives, air photographs and satellite imagery. There is potential for a very powerful, integrated information retrieval system to be established. There are plans to link the CARTO-NET map retrieval system directly to a related suite of software packages called PHOTO-NET which has also been developed by GIS Applications. PHOTO-NET allows the user to search for all vertical and oblique air photograph cover of a particular area of the U.K. It could also be adapted for other countries where detailed digital backgrounds were available.

Cataloguing of all map sheets will be a major, but worthwhile task since it will enable map collections to be used more fully and direct readers quickly to where particular map sheets are located. It is often the case that one institution will have some maps of a large series while others will be held by another. Many collections have over one million individual maps but few can afford to automate the catalogue record of each and every sheet, although this is highly desirable in order to use the collection fully.

The British Library Research and Development Department supported a study from 1987-88 on the feasibility of setting up a co-operative map cataloguing network which would have the aim of sharing out this estimated 100 man-year task between many map libraries within the UK and avoiding duplication of data input. One of the obvious advantages of such an union catalogue would be the sharing of cataloguing effort between participating libraries as many collections have overlapping holdings.

Three possible scenarios for the implementation of a cooperative cataloguing system were investigated; firstly where data would be managed centrally with one host machine holding all the records and users having access through a modem, the Packet Switching Service (PSS) or the Joint Academic Network (JANET). This is currently the favoured solution although it might be implemented in conjunction with the second. This second scenario would involve individual sites checking a central datastore to see if a record already existed before entering it in a local microcomputer-based system. Local records could later be loaded into the central database. The third alternative would be to use distributed database facilities. This is not realistic at present as very few institutions have access to such facilities. In the longer term it would be the preferred solution. It would appear to the user that all data were held centrally, but would actually be held on a network of computers around the country. Any number of other sites could dial in to interrogate the distributed data without being involved in the input operation. The results of this feasibility study on networking were published by the British Library in October, 1988. International telecommunication standards were observed during the study so that the network could be extended overseas beyond the U.K. at some future date.

Following the positive results of this feasibility study, a Working Party of the British Committee for Map Information and Cataloguing Systems (BRICMICS) was set up to plan the implementation of a UK Cartographic Records Database. New standards were drafted by staff in the British Library, Royal Geographical Society and the University of Manchester for the description of Sheet Level records which could be used as an extension of the UK MARC format for the exchange of bibliographical records. These standards emerged after evaluation of the CARTO-NET project. The CARTO-NET system will be considered, along with any other systems in existence, as the basis of such a Union Catalogue.

CARTO-NET is also under consideration in its present form for the control of series mapping and of individually published maps in many overseas countries. A joint application for funding for further development of the graphics handling capability is being submitted in the United States by GIS Applications and the Research Library Group (RLG) in Stanford, California. This would be an extension of the project already under way at RLG for the University of California at Santa Barbara.

Rather than use special-purpose library software which has proved unsuitable for cataloguing complete map collections, or developing all the software in-house, it was decided to build interfaces between commercially available software tools. This technique has allowed a complex system to be built relatively quickly. CARTO-NET records are held in the ORACLE Relational Database Management System. ORACLE is one of the most widely used systems in the world and uses the SQL query language. SQL is an ANSI standard. The catalogue data held in ORACLE is linked with graphics software to allow the user to carry out an exhaustive on-line search over a wide range of material. This approach produces many more hits than has ever been possible with the traditional method employed by map librarians of searching with a combination of card catalogue, map coverage diagram and personal knowledge of their collection. Some of the graphics software used in the CARTO-NET application, such as GIMMS, has been commercially available world-wide for many years; other packages have been specially written in Edinburgh for the map and air photograph library automation systems but are sufficiently general-purpose for use in other applications and can be licensed as separate modules from CARTO-NET.

A menu offers many ways of searching the database but since all the material catalogued in CARTO-NET can be assigned a spatial, or geographical reference in terms of latitude and longitude, many users of the system have stated their preference for making the initial search of the database graphically. Only after the area of interest has been established by zooming into a digital outline of the world which is displayed on a graphics terminal would the search be further cut down by a combination of the catalogue fields. They could include any selection of aspects of the material which have been recorded in the catalogue such as subject, date of publication and surveyor. Once the user is satisfied with the results of the search a digital plot can be generated to accompany the listing. A search can take place across a wide range of other geographically-referenced datasets held in ORACLE. These might include census returns, gazetteer records, archival material, manuscripts or aerial photographs. For example, archaeologists are using CARTO-NET to link site records with map and air photograph cover.

CARTO-NET has been installed in universities and government departments within the United Kingdom within the last year. Both military and civilian versions have undergone extensive benchmarking. CARTO-NET has also been demonstrated on-line in the United States and Canada. There is a perceived need in North America, Europe and Australia for a National Cartographic Records Database which would be internationally compatible. It is envisaged that such databases would be built up using a co-operative cataloguing network.

Although the system was originally developed and tested on a range of Digital Equipment Corporation VAX computers, evaluation studies have shown that CARTO-NET is portable and can be mounted on a variety of other manufacturers' computers within large organisations.

Many map libraries are small and isolated with no access to mainframe or mini-computers. They would benefit, nevertheless, from an automated cataloguing and retrieval system. In order to make CARTO-NET more widely available development work is currently under way to produce an IBM PC version. This may either be used on its own for local cataloguing or linked through local area networks to a central database of map catalogue records which could be searched and updated from time to time. The IBM PC could also be used as a node to a national database. This is being considered in the U.K. For those libraries with PCs and no access to a network, update disks could be posted at regular intervals.

The CARTO-NET software has been under development by a team in Edinburgh University Geography Department for the last ten years. Those who have been involved include Alan Alexander, Darius Bartlett, Frances Donegan, Steve Dowers, Janet Gibson, Richard Healey, Jim Irvine, Barbara Morris and Tom Waugh. The project had financial support from the British Library Research and Development Department between 1985 and 1988.

Figure: Graphic Index of Different Map Series Covering Spain and Portugal, Normally Displayed in Four Colours. The On-Screen Menu is Used to Construct the Geographical Part of the Search

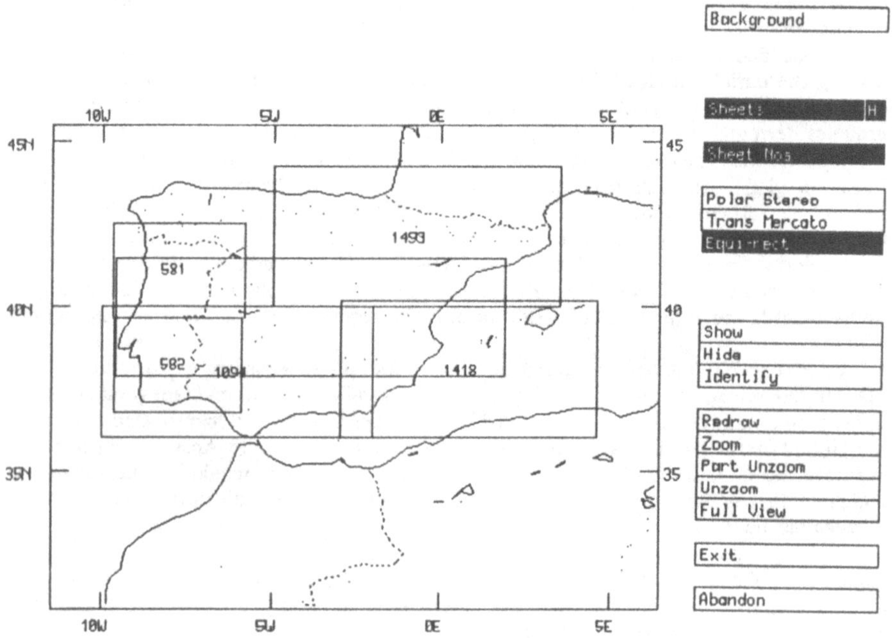

ACKNOWLEDGEMENTS

The author is grateful for continuing support from the Department of Geography, University of Edinburgh and the British Library, Research and Development Department. The development of CARTO-NET owes much to the team which has been involved in it from time to time over the past seven years, including Darius Bartlett, Steve Dowers, Janet Gibson, Bruce Gittings, Richard Healey, Jim Irvine, David Munro and Tom Waugh. Peter Milne and Margaret Wilkes of the National Library of Scotland Map Room have acted as the front-line of the evaluation sites. Other organisations mentioned in the text have also contributed greatly to the project's success.

REFERENCES

BARTLETT, D.J.; IRVINE, J.J.A. and MORRIS, B.A. (forthcoming). "The Map Curator in the computer age: the World at your fingertips", in: Wood, M. and Stone, J.C. (eds.). *Cartography - The Way Ahead.* Geobooks

BRACK, E.V. and CHIBNALL, J. 1985. "Map use in a small academic library." *The Cartographic Journal* 22(1), 45-48

British Library. Bibliographic Services Division. 1980. UK MARC Manual, 2nd edition, London. Amendments to 6/1986

Central Intelligence Agency 1977. CAM- Cartographic Automatic Mapping Program Documentation. 5th edition. Central Intelligence Agency: Washington D.C.

HEALEY, R.G.; DOWERS, S.; IRVINE, J.J.A. and MORRIS, B.A. 1988. "Developments in CARTO-NET - an automated system for map cataloguing and retrieval." *Proceedings of the GIS Conference of the Natural Environment Research Council*, NCS Report No. 8, June 1988

HEALEY, R. and MORRIS, B. 1987. "CARTO-NET: A relational database approach to automated map cataloguing." *The Cartographic Journal* 24(1), (forthcoming)

MORRIS, B. 1987. "CARTO-NET: A Cartographic Information Retrieval System." *British Library Research Report* No. 33, British Library, London

MORRIS, B. 1988. "CARTO-NET: Graphic retrieval and management system in an automated map library bulletin." *Special Libraries Association, Geography and Maps Division* No. 152, Washington, D.C.

MORRIS, Barbara. 1988. "CARTO-NET: Networking Map Catalogue Records." *British Library Research Report* No. 53, British Library, London

MORRIS, B.A. 1984. "Computer generated map indexes, cartographic information retrieval using the ORACLE-GIMMS software interface." *SUC Bulletin* 18(1), 25-28

MORRIS, B.A. 1986. "CARTO-NET British Library Research Project on Map Library Automation at the University of Edinburgh Department of Geography." *SUC Bulletin* 20(1), 31-32

MORRIS, B.A.; HEALEY, R.G. and WAUGH, T.C. (forthcoming). "From map catalogue to database with graphics in view." *LIBER Bulletin* 28, 1986 (Ligue des bibliothèques européenes de recherche)

STIBBE, H.L.P. (General Editor). 1982. *Cartographic Materials. A Manual of Interpretation for AACR2.* Chicago, Ottawa, London

WAUGH, T.C. and Healey, R.G. 1986. "The GEOLINK system: interfacing large systems." *Proceedings AUTOCARTO.* London

WAUGH, T.C. and McCALDEN, J. 1983. *GIMMS Reference Manual.* Release/Edition 4.5. GIMMS Ltd., Edinburgh

CONSIDERATIONS ON THE USE OF AN EXPERT SYSTEM TO SUPPORT ECONOMIC AND SOCIAL PLANNING

R. Arrus, B. Gronquist, D. Lelis, M. Ollivier, Z. Tari
Centre de Récherche en Informatique Appliqué aux Sciences Sociales
Université de Grenoble II
France

I. A Need of Planners: Exploring the Domains of Planning and Programming Actions

The activity of planning implies knowledge of what specific *elements* one must consider to solve a given problem and what *type of links* exist between them. It is also determining the level of coherence of the solution and, thus, carefully bounding the *planning domain*. The complexity of this domain depends on the desired level of refinement.

Exploration in this domain is based on the presence of relationships between the elements established by experts. The domain is updated interactively from an *entry point* (an element examined by the user), by successive refinements of sub-domains and it is represented by a graph whose arcs are the source elements and the target elements, the intermediate situations being made up of relay elements.

The originality of the method is demonstrated by the fact that while the entry point is in a given field, the domain-based coherent solution is *domain-wide*. This allows intervention on a set of elements which did not seem to be related to the *entry point* a priori. This approach provides a satisfactory solution to the given problem.

Once the *planning domain* has been determined, the second phase consists in programming actions. Each element is associated with a corresponding series of possible *actions* determined by the experts in each respective field. The diversity of the fields requires the combined knowledge of several groups of experts. The planner must program a series of coherent actions with respect to various political scenarios, both economic and social, which he has defined. It is in this context that the usefulness of computer-based assistance is best demonstrated.

II. The Advantage of an Expert System Assistance

We propose the use of an *expert system* approach to assist the planner. The goal is not to replace the planner, but to provide a *decision-making assistance system*. The system is designed so, as to allow the user to query, ask for explanations, modify data, select parameters etc. and let the user make the final decisions.

* Such an expert system is not limited by its design to a specific or restricted domain; it provides methodological support which can be adapted to the desired domain.
* It allows the user to enter data corresponding to his particular problem and to specify his own goals.
* The descriptive nature of the system facilitates simulation of planning scenarios.
* It offers powerful mechanisms to represent and use planning data from both,

quantitative and qualitative points of view.

* This technique allows integration of different levels of abstraction depending on the required refinement. It allows integration of methodological knowledge and application domain specific knowledge.
* A user can enter his own experience into the system and benefit from accumulated experience. The system can expand its knowledge base in the absence of a particular reasoning step or data while in use.
* Finally, the approach is modular and allows progressive integration of the necessary knowledge bases.

III. Design Choices and Proposed Techniques

a - Structured Knowledge Representation

The representation model in our system is based on *schemata*. The main reason is the nature of the knowledge itself. For most types of knowledge in our domain is manipulated (characteristics of problems and actions, general rules and specific action rules, coherence and compatibility rules...), we think that schemata have advantages with respect to factorization of knowledge and managing of the knowledge base. In addition, they allow grouping of rules based on their application context.

b - Explanation Capabilities

The goal of early expert systems was to approach the performance of human experts without worrying about the *user aspects*. In our domain, this aspect is important since it allows the development of a system which adapts itself to different users (decision maker, planner...). In general, the explanation is based on the use of a *unique trace*. This trace contains, in one structure, several types of knowledge: knowledge about the method (methodological) and knowledge about the application domain (factual knowledge). These two types being on the same level, make it easy for the user to confound them. One solution is to distinguish them: method (series of tasks) and domain knowledge (all of the relationships between problems and their characteristics). The use of these two types of knowledge by the *knowledge exploitation mechanisms* (K.E.M), which is a specialized inference engine, engenders *two types of traces*: the trace of the method (the user actions) and the trace of the domain knowledge producing distinct explanations for these two domains.

c - A Refined System for Knowledge Management

With regard to the K.E.M, we foresee the difficulties pertaining to the semantics of the elements taken into account and the manipulation of these elements. Surmounting these difficulties by designing and implementing the appropriate software modules makes the knowledge *operational*. For example in planning, when looking at the method proposed by experts to solve a given problem, we are confronted with several difficulties such as loops in the graph of elements or the absence of data that would allow the association of one or more types of actions for a problem. Once the problem of the difficulties of getting the knowledge operational is solved, the next problem is the *programming optimization* of the expert's method.

The last problem is the *modification of knowledge*. A user could choose between the use of fragments of know-how provided by the expert (in our case this implies the updating of attribute values for one or more schemata) or the multi-evaluation of schemata or a change in the chaining of the know-how fragments.

The K.E.M could also be used as a tool to construct a *data base*, which would allow the possibility of both, qualitative and quantitative levels. It can also transform a representation consisting of production rules or a semantic network into a strict representation (i.e. the schemata) defined by the formalism of the knowledge base. *This feature allows the user to represent his knowledge using that one of the three formalisms which suits him best.*

Presently, the C.R.I.S.S is working in two application domains (water and health), one of which is particularly advanced: SAPH2O (Système d'Aide a la Planification des ressources Hydrauliques).

IV. An Application: SAPH2O

The first question is: how can we rationalize the programming of the investments in the various sectors concerned by water resource mobilization, transport and use?

Figure 1: Water Resources Management Field

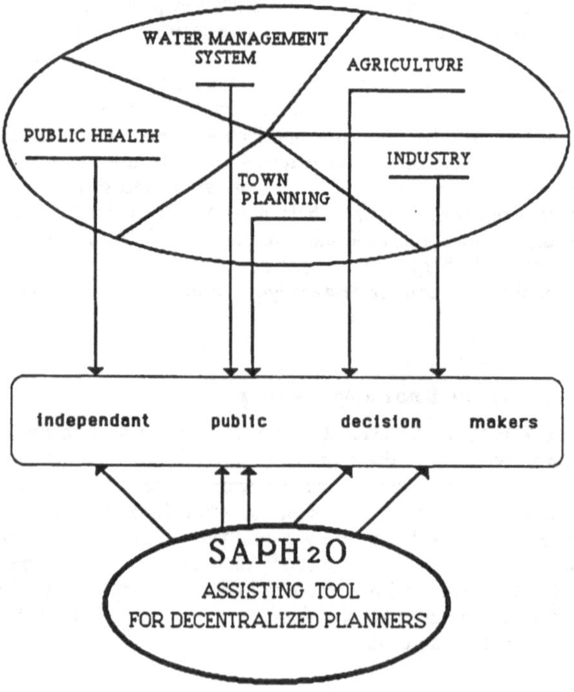

The domain of the water cycles concerns various sectors of activity: the water management system itself, but also the public health services, the energy production sector, the agricultural sector and the industry and town planning sector. In every sector we find independent decision makers, whose actions determine the behaviour of the global system. The problem is, how to rationalize the sector-dependent decisions in order to improve the behaviour of the system.

In each sector of the domain, the experts made a complete inventory of the environmental problems. From the point of view of its malfunctioning linked with the management of water resources: for instance, in the public health sector they found various human diseases; in the industrial one different types of pollution, in the agricultural sector problems of soil erosion and so on. The experts identified 150 types of problems in the six sectors of the domain:

Sector	Number of Problem Types
ENERGY	12
INDUSTRY	25
HEALTH	28
HYDRAULIC	32
TOWN PLANNING	20
AGRICULTURE	32

For each of them, they summarized their knowledge in three categories of information:

* the first one concerns the relationships between the different problems,

Figure 2: Linked Problems

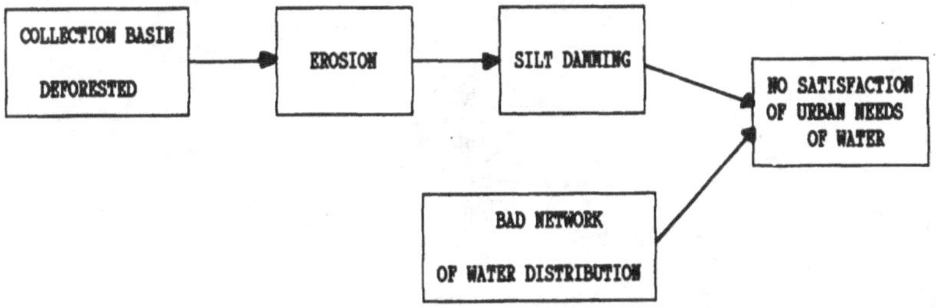

* the second category of information contains the specific characteristics of each problem,

* the third category of information contains, for each problem, different actions able to solve the problem or reduce its harmful consequences.

Figure 3: *PROBLEM CARD* and *TECHNICAL INTERVENTION CARD*

PROBLEM CARD		TECHNICAL INTERVENTION CARD	
Name of the Problem		*Name of the technical intervention*	
1	State of the problem	1	Short description of the technical intervention
2	Scope of the problem	2	Level of application
3	Spatial localization	3	Executive agent
4	Type of habit of the population concerned	4	Necessary technical means
5	Spatial results	5	Cost
6	Social classes concerned		
7	Effects on health		
8	Effects on economy		
9	Problem Control		
10	Overall length of treatment		
11	Results of treatment		

Figure 4: Associated Graphs of Characteristics and Actions of a Problem

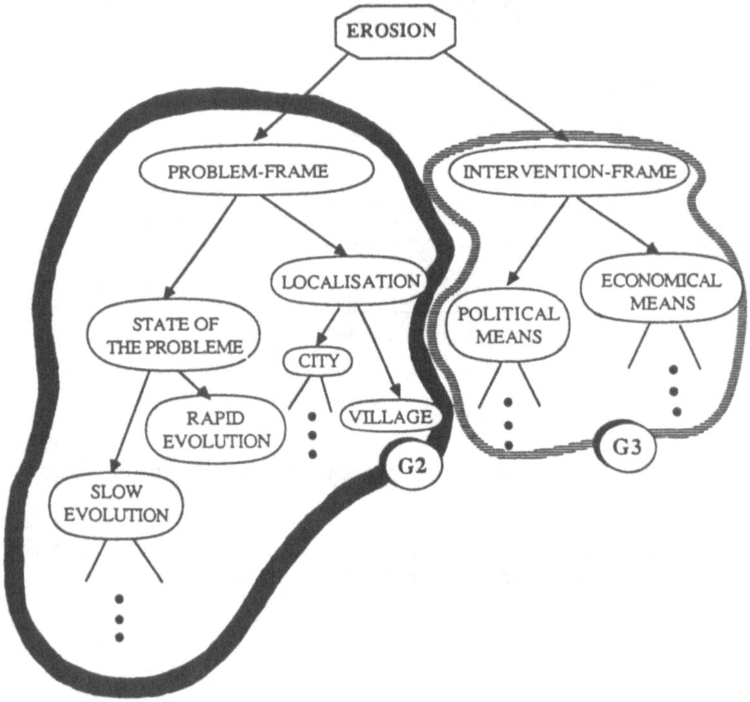

All of these information were stored in the knowledge base. Two graphs are associated with each problem. The first graph represents specific characteristics (see G2 in figure 4) and the second one represents the successive actions needed for its solution (G3 in the same fig.). This structure permits a partitioning of the knowledge base into three levels (see figure 5). The first level, G1*, describes the links between the problems, the second level G2* contains the graphs describing the specific characteristics of each problem and, finally, the third level G3* contains the necessary actions for the solution of each problem.

Figure 5: Knowledge Base Structure in Three Levels

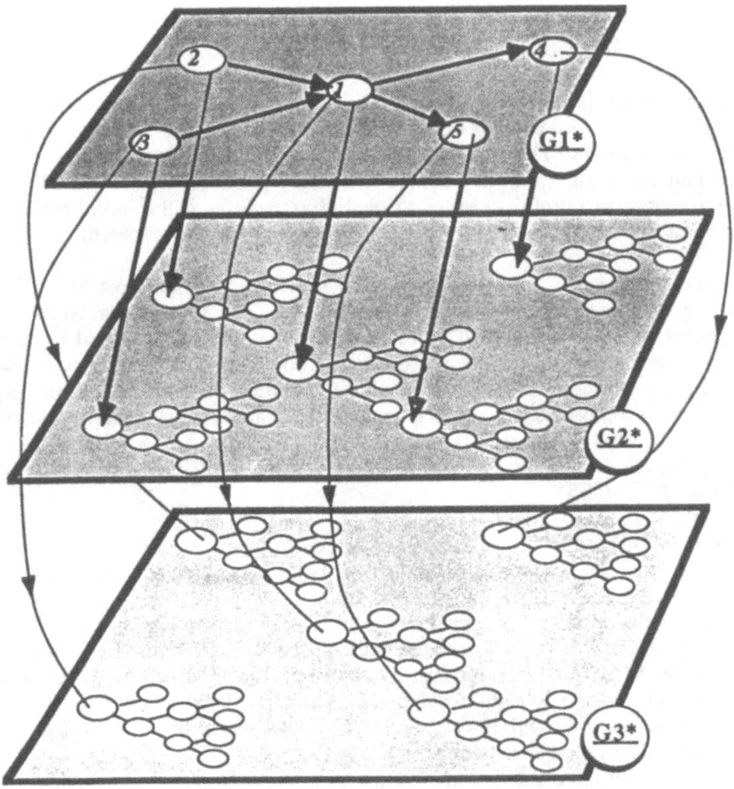

How does the system work?

The general system can be divided into three parts:

Figure 6: Architecture of the System

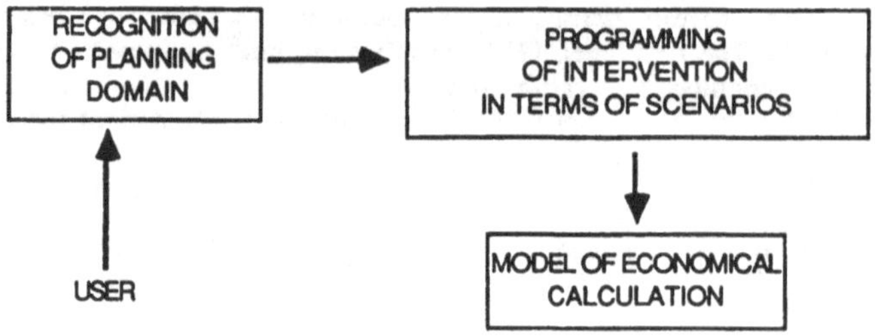

The system SAPH2O works to assist the user with two phases.

1. The first phase is the recognition of the planning domain: the system informs the users on all the potential relationships between the initial problem and the other problems it knows. The user has to select among these potentialities the relevant ones and by doing so, he constructs the actual planning domain or planning field where actions are useful in order to deal effectively with the initial problem. He is informed on the down-stream effects of a solution of this problem.

2. The second phase consists in building the program of actions corresponding to the planning domain. The system informs the user on the various types of actions suggested by experts for each problem of the planning domain and helps to select among them according to the preferences or the capacities of the user. He has to choose, for instance, between local or national actions, between capital or labor-saving actions, short or long term actions and so on. Finally, the process is constituted by six steps: ENTRY - FACTS BASE - PLANNING DOMAIN - TECHNICAL INTERVENTIONS CONCERNING A PROBLEM - SCENARIOS - CONSEQUENCES.

At the end of the process, the user is supposed to have an information on the global salient features of the system large enough to build a program of action more rational than it could have been if he had worked from his own narrow point of view.

In this application case, our planners' assistance tool was implemented in a specific domain, that of water resources management, with a specific knowledge base under the specific name SAPH2O. But it must be stressed that the software supporting this implementation is not application dependent. Its name is SADE (Système d'aide a la Decision en Economie) and it can be used to develop other knowledge bases with another type of knowledge structure.

In order to illustrate this possibility, we give the example of a complex production line, where the final product is the result of various industrial processes, associating several independent firms. In such a situation, the global efficiency of the system could probably be improved by using a decentralized information system like SAPH2O, where the knowledge base would be structured according to the requirements of the users.

From the computer techniques' point of view, we insist on some points:

Knowledge Representation

The representation model in our system is based on frames. The main reason is the nature of the knowledge itself. For most of the items of knowledge in our domain is manipulated (main features of problems and actions, general rules and specific action rules, coherence and compatibility rules...), it is the case that, being manipulated, frames have advantages with respect to factorization and managing of the knowledge base. In addition, they allow grouping of rules based on their application context.

Structure of the Knowledge Base

Early Expert-systems were designed as systems whose Knowledge Bases were completely unstructured. This lack of structure eased the changes of the content of the base, but they had to be of small size to avoid the saturation, more precisely, the overflow of the memory due to stack growth.

Usually, the Expert-system designers tried to overcome this problem with the sophistication of the inference engine. We have used heuristics to improve the performances of our prototype and we introduce an innovation by offering the possibility to reduce the search space of the inference engine through a specific structuring of the Knowledge Base. We give the name Knowledge Exploitation Mechanism to the packages of programs which deal with this problem.

The Explanation Module

The goal of early Expert-systems was to model the behaviour of human experts without worrying about the users requirements. We pay greater attention to this aspect in order to ease the accessibility of our system to different users.

A first step in that direction is to improve the management of dialogue between the system and the users by a specific man/machine interface; another way is to develop the explanation facility of the Expert-system. In the early Expert-systems the explanation is based on the use of a unique trace reflecting the work of the inference engine. This trace contains several types of knowledge about the domain (factual knowledge) as well as the methodology (meta knowledge). We decided to separate the different kinds of knowledge into different traces, Object trace and Meta trace, producing different explanations to the users and improving the interactive capabilities of the system.

Finally, the Knowledge Exploitation Module allows the system to render the knowledge operational, to modify the knowledge by updating the attribute values of one or more frames, to construct the data bases of the system and to represent the knowledge in one of the three available formalisms, depending on which of them suits a specific view best.

Figure 7: Different Traces

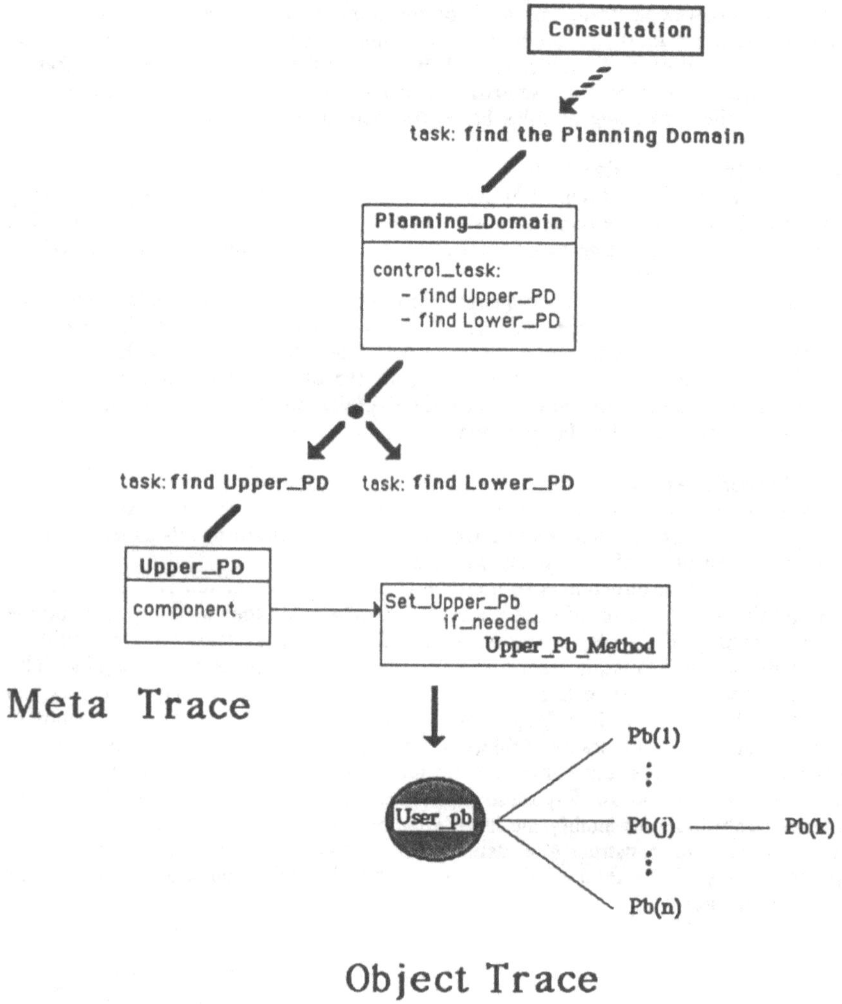

REFERENCES

ARRUS, R. and OLLIVIER, M. 1977. *Étude sur la politique nationale de l'environnement en ALGERIE*. CRISS, Alger, 270 p.

ARRUS, R. 1987. *Éléments pour la réalisation de SAPH2O*. CRISS, Université Grenoble, 30 p.

ARRUS, R. 1988. *SAPH2O: système d'aide a la planification de l'eau*. 1st Water Computer Conference in Africa. RABAT (Morocco), 14 p.

ARRUS, R.; LELIS, D. and TARI, Z. 1988. *SAPH2O, Système d'aide a la planification de l'eau*. Colloque international sue les systemes experts, AVIGNON, 25 p.

CLANCEY, W.J. 1983. *The advantages of abstract control Knowledge Design*. Report STAN CS 83 995, Stanford University

CLANCEY, W.J. 1983. *Strategic Explanation for Diagnostic System*. Report STAN CS 83 996, Stanford University

SWARTOUT, W.R. 1983. "XPLAIN: a system for creating and explaining expert consulting programs." *Artificial Intelligence 21*, 285-325

TARI, Z. 1988. *Représentation et explication dans les systèmes experts*. CRISS, Université Grenoble

LEGAL DATA BASES AND EXPERT SYSTEMS IN THE EUROPEAN COMMUNITY
THE POSSIBLE INTEGRATION OF INFORMATION RETRIEVAL AND ARTIFICIAL INTELLIGENCE

Antonio Maria D'Amico
Universita di Camerino, Roma
Facolta di Giurisprudenza
Italy

Abstract

The first part gives an introduction to the development of legal computer science in Europe. Considering information retrieval (IR) and artificial intelligence (AI) as different generations in computer science, we define the principal features of data bases (DB) and expert systems (ES). Several prototypes of Expert Systems are presented. In the second part, the idea of continuity between DB and ES is stressed and emphasis is laid on the sectors in which results of the application of IR could be improved. The focus is concerned with the increase of the market of CD-ROM and with the possibilities that applications of expert systems provide in the utilization of data bases. Some possible applications are studied here.

Part I

Introduction

The scientific discipline of legal computer science deals with the development of information technology and its applications in the field of law; it began in Europe between 1965 and 1970.

In terms of generations in computer science we can present this development by dividing it in the following way:

* the generation of information retrieval (IR) that is the years 1965-1975 when in the European countries the major part of legal data bases were created,
* the generation of artificial intelligence (AI), starting in 1975 with the development of prototypes of expert systems (ES).

As in all classifications, these limits in time as well as in generations are obviously much less precise than it seems to be. This becomes particularly clear in the literature which aims to associate specific realizations with either generation, whether IR or AI.

The divergencies in classification result in part from an inaccurate use of the information concept. According to some authors, the concept of information is defined in relation to general operations which include the application of computer science in the field of law. According to others, the concept of information should necessarily present a cognitive content.

Therefore, a classification of information systems according to the way they treat information will arrive at a typology consisting of *legal data base information systems* and *knowledge based systems.*

The first type of systems can be characterized by non-intelligent operations, whereas the second type is capable of interpretative processes according to specific levels of knowledge usually associated with "intelligent" human behaviour.

The Legal Data Bases

The first years of computer science development in the field of law were those governed by the great necessity to get acquainted with and to codify already existing information.

During this first period, the research activities concentrated on the realization of systems for the collection, treatment and diffusion of legal information.

Numerous data bases and data banks were created in the European countries; the level of research and application had to tackle and resolve problems above all related to the technical aspect of information retrieval.

We do not think it necessary to present in particular a detailed description of the most important data bases which exist in the Community countries because the respective literature is very voluminous and widely disseminated.

We will limit ourselves to recall that each member State has developed one or more systems on the national level. The best known are CELEX for Community law, CREDOC (Belgium), ITALGIURE (Italy), JURIS (Germany), CNIJ (France); all of them are national systems. It might be interesting to stress that the respective software used are MISTRAL, STAIRS, FIND, GOLEM and QUESTEL PLUS - that is five packages for five systems!

During recent years, however, data banks have entered - though slowly - the cultural background of legal professionalists, notwithstanding considerable resistances. According to a first review of literature it seems that data bases already are part of a reflected experience, results and useful applications may be derived from. Moreover, the same emerges from a summary analysis of the fields in which legal computer science develops. Actually, the present generation of legal computer science revolves mainly around the development and application of artificial intelligence, and all European laboratories move towards the realization of expert systems.

Therefore, one has the impression that information retrieval systems and the practical experiences with data banks and data bases are a technical level generally acquired.

Nevertheless, some aspects as

* utilization of query language,
* management of data base systems,
* compatibility between different systems,
* and finely, compliance with common standards on the Community and international level, could be solved in a better way.

One of the most recent publications which gives an extremely clear picture of the situation is Michael Lloyd *Legal Data Bases in Europe - User attitudes and supplier strategies.*

Dealing with the situation of utilizing data bases in Europe, the author states that the present level of utilization is unsatisfactory. The results of his research show how legal professionalists, although recognizing the theoretical utility of data bases, indicate a number of limitations being disincentives to their utilization.

These handicaps concern in particular:
1. the content of the data bases and the absence of information of supplementary value
2. the modes of utilization.

Recently, the Council of Europe has shown a particular interest in this problem and the principal consultant, Mr. J. Bing, underlined the aspects to be improved in his report *Les systemes de recherche de donnees juridiques: l'etat actuel des choses et ses insufficiences.*

In fact it seems that the structure of data base systems remained unchanged with respect to the developments that took place in the 1960s and, as a result, this structure does not allow to tackle the problems caused by the developments in recent years in a positive way. Therefore, the concepts that need continuation of work are "integration", "compatibility", "compliance with common technical standards" and "improved commercialization". But as long as there will be five different packages for five systems, all this will remain unrealizable. Only if more than one data base can be accessed - also because they are often complementary - the initial investment in human and economic costs will finally be used to capacity.

This situation gave raise to the phenomenon of intermediaries of information; but this may only serve as a makeshift.

CELEX, the system for Community law, deserves special attention: beyond its role as trans-national system, the possibility of easy access to Community law depends on the efficiency of this system; in the 1990s, 90% of the legislative drafting in each Community country will be based on Community law. Nevertheless, legal professionalists indicate difficulties in accessing this system. Despite new marketing politics of the European Commission planning for direct distribution, the legal information system of the Community will remain elite oriented, distant and not integrated into the national information systems. At present, one tries to find remedial measures for this shortcomings by reproducing the stock of Community law within the national systems. This is done by the project of the Centro Elettronico di Documentazione of the Corte Suprema di Cassazione Italiana, even though a solution based on the compatibility of the two data bases would have been preferable to the creation of a duplicate of the documentary holdings.

Among the publications on the data bank problems just mentioned, we want to recall the report to the Prime Minister by Mr. Leclerq, the works of L. Barbet, J.C. Meunier and of D. Gibert; for information purposes see also the guide to EURONET/DIANE 1985.

The Treatment of Information in Data Bases

As we have outlined before, data bases and data banks respond to the need to handle information. By using a query language a number of operations are possible and are executed strictly in the sense they were given. With the help of keywords and Boolean operators the computer makes a comparison between the keywords used for the query and those in the documents stored. In most cases an archive file is used to execute this comparison. The language may be natural, sometimes restricted to descriptors, but generally (the translation) takes place automatically with a thesaurus.

The response given consists in the documents containing the words or the corresponding syntagma used for the query. If the results are too extensive and give access problems or if they are unsatisfactory in some other way, the user may decide to continue his search by using more general or more specific expressions. If the answers are satisfactory the results may be visualized, printed or transferred to other storage media.

As we will show below, the application of artificial intelligence in information retrieval will be able to improve the results one can obtain from the interrogation of a data base and also solve some of the current problems.

The Legal Expert Systems

Since 1975, a major part of research in legal computer science has been absorbed in the field of artificial intelligence and the realization of prototypes of legal expert systems. The concept of an expert system emerged from the possibility to assign to some information management systems those operations which normally are executed by the human operator.

The field of expert systems is only one field of artificial intelligence which comprises

* reproduction of cognitive processes
* treatment of natural language
* recognition of voice
* recognition of images
* simulation of learning
* automatic programming
* computer-supported instruction.

The realization of an expert system has the following phases:

1. acquisition of knowledge
2. representation of knowledge
3. utilization of knowledge

1. Acquisition of Knowledge

The number of operations necessary to extract knowledge from a human expert for inclusion into a computer based system presents at the moment a lot of problems. The realization of the expertise which includes heuristic knowledge does not dispose of an efficient and generally accepted methodology. This situation seems to improve in specialized or sectoral projects where it is easier to describe and control the knowledge.

2. Representation of Knowledge

In this stage, the differences between the realization of a data base and an expert system become particularly clear. In data bases the documents are memorized according to standards that allow the computer to read them and they are retrieved by a mechanism of comparing similar words. In an expert system the elaboration is more complex and provides the treatment of facts and logical rules in an autonomous way.

From a theoretical point of view, the realization of an expert system should confront - in an even more profound way than in the case of a data base - the objective to evaluate the fundamental concepts of law and to define a system of rules underlying juridical reasoning. Already in 1666, Leibnitz stated in his *De arte combinatoria* the problem whether reasoning could be reduced to a form of calculus. The end product of this approach is the algorithm, a predetermined procedure which allows in any case to achieve a unique solution.

It is indispensable to confront such problems in order to find a better reformulation, as some authors say, or a rational reconstruction, as others say, of the corpus juris. Such a theoretical model might resolve the problems we face now. At present, there are several logical approaches to the representation of knowledge which are used individually or complementarily in the same system. The logical model of representation may be procedural or declarative. Among the latter the most widely spread are:

a. first order logic,
b. rule of production,
c. frames (object oriented programming),
d. semantic networks,
e. scripts.

3. Utilization of Knowledge

This part should be defined precisely. An a priori study of the needs an expert system should satisfy is required. The problems arise in relation to the social and juridical impact which the utilization of the expert system has; more specifically:

* the type of user, whether professional or non-professional, whether end user or intermediary,
* the possibilities of access to the system and the user interface,
* the level of transparency of the system and its capacity to provide explanations about the operations.

Some Prototypes of Expert Systems

We will now present some legal expert systems which have been developed in Europe. These systems represent only a part of the existing ones and should not be taken as exhaustive examples of the research activities in artificial intelligence. We only want to sketch the thematic lines of the activities in this field.

Analysis of some Expert Systems

In Belgium, at the Universite de la Paix, Namur, a prototype of an expert system is beeing developed which should support the elaboration of judicial decisions. The competence of this system lies in the search of documents and the evaluation of the coherence of a legal decision. The documentary part allows for consultation and updating of the data base; the evaluative part allows to verify the internal and external coherence of an argument. For the realization of this prototype DBMS, DBase II was used which allows the management of relational systems.

In the German Federal Republic a system for law of contract is developed at the university of Konstanz (BDJUR Juristisches Datenbanksystem für Experten und internationale Verträge). This system analyzes the respective legislation and jurisdiction and is intended to assist in the editing of contracts; it may also be used for instruction in law of contract. The system can be used on PC and allows the pleasure of natural language.

Still in the German Federal Republic, at the university of Tübingen, the system LEX (Legal Expert System) is intended to assist in decision making; in natural language it is geared towards professional and didactic uses. The prototype is realized using a program "Natural Language Analyzer", which provides the following components;

* a representation of the semantic structure of the German language,
* a mechanism to represent such structures on the base of 1st order logic predicates,
* a base of legal knowledge,
* a formalized conference engine,
* a user interface.

So it focuses upon the needs of the user and tries to guide him to the information.

In France, at the university Montpellier I, several systems were developed, among them NAZIONALITA, intending to provide assistance in decisions about granting the national status. The system works with PATROCLE, it runs on PC and is extremely user friendly.

In Italy, the system METHODUS is developed at the university La Sapienza, Rome, with the principal purpose to normalize language in the field of law. For the authors of the system, normalization of language is a particularly difficult phase and the automatic analysis does not seem capable of solving problems related to propositions with deontic connotations.

In the Netherlands, the system PROLEX (PROtotype of a Legal EXpert system) at the Vrije Universiteit of Amsterdam intends to be a 'user oriented expert system'; the system should recognize which norms and basic concepts are applicable to the given facts of a case and guide the user towards a solution.

In the United Kingdom, the system LEGOL, developed at the London School of Economics tends to the analysis of language in the field of law and to the formalization of concepts expressed in this language; the elaboration of information takes place only in the subsequent phase. The prototype translates the natural language into a formal language, an operation usually done by a human expert with a lot of time and extremely high costs.

Problems presented by Expert Systems

The market for expert systems is fluctuating at the moment, at least that for legal expert systems. In order not to repeat the same mistakes that occurred in the development of data bases some points should be considered with utmost care, when realizing instruments of practical efficiency and practical utility. Above all, the role of the user should be considered already in the planning phase in order not to create systems of limited or non-existing utility. Given this purpose it is important to define which task the expert system should have. That is: assistance in judicial decision making, assistance in consultancy of a lawyer or computer-aided instruction imply models and competencies which, although complementary, are primarily specific to their environment of operation, to the professional competence of the user and to the consequences a non-valid decision may generate.

When analyzing the various prototypes of expert systems it is possible to identify a typology of the two most prominent approaches. We have seen in fact that some prototypes operate in a specific field of law whereas others try out the possibility of formalizing the juridical reasoning in general. The great quantity of different approaches, however, creates problems of evaluating the operation of the systems, in particular from a user's point of view who will not always be able to evaluate in an autonomous way the soundness of what the system provides. Jurisprudence, moreover, seems too often to be penalized by its more human than juridical mode of operation, by the difficulty and the eventual irregularity of its statements.

Part II

The Interest to Integrate Data Bases and Expert Systems

Given the points mentioned in the first part and after having presented a panorama of the existing expert systems we want to analyze the possibilities we have using expert systems in direct relation to data bases.

In fact, despite the multiple facets of artificial intelligence that may be used to improve the performance of data bases, applications in this field between information retrieval and artificial intelligence are very little developed, yet.

On the whole, information retrieval should become more "intelligent" and capable to adapt better to the needs of the end user; this would increase the utility of data bases transforming a tool for the elite into a tool for the mass public.

The most important aspects concern

* easier access for the end user to CD-ROM data bases,
* valid information in shorter time,
* a greater variety of products and services.

The actual information retrieval systems may be considered as "passive" and are not yet able to

* provide supplementary information to the user,
* give the user hints on how to improve the results of an unsatisfactory query,
* help the user to formulate queries.

Systems for the treatment of language and computer linguistics, could moreover be used with benefit in the field of traditional information retrieval. Technologies for reproducing knowledge could improve the query phase and several models of behaviour could be inserted into these systems. We would like to stress this point for two reasons. Primarily, because the phase of utilization of data bases and of expert systems is important as here, the user and the producer of the systems get in contact. Second, we should not forget that the know-how of expert systems represents a precious scientific treasure to improve the utilization of data bases; in addition, these two fields of research in legal computer science seeming to develop extremely autonomously would get closer to each other.

The preliminary observations are the following:

* It emerges that during the last years the market of CD-ROM expanded considerably and allows for a better treatment of information.
* Legal computer science could not keep pace as far as the utilization of information actually accessible is concerned.

From an operative point of view, the evolution of the information sector allows at least

a. a new approach for analysis and retrieval of documents. Overcoming the limits set by formal languages, software implements file searches and the Boolean operators with much greater user friendliness and tends more and more towards the use of natural language.
b. progress in logical programming gives access to parts of a document or to parts of a data base through the creation of inferential dictionaries, automatic dictionaries etc.
c. the technology of CD-ROM makes possible intelligent information retrieval systems in a functional and economic perspective.
d. greater user friendliness, control of the system operations, man-machine interaction etc.

Moreover, these systems could be experts at different levels and represent a kernel of more or less important expert systems.
At a first level, there are "query-response systems", the classical systems of documentation.

A second level is represented by "intelligent documentation systems" using natural language which modify the queries but on a "surface" level and can be used by the end user. The relations between these systems and those of the first group are still very strong.

On the third level, we have systems capable to select the data base, that is they handle a certain amount of knowledge automatically and structure the documentary bases according to their importance.

Analysis of some Experiences

The integration of data bases and expert systems is a field of legal computer science which merits broader development. The experiences we present here, do not come from the field of legal computer science but are, nevertheless, of considerable interest to applications in this field.

n°. 1 - "Intelligent" Search in Full Text Data Bases

Prototype developed by Susan Gauch and John Smith, M.I.T.

Executing a data base query is still perceived by the user as an obstacle. Experiences show that videotext bases can not be regarded as a model usefully applicable in the field of law. The procedures of the query (link-up and use of codes) are not yet standardized; the additional need to use more than one data base puts the user in a situation where he must know a series of link-up procedures and query languages. All this means a loss of time which is unacceptable in the time of computer science.

The development of an intelligent interface, a help tool for queries, could carry out these operations automatically. The intelligent system could reformulate automatically Boolean operators and improve the results of the query.

The objective of the working team at M.I.T., therefore, is precisely to realize an intelligent system that can operate with a large textual data base.

The prototype would operate with a data base of great dimensions and represent a retrieval instrument that can handle the characteristics of several query languages, modify the searching strategy, handle algorithms and present the results. The

implementation of a menu seems to give additional advantages.
It facilitates the procedures of
1. data base selection,
2. linkage and
3. selection of query terms.

The query could be made in natural language, which the system would transform into the appropriate Boolean operators.
The architecture of the system provides for
* a data base with integral text (full text data base)
* an inherent thematic thesaurus
* an expert system which can
    - interpret and modify the user's query
    - control the retrieval process
    - analyze the validity of the retrieved documents
    - present the final results (see figure 1)

Figure:

			Thesaurus ↑		Data Base ↑	
User	———> <———	user interface	———> <———	expert system	———> <———	information retrieval system

The procedure:
The user communicates with the expert system in natural language, the expert system formulates the question using Boolean operators and semantic equivalents with the help of the thesaurus and communication with the actual retrieval system; finally, the expert system evaluates the relevance of the responses, modifies the query or supplies the results to the user.

n°. 2 - Very user friendly Information Retrieval
prototype developed by S. Chang and A. Chow, GTE

The most interesting aspect of this system consists in its capacity to evaluate the validity of responses received through an intelligent handling of recall/precision functions. The prototype provides also a user friendly environment in natural language; it does not need an indirect or retrieval file and runs on PC.

The actual information retrieval systems can solve recall/precision problems in the response phase. For this purpose, they use combinations of Boolean operators and/or weighting expressions directly managed by the user; sometimes, these instruments turn out to be extremely rigid as for example the treatment of certain not well defined conceptual associations.

The underlying idea of the system is to improve this phase by introducing into the system an automatic evaluation so that the output presents the responses according to their validity. Therefore, the user may only select the first documents without having to analyze all documents retrieved. The user may also specify his own rules for the evaluation according to his proper needs and he may assign a weight to each query term.

Access to retrieval is also possible via a menu, in natural language and directly to the main data base (without using a retrieval file).

n°. 3 - Gateway System to access more than one DB
prototype developed by Allan D. Kuhn, D.T.I.C.

The experience to allow multi-base access has to consider above all normative standards in information retrieval and artificial intelligence. Despite the activities of the European Council, of the International Organization of Standardization and of the respective national committees the application of established standards is very scarce. Because of this situation the possibility to make more data bases compatible is reduced.

The prototype of this project tries to solve these problems by the creation of a system that can handle a variety of query languages.
The aim here is to implement an on-line system that can:

1. identify the content of several data bases
2. carry out the link-up procedures
3. retrieve and analyze data coming from different and heterogeneous data bases.

The application of a Common Command Language (CCL) will contribute to the solution of these problems.

Conclusion

With this contribution the author wants to put the development of legal computer science back into a broader social context. For this purpose he wanted to propose lines of reflection that may contribute, although in minimal part, to the creation of an computer science culture which will allow the development and the utilization of technologies in respect of the fundamental values of society.

REFERENCES

BARBET, Luis. 1982. "Les banques de donneés juridique en France." *Juriste International* 2, 35

BASSANO, Jean Claude. *Systèmes experts et systèmes documentaires intelligents - État de l'art er perspectives*. Conferenza di Avignon 87 su "Expert systems and their applications".

BING, J. 1984. *Handbook of legal Information retrieval*. North-Holland, 504p.

BING, J. and Harvold, T. 1977. *Legal decisions and information systems*. Universitetsforlaget, Oslo, 257p.

CHANG, S. and CHOW, A. 1988. "Towards a Friendly Adaptable Information Retrieval System." *Atti della Conferenza "User-Oriented Content-Based Text and Image Handling". M.I.T., Cambridge MA, 21.-24.03.1988*, 172-182

Consiglio dell'Europa. 1985. *8° Simposio sull'Informatica Giuridica in Europa; l'accesso alle banche di dati giuridici in Europa*. Lussemburgo, 12.-14.06.1985

FAUVREAU, Bertrand. 1986. "L'informatique judiciaire: pour quoi faire?" *Gazette du Palais*, 1° trim., 208/212

FOX, E.A.; WEAVER, M.T.; CHEN, Q. and FRANCE, R. 1988. "Implementing a distributed expert-based information retrieval system." *Atti della Conferenza "User-Oriented Content-Based Text and Image Handling". M.I.T., Cambridge MA, 21.-24.03.1988*, 708-723

GAUCH, S. and SMITH, J.B. 1988. "Intelligent Search of Full-Text Databases." *Atti della Conferenza "User-Oriented Content-Based Text and Image Handling". M.I.T., Cambridge MA, 21.-24.03.1988,* 162-171

GIBERT, Dominique. 1983. "Les banques de données juridiques francaises." *Quadrature*, Mai 1983

KUHN, A.D. 1988. "DOD Gateway Information System (DGIS) Common Command Language: Decision on Artificial Intelligence." *Atti della Conferenza "User-Oriented Content-Based Text and Image Handling". M.I.T., Cambridge MA, 21.-24.03.1988,* 863-881

LIMONE, D. 1988. "Ricerca giuridica e sistemi esperti." *Atti del 3° Convegno Triveneto "Informatica e Uomo" su "Conscienza, Professionalità e Intelligenza Artificiale".* Ediz. Padova, 12.03.1988, 78-94

LIOYD, M. 1986. *Legal databases in Europe. User Attitudes and Supplier Strategies.* North-Holland, 203p.

LOSANO, M. 1985. *Informatica per le scienze sociali. Corso di informatica giuridica.* Einaudi, Torino, 461p.

MEUNIER, J.C. 1985. "Evalution et perspectives de l'Informatique document. Jurid." *Gazette du Palais* 48639, du 21.11.1985

PIETTE-COUDOL, Thierry. 1987. *Informatique juridique: beaucoup de bruit pour rien.* Expertise n° 96-Juin 87, 250/252

SUSSINK, R.E. 1986. "Expert Systems in law: a jurisprudential approach to artificial intelligence and legal reasoning." *The Modern Law Review* 49, 2, March 1986, 168-194

SVOBODA, W.R. (ed.). 1981. *Users of Legal Information Systems in Europe.* München, 273p.

A SHELL - BASED LEGAL EXPERT SYSTEM PROTOTYPE FOR LEGISLATIVE DRAFTING

Antonio Cammelli, Fiorenza Socci
Istituto per la Documentazione Giuridica, Florence
Italy

1. Legal Language and its Formalization

The use of computer technology in the law has also developed chronologically by adopting the contraposition mentioned already in earlier papers of these authors between norm-making and decision-making: the former certainly refers to documentary legal informatics, meaning the capacity to store, save and utilize information whilst the latter refers to legal informatics and decision-making, meaning not only the creation of rules (legislation, court decisions, etc.) but also the need for interpreting these rules, so they can be enforced. It is easily understandable, therefore, what a valuable contribution the computer when correctly guided by the lawyer can make.

Firstly, the need to transfer the language of the norms into a new and appropriate language for the computer makes it necessary to formalize the text as an obligatory step towards further processing and also towards a codified font which even now let us perceive that a logical structure does not always govern legal sentences.(1)

Even the text of the normative corpus examined in our research, leads to considerable confusion which can already be seen in an initial textual-linguistic analysis. Semantic ambiguity, however, is often defended as a useful tool provided by the drafter so that situations which are not currently foreseeable can be regulated.

The formalized language of the normative text has, in our view, the same expressive richness as the original legal language. In fact, it has a level of abstraction, on the one hand, which guarantees precision and homogeneity in its representation and preserves all the characteristic traits of natural language, on the other. The formalization of a legal base cannot, of course, leave a preliminary, accurate and precise interpretation of the scope of the sentence, of the text and the "significant" sentences out of consideration. Propositional logic allows the logical structure of legal propositions to be identified and represented; the logic of predicates analyses the individual components within a sentence.

The fundamental logical structure of a norm is represented as implication where the antecedent expresses one or more conditions and the consequent expresses a legal solution.

The system used for our prototype is of the declarative non-procedural type and is written in natural language. In this way, the lawyer can write and construct a knowledge base using a technique which is familiar to him, avoiding writing programs in traditional language which, inevitably, require the assistance of a computer expert. In fact, the knowledge base in Xi plus, as we shall see later, is structured in rules integrated with questions and facts.

2. The LEXIS Project: The Xi Plus System

Our choice was determined by evaluating the features of the tool in relation to the need to represent a knowledge base in the field of legislation. It appeared to us that Xi plus(2) produced by Expertech, unites ease in use and a userfriendly interface with the capacity to represent even considerably complex knowledge structures thanks to several facilities such as control rules, classes of knowledge, the possibility to alternate reasoning strategies through backward and forward chaining.
The knowledge base is divided into various elements:
* rules (including demons or when/then rules);
* questions;
* facts;
* queries.

The rules express essential knowledge and are written in natural language with the if...then formalism;

Example: if <identifier> is <value>
then <identifier> is <value>.

The first term appearing after "if" indicates the object to which a value must be attributed, the verb identifies the relation and the last part is the value attributed to the identifier.

Although the system only provides some verbal forms: is; is not (for single values); include; includes; is a; do not include; does not include; is not a (for multiple values), any verbal form can be utilized as long as it is predefined by the user in the "language" sector. In the absence of any information about the values, pre-established values (defaults) can be used.

Demons are a special kind of rules expressed in the "when...then" form. They have precedence over normal rules and are activated by forward chaining, as soon as the conditions contained in them arise.

Apart from the rules which, along with the demons and the facts, organize the primary knowledge base, there are the questions which help to obtain the information from the user about the values to be given to the identifier. They are made up of the same identifier appearing in the rules, of the values which have to associate with this (which may be single or multiple) and of a part in free text which will appear as a question to the user in the search phase.

Example: separation is
* judicial
* consensual
* de facto
* no separation

The question in free text: What kind of separation has
occurred between the parties?

It would be up to the user to make one of the choices given as a value for the "separation" identifier; the final value attributed can be either assigned by the user or inserted as a default value.

The facts represent true assertions for all the conditions.

Example: of age < = 18;

This means that the assertion given as a fact, is to be considered true in the whole domain of the knowledge base in question, and is activated in the rules for integrating the data of the knowledge volunteered by the user in his answers to the questions.

The queries identify the objective. They contain the chosen identifier to which the system in the decision-making phase must attribute a value, once the inference engine is activated.

Besides these elements, some help and report facilities can be activated.

2.1 The Knowledge Base

The conceptually harmonized legislative corpus contained in Arts. 84-92 of the Italian Civil Code on the "Conditions Required for Contracting Marriage" and Law No. 898 of 1st December 1970 on the "Regulation of the Dissolution of Marriage" as recently amended by the Italian Parliament were chosen for our prototype.

The research group working on the "Automated Analysis of Legislation"(3) at "Istitute per la documentazione giuridica" of the Italian National Research Council had already previously done research on norms relating to marriage and this seemed to us to be a valid motive for evaluating whether this new trend in technology was capable of reaching better results. Moreover, an Act had been added to the text of the Code and represented one of the possible ways to improve it and which, from the way it had been enacted, seemed appropriate for being tested most effectively, both, from the point of view of its formalization and for its computer-aided reconstruction.

As we have already mentioned, an objective which we will define as a query according to the formalism of Xi plus, has to be identified within the set of norms constituting the conditions required for contracting marriage, namely an identifier which constitutes the goal of the search with an attributed value. This query identifier was assigned the term "marriage".

At this point, the normative text is subdivided into a number of conceptually homogenous units denoting the various logically grouped conditions which, once they have been ascertained, compete to attribute the final value to the query identifier (for example, permitted, forbidden, etc.).

It is obvious that in this phase, the textual reconstruction, which is certainly easier in the Civil Code, is of fundamental importance. In this specific case, the first level of the condition to be reached is represented by age.

In fact, Art. 84 lays down 18 years, the age of majority, as the requirement for contracting marriage or, for serious reasons, 16 years. We can, therefore, represent the normative sentence as follows:

a) - party > = 18
- party > = 16 authorized by the court
age requirement met

b) - party > = 16
- party > = 16 not authorized by the court
age requirement not met

In order to effectively represent subsections 3, 4, 5, and 6 which lay down the procedure whereby the court can permit a minor to marry, as well as the appeal procedure, the user can utilize the report or help commands. For the purpose of representing in Xi plus that which has been expressed in points a) and b) above, we will have the following rules in the formalism of the system:

point a):

if the age of the party > = 18
then the party is of age
and the age requirement is met

if the age of the party > = 16
and the authorization of the court is granted
then the age requirement is met

These two rules will be activated when the user has provided the information pertinent to this matter, namely an age of the party at least equal to 18 years, or an age not less than 16 years which must, however, in this case, be accompanied by a positive answer to the question relating to whether the minor has, or has not been granted the authorization of the court. As we can see, the "marriage" identifier does not appear in the consequent, because age is not the only condition, but rather only one of the conditions which must be met in succession in order to contract marriage. For this reason, these are called intermediate rules and as we shall see, must reappear in the top rule where the query identifier will appear.

As far as point b) is concerned, the following will appear:

if the age of the party < 18
then the party is a minor

if the party < 16
then the marriage is prohibited

if the age of the party > 16
and the authorization of the court is not granted
then the marriage is prohibited

It will be noted that in these rules, the "marriage" query identifier appears as associated with the "prohibited" value: it is not necessary here to check the other conditions and for this reason, the search is completed promptly, avoiding the scanning and evaluating of other levels of conditions which are, therefore, superfluous.

What happens instead within ambit a) if the user is asked a question with a response at the second level of conditions which, in this case, is represented by Art. 85: mental incapacity. Both, this article and the one following which deals with the freedom to marry, can be easily formalized: if the response is negative, the two conditions are met and the system continues scanning in sequence, otherwise two conclusive rules of the following kind are activated:

if the party is interdicted for mental infirmity
then the marriage is prohibited

if the party is bound by a previous marriage
then the marriage is prohibited.

As explained previously, two rules having the word "marriage" as identifier in the conclusion will prevent further paths being followed by responding negatively to the proposed goal.

The fourth level of the conditions concerns kinship (Art. 87) which presents a situation that can logically be represented by using an analogous formalism to that we have already described for Art. 84 (the age condition). Art. 87 sets out a whole series of prohibitions concerning persons connected by consanguinity, affinity, etc. but, along with cases such as those in subsection 2 (regarding brothers and sisters whether of full or half blood) where there is an absolute prohibition, there are also cases like those in subsection 3, for example, (uncle and niece, aunt and nephew) where the prohibition is conditional on the authorization of the court. In the case of subsection 2, the situation will be treated in the same way as Arts. 85 and 86, whereas in the case of subsection 3, the situation will be treated like that discussed earlier of the minor permitted to marry by the court.
This appears as follows:

if the parties are uncle and niece, aunt and nephew
then the impediment is conditional

if the impediment is conditional
and the authorization is granted
then the kinship requirement is verified

The two rules expressed have the rank of intermediate rules because, as we have already explained, they meet one of the conditions required for contracting marriage.

When there is an affirmative response to a question regarding absolute prohibition, the following top rule will be activated:

if the parties are brother and sister
then the marriage is prohibited

The subsequent level of the conditions to be examined is represented by the condition relating to crime (Art. 88). This prohibition concerns persons found guilty either of attempted murder or murder of their spouse. Even in this case, the following kind of intermediate rule is activated by a negative question:

if the crime or attempted crime is no
then the crime requirement is verified

where it is shown that the condition has been met and, therefore, that the system can proceed with another scanning of the conditions to be checked. In the opposite case, also in consideration of the fact that we are faced with an absolute prohibition, the following kind of conclusive rule is activated:

if the crime or attempted crime is yes
then the marriage is prohibited

The conditions relating to a male party wishing to contract marriage end with Art. 88. In fact, Art. 89 (temporary prohibition of a new marriage) provides for a temporary prohibition on a female wishing to contract a new marriage: 300 days from the dissolution of the previous marriage need to have passed except when that marriage was declared void on the grounds of the impotency of one of the two spouses.

In this specific case, it is necessary to ask the user whether the party is male or female and in the latter case, the formalization must take into account both, the number of days which have passed since the previous marriage and any annulment for impotency which, of course, extinguishes the condition relating to the three hundred days. The formalization here is rather complex, as it must be remembered that apart from the conditions cited previously, the court may authorize the marriage when there is no pregnancy or where it is, nevertheless, shown that the husband has not cohabited with the wife during the three hundred days prior to the dissolution of the marriage. Therefore,

if the party is a female
and there is dissolution or annulment of the previous marriage
and days < 300
then the required condition is met

this is, therefore, an intermediate rule such as the following:

if the party is a female
and there is dissolution or annulment of the previous marriage
and days > 300
and the previous marriage is void for impotency
then the required condition is met

The legislator has, however, also provided for the case mentioned above, where the three hundred days have passed before the dissolution or annulment, in which case the court must certify what has been declared. In particular:

if the party is a female
and pregnancy is no
and authorization is yes
then the required condition is met

Or:

the party is a female
and cohabitation during the 300 days prior to
the dissolution or annulment is no
and the court decision is yes
then the required condition is met

of the top rule as illustrated in the following example:

if the age requirement is verified
and the infirmity requirement is verified
and the previous marriage requirement is verified
and the kinship requirement is verified
and the crime requirement is verified
and the conditions requirement is verified
then the marriage is permitted

In cases like this, although the terminology can be improved even more, the examples set out here are conceptually useful for measuring exactly the way the system's inference engine operates.

3. Preliminary Evaluation of the Prototype

Whilst we consider the current prototype to be merely a stage (even if an important one) in a more ambitious project, we are able to make some predictions about its future.

Firstly, about the tool in general: it has proved reasonably flexible and adaptable even for representing complex and articulated knowledge bases, such as those in the field of legislation. The fact that there is no operator "or" among the conditions (only the values can be related by "or") is not very serious and can be got around, although this requires extra work in structuring the system. The same can be said for negation which is provided for only in the antecedents and not in the conclusions, forcing the programmer to find alternative but not always the best solutions. It is true that although the choice of these solutions is facilitated by using reports, a future version could profit from the addition of these options.

The user interface, even if it is acceptable in the present version, could also be improved: this is not only an aesthetic but, sometimes, also a functional requisite. The wider use of windows in the last update of the program is a welcome addition.

As far as the actual application of the system to the legal domain is concerned, it must initially be said that the work of the expert (in this case, a lawyer) is fundamental in the knowledge base construction phase if the tool is to be used to its fullest advantage. This means, as we explained previously, making the lawyer the central figure in projects of this kind.

The best strategy with Xi plus is to begin, in implementing it, with a small number of rules which can be tested rapidly with the tool's facilities (Checker, Charter). The knowledge base can, therefore, be further incremented relying on a basic structure which has been tested and checked. This is one of the advantages of rule based systems in comparison with traditional procedural systems which allow for testing only after programming is finished.

Based on the assumption that the Xi plus system is backward chaining, it is advisable to begin with the so-called spider diagrams which assist in representing the concepts and their principal implications. The query (or objective) is in the centre of the diagram and the different conditions required for giving the query a value or even the various and eventual subconditions are set out in a clockwise direction.

In this way, the gaps and contradictions existing in the universe of the chosen normative domain, can be pointed out through a proper selection of linguistic terms which ought to mediate between adherence to the text and the univocal connotation of the language.

In the desired endeavour to draft legislation better, the legislator should begin with a formal-logical reconstruction adapted for its reproduction in rules. This seems to us to be a small but fundamental contribution to certainty in the law.

NOTES

1. On the formalization of legal texts see Mariani, P. et alii. 1981. "Metodologie di normalizzazione del linguaggio giuridico." *Informatica e Diritto*, X, May-August, 2, 307-320
2. The product works on an IBM Personal Computer or IBM compatibles, requires at least 512 K of memory capacity and preferably a hard disk, is written in LPA Microprolog and Assembler. For a critical analysis of the potentiality of Xi plus see Forsyth, R. 1987. "Expertech Xi plus." *Expert Systems*, 4, February, 1, 48-51.
   We would like to mention the valuable collaboration we have had with Elea S.p.A., who are exclusive distributors for Xi plus in Italy and, especially, for the assistance given by Elisabetta Tesi and Laura Arrigoni during the various phases of the work.
3. With regard to this, see the internal report of the Istituto per la documentazione giuridica, which collects several papers on the subject together: *Automated Analysis of Legislation, Trends in Research from 1981 to 1984*, IDG, December, 1984 as well as the volume: A.A. Martino, F. Socci (eds.). 1986. *Automated Analysis of Legal Texts*. North-Holland, Amsterdam, which contains the most important contributions on the subject, presented at the II International Conference on "Logic, Informatics and Law", held in Florence, Italy in September 1985.

EXPERT SYSTEMS AS AN AID TO LEGISLATIVE DRAFTING

Paola Mariani, Daniela Tiscornia
Istituto per la documentazione giuridica (IDG) of Florence
of the Italian National Research Council (CNR)
Italy

1. Introduction

The characteristics and the functions of a legal expert system prototype (ESPLEX, Mariani, Tiscornia, 1988) will be illustrated in this article. Expert systems are generally utilized in problem solving and, therefore, as advisory systems in the legal field. Legislative planning is, however, an environment where, in our opinion, the application of legal expert systems could be valuable in contributing to the rationalization of legal drafting techniques.

It is no secret, even to public opinion that legislation is often badly drafted: a legislative text is often almost incomprehensible to anyone who is not a lawyer and also creates serious problems in interpretation and application even for those who are lawyers.

There is a considerable amount of scientific documentation available today, at both national and international level, on the results of research carried out by legal experts who have analysed the causes of the poor state of legislation and have proposed solutions.

Broadly speaking, three classes of defects on which to blame the difficulties involved in the enforceability of legislation emerge from this research:

1. at the level of legislative drafting, purely formal defects (obscure or ambiguous linguistic expressions, contorted literary forms, rhetorical expressions, etc.);
2. at the level of the legal system, normative overlapping: each legislative innovation is grafted onto an extremely complex system where it is often very difficult to identify and define the relationships between new and pre-existing norms;
3. at the level of application, the failure to verify in advance the conditions relating to applicability: here, economic (funding), organizational (qualified personnel), social and political factors come into play.

We can see three possible levels of intervention, creating, therefore, three integrated systems:

1. a system to aid in the drafting of the text (a text editor) which carries out checks at the lexical and structural level;
2. a system capable of simulating the application of legislation in abstract cases through a model and, therefore, of checking and evaluating it on a legal-logical level;
3. a system capable of simulating, again through a model, the actual application of the legislation, introducing those extra-legal elements (economic, statistical, financial, etc.) which can be identified and formalized. In this way, the effects of the simulation would be ascertained and the enforceability of the new legislation could, therefore, be gauged.

The most obvious thing about this tripartition is that the first step is taken by acting directly on the text whilst the other two subsequent steps mean changing the object of the investigation, namely by going from the original to the model. It follows that the results can be applied to the legislative text through a "feed back" process, and the closer the model is to the original, the more relevant and utilizable the results will be.

In order to make this idea easier to understand, we have drawn up a very simplified diagram of the procedure in the following figure, which the proposer of a bill could follow in producing a "rationalized" text as output.

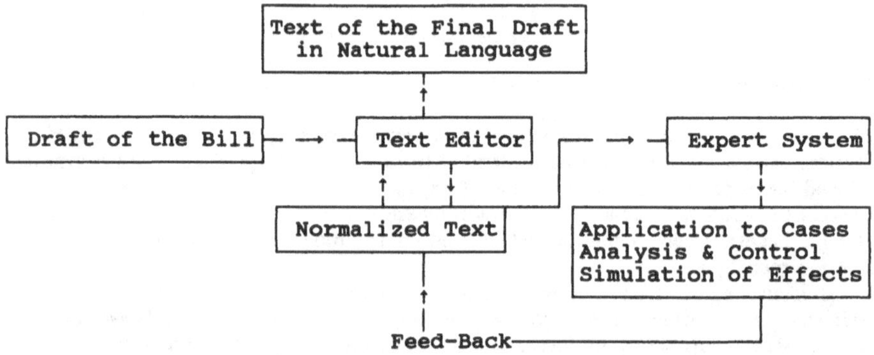

We will not discuss our specialized text editor here; we will, instead, illustrate our research which has as its objective the designing of an expert system prototype. The functions of the system are centred on the application of norms to cases with special attention paid to the user interface and the internal knowledge representation.

2. The Automated Analysis of Legislation

The basic theoretical idea is that a legal subsystem (a set of all the legislation in force relating to a specific domain) can be represented in a logical model: this permits the kinds of relations existing between the norms (or, to be more precise, between normative sentences) to be explained, the organizational structure of the system to be rationally reformulated and the abnormal relations (contradictory norms, normative gaps, redundancy) which may be created to be identified.

This actually means working with a formal model which reproduces a part of the normative system (for example, a new piece of legislation and the legal rules it refers to), by simulating its application to all possible cases and checking the consistency and completeness of the legal rules defining this part of the normative system.

As we are concerned with legislative texts, an attempt is made to explain the various steps in interpretation through which the written text acquires its normative meaning; the project we will illustrate aims at isolating the phases in interpretation based on ordinary linguistic rules from all the complex activities carried out by the lawyer according to the actual rules of law and other extra-legal factors. As we have only dealt with the formal aspects of the legislation, our analysis is, therefore, limited to the legal language in which the text is expressed.

An important requisite for any model analyzing legislative texts is that its representation language should be as close as possible to the natural language of the

legislation.
It follows that it should be:

* rich, for representing all the expressive nuances of the text;
* diversified, for expressing classes of sentences having different characteristics and aims with different formalisms;
* legible, so that the knowledge base can be updated even by the user;
* defined, both on a syntactic level for explaining any ambiguities and on a semantic level.

3. The Corpus

We have chosen the rules on agricultural tenancies as our research field. These are taken from an Act of 1982 which regulates the leasing of rural land and the conversion of other kinds of agricultural tenancies into leases. This Act (comprising 63 sections) refers to other earlier legislation on agricultural tenancies as well as several articles in the Italian Civil Code dealing with contracts in general and in the Italian Code of Civil Procedure.

We believed that it was necessary to add information about the legal regulamentation of contracts in general to the normative knowledge contained in the corpus. This was not taken from specific legislative texts but from the structural organization of contract law as given in jurisprudence. From this point of view, we also considered our choice of contract law to be a good one as jurisprudence is well established in this field.

The knowledge to be represented was, therefore, divided into explicit and implicit knowledge. Explicit knowledge is that contained in the legislation itself whereas implicit knowledge is not knowledge contained in the legislation but is useful for understanding it: the two kinds of knowledge are represented separately in the knowledge base.

We have expressed the strictly regulatory content of the normative knowledge (explicit) as logical implication (if...then). This part of the knowledge in ESPLEX can be defined as dynamic or explicit or normative in as far as it constitutes the explicit message of the legislator expressed through the legislative text.

We then defined and expressed all the knowledge missing in the text (implicit knowledge) being essential for its comprehension as the definition of objects and concepts. This is not, in fact, expressed by the legislator but is believed to be already known or possible to be deduced from common sense or, above all, from jurisprudence.

4. Building the Knowledge Base

We will illustrate the phases in the passage from natural language to the formalized model. The translation of the legislation chosen for research purposes (mainly done manually) required a considerable amount of time, even taking into consideration that the methodology was defined contemporaneously. This is a critical issue as far as the actual utilization of these tools is concerned which could partially be overcome by computerizing the largest possible number of phases in the formalization. It can be foreseen, once the entire system is perfected that the input for an L.E.S. could be a legislative text in natural but "normalized" language.

4.1 Text Composition

We, therefore, presume that the new text of the legislation is computer-generated by utilizing a specialized editor and is submitted to an automated checking procedure which guarantees:

* the absence of spelling mistakes;
* the progressive numeration of the sections and subsections;
* the standardization of the partitions above the level of the sections;
* the standardization of abbreviations and acronyms;
* the codification of internal and external legislative citations (for example, through the use of standard linguistic expressions);
* the addition of norms in the text which were previously the subject of amendment;
* the explanation and unambiguity of the syntactic structure of the sentence.

All points listed here, except for the last, are the subject of the rules laid down in the Circular of the Speaker of the Italian Chamber of Deputies of 19 February 1986, which has been applied to the most recent legislation. Although the last point was not dealt with by the Parliamentary Commission (which, however, pointed out the complex and ambiguous syntactic structure of legislative texts as being defects), it has been the subject of research by logicians and lawyers, who have proposed valid solutions.

The analysis and transformation of the syntax which connects the individual sentences within a legislative section is the first step in interpreting the text and will, therefore, be dealt with separately.

4.2 Syntactic Normalization

The "universal norm form" created by L.E. Allen for explaining and eliminating ambiguity from legislative texts by using expressions in non-defined natural language is well known (for example, the use of the connective "or" between two sentences meaning "vel" or "aut" without distinction, of "after" and "before" to introduce conditions and non-temporal qualifications and of "unless" in both, a weak and strong sense, etc.).

Allen's universal norm form is based on the rewriting of the text, keeping the linguistic form of the sentences unaltered but substituting the syntactic connectives of the traditional logical operators ("and", "or", "not") and linking the conditions to the consequences as a logical implication ("if...then"). This allows the relations joining the legal sentences to be represented in a non-ambiguous way or, at any rate, prevents more than one interpretation to be made.

The normalization of a text cannot be totally computerized as the logical structure must be introduced by a human expert, although the computer is capable of simplifying its complex logical structure and of providing several normalized versions of the same section in accordance with the different logical interpretations.

Based on the author's objective to represent and analyse the logical relations between sentences, the normalized form is a formalism for the representation of the knowledge which an expert system may directly utilize for drawing inferences.

In fact, a representation model of the text is, therefore, attained in this way which explains an initial level of interpretation restricted to the syntactic relations between sentences. In logical terms, this means constructing a logical model at a propositional level and, in legal terms, representing the relations between the constituents (conditions and consequences) of a prescription. By activating the rules, it is possible to evaluate whether the prescriptive effect is actually the one desired or to choose the anticipated interpretation from among the various different interpretations, substituting the ambiguous expression with a defined connective in the text.

According to the well-known definition given in 1984 by T. McCarty, such a system should be "shallow" as opposed to systems based on "deep conceptual" models. Whilst systems based on superficial knowledge reach conclusions to queries by merely applying an inferential process to the rules, a system built on a conceptual model is capable of understanding and, therefore, of also dealing with the concepts contained in the rules and of coming to a decision about the relevant rules and of justifying its reasoning in an intelligent fashion.

The propositional level has proved totally unsatisfactory in attempting to utilize the model for the evaluation of the characteristics of the text as it does not allow for any kind of analysis within the sentences. The system must, therefore, be provided with tools for reaching a partial understanding of the meaning: this means moving on from the syntactic level to a (reduced) semantic interpretation model.

4.3 The Semantic Level

The problems related to AI research in the field of natural language understanding demonstrate the extreme caution required in dealing with the semantic aspects.

The criteria giving a partial and as "objective" as possible understanding of the sentences were identified. A distinction was made between: a) a classification of the sentences according to their expressive characteristics; and b) a definition of the relevant concepts contained in the sentences.

The knowledge base is, therefore, made up of:

a) rules, which reproduce the specific norms contained in the legislative text as formulae of first order logic, where the predicate identifies the type of sentence (prescriptions in the narrow sense, definitions, procedural norms) and the subject matter corresponds to the important elements of the norm (parties to the contract, object, legal actions or events relating to the contract);
b) semantic networks containing the abovementioned elements which have been structured and organized within a more general conceptual field (contract law).

Rules

```
goal    (rescission, tenant, tenancy):-
        cond (the party is the tenant),
        def (he is a small tenant farmer, party)
        proc (rescission, tenancy).
goal    (termination, landlord, leasing of the land):-
        cond (the landlord is the party),
        def (serious breach of contractual duties, tenant),
        proc (termination, tenancy),
        not (cond (the tenant has remedied the breach)).
def     (he is a small tenant farmer, party):-
        cond (the party cultivates the land himself),
        cond (the work force constitutes a third of that
        required for cultivating the land).
```

```
proc    (rescission, tenancy):-
        cond (tenant simply gives landlord notification),
        cond (form, by means of, registered letter),
        cond (time, by means of, a year before the end
        of the agricultural year).
```

Let us look now, for the purpose of explaining the rules described above, at both, the name of the predicates and at the arguments of the expression.

The name of the predicates gives us an idea of the type of sentence it represents. An attempt has been made, in choosing the terms of the expression to provide the greatest amount of information possible: legal actions (first term of the expression), active parties in the action (second term), passive parties or objects in the action (third term). The number of the arguments is, however, variable. A variable, which represents the value to be calculated (for example, the duration of the tenancy or the rent) is often added. It should be noted that all the terms of the rules make up part of the nodes in the semantic network.

The semantic network is implemented in the knowledge base by binary relations: it is structured in such a way that the lack of precision of the information based on relations is limited only by meaning. The parameters for organizing and making the knowledge more specialized are based on the legal order (contractual parties and objects, types of contracts, legal actions and events relating to them).

5. Searching the Knowledge Base

An important feature of ESPLEX is that the knowledge base is separate from the management system and that both are implemented in the same language, Prolog, used on the one hand in its declarative function (in the knowledge base) and in its procedural function (in the inference engine) on the other.

ESPLEX can, therefore, be considered as a shell for a legal expert system because its inferential engine (or interpreter) can be utilized for managing any knowledge base with a predetermined structure. This includes:

* a series of instructions for the calculation of the legal consequences making use of Prolog's problem solving mechanism;
* a program for the reconstruction and management of the semantic network;
* a user interface permitting:
  i) facts to be inserted;
  ii) access to information.

5.1 Information Access: Searching the Rules

Two types of access for searching the knowledge base are provided: through the rules and through the network.

1. Searching the rules by choosing between the possible goals and calculating the normative consequences.

The selection of the rules permits the different types of sentences (prescriptions, definitions, procedures) and relevant elements (parties, contractual objects, contractual events and other legal actions) to be combined.

The search can be carried out, as follows:

a) by justification; that is, by displaying the pattern of reasoning as followed: listing the rules retrieved, or the elements thereof (atomic and complex conditions, definitions, procedures, and facts which have been used);
b) by retrieval of the sections (of the legislative text) applied to solving the problem. The normalized versions of the sections may also be examined;
c) by detailed analysis of the type of action, of the active parties, of the passive parties, and of the legal objects involved in finding a solution to the case (for example, which legal procedures must be performed by the owner, which must be carried out by the landlord, etc.).
d) by access to the network, guided by the main concepts contained in the rules consulted, in order to better justify the solution.

2. *Searching the network, once the user has identified the node or concepts he is interested in.*

An aspect we have not as yet discussed relates to the representation of the case: the conversational search strategy, as we have already mentioned, allows the user to define the case. It is not, however, possible to do this freely with the computer by simply describing the factual situation in natural language. In order to facilitate the representation of the case we could, however, enrich the implicit knowledge by defining (common) objects and concepts for "accessing" the knowledge base, relating to the world regulated by the norms, in the non-legal lexicon. The world (lexicon) of the legislation has partially been augmented by the description of the world (lexicon, its definitions and its relations), which are its equivalents in jurisprudence: The same operation can be carried out in the opposite sense, in relation to the ordinary (real) world.

5.2 Legal/Logical Analysis

Operating the inferential process on the rules, therefore, permits a rigorous check to be made on the normative amendments and additions in the new text as compared with regulations previously in force. Apart from this, the analysis could also be refined, by providing the system with additional functions.

Three main phases have been identified:

1. the checking of normative consistency and completeness: this requires the adoption of a normative logical system and the definition of a consistent and complete system within it. To achieve this, it is necessary:
   a) to be able to carry out "normative" calculations, that is, to take into account the modal operators of deontic logic and
   b) to optimize the forward-chaining and multiple goals of the search strategy;
2. the processing of meta-level norms: those norms which, within the legislative text, regulate validity in terms of time and space must be managed at a higher level than the other norms within the text. This phase would be the first step in coming to terms with the complex issue of the hierarchic relations between norms.

REFERENCES

BIAGIOLI, C.; MARIANI, P.; TISCORNIA, D. et al. 1983. "Un modello automatico per l'analisi dei sistemi normativi: una proposta sperimentale." *Proceedings III International Conference on "Legal Informatics in the National and International Communities"*. Rome

BIAGIOLI, C.; MARIANI, P.; TISCORNIA, D. et al. 1984. "Automated Analysis of Legislation", in: Peczenik, A. (ed.). *Theory of Legal Science*. Reidel Publishing Co., 587-605

BIAGIOLI, C.; MARIANI, P. and TISCORNIA, D. 1987. "ESPLEX: A Rule and Conceptual Model for Representing Statutes." *Proceedings of the First International Conference on Artificial Intelligence and Law*. Boston, May 1987, ACM Press, 240-252

BIAGIOLI, C.; MARIANI, P. and TISCORNIA, D. 1987. "ESPLEX: An Expert System in Contract Law." *Proceedings of the International Conference "20 ans informatique et droit"* (Strasbourg, 15-17 October, 1987)

BIAGIOLI, C.; MARIANI, P. and TISCORNIA, D. 1988. "ESPLEX: An Expert System for Representing and Analysing Statutes", in: *CC-AI* 1.A. (ed.). *Theory of Legal Science*. Reidel Publishing Co., 587-605

MARIANI, P.; MARTINO, A.A., TISCORNIA, D. et al. 1986. "Knowledge Base in the Automated Analysis of Legislation", in: Martino, A.A. & Socci, F. (eds.). *Automated Analysis of Legal Texts*. North-Holland Publishing, Amsterdam, 281-307

MARIANI, P.; MARTINO, A.A. 1986. "'Sistema Esperto' per il diritto." *Proceedings of the Conference A.I.C.A. "Expert Systems and Business Applications"*. Milan

MARIANI, P.; TISCORNIA, D. 1988. "I Sistemi esperti di supporto alla redazione di testi legislativi." *Proceedings of the IV International Conference held by the Corte Suprema di Cassazione on "Informatica e Regolamentazioni Giuridiche*. Rome

MARIANI, P.; TISCORNIA, D. (eds.). 1988. *Sistemi Esperti Giuridici*. F. Angeli, Milano (forthcoming)

NEW DEVELOPMENTS IN THE LEGAL BIBLIOGRAPHICAL DOCUMENTATION

Rosa Maria Di Giorgi, Roberta Nannucci
Istituto per la Documentazione Giuridica of
the Italian National Research Council, Florence
Italy

1. Introduction

The rapidly increasing growth of information technology already widely in use in all public and private areas of social life has led to enormous changes in scientific research work. The potentiality for accessing a huge amount of data constitutes a real revolution involving all areas, ranging from the humanities to technical research. Both, factual and bibliographical databases have become an essential component in a thorough and systematic approach to any sector of scientific research.

The problems related to bibliographical information are examined here, because it is in this area that developments in computer technology have had the greatest impact. Initial use of computer technology aimed at processing data to create bibliographies which were, however, distributed only in a traditional form (printed publication).

The subsequent step in the evolution of the automated management of documents was to supply the user with bibliographical information directly online. This development led the majority of bibliographical services to gradually abandon distribution on paper in favour of online dissemination.

At present, the widest and most useful application of modern technologies seems to be that of disseminating bibliographic information through different media (in print, on magnetic tape, on floppy disk or on CD-ROM), taking into account recent progress in distributed and personal informatics. The exploitation of personal informatics in the management of bibliographical databases appears to be very stimulating as it allows database producers to create bibliographical files for special purposes or for clearly defined user groups.

2. Database Systems: Development Trends

Current systems for managing databases can be subdivided into two major groups: the so-called Database Management Systems (DBMS), which largely process formatted data and Information Retrieval Systems (IRS), which process textual data.

The former group, in continual evolution since the '70s, can, in turn, from the architectural point of view, be divided into three different categories: hierarchical, reticular and relational. Whilst the characteristics specific to each of these categories are not discussed in detail in this paper, we will, instead, concentrate on the one feature they have in common: the capacity to manage formatted data mainly directed towards applications rather than users. This is the reason for their wide utilization in traditional management applications where only the programmer understands the functioning of the DBMS. Only with the most recent generation of relational databases even the non-expert user can manage the various tools available for the research and display of different kinds of data.

Information Retrieval Systems represent the second major group of systems for managing data. Their evolution has taken place in areas quite different from those where DBMS are used. This is easily understandable when the largely textual nature of the data being processed is taken into consideration. These systems have, therefore, spread as automated documentation systems in applications such as the searching of factual and bibliographical databases through local terminals or telecommunication networks.

Advances in microelectronics have also brought about enormous changes in data processing and communication systems in terms of both, quality and cost. By replacing electromechanical with electronic systems, telecommunication networks managers have encouraged the spread of intelligent workstations, capable of processing and storing data at reasonable costs and of communicating with each other through local networks (LAN) or with large computer centres through public networks.

In the meantime, it became clear that if data was to meet the needs of a wider user group, it had to be disseminated in more varied ways such as formatted, textual, graphic and voice data. These so-called multimedia systems cannot, however, be structured according to the architecture used for managing DBMS requiring preset keys to access data. On the contrary, IRS systems are far more functional here, as they are suited to more freely searching. An integrated information network which permits the maximum utilization of the tools and technology currently available is, therefore, anticipated.

Although the information patrimony will be traditionally managed through large computers, the potentialities of information systems will, at the same time, be enriched by utilizing personal informatics which is also decentralized and more accessible. In fact, users with multimedia workstations are able to simultaneously manage different kinds of data with adequate and autonomous processing power, to have access to data of interest to them, to define their own search strategies, to reprocess the retrieved data and to make it available in reply to an increasingly specialized demand.

3. From Traditional Bibliographies to Multimedia Information Systems

3.1 A Bibliographical Documentation Project on PC

Trends in personal informatics and videodisk technology as well as the increasing applications of artificial intelligence are being conditioning the methods used for disseminating information.

Professional users who have turned to personal informatics as a solution to their in-house problems relating to information or management are also generally interested in consulting databases. The same may also be said for the Public Administration which, by utilizing computers already in its possession, could, with a relatively limited increase in hardware and software, begin querying databases produced by other public bodies. This could prove very useful for internal management or as an aid to research and planning.

It is for this reason that a project is currently underway at the *Istituto per la documentazione giuridica (IDG)* of the *Italian National Research Council (CNR)* aimed at making bibliographical data available through various different kinds of media. The project concerns the *International Bibliography on Computers and Law* presently distributed in a traditional way (on paper) - appearing as a special issue of the international journal *"Informatica e diritto"* edited by the *IDG* - and as an online database retrievable in the information network of the *Italian Corte of Cassazione* and in that of the *Italian Chamber of Deputies.*

The initial part of the project is concerned with the improvement of data acquisition. The International Documentation Centres are required to provide the data directly on floppy disk by utilizing their own personal computers. The bibliographical data acquired in this way is to be processed and phototypeset and will subsequently have different types of output: on magnetic tape for its utilization in large information networks; on film strips for printing, on floppy disk for particular user groups and finally, on compact disk.

The phase of data 'reacquisition' from the original forms produced by the Documentation Centres is then avoided. As a result, this would also mean a considerable cut in production costs, which are often very high for those who produce bibliographies.

An important advantage would be the consistent improvement in the quality of work, thanks to the automated acquisition of bibliographical material.

Some difficulties may arise if the Documentation Centres would be without the proper tools required for this new production cycle, meaning they would, therefore, be unable to provide bibliographical data on magnetic media. New optical scanner technology (OCR: Optical Character Readers) may be of assistance in solving these problems.

Optical scanners are different from image scanners because they interpret the dots they digitize and reduce them to alphanumeric characters. Image scanners merely transform the text into a new dot matrix without distinguishing between text and image, whilst text scanners transform the text into a sequence of ASCII characters. Thanks to laser scanning systems and ICR (Intelligent Character Recognition) technology, the results are more than satisfactory. By using artificial intelligence, the system is able to recognize various 'fonts' of characters and to analyze the geometrical and topological features of the characters comparing them with those already stored. New methods available on the market guarantee a low percentage of errors and only a marginal need for the operator to intervene.

With regard to data dissemination, we have already mentioned that apart from the kinds of output which have been in operation over the years (magnetic tape and publication in print), the new organizational structure proposed envisages making the documents available on floppy disk and creating a current subscriber service to individual sections of the database or to personalized and specialized bibliographies.

It is worth, in this context, focusing our attention on the role of the bibliographical editors which is in a phase of rapid evolution. Having begun as information producers, they are now being called on to become information brokers. Their new role will in fact assume another function, that of database counsellors, able to search the database so that users can be supplied with specialized products meeting their personal needs as far as content and format (in printed form or on floppy disk) are concerned.

Information technology in recent years has developed new (software) tools which allow very interesting work to be done on databases. These include interface programs, which are more or less user-friendly for accessing, querying and locally transferring the output of user searches. After the user has carried out a particular search strategy, he can easily store it in his personal computer, regardless of his link up with the host computer where the data is housed. This strategy may require some adjustments, even in stages, but it is, nevertheless, permanently available.

When the bibliographical units useful for a specialized bibliography have been identified, downloading can be carried out by loading the documents retrieved in the search onto the hard or floppy disk.

Although of technical nature, the problem that may arise is connected with the document organization which presumably has a format the user is able to manage with his personal computer. It is, therefore, necessary to work on the record structure that is to 'reformat' the data or, in other words, to give it a structure which can be managed locally on a personal computer.

The interface permits the various kinds of printed record to be restructured in accordance with instructions previously given by the user. A powerful text editing function strongly increases the possibilities of manipulating the output of the search online, allowing the editors to eliminate any documents which are not considered pertinent and to add information deriving from other sources.

Once the most useful interface for the purpose has been identified (interfaces for accessing specific databases, interfaces linking up with the host computer and general-purpose interfaces are already in existence), different potentialities become clear.

A new kind of database producer is, therefore, emerging, alert to technological advances and ready to measure up to an increasingly specialized demand and to the needs, in general, of users who, more and more frequently, have their own tools for accessing information.

The development of user-friendly techniques is of great interest. These include simplification of search procedures and greater compatibility and integration between the various different services for the purpose of making the information on hand as complete as possible.

Some legal problems caused by resort to the technique of downloading discussed here must be mentioned. The first legal issue arising whenever there is no legal agreement between the user and the database producer is, whether an infringement of copyright is involved.

A similar problem is created by photocopying, as the real owner of the material does not, in effect, know if and when his work is photocopied. The database producer finds himself in a similar position, whenever the user fails to make a formal application for a specific data format to which, eventually, the downloading operation can be traced. Although exact information about the number of "records" retrieved by the user can be ascertained, no data is available about how the retrieved data is used (printed, only read on the screen or downloaded).

Whilst it is, of course, important to examine problems of this kind and to make them the subject of computer law research, it is no less important to give the proper weight to the positive results arising out of resort to this technology which could, in the long term, prove advantageous even for database producers.

It is without doubt that from the moment when the retrieved information is reprocessed, the intermediary adds value to it. He, in fact, personalizes the information for the user who has asked him for it. User satisfaction is higher and, therefore, the database is fully exploited through tools designed and built only to meet the user's specific needs.

As far as the view that growth in the use of downloading technology could lead to a reduction in the demand for information through direct link up with the host computer is concerned, it can be argued that the need for up-to-date information will force the user to link up periodically.

Independently of all this, something else has to be said. Existing databases are extremely numerous and well structured and given the progress made in recent years in user interfaces, can relatively easily be searched. But it is an established fact, proved by the analyses carried out by researchers from various different disciplines that the use of online information plays no fundamental role in the methodology of scientific research as it should do.

Many research studies argue that the reasons for this disappointing impact of information retrieval on the international scientific community are due, on the one hand, to the primordial repulsion of the keyboard and to the uneasiness caused by the cost involved in linking up with the host, on the other.

Technology directed towards integrating already experimented methods for online retrieval with those aimed at the local reorganization of the retrieved data must, therefore, be developed in the interests of database producers and professional operators in general. Further research into this kind of development trend would allow a different kind of relationship to be established between the user and the information source and would guarantee an adequate use of resources too frequently underutilized.

In the light of what has been said so far, we would like to make some comments about several proposals circulating in the world of online information. Firstly, users could pay a higher tariff per record when downloading is carried out for them. This would, of course, only apply when the user states that he wishes to use this function. A further proposal may concern the managers of host computers who, taking into consideration the number of users able to download, could adjust their tariffs but at the risk of negative reactions from ordinary users who are not interested in this kind of activity. The final solution would be provided by stipulating downloading contracts on the payment of a fee.

3.2 The New Frontier: CD/ROM

Research into new strategies for data distribution cannot leave out of consideration an analysis of videodisk technology through which the current restrictions on storage found in conventional computer tools have been lifted.

The CD (Compact Disk) for information technology applications is a truly innovative tool in the mass memory area. There are three different kinds of CD: read only, write only and read and write. 'Read only disks' can only be read by the user, 'write only disks' simply allow for storage whilst 'read and write disks' can be utilized in the same way as any floppy disk, that is, to record data and subsequently erase it. Only the so-called CD-ROM (Compact Disk-Read Only Memory) are currently on the market and can be used in conjunction with personal computers. Data is stored in digital form on non-erasable ('drive write once') disks: 'read only disks' where, once the information has been recorded, it cannot be modified.

Apart from CD-ROM, which are easily managed by a PC and by an optical scanner and permit a consumer-type utilization (for example, an immediate search, on easily accessible tools, of very large databases), WORM (Write Once Read Memory) disks are also available. These allow data to be recorded and stored through a special type of drive without, however, giving the possibility of erasing it.

The storage capacity of CD-ROM is enormous: 300,000 typed pages in a plastic covered aluminium disk 12 cms. in diameter. There are already scanners on the market with an interface linking them to the most popular marks of PCs. So multi-key research can be carried out, correlations built and extracts of documents to be word processed selected.

The special feature of this technology is, however, its capacity to store not only text but also graphs, figures, programs, sound and speech. CD/ROM permits multimedia documents or, in other words, files containing binary (programs) and ASCII-type information as well as graphic (images) and audio information (music and speech) to be processed. The software for scanning these disks is, of course, specifically designed to synchronize the presentation of the different kinds of information.

These brief comments give some idea of the revolutionary nature of such a tool: electronic information is no longer confined to texts in ASCII characters and, therefore, the interaction between man and machine can reach a very high level. The CD-ROM reader market is growing rapidly and we can, therefore, predict that many applications of the widest possible variety will be based on the use of such an advanced tool.

Costs which are still fairly high for the creation of the MASTER (the disk with all the information on the data format) are to be compared with the cost of the copies, which is inversely proportional to their quantity. Difficulties in the propagation of this new technology are connected with the question of standards: the larger the number of users able to exploit CD by carrying out only minor adjustments to the hardware already in their possession, the greater the possibilities will be for it to spread in the information market.

The industry in this sector has, at worldwide level, directed its attention to defining a logical structure which will allow the majority of PCs to read optical disks.

A standard CD must define the structure of the disks, the data format and addresses as well as the error correcting codes. The standards which are becoming increasingly accepted (Microsoft's High Sierra CD-ROM File Format standard seems to be moving towards a prime position) give information producers, from software houses to hardware manufacturers, the opportunity of releasing compatible products based on CD-ROM. Any standard which becomes accepted internationally will, in the short term, lead to the production of CD-ROM disks which have a single format and are easily readable by computers with different drives and operating systems.

Videodisk technology, precisely because of its features described here, is a considerable aid to the diffusion of advanced hypertext systems. The problems connected with available hardware and the occupancy of storage have hindered the development of the systems based on non-linear documents, constituted by fragments of information which can be linked together in the most varied fashion.

A hypertext system is the tool for displaying all the information on a (specially prepared) screen about the relationships between possible 'accesses' to it (for example, the reference from one heading in an encyclopedia to another connected with it) united by a series of nodes which provide more than one access, even of a horizontal kind, to the information.

The information is richer and numerous applications are possible in the various sectors. Progress in videodisk technology will allow data base producers to study the format of information, so it can be made more accessible and visually more attractive to users thanks to the utilization of CD graphic functions (apart from the less probable, but nevertheless possible, audio applications). Furthermore, by adding intelligent retrieval software to their product, they will be able to provide the user's PC with the same advanced information retrieval capacity which very large databases currently have, only on mainframe.

4. Conclusions

Research into information systems and new information dissemination methodologies has in recent years reached a considerable level of integration. The most immediate need is to improve traditional information retrieval systems giving users online access, through telecommunication networks, to distributed information with their personal computers.

The computer terminal will gradually be substituted for a PC providing the user with a more functional and personalized approach, being able to reprocess the information adapting it to his individual needs.

Systems for accessing the databases, defined as 'intelligent interfaces', are being developed keeping the increasingly more diversified demands of users in mind. Retrieved documents, processed with the functions offered by modern electronic publishing systems, reach the end user with considerable added value. Database producers and host computer managers are faced with the necessity of adapting themselves to the new rules created by the spread of personal computing and with providing tools which substitute or supplement already consolidated systems.

It is within this framework that new methods for information dissemination are developing, from the floppy disk to CD-ROM and from CD-ROM to multimedia information systems, whose main and absolutely innovative feature is their strong integration and highly transparent communication between man and machine, with a great capacity for managing documents and multimedia data.

REFERENCES

AGOSTI, M. 1986. "Information Retrieval: stato dell'arte." *Informatica oggi* 18, 34-42

AGOSTI, M. and SPILOTRO, F. 1986. "Tendenze nello sviluppo di sistemi di Information Retrieval (IR) e di sistemi che incorporano funzionalità IR." *Rivista di informatica* 2, 163-173

BIANCHI, G. and PACI, A.M. 1986. "Funzioni, caratteristiche e finalità delle interfacce per la ricerca in linea." *Quaderni* 17-18, 111-125

BING, J. 1984. *Handbook of Legal Information Retrieval*. North-Holland

BRACCHI, G. and LOCHERMAN, P.C. (eds.). 1986. *Information Systems Technology*. Springer-Verlag

BURNS, A. (ed.). 1984. *New Information Technology*. Ellis Horwood

BURTON, P. 1986. "The Use of Microcomputers in Libraries and Information Services." *Law Librarian* 1, 19-23

CIRILLO, M. 1986. "Il futuro in CD-ROM." *Industria oggi* 1, 84-90

COCOLA, F. 1987. "Una nuova frontiera." *Sistemi e automazione* 281, 457-460

CORDES, R.; BUCK-ERNDEN, R. and LANGENDOERFER, H. 1988. *Multimedia Information Management and Optical Disk Technologies as a Basis for Advanced Information Retrieval*. Proceedings of RIAO 88 Conference on *User-oriented Content-based Text and Image Handling* (Cambridge, 21-24 March 1988)

CURTICE, R.M. and CASY, W. 1986. "Cosa ci riserva il futuro delle basi di dati?" *Zerouno* 54-55, 61-67

DI GIORGI, R.M.; FAMELI, E. and NANNUCCI, R. 1983. *La documentazione nel campo dell'informatica giuridica e del diritto dell'informatica e la Bibliografia internazionale d'informatica e diritto*. Proceedings of the 3rd International Conference on *Legal Informatics and National and International Communities* (Rome, 9-14 May 1983)

GATTI, M.; OCCHINI, G. and SALVATORI, M. (eds.). 1988. *Memorie ottiche per una nuova editoria*. Masson

JANSEN, A.A.J. 1984. "Problems and Challenges of Downloading for Database Producers." *Electronic Library*, 42-43

LLOYD, M. 1986. *Legal Databases in Europe. User Attitudes and Supplier Strategies*. North-Holland

MARASCHINI, F. 1988. *L'accesso intelligente alle basi informative*. Pre-proceedings of the 4th International Congress on *Law and Computers* (Rome, 16-21 May 1988)

MAZZONI, R. 1986. "Nuove luci sull'info-retrieval." *Informatica oggi* 18, 50-61

QUINEY, L. 1986. "Recent Developments in Information Retrieval: An Overview." *Law Librarian* 1, 7-13

SALTON, G. 1986. *Recent Trends in Automatic Information Retrieval*. ACM SIGIR Conference Proceedings

SMEATON, A.F. 1988. *Information Retrieval Advances in the Last Five Years*. Pre-proceedings of the 4th International Congress on *Law and Computers* (Rome, 16-21 May 1988)

WALKER, J. 1987. "Document Examiner: Delivery System for Hypertext Documents." *Hypertext '87 Conference Proceedings*

WINDER, J. 1986. "The Value of Downloading for Database Users and Database Producers." *Aslib Proceedings* 11/12, 411-416

THE APPLICATION OF TERMINOLOGY-BASED KNOWLEDGE DATA BASES IN THE HUMANITIES AND THE SOCIAL SCIENCES AND ITS IMPACT ON RESEARCH METHODS

Gerhard Budin
Infoterm, Wien
Austria

1. Introduction

Since the use of modern information technologies has become quite common in the social sciences and the humanities, the need for terminology work and knowledge engineering based on terminological principles has become more and more evident. This paper is an attempt to demonstrate the importance and usefulness of a terminological approach to the establishment of terminological data bases and knowledge bases designed for research in the disciplines in question.

2. The Aim of Terminology Research

Originally conceived by the Austrian engineer E. Wüster as early as in the 1930s for the harmonization and standardization of concepts and terms in engineering and technology, the General Theory of Terminology and its practical application - terminology work - have proofed to be successful tools to overcome or at least minimize barriers and conflicts in specialized communication (Wüster 1974, 1979). This approach is concept-orientated, this means that every piece of information is related in some way or another to the concepts formed and used by scientists. The reason for this is quite simple: the number of concepts formed in every subject field is rising exponentially, whereas the number of terms representing these concepts is limited (even taking into account compounding, derivation etc.). Therefore, many concepts are represented by other signs (e.g. graphical symbols).

The more or less systemic character of scientific knowledge requires an appropriate approach to the recording, processing, retrieval and application of all kinds of data. Therefore, the interdependencies and relationships between concepts are reconstructed and recorded, which in turn requires the delimitation of these concepts from each other by definitions. This structured set of concepts and the terms assigned to them constitute a terminology.

3. The Structure of Terminologies in the Social Sciences and the Humanities

According to various authors in the theory of science and related fields and to my own investigations into the nature of social science terminologies (Budin 1988), the following peculiarities, constituting the cause of many problems in specialized communication in these disciplines, can be observed: since the majority of objects of investigation in disciplines such as sociology, political science, economics, history etc. are human behaviour and its - mostly abstract - results such as different kinds of social systems and structures, psychological phenomena, historical facts etc., these objects "exist" only through the "construction" by concepts. In other words, most parts of disciplines of the social sciences and humanities are constituted by a cognitive reality, i.e. a conceptual reality (e.g. law). Terms, symbols etc. assigned to these concepts are the only way of communicating about these objects and the only access to scientific knowledge on them. Therefore, the terminological treatment of these concepts and terms is essential for efficient processing, storing and retrieval of specialized knowledge. Since most of these objects described above constantly change (especially in sociology, political science etc., but certainly not in historical disciplines), empirical and - as a consequence - also theoretical concepts are modified in order to represent these objects adequately. Therefore, a certain degree of inherent fuzziness cannot be prevented. But even if social, historical etc. objects remain the same, investigations, studies, empirical observations and their results inevitably lead to conceptual change, since these concepts are theory-laden. The interdependency of conceptual change and the modification of hypotheses, theories etc. during the research process is accompanied by another phenomenon typical for the social sciences and the humanities: unlike natural sciences such as physics etc., these disciplines do not have any predominant paradigm (in the sense of T.S. Kuhn) but rather a plurality of theories, hypotheses, schools of thought etc. concerning the same "objects". This means that several differing concepts are formed about the same object according to the framework of the respective theory.

There is another typical phenomenon regarding concepts and terms formed and used in the social sciences and humanities: due to the epistemological vicinity of many of these disciplines, they have the same object of investigation seen from different points of view and as a consequence, many concepts are taken over from neighbouring disciplines. During this conceptual shift the term representing the concept remains the same, which is the reason for many communication conflicts among researchers, since they often do not realize the reason of their misunderstandings.

The disciplines in question show a low degree of structurization and hierarchization of concepts and of knowledge in comparison to natural sciences (some of them have highly sophisticated nomenclatures). Clear-cut concept systems are rarely to be found, instead, conceptual fields with loose relationships predominate. Furthermore, hardly any definition of the concepts used in publications can be found; sometimes the only conceptual description is given by the context, which is a very important factor for terminology work in these disciplines.

4. The Terminological Approach to Information Management in the Social Sciences and the Humanities

The consequences of these aspects for the construction of data bases, i.e. the processing of terminology and of knowledge are manifold. Information management in this sense means the systematic extraction, recording, processing, condensation, structurized combination and application (dissemination) of all kinds of data needed for certain purposes.

A distinction of 3 data groups has proofed quite useful in the computerized handling of terminologies and knowledge and in the construction of terminological data bases:

1. *Bibliographic data*: This first group of data is primarily used for documentation purposes, thus, these data categories are indispensable for the identification of documents (or parts of them) containing relevant information. While the formal handling of documents includes a unified (standardized) way of recording data such as author, title, location etc., the contents-orientated handling means the provision of condensed information on the contents of documents: e.g. abstracts, extracts, and all kinds of so-called documentation languages such as thesauri, classification systems, keyword lists etc. for the ordering of knowledge provided by documents.

The documentation of objects becomes more and more important, especially in disciplines like archaeology, art history etc. Efforts for standardization of data categories are taken now.

2. *Terminographic data*: This group of data categories can be divided into terminological and administrative data categories. Terminological data can be concept-orientated (e.g. description of the concept) or term-oriented (e.g. variant of the term). In this group, there are data categories such as picture, graphic, formula etc. representing a concept or an object. It is very important to record any change in every category. Especially the structure of the characteristics of a concept may constantly change (see above). For disciplines such as history categories covering diachronic aspects are essential (concept history etc.). Since terminology work is concept-oriented, the problems of synonymy and phraseology can be handled with a number of terminographic data categories.

3. *Factual data*: This group is situated on the level of predicate logic and compromises any data category covering all kinds of propositions (formed by concepts), e.g. theories (a proposal for the documentation of theories has been made by OHLY 1988), hypotheses, empirical results of tests etc. (e.g. the concretization of metrical concepts etc.), any kind of historical facts, complex symbols, pictures, graphics representing events, actions, attitudes, propositions.

In every group a number of administrative data categories is necessary for documentation and handling purposes.

Expert knowledge on a certain "object" of social (etc.) reality can be seen as a combination of these three groups of data (and a combination within these groups), e.g.: certain concepts and terms (group 2) are used in propositions, constituting a theory (group 3) in a certain document located somewhere (group 1). Information on all three groups of data is necessary for efficient research, since the scientist could not identify the document without bibliographic data; he would not know what the object of investigation is without terminographic data and could not evaluate existing theories etc. or create new ones without factual data. Thus, the availability of all three kinds of knowledge is essential for research.

Accordingly, data bases used for efficient information management in disciplines such as sociology, political science, history, philology etc. should be designed in such a way that - depending on the specific purpose - a highly complex structure of data categories is defined in order to be able to establish all the necessary links between data to generate usable information. Furthermore, the architecture of such data bases should prevent the generation of redundant or irrelevant information, since - according to Herfurth - the evaluation of such information is as time-consuming as that of relevant information (Herfurth 1988).

Therefore, the goal of multifunctionality of data bases containing bibliographic, terminographic and factual data on research objects in the social sciences and the humanities can only be reached by certain combinations of data categories tailored to specific user needs. This selective retrieval of information from data bases can easily be reached in the programming structure, but it has to be established in theory beforehand.

In other disciplines and mainly for translation purposes, terminological data bases have been established functioning along a similar (less complex) data structure. Taking into account the complexity of data categories necessary for the exact description and documentation of research results, such terminological data bases can also be created for the disciplines in question.

5. The Impact of the Application of Terminological Data Bases on Research Methods in the Social Sciences and the Humanities

According to Oeser, science can be seen as an information system having the functional property of organizing communication processes (Oeser 1987). The state-of-the-art of a scientific discipline is represented by those documents actually used by the representatives of this system. Since the amount of information produced in every scientific discipline is rising almost exponentially, various mechanisms have to guarantee that redundant information is eliminated. According to the principle of economy empirical knowledge can be condensed by modern information technologies (increase of storage capacity), whereas theoretical-structural knowledge has to be evaluated according to established criteria. The greatest problem in highly complex information systems is not the perfection of information channels, but the improvements of internal processing and selection mechanisms (Oeser 1987; Herfurth 1988). As far as terminological data bases are concerned, this requirement can be fulfilled by efficient data management with the obsolete ones being deleted automatically.

Computerized communication networks in the social sciences and the humanities have to be structured in such a way that bibliographic, terminographic and factual data are recorded and processed only after having been carefully selected. In this connection, there is a problem typical of this kind of scientific disciplines: According to Herfurth (Herfurth 1988) and other authors sociology, for instance, is highly particularized and individualized with many researchers barely taking notice of methods, results, hypotheses etc. of colleagues from other countries and/or other schools of thought. There is a negative interdependency of communication barriers because of differing and unclear concepts being used. This vicious circle can only be broken by an information management strategy covering both sides at the same time:

1. Availability of terminographic data (on concepts, their description, conceptual relationships, terms, synonyms etc.) with an indication of the theory etc. the concept(s) in question belong(s) to.
2. Availability of factual data including propositions of all kinds belonging to the theory etc. in question containing certain concepts.

A network of data bases designed to fulfil these requirements could then be used by sociologists, historians etc. and would affect their research methods by an increased availability of information on concepts, terms, theories etc. formed and used in their subject fields (and related disciplines). Retrieval methods have to be structured in a user-specific way in order to avoid the retrieval of unwanted or redundant information. Such networks would reduce communication barriers among individual disciplines of the social sciences and the humanities on the one hand and among individual schools thought, paradigms and individual researchers on the other. This could initiate a new phase in the evolution of this type of scientific disciplines.

New technologies and methods (active book, electronic library etc.) are developments which should be used for reaching the goals described above. Otherwise, there is the danger that electronic libraries etc. are badly designed in terms of the documentation language(s) being used, their structurization, linking of data etc.

6. Conclusions

An information strategy based on terminological principles would lead to some kind of harmonization of concepts, terms etc. and to a higher degree of structurization of the knowledge formed in these disciplines. The negative interdependency mentioned above can now turn into a positive loop: knowledge on concepts used in other theories etc. increases knowledge on the theories etc. and vice versa. This process could be a sound basis for highly efficient interdisciplinary research. Using the experience of other sciences this means that the bad performance of certain data bases, e.g. traditional term banks for translators or some data bases in the natural sciences that were not structured in a knowledge store, should be reason enough to raise the awareness of terminological problems, which actually are vital problems of many disciplines of the social sciences and the humanities. One should start to solve these problems as soon as possible for the sake of scientific progress.

REFERENCES

BUDIN, G. 1988. *Möglichkeiten und Grenzen der Terminologieforschung in den Sozialwissenschaften* [Possibilities and limits of terminology research in the social sciences]. Wien, 269 p. (doctoral dissertation)

HERFURTH, M. 1988. "Notationen soziologischen Wissens. Ein Beitrag zur Architektur sozialwissenschaftlicher Wissensbasen" [Notations of sociological knowledge. A contribution to the architecture of social science knowledge bases], in: Hermes, H.-J.; Hölzl, J. (eds.). *Wissensorganisation im Wandel. Dezimalklassifikation - Thesaurusfragen - Warenklassifikation.* Proceedings 11. Jahrestagung der Gesellschaft für Klassifikation, Aachen, 29.6.-1.7.1987. Frankfurt/Main: INDEKS Verlag, 82-93

OESER, E. 1987. *Der Informationsbegriff in Philosophie und Wissenschaftstheorie* [The concept of information in philosophy and the theory of science]. (in print)

OHLY, H.P. 1988. "Sozialwissenschaftliche Theorien als Gegenstand systematischer Dokumentation" [Social science theories as objects of systematic documentation], in: Hermes, H.-J.; Hölzl, J. (eds.). *Wissensorganisation im Wandel. Dezimalklassifikation - Thesaurusfragen - Warenklassifikation.* Proceedings 11. Jahrestagung der Gesellschaft für Klassifikation, Aachen, 29.6.-1.7.1987. Frankfurt/Main: INDEKS Verlag, 94-102

WÜSTER, E. 1974. "Die Allgemeine Terminologielehre - ein Grenzgebiet zwischen Sprachwissenschaft, Logik, Ontologie, Informatik und den Sachwissenschaften" [General Theory of Terminology - a border field between linguistics, logic, ontology, information science and the subject fields]. *Linguistics* no. 119, 61-106

WÜSTER, E. 1979. *Einführung in die Allgemeine Terminologielehre und Terminologische Lexikographie* [General Theory of terminology and terminological lexicography - an introduction]. Wien/New York: Springer (Schriftenreihe der Technischen Universität Wien, Bd. 8, vol. 1, 145 p.; vol. 2, 70 p.)

CONSTRUCTION OF AN INDIVIDUALS IDENTIFICATION HELP SYSTEM

Caroline Bourlet, Agnès Guillaumont
IRHT (CNRS), Paris
Arlette Faugères, Michelle Magdelaine
IHMC (CNRS), Paris
Marion Selz-Lauriere
LAS (CNRS), Paris
France

Presentation

Historians are often faced with the necessity of identifying individuals through a variety of historical sources. This is always a delicate process for at least two reasons: until the XXth century, there is no fixed means of identifying individuals (as the INSEE code in France) and the sources never point out all the necessary elements for a reliable identification of each person. On the other hand, and this is particularly true concerning the time prior to the XIXth century, the spelling of information, especially of names, varies tremendously. In order to avoid difficulties caused by spelling variation one can normalize occupations and firstnames, although difficulties arise here when these are French translations of foreign firstnames, but is out of the question for nicknames and patronymics. A strategy must, therefore, be set up to compare nicknames and patronymics despite the spelling variations. It is only this aspect of the problem, with which we shall deal here after having quickly described the sources and presented the main principles on which the phonetic rules concerning our respective sources are based.

The Sources

Our sources date from two historical periods. Medieval: the seven Parisian tax rolls dating from the reign of Philippe the Fair(1) (end of the XIIIth - beginning of the XIVth century) and modern: documents concerning the huguenot refuge at the end of the XVIIth century. Gathering characteristic information on each individual mentioned in the various sources is necessary for any prosopographical study of whatever period: the craftsman and tradesman in the Middle Ages, the various socio-professional groups of huguenot refugee or the persons participating in any migratory movement. This gathering is based on the comparison of the various information elements existing in the registers paragraph. In the tax rolls, these elements are always of the same kind: date of the register, location in a parish, a street..., personal appellation (first name, surname, occupation, sometimes a title, family or craft relationship), taxation (livres, sous, deniers).

It is different for the huguenot refuge. The documents are of very different kinds: lists of refugees to which assist, parish registers, judicial, hospital, military archives. Sometimes, they give numerous details on each person: name, firstname, occupation, family situation, geographic origin, itinerary, date, etc...; sometimes they give much more succinct information.

In both cases, all the elements intervene in the identification of a person. However, their function and weight in the general identification system depend on factors such as their frequency in the sources, the degree to which they have been permanently applied during the whole of an individualy life and their discriminating aspect. In fact, the way to designate individuals evolved between Middle Age and Modern times. Therefore, the weight of the various elements of identification cannot be identical from one period to the other. For example, the anthropomorphic system in Paris during the XIIIth century is very far from being what it is today. The two terms denomination system, i.e. christian name plus surname, is well established but the christian name is frequently the sole element mentioned in the sources: it is the more fixed element to designate a person during his or her life. It follows that for the period, when one wants to restrict the number of individuals in a population, which have to undergo comparison, the first name is a more reliable criterion than the surname often missing or ambiguous. However, because of the lack of comparison elements available, comparison of surnames must be made where it is possible.

During the XVIIth century, patronymics are fixed, whereas their spellings are not. It is not unusual that in a baptismal register one finds the same patronymic written in three different ways. Especially, when the documents come from different countries, written by scribes who were not necessarily speaking French.

Review of the Patronymics Processing

This problem of processing spelling variants is not new. A very effective method has been developed by demographers and historical demographers: That is, the reduction of words to a framework (or skeleton) and, thus, comparison of the characteristic part of patronymics. Reduction to a framework is done through the use of an established code according to phonetic rules and other observation criteria. The Russel soundex code is the first and most well known of these codes. However, it is not altogether suitable for processing of French patronymics.(2) For this reason, special codes have been developed which respond to the characteristics of the French language. There exist, at present, several phonetic transcription codes as well as several reduction codes. In the sixties, Louis Henry developed a first method based on the soundex Code which had to be modified in order to get more satisfactory results.(3) FONEM(4), also inspired by Louis Henry(5), was created in the seventies by a Canadian research team. It has the advantage of expressing clearly not only the phonetic transcription rules but also the rules about the application priorities.

General Rules of our Patronymics Identification System

The method employed by our project is based to a large extent on the previous patronymics processing codes. However, we could not use them without modifications for two reasons:

1 - Those phonetic codes were developed to process documents well defined in space and time and reflect in a certain way the state of language of the space and time studied. This is a necessary condition for their effectiveness. Therefore, they are not universal.(6) We have, thus, developed phonetic codes which fit our respective sources

and the state of language they reflect.

Old French was essentially a spoken language which had not been normalized by a grammar such as it is today. Two important consequences for our subject result from this:

* the spelling refers to sounds.
* there is much freedom in the choice of spelling to represent one sound: the nasalized diphthong **oi** (oin) is written **ouin, oin, oen, ouen, ouain, oyn, ouyn.**
* there are tendencies specific to the Parisian dialect.(7) Take for example the pronunciation of a yod after an occlusive consonant (b, p, t, d, k, g). The Parisians pronounce *biau* for *beau*, *guiet* for *guet*, etc...
* Finally, a large variety of alternative pronunciations are found in Paris at the end of the XIIIth century. The result is a large variety in the written transcriptions of one word. The pronunciations **è-oè-oa** coexisted in Paris under Philippe the Fair and allowed Le Tréport to be written: *tresport* or *troisporz*, the town of Troyes: *Troas, Traies, Troie, Troies, Trois*. The rules we elaborated to process the medieval corpus take into account all these aspects.

The database concerning the Huguenot refugee is partly similar and partly different from the medieval corpus of Parisian tax-rolls: The language of the sources is French and one can find spellings which correspond to sounds. For example *Heiltz-le-Maurupt* is often written *Helmoru* or *Elmoru*, *Sainte-Menehould* is written *Sainte-Menou* and one can find *Surtille* for *Is-sur-Tille*. As these examples are place names, it is easy to recognise them through the spelling transcribed by the secretaries. Nevertheless, when patronyms do not refer to place names, one has no means of recognising them through different spellings without referring to phonetic rules. Those, who migrated to Frankfort came from different parts of France. This pronunciation followed the dialectal habits of their native country. The secretaries lived in a very different linguistic background, they belonged to the French Church and were French speaking, but they were from the north of the country or from the Spanish Lowlands. They were often incapable to transcribe the sounds they heard when pronounced by "provençal" or "gascon" people. Misspellings are sometimes very simple: *Bourcette* for *Bourcet* which is not the feminine of a patronymic but the phonetic transcription of a stressed end consonant, or *La Tour d'Angalm for La Tour d'Angalin*. A minor difficulty being the spellings *Lacroix, La Croix* or *Croix* for *Delacroix*. We had to take into account the linguistic characteristics of northern and southern France. The yod can be spelled -ill or -lh: *Brouillet* or *Broulhet*; the confusion of "b" and "v" in the South-West: *Fabre* or *Favre*; the "a" which, in the north becomes a stressed "e": *Fèvre, Febvre*. We, therefore, established general rules, applicable to the entire corpus, and specific rules for each country.

2 - Those systems integrate the Patronymics Identification Automatic System into the more general Record Linkage system. It is not possible to use only the module for the phonetic name transcription in an independent and convivial way. We, therefore, decided to build an independent module for the patronymics identification which could be used by medievalists as well as by modernists that is a system which allows the historian to enter and to test the phonetic rules adapted to his corpus and their application priorities and which is independent of any Record Linkage system.

The Skeletonizing Program

The purpose of this program is, to simplify each surname so that its spelling variations are merged. It reduces the surname to a "skeleton" through a number of transformations, which vary according to the time and the place of the studied corpus, but are always a set of rules taken from the following:

* removing a prefix at the beginning of the name (example: remove *la* so that *Lacroix* and *Delacroix* equals *Croix*).
* substituting a character string for another one, either at the end, or within the word (example: substitute *o* for *eau* and for *au* everywhere; substitute *o* for *eault*, *eaux* and for *aux*... at the end of the word).
* ignoring letters either at the end (ex.: *s*) or in the word (ex.: *h*).
* undoubling double letters (example: *Challier* = *Chalier*).

Prefixes, suffixes, letters to be ignored and equivalent groups of letters depend on place and time; but the basic operations are always the same. Thus, we programmed these basic operations (or rules) so that anyone could easily change their parameters and modify the order of their execution and so be able to adapt them to the various corpus to be dealt with.

Example of transformations:

Carriere: remove-ending (*e*) -> *Carrier*
double-letter (*r*) -> *Carier*
substitute-ending (*er* -> *r*) -> *Carie*
remove-ending (*e*) -> *CARI*
Charie: remove-ending (*e*) -> *Chari*
ignore-letter (*h*) -> *CARI*
Charrier: substitute-ending (*er* -> *r*) -> *Charrie*
double-letter (*r*) -> *Charie*
ignore-letter (*h*) -> *Carie*
remove-ending (*e*) -> *CARI*
Charriere: remove-ending (*e*) -> *Charrier*
substitute-ending (*er* -> *r*) -> *Charrie*
double-letter (*r*) -> *Charie*
ignore-letter (*h*) -> *Carie*
remove-ending (*e*) -> *CARI*
Charieres: substitute-ending (*eres* -> *er*) -> *Charier*
ignore-letter (*h*) -> *Carier*
substitute-ending (*er* -> *e*) -> *Carie*
remove-ending (*e*) -> *CARI*

As far as we know, it is impossible to find a set of rules which yields a same skeleton for a various spellings of a same name, without ever producing the same skeleton for two really different names.

In the same way, it is impossible to find a set of rules which yields distinct skeletons for all really distinct names, without also producing distinct skeletons for different spellings of a same name.

> Example: the set of rules which, in a proper way, turn *Carriere, Charie, Charrier, Charriere* into *Cari* - or *Dufour* and *Four* into *For* - also transform *Cher* and *Duc* into *C*, which is of course not correct.

Finding a skeleton, we have to conciliate two conflicting purposes: get rid of irrelevant differences, and keep relevant differences.
A compromise has to be found between both solutions:

* either emphasize the unification of spellings, even though different names may get the same skeleton;
* or emphasize the differences, even though two spellings of a same name may occasionally get different skeletons.

The choice has to be made according to the corpus: if the surname is a fixed element of the name, then it may be used as a sorting key, in order to reduce the number of comparisons. The unification may be emphasized. In the case of a medieval corpus, as surnames are not fixed, they are only an element of comparison; the differences must be maintained.

In the modern corpus (the huguenot refuge), we gave precedence to the first solution. Consequently, two really distinct names may have identical skeletons; other information (such as geographical origin, profession...) will make it possible to distinguish between persons who are called by these names.

But even in this case, specific variations are difficult to take into account: the rules which would merge them would wrongly merge a good deal of other names.

> Example: to let *Archambaud*, *Archebaud* and *Archimbaud* get the same skeleton, it would be necessary to set an equivalence between *am*, *e* and *im*, which would in most cases be incorrect. We made a decision to accept that these cases cannot be solved automatically. Sorted lists may enable us to locate some of such cases. As for the remaining cases, usual names will easily be located by the scholar and their skeletons manually merged; unusual ones will remain unchanged; we assume that the impact of this decision on the general analysis of the data base will be weak.

The order in which the rules are executed is not insignificant. Successive transformations may produce unexpected results, and it is necessary to foresee and to control these chain transformations. This may not be easy, as there is no tool to test the coherence of the rules. For example, if *eau* and *au* have to be changed into *o*, it is necessary to have the transformation *eau->au* executed first; otherwise, the result would be *eau->eo*.

The skeleton may be quite different from the original name, in its written form and in its phonetic. But it does not matter, as the only aim is to compare the skeletons.

Implementation

Choice of the Prolog language.
We decided to write the skeletonizing program in the programming language Prolog for the following reasons:

* this language is available on a great number of computer systems; thus, our program is either portable or easily adaptable. Two versions of the program exist at present:

the first one written in Prolog-Criss on a micro-computer running Unix, the second one in Prolog-VM on mainframe running HVM/CMS (the *Centre Interrégional de Calcul Electronique -CIRCE-* at Orsay, France).

* Prolog is a language which is widely used in the field of artificial intelligence, especially by linguists to program grammars, and it is well adapted to writing transformation rules.
* it is a declarative language, which means for us that the basic functions are defined independently of each other. The advantage of such a modularity is that it is easy to modify functions and to create new ones without affecting the others. For the programmer, a Prolog program may be very short, especially by the use of recursion (i.e. a function may be defined in terms of itself).
* the transformation rules that are appropriate to a given corpus are also written in the Prolog language, but in a module which is distinct from the function definition. The same goes for the order of the execution of rules.

As the words of the natural language may be used as function names, this part of the program is clearly understandable to a non-programmer (cf. Appendix A). The historian himself, without the intervention of a programmer, can write and tune his rules. It is not necessary, as is generally the case with most programming languages, to write a user-oriented interface.

Independence of the skeletonizing module.
As we already said, we wanted to make the system as independent as possible of the specific format of a given software or DBMS. It was also important to be able to call upon the reduction of the spelling variations of surnames at a precise point according to the corpus under study. That is why the program has been designed to process a file of surnames (which one can always extract from a data base consisting of personal data); it produces as a result a file linking each surname to its skeleton. It is then easy to incorporate these skeletons in the data base.

Appendix: Transformation Rules (Medieval Corpus), as Written in the Prolog Language

```
debut-champ("des-").
debut-champ("d_").
debut-champ("de-la-").
debut-champ("de-l_").
debut-champ("de-").
debut-champ("du-").
debut-champ("le-").
debut-champ("la-").

subst-fin-mot("eur","or").
subst-fin-mot("iau","el").
subst-fin-mot("eau","el").
subst-fin-mot("x","us").

substitution("ngn","n").
substitution("ng","n").
substitution("gn","n").
substitution("st","t").
```

```
substitution("sp","p").
substitution("sc","c").
substitution("sl","l").
substitution("sn","n").
substitution("cq","q").
substitution("ll","l").
substitution("ci","si").
substitution("ce","se").
substitution("ai","oi").
substitution("ay","oi").
substitution("oy","oi").
substitution("aa","a").
substitution("ou","oo").
substitution("mm","m").
substitution("nn","n").
substitution("cc","c").
substitution("ff","f").
substitution("mont","mon").

a-ignorer-fin("fcgsz").

lettres-a-ign("jiuvyh_-12345").

lettres-meme-poids("ckq").
lettres-meme-poids("dt").
lettres-meme-poids("ae").
lettres-meme-poids("mn").
lettres-meme-poids("gw").
lettres-meme-poids("sz").

resol-graphique(_chaine,_squelette):
                        ignorer-debut(_chaine,_res1) &
                        substituer-fin-mot(_res1,_res2) &
                        substituer(_res2,_res3) &
                        ignorer-fin-mot(_res3,_res4) &
                        ignorer(_res4,_res5) &
                        meme-poids(_res5,_squelette).
```

NOTES

1. Four of them are published. H. Géraud published the tax roll dating from 1292 in 1837, and those dating from 1313, 1296, 1297 were published by Karl Michaelsson respectively in 1951, 1958, 1962.
2. SOUNDEX is more an algorithm than a real phonetic code. It had, therefore, to be adapted to patronymics processing as well in English as in French in order to be more conform to phonetic rules of each language. See Wrigley, E.A. 1973. *Identifying People in the Past*. Cambridge; Winchester, I. 1970. "The Linkage of Historical Records by Man and Computer: Techniques and Problems", in: *Journal of Interdisciplinary History*, I, 107-124; Charbonneau, H.; Lavoie, Y. & Légaré, J. 1972. "Etude des caractéristiques nominatives dans l'état civil et les recensements Canadiens du XVIIIe siècle", in: *Annales de Démographie Historique*, 269-295
3. Blayo, Yves. "Names variations in a village in Brie, 1750-1860", in: Wrigley, E.A. 1973. *Identifying People in the Past*. Cambridge, 57-63; Charbonneau and alias, article cité précédemment.

4. Bouchard, Gérard; Brard, Patrick & Lavoie, Yolande. 1981. "FONEM: 'un code de transcription phonétique pour la réconstitution autmatique des familles saguenayennes'", in: *Population*, 6, 1085-1104
5. Henri, Louis. 1976. "Projet de transcription phonétique des noms de famille", in: *Annales de démographie historique*, 201-204
6. Cf. Henri, Louis. 1976. Bouchard and alias, 1981
7. Straka, Georges. 1952. "La prononciation parisienne, ses divers aspects et ses traits généraux", in: *Bulletin de la faculté des Lettres de Strasbourg*, 1-45; Michaelsson, Karl. 1956. "Quelques variantes notées dans la prononciation Parisienne au temps de Philippe le Bel." *Actes du 8e Congrès d'études Romanes*. Florence, 287-297

THES GIUR:
AN EXPERIMENTAL THESAURUS OF LEGAL TERMS

Antonio Cammelli, Luigi Parenti
Istituto per la Documentazione Giuridica, Firenze
Italian National Research Council
Italy

1. The Purposes and Functions of a Legal Thesaurus

The "Istituto per la documentazione giuridica" (IDG) of the Italian National Research Council (CNR) started at the beginning of 1976 building a data bank of legal data which was subsequently stored and processed for data base management utilizing STAIRS/VS.

The purpose of our work is to construct a thesaurus as a research aid for this data bank.(1)

The building of a "thesaurus" (the structured organization of keywords) is seen as a natural step in the development of any documentation retrieval system.

By documentation we mean the whole field encompassing the acquisition and processing of documents so that certain individual items of data out of a mass of potential information give exact answers to specific queries. Ours cannot, however, be considered a classical "thesaurus", or, in other words, an instrument which has the dual task of indexing and retrieving documents during searches, but as a documentary base and an instrument permitting free full text searches of documents being already available. It is our aim to create a further research tool which will guarantee greater precision in information retrieval.

Thesauri have played a prominent role among the traditionally more effective tools for improving quality of the information retrieved, both, in relation to recall and precision.(2)

There have been many definitions of "thesaurus" and still others could be given, depending on the particular aspect of a thesaurus which is being underlined. One of the definitions which, in our opinion, most clearly expresses the intention (intentional aspect) of the concept is the following: an ordered set of signs (descriptors) which constitutes an open system designed to classify and organize concepts or terms according to subject matter, problems or some other criteria.

This definition has, perhaps, the advantage of unifying the two functions which co-exist in any genuine "thesaurus", namely the classification and organization of concepts.

As classification system it attempts to allocate an univocal and reciprocal concept to each descriptor. As an organizational system it attempts to identify relations between concepts through a relation between descriptors. This means that a "thesaurus" is made up of a set of descriptors and a set of relations between those descriptors.

2. A Thesaurus "on line"

Because of the flexibility of natural language, the meaning of a word varies according to the context in which it is used. In order to make an information retrieval system and to identify the inflexions of a word, different keys must be used for each inflexion. Consequently, when a key is searched during a session at the terminal, only the documents relating to the particular inflected form are retrieved from the data bank. This sometimes gives a reply which does not altogether satisfy the user's needs.

This is not so with data banks such as the one under consideration where the information made available to the user begins with the text of a document written in natural language without using different keys to denote the inflexions of words.

Nevertheless, experience shows that when a considerable quantity of data are involved, there are different terminologies used to express the same concept. It frequently results in a system which is incapable of giving the user comprehensive replies to his queries.

This is the reason why an information retrieval system needs backing up with an instrument such as a thesaurus which, as it is built up from relations between terms in the data bank, becomes a very useful aid to users of a documentation retrieval system, regardless whether it is an expert system, as it improves information search strategies.

The actual implementation of decisions taken concerning language analysis led to the utilization of the STAIRS/VS - Integrated Thesaurus and Linguistic System (TLS) which is an extension of the STAIRS/VS retrieval system.

Once the thesaurus has been implemented in TLS, the user can gain access to it by formulating pertinent queries and then by passing them to the STAIRS retrieval system.

In the TLS the term "thesaurus" does not refer to the vocabulary of the documents in the data bank that is, the set of all the words which occur at least once in the text of the documents, but it refers to a set of terms connected to each other by indicators where these connections are determinated by relations defined through the terms themselves. All thesauri have in common the fact that relations are defined by a number of descriptors, called thesaurus entries and that each descriptor can be related to one or more codescriptors. The relations are based mainly on semantic considerations depending on their particular usage.

Relations are defined by their names, identifiers and properties (symmetry, existence of opposites, transitivity, etc).

Subsequently, the relations between descriptors and codescriptors are written in a format acceptable to the generator programmes. Starting from this input and the table of definitions of the relations, these programs are able to generate automatically all the other relations which are the logical consequence of the ones which were actually entered.

3. Legal Thesaurus and Linguistic Problems

Our experiment was carried out in two phases: initially we used the mainframe of our institute. Afterwards, a specific program capable of functioning on a PC was constructed, by utilizing the entire linguistic structure which had already been processed,.

Lexical, semantic and syntactic relations were chosen and implemented. To these, we added the so-called Multiple Word (MW) which is written in the program and, therefore, automatically generated by the system.

The list of implemented relations is this:

name	Identifier
MULTIPLE WORD	MW
EQUIVALENTS	EQ
SYNONYMS	SN
RELATED TERMS	RT
HOMOGRAPHS	OM
NARROWER TERMS	NT
BROADER TERMS	BT

In particular, the definition "equivalent" (EQ) indicates those lemmata which have the same morphological roots and which, by the use made of them, can modify the syntax of a phrase but not the meaning. This lexical relation appeared to us to be useful not only in widening naturally the user's field of inquiry but, above all, because it could make material of an even richer linguistic quality available in the processing of legal language where placed in different semantic levels (e.g. "adozione" (adoption), "adottabilità" (adoptability)).

As far as semantic relations are concerned synonyms (SN), narrower terms or hyponyms (NT) which have inverse broader terms or hyperonyms (BT) were defined and implemented. In case of synonymy definition of a difficult linguistic concept, we confined ourselves to those relations indicated as synonymous by the "Dizionario macchina dell'Italiano" (DMI).(3)

It is also of fundamental importance for the structure of a "thesaurus" to define its semantic hierarchy which, in this case, we identified with BT and NT to signify respectively "Broader terms" and "Narrower terms". A satisfactory definition was in fact arrived at through a critical analysis of the DMI propositions. For example in reference to the term "contratto" (contract) there is

BT convenzione (agreement)
intesa (understanding)
impegno (undertaking)

NT abbonamento (subscription)
assicurazione (insurance)
concordato (deed of arrangement)

The related terms (RT) relation denotes those terms which are not linked either lexically or semantically, but are linked by ideological and conceptual connections. This involves a reasonable area where legal language is concerned (e.g. the lemmata "contratto" (contract) can be linked to the terms: "disdetta" (notice to quit), "socio" (partner), "liquidazione" (winding-up), società (company), "caparra" (deposit).

4. Implemented Relations

Relations we have defined along with their respective properties are given below:

- EQ (equivalents) having the following properties:
  * transitivity: if "a EQ b" and "b EQ c" then "a EQ c";
  * symmetry: if "a EQ b" then "b EQ a".
- SN (synonyms) having the following properties:
  * transitivity: if "a SN b" and "b SN c" then "a SN c";
  * symmetry: if "a SN b" then "b SN a".
- RT (related terms) having the following properties:
  * symmetry: if "a RT b" then "b RT a".
- OM (homographs) having the following properties:
  * symmetry: if "a OM b" then "b OM a".
- NT (narrower terms) having the following properties:
  * there is inversion: if "a NT b" then "b BT a".

Using this information we can compile the following table of definition:

1	2	3	4	5	6	7	8	9
MULTIPLE WORD	MW	010	N		N	*	N	0
EQUIVALENTS	EQ	030	Y		Y		N	0
SYNONYMS	SN	031	Y		Y		Y	0
RELATED TERMS	RT	032	Y		N		N	0
HOMOGRAPHS	OM	033	Y		N		N	0
NARROWER TERMS	NT	034	N	BT	N		N	0
BROADER TERMS	BT	035	N	NT	N		N	0

1 Relation description

2 Relator

3 Internal relation code

4 Symmetric relation? Y/N

5 Relator of converse relation

6 Transitivity Relation? Y/N

7 System Relation

8 Cycles Allowed? Y/N

9 Number definition schemes

In the second phase a specialized sector (the criminal aspects of taxation law) was identified within the Institute's data bank and we are testing a specific program capable of functioning on a PC. Our aim is to build a single thesaurus based on specialized data bases. The advantages include user friendliness and a great ease in management which can be translated into better results for the user.

NOTES

1. On this aspect see Cammelli, A. et alii. 1986. *Thes Giur, definition of an experimental legal thesaurus in TLS. Automated Analysis of legal Texts.* (A.A. Martino and F. Socci, editors), North Holland, Amsterdam, 361-384
2. On thesauri generally and on questions concerning the formulation of legal thesauri see Knapp, V. 1979. "Alcuni problemi relativi alla costruzione di un thesaurus giuridico." *Logica, Informatica, diritto* 5, 1, 175-195
3. *Dizionario Macchina Italiano* (DMI), edited by A. Zampolli and others. Istituto di Linguistica Computazione of the CNR, Pisa, Italy; see also Calzolari, N. et alii. 1983. "Documentazione sui tre nastri contenenti il DMI." *ILO-DMI* 2, Pisa

STATISTICAL MODELLING

Johannes Gordesch
Institute for Sociology
Freie Universität Berlin
FRG

Introduction

Classical statistics in the social sciences and humanities was looking for a significant relationship the nature of which was "hidden" in the test procedure (e. g. comparison of means), whereas in the natural sciences explicit mathematical modelling has been standard. During the last decade, however, various statistical modelling techniques in the social sciences and humanities have been disseminated and most of them heavily ground on modern computing techniques.
Let us start with the simple model:

> I set of texts; J set of key words;
> k(i,j) number of times key word j is found in text i.

Then, for fixed i and $j \in J$, k(i,j) characterizes text i. Various hypotheses concerning texts out of I (equality etc.) may be formed, e.g. by computing frequencies of key words in text i_1 as a linear combination of frequencies in text i_2.

Most empirical theories follow this guideline of operationalization of concepts by sets of indicators and of their interrelation by systems of (linear) equations.

Operationalization and Linear Models

An adequate generalization would identify concepts with vectors, indicators with coordinates and hypotheses with endomorphisms of linear vector spaces.
Let us recollect the definition of vector spaces:

A ***vector (linear) space*** E over the field F is a set of elements x, y, ... called vectors bearing the following algebraic structure:

1. E is an additive group, i.e. a mapping $E \rightarrow E \times E$ satisfying the axioms:

1.1 $(x+y)+z = x+(y+z)$ — associativity
1.2 $x+y = y+x$ — commutativity

$1.3\ x+0 = 0+x = 0$ zero element
$1.4\ x+(-x) = 0$ inverse element

2. There is a mapping $F \rightarrow E \times E$ satisfying the axioms:

$2.1\ (\alpha\beta)x = \alpha(\beta x)$ associativity
$2.2\ (\alpha+\beta)x = \alpha x+\beta x$ distributivity
$\alpha(x+y) = \alpha x+\alpha y$
$2.3\ 1.x = x$ unit element

Axioms 1.1 - 1.4 (addition and subtraction of vectors) guarantee aggregation of data, while axioms 2.1 - 2.3 provide for a change of scale (each element, however, transformed by the same factor). Each coordinate x_i corresponds to one indicator and the whole set of indicators is identified with the concept that the indicators operationalize.

Modelling

Once the operationalization of all the pertaining concepts has been achieved, the (linear or non-linear) model must be conceived and accomplished. At least the following six steps are required:

1 Collect: In a first step, all the relevant factors (variables) are listed. The variables x_1 ... x_n determine an n-dimensional vector space.

2 Select: Then related variables are grouped together, thus forming submodels. Mathematically spoken, the n-dimensional vector space is partitioned into subspaces x_1 ... x_{r1}; x_{r1+1} ... x_{r2}; ... Their intersection is not necessarily void.

3 Combine: Next, the within-structure of the submodels has to be elaborated. The submodels generated in step 2 are made up from single equations (the subspaces are generated by cutting hyperplanes).

4 Connect: Now the interrelation of the submodels (the between-structure of subspaces) is established, i. e. homomorphic mappings of pairs of subspaces, $S_i \rightarrow S_j$, are constructed.

5 Interpret: In a rather laborious step the formal model is "interpreted" by its connection to real world data. The hither unknown parameters of the mathematical model are estimated according to some appropriate statistical procedure. This presupposes the prior knowledge of the underlying structure, the type of measurement, etc.

In the past, various specialized techniques had been developed. One should mention among sundry others:

Path Analysis (Wright 1934)
Causal Models (Wold 1960)
Correspondence Analysis (Benzécri 1973)
Generalized Linear Models (McCullagh - Nelder 1983)
Graphical Chain Method (Lauritzen - Wermuth 1984)

6 ***Infer:*** Eventually, the formation and testing of hypotheses take place. The central problem is that of statistical inference, which means the generalization of findings from the sample to the population.

Nonlinear Models

Nevertheless, nature and society seem to be inherently nonlinear. Catchwords like catastrophe theory and chaos theory have attracted the public, while engineers and physicists prefer to speak of nonlinear dynamics, dissipative systems, or fractal geometry. The core of these theories is that small changes in the independent variables may cause large variations in the dependent variables and that the uniqueness of the solution of the functional equations can no longer be guaranteed.

The main steps of modelling remain the same as in the linear case. Despite the challenging features of these models, hardly any statistical method has been designed yet to cope with this new approach.

A very simple nonlinear model is given by the quadratic first order difference equation known as Verlhust's law (1845):

$$x_{t+1} = r.x_t.(1 - x_t),$$

x_t resp. x_{t+1} population at time t resp. $t+1$
(normalized to $0 \leq x_t \leq 1$),
r rate of growth.

The parameter r may be estimated by similar methods as in the linear case. Small changes in the rate of growth, however, may entail an entirely different behaviour in the limit (convergence to one point, to a finite set of points between which the solution oscillates, to a patternless chaos).

Catastrophe theory in the strict sense of René Thom is a qualitative theory of particular systems of differential equations:

$$d\mathbf{x}(t)/dt = - \text{grad } V(\mathbf{x}(t);\mathbf{u}(t);t),$$

t time, $\mathbf{x}$ state variables, $\mathbf{u}$ input variables,
V potential function.

$\partial V/\partial x_i = 0$ yield the stationary solutions (maxima, minima, saddlepoints) of the surfaces V = const. Minima lead to stable states. If, in addition, the Hessian determinant equals zero,

$$\det(\partial^2 V/\partial x_i \partial x_j) = 0,$$

then the system is not stable, since the trajectories are very sensitive to small variations δV. Thom had classified catastrophes up to diffeomorphisms for a number of control variables less than five (the seven elementary catastrophes). These models are rather restricted, for the f_i must satisfy the conditions

$$\partial f_i/\partial x_j = \partial f_j/\partial x_i.$$

Let us describe a system by a probability surface

$$P(\mathbf{x},t;\mathbf{u}).$$

A deformation of the surface corresponds to a variation of the system. P is obtained by solving functional equations and imposing the boundary and initial conditions. Then, under mild restrictions, a stochastic system possesses a unique asymptotic stationary distribution $P^0(\mathbf{x};\mathbf{u})$.
In the special but for practical purposes sufficiently general case:

$$f_i = - \partial V/\partial x_i,$$
$$\partial P(\mathbf{x};t;\mathbf{u})/\partial t = - \Sigma\partial(f_i P)/\partial x_i + \tfrac{1}{2}D\Sigma\partial^2 P/\partial x_i^2$$
(Fokker - Planck equation),

P^0 is given by:

$$P^0(\mathbf{x};\mathbf{u}) = N^{-1}\exp[(-2/D)V(\mathbf{x};\mathbf{u})],$$
V potential function of the deterministic model,
D, N constants.

Thus, the topology of the probability surface and of the potential function are identical (except sign, i.e. maxima and minima are interchanged). This result is of importance, for parameter estimation is often more robust in the case of distribution functions (when the type of the distribution is known) than in the case of nonlinear difference or differential equations.

Let us consider an example. The Pearsonian system consists of the functions $\Phi(x)$ which satisfy the differential equation

$$\frac{dy}{dx} = - \frac{(x - a)\, y}{c_0 + c_1 x + c_2 x^2} .$$

The solutions are found by immediate integration; thus,

$$\log y = - \int \frac{(x - a)}{c_0 + c_1 x + c_2 x^2} dx .$$

The shape of the curves $y = \Phi(x)$ (usually twelve types of Pearson curves are distinguished) depends on the discriminant of the quadratic in the denominator.

If, however, the type of the distribution is known, the parameters can be estimated easily, and qualitative as well as quantitative predictions made. Cf. the following example of a biquadratic potential function:

$$P^0(x_1,x_2;u) = A(x_2/x_1)\exp[a(x_1^2 + x_2^2) - b(x_1^2 + x_2^2)^2].$$

The maxima lie on a circle of radius $\sqrt{(a/b)}$.

Identifying "state variables" with "historical phenomena" and "control variables" with "causes of historical development", we obtain a rather flexible type of model for quantitative historical research. Formulating the model, solving the functional equations and estimating the parameters of a distribution function not being of standard type, requires much effort and skill. It promises, however, not only to reproduce the data but to reflect the genuine structure of the object under research.

Conclusion

Statistical methodology depends on its inner development, on the scientific disciplines it is applied to and on the development of society itself. Mathematical statistics still adheres to its old problems (mostly of estimation and testing), which become of less and less importance. The social sciences are leaving approaches like Lazarsfeld's paradigm of empirical social research, which never could really cope with time and evolution. Facing a world threatened with hunger, war, environmental destruction and endless social conflicts, social sciences reluctantly reach for that which the superior natural sciences seem to possess: a theory to manage life's inherent instability and uncertainty. Thus, a change from traditional empirical (linear) theories to nonlinear, thought to be more adequate to reality, is in the offing. This, however, is often done at the price of abandoning a really quantitative theory for a heuristic one.

REFERENCES

BENZECRI, J.-P. et collaborateurs. 1973. *L'Analyse des données*. Paris: Dunod

STEWART, J.B. and THOMPSON, J.M. 1986. *Nonlinear Dynamics and Chaos*. Chichester: Wiley

EBELING, W. und FEISTEL, R. 1982. *Physik der Selbstorganisation und Evolution*. Berlin (DDR): Akademie-Verlag

GORDESCH, J. 1972. *Multivariate Verfahren in den Sozial- und Wirtschaftswissenschaften*. Wien: Physica

HAKEN, H. 1981. *Synergetics. An Introduction. Nonequilibrium Phase Transitions in Physics, Chemistry and Biology*. 2nd expand. ed. Berlin: Springer

LAURITZEN, S.L. and WERMUTH, N. 1984. *Mixed Interaction Models*. Res. Rep. R-84-8. Institute of Electronic Systems. Aalborg University

LU, Y.C. 1976. *Singularity Theory and an Introduction to Catastrophe Theory*. New York: Springer

MCCULLAGH, P. and NELDER, J.A. 1983. *Generalized Linear Models*. London: Chapman and Hall

MANDELBROT, B. 1977. *The Fractal Geometry of Nature*. New York: Freeman

PRIGOGINE, I. 1985. *From Being to Becoming - Time and Complexity in Physical Sciences*. San Francisco: Freeman, 4th German edition, München: Piper

RAND, R.H. and ARMBRUSTER, D. 1987. *Perturbation Methods, Bifurcation Theory and Computer Algebra*. New York: Springer

THOM, R. 1972. *Stabilité Structurelle et Morphogénèse*. Reading, Mass.: Benjamin

WOLD, H. 1960. "A Generalization of Causal Chain Models." *Econometrica* 28, No. 2

WRIGHT, S. 1934. "The Method of Path Coefficients." *Ann. Math. Statist.* 5, 161-215

REAL TIME MODELLING

Norbert Müller, Bernd Thober
Systems Research Working Group, University of Osnabrück
FRG

PART I: Introduction

Problems Connected with the Description of Social Units

To understand the behavior of social systems requires an understanding of the behavior of large scale social units such as towns, countries and so on. Science-based understanding needs a descriptive fundament. Description should be model-controlled. Modelling of large scale social units, however, is confronted with three problem areas: large organized complexity, structural change and self-referentiality. Unfortunately, these problems generally interact leading to an extremely complicated research situation.

It is important to recognize that in social science all we want to describe are phenomena produced by social actors. Hence, we can regard data as outputs of data generators. A set of descriptive statements must identify the relevant inputs and especially the transformation mechanisms leading to these outputs. If a formalized model is used, then let this set of statements be labelled a "descriptive model".

It can be assumed to hold for all types of civilization that a large number of considered outputs are produced by organized output generators which we call decision centres (DCs); for details see (1). Thus, to a growing degree, complexity can be regarded as produced by DCs. This holds even more for structural change because of the change agent role of DCs. As a result, the principle can be derived that structure and functioning of large scale units can be expressed to a large and growing extent by the structure and functioning of the associated DCs. Let this be a first tentative self-referentiality concept of large scale social units; for an introduction see (5).

Therefore, in societies where DC systems are of great importance, and this maintains for all modern civilizations, complexity, rapid structural change and self-referentiality are mutually enforcing by virtue of the fact that all these properties are built-in properties of DC systems.

Structural Ruptures and K-Stationarity

To analyse the consequences of rapid structural change more precisely, I proposed the concept of K-stationarity.(1) In summarizing this problem of dynamic systems description, outputs Y (t) must be at least weak stationary, as for instance to ANDERSON.(2) Testing for this property, however, requires that the stochastic process Y(t) is unbroken within a time interval of a minimal length. Let this minimal length be labelled K, and the property of stochastic processes K-stationarity. K depends on varying circumstances, among others on qualifications set upon the autocorrelation function by the researcher.

As a consequence, the construction of dynamic descriptive models for any part of a large scale social unit must take into account that within those time intervals of length

K a structural rupture can occur. According to results of the mathematical theory of stochastic processes, as for instance to (2) and to practical experience, a certain number of unbroken time series data is necessary to perform the time series analysis required for dynamic model building. As a rule, a number of less than 10 time series data is in any event too small. Dependent on the time steps chosen, we can identify critical K, for instance, in the case of monthly data $K>1.5$ and so on, where K denotes years.

To provide evidence upon the question of K-stationarity probabilistic models and the results of empirical studies of social units have been compared:

For a realistic large scale social unit model the probability of observing at least one structural rupture per year is greater than 50% so that one structural rupture is expected nearly each year; for details see (1).

Real Time Modelling

We can summarize as follows: Rapid structural change is not the exception as it may be in most natural sciences but it is the rule in social sciences. Therefore, it seems to be appropriate to develop instruments able to cope with this characteristic of social units explicitly. Structural ruptures can be of two types, change of parameter functions and change in the state space. In the case of model systems a structural rupture can result in a total submodel having to be rewritten.

One obvious approach could be to develop a technology enabling the researcher to arrive at new or rewritten models quicker than the next structural rupture occurs. Analogous to the problem of real time computing let this be called the problem of real time modelling.

Rapid Modelling

What is needed, therefore, is a technology of RAPID MODELLING. "Rapid" means - according to the analytical and empirical results mentioned above - that the new or rewritten (sub)model should be finished in a time interval significantly shorter than one year. Referring to the engineering half-period rule of thumb, the technology of rapid modelling should be designed such that new or rewritten models are finished within a time period of less than half a year.

Some details of such a technology are procured in the second part of this paper by THOBER. Let me only sketch some prominent properties briefly. Two properties are widely accepted: hierarchical design and modularization of frequently used model parts. However, these characteristics are mainly regarded from a technical point of view overlooking that hierarchization and modularization must also be appropriate with respect to real structures of social units under consideration.

This lack of substantial orientation applies even more for two further aspects of rapid modelling, so far mostly neglected:

* Rapid modelling needs rapid model oriented communication within the research field, mainly with DC personnel.
* Model support interfaces must be communicable to DC personnel.

Both aspects require a high degree of acceptance by DC personnel. A necessary condition for this is that the structure and results of models can be made plausible to these persons, that is that structure and results fit in with their experiences. Thus, models of a special type are required which we labelled REAL STRUCTURE MODELS (RS-models), as in (1), (3); for some preliminary studies regarding real structure decision support interfaces, see (4).

Rapid Prototyping and Updating

Modules of an RS-module base system can serve as prototypes of the corresponding subsystems or DCs. Such proto-modules can help rapid modelling. Concerning the sophistication of a module, we distinguish three levels:
VERSION (1.01) - (1.99): The module produces logically consistent outputs (e.g. no negative number of population),
VERSION (2.01) - (2.99): the module produces outputs falling into plausible ranges,
VERSION (3.01) - (3.99): the module is validated under real conditions of confrontation with data or application.

Experiences from a rapid modelling attempt(6) in the field of water management coping with nitrate in drinking water brought the evidence that a module must be lifted to a version of (3.xx) to be valid and efficient for practical purposes. As soon as having reached a (3.01) version, updating the module to the final version is generally rapidly performed, as is expected from RS-modelling principles. Thus, what we need is a technology for rapid prototyping (versions 1 and 2) and of rapid updating (version 3).

Rapid prototyping of an existing model of version 2.02 to a version 3.01 and rapid updating to the final version 3.06 took .35 man-years, which is markedly below the rapid modelling period of half a year mentioned above. The time necessary can presumably be significantly reduced by making use of graphically supported instruments for rapid modelling on work stations. These were not used in the outlined example.

Nevertheless, there is a multiplicity of deep problems connected with rapid modelling some of which are broached in (1). They stem mainly from the fact that real time modelling has to be "implemented" in the research field. In difficult cases such a research field is characterized by DC-overcrowding, strategic interactions, structural rupture surprises, collapses of hierarchies and so on. It must be left to the future whether real time modelling can be implemented also in such research fields.

The water management example, however, was chosen as an extremely simple one, where the research object was only affected by rapid structural change. In this simple example, real time modelling based on real-structure modelling was efficient.

Computer-Human Expert Interaction in Real Time Modelling

A further result of our modelling experiences in the field is of high importance: it would be seriously misleading to attempt at the replacement of the human expert by software systems. On the contrary, software systems must be designed such that the human experts' facilities are optimally used. This holds in particular with regard to real time modelling in the social sciences which depends heavily on bringing in the human expert as was pointed out above.

Therefore, what we need are optimal support instruments for computer-expert interaction. This requires some kind of an operation pre-analysis of the field under consideration. Also for this pre-analysis Real Structure Modelling can help.

Owing to our experiences, it would be more promising to speed up prototyping and updating of models than to focus on "expert systems" in the field of social-scientific modelling. Such a speeding up can be realized with available technologies and possibly leads to a significant reduction of time schedules in this modelling field, whereas "expert systems" would have only a neglectable additional effect.

PART 2: Environments for Real Time Modelling

In this part some hard- and software aspects shall be discussed from the point of view of model builders. Our ideas are the result of some years of experience in the field of socio-economic and ecological modelling.

Trends in Hardware and Software Developments

In the past, large scale modelling and the use of model and method bases were oriented towards the properties of mainframes. At present powerful workstations and micros are available enabling new modelling technologies running with graphical support and, probably, with distributed model application in the near future.

Real Structure Model Systems

Faced with the idea to develop an environment for real time modelling we have selected some important aspects. We will not restrict ourselves to socio-economic models alone but also consider interdisciplinary model systems. Natural science models are considered to be based upon well accepted and established theories. Socio-economic models are either so called MASS PHENOMENA models (MPM) or DECISION CENTRE models (DCM). We will concentrate on the last model type.

Expert Systems and Human Knowledge

Due to the problem areas mentioned above by MUELLER, i.e. large organized complexity, structural change, and self-referentiality, human knowledge is indispensable in the modelling process. Expert systems cannot reach the power of human knowledge. Neither the model builder nor the human decider in a DC can be replaced by an expert system. Therefore, useful software tools should be created in order to support the human contribution in modelling, especially, to arrive at modelling, validation or application results in time.

Software Requirements and Proposed Software Tools

To define the necessary features of an RTM approach we will discuss the topics model design and production, user interfaces and field monitoring.

Model Design and Production

We will confine ourselves to that model type which has the shortest life cycle, i.e. the DC model. Model design and production of a DC model consists of five steps:
1. Gather information from field experts (FEs)
2. Develop a model concept based upon (1)
3. Coding (Translation of the model concept into statements of a Simulation language)
4. Running the prototype model
5. Inspection of model results

The first three steps can contain errors like inappropriate investigation of reality, inappropriate conception, or incorrect coding (Syntax errors). Errors in Step 3, which can urge the model builder to spent a significant amount of modelling time, will inhibit the following steps and have to be corrected as quick as possible. Having corrected the syntax errors inappropriate model components must be identified after the completion of step 5. Also this can afford a significant amount of time.

Software tools are necessary in order to create a syntax error free code, to generate graphical model representation, to support the composition of model parts and to assist model application (run time support).

Model coding and representation tools will help to create a model coded in a simulation language. An advanced tool pack should have the capability of autocoding, i.e. quick generation of an errorfree model code. Syntax may be controlled by simulation language intelligent editors, a feature which is well known in the field of compilers. Graphical representation of model structure and functional relationships provides a visual component useful to understand a model's logic. For certain simulation languages, defined symbols allow the construction of flow charts representing nearly the whole model code. A simulation system should allow to code the model either by graphic or alphanumeric input and automatically generate the other form of representation.

Support of model composition is a helpful tool since models under consideration often contain substructures (standard structures) already defined in other models or predefined as prototypes. Therefore a modelling system should have the capability to generate, to import and to export such building blocs. In the case of RSM we distinguish a structural kernel of hard relationships between variables from the soft relationships. It would be helpful to conserve the hard kernel as a prototype. Thus, modelling can concentrate on the solution of the specification of the soft relationships.

Run time support for models is needed to detect logical errors and to explain invalid results. This can be done by the aid of range control for variable values and backtracing. In order to detect why variable values violate defined ranges a debugger with backtracing features would help to detect model errors. A more advanced tool should enable the user to observe the computing process supported by windows containing the respective parts of the model in desired representation forms (graphic or equation based).

All the tools defined above should be integrated into an overall system handler based upon window technique, enabling the user to inspect results, detect misleading results and immediately update models.

User Interfaces

Since model application is one way to detect inappropriate model parts the design of user interfaces plays an important role with respect to rapid modelling. An advanced user interface has to assist the user supporting input, output and explanation of the model. From a technical point of view, input and output support are standard properties of well designed simulation languages. In the case of DC models these properties have to be complemented with DC-specific contents in order to arrive at a high correspondence of the real decision environment and the simulation environment. A user interface containing only input and output windows leaves the model in the state of a black box. It is desirable to assist users to understand the model structure and therefore an advanced user interface should contain routines to explain model structures. Especially in the case of DC models this feature can help to detect logical errors and activate the knowledge of the field expert for update purposes. Two problems shall be mentioned here:

* Different user types may require different types of interfaces.
* Semantic problems may arise which are far from being solved at present.

Field Monitoring

Field monitoring is an important task in the application phase of a model or model system. It must be used to detect structural ruptures as early as possible and, therefore, signals the necessity for model update and refinement. Local application of a model or a submodel and central supervising require a decentralized equipment for information gathering, processing and analysis.

Abbreviations:

RTM: Real Time Modelling
RSM: Real Structure Modelling
DC: Decision Centre

NOTES

1. MÜLLER, N.; SCHÖN, K.-P. and THOBER, B. 1987. *Real-Structure Modelling - A Simulation Based Methodology for the Description of Large Scale Social Units.* Köln, TÜV Rheinland
2. ANDERSON, T.W. 1971. *The Statistical Analysis of Time series.* New York: Wiley
3. MÜLLER, N. 1985. "Real Structure Modelling: A Methodology for the Description of Large-scale Social Units." *Social Science Information* 24, No. 3
4. MÜLLER, N. and THOBER, B. 1985. *Real Structure Decision Support Interfaces for Ecological Problems.* Unpublished paper delivered at the status seminar on decision support systems for ecological policy making. IIASA: Laxenburg, Austria
5. WILLKE, H. 1983. *Entzauberung des Staates - Überlegungen zu einer sozietalen Steuerungstheorie.* Königstein: Athenäum
6. MÜLLER, N. n.d. *Valid Modelling of Institutions Challenged by Rapid Environmental Change* - The case of a waterworks coping with nitrate in drinking water, to appear Env. & Planning A

COMPUTER SIMULATIONS IN THE SOCIAL SCIENCES

Heinrich Siegmann
Max-Planck-Society, Starnberg
FRG

Computer simulation has become an established field in computer science and its technical applications. This is not (yet) so in the social sciences but progress has been great in specific areas. This paper does not attempt to provide a comprehensive overview but summarizes examples of social-science-related computer simulation modelling with efforts which the author has worked or been exposed to in the past. They are

1. Global or world modelling (an overview)
2. A specific global model: GLOBUS
3. "Politics among Hexagons"
4. A model of the French revolution
5. Simulating conventional defense options

1. Global or World Modelling: An Overview

Since the late 1960s, various so-called global or world (simulation) models have been developed as interdisciplinary efforts (often with a strong social science component) around the globe. The author has summarized 27 such modelling efforts (model assumptions, structure, findings, impact, implementation, usage, etc.) in a report to UNESCO (Siegmann 1987a) that forms a convenient base for an overview of the state of the art of global modelling.

In the words of notable global modellers, "global modelling is just computer modelling done to investigate social questions or problems of global scale" (Meadows et al. 1982). A global problem tends to be long- term, persistent, pervasive, affecting many people, the "ownership" of the problem is difficult to establish, the characteristics of the "solution" are unknown, and the proposed solutions require new styles of cooperation. The main purpose of global modelling is not prediction but better understanding and more informed decision-making of complex interrelationships as a result of rigorous analysis and assumptions stated explicitly. In addition, modelling efforts (such as "The Limits to Growth" (Meadows et al. 1972)) have increased public awareness and served as educational tools.

Global modelling as an emerging scientific field can look back to three distinct origins: the modelling of East-West military antagonism (Guetzkow), System Dynamics (Forrester) and Econometric Modelling. Today, global and regional models encompassing often thousands of economic, political and social variables and equations exist on all continents and are themselves closely intertwined in terms of sponsorship, initiators, modellers, shared data banks and approaches. After almost twenty years, global models have tended to be of shorter time horizon, are geographically more disaggregated, focus on more specific concerns, include increasingly political variables and international econometric modelling and are designed for easy and interactive use. In many instances, PC-versions exist and, thus, allow for fast dissemination and usage for educational purposes.

2. A Specific Global Model: GLOBUS

One of the most advanced global models is GLOBUS (Generating Longterm Options By Using Simulation) developed at the Science Center Berlin (Bremer 1987). Unlike most other such models, political variables play a major role in it and individual nations are the units of analysis. Moreover, a well documented micro-version for personal computers is available (Bremer, Gruhn 1988).

The GLOBUS world is made up by 25 states (7 from the West, 4 from the East, 9 from the South and 5 from OPEC). These countries represent 74% of world population, 80% of world production, 85% of world military expenditures, 68% of world inter-national hostility involvement, 57% of world political protest and 67% of world exports. The rest of the world is treated as a 26th actor. Each national model has five sectors (government, domestic economic, domestic political, foreign economic and foreign political) that interact among one another with the government sector being the centerpiece. The 25 national models are linked to each other by two transmission mechanisms for dyadic flows of hostility and cooperation, and of trade and foreign aid. Foreign policy flows result from national predispositions toward other nations in response to internal and external developments. Governments continuously monitor their international political environments and tend to counteract perceived threats by adjusting their military capabilities. Dyadic economic flows are modeled for six commodity groupings (services, raw materials, primary energy, agricultural products, manufactures, and armaments) and bilateral foreign aid.

In a sense, GLOBUS can be considered a laboratory for examining possible global behavior under a wide range of assumptions and scenarios. I will refrain from reporting any specific "results" here but rather list a few questions that have been investigated:

* What are the possible national and international long-term consequences of alternative Western defense postures?
* Who is likely to gain and who is likely to lose from imposition of protectionist measures by nations of the West?
* What are the socioeconomic implications of alternative assumptions about long-term population growth?
* Under what conditions can foreign aid accelerate development in the Third World?
* Can a combination of arms reduction measures in the North and increased aid flows to the South reduce both East-West tension and the North-South gap?

GLOBUS is written in Fortran 77 and was implemented on a CDC Cyber 170, a Cray-MP and, as "Micro-GLOBUS", as a PC version. It consists of more than 10,000 lines of code and comprises 40,000 parameters and variables. It relies on data compiled in the World Handbook of Social Indicators and on UN, IMF and World Bank data collections. For the Micro GLOBUS version, a source code is even made available in order to being utilizable as a global laboratory.

3. "Politics among Hexagons"

Another type of simulation of the international system was conducted by Bremer and Mihalka (1977). They simulated the development of a hypothetical 98-nation state system under certain decision-rules for conflictual and alliance behavior. This model was amended in interesting ways by Cusack and Zimmer (1986).

The model assumes a hypothetical multistate system in which each of the 98 states has the shape of a hexagon. Thus, most states have six contiguous neighbors. Each state has an initial amount of military power and territory and some (but not certain) knowledge of the other states' power. State behavior is governed by a set of decision rules vis-à-vis the inter-state system resulting in attempts for territorial conquests and alliance formation.

The basic question the model is designed to address is: How and under what conditions do multistate systems achieve stability or are transformed into empires?

Proceeding from an initial system of equally powerful states, the simulation moves through usually several hundred iterations until a stable pattern of states emerges. In each iteration, a state with hostile intentions toward a neighbouring target state is selected (initially at random, later as a function of power) and a fairly complex set of decision rules is invoked. Depending on the outcome of estimations of the other side's power, the initiator and/or the target may, or may not, seek to assemble offensive and defensive coalitions. The accuracy of power estimation is an important parameter. Third, party states may, or may not, choose to join coalitions. After elaborate coalition formation procedures, the initiator will decide to go to war or refrain from taking action. The outcome of war is stochastically dependent upon the relative actual (not estimated) capabilities of the initiator (and its allies if there are any) and the targets (and its possible allies). The winning party will gain territory at the cost of the losing side but both sides will suffer a loss of power (per unit of territory) reflecting war costs. Then the next iteration begins.

The overall result of the simulation exercise is a clear movement towards empires. Three distinct phases have been observed: following a phase of political unification in which the number of states drastically declines the system enters into a second balance of power phase that is usually succeeded by the final phase of imperial consolidation. For some time, self-organizing processes seem to prevail maintaining stability without any actor actively pursuing it. Stability tends to be enhanced when power estimation is more uncertain.

4. Simulating the French Revolution

A simulation model of historical events deals with the French revolution (Siegmann 1987b). This heuristic simulation model was designed as a vehicle for exploring methodology in the area of social structure formation.

The computer simulation model has a system-dynamics-type set of interconnected state variables at its core and a political control mechanism put in use under certain conditions. The state variables are political ("religious freedom", "protection of property", "degree of feudalism", "electoral system", "institutional transparency", "democratic rights") and economic ("basic needs satisfaction", "economic infrastructure", "price stability", "state finances", "taxes"). This heuristic model is capable of producing in the aggregate "meaningful", i.e., non counter-intuitive, results. Under certain parameter constellations, the system of state variables produced ten years of fictitious French revolution which, without any claim of model validity, very roughly corresponded to the historical pattern. While looking at individual variable curves was rather meaningless, the aggregate behavior was quite erratic in the first revolutionary years, indicating a turning point after about five years (corresponding to the end of the Jacobin terror) and stabilization after about 6-7 years. This pattern held for a limited set of parameter constellations and model (version) configurations. Under different assumptions, the variables behaved rather arbitrarily without any resemblance to reality.

Structure formation is contained in this model in an explicit and in an implicit way. Explicitly, new structure is formed if a variable indicates system overload and a new variable is created and interconnected with the others. Implicitly, structure formation, presumably occurs if the change of the system state (viewed as the combined behavior of the state variables) follows a discernible course distinct from strictly random behavior or from no change at all. The patterns observed, we believe, show structure formation and change according to the implicit definition. Achieving great historical accuracy was *not* the purpose of this modelling exercise. Had that been the case, the model would have required empirically grounded time series analysis, parameter estimation and historically valid decision rules. Historians are invited to engage in computer simulation to pursue this line of research further.

5. Simulating Conventional Defense Options

Rounding up our simulation tour d'horizon brings us to defense policy (which, at least in the anglo-saxon tradition, is subsumed under the social science header). A highly aggregated model examining the effects of different force structures in Central Europe on stability was constructed by the author (Siegmann 1987c).

Modelling of this kind presupposes that ultimately military capabilities rather than intentions should underlie military force planning and arms control. The question has been posed whether the force structures that have evolved over the past decades on both sides of the Central European front are militarily effective, cost effective, conducive to conventional arms control and enhance stability even under crisis conditions. Clearly, trade-offs among these criteria must be assumed to exist. In recent years, in NATO and Warsaw Treaty countries proposals have mushroomed advocating a decoupling of offensive and defensive capabilities. These proposals claim that a defensive restructuring of military forces would be superior to current structures in terms of most (if not all) of the above criteria.

I built a simulation model of ground forces in Central Europe that in a first version allows to distinguish among various force dispositions in terms of their offensive and defensive characteristics. Other parameters are the mobilities of offensive-prone and defensive-prone forces, the delay with which the defender reacts to enemy force movements, the effectiveness of barriers and other obstacles the defender may use, hold factors (the ratio defending/attacking forces sufficient for successful defense) and break factors (the ratio attacking/defending forces assuring break-throughs).

Three basic scenarios were used: (1) force dispositions in which both sides have more offense-capable than defense-capable forces (mutual offensive preponderance), (2) a mixed case in which one side is basically offensive-oriented and the other side defensive-oriented (unilateral defensive preponderance) and (3) the case of mutual defensive preponderance. Under these scenarios, various runs have been made altering total force strengths, assault widths, assault locations, mobility, hold and break factors.

The following conclusions have emerged: Under the mutual offensive preponderance scenario, most parameter constellations allow for successful attack. The more concentrated the attack, the better is the chance of success to the attacker. The defense is successful for very limited attacks (since defense forces present suffice) or very large attacks (since the defender has time for taking countermeasures). In case of unilateral defensive preponderance, only for about half of the runs the attack will succeed. But carefully selected attack options of small width and not too high concentrations still would look promising to the attacker. For higher force concentrations, the barrier will cause substantial losses. In case of mutual defensive preponderance, the defense mostly prevails. Massive attacks are not possible because offensive forces are insufficient for standard hold and break factors. Only surgical narrow-scope, limited attacks promise success.

REFERENCES

BREMER, S.A. and MIHALKA, M. 1977. "Machiavelli in Machina: Or Politics among Hexagons", in: Deutsch et al. (eds.). *Problems of World Modeling*. Cambridge

BREMER, S.A. (ed.). 1987. *The GLOBUS Model - Computer Simulation of Worldwide Political and Economic Developments*. Frankfurt:Boulder, Westview:Campus

BREHMER S.A. and GRUHN, W. 1988. *Micro GLOBUS*. Berlin: Edition Sigma

CUSACK, T. and ZIMMER, U. 1986. *The Bases of Multistate System Endurance*. Mimeo, Wissenschaftszentrum Berlin

MEADOWS, D. et al. 1982. *Limits to Growth*. New York: Universe Books, A Potomac Associates Book

MEADOWS, D.; RICHARDSON, J. and BRUCKMANN, G. 1982. *Groping in the Dark. The first decade of global modeling*. London: Wiley

SIEGMANN, H. 1987a. *Recent Developments in World Modeling*. UNESCO, BEP/GPI/2, Paris

SIEGMANN, H. 1987b. *Modeling Structural Change in Social Systems: The French Revolution*. Mimeo, Program on Stability-Oriented Security and Defense Policy, Max Planck Gesellschaft, Starnberg

SIEGMANN, H. 1987c. *A Simulation of Defensivity in Central Europe*. Paper prepared for the Sixth Workshop of the Pugwash Study Group on Conventional Forces in Europe, Bari, Italy, October 1-4

AUTOMATIC LEMMATIZATION OF LATIN TEXTS

Andrea Bozzi, Giuseppe Capelli
Istituto di Linguistica Computazionale, CNR, Pisa
Italy

1. Preface

The project for the creation of a Latin Lexical Database (RELAL)(1) was started in 1981. The first draft of the project was presented during the International Workshop on "The Possibilities and Limits of the Computer in producing and publishing Dictionaries" (Pisa, May 1981) and later extended so as to form the Latin Informative System (SIL), which now includes the following:

a. a *text archive* organized in the form of a database;
b. a series of computational modules for the linguistic analysis of the forms (*morphological analyzer*);
c. a *lemmatization module*;
d. a *comparison module* for already lemmatized, non-homogeneous texts, in view of the creation of a single uniform archive;
e. a an *editing module* for the entries of a "Thesaurus Mediae et Recentioris Latinitatis".(2)

This paper describes modules b) and c) which form the main part of the machine dictionary.(3) The modules were first written in PL/1 running on the mainframe of CNUCE (Centro Nazionale Universitario di Calcolo Elettronico).

A second version was implemented in collaboration with Manfred Thaller of the Max Planck Institut für Geschichte in Göttingen.(4) It is written in the 'C' language which operates, among other operating systems, under MS-DOS on a personal computer.

2. Morphological Analyzer

The analysis of the Latin forms is performed by a morphological analyzer which uses the following: a basic dictionary (LES); a table of suffixes (SM); a table of endings (SF); a table of postfixes (SPF).

a. The basic dictionary (LES) is formed by approximately 57,000 entries providing three types of information:
   * An *identification number*. This number is not used univocally to label each entry but it refers to all those basic segments which, although related to different headwords, have at least one in common. For example the bases FAC FEC FACT have the same number because, although related to FACIO, FECI, FACTUS respectively, they have the headword FACIO in common.
   * A code of *graphical alteration*. The bases which are likely to undergo graphical changes appear with an alteration code. The system is thus able to verify which type of transcription must be performed so that the analyzed form can be related to the base recorded in the LES.

This makes it possible to reduce the number of entries to be included in the LES dictionary. As all the possible variations of the Latin prefixes (SI) are divided into several groups, the number of false homographs have been reduced. This method has proved particularly suitable to relate automatically to the same entry all the Latin words which appear in both assimilated and dissimilated form. The same criterion is used to automatically check the spelling with "H" at the beginning or in the middle of a word: in this respect, a transcription code "H" informs the analyzer that the base can also appear with an aspiration.

* A *compatibility* code. This value is used by the segmentation system to check the compatibility between the different parts of a word which has been broken up into segments. Segmentation can be considered correct when the separated elements are compatible. It must be noted that the compatibility code (which may be considered as the grammatical code of the base provided with the most information) and the code of the headword developed by that base are not the same. This difference is based on the distinction between the segmentation module (the data and codes of which are organized so that the algorithm of morphological analysis can work at its best) and the lemmatization module the data of which (the headwords produced by the relative grammatical codes) are linguistically consistent.

  As an example, if the base FOEDER is classified as N3N1, the headword it produces will be FOEDUS N3: the first code has an operational value while N3 is the grammatical code classifying all those words grouped in the third nominal declension. See the compatibility codes used for the bases in Table 1.

b. The system also uses a second group of data formed by suffixes (SM): these are always provided with two indications necessary to check compatibility with both the preceding and the following elements.

   A suffix can be considered as such only under the two following conditions:

   * when there is equivalence between its own compatibility code and the one which identifies the base or any other suffix placed on its left-hand side;
   * when there is equivalence between its second compatibility code and the one which identifies the ending or any other suffix on its right-hand side.

   The balancing between compatibility codes has offered two advantages: on the one hand it has been possible to avoid including the form with a suffix as a new entry in the basic dictionary (saving time and money); on the other hand it has been possible to optimize more easily the segmentation procedures which run with almost 100% success.

c. The third group of data includes the flectional endings (SF), each identified by the code which enables the system to check compatibility with their preceding left-hand side elements (base or suffix).

d. We are now organizing a fourth group of data including postfixes, i.e. the enclitics and those elements which are generally used for the creation of some pronouns, both placed after the endings.

   With regard to the first kind, let us consider, for example, -QUE, -NE, -VE and, for the second kind, cases like -NAM, -LIBET, -LUBET, -LIBEAT, -LUBEAT, -VIS, -CUMQUE.

Segmentation is performed by checking compatibility between contiguous elements until the base which forms the dictionary entry is found.

The system makes it possible to perform all the segmentations which are compatible with rules concerning isolated segments.

Example: Segmentation and compatibility check in PULCHERRIMOS, AMANTIORES, DELEVISTI, AUDISTI

LES		left	SM	right	left	SM	right	left	SF
PULCHER	N6	N6	RIM	N6				N6	OS
AM	V1	V1	ANT	N7	N7	IOR	N3	N3	ES
DEL	V2	V2	EV	V7				V7	ISTI
AUD	V4	V4	I	V7				V7	STI

The system fails to recognize LES only when encountering a new word: in this case the morphological analysis is still performed so that it is possible to print out all the segmentations obtained. The user must then choose the correct segmentation(s) among those proposed by the computer. This process is also useful to update the dictionary.

The base is a conventional entity, containing the necessary information for a constant control of the reliability of the segmentations performed and also for lemmatization.

3. Lemmatization Module

The lemmatization system has been structured according to the following fundamental rule: let us consider as headwords only those forms which have their own morphological unity with no distinction between the function of nouns as adjectives or as substantives; the verbal nouns are separated from the verbs. The lexical entities created by the lemmatization module are thus divided into N(ominal), V(erbal) and I(nvariable) forms.

In accordance with this principle our lemmatization rules produce the nominative singular for the nouns and the first person of the present indicative for the verbs.

The lemmatization rules use the following data: grammatical codes or information given for the base; reference codes (V).

a. Grammatical codes. When the segmentation process has isolated the base and all the compatibility tests have given positive results, the system activates the lemmatization module. It identifies the grammatical code which, as already said, can be different from the compatibility code of the base. The grammatical code, recorded in a specific field of the basic dictionary, represents the rule for the production of the headword. The system can also produce the headword by:
   * only using the information represented by the *grammatical code of LES*. E.g. AM V1 is sufficient to develop AMO V1 automatically.
   * verifying if the isolated LES has some peculiarity which makes it necessary to use *particular rules* for lemmatization. This generally happens when the headword is different from LES or has a different ending than the one envisaged by its grammatical code. E.g. the N3 and N7 bases ending in -C, -G, -ON, -IN, -D, -T, -IUS, -IOR, -NS automatically produce headwords ending in -X, -X, -O, -O, -S, -S, -IOR, -IS, -IS respectively.
   * checking if the isolated LES is followed by *particular information* for lemmatization. This occurs when our headword is quite different from the one

generally written in the dictionaries. E.g. ABBA/ABBAS is our headword for ABBA and ABBAS or ABOMINO/-OR for ABOMINO and ABOMINOR.
The grammatical codes used by the lemmatization module, namely the codes which accompany the headwords produced by the system, appear in Table 2.

b. The lemmatization module also operates according to the reference code (V) when one or more reference headwords must be placed next to the headword created for a given form. This indication has been used in the following cases:
* different bases in the verbal paradigm: for example, in addition to the headword FECI VP, the form FECITI is also provided with the headword FACIO V5, because of the reference code (V) indicated in the LES dictionary;
* allographs unsuitable for control according to the graphical variation codes: for example, the form RACANAS is lemmatized as RACANA N1. The 'headword-added' code produces a second headword RACA N1.

Therefore, the lemmatization module operates according to a double scheme: from the wordform to the headword (the system generally used by the automatic and/or semiautomatic lemmatization tools) and from the wordform to the **lemmatic constellation**. The morphological criterion on which the segmentation algorithm is based and which consists in grouping several basic forms under the same reference number, also produces several important effects in the lemmatization process.
The numerical indication, in fact, obliges the system to construct for the bases isolated by the morphological analyzer, a constellation of as many headwords as the bases identified by the same reference number. The headwords thus produced are organized in hierarchical form. In order to provide the utmost flexibility of analysis, the hierarchy in which the headwords of the constellation are organized is not fixed. Responding to the instructions provided by the menu, the reader can always shift the level beginning from which some elements of the lemmatic constellation are considered as reference headwords.(5)
According to this principle, a lemmatic constellation produced for a form of the past participle, which at present hierarchically includes first the past principle (nom. sing.) and secondly its verb (1st pers. sing. ind.) can be changed. It will in fact be possible to invert this standard hierarchy or to suppress one or more elements. This change will thus produce a different visualization on the screen or on the printout of the results of the lemmatization module.

Table 1: Compatibility Codes

a) Verbal Bases

	1st conj.	2nd conj.	3rd conj.	4th conj.	E/I conj.	anomalous	perfect
active, passive	V1	V2	V3	V4	V5	V6	V7
active only	V1S	V2S	V3S	V4S	V5S	V6S	
Deponent	V1D	V2D	V3D	V4D	V5D	V6D	
Intransitive	V1I	V2I	V3I	V4I	V5I	V6I	
Impersonal	V1E	V2E	V3E	V4E	V5E	V6E	V7E
Syncopated							V8

b) Nominal Bases

N1	1st decl. nouns
N1	1st anomalous inflection
N2	2nd decl. masc. and fem. nouns
N2N	2nd decl. neuter nouns
N2E	2nd anamalous inflection
N21	gerunds
N3	3rd decl. masc. and fem. nouns (gen.pl. -UM/-IUM)
N31	3rd decl. masc. and fem. nouns (gen.pl. -UM only)
N32	3rd decl. masc. and fem. nouns (gen.pl. -IUM only)
N3N	3rd decl. neuter nouns (gen.pl. -UM/-IUM)
N3N1	3rd decl. neuter nouns (gen.pl. -UM only)
N3N2	3rd decl. neuter nouns (gen.pl. -IUM only)
N3E	3rd anomalous inflection
N4	4th decl. nouns
N41	supines
N5	5th decl. nouns
N6	1st and 2nd declension adject., numeral adject., superlatives, perfect and future participles, gerundives
N6P	pronominal adject.
N7	3rd decl. adject., present participles
N7C	comparatives

Table 2: Grammatical Codes for Headwords

ENC	=	enclitic
I	=	invariable
N	=	indeclinable noun
N1	=	1 decl.
N2	=	2 decl.
N2/1	=	1st and 2nd decl. adjectives, superlatives, numerical and pronominal adjectives, perfect and future participles, gerundives.
N2G	=	gerund.
N3	=	3 decl. (substantives and adjectives), comparatives and present participles.
N4	=	4 decl.
N4S	=	supine
N5	=	5 decl.
P	=	pronoun
SEP	=	separable syntagma
V1	=	1st conj.
V2	=	2nd conj.
V3	=	3rd conj.
V4	=	4th conj.
V5	=	-io conj.
VA	=	anomalous verb
VP	=	"perfectum" all conj.

NOTES

1. The Italian acronyms are used for uniformity with the indications given in the software.
2. See GREGORY, T. 1979. "Pour un Thesaurus Mediae et Recentioris Latinitatis", in: *Ordo. II Colloquio Internazionale del Lessico Intellettuale Europeo. Atti a cura di Fattori M. e Bianchi M.* Roma, 733
3. For the description of points d) and e) see BOZZI, A. and CAPPELLI, G. 1987. "The Latin Lexical Database and Problems of Standardization in the Analysis of Latin Texts", in: *Datennetze für die Historischen Wissenschaften?* Graz, 28-45 and BOZZI, A. and EMMANUELE, S. 1983. "Thesaurus Mediae et Recentioris Latinitatis. Sistema per la redazione semiautomatica delle voci", in: *Spiritus. IV Colloquio Internazionale del Lessico Intellettuale Europeo. Atti a cura di Fattori M. e Bianchi M.* Roma, 567-577
4. This collaboration consists in a bilateral agreement of scientific cooperation for the exchange of data and software between the Istituto di Linguistica Computazionale - CNR, Pisa (ILC) and the Max-Planck-Institut für Geschichte in Göttingen.
5. This option will be implemented in the version which should be ready by December 1988.

RELATIVE INDEXING OF DOCUMENTS IN MICROCOMPUTER SYSTEMS PRINCIPLES, TESTING AND EVALUATION

Kazimierz Choroś
Technical University of Wrocław
Department of Information Systems
Poland

Introduction

The main aim of document retrieval systems is to provide, in an effective way, documents containing the information satisfying the specific information needs of a given system user. Such documents are called pertinent documents. The basic element of an information system is the information retrieval language, which is also called the indexing language. This language is used to form document and query representations, i.e. document and query search patterns during the indexing process. The effectiveness of the indexing language has the greatest influence on the performance effectiveness of the entire system. In computer information systems descriptor-type languages are the most frequently used (Salton and McGill 1983). A document is represented by the set of descriptors from the text of the document. In this case, each descriptor has the same importance in representing the document content, and as a consequence, a given set of descriptors can describe documents which concern the same problems, doing so to a different extent, though. The introduction of descriptor weights, which are the numbers qualifying the importance of a given descriptor in the document search pattern, makes it possible to differentiate the importance of descriptors in representing the document content and to retrieve documents more effectively.

Unfortunately, the descriptor weighting methods proposed up to the present have not been applied in practice, mainly because of the considerable cost increase of the system. These methods were generally based on the frequency of the descriptor in a document. In order to calculate this frequency, it would be necessary to introduce the entire text of a document into the computer memory and to apply linguistic tools to analyse the document text in a natural language. Such a process is time-consuming and not effective enough.

The inefficiency of these methods is due to the fact that indexing has been treated only as a process of the formation of document representations on the basis of a document content analysis. The results of such an analysis, however, are not always consistent with the preferences of system users. The weighted descriptor indexing of documents is therefore relative in nature (Choros 1981). Especially, the assignment of weights to descriptors in document search patterns should be considered in view of the interests of a specific view of the system.

The system can be oriented to the user if it provides the information for a homogeneous user population that is for a group of users with similar information needs and similar preferences. Such a situation is more and more common because of the wide application of microcomputers and the organization of local systems of information retrieval for a particular group of users (Choros 1983, Choros & Sieminski 1987).

Relative Indexing

Relative indexing is an indexing method substantially oriented towards individual information needs and user preferences (Choros & Danilowicz 1982). This method consists in the modification of document search patterns based on the user pertinence assessments of the documents retrieved. Hence, the descriptor weights play an important role in the system adaption to the user information needs and in reflecting user preferences.

The idea of relative indexing is based on the following assumptions determining the conditions which should be satisfied by the descriptor weight in a document search pattern:

1. The descriptor weights in a document search pattern are dependent on the document usefulness for the user.
2. The descriptor weights in a document search pattern are a value changeable over time.
3. The descriptor weights in a given document search pattern are independent of each other.

The relative indexing method can easily be introduced into the models based on the theory of fuzzy sets which seems to be the most adequate to the description of information retrieval systems (Radecki 1983).

In a fuzzy model of a document retrieval system (Radecki 1979) documents are described by the binary fuzzy relation F determining for each ordered pair $<d,t>$ the importance of the descriptor $t \in T$ in the search pattern of the document $d \in D$:

$$F = \{ < d,t, \mu_F(d,t) > \mid d \in D, t \in T \}$$

where D is a set of documents, T is a set of descriptors and

$$\mu_F : D \times T \rightarrow [0,1].$$

The relative indexing method modifies document search patterns on the basis of user assessments of the documents retrieved. Among the documents retrieved the user can distinguish pertinent documents, non-pertinent ones, and also, if there are slightly pertinent documents, it is possible for the user not to decide whether they are pertinent or not. Such documents remain unjudged.

In the presented system model, taking into account the principles of the relative indexing, it is assumed that in the search patterns of documents being introduced to the document collection, the descriptor weights take the a priori established value. For example, all descriptors in the document search pattern have weights equal to 0.5.

During the relative indexing process document search patterns can be modified immediately, i.e. after each assessment of the system response by the user, or after a certain number of requests. In the second case (for its detailed description see Choros & Danilowicz 1982), the user assessments are first analyzed and then document search patterns are modified on the basis of the averaged assessments. This may lead to the reduction of faulty modifications.

Current Modifications

The information about the pertinence of the documents being retrieved in response to a given query causes the modification of the relation of document description as follows:

$$F^* = \{ < d,t,\mu_{F^*}(d,t) = \begin{cases} \mu_F(d,t) + \alpha(1 - \mu_F(d,t)) > & | \quad d \in P,\ t \in T_q \\ \mu_F(d,t) - \beta\mu_F(d,t) > & | \quad d \in N,\ t \in T_q \\ \mu_F(d,t) & | \quad d \in O,\ t \in T_q \\ & \text{or } d \in D,\ t \in T \setminus T_q \end{cases} \}$$

where: P, N - sets of documents judged by the user as pertinent and non-pertinent
O - a set of documents slightly pertinent and of documents not judged
T - a set of descriptors used to formulate a query
α, ß - parameters.

It was assumed that a query search pattern is a Boolean expression formed of a subset of descriptors and the two Boolean operators: AND and OR.

The search patterns of both, the pertinent and non-pertinent documents are modified. However, the weights of only those descriptors are changed which occur in a query. The weights of the remaining descriptors are not modified, according to the postulate of the relative indexing that the descriptor weights in a document search pattern are independent of each other.

The parameters α and ß are established on the basis of experimental studies of the system and can be changed during the functioning of the system.

In both cases, i.e. in the case of current or averaged modifications, descriptors occurring only in the query are introduced to the adequate document search patterns (i.e. of pertinent documents) according to the modified relation of document description with the initial value α. Whereas the weights of descriptors in search patterns of non-pertinent documents, due to the successive modifications, tend to zero which eliminates these descriptors from the search patterns of non-pertinent documents.

Tests

The relative indexing method has recently been verified in the research system SINTBAD (Choros 1988). The name SINTBAD is an acronym of its Polish name *BADawszy System wyszukiwania Informacji Naukowo-Technicze j* (*Research System of Scientific and Technical Information Retrieval*). The SINTBAD system is based on a fuzzy model of information retrieval but it also allows Boolean retrieval, retrieval based on a vector space model (like the SMART) as well as mixed retrieval (like the SIRE).

The data base of the SINTBAD system consists of 4128 INSPEC abstracts in a specific field received during 2 years from the SDI system. A user group of a particular staff presented 64 requests. The requests of 4 users formed one round of the experiment. The users made about 2 thousand assessments. 3 rounds of requests enable us to observe the influence of relative indexing on the system performance.

In the experiment the following measures of retrieval effectiveness were applied to estimate the usefulness of relative indexing:

* number of pertinent documents retrieved by the system (proportional to the system recall)
* macroprecision
* macroprecision for the responses whose sizes have been limited to the numbers of documents which would have been retrieved without the relative indexing method
* microprecision
* microprecision for the responses whose sizes have been limited to the numbers of documents which would have been retrieved without the relative indexing method
* rank recall
* number of pertinent documents retrieved up to the first non-pertinent one.

For the definition of macroprecision, microprecision and rank recall see (Salton & Mac Gill 1983).

Table 1: Increase (in Percent) of the Values of Retrieval Effectiveness Measures in the SINTBAD System

Measure of effectiveness	Round I 4 users 25 requests	Round II 4 users 17 requests	Round III 4 users 22 requests
Number of pertinent documents retrieved	+ 18.73	+ 51.52	+ 53.59
Macroprecision	- 14.65	- 14.25	- 6.86
Macroprecision for the limited response	+ 1.10	+ 1.73	+ 13.04
Microprecision	- 5.98	- 2.99	- 6.74
Microprecision for the limited response	+ 0.78	- 1.00	+ 5.62
Rank recall	+ 2.85	+ 12.81	+ 8.44
Number of pertinent documents up to the first non-pertinent	+ 18.07	+100.00	+ 97.85

Table 1 presents the increase of the values of retrieval effectiveness measures in the system after the application of relative indexing. The improvement of the system effectiveness is extremely significant. For the last requests, i.e. of Round III, when the influence of relative indexing is of course the strongest, the increase of the recall is greater than 50%, whereas the precision has decreased only by 7%. When this precision is compared with that of the responses whose sizes have been limited to the numbers of documents which would have been retrieved without the relative indexing method, we observe its definite increase. The rank recall has increased more than by 8%. The most significant fact is that in the case of 27% of the system responses the number of the pertinent documents retrieved up to the first non-pertinent one was greater than the number of all pertinent documents which would have been retrieved without the relative indexing method.

Final Remarks

The relative indexing method has been introduced into the fuzzy model of a document retrieval system. In the fuzzy models no indexing method has been considered as yet which would enable us to assign to descriptors the weights consistent with the logic of fuzzy operations. The methods presented in the paper completes these models and permits us to apply fuzzy retrieval methods in practice.

The relative indexing methods accepts data bases whose documents are indexed in a standard way, i.e. with the use of indexing languages of keywords potentially enhanced by thesauri. Furthermore, the relative indexing method does not require to re-index the existing bibliographic data bases.

The relative indexing method is one of the recent achievements in information science and when applied in information retrieval systems, mainly microcomputer systems, it should improve their performance.

REFERENCES

CHOROŚ, K. 1981. "Weighted descriptor indexing of documents." *Aktualne Problemy Informacji i Dokumentacji* 26, 22-26

CHOROŚ, K. and DANILOWICZ, C. 1982. "Relative indexing. Weighted descriptors and relative indexing in a document retrieval system model." *Information Processing and Management* 18, 207-220

CHOROŚ, K. 1983. *Relative indexing in a fuzzy model of a local system of information retrieval*. Reports of BGiOINT, Technical University of Wroclaw, Ser. PRE, No. 51

CHOROŚ, K. and SIEMINSKI, A. 1987. *Retrieval indexing in microcomputer systems of information retrieval*. Katowice: Proceedings of the International Symposium on the Application of Microcomputers in Scientific Information, 69-79

CHOROŚ, K. 1988. *SINTBAD*. Reports of BGiOINT, Technical University of Wroclaw, Ser. SPR, No. 111

CROFT, W.B. 1983. "Experiments with representation in a document retrieval system." *Information Technology: Research and Development* 2, 1-21

PARKER, L.M.P. 1984. "An experiment in document representative modification." *Journal of information Science* 8, 1-6

RADECKI, T. 1979. "Fuzzy set theoretical approach to document retrieval." *Information Processing and Management* 15, 147-259

RADECKI, T. 1983. "A theoretical background for applying fuzzy set theory in information retrieval." *Fuzzy Sets and Systems* 10, 169-183

ROUSSEAU, R. 1985. "On relative indexing in fuzzy retrieval systems." *Information Processing and Management* 21, 415-417

SALTON, G. and MC GILL, M.J. 1983. *Introduction to Modern Information Retrieval*. New York: Mc Graw-Hill

SPARCK JONES, K. (ed.). 1981. *Information Retrieval Experiment*. London: Butterworths, 1981

ELECTRONICALLY PROCESSED TEXTS OF EXOTIC LANGUAGES IN FAVOR OF THE INTEGRATION OF DESCRIPTION INTO LINGUISTIC DISCUSSION

Otto Esser, Franz Potyka
Institut für Afrikanistik, University of Cologne
FRG

Descriptive linguistics as the fundament for any further branches in the linguistic science is one of the fields where the redemption of age-old challenges now becomes possible with the help of electronic data processing. Descriptive (and historical- comparative) linguistics - as other sciences of social systems - offer in several ways the so-to-speak classical problem of where the computer applies: the mass problem. How this problem is ingrained in descriptive linguistics should be examined more closely.

The aim of a grammarian is, to find out the basic algorithm of a language which can be formulated in a handful of rules. It is true that the rules of a language are represented in speech acts (texts), but these rules are not acquired by explanation but by conditioning. They are internalized and mastered but not transparent for the speaker (as everyone knows; hence it has become the object for science). The task of the descriptive linguist is, to work through the language from the every-day-speech-level with its prescriptive rules step for step up to the final abstract basic rules each language is built on.

In our approach to hitherto unknown languages, abstractness of rules and quantity of data background are in proportional ratio to each other: The more general the scope of a hypothesis is, the more complete the incorporation of the textual corpus has to be. This sounds trivial, but the reality shows that the above-mentioned proportion is very often turned to the inverse ratio and we assume that the reason for this is, in many cases, more a non-accomplishment of the mass problem rather than pure intention: also a data oriented linguistic work is continually menaced. The inclination to economize an unsurveyable amount of data with already existing theories at too early a stage is prevalent. The problem with this premature theory is not only its potential inadequacy, but its potency for feedback: it functions in a prejudiced way and, thus, precludes the exposure of the true conditions and, therefore, the formulation of a more adequate hypothesis.

The relevance of this problem is even further aggravated by the fact that descriptive linguistics is still a subject where findings are rather announced than put up for discussion. The reason for this is to be found in the situation in which the exotic languages of the world and their study are: their social relevance can be denied in a modern context, their loss can be forgotten, their study is relevant only for the history of mankind and irrelevant for the security of the finally adopted way. Keeping in mind the constant decrease of demand for causality, nobody will marvel that the study of exotic languages is not in the centre of public interest, i.e. the want of financing. The self-evident consequence is that there are still many undescribed languages and the name of languages which are studied by only a single expert is legion.

The problem of "universalizing" a language by the lack of an adequate theory or by the lack of scientific communication can be solved with the help of electronic data processing. The desideratum is a tool which allows the continuous grasp to the language data of interest from the first examination of the transcribed texts by the specialist over the different stages of description and analysis to the rendering of a scientific work to the public - and beyond that point. The scientific community is then confronted with two different but complementary objects, both born in a single working procedure: an analytic description based on a corpus of texts and the corpus of texts in processed form documenting the exotic language. (The former can also, of course, be published in printed form; the latter should be published on electronic storage media, for example disks.) Any competent recipient, thus, has his own access to the exotic language without the necessity of becoming a specialist himself. With the publication of the - up to this point - complete knowledge of the exotic language, a developable platform for its discussion is established.

To make the desiderata and our answer in this connexion more vivid, we will open the description of our software not at its natural starting point, the module for input of data, but at a potential endproduct: we assume that a grammar of several hundred pages or one of those standard-sized articles has been written. Both have a background of data whose printing does not only go beyond the quantitative frame of the respective category of text, but would be useless for linguistic access to a large extent if merely printed - even with interlinear translations. It would merely be an impenetrable block of data or - to use another picture - the haystack in which the needle must be searched for. A completely different situation grows from the fact that the data - irrespective of its quantity - can be presented in electronic processed form. The scientific recipient - equipped with a software for personal access - is not only in the position to verify the hypothesis offered by his colleague, but also to work on the language himself. The effort of familiarizing oneself with the unknown exotic language is comparatively low. The reason why the level of information sufficient for a discussion between colleagues of different specialization areas can be produced so easily, is the fact that the pioneering work of the specialized linguist is offered as a complete volume and - equally important - that the non-specialized recipient can make a selection according to his own criteria. The scientific recipient profits from a highly processed material whose origin can be explained very simply: the accessibility of the data is a by-product of the former computer aided descriptive and analytic work done by the specialist.

Having mentioned aspects of the endproduct of the work with SRTEXAN - which in our conception is more an accelerator of scientific discussion rather than an everlasting product - we will now come to the proper start of electronic data processing in descriptive linguistics and the designing details of SRTEXAN. How is the input of data organized? This is, of course, hard work because the linguist has to type. The alternative, an OCR-scanner is out of the question for reasons of linguistic work and economy. An OCR-scanner is due to its shape/pattern comparison unable to read handwriting. Pre-typing would contradict the motive for the employment of a computer: All effort must be optimized, all results must be able to be recalled in any optional context. The typing of the text i.e. the laying out of the database, is very much the linguistic segmentation which is indispensable for any further linguistic work (as everybody knows). The feeding procedure of SRTEXAN is - in harmony with widespread linguistic practice - based on the sentence as the segmentation unit for the input. Provided with an identification number which cannot be used twice, the sentence is the context presented by the system to the user in any later operation. Specific phonetic signs can be used in printing (download), characters to backspace, the signs for morpheme boundaries (whitespace) and end-of-sentence-markers are user definable. In a further step, the vernacular sentence on the screen can be commented with supplementary information on a line below. This part of the input, its stringency and function, has been very hotly debated. We will come back to it after having shown all the other parts of the program. Following, this is the interlinear translation and the accumulation of lexicon as its by-product. One word of the vernacular sentence after the other is offered by the computer on screen, either together with an already stored translation which can be affirmed by pressing a single key or - if the word appears first time - in a field for adding a translation. The sets of morphemes, consisting of vernacular line, supplementary information line and interlinear translation line, are assembled anew to a now three-line-sentence on the screen, each set left adjusted. Furthermore, a free translation can be added. As previously indicated, the lexicon is accumulated by the system during the interactive translation of the vernacular text as its by-product. No additional effort by the user is necessary. The amount of translation entries for a single vernacular item is not limited; the offered space for translation is more than needed.

Having touched the elementary necessity for electronic data processing, the input of the foundation of data, we will come to the more sophisticated parts of the program. We already mentioned the ability of SRTEXAN to master a process of linguistic analysis in its entirety. That means the possibility of the input of raw material with makeshift segmentation. For the continual actualization of the data according to the latest findings, we offer two independent editors, one for the texts and one for the lexicon. The text-editor presents a single sentence on screen, selected either by browsing through the database or by purposeful aiming by means of an identification number. Corrections affect the database and are carried out by screen control. All further occurrences of the corrected item can be traced through the entire corpus. In the lexicon-editor, the entry designated for correction will be found by the computer after the input of the vernacular item.

The essential core of SRTEXAN is the module for retrieving procedures. In our conception of linguistic reasoning, attestation of data, which must comprise the complete corpus plays a central role. The different possibilities in the output mode also ensure the quantitative measuring: whether a construction is marginal or central can be highly significant. The possibility of specifying the retrieval-order in SRTEXAN generally exceeds the necessity. This means that also the most delimited question can be answered in less than no time. Technically spoken, SRTEXAN works with wildcards and logical connexions (AND/OR) within the three lines of the interlinear text blocks.

An additional programm for counting phonemes, phoneme environments and the frequency of words should be mentioned. Furthermore, some self-evident possibilities: The output of the interlinear text blocks is possible in any desired volume. A wildcard of identification numbers allows an output from simply a single sentence up to the entire stored data. Whether the output is on printer or on file in wordprocessor format is a matter of choice. Command sequences are defined according to the respective wordprocessor. The output of the lexicon may be routed to file or to the printer at any time and can be sorted either by vernacular item or by translated meaning using a user definable sortkey. Other points in the menu are programs for maintaining the database, for providing security copies and for restoring the data.

Having given a rough overview over the software we offer for linguistic text analysis, we now come back to our conception of linguistic work in collaboration with a computer.

We have tried to make clear that the inevitable mass problems in language description can be made to bear fruit for the progression of linguistic research, and also the problems which arise when the members of the scientific community are isolated specialists. We have not yet discussed our designing conception with regard to our target group. We did not design a programm for all those who are concerned in one way or another with a foreign language. The starting question was, how to handle an unsurveyably large corpus of texts as easily and accurately as a small story. This question had to be answered with regard to the process of analysis as well as the procedure of publication. First of all, one has to recognize the financial preconditions of the target group which are more in a frame with dimensions that could be called private but those of institutes with generous provisions. This, and the compatibility to other software were decisive for PCs with a hard disk. Although their capacity (see technical specifications at the end of this article) is enough for most of the available corpora of exotic languages, we had to think of the storage capacity consumed by detailed linguistic notations, for this is the only division of the storage of the designers free disposition. One cannot, of course, shorten the vernacular text and one should not restrict the interlinear translation to too high an extent. These are the two obligatory parts of a set worked with and combined again and again. All other potential parts of the set are non-obligatory but have consequences for the speed and the flexibility of the system. We decided for the primacy of speed within the proper process of linguistic analysis. In consequence, there is only a single, but important supplementary line (the above mentioned hypotheses line between vernacular and translation line) with a scope on the word not as a member of the lexicon, but in the concrete environment of the sentence. It is intended as an open line filled according to the needs of the moment. It is more a bench in the linguist's workshop, but the vitrine for deliberate solutions. The latter can easily be added for publication in any conventional wordprocessor or with the help of a publication program.

To summarize: Our conception of a tool for linguistic text analysis emphasizes the dynamic fluxion of heuristic progression. The tool (the software) is designed to be incorporated into the material (data of language) or, vice versa, the texts of a formerly unknown language are structured by SRTEXAN for complete access not only by the specialist but by the entire scientific community.

NOTES

Technical specifications

system requirements: XT/AT compatible computer - MSDOS/PCDOS / 512 kB main memory / Harddisk/ Hercules (compatible) graphics adapter (EGA in progress) / printer (for self-defined symbols it must support download) / optional, but recommendable: RAM-disk (>=384 kB) as buffer drive

technical specifications of current (beta-)version:
text: > 2,000,000,000 text units / lexicon: 15,000 words and their translations / sortkey definable / text & lexicon: 8-bit extended ASCII-code / diacritics supported / printer download supported / user definable: various whitespace characters (end of word/morpheme) / various end-of-sentence-markers / characters to

backspace for output / download switch sequences / print attribute sequences / word processor dependant sequences / reserved characters: ' " * $ # =

Development-system configuration: PC/AT (80286) - MSDOS/PCDOS 3.3 / 640 kB main memory / 384 kB RAM-disk (virtual disk drive) / 40 MB Harddisk / Hercules compatible graphics adapter / printer (24-pin dot matrix)

SRTEXAN is designed by Otto Esser, Institut für Afrikanistik, University of Cologne, Meister-Ekkehart-Strasse 7. e-mail: AMA02@DK0RRZK0.bitnet

AN EXPERT SYSTEM THAT USES ABSTRACT FEATURES OF A POEM TO IDENTIFY ITS MOST PROBABLE AUTHOR

Wilma Knoppert
TNO Institute of Applied Computer Science
Department Knowledge Based Systems
The Netherlands

Abstract

It is important to investigate the structure of expert knowledge poetry. The results of this research can be used for further theoretical investigations and in the education about poetry. Expert knowledge of poetry can for example help in the classification of poems by identifying their author. An expert system was made to learn more about this classification process and to extend the possibilities of using a computer in poetry analysis. Often this usage is limited to applications that are only interesting for a few specialists in the field and not for a normal reader. This system should reduce the gap between questions of a poetry reader and the information supplied by the computer.

The system uses the features of the work of twenty Dutch poets to select which of them is the most probable writer of a certain poem. The user of the system has to answer a series of questions about the content and form of the poem. When all questions are answered the system generates a list of possible writers of the poem. Each name is followed by an indication of the probability ('low', 'medium' or 'high') that the answer is correct.

The knowledge of three experts holding academic qualifications in modern Dutch poetry was used to set up the knowledge base. They had to execute several tasks to show different aspects of their knowledge base. Some tasks concentrated on one poem and on the effect of a single feature in deciding which writers were more or less probable, others on the characteristics of the complete works of a poet.

The choice of the features depended partly on the difficulty the user of the system would have in answering a given question. Questions were excluded when they were likely to generate little consensus between users, or when they needed an explanation that was too difficult to understand for a person who had been educated to A-level standard.

The system was made in a simple expert system shell (KES.HT) and its preliminary results are encouraging; in many cases, including users with little knowledge of poetry, the correct poet was identified by the system with probability indication 'high'.

INTRODUCTION

The Structure of Expert Knowledge of Poetry

It is psychologically interesting to investigate what it means to have expert knowledge, in general and about the work of some poets in particular. For fields like chess and medicine, psychologists already did research work to find the differences between experts and novices. Those investigations have shown that experts store knowledge in a structured form which makes it easy for them to understand and remember examples in their domain of expertise. For example, chess masters can reconstruct the position of all the pieces on the chess-board, because they remember the position of one piece in relation to that of other ones. An expert in poetry should also have knowledge in a structured form. The words 'experimental' or 'traditional' for example should have a number of connotations that arise automatically when an experimental or traditional poem is read. When the expert reads a poem that is familiar to him or her, the name of its author will probably be activated in the same automatic way.

Because experts have structured knowledge, several different units of knowledge for a novice can be one unit of information for the expert. This is important because the human Short Term Memory (STM) that is the part of our memory that we need to use our knowledge in practical situations, has a limited capacity of about 7-9 units.

To use this small capacity as efficiently as possible, for example in making a decision, it is not enough to organize the knowledge well. It is also important that the units are only filled with the most important information. Here, a second difference between experts and novices shows itself: experts have much more experience in selecting the relevant aspects of a case (Schraagen, 1986, p. 22).

Although their knowledge is better structured and they are better in selecting relevant features, even for experts the limited capacity of their STM makes it difficult to combine many different features into one conclusion: To prevent an overload of the STM, attention is only paid to a few aspects at the time.

Because expert knowledge consists of complex structures, it is difficult to understand it and to isolate small parts of it. Yet it is important to get insight in the knowledge, for example to help students in developing their knowledge and to analyse differences between experts. To learn more about expert knowledge of poetry, a computer model of a small part of this knowledge was made in the form of an expert system.

An Expert System for Poetry Classification

The expert system contains knowledge necessary for the classification of poems by identifying their author. The system asks a series of questions; when the user has answered a question, the system combines the given answer with information obtained earlier in the session and with the knowledge that is permanently present in the system. When enough questions are answered the system shows its conclusion. The knowledge of the system is in the form of abstract features of the work of several poets, the questions are about a poem read by the user of the system, and the conclusion consists of a list of names of possible authors of the poem.

The first purpose of building the system is already explained; we want to learn more about expert knowledge of poetry. The second purpose of the system is to extend the possibilities of using a computer in poetry analysis. Often this usage is limited to generating statistical information concerning for example the occurrence of special words and of linguistic structures in the work of a poet. Although such information can be important for the specialist, a student in literature or a person who reviews the poet's work will concentrate on other aspects. This system should reduce the gap between the knowledge stored in the computer system and that of a poetry reader.

Much attention was paid to the knowledge acquisition, the extraction of knowledge 'out of the head' of the expert.

KNOWLEDGE ACQUISITION

The Problem of Extracting Expert Knowledge of Poetry

If we intend to make an expert system based on expert knowledge of poetry we have to find a way to make the experts show their knowledge. For poetry experts this is rather unusual; a doctor has to come to the right diagnoses, a chess master has to win his or her game, but an expert in poetry will demonstrate his knowledge only in rare cases.

We can of course force the experts to show their knowledge by giving them a problem to solve. For example, they can be asked to give the author of a poem they have never read, if they have read much other work of the same poet. This is, however, not really a solution of the problem of understanding the structure of the knowledge of the expert, because the expert will often automatically come to the choice of a poet or a small group of poets. Of course, they should be able to give a motivation of their choice by pointing out the correspondence between the poem and other work of the same poet, but in this motivation they will probably forget aspects that are less striking, even if they did play a role in the decision.

Knowledge as Lists of Features and Values

To get a better understanding of the features that belong to their knowledge structures, the experts should be forced to slow down their process of classification.

One way to do this is by telling them about the different aspects of a poem one by one, without showing the poem itself. After each new part of information the expert should state how this part influences the choice.

To perform such kinds of tasks we should know first what kinds of aspects of a poem could be useful in choosing a poet. Therefore, we want to come to a list of features to analyse a poem, independent of the poem and its author. This *general list* can contain features of the content and form of the poem. We can use this general list not only to analyse separate poems, but also to describe the work of each poet in general. For each poet, those features can then be written down, together with information about the frequency with which they are used by the poet. This means that every poet gets his or her own list, where features of the general list are combined with values that are characteristic for the work of that poet. Thus, the general list is a list of *features* and the lists of the poets are lists of *feature-value combinations*. It was decided that such lists would be made for twenty important Dutch poets from 1880 until 1970, both traditional and experimental ones.

One can use these lists independent of the expert to identify the author of a poem, provided that two conditions are satisfied:

* a person, the *user*, exists who analyses the poem the author of which has to be identified.
* a *measure* exists to compare the list of the poem with the lists of the poets.

It should be clear that the central idea of comparing the list of a poem with the lists of poets is independent of a computer implementation. Therefore, we will first concentrate only on the acquisition. For this problem the knowledge acquisition concentrates on the selection of features for the general list and on the choice of values to fill the lists of the work of the twenty poets. Two important aspects of the knowledge acquisition were the criteria for feature selection and the tasks that were used.

Criteria for Feature Selection

Two things have to be kept in mind when we think about the features on the list. In the first place: the choice of the features is a kind of compromise between the experts and the users. The experts are used to broad knowledge structures; a broad question (for example: 'Is the poem traditional?') can help them to come to a decision. Most users do not know much about poetry and will prefer smaller questions that are easier to answer than general questions.

In the second place: the general list of features and the corresponding lists of feature-value combinations for each poet are based on the opinion of the experts. This means that we cannot expect exact statistics about the frequency of occurrence of certain features in the complete works of the poet. The experts will probably remember more about the better and most characteristic work of a poet and, even for this part of the poet's work, the way the experts have structured their knowledge has influence on the features and values they remember.

Three criteria were used in the feature selection.

1. The questions should really help the expert in choosing a poet. Sometimes a question was excluded or changed because the experts did not expect it to be informative, sometimes because the experts simply did not know the value of the feature for each poet. The second situation occurred especially with questions for numerical values, for example the question which percentage of the total work of a poet was made of one stanza. The difficulty the experts had with this question does not mean that the experts have no knowledge at all about the amount of stanzas, but only that they do not know or use such exact information. We see here the difference between seizing the characteristic aspects of a poet through the 'filter' of the knowledge of an expert and a direct evaluation of the complete works of a poet.
2. A second criterion was the difficulty the user of the system would have in answering a given question. Questions were excluded when they needed an explanation that was too difficult to understand for a person who had been educated to A-level standard. An example is the question whether the metre of a poem is regular. Even for experienced people this question is not always easy to answer.

   To make the answering as easy as possible sometimes one comprehensive question was reduced to several smaller questions. For example, the question whether the poem had a traditional form was not put in the system, but questions about the use of rhyme, of grammatical language and of a normal interpunction were put in. In most poems with a traditional form, rhyme is used frequently, the language is grammatical and the interpunction is normal. Therefore, those smaller questions are useful in making a distinction between more traditional and more experimental poets.

Although it is much easier to agree about the form aspects of a poem than about its content aspects, both kinds of features are necessary if we do not want to neglect a large part of the expert knowledge. This difficulty to answer questions about content is of another kind than for example the difficulty to find the metre of a poem. With content questions different interpretations are more important than differences in experience. To prevent a situation in which the interpretation of one feature will have too much influence, we can ask more than one question about related features.

3. A third criterion was that features should be general enough to be meaningful for more than one poet. Therefore, questions about specific words used by one of the poets were not allowed. One problem with this exclusion is that in some cases the experts probably will use those words as an indication that a poet is the right one, but that each expert will have other words with this function. To put some knowledge of the words being used by the poets in the system, features such as for example the use of archaic words and of neologism were included.

Different Kinds of Tasks

The criteria for feature selection are only useful if we can choose from enough features. Therefore, we should first think of features that could be used and, thus, about tasks to find theses features. Figure 1 shows two dimensions in which these tasks can be sorted.

Figure 1: Tasks for Knowledge Acquisition

	ORIENTATION	DIRECTLY USABLE
SEPARATE POEMS	Combine lines of poems (A)	Find author with few questions (C)
ALL POETRY	Striking features for each poet (B)	Combine parts of lists and names of poets (D)

* *Separate poems and all poetry*: We can look in handbooks about poetry analysis or ask the expert what he remembers of the work of a certain poet, but to grasp all the important features this approach is not enough.

  Seemingly minor characteristics, for example aspects of the interpunction that are typical of the work of a poet, will probably be overlooked in that way. To find such features we have to look at separate poems. Therefore, tasks that use separate poems or parts of them, as well as tasks about all poetry of a certain poet are necessary.

* *Orientation and directly usable tasks*: We can split the tasks in another way by making a distinction between orientation tasks and tasks that result in information that is directly usable in the system. The orientation tasks have two functions. First, to suggest features that can be useful in the system, second, to make the experts sensitive about the knowledge they have. The last function is important because, as mentioned earlier, the experts are not used to demonstrate their knowledge. It is clear that orientation tasks alone do not give enough information to fill in the lists; therefore, we also need tasks which systematically examine the features of the work of the twenty poets.

Procedure

The knowledge acquisition started with orientation tasks; the result of these tasks was a first version of the general list. The rest of the tasks were necessary to fill this list with the right values and to learn something about the relative importance of the features in deciding which poet had written a poem.

Three experts with academic qualifications in modern Dutch poetry were used for the total series of nine tasks, but none of the tasks was finished by more than two experts. Often one task was used to check the information given earlier in another task. In that case sometimes the same expert could be used for both tasks, but mostly different experts were necessary to get a proper check. For example, two experts filled the general list for each of the twenty poets and the third has evaluated their answers. It is notable that the experts had almost the same opinion about the features that should be in the general list, even if they were given different tasks to arrive at the features.

Examples of Tasks

Most tasks were used to get new information and to check information that was obtained earlier. One example of a task for every part of the scheme is:

* *Separate poem/orientation (Task A)*: Two experts had to combine lines that belonged to the same poem. They got eight third lines and eight ninth lines and had to think aloud while motivating their choice. This task showed the importance of seemingly minor aspects of interpunction and metre.
* *All poetry/orientation (Task B)*: One expert gave for every poet a first short list of features that could be interesting in the system. This resulted in the first version of the general list.
* *Separate/directly usable (Task C)*: One expert had to ask as few questions as possible, chosen from the first version of the general list, to find the author of a poem.
* *All poetry/directly usable (Task D)*: One expert had to combine the names of the twenty poets with parts of the lists of feature-value combinations of the twenty poets. He was given feedback about the faults he had made and could suggest improvements in the lists.

Task C is especially interesting, because here, the expert had to perform something like the task of the future expert system. This task was difficult for the expert; he found the right poet in only one of the five cases. In one case he could not find an answer at all, in one case he named a poet totally different from the writer of the poem. In the other two cases the wrong choice was understandable because the work of the chosen writer and of the one of the right answer had a large amount of resemblance.

When the task is so difficult for the experts themselves, we cannot expect the system to work perfect, even with an 'ideal' user. When the system does not have the right answer as the first choice we should inspect the alternatives it has chosen. When those alternatives are understandable, changing the system is probably not useful. When they seem very strange, we should think of improvements of the system.

The Result of the Knowledge Acquisition

The general list that was formed after the orientation tasks consisted of three parts: Subject, Form and Atmosphere. For each subject on the Subject-part of the list the experts had to answer with 'yes' or 'no', whether the subject occurred in the work of the poet and whether it was an important subject for the poet. The questions about form and atmosphere had to be answered with a value from 0 to 4 indicating how frequently the feature was used by the poet. The resulting lists were used as a basis for the implementation of the expert system.

IMPLEMENTATION

The Expert System Shell KES.HT

The system was implemented in the expert system shell KES.HT, one version of three different shells that have been brought out under the name KES (KES.HT, 1987). Expert system shells provide their own question-generating mechanisms and have their own way to evaluate the answers. This makes the programming of an expert system much easier than in a plain programming language. To use the shell KES.HT it is enough to put the feature-value lists for each poet in the right format, to list the questions asking for the value of each feature and to provide some extra information about relations between features. Then the order in which the questions are generated is clear, as well as the way some questions depend on answers given earlier during the session.

When the question generation is finished (and when all generated questions are answered) the shell provides a list of poets that are possible, with an indication of the probability that the choice of that poet is correct.

Description in KES.HT

The list of feature-value combinations for each poet was put into a *description*. A simplified example of a description is shown below:

Certainty Factors Instead of Values in the Lists of the Poets

In the description every value is followed by a so-called *certainty factor* marked by the words between the brackets. This certainty factor forms an indication of the probability that the value will occur in a poem. One can choose between five certainty factors: never, low, medium, high and always.

WRITER: **Lucebert**

DESCRIPTION:

FORM	rhyme	= hardly not (high), sometimes (medium), much (low)
	each line with capital	= no (always)
	normal interpunction	= yes (low), no-period (high), no-general (low)
	spoken language	= word-no(high), sentence-no(high), wordsentence-no (medium), spoken-yes (medium), written-no (medium)
	assonance	= hardly not (low), sometimes (medium), much (high)
	metaphorical language	= no (low), yes (high)
	wordlyrical	= no (medium), yes (high)
SUB-JECT	fantasy	= no (medium), yes (medium)
	desire	= no (medium), yes (medium)
	contrast	= no (medium), yes (high)
	'I' occurs	= no (medium), yes (high)
ATMO-SPHERE	concerned	= no (low), yes (high);
	way of concerned	= politically committed (high), critical (high), no (low);
	resigned	= no (medium), yes (low);

The transcription of the lists of feature-value combinations that were the result of the knowledge acquisition into the feature-value combinations of the descriptions was rather straightforward. For example, subjects that were judged as important for the poet usually got a certainty factor 'high' for the subject-'yes' combination and a certainty factor 'medium' for the subject-'no' combination. For the two other parts, Form and Atmosphere, the values 0 to 4 that indicated how frequently a feature-value combination occurred, had to be changed in certainty factors. Here, the values 1, 2 and 3 were often at first 'translated' in 'low', 'medium' and 'high', respectively, although a number of other factors had influence on the final transition.

In most cases it is impossible to state that a certain feature-value combination will never or always occur in the work of a poet. Therefore, even if both experts gave a 0 (= this occurs never or almost never) or 4 (= this occurs always or almost always), usually this did not result in a certainty factor 'never' or 'always'. The only place in the description of Lucebert where one of the two ('always') is used, is with the question: 'Does every line in the poem start with a capital, even when no new sentence starts there?', and even for such straightforward feature it is possible that there are some exceptions. Perhaps the writer wanted one of his poems to look old-fashioned, in which case starting every line with a capital could be useful.

The system was built step by step; after adding some questions-value combinations to the descriptions, a few poems were used to test the system. When the system failed, this could cause changes in the certainty factors in the descriptions for some poets. The poems used to test the system were not chosen at random from the complete works of a poet, but from his or her more characteristic work. When, for example, an anthology of the work existed, this was used as a source for the poems to test with. An interaction with several users was necessary to test the system.

Interaction with the User

For every feature a question to the user is formulated; and in most cases every value also needs some explanation in the form of a possible answer to the question. One example of a feature with its values and the corresponding question with its answers is:

```
feature:      spoken language
   question:  Is this poem written in usually spoken language?

value:        word-no
   answer:    No, it contains words that do not belong to the
              usually spoken language

value:        sentence-no
    answer:   No, the words are from usually spoken language,
              but the sentences are constructed differently.

value:        wordsentence-no
    answer:   No, there are words in the sentence that do not
              belong to the usually spoken language and the
              sentences are also constructed differently.

value:        spoken-yes
    answer:   There are sentences in the poem that are typical
              for spoken language.

value:        written-no
    answer:   No, there are no uncommon words or sentences in
              the poem, but the used language is more written
              language than spoken language.
```

Remarks About the Questions of the System

The user has to answer all the questions that are asked about a certain poem to make the system identify the author. To make this as easy as possible much attention was paid to choosing the best question to ask about each feature. Especially for concepts that are often used by experts, but mostly without a careful definition, this was often rather difficult.

An example of such a concept is 'lyrical', which says something about the form and the content of a poem; about the form, because in a lyrical poem often much adjectives are used, and about the content, because in a lyrical poem the emotions of the poet are important.

Another problem was the choice of the optimal amount of questions. More features and questions can perhaps help in the decision process, but answering too much questions might bore the user. Sometimes the amount of questions could be lowered by using relations between concepts. For example, when the user answers that a poem does not show that the writer is concerned about his or her subject, the system should not ask in which way the writer is concerned.

The system was built step by step and sometimes, when the system failed, the wording of questions was changed or new questions were added. The amount of questions in the last version of the system depended party on the answers given by the user; therefore, it varied between 25 and 30.

How the System Comes to a Conclusion

The description and the answers of a user are combined to come to a conclusion. Until the first question is answered all poets have an equal probability of being the author of the poem. While the questions are being answered a poet can be excluded from the range of possible authors, but this is only possible when the user gives a value to a feature that never occurs according to the description or when the user does not give a value to a feature that always should occur, according to the description. As we saw earlier, this situation does not occur often because 'never' and 'always' are seldom used in the descriptions. Most questions do not exclude answers, but only change the relative probability of the poets by comparing the answer given for a poem with the descriptions.

When all necessary questions are asked, the expert system generates a list of all poets that were not excluded with an indication 'low', 'medium' or 'high' that the answer is correct. In most test-cases the amount of poets with indication 'high' was about three. When 25 questions can be answered in 2 different ways, then the amount of possible different sets of answers is 2^{25} that is about five hundred million. Therefore, it is impossible to evaluate systematically which series of answers lead to which solution. It is also difficult to evaluate the influence of minor changes in the descriptions for the decision process.

RESULTS

During the building of the system, about fifteen users interacted with the system for one or two poems. In many cases, including users with little knowledge of poetry, the correct poet was identified by the system with the probability indication 'high'. Often the system was slightly changed after an interaction with an user; therefore, these positive results with different versions of the system are not more than an encouraging start.

One problem with all tests is of course that the values given for a poem depend on the user who reads the poem. For example in testing one version of the system, it happened once that the same system and the same poem resulted in two different conclusions for two different users. In the conclusion for one user the correct poet got the probability indication 'high', in the other conclusion this poet got the indication 'low'. A proper test should therefore work with a substantial amount of users for the same poem, in order to get a clear impression of the quality of the system.

Although this is somewhat disappointing, the objectives of building the system, as discussed in the introduction, were to learn more about expert knowledge of poetry and to bridge the gap between the information supplied by the computer and the questions of a poetry reader. For these purposes a test of the last version of the system is not absolutely necessary. For the moment it is enough that the system consists of features that are relevant for the poetry expert and that a user of the system with little knowledge of poetry can work with the system.

IMPLICATIONS

An interesting test would be to combine this expert system with a kind of database system to analyse poetry on the word-level and to compare the results of this combination with those of the database system alone. The expert system alone has also interesting implications, both practically and theoretically.

Practically, the system can be used for education purposes to help students to concentrate on one aspect of a poem at a time and to draw their attention to similarities and differences in the work of several poets. The feedback they are given will probably stimulate them to think more carefully about their answers. For such applications much care should be paid to the selection of those descriptions of the features that provide the clearest questions to the user.

Students who are interested in programming and in poetry can also change parts of the system themselves and use other students to test whether the system is really improved by their work.

Theoretically, different versions of the system can be compared to see which combination of abstract features and which formulation of the questions render optimal results. Of course, it is probable that the optimal combination is not the same for every user. It would be psychologically interesting to compare the knowledge structures of different experts and to investigate the differences between the behaviour of the system and the ways experts come to a decision, when they are given the same information as the system.

REFERENCES

KES.HT. 1987. *Knowledge Base Author's Manual.* Updates 2.4, Software Architecture & Engineering, Inc., Sussex Suite, City Gates, 2-4 Southgate, Chichester, West Sussex, UK

SCHRAAGEN, J.M.C. 1986. *Expert-novice differences and their implication for knowledge elicitation techniques.* Soesterberg: Rapport TNO-IZF nr. 34

COMPUTER-ASSISTED INTERPRETATION OF DETECTIVE STORIES
(CID - COMPUTERGESTÜTZTE INTERPRETATION VON DETEKTIVROMANEN)
A RESEARCH PROJECT

Volker Neuhaus et al.*
Germanistisches Institut, University of Cologne
FRG

In our research on the use of data processing methods for literature analysis we decided to use the mystery or detective story as our subject, because this genre is one of the still remaining productive specimens of a type of literature form, which is governed by a fixed set of rules and generates variations of a fixed pattern.

Till about 1750 the production of literature in general was regulated by stable genre codes. Consider for example the extensive "examens" and "préfaces" of French Classical Tragedy, in which the authors deal at length with the genre traditions and describe the present work's place within these very traditions and their complicated codes. The success of such a drama depended entirely on its sticking to the rules on one hand and being innovative at the same time without stretching or even breaking these conventions.

The poeta doctus as author and the connaisseur as listener, spectator, or reader were taken for granted in all periods of literature from ancient Greece, or the minnesingers to the literature beginnings of Goethe.

For the detective story this continues to be true even in our century. We do not know of any author of the so-called >Golden Age< of the mystery story who did not have a thorough knowledge of all the relevant production of his predecessors and his competitors, and who did not dream of "the alert student of mystery tales" as his ideal reader, as Ellery Queen put it. With the final establishment - in the nineteen-twenties - of the code regulating both production and the readers' response, we encounter the first explicit codifications of definite rules by Ronald Knox and S.S. van Dine.

By employing CID, we aim to extract the entire set of rules which guide the author's narration and the reader's response, from the micro and macro structuring of the texts, and to verify them by empirical means.

If you ask several individuals to give you a condensed version of a mystery story, approximately half of them will tell you about the murderer, his plan, and its execution, and the others will tell you about the discovery of the corpse, the detective's activities, and so on.

It was on this observation that Dietrich Weber based his Habilitation thesis "Theorie der analytischen Erzählung". On Weber's so-called >first level<, we are told in an analytically structured narration what the characters, in the first place the detective, experience - beginning with the discovery of the corpse, continuing with the detection and sorting-out of clues, and ending with the identification of the murderer.

While reading this story of an experience, the reader accompanies the detective in making up a construct which arranges all of the facts mentioned in the course of the story in a neat chronological sequence, and which offers a chain of cause and effect for the initially unrelated and mysterious facts. On this level, Weber's >second<, the murderer and not the detective is the leading figure; the >second level< is dominated by his plan and its execution, the detective appearing only at the very end.

The >second level< establishes itself first and foremost in the reader's mind, but it also appears, in a condensed form, in the mystery story itself, viz. in the concluding summary of the detective in the final chapter.

Main subject of our research is the so-called >orthodox< or >classic< mystery story of the Anglo-American School.

Right now, the CID project comprises four separate research groups, with each having its particular objective and focusing on the corresponding level of Weber's model.

The >second level<, being in its essence a construct in the reader's mind, is converted into tangible form as a summary of contents which lists all relevant facts mentioned in the story in their chronological sequence and numbers them accordingly.

The >first level<, representing the genuine experience of reading a mystery story, is documented in a description of the scenario, giving in coded form narrative time, narrative level, narrative situation, narrative medium, persons >on stage<, time, place and type of action, and also providing a reference to the corresponding section of the summary of contents.

Into this scenario we can integrate by appropriate codes the results of the other research groups, which deal with elementary structures of fiction in general and mystery stories in particular. These groups - personage typology file, sociogram, crime typology file - analyse Weber's >second level< that is what really did happen, with other words: what the reader definitely knows after having finished his reading.

We use a permanent Personage Typology File (PTF) to make apparent the elements and methods of building fictitious persons. For this purpose we set up a matrix comprising all possible features of a person. It is structured on the basis of logical and systematical definitions and can be expanded as necessary.

At this stage it comprises about 2.200 different codes, ranging from entries like >tall< or >unusually short middle finger< or >from a well-to-do family< to >unpredictable behaviour<.

This permanent PTF serves as a guideline for the individual PTF: A special program stores the individual features of a fictitious character into their proper places within the permanent PTF. Additional statements, facultative or obligatory, serve to analyze the narrative techniques or to document the process of recording.

There are many ways of exploiting these data: determination of prototypes, methods of presentation, qualitative and quantitative standards, characterisation, analysis of a single or comparison of several characters.

While the proper scholarly work has still to be done by the researcher, the necessary time-consuming and error-prone business of structuring, assorting and filing away can be done by PTF. So, we minimize the risk of selective that is restrictive perception of given data and put this special aspect of our research on an objective basis by means of a separate and structured procedure. On an average, we have one to two hundred entries per story for leading characters like the murderer or the victim.

Of course PTF is not in any way limited to mystery stories, but can be used in the analysis of all types of fiction.

SOC (Sociogram) codes and analyzes all bi-, tri- and multilateral relations in a given mystery story. It is based on:

1. a wide, comprehensive set of categories (i.e. code lists) which comprises all kinds of general relations (family, emotional, social etc.) as well as those specific to the genre, like criminal-victim, witness, intentional or accidental accessory etc.

2. a program which converts the code-list-based static and dynamic data, resulting from our text analysis, into ASCII textfiles. Here are some of the questions which we believe can be answered by CID: How closely does the narrator interact with the novel's personnel, or - genre specific - how often do nephews murder their rich uncles because of the specific British laws of inheritance?

CTF (Crime Typology File) standardizes 'crime', the constitutive phenomenon of the mystery story, in its entire complexity and relevance, and converts it into a DP(data processing)-suited format. The data acquired may then be used to analyse - via quantitative or qualitative parameters - the particular features of a given text or of the genre as such.

For PTF, SOC and CTF, we are following the same routine: After having carefully read the text, we extract the typology-relevant data and input them in clear via a screen-displayed menu. The active acquisition program automatically allocates the data to the corresponding typology fields. Currently the data are stored in ASCII text files; in future we will use a relational database.

Crucial from a basic point of view and for mystery story analysis in particular is the precise distinction between the giver or transmitter and the receiver of a piece of information. The model developed by Fieguth is generally recognized as the most exact description of the transmitter/receiver interlacing.

The special relevance of this model for the mystery story seems quite obvious: With regard to the transmitter side it is important to know who gives a particular piece of information: the characters in a story may lie, the figural narrator is allowed to make mistakes, which the authorial narrator may not do. The precise identification of the persons receiving a piece of information makes it possible to determine for each point in time of the narrated story what - according to the reader's knowledge - a particular person knows or does not know.

For that reason, the scenario description records, with reference to page and line, who gives which information to whom.

By this method it becomes possible to lay open the specific obscuration and revelation techniques of the mystery story: Although it is its main objective to build up tension founded in mystery and secret, it is an inviolable rule of the genre of classical mystery stories to present the reader with all and any of the clues necessary for the final solution. It is well known that writers at being received into the Crime Writers' Association are required to swear an oath "never to hide a vital clue from my readers".

For this reason, the author has to separate the clue as far as is possible from the question it may help to solve. Our method of assembling and storing data allows us to give precise information on obscuration and revelation techniques; correlation between the three typology files and the scenario description is an especially helpful tool in this respect.

In our presentation of the project we use Agatha Christie's "Death on the Nile" as an example.

A wealthy heiress - whose life various people are after for various reasons as the reader, in part, knows, - is murdered during a steamer trip on the Nile, approximately in the middle of the book. The second part of the novel deals with Hercule Poirot's investigation among the closed circle of people on board the ship which, after the murder, nobody can leave.

The personage typology analysis shows a high density of personal data on the victim and all suspects. Other than in most detective stories which begin with the discovery of the corpse, most of the victim's data are disclosed while the heiress still lives, and not by "hearsay evidence" after the murder.

The same is true for the victim's sociological relations, as listed in the sociogram. On the other hand, "Death on the Nile" in this respect comes near to the typical "Whodunnit", where the victim is placed in a close net of "deadly" relations, among which the detective has to find the right one.

With regard to the central crime, the crime typology evidences that it belongs to a clearly defined subclass of the detective story: The concealment of the perpetrator is achieved by a simple, but extremely effective faking of an alibi, which results in the classical "Howdunnit".

The characteristic feature underlined in the personage typology analysis, viz. that events anteceding the murder are told in all detail, becomes also apparent in the description of the scenario, by the largely linear narration of the plot, without having recourse - otherwise typical for detective stories - to untold anteceding events. This is reflected in the narrative technique which makes use chiefly of the figural narrative situation and scenic presentation, with authorial interventions now and again.

These observations, both on the structuring of "Death on the Nile" and on the formation of subclasses in the genre, are statistically substantiated within the CID project, and thus can be verified intersubjectively.

In addition to obtaining an account of the micro and macro structuring of the orthodox mystery story, we can use CID to follow the genesis of the genre and its constitutive elements in Germany, France, England and the U.S. in the 19th century, as well as to describe the disintegrative process which has become apparent for instance in France, Germany and Sweden since the fifties.

Beyond our immediate subject, our project will result in statistically confirmed insights into the structuring of fiction in general.

Figure:

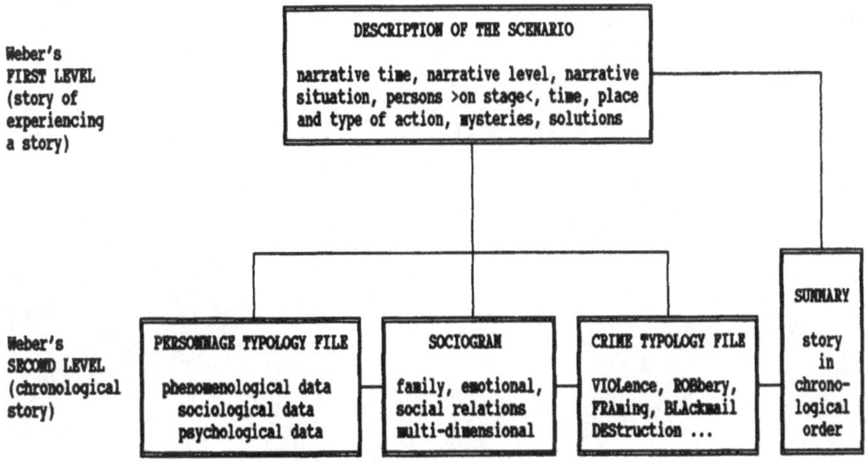

NOTE

* Volker Neuhaus, Harald Böhm, Doris Deinet, Martina Gierling, Wolfram Gierling, Daniela Hermes, Rainer Lippke, Andrea Maushagen, Dagmar Schier, Anne Thurnburg, Petra Trinkaus

REFERENCES

CHRISTIE, A. 1956. (First published 1937). *Death on the Nile*. Harmondsworth, Middlesex: Penguin
FIEGUTH, R. 1973. "Zur Rezeptionslenkung bei narrativen und dramatischen Werken." *Sprache im technischen Zeitalter* 43, 186-201
WEBER, D. 1975. *Theorie der analytischen Erzählung*. München: C. H. Beck

A NEW LITERARY CLASSIFICATION METHOD: THE CASE OF JANE AUSTEN

Cheryl M. Upchurch, Robert L. Oakman
University of South Carolina
USA

Of special interest to linguists, those interested in the humanities and computer sciences is the use of the computer to process text or natural language. Information retrieval systems are used to retrieve natural language information items. Computers are used to develop word indexes, concordances, dictionaries, thesauri and abstracts from natural language input. Computers are even used to attempt to prove or disprove authorship of some literary works. These applications require grouping of similar information in some form. This process called clustering is pertinent to the study of natural language.

For this project, we plan to illustrate that a classification method developed by Robert Ehrlich, University of South Carolina, and William E. Full, Wichita State University, for use in the field of geology, will classify text as well. We compare this algorithm with the theoretical properties of other clustering available today. What are the problems or downfalls of other algorithms? Cân the proposed algorithm theoretically eliminate these problems? The texts we will use for analysis are all six of Jane Austen's novels, plus *Sandition*, which was left unfinished at her death and completed later by another woman.

In the field of geology, most samples are actually mixtures of simpler components. For example, a rock could be made up of several different components, rather than a pure sample comprised of one element. This had been tested and proven in several branches of geology: sedimentology, paleontology and petrology. The goal of the geologists is to unmix the samples. Ehrlich and Full's algorithm defines "sub-populations" that, when mixed together in various proportions, can reproduce the original data set.(1)

In the case of natural language, we intend to show that language, too, is a mixture of components. In order to classify or cluster the text, three parameters need to be determined:

1. Number of components in the sample (in our case, chapters)
2. Identify of each component
3. Relative proportions of each component in each sample.

The only assumption for this project is that the frequency of words is non-random in language. Some words are characteristic of the domain in which they appear, i.e. culturally determined.

The input to the algorithm is word frequency, as expressed in the form of percentages. Then we construct a matrix; columns consist of selected words, and rows include frequency percentages of the words within selected chapters. The column vectors sum to a constant.

The new algorithm itself is divided into two parts. The first determines the number of components in the sample. It does this by taking the constant-sum matrix and determining the number of eigenvectors necessary to maintain the relationship between the original frequency vectors. The number of eigenvectors equals the number of components in the sample.

In the second part, the compositions and the frequencies are determined. In simple terms, the second stage builds a geometric object (cluster) to enclose the data vectors. This is done by either EXTENDED QMODEL or FUZZY QMODEL. Both are iterative procedures which start with an initial polytope, a straight-sided geometric figure. The polytope is then enlarged and rotated until a convergence occurs. The two procedures differ in how the initial polytope is found. EXTENDED QMODEL determines the number and position of the components which are the most mutually extreme samples for the initial polytope. FUZZY QMODEL defines the initial polytope by the general dimension of the sample. The output of both procedures indicates which words belong together as a component and what the rations are. It is defined in terms of the original words.

This algorithm is expected to eliminate many problems associated with existing clustering algorithms for the reasons cited below.

1. Any step of the proposed analysis can backtrack and retrieve all data. Since it destroys no information, it reports on true data.
2. The determination of sub-clusters is mathematically sound and valid.
3. It has the strength of fuzzy clusters.
4. It assumes no initial distribution of data; that is, it possesses no required or predetermined data structure.
5. It does not calculate cluster centers as a frame of reference.
6. It is based on linear combination and a true columns and rows matrix.

We plan to test the validity of the algorithm by checking the results of this method with well known documents of sufficient length. The documents chosen are all six of Jane Austen's novels, plus *Sandition*, which is written partially by Austen and partially by another woman. We analyzed the results to see if the clusters formed will reveal the following:

1. *The chronology of the novels*
   Although the chronology of the first three novels is undecided, we hope to establish publishing order with our method. The publishing date of *Northanger Abbey* shows it to be the last published in full, but it was the first to go to the publisher (1803). Following is a list of Austen's books, the date she began writing them, the date she finished them, and the publishing date:

	BEGINNING DATE	COMPLETION DATE	PUBLISHING DATE
A. *Emma*	Jan. 1814	Mar. 1815	Dec. 1815
B. *Mansfield Park*	Feb. 1811	1813	May 1814
C. *Northanger Abbey*	1797	1798	Dec. 1817
D. *Persuasion*	1815	Dec. 1816	Dec. 1817
E. *Pride and Prejudice*	Oct. 1796	Aug. 1797	Jan. 1813
F. *Sandition*	Jan. 1817	Mar. 1817	1925
G. *Sense and Sensibility*	Nov. 1797		Nov. 1811

With our method, can we discern a difference between the novels' publishing order and the order Austen wrote them? Is there any overlap among the novels? For example, did the author perhaps work on more than one at a time?

2. *What chapters belong to which novel*
   Given numerous chapters from various novels, do the clusters generated reveal which novel the chapter belongs to?

3. *The mood or contents of the chapter*
   Can the algorithm group the chapters according to their content? For example, will all love scenes be in the same cluster?

4. *The text written by Jane Austen versus the text written by The Other Lady*
   Austen started her novel *Sandition* in January 1817 and worked on it until March of that year. When she died in July 1817, only part of the novel was complete and part in summary. Another author tried to imitate Austen's style in completing the novel. Reverend Andrew Queen Morton uses samples of *Sense and Sensibility, Emma, Sandition* (Jane Austen) and *Sandition* (The Other Lady) to show that there is a difference in the two ladies' style. For his test, he computed chi-squares for function words such as "a", "and", "the", "this", "with", and "very". Our study will investigate for *Sandition,* whether the chapters can be clustered according to author. Which chapters were written by Jane Austen and which by The Other Lady?

5. *How Austen's style changes*
   Can the clusters indicate any change of style as Austen's career progressed?

6. *How the choice of words used affects the results*
   Is it better for stylistic purposes to choose content words or function words? What is the difference between high frequency words and low frequency words?

Not only are we introducing a new method of literary classification free of many of the troublesome assumptions of other schemes; but with the Austen analysis, we are also testing its usefulness for further stylistic investigations. If the results are promising, we will have introduced a revolutionary classification method to literary analysis.

NOTE

EHRLICH, Robert and FULL, William E. 1987. "Sorting Out Geology - Unmixing Mixtures", in: SIZE, William (ed.). *Use and Abuse of Statistical Methods in the Earth Sciences*. London: Oxford University Press

THE GENERAL INQUIRER III

Peter Ph. Mohler, Cornelia Züll
ZUMA, Mannheim
FRG

Outline

The General Inquirer III contains programs and highly sophisticated classification schemes for an automatic content analysis of texts by a computer. Despite its age, it features some characteristics which make it superior to many more modern programs for literary and other textual computing in the humanities. Among these features are its high speed performance, the availability of tested classification systems, its power in disambiguating ordinary word senses and the possible connection to other text analysis programs or statistical packages. The GI III runs on IBM mainframes and is now distributed to the academic community for a nominal fee. We will sketch out some of these features in the following paragraphs.

Classification Schemes (Dictionaries)

One of the main features of the GI are the classification schemes (content analytic dictionaries) designed for the GI programs. Three major dictionaries, each containing more than 5000 entries (word roots) are now available. The first two are different releases of the well known HARVARD dictionaries developed since 1964 by Philip Stone and his associates. The dictionaries aim to map every single text word into a general socio-psychological frame, where the underlying theory is a compound of Parsonian and Freudian categories. The third dictionary is named the Lasswell-Value-Dictionary (LVD) developed by Zvi Namenwirth and associates. Here, the underlying theory is taken form Lasswell's value theory. While the LVD was designed especially for political texts, the HARVARD dictionaries are more appropriate for fiction and other literary kinds of texts.

By their high complexity the dictionaries provide powerful tools for multivariate analyses like factor analysis, multidimensional scaling or structural modelling. However, this complexity does not facilitate simple, straightforward quantitative analyses. Here, small user defined dictionaries seem to be more appropriate. Thus, the GI III contains special programs which facilitate the design of the users' own dictionaries.

Disambiguation

The philosophy of the afore mentioned dictionaries asks to classify as many text words as possible according to the general scheme of the dictionary. Thus, the GI programs have to resolve ambiguities like "look" (to look, a look), i.e. handle homographs. Kelly and Stone developed a special disambiguiser for the GI which balances well the requirement for accurate classification and good performance of the program. The Kelly-Stone-Disambiguiser works on a sentence by sentence basis. It assigns in an iterative, context sensitive procedure definite word meanings to all homographs listed in the dictionary. The rules for the look up and the definition of word-meanings can be changed by the users of the GI III. The accuracy of the disambiguation is in general higher than 85% compared to manual checks. The speed of the procedure is still high above all other disambiguisers known to us.

General Performance of the GI III

To perform an analysis with the GI and its dictionaries is straightforward and easy to handle for those who are acquainted with IBM mainframes and the IBM JCL. The first step is to format the text into the GI input format, which can easily be done by wordprocessors or special programs like the TEXTPACK program REFORM. Then the text file is read and transformed by a special procedure into an internal GI format (system file). The system file is then input into the main program TAGGER which disambiguates and classifies the text. The output from TAGGER are counts of the categories plus some other information (like a file containing the disambiguated text). These counts can then be manipulated by a GI program named TALLY or via program CONNECT be input into standard statistical packages like SAS or SPSS for multivariate analyses.

In addition to this, the users may re-design the dictionaries according to their purposes or design entirely new dictionaries. To do this asks, however, for some knowledge of the general principles of programming.

There are some limitations to the GI III, namely the number of categories, which can be handled in one single run. This number is fixed to 256. But there are no restrictions to the length of text input into the program other than system restrictions as for example shortage of pub space.

Distribution

The GI III is a consolidated version of the several not at all or not sufficiently documented earlier versions. This version contains all major programs which are necessary to perform content and text analyses as described by Stone et all. (1966).(1) Together with R.P. Weber of the Harvard University we prepared a detailed documentation of the GI III.(2) The GI package and its documentation is now distributed to the academic public for IBM mainframes by ZUMA, the Center for Survey Research and Methodology at B2,1 6800 Mannheim (West Germany) for a nominal fee of $ 100.

NOTES

1. Stone, Philip J. et al. 1966. *The General Inquirer*. Cambridge/Mass.: University Press
2. Züll, Cornelia; Weber, Robert P. and Mohler, Peter Ph. 1988. *Computational Text Analysis - The General Inquirer III*. Mannheim: ZUMA

CAN WORDCRUNCHERS ENABLE THE USER TO ASK SIGNIFICANT QUESTIONS ABOUT LITERARY TEXTS?

Estelle Manette Raben
Department of English, Queens College
City University of New York
USA

In the near-decade since the inception of the International Conference on Data Bases in the Humanities and Social Sciences, a major transformation has occurred. The availability of personal computers has placed in the hands of thousands of individuals the power to perform operations which formerly required not only access to mainframes but extensive programming. Now, in the same spirit that produced standard word processing and spreadsheet programs, we are being offered concordance programs. It is appropriate for us to ask just how useful these programs are, and specifically how well they fit with the current interests of the humanistic community which is being asked to adopt them. In other words, do humanists need word crunchers?

There is, of course, no question that humanists are concerned with words, and that any means of understanding them better (whatever "understanding" means) is a desirable addition to the reader's perception of written art. Thus, we are indebted to the compilers of dictionaries of all sorts, including historical. Some of the enhancements made feasible by computers, like chronologically structuring the headwords in the Oxford English Dictionary (OED), as was done some years ago at the University of Muenster, demonstrate the computer's ability to generate in a relatively simple way the kinds of information that can be of use in understanding literature. We are promised much more help of this kind by means of the CD ROM version of the OED. But the help provided by dictionaries has not yet created any significant new bases for critical insights.

The epoch-making critical works of earlier generations did not rely on the type of verbal information that computers are presently offering. One major critical study, Caroline Spurgeon's *Shakespeare's Imagery*, called attention for the first time to major concatenations of images in the plays, but there is no evidence that she used a concordance to locate them. Another highly regarded study, John Livingston Lowes' *The Road to Xanadu*, located many of Coleridge's images in the books he is known to have read before composing two of his best poems, but Lowes describes his method as simply reading those books and recognizing the source passages. And in our own generation, there is no record of major critical voices crediting concordances (or any other reference work of that type) with insights into the texts they are analyzing.

The current scene in word-crunching is dominated by a general type of program that is recognizably derivative from traditional printed concordances. Most, in fact, promise that printed versions can be produced, even in exotic type faces and alphabetized according to the conventions of many languages. The editors of concordances, locked into a system that rewards only conventionally published volumes of scholarship, are presumably content with programs that satisfy their needs. And so a totally new technology is restricted to functions which can be justified only in terms of antique conceptions.

It is not surprising that computer-based concordances still exhibit many archaic characteristics, since these reference works date back several centuries to the early Renaissance. In all those years, not only has there been no fundamental change in their format or method of compilation, but no one appears to have challenged the concept that an alphabetized listing of an author's vocabulary would reveal aspects of his art and thought that would otherwise remain obscure. (The use of the masculine pronoun is intentional here, for to my knowledge only one woman poet - Emily Dickinson - has been honored with a concordance.) In other words, the computer has merely replaced two key elements in the production of concordances: the drudges who copied citations onto slips and then alphabetized them and the typesetters who reproduced the whole manuscript for printing.

More important than this extension of ancient attitudes into the computer age, however, is the failure of concordances - whether produced by hand or by computer - to support the sorts of analysis that relate to contemporary critical concerns. In their concerns and approaches, the literature on computer studies and on literary studies are as far apart as, say, sociology and psychiatry. Literary conferences usually have no papers on computer applications (or if they do, segregated sessions are established); computer conferences similarly devote little or no time to literary questions. If computer-based methods, and particularly concordance programs, are to fulfill the expectations of their advocates and establish themselves as respected and legitimate tools of scholarship, these gaps must be explored and, if possible, eliminated.

Much of the current hope that concordances will provide keys to deeper understanding of literature is a residue of their original purpose, which was the study of Scripture. A brief review of the concordance's early history reveals an initial enthusiasm matched only centuries later by the early converts to computer-based compilations. It was at the end of the Middle Ages that the spirit of inquiry which generated the scientific and industrial revolutions led to a critical examination of the New Testament. The discrepancies among the four accounts of the life of Jesus troubled those who devoutly wanted to accept this purported historical record. One possible explanation of their dilemma was that the historical truth had been buried under layers of unhistorical additions over years of oral transmission. If only the "core" could be identified, the sacred and indisputable facts could be established.

To achieve this scholarly goal, theologians sought to isolate each word in the four Gospels, on the assumption that any word that appeared in all four was authentic. This quest was pursued for centuries, with the support of popes and kings. Elaborate concordances, now including the Old Testament as well, were major products of the new printing industry, often with such impressive titles as *The Way of Light*. Thus was firmly established the high seriousness of concordance-making and its implied promise of spiritual insights into inherited texts.

By the nineteenth century, this quest for truth spread to include literature that was not considered sacred but was thought to have exalted moral value. It was not uncommon for a dedicated individual to spend as much as a quarter century in the copying and sorting required to produce a single concordance. Among the first authors to be honored in this way were Milton and Shakespeare, followed closely by Wordsworth and Browning. When Steven Parrish began his important series of computer-generated concordances at Cornell University, the poet he selected for the inaugural volume was Matthew Arnold. The Italians at Pisa just as naturally chose Dante as their first poet to achieve a computer-based concordance. Implicit in the dedication of so much energy was the belief that obscure truths lay hidden in a linear text. By drawing out its underlying paradigms, a concordance could lead to a profounder understanding of such a text.

Although very little of this attitude has been explicitly stated since computers came to the aid of concordance-makers (or inspired them in the first place to attempt such projects), it is certainly implicit in the works chosen. Noble assaults have been launched against such indomitable targets as Melville's *Moby Dick* or even the complete novels of William Faulkner. Father Roberto Busa's lifelong analysis of Thomas Aquinas and the writers associated with him obviously derives from a veneration for the saint's teachings. Just as the originators of the concept created concordances to plumb the heart of sacred writings, so their modern followers have canonized authors and texts by implying the same hidden truths awaiting revelation.

Thus, in all of these projects that we are aware of, the flow of information has inevitably been one-way: from the text to the reader. In dealing with sacred materials, one may learn much *from* them but one does not communicate *to* them. The function of the concordance has accordingly not been to change that direction but only to speed the flow and to codify the information. By consulting a concordance, a reader can locate all the occurrences of a particular character string without having to search the entire text. Since the computer has been employed in this work, it is now possible to perform some elementary calculations, such as a word's frequency in relation to the total vocabulary in a text. None of this information, though, relates to the two-way communication between reader and author that is the concern of modern literary criticism.

This generalization holds for all the programs being offered now to put concordance-making power into the hands of anyone with access to a personal computer. The one with the longest apparent history is the Oxford Concordance Program, the latest avatar to be offered by a group at Oxford University whose prime interest appears to be Classical and Oriental languages. Several individual efforts, like that of Philip H. Smith at Waterloo, provide a limited ability to search for character strings. And the latest, WordCruncher, a descendant of the BYU Concordance Program, proclaims its capacity for scanning whole volumes, once they have been properly indexed in a lengthy procedure. The variations among these and others announced as available or forthcoming seem superficial, for they all concentrate on the author's diction and the reader's need to codify it.

This emphasis on the presumably objective element in literature may represent the current status of computer applications in the study of literature. Few scholars trained in the humanities are truly competent programmers, and few competent programmers are truly trained in the humanities. The programs produced by the joint efforts of these two groups are likely to reflect the orientations of the computer scientists more than the humanists. Their overall design and detail show their concern with isolating "key words" and "key phrases." These, of course, are the diction of the author; in other words, the search is for authorial intent, conscious or otherwise.

The discrepancy between the author's intent and the reader's perception lies in the variety of ways in which an idea may be expressed and perceived. What may be key words for the reader may not have been intended as such by the writer, and vice versa. It is even possible that key words are those which do not appear at all. For example, in two major American novels, *The Scarlet Letter* and *Huckleberry Finn*, a key theme is sex, consummated in the first and anticipated in the second. In neither one, however, is that word or any synonym present. In the dialog of *The Scarlet Letter*, the sexual connection between Hester Prynn and Arthur Dimmsdale is alluded to in the most oblique way. *Huckleberry Finn*, written as if by the central figure, who is an adolescent struggling to understand himself, restricts itself the vocabulary available to such a boy and considered by him to be proper in a book. No concordance is likely to reveal how prominent this theme is in these two masterpieces.

Since many concordance programs are created by individuals with credentials in computer science rather than in literature, their shortcomings may be attributed, at least in part, to varying attitudes toward precision in language. In non-literary diction, like that of the sciences and all activities based on them, precision is a paramount concern. Vast amounts of money are invested in establishing rigid semantic boundaries around scientific words, in creating new ones to match evolutions in discovery and technology, and in translating these terms among languages. The entire effort is directed to eliminating ambiguity, which may derive from different cultural perspectives or the passage of time. With literary diction, on the contrary, writers and poets strive deliberately to enrich the meanings of words, to use them in startling ways, to combine them in a manner that will strike the reader's imagination.

This point can be illustrated easily by briefly examining the short opening paragraph in James Joyce's short story "Araby" from his collection *Dubliners*:

> *North Richmond Street, being blind, was a quiet street except at the hour when the Christian Brothers' School set the boys free. An uninhabited house of two storeys stood at the blind end, detached from its neighbours in a square ground. The other houses of the street, conscious of decent lives within them, gazed at one another with brown imperturbable faces.*

The paragraph functions on at least two levels: it is simultaneously informative and suggestive. On the first it communicates the factual information that at the end of a street which in the United States is called a "dead end," in France a "cul-de-sac," and in Germany a "Sackgasse," there is a two-storey house separated from those nearby. While all the others are matched in pairs down the sides of the street, this one stands alone. Objectively, the street is quiet, the houses ordinary. But Joyce has employed a number of words that communicate much more. Starting with the opportunities offered by the British term "blind street," he speaks of the house having "neighbours" who were "conscious" and who "gazed ... with brown imperturbable faces." By the time he reaches the end of this very short paragraph, he has imbued the street and its houses with distinct personalities, identical (we are to learn later) with those of their inhabitants.

"Araby" is a brief anecdote about a pre-adolescent boy who wants to behave nobly toward the first girl who is the object of his burgeoning, unrecognized sexuality. In this attempt he is frustrated by his environment of unfeeling adults. By endowing the street with human characteristics, Joyce succeeds in making the entire neighborhood a character. The houses and their inhabitants reflect one another. The buildings are as respectable but unresponsive as the people who live in them. This was Joyce's feeling about the whole city of Dublin, which he regarded as sterile, unsympathetic, unseeing. All the stories in *Dubliners* dwell on the paralysis of spirit that Joyce felt had driven him from Ireland into exile on the Continent.

But are the words in this paragraph "key terms"? Would a search through the rest of Joyce's short stories and novels reveal a special significance in "blind" and "conscious" and "gazed"? At this point, we can only conjecture what such a search would produce, since the machine-readable text of *Dubliners* has not been edited for scholarly use. But it is a fairly safe conclusion that the particular effect that Joyce creates in this short passage derives from an artistic juxtaposition of words and not from any particular one or even a particular phrase.

That juxtaposition occurs in only one place, the reader's mind. The recognition that the houses are being described as if they were people, that in a sense there is little difference between houses and people, that just as the houses reflect the personalities of their inhabitants, just so the people have taken on the stodginess and brownness of the houses - none of these is implicit in the words themselves. The crucial perception that raises this paragraph from objective reality toward art must function in each individual reader. If no such perception occurs (as happens frequently when young, inexperienced readers first encounter this story), then no meaningful communication can be said to have been established between the author and his audience.

Thus we are led back to the critical disjunction between the efforts of concordance-makers and the concerns of present-day literary critics. In the tumultuous context of shifting sex roles, recognition of non-European literatures, and perspectives from economic, psychological and social positions that were ignored until recent times, a methodology of analyzing literature that was not adequate even when it was developed centuries ago cannot be expected to identify those aspects of literature which really concern readers and critics.

To connect computer-based studies with current critical concerns, developers of utility programs will have to consider such aspects of literature as the changing role of women in Western society, and the consequent outpouring of feminist criticism. For centuries, the very word "woman" denoted inferior status, as in "woman in waiting," "woman of the streets" or "cleaning woman". Derived terms, like "womanish," denote weakness. Synonyms tend to attract the same pejorative values: "lady," once a designation for the high-born, now is generally found in such phrases as "scrub lady". Similar associations relate to race, ethnicity, national origin and social class. To the extent that recent criticism focuses on words, it considers diction in this perspective.

Whether or not traditionally oriented concordances can be enhanced to achieve the sophistication necessary to incorporate this semantic level is a question beyond the scope of this paper. Only speculative possibilities suggest themselves: could the Oxford English Dictionary on a CD ROM be coupled with a concordance program so that meanings appropriate at least to a particular century would be associated with each word being examined? Could the synonyms and antonyms provided by a thesaurus create a semantic environment for every key word? In efforts such as these, however, one fundamental reality persists: as long as computers cannot understand a text, there will always remain a doubt about their capacity to generate data of real value to criticism.

This is not to say that concordances do not have their uses. They can continue to serve in a limited way without being considered tools for literary criticism. Just as dictionaries are reliable reference works, concordances can provide a variety of interesting and potentially worthwhile information. Of course, there must be substantial improvements over what is currently available. There must be a real library of reliable and accurate electronic texts. There must be reasonably simple and straightforward concordance programs. These must provide true interactivity between the user and the text. We must ask, however, whether the results likely to be obtained will justify the expense of time, cash and human energy required to produce them.

The arrival of the computer itself has forced some hard decisions on the academic community. The types of software being offered complicate those decisions, to the extent that they offer users a path that leads away from mainstream literary activity. The promise of the computer has always been certainty and specificity: the accumulation of hard data that would support irrefutable conclusions. Literary criticism has never functioned this way, and never can. Simply refining the techniques for producing a time-worn tool will do little to persuade the world at large that computers and the concordances they generate can truly contribute to the better understanding of literature.

RELATIONAL DATABASES FOR TEXTUAL DATA?

Hans Pruyt
Faculteit der Sociale Wetenschappen
Erasmus Universiteit Rotterdam
The Netherlands

This paper deals with some of the problems that arise, when relational database systems are used for textual data. A strategy to overcome these difficulties will be illustrated. This is done by describing the program Interview Streamliner. This is a database application for use in qualitative social research.

Basic Problems

Relational Database Management Systems are basically designed for processing administrative data. This is reflected in the predominance of fixed length fields, limited to a few hundreds of bytes. Variable length fields are usually not supported. If variable length fields are supported, this support is usually not complete. The methods of indexing are also geared to the world of customer names and part numbers. Index keys are based on entire fields, or in the most flexible arrangements, on fixed parts of fields.

These characteristics limit the usefulness of relational database management systems for processing textual data. Two basic problems arise:

1. Text tends to lack the kind of structure that is needed to fit into fixed length fields,
2. In textual data, index keys that are needed to speed up retrieval can be found everywhere in the fields. This means that the index methods based on whole fields, or on fixed parts of fields, can not be used. Or at least, they can not be used directly.

Interview Streamliner

Relational database management systems have come to dominate the database field. This is probably caused by the conceptual simplicity and elegance of the relational model. This dominance explains why, in spite of the two basic problems mentioned above, relational systems are being used for textual data. An area in which large amounts of textual data are manipulated is qualitative research.

Qualitative research often entails the following procedure:

* semistructured interviews are made and taped,
* the complete text from the interviews is typed,
* the text is split into fragments,
* a first thematic ordering of the material is made. No clear cut logic will be found, which means that there will be many cases, where a fragment will fall into different categories.
* this ordering is changed and refined as new ideas and concepts arise.

The last steps are an iterative process until a framework for a final report has been developed, which contains an interpretation illustrated with striking quotations from the interviews. Accomplishing this task manually might be stimulating, but it is tedious when a large dataset is involved. Because of this, we were not surprised when two researchers, having to deal with nearly two megabytes of interviews about intercultural education, approached us for a computerized solution. We felt that a relational database application could be appropriate for this problem. After 2600 lines of code, we had *Interview Streamliner*, a Clipper program that proved to meet the requirements. Clipper compiles relational database applications into stand alone executable code. As far as we know, it was the first system to support variable length fields that can be searched and edited. Choosing this compiler as the development tool went a long way in taking care of the first basic problem (the problem of field length). Working around the second problem - the lack of indexing support - accounts for most of the complexity of the application. It would have been possible to do without indexing altogether, and to rely on sequential searching for selecting records. This would mean, as database size increases, a degradation of performance. But this was considered not acceptable.

The Interview Streamliner Approach

Interview Streamliner accepts ASCII texts as input. First, the texts must be prepared using a wordprocessor.

* the borders of fragments are indicated, by inserting a special symbol,
* keywords are added to the text. The keywords are identified as such, by using a special symbol as well.

The prepared text looks like this:

```
@
_keyword A_  _keyword B_  _keyword C_
Text fragment .....................
...................................
..................text.............
@
_keyword B_ _keyword C_
Text fragment ....................
..................................
..................................
.....................text.........
@
```

Interview Streamliner adds this text to a database, which is based on the relational model. The structure of an Interview Streamliner database is as follows:

Figure 1:

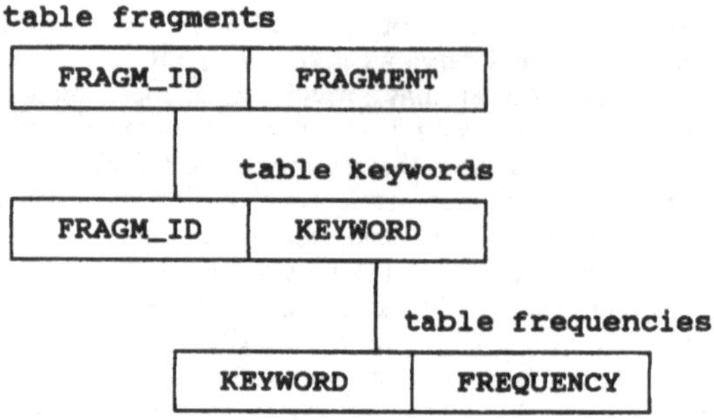

- The table *fragments* contains a variable length field in which the fragments, including keywords, are stored.

The maximum length of a fragment is 32kb.

- The table *keywords* contains all occurrences of keywords.
- The table *frequencies* is a list of all keywords and their frequencies.

Retrieval starts with selecting one or more keywords. In order to view and select keywords, we can browse through the table *frequencies*.

Browsing through the table *frequencies*:

Figure 2:

AI
CAD/CAM
→ Taylorism
computers
contradictions
control
creativity
data bases
degradation
→ expert systems
hardware
humanization
office work
power
→ program generator
security
upgrading
user participation
women
AI

SPACE to select, X to stop

Let us suppose that we want to see those records about expert systems of program generators, connected to Taylorism. The first step is to select the appropriate keywords, then to press *X*. A window appears, showing the selected keywords. The program assigns to every selected keyword a number from 1 to 30. The next step is to enter the query. Instead of the usual command line arrangement for querying textual data, forms are used in Interview Streamliner. In these forms, the numbers referencing the selected keywords can be entered. Because we want to make a complex query in this example, the form *Profile* is chosen.

Figure 3:

```
selected keywords
 ------------------------------------------------------------
| k1 AI                                          count: 24   |
| k2 AI                                          count: 24   |
| k3 AI                                          count: 24   |
| k4 AI                                          count: 24   |
| k5 Taylorism                                   count: 11   |
| k6 expert systems                              count: 13   |
| k7 program generator                           count: 10   |
|                                                            |
 ------------------------------------------------------------

Search  And  Profile  List  Select  1  2  3  X=eXit
--------------------------------------------------------------
Search for one keyword.
```

The form is completed by filling the appropriate spaces with the numbers referencing the selected keywords. If we do not only want to see the output on the screen, but written to a file as well, we can add an option *f* (see Figure 4., page 422).

The output file can later be edited with a word processor. After leaving this form, the selected records that match the search condition are presented. If we want to change a record, for example to add or delete keywords, we press F2. This drops the selected record into a full screen editor, where the required changes can be made. If the changes involve addition or deletion of keywords, the *keywords* and *frequencies* tables are automatically updated.

The approach based on form was chosen because this makes it easier to program procedures that speed up the selection process. The information from the table *frequencies* is used to find the quickest path to the data. For example, when the numbers of the selected keywords are entered in the last form, the row with the lowest total frequency is determined. Then, only the records in the table *fragments* containing the keywords from the row with the lowest total frequency have to be searched. This can save a lot of disk access time. Query optimizing techniques like these were used to minimize the degradation of performance as database size increases.

Figure 4:

```
selected keywords
```

```
k1 AI                                          count: 24
k2 AI                                          count: 24
k3 AI                                          count: 24
k4 AI                                          count: 24
k5 Taylorism                                   count: 11
k6 expert systems                              count: 13
k7 program generator                           count: 10
```

```
(k1  OR k2  OR k█  OR k█  OR k█  OR k█  OR k█  OR k█ )
AND
(k3  OR k█  OR k█  OR k█  OR k█  OR k█  OR k█  OR k█ )
AND
(k█  OR k█ )
AND
(k█  OR k█ )
AND NOT
(k█  OR k█  OR k█  OR k█ )
                                  options: █ (? for option list)
```

Conclusions

Much of the complexity of this application was caused by having to deal with the second basic problem of relational databases: the unsuitability of the provided indexing mechanisms for handling textual data. Interview Streamliner's way to overcome this weakness is by using keywords. This strategy supports the type of qualitative social research that involves interpretation of interview fragments. Of course there are limitations of the keyword approach. Some of the limitation are outlined by Desirée Schipper in her paper *A plea for incorporating a textual datamodel in relational databases*, elsewhere in this volume.

A PLEA FOR INCORPORATING A TEXTUAL DATAMODEL IN RELATIONAL DATABASES

Desirée Schipper
Erasmus University, Rotterdam
The Netherlands

I. Introduction

This conference has shown once again that more and more historians call upon the assistance of computerized techniques in conducting their research. It is also evident that it is not always easy to apply computers to historical sources. Although there is abundant supply of standard software packages that historians can use, it is sometimes necessary to write special made applications. Sometimes because they are using techniques that are not so common in other sciences, like for example record linkage or automated family reconstruction.(1) Most of the time, however, the problems are caused by deficiencies in standard software packages, which are almost exclusively developed for business use.

One of the main problems historians encounter while computerizing their research is to be found in the nature of their sources. Unlike most social scientists, most historians use a lot of qualitative or textual data. Just a minority of historians deals exclusively with quantitative or serial data. I do not mean to say that social scientists do not use textual data at all. However, I do think they often use them in a different way and are also able to employ different techniques. For example, the qualitative data sociologists deal with are often derived from interviews. Here is one essential difference with historians. Their sources are almost unlimited. In principle, they can ask their respondents all the questions that are relevant to their research. So, one could say that to a certain degree they have control over the origination of their sources. Historians, however, do not have any such control. Historical sources are limited in amount and fixed in content. Historical sources have been created in the past with other purposes in mind than historical research. Therefore, the information that has been recorded in many cases falls short of answering the research questions of the historian. Therefore, they have to extract as much information as possible from the available sources. This often means combining information from several sources into one project. It also implies combining information from sources with entirely different structures and different types of data. This poses real problems because most software packages only deal with one datastructure at a time. For example, statistical programs are less suitable for textual data. Also free-text systems do not have facilities for the processing of numerical data. Likewise, databases are very well adapted to numerical and serial data like names, professions etc., but have almost no facilities for handling large bodies of textual data.

Recently, some software applications have been developed for the analysis of qualitative data.(2) One of these programs, INTERVIEW STREAMLINER, developed by my colleague Hans Pruyt is discussed elsewhere in these proceedings. During the conference I have already discussed some of the advantages of this program. Both programs have been developed as a tool for analyzing qualitative data from the social sciences. They do so by using keywords to retrieve information. This method is extremely suitable for analyzing, for instance, interview data. Historians, as I already mentioned, use a lot of qualitative data. As a historian, I wondered whether this program would be very helpful to historians, too.

I think that these programs can be very helpful to historians when using certain kinds of qualitative data. Qualitative data in which it is possible to discern keywords in, or add keywords to the text. Furthermore, all the data used by the historian have to be of a qualitative nature. The fact that these programs operate by the use of keywords restricts their applicability to certain kinds of historical sources. It is not always possible to use keywords with certain kinds of historical data. In the next paragraph I will discuss the limitations of methods that use keywords to retrieve information. In addition, I will pay some attention to the problem I already mentioned before; the difficulties we encounter when we want to compare qualitative sources with numerical or serial sources.

II. The Limitations of Using Keywords

I will illustrate the limitations of applications that use keywords to retrieve data by means of a prosopographical research project that is being performed at the University of Leiden.(3) This project aims at combining data from several different sources to infer the characteristics of the urban elites of Leiden, the so called "Patriciaat", at the end of the Middle Ages. This is done by reconstructing the lives and careers of seven "patriciers families". Information about the "Patriciaat" is found in sources that contain data of a serial and/or quantitative kind like censuses, tax-registers, parish-registers etc., as well as in sources containing running text like criminal reports, letters, chronicles, diaries etc. These texts contain information about persons (names), relations between persons, occupations, official functions and the like which are to be compared with the data in the serial sources.

One way to do this would be to extract the information that is thought necessary and to store it in fields in a database. Prerequisite is that one should have a certain idea about which information is important and which is not. In reality, information that did not seem useful in the beginning turned out to be very important once the research was started. Even if it would have been possible to decide at the beginning of the research project which information would be used, this would still have meant a great loss of potential information. This would render the machine readable data useless for secondary analysis. Therefore, it was decided to store the integral text.

Although part of the information now is available in machine- readable form, it still has to be compared with the more serial data stored in database-files. For example, we would like to search the running text for names that occur in, amongst others, the censuses. What is needed is some procedure to locate the required information in the running texts and perhaps store them in a database field. Using a program like the ones mentioned before requires that the names that have to be located are indexed. They are not, however. It is useless to try to index all the names that occur in the text at the beginning of the research. We would have to search the file manually, locating the names and setting them apart. But that is just what the computer should do.

An alternative approach would be to locate the names with a special text-retrieval package. But there are some major drawbacks to this method, too. Using a text-retrieval program only solves our first problem. We are no longer confined to the use of keywords. Text-retrieval packages do not offer a solution to the other problem. Comparing sources containing different kinds of data still is very difficult to accomplish when we use a text-retrieval program. Suppose we would like to compare a database containing data from a census-list with criminal reports in order to locate names from the census in the reports. After a name has been located in both sources the positions where the names occur have to be related. Perhaps information from the criminal record has to be transferred to the database. Besides the plain transfer of information, the name and its position in the criminal record (or other text) have to become permanently linked to its corresponding name in the list. We could pick one name from the list and use a text-retrieval package to search for the corresponding name in the text. If we actually located a corresponding name we would have to mark this in the database and transfer the information we might need from the text to the database. Then, we would have to go back to the list, get the next name and start all over again. This procedure has two major disadvantages: the searching happens interactively and although information is transferred from the text to the database, the occurrence of the name in the text is not permanently linked to the name in the list. It would be far more efficient if we could let the computer process all the names in the list consecutively without interference of the user. Since the two names are not permanently linked we will have to start searching all over again if we want to extract more information about the person.

III. Towards a Textual Data Model for Relational Databases

It is much more convenient if it would be possible to store both the list and the reports in a database (or connected datasets) and have the program search the text for occurrences of the names that are in the list. Every time a corresponding name is detected in the text it can be marked in an index or catalog so that it would be permanently linked to the name in the list. In this way the names can be located very easily, if additional information from the text is required. I have tried to visualize this in picture 1. The double arrows in the picture indicate the relations as they would be marked in the index or catalog. The relations marked in the catalog serve as pointers towards the position in the text where, if needed, additional information about the person can be found. An other advantage of this method is that we do not have to keep duplicate information. This will avoid both the risks of redundancies and inconsistencies in our data.

If we look at the present state of software technology it is evident that almost none of the existing database management systems is well equipped for handling textual data. Although most packages have some facilities for handling short or medium sized strings of a fixed length, most database management systems have difficulty in handling very long strings of variable length. In my opinion this is not because it is impossible or too difficult to build in a good textual data-model, but because database management systems are primarily designed for business use. To overcome these basic weaknesses in standard software, historians have to build their own applications. In doing so, however, they are constantly reinventing the wheel. Therefore, it would be very convenient if standard databases could handle large amounts of textual data. They should also have some of the features of text-retrieval systems built in. This would facilitate the process of searching within the text.

If we are able to incorporate a textual data-model, with the facilities of a textindexing- or textretrieval-system in relational databases we can have the best of two worlds. On the one hand we could use all the extra facilities databases have to offer in the handling of structured and (semi-) numerical data, like mathematical functions, aggregation, quick sorting, retrieving, rearranging etc. On the other hand we could store our textual data in an efficient way without having to use several different software packages. Then it would be very easy to extract relevant data from running texts and store them in database fields. Subsequently, we could compare them with more structured data. There would be no necessity of coding the data in advance which could cause a great loss of potential information. What is more, we would not have to bother about the output of one software package not fitting the input requirements of others.

Figure:

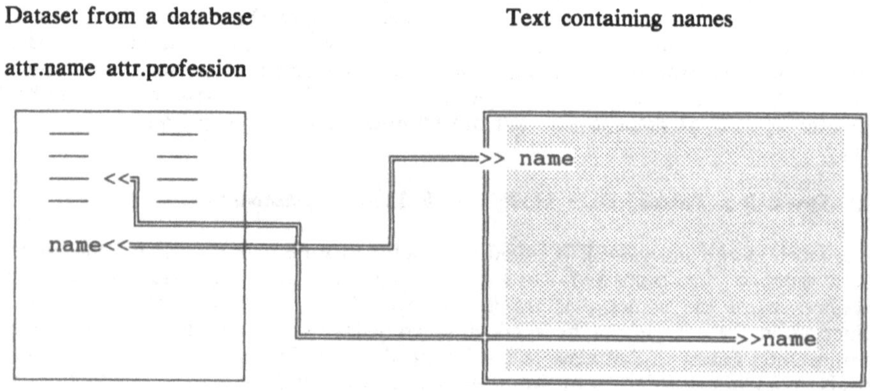

NOTES

1. Although both techniques are applied in other disciplines, too. For example record linkage in medicine and family reconstruction in demography.
2. PETERS, V.A.M. 1988. *De computer als hulpmiddel bij kwalitatieve analyse*. SURFen met een toetsenbord, een congresverslag. Delft, 335-349
3. Brand, A.J. 1987. *IN POLITIEKE KRINGEN: de familie Paedze van Sonnevelt en de verdeling van de macht in Leiden aan het einde van de middeleeuwen*. Leidschrift. Leiden, June 1987, 40-65

MOLLUSCS - A PACKAGE FOR POETRY

Charles Whitaker
United Kingdom

Who but a poet can convey
The subtle nature of a living day,
The world of our most careful thought,
That sensitive experience which ought
To illuminate the darkest night
With understanding of our human plight
And sympathy with different aims -
All that our best devotion claims?
When words are notes and chords of music,
Their impact and their sense intrinsic
In a whole we mean to know:
Waves of delight and tides below -
Fast, detailed digital machines
Alert us to aesthetic themes,
Explore subconscious writing arts
And free us to perceive those parts
Which attune and harmonise perception
Closer to our poets'intention -
To appreciate, enriched, their mind
Through revelations more refined!

The general purpose of *Molluscs* is to cluster all usable powers of the machine round our favourite poetry and stylish prose, and so discover elements of meaning, significant nuances of expression, changes of key or of harmony, communicative techniques which illuminate the interpretation, melodies which enrich, rhythms which emphasise, oral enunciation which simulates or even inspires parallel emotions.

In short, the machine unconsciously reveals riches of which we ourselves were unaware. How is that possible? Perhaps because the machine has no axes to grind,prior assumptions or oriented sensibilities? Neither have we! It must be the infinite patience, faultless accuracy, astonishing rapidity with which every detail can be compared, located, counted, tested, listed, noted and reported. It must also be as userfriendly as it is possible to make it - at all levels of the mechanisms - and that it already is, surely, to a wonderful degree.

For appreciation and understanding of poetry, the critical question is how creatively interactive our use of the friendly machine can be. Insights into meaning and responses to artistic communication often occur unpredictably, stimulated by a different angle of view or a change of attitude, alerted by a detail, perhaps, at the turning of a page. Certainly the machine can raise the probability of fresh thoughts surfacing, provided that it is collaborative (and collaborable) enough. If all applicable facilities are to hand while we have our mind on the poem and our ideas can be noted on screen straight away, attached to the feature which aroused them, there is a good prospect of progress!

To maximise interpretative opportunity, so to speak, word lists, concordances, word counts, random syllable matching, linear graphic alliteration statistics, flexible search routines, overall graph frequency surveys, pitch and tone musical diagrams, rhythm, metre and style pattern coding and analysis - all work together (With a file management register to hand and index our vocabulary programs alongside) directly accessible for application to the piece of pieces being studied (or groups of pieces, selections by alphabet, line numbers or labels, with individual character in plays isolable, individual odes in books of poetry separable) - in a single system with fully selective output and direct on-screen annotation (and disc output storage with further selection when printing, if required).

This is what *Molluscs* is intended to provide, and I am keen to ensure (by quick response to any problem encountered) that it really des so. It is available free for charge to academic institutions (and individual academics); please contact me at the address given below if you are interested!

The system is also designed to be self-explanatory; that is to need no supplementary paper work, because all demonstrations are built in an accessible while working. Because all output can be stored (on the hard disc for transfer to personal discs by automatic procedures at the end of the session), printing can be done at more convenient times, or temporary problems of access to printers can be overcome; concentration is not distracted, use can remain fully interactive, incipient ideas live on and investigations are kept intelligibly related.

By the way: if it would be useful to reshape presentation of the output to suit a text in literary criticism, then as the material on hard disc is about to be transmitted to personal discs, put TRANSTOR into TXT mode (press T!) and it will go wordprocessable. Similarly, when texts are available on standard TXT discs, they can be transmuted (selectively, with screen display and opportunity for correction) into *Molluscs* files. If one has several dozen short poems in each of a number of books, no problem! They can be in one file with line numbers including references, which the line selection routines can recognise when individuaL poems or groups of them are to be separated out for processing. Suppose areas of interest are scattered over a text and need examining individually and collectively labelled at speed and programs directed to take up lines with one particular label or a group of them.

All operations are menu-driven: that is, instructions are given to the machine as choices of number, character or symbol, and current processes are controlled by keys specified in message lines. In this way, menus and messages map the route and options available at any point are shown on the screen.

The diagram at the end of this abstract shows the central menu as it appears on the screen (please regard the thicker lines as equivalent to double lines on the machine). The options fall broadly into three categories: Management (a-n), Processing (o-v) and Information (1-5). Management seems sufficiently clear in the menu; May I briefly describe the other two sections?

MELODY (o) enhances perception of sound effects by showing vowels or consonants on quasi-musical staves. Precision with accented vowels is adjustable for French and German. Corrections for divergence of spelling from natural phonetics are easily made. Screen reference gauges and a panel for three lines of notes help preserve insights and inspired thoughts with disc storage or printing.

CARA (p) and CODAC (q) provide diagrammatic line labelling with ten symbols at four levels - for metre and rhythm only, or for all forms of analysis. The diagrams are translated automatically into machine-processable letter codes for examining features and recurrent patterns. They may be included in a special convertible code, if you wish, for easy recall, and stored or printed for visual comparison.

FINDTEXT (r) and FINDCODE (s) are for searching; precise or partial letter patterns may be found within lines, or regarding the file as a single line. In DECO mode they survey complete files or file sections in precision graph counts to show relative frequency or choose areas of interest for further investigation. Onflowing lines may be viewed incidentally.

WORDLIST (t) derives a key file from which full concordances, word lists, percentage or plain word counts, with totals and maximum lengths noted, may be produced. Pages or individual lines of concordances may be selected and annotated on screen for disc storage and review or direct printing. Labels may be used to limit them to particular characters in plays or areas of interest in the text.

MATCH (u) takes the number of characters you specify and finds which groups that length recur anywhere in the file or file section. Line ends may limit this random matching, or be disregarded. Word divisions are ignored. This is invaluable for detecting unsuspected effects, even in thoroughly familiar poetry, often revealing more meaning and subtlety.

ALLIT (v) makes comparative graphs of alliteration in two files or sections of files, simple graphs and precision count tables with percentages. For individual lines, it gives reports on all repetitions of letters above the minimum count you specify, numerically or in row displays. Selection and annotation of pages or lines preserves perceptions!

For information options (1-5) no disc is needed in drive A: that is, you do not have to be a user to find out about it (or if the system is in use with a personal disc installed, it does not need to be removed when taking these options). Option 6 (FLEXibility) does need a disc of course, because its purpose is to put useful material on it!

FACILIST (1, facilities list) is effectively a central menu for the information options designed to make *Molluscs* self-explanatory. System checklists are available here, too.

BRIEF (2) gives single panel descriptions of all the main programs. This is available on paper, too; please write, if you would like a copy.

ROVE (3) provides a tourist visit to all the menus contained in the programs to see how the system works without actually using it!

APPLY (4) lists 75 words familiar in descriptions of literature and language. Opting for one of them puts a five line note in the panel display suggesting which programs might be used to analyze in that area.

SELECTION (5) gives full details of Selective Printing and Annotation and other ancillary facilities intended to be responsive to the critic at work with the machine.

FLEX (6) puts on one's personal disc a selection of short poems in eight languages.
or the Disc Output Storage FLOPSTOR to review or print output on the disc independently of *Molluscs* - that is, on any available machine!

To sum up: how is the function of the machine best described in this approach to the appreciation of poetry? Surely not artificial intelligence or sensibility until machines can weep, choke with anguish, grind with wrath or glow with bliss? Perhaps the artificial subservient intelligence of a poetaster's secretary? This seems a perversely poetic description of a PC!

Should the question rather be how the critic experiences the relationship - as enhanced awareness, sophisticated discrimination, alerted response, angled perspective or even contorted recognition? Is not that artificial presumption, machine arrogance? Where is the professional deference and discretion?

In the menus! The machine is menu-driven, the critic menu-resourced: applications are at his discretion, interpretations through his discernment. There is almost always more to learn because, as Wassily Kandinsky wrote:

"Every work of art comes into existence, from a technical point of view, exactly as the universe came into existence - through a series of catastrophes which began with chaotic rumblings and ended in the symphony we all call the music of the spheres."

And there is no substitute for the intimate personal rapport Marc Chagall paints in "I and the Village". This is the poet's and his critic's private world, where a PC must evince machine modesty or contaminate the natural environment!

The name *MOLLUSCS* is an approximate acronym for *MO*dern *L*anguages and *L*atin *U*ser-friendly *S*ystem for *C*oncordances and *S*uchlike, and was inspired by the sight of the creatures clustering under water round a North Sea Oil Rig in a Shell television advertisement. The company was actually promoting a chemical preparation to dissuade them from clinging to such apparatus, but that seemed incidental, and even focused the mind on a need for exploratory procedures to be clustered round a poetic (or prosaic) object of interest! The accent sets (on function keys plus codes) cover Old English, French, German, Italian, Portuguese and Spanish. *Molluscs* has been in use for four years now, though it is becoming much more developed (dare I hope sophisticated?) than it was at first. If there are any questions anyone would like to ask, I should be delighted to try to answer them, and to help in any way I can with applications.

Figure: MOLLUSCS - Central Menu Diagram

OPTIONS in MOLLUSCS   Output Mode: Disc Store   Printer

a TEXT, entry or edit	b TRANSFER, .TXT files	source	c DOS sequential disc copies
d INCARD, index entry	e INCALL, index output	lists	

f REGISTER, check the lists of files on personal discs g FILEVIEW, inspect or print out files on personal discs h CONVERT, modify files (reverse, recode, join, back up)	management of text & code files
i FLOPSTOR, j HARDSTOR, output review or print	k TRANSTOR < output l check store space m Check floppy disc
o MELODY, tone patterns p CARA, rhythm code	n system checklist
q CODAC, analysis code r FINDTEXT, s FINDCODE, search	
t WORDLIST, concordances, word counts or lists (% option)	spacer bar to STOP
u MATCH, list all repeats of n characters in text or code	
v ALLIT, count or graph reports on lines or whole texts	

1 FACILIST	2 BRIEF	3 ROVE	4 APPLY	5 SELECTION	6 FLEX	review

please key in the marker of your choice   (w notes on disc formatting)

Machines: XT, AT & networks (5.3" discs: 8 DD or 4 HD) PS/2 model 50 upwards (3.5" discs: 4 DD or 2 HD). Hard disc space needed: 2.5 Megabytes with 1 more for Output Storage.

Address: Charles Whitaker, 12, Heatherdeane Road, Highfield, Southampton S02 1PB UK (0703) 554068

TUSTEP

Wilhelm Ott
Zentrum für Datenverarbeitung
Universität Tübingen
FRG

Among the first large humanities computing projects supported in the late 60s and early 70s by the Computing Center of the University of Tübingen were the "metrical analysis of latin hexameter poetry" and the "Concordance to the Vulgate". Experiences gathered with these and other projects showed us that despite the special requirements of each project there are many common functions which are needed whenever, in humanities applications, texts are to be handled or analyzed by computer.

These experiences induced my group to give up programming for single projects and to develop a series of systematically interrelated programs for the reocurring basic functions of text data processing. In the meantime, these programs are known as the "TUebingen System of Text-Processing Programs", TUSTEP. This development was made possible by the fact that the University of Tübingen had created, in 1970, at its Computing Center a Department of "Literary and Documentary Data-Processing".

TUSTEP consists of a set of closely interrelated programs for the most important basic operations of text data processing. The functionality of the single programs may further be specified by user-supplied parameters. The programs themselves may be combined in manifold ways to solve problems of the most diversified kind (e.g. in the fields of information and documentation, scholarly editing, philological sciences, historical sciences). They cover all steps of processing, from the input (including the support of optical scanning techniques) up to the output in letterpress quality by photocomposition.

The term "text data processing" has been chosen in order to distinguish the typical field of application of TUSTEP from what is commonly understood when speaking of text processing or word processing. Of course, also the functions required for document preparation (like inputting, correcting, formatting, printing texts) are available in TUSTEP; these are functions which are required for the preparation of publications and for documentation in the whole field of scholarship, including both humanities and sciences. TUSTEP, however, has been developed as a tool for that part of the scholarly world where texts are the object of scholarly research: philology, literary studies, linguistics, historical sciences, librarianship: i.e. fields of research where not only new texts are to be produced and published as the result of scholarly work, but where existing texts (including literary texts and historical sources) are to be saved for the future by new critical editions, to be analyzed concerning language, style, contents, or to be catalogued in bibliographies.

The tasks which are processed with the help of TUSTEP range from typing a seminar paper to the preparation of large bibliographies, lexica, indexes, concordances, dictionaries, critical editions and - of course - monographs; the final output is normally prepared by photocomposition in a quality to which one is accustomed to from letterpress printing. Beyond the normal word processing functions, these tasks require programs for decomposing texts into elements (governed by rules provided by the user), for building logical entities consisting of more than one line of text, for sorting such elements or entities (allowing also for rules of non-latin alphabetic order and other sorting criteria), for automatic collation of different versions of a text, for extracting numerical information contained in a text, etc.

Basic Operations of Text Data Processing in TUSTEP

The most important operations of text data processing covered by TUSTEP programs include:

EDITING
Entering, modifying, replacing and searching of text data with the text editor at a data display device [#EDIT]
Automatic correction of text data with the help of correction instructions previously defined by the user (e.g. in cases in which an interactive correction with the editor is not efficient) [#CORRECT]

COMPARING
Comparing of different versions of a text; protocolling and storing of identified differences [#COMPARE]
Listing, in synoptic lines, the basic text and the differences contained in the other versions [#COLLATE]

PROCESSING
Selecting, substituting, rearranging, completing, compressing and comparing of text parts on the basis of given rules and conditions; calculating with numerical values (including calendar-dates), which are already given in the text or can be derived from it; output in various formats (also for subsequent processing outside of TUSTEP) [#COPY]
Maintaining and actualizing of cross-references [#NUMBER]

PREPARING INDEXES
Preparing index entries by decomposing text units into their elements or by extracting marked text parts; if necessary, by additionally completing and modifying text parts; defining the sort criteria and the sort alphabet; completing the reference; distinguishing different types of entries [#PINDEX]

PRESORTING
Combining text parts which logically belong together in order to form sort units; defining the sort criteria (selection and sequence of certain parts of the text units) which can freely be chosen; defining the sort values for any string of characters and defining the sort alphabets, which will be used to determine the sequence of the text units to be established by the subsequent sorting [#PRESORT]

SORTING
Rearranging the sort units prepared by programs like #PINDEX and #PRESORT [#SORT]

GENERATING INDEXES
After SORT, reducing multiple and perhaps hierarchically structured index entries or text units to single entries; completing and substituting text parts and references;

distinguishing different types of entries; calculating absolute and relative frequencies [#GINDEX]

GENERATING LISTINGS
Preparing output for line printers, daisy wheel printers, dot matrix printers, laser printers and microfilm recording devices

* in the form in which the data are recorded on the file (control characters are not interpreted but printed) [#GLISTING]
* in a format and an arrangement which can be defined by control characters contained in the text, using the whole inventory of typefaces and characters which is available for the selected printer, with automatic hyphenation and automatic line division and page make-up, including line justification and placing of footnotes [#FORMAT]
* for predefined forms (e.g. address stickers, catalogue cards, standardized letters, office forms) [#GFORMS]

PHOCOMPOSITION
Transforming text data into a form required by a photo composition device (presently DIGISET and Monotype LASERCOMP), including automatic line division (with and without line justification and tabular setting) and automatic page make-up with running titles, headings, text, insertions in smaller type, marginal setting, footnotes and up to nine critical apparatuses at page bottom; great variety of typefaces and special characters [#COMPOSITION]

(The names preceded by # in the above list of basic operations are the translation into English of the respective TUSTEP command names. In the actual version of TUSTEP, which speaks and understands German only, they are, in the above order: #EDIERE, #KAUSFUEHRE; #VERGLEICHE, #VAUFBEREITE; #KOPIERE, #NUMERIERE; #RVORBEREITE; #SVORBEREITE; #SORTIERE; #RAUFBEREITE; #DVORBEREITE, #FORMATIERE, #FAUFBEREITE; #SATZ.)

Each of these programs covers more or less one basic operation of text handling only; these basic operations may be adapted to the specific requirements by user supplied parameters. The programs may be freely combined according to the needs of the respective application.

This approach did not only save us a lot of project-specific programming, but also allowed us to make the humanities scholar independent of the knowledge of programming and job control languages and of the help of programmers: the handling of TUSTEP is easy enough, the parameters are problem-oriented enough to allow the scholar himself to solve also non-trivial data processing problems.

File Handling and Job Control in TUSTEP

In order to make the user independent also from the specialities of different operating systems, TUSTEP contains, in addition to the above-mentioned programs for text data processing, all the necessary organizational functions like file handling and defining new commands, functions which are normally covered by the job control language (JCL) of the operating system (OS). Thus, an identical user interface independent of the computer and its OS is provided. Thereby the user not only saves to relearn when passing over to a new computer with a different operating system, but he is also able to adopt unchanged sequences of already existing TUSTEP commands.

The most important respective functions include:

DATA TRANSFER
Transformation of text data in the host's native format (e.g. ASCII-files) into TUSTEP format and vice versa [#CONVERT]

FILE ADMINISTRATION
Creating, cataloging, opening, closing, renaming, deleting files
[#CREATE, #OPEN, #CLOSE, #RENAME, #ERASE]

MAGNETIC TAPE HANDLING
Reading from and writing to magnetic tape (also for compatible data transfer between computers with different operating systems); providing information about the contents of magnetic tapes [#MTREAD, #MTWRITE, #MTCOPY, #MTINFORM]

JOB CONTROL
Executing and controlling sequences of commands and programs; defining and executing user-specific commands ("macros")
[#EXECUTE, #MACRO]

(The actual German command names are, in the above order:
#UMWANDLE; #DATEI, #ANMELDE, #ABMELDE, #AENDERE, #LOESCHE; #MBEINGABE, #MBAUSGABE, #MBKOPIERE, #MBINFORMIERE; #TUE, #MAKRO.)

Working with TUSTEP

The design of TUSTEP starts from the fact that the whole responsibility for the data processing part of a project must remain at the user. So, TUSTEP is far from offering turnkey solutions (it happens that TUSTEP users provide them for other users with similar problems; one of the better known examples is a sophisticated procedure for the preparation of professional bibliographies, which has been prepared by a scholar from the university library on the basis of TUSTEP programs and which may be used almost without any deeper knowledge of TUSTEP).

TUSTEP is a toolbox which requires - and enables a user to do so - to learn how to solve also complex problems in small and controllable steps; the modularity of TUSTEP provides the possibility to perform each step separately and to control the results before executing the next one.

Once the procedures are tested, they can, of course, be run in a single batch, if required, or if the same task occurs again. A large number of projects work like this, e.g. the periodicals "Germanistik" and "Romanische Bibliographie" which since the volumes for 1978 (Germanistik) resp. 1975/76 (Romanische Bibliographie) are prepared and published using TUSTEP; other examples are large editorial projects: the procedures which have been developed and tested for the different steps in the preparation of a volume (input and correction; control of emendations made to the text; establishing of apparatuses; preparation of different indexes used only for the editorial work and of other indexes to be published with the text; automatic composition and pagination; etc.) are used for years - without alteration or in a modified way - for the preparation of further volumes of the same series.

One of the most important requirements of a toolbox like this is to provide continuity over many years and compatibility between different hardware environments and different generations of technology. A user working on a large project can not change everything each time when new hardware appears or when a new operating system is introduced, when he changes the university or when he wants to cooperate with colleagues at other sites. We therefore invested much effort to hide from the user the differences (except, of course, in speed and space) between e.g. PC and mainframe, between an ASCII based and an EBCDIC based hardware. The user should have the possibility to concentrate on his problem, not on the technical environment in which he solves it. He must have the possibility to transport data and programs without difficulty to different places and sites, and to new hardware when technological progress requires it.

The Availability of TUSTEP

We started to develop TUSTEP for our own convenience when supporting humanities projects at the computing center of the University of Tübingen. Our approach described above has been as successful that since 1976 we were asked to make it available also outside of Tübingen. A great number of humanities projects have been carried out or are presently run on the basis of TUSTEP. Almost 600 volumes of books and periodicals which up to now have been published with the help of TUSTEP witness its broad field of application.

Though primarily developed for the use at the University of Tübingen, TUSTEP is in the meantime available at quite a number of other universities. A grant received from the Land Baden-Württemberg for the years 1985-1989 helps us to make it still more useful for new fields of application and more portable to other places. At present TUSTEP is running under the operating systems MVS (IBM), VM (IBM), VMS (DEC VAX), MS-DOS (IBM PC and compatibles). Implementations for further operating systems (presently planned for Siemens BS2000 and for UNIX) will follow.

Figure:

Transkription der griechischen Schrift für TUSTEP

q	w	e	r	t	z	u	i	o	p
	ς	ε	ρ	τ	ζ	β	ι	ο	π

Q	W	E	R	T	Z	U	I	O	P
		Ε	Ρ	Τ	Ζ	Θ	Ι	Ο	Π

a	s	d	f	g	h	j	k	l
α	σ	δ	φ	γ	η	ξ	κ	λ

A	S	D	F	G	H	J	K	L
Α	Σ	Δ	Φ	Γ	Η	Ξ	Κ	Λ

y	x	c	v	b	n	m
υ	χ	ψ	ω	β	ν	μ

Y	X	C	V	B	N	M
Υ	Χ	Ψ	Ω	Β	Ν	Μ

(dies entspricht der Tastatur-Anordnung auf der griechischen Schreibmaschine). Dazu: ᾳ ῃ ῳ *(mit iota subscriptum).*

Beispieltext:

Επειδήπερ πολλοὶ ἐπεχείρησαν ἀνατάξασθαι διήγησιν περὶ τῶν πεπληροφορημένων ἐν ἡμῖν πραγμάτων, καθὼς παρέδοσαν ἡμῖν οἱ ἀπ' ἀρχῆς αὐτόπται καὶ ὑπηρέται γενόμενοι τοῦ λόγου, ἔδοξε κἀμοὶ παρηκολουθηκότι ἄνωθεν πᾶσιν ἀκριβῶς καθεξῆς σοι γράψαι, κράτιστε θεόφιλε, ἵνα ἐπιγνῷς περὶ ὧν κατηχήθης λόγων τὴν ἀσφάλειαν.

Transkription der hebräischen Schrift für TUSTEP

q	w	e	r	t	z	u	i	o	p
	ש		ר	ת	ז	ב	י		פ

Q	W	E	R	T	Z	U	I	O	P
			ר	תּ	זּ	וּ	יּ		פּ

a	s	d	f	g	h	j	k	l
א	ס	ד		ג	ה	ט	כ	ל

A	S	D	F	G	H	J	K	L
א	סּ	דּ		גּ	הּ	טּ	כּ	לּ

y	x	c	v	b	n	m
ע	ח	צ		ב	נ	מ

Y	X	C	V	B	N	M
ע	ח	צּ		בּ	נּ	מּ

Beispiel ohne Vokalisierung:

אשרי האיש אשר לא הלך בעצת רשעים ובדרך חטאים לא עמד

Beispiel mit Vokalzeichen:

אַשְׁרֵי־הָאִישׁ אֲשֶׁר לֹא הָלַךְ בַּעֲצַת רְשָׁעִים וּבְדֶרֶךְ חַטָּאִים לֹא עָמָד

Syrische Schrift (Estrangelo) in TUSTEP

alleinstehend:

nach links verbunden:

nach rechts verbunden:

beidseitig verbunden:

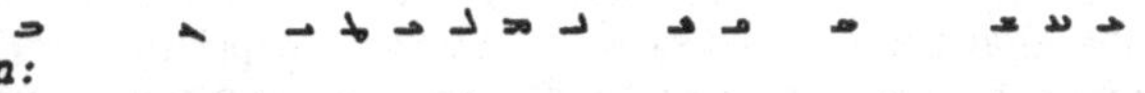

Beispiel:

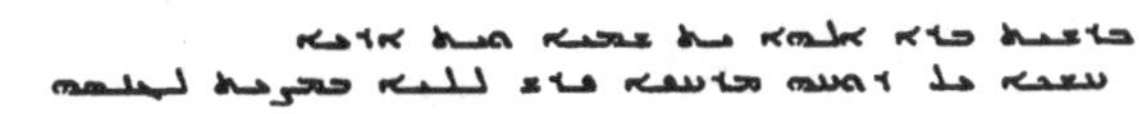

THE SOCIAL IMPLICATIONS OF COMPUTING IN STUDENT RESIDENCES

Philip Brady, Richard Startup
University College of Swansea
United Kingdom

Introduction

This paper reports on our experiences at University College, Swansea where clusters of computer terminals have been provided in student residences. This development was partly inspired by the U.K. Nelson Report (Working Party on Computer Facilities for Teaching in Universities, 1983) which laid great stress on the rapid increase of availability of workstations in universities for student use and their accessibility on a 24 hour per day basis. The Swansea initiative is in line with experience in the United States where during the 1980's there has been a tendency for university computing facilities to be decentralised (McCredie, 1983, pp. 8 and 207).

Computing at Swansea

Until August 1987, the main academic computing service at University College, Swansea - a campus of the University of Wales - was based around a PRIME 750 used mainly for undergraduate teaching and an ICL 2966 used mainly for research. For a number of years the demand for the PRIME 750 service had outstripped its capacity and the problem had become especially acute due to an increase in first year Computer Science student numbers from 80 to 240 in two years. The 1985/6 usage chart - showing the number of terminal hours each week for the first two academic terms - indicated severe 'peaking' as a problem - the peaks occurring as students sought to meet project deadlines. Many steps had been taken to alleviate this overload, such as memory and disc enhancements, but demand still remained unacceptably high, so the College embarked upon its first venture into 24 hour undergraduate access. It initiated an exploratory study into the use of terminals in residential areas by placing them in an on-campus hall. Curiously perhaps there was some unexpected hostility. The porters in the hall made very gloomy predictions of equipment being vandalised. The safety officer complained that one enterprising student had thrown cables out of his tenth floor window to connect his own micro to the network. Computer Science staff complained of 'hackers' using micros in the hall. But these initial problems were soon resolved. Vandalism and theft have been noticeable by their absence. The facility quickly achieved popularity and attracted heavy use. However, there was some resentment by students living elsewhere that they were relatively deprived. This was dispelled when shortly afterwards, further College funds were used to create a terminal room in the Computer Centre itself which could be accessed 24 hours per day. The door of this room has an electronic lock operated by a card, use being automatically logged.

An encouraging reaction to these developments led to a successful application for funds for further expansion to more remote residential areas, under the 'Computers in

Teaching' initiative of the U.K. Computer Board and University Grants Committee (Slater, 1986a and 1986b). The two year study of the implications of this provision has been jointly carried out by the Computer Centre and the Department of Sociology and Anthropology.

Accommodating the Facilities

The residences involved in the expansion were a pair of off-campus halls which are situated together a mile away from the main campus, and a student village which is about a mile and a half distant. These residences presented rather different operational and managerial problems. The pair of halls is self contained with 320 student places in separate men's and women's buildings and there is conventional management by a warden. The terminals were placed in the women's hall in what was formerly a reading room off the library. Thus a valid excuse was provided - were it needed - for men being in a women's building for 24 hours a day! These halls have an isolated location reached by a dark lane which had become infamous for the presence of a 'flasher', so our innovation was highly popular since it avoided the need for women to travel to the main campus on dark evenings to do their computing.

The student village - to which terminals were also extended - is rather different being home to well over 1000 students and consisting of houses containing from 7 to 11 persons. It lacked the equivalent of a warden and was a much less integrated community. Given the pressure for accommodation in the village there was no possibility of using any existing living space to house the terminals, so it was decided to purchase a secondhand portacabin. This was then specially fitted out as a terminal room. This involved sacrificing car parking space but this does not seem to have been resented by the inhabitants of the village. To cope with the security problem at the village students using the facilities were issued with their own keys.

Initially in each residence a group of from three to five terminals was installed. As regards provision of printers, software for remote printing was not initially available; also there were fears about security. However, suitable software was later developed and fears on the latter score were allayed so printers too were made available.

The Student Response

A steering committee had been set up to oversee and evaluate the project. Early on the committee recognised the importance of appointing student representatives with whom they could liaise in the residences. Three main methods were used for assessment purposes: automatic monitoring, surveys in the residences, and informal inquiries.

It was noted that a new peak of total usage on the PRIME was achieved as students struggled to reach their deadlines on Friday, 29th of November 1985. However, when the figures for the 24 hour areas (the residences and 24 hour room) were extracted it was apparent that use was evenly spread throughout the day and night. Indeed even on the following day - Saturday - a similar pattern was evident (with one of its minor peaks at 3am!).

When surveys were carried out in the on- and off-campus halls and in the village there were rather different response rates of 61.5%, 77.8% and 40.0% respectively. The low response at the village probably reflects its dispersed nature and a correspondingly lower level of 'community spirit'. Altogether about 40 per cent of those responding had used the facilities. The figure claiming to have done so at the village did indeed correspond to the number of portacabin keys issued. The use figures varied by faculty and were highest in the Applied Sciences (see table). The systems used were as expected - the emphasis being on the PRIME 750. Particularly gratifying was the substantial use made - especially by arts students - of remote terminal access to the library catalogue. Indeed, pressure on the computer facility in the library itself was so great that some preferred routine access from the residences. It was of particular interest that almost one in five of those who had used the facilities stated that the overall pattern of their work had been significantly affected thereby. The greatest gain appeared to be sheer flexibility; as one respondent said, "my favourite time for computing is now at weekends". (See also Startup et al. 1988.)

It can be shown from the survey that the use made of the terminal facilities was affected by students' changing knowledge of, and attitudes towards, computing. Two thirds of respondents had some previous experience of computing before coming to the university. A clear majority - of 59 per cent - had a predominantly relaxed attitude to computing even before coming and as a result of their university computing experience this figure increased to 73 per cent. The proportion who expressed liking for computing also increased slightly, as a result of university experience, from 51 per cent to 59 per cent. But it is important to note that the residence facilities made a positive contribution in both these respects: they caused favourable attitudes to become even more widespread.

From informal reactions and the responses of student representatives it is apparent that the problems have been mostly those of success. There were fewer complaints about the computing service than previously and students enjoyed being able to work when they wanted to. The facilities were thus well received but users wanted more of everything and generally enhanced facilities. On the word processing front, it was not possible to provide this facility to undergraduates on a mainframe basis with the resources available but more recently a networked microcomputer facility has been provided in the Arts building specifically targeted at word processing.

A particularly striking development has been the considerable growth in the use of electronic mail. To some extent this was regularised in that users were encouraged to seek advice electronically from their lecturers, but it was informal too for help was frequently sought from fellow students on other sites. There are points of similarity here with the recent innovative use of mail and electronic conferencing by the British Open University. (Butcher 1988). Electronic communication can powerfully supplement, but also to a degree reduce the need for, face to face contact. It can also be used by staff for administrative purposes. A further common theme is that students quickly learn to use mail to help organise their social lives.

The clustering of terminals in residences and their heavy use outside the ordinary working day encourages students to assist each other with their computing. On all three sites at Swansea there were in fact computing 'experts' among the students, persons who were widely referred to when problems arose. However, there were not many students whose knowledge and experience of computing were great enough for them to operate freely across system boundaries. Nevertheless, new and useful relationships were frequently forged from computing. (Auld et al. 1981)

Benefits and Challenges

A number of benefits have resulted from the innovations. The new service offered has allowed a dramatic increase of central computer throughput, at comparatively modest cost and with few operational problems. Students have been able to adopt a more flexible approach to their work schedules and work at times when the computer response is faster. Staff, of the Computer Science department particularly, feel that the facilities encourage their students to write programs in an evolutionary manner and that their projects show more polish as a result. The achievements of Swansea students in the British Computer Society team programming competitions in recent years - among the medallists four years running - suggest the techniques being instilled have some merit.

The Computer Centre has had several indirect gains. In particular it has had to become more outgoing in its attitude, and has needed to develop a closer relationship with students in order to make the facilities run smoothly. To ensure the success of this type of innovation it is necessary to have a clear understanding of, and co-operation from, the management of the various residential areas. In addition, it is vital to appoint student volunteers to represent their residences and to initiate any local actions which become necessary. In this case representatives have published newsletters, as well as badgering for resources - including additional free documentation - and even on one occasion suggesting an opening ceremony with wine!

Figure: Use of 24 Hour and Residential Facilities, 17 November 1987

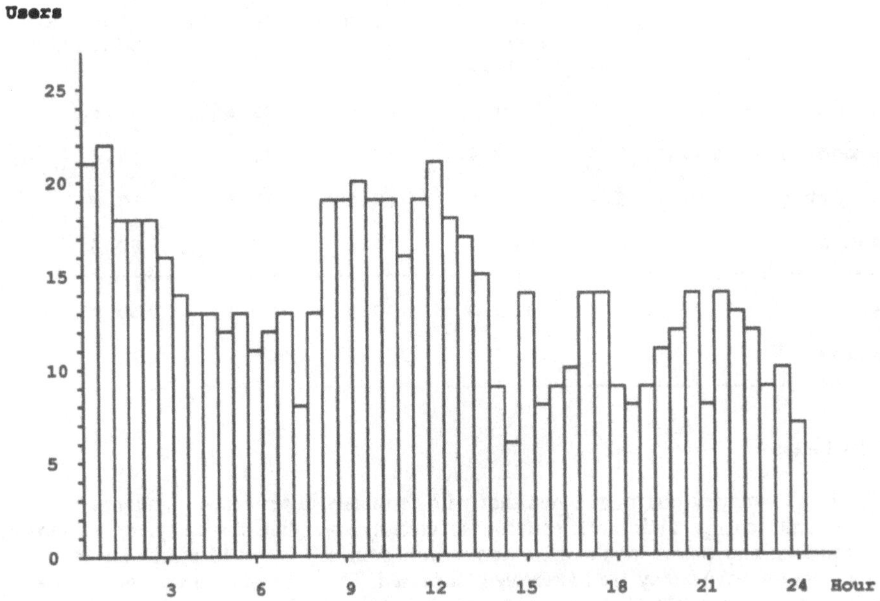

Nevertheless, remote facilities will always be harder to manage than local ones (Brady and Startup 1988). They are remote both in the sense of being distant and in being heavily used when Computer Centre staff are off-duty, but a combination of methods can alleviate the difficulties. The provision of fault diagnostic instructions can enable students to rectify most of the more common faults themselves. Remote monitoring of communications equipment certainly plays a vital role. At Swansea it was also necessary to develop a housekeeping task for both main systems which automatically initiated actions at appropriate times to clear disc space, keep usage statistics, monitor and reschedule batch jobs, and generally keep them running as sweetly as possible in the absence of operators. But at the end of the day great emphasis is placed on the reliability and resilience of computing and communications equipment continuing to operate in unattended mode.

It may be wondered whether the patterns and solutions discussed here are basically relevant to overloaded systems. We doubt this. In August 1987 there was mainframe replacement at Swansea and we now have a Vax 8700 and a Pyramid 9820, with new terminals and an enhanced communications system. There is at the moment no tendency towards system overload. However, student behaviour approaching project deadlines has not altered that much, as can be seen from the figure which shows the intensive use of terminals throughout the day in the 24 hour room and residences at the 1987/88 peak time. In fact the Computer Centre's problem now is insufficient terminal availability.

Table: The Use of the Facilities by Faculty (Percentages)

	Arts	Economic and Social Studies	Pure Sciences	Applied Sciences	All (including Education)
A lot	1.1	3.5	22.5	23.8	14.6
A moderate amount	3.2	2.4	10.3	28.2	12.6
A little	6.9	4.7	17.6	14.6	12.0
Not at all	88.9	89.4	49.5	33.5	60.8
All	100.1	100.0	99.9	100.1	100.0
Number	189	85	204	206	691

Conclusion

Finally in summary one must stress that with terminals in residences, students will not infrequently change their work patterns, so usefully spreading the computer workload. At Swansea and elsewhere there is a move from centrally provided computing facilities to a situation where they are increasingly dispersed. The increasing use of micros is also part of this pattern. The Swansea experience helps to provide a model of how to expand

and decentralise computer facilities. This project has also been fascinating in the way it has brought together computer experts and sociologists to explore the relationship between the technical on the one hand and the social and educational on the other.

REFERENCES

AULD, R.; LANG, K. and LANG, T. 1981. "University computer users: characteristics and behaviour", in: Coombs, M.J. and Alty, J.L. (eds.). *Computing Skills and the User Interface*. London, Academic Press

BRADY, P.R. and STARTUP, R. 1988. "Expanding student access to computer facilities - the way forward?", in: *University Computing* 10(2), 86-91

BUTCHER, P.G. 1988. "Development and delivery of educational software: an institutional approach." *The CTISS File* 6, 64-67

McCREDIE, J.C. (ed.) 1983. *Campus Computing Strategies*. Bedford Mass.: Digital Press

SLATER, J.B. 1986a. "An introduction to the University Grants Committee/Computer Board joint computers in teaching initiative." *The CTISS File* 1, 4-5

SLATER, J.B. 1986b. "An introduction to the UGC/CB teaching initiative." *University Computing* 8, 161

STARTUP, R.; BRADY, P.R. and GILMOUR, A. 1988. "The value of computing facilities in student residences". *Studies in Higher Education* 13(3), 309-16

Working Party on Computer Facilities for Teaching in Universities 1983. Report ("The Nelson Report"). London, The UK Computer Board for Universities and Research Councils

COMPUTER-AIDED INSTRUCTION AND COMMUNICATION-SKILLS

Dieter Euler
University of Cologne
Lehrstuhl für Wirtschafts- und Sozialpädagogik
FRG

In the educational field, computer-aided instruction (CAI) is a controversial topic. Proponents argue that it is a powerful method of teaching - one with the capacity for conveying the necessary qualifications for the coming years. Others say that future qualifications such as skills for communication, participation or cooperation require teaching methods based on a social relationship with a personal teacher rather than a personal computer. That was one of the starting points for my research. I have tried to find out more about the implications CAI as a type of man-machine-communication has on the acquisition of communication skills. As to CAI, I will focus on the narrow application of a pure learner-computer communication. Although CAI may be embedded in social interactions, for the purpose of learning on its potential it seems appropriate to analyse an extreme type.
I am going to elaborate on the following questions:

1. What potential for communication is immanent to CAI?
2. In what respect are there any differences to social communication and to what extent can CAI contribute to the acquisition of communicative skills?

How does CAI work and what basic communication structure is in operation? I am going to sketch this structure by way of a "tutorial". As to the communication structure, this strategy is hardly different to other CAI-strategies such as "drill-and-practice" or "simulation".

Figure: Tutorial as a Basic Strategy of CAI

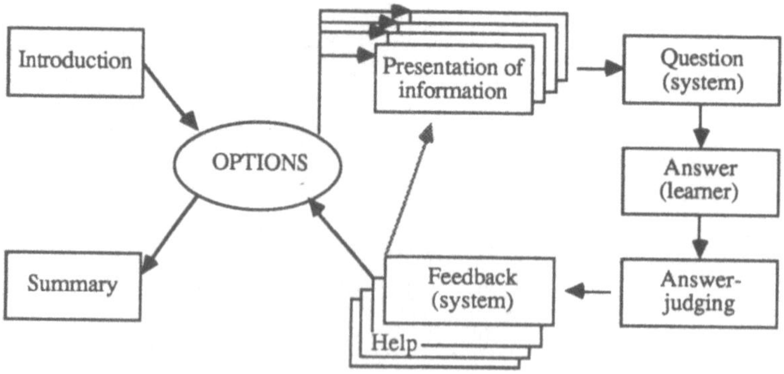

In communication it is important to point out that a learner-computer-dialogue basically constitutes a sequence of four components:

1. Presentation of information.
2. Question-answer pattern.
3. Feedback of the system.
4. Decisions on branching, either taken by the program or by the learner.

Within this context, the following problems of Learner-Computer-Communication can be outlined:

1. Due to a limited screen size, information is presented in a sketchy manner with less redundancy!
   ... which in turn means that there is a higher risk for the learner of being left alone in cases of comprehension difficulties.
2. In cases of comprehension difficulties the learner may only draw on those help-information the author has anticipated!
   ... that is to say, if such difficulties cannot be resolved, the learning-process may be jeopardized and probably will be finished prematurely.
3. In response to open questions, the learner is bound to the limits of the authoring software!
   ... which in practice means filling in a gap of a maximum of some 120 characters (approx. 2 lines).
4. The more openly a question is put to the learner, the less the system is able to judge the answer adequately - the less it is possible to provide corrective feedback!
   ... open questions allow a great number of (right or wrong) answers. In practice, it is hardly possible for the courseware author to comment on any conceivable answer with a corrective feedback. That is why...
5. Many answers inevitably will be followed by "stock responses" which are neither corrective nor acceptable to the learner!
   ... feedback such as "Try it again" or "Sorry that missed the point" may be puzzling to the learner and, in result, may leave him back in anger or frustration.

The second questions requires an investigation of the main differences between Learner-Computer-Communication and social communication in order to find out to what extent CAI can contribute to the acquisition of communication skills. As 'communication skills' is quite an ambiguous term used in all kinds of contexts, one has, at least, to give a sketchy view of one's own understanding. In the frame of my investigation, "communication skills" represent the ability:

... in situations characterized by a different degree of anonymity;
... with respect to topics of the personal, interpersonal and objective world of an actor;

* to express oneself;
* to interpret utterances of other people;
* to explore and to stand conflicts in order to reach a compromise on controversial views;
* to participate in common enterprises;
* to responsibly stand up for those not able to advocate their case.

The results of my analyses can be sketched by the following theses:

Learner-Computer-Communication

1. can only focus on clear-cut and definite facts, i.e. only topics of the objective world can be addressed!
   ... personal feelings, individual values or the negotiation of interpersonal relationships cannot be addressed within a Learner-Computer-Communication.
2. is a type of communication completely planned by the author! Questions and experiences introduced by the learner cannot be considered!
   ... CAI is frozen communication which has to be defrosted in the learning-process. But there cannot be more than was originally planned.
3. is only able to resolve comprehension problems of the learner if the author has anticipated them!
   ... comprehension problems can be met with help-information files or corrective feedback - but again, only if they had been anticipated by the author.
4. is basically anonymous communication! In principle there is no relationship between the author and the learner. Some learners see the computer with human characteristics!
   ... CAI has no emotional platform - author and learner usually do not know of each other. If emotions do come in, they refer to feelings the learner builds up with respect to the computer. Some learners describe the computer in psychological terms: they treat him "as a friend", they "place confidence in him" or tell him intimate and personal experiences. One extreme are the reports of Weizenbaum, introducing cases in which people try to reveal their very personal feelings to the computer while at the same time refusing to open up towards other people.
5. limits the spectrum of articulation for the learner to either clicking pre-structured options or feeding the computer with few words!
   ... In doing so, the learner is forced to adjust himself to the formal structure the courseware is able to analyse.
6. limits the spectrum of interpretation on the part of the learner to the factual information. Contrary to social communication both, the underlying intentions of the other and the implications of one's action on the other remain out of focus!
   ... if one interprets actions of other people, this interpretation reflects many dimensions. CAI is limited to address just one dimension, namely the interpretation of factual information.
7. remains static. As computers do not build up experiences, communication consists of question-answer-patterns which lack a dynamic development!
   ... social communication constituents a dynamic development: former statements bind later ones. As the computer is not able to learn, CAI represents a succession of more or less unconnected dialogues.
8. cannot negotiate conflicts!
   ... Skills for setting conflicts require some openness on the part of the opponents, computers require just programmed dialogue patterns.
9. does not require any responsibility on the part of the learner!
   ... the computer does not ask the learner for explanations or justifications for what he has entered. The computer regards the learner-responses as a neutral piece of information. He does not understand, he simply functions!

In summary, one may say that - compared to social communication - communication with a computer is extremely reduced. Analyzing the limits of Learner-Computer-Communication reveals the great variety of social communication, or how Crombach put it: "Once interactions are involved, one enters a great hall of mirrors that extends to infinity".
For educational processes two main implications can be drawn:

1. CAI should be confined to objectives aimed at cognitive dimensions of the individual. Communication skills cannot be advanced by CAI!

2. As communication skills are of increasing importance in the next years, CAI should be integrated in social arrangements. The computer should remain an instrument rather than a condition of learning.

REFERENCES

EULER, D. 1989. *Zum Einfluß von computerunterstütztem Lehren und Lernen auf die Bewirkung sozial-kommunikativer Lernziele.* In preparation

Special attention is to be drawn to:

ALESSI, S.M. and TROLLIP, S.R. 1985. *Computer-Based Instruction, Methods and Developments.* Englewood Cliffs - New Jersey

BELL, M. 1985. "The Role of Instructional Theories in the Evaluation of Microcomputer Courseware." *Educational Technology* 3, 36-40

BERNOLD, T. and FINKELSTEIN, J. (eds.). 1988. *Computer Assisted Approaches to Training.* Amsterdam - New York - Oxford - Tokio

BÖLLERT, G. und EULER, D. 1987. *Arbeitsleitfaden zur Entwicklung von Courseware mit Hilfe des Courseware-Entwicklungsmodells.* Unveröffentlichtes Manuskript, Köln

BORK, A. 1986. *Interaction - Lessons from CBL.* Irvine (Ca.)

BOSTROM, R.N. (ed.). 1984. *Competence in Communication.* Beverly Hills - London - New Delhi

EISSNER, E.W. 1969. "Instructional and Expressive Educational Objectives: Their Formulation and Use in the Curriculum." *AERA Monograph Series on Curriculum Evaluation* 3, Chicago, 1-18

EULER, D. 1987a. "Didaktische Reflexion: Möglichkeiten und Grenzen des computerunterstützten Unterrichts im Hinblick auf die Gestaltung der Lehr/Lernmethoden", in: Euler, D. u.a. 1987. *Computerunterstützer Unterricht, Möglichkeiten und Grenzen.* Braunschweig - Wiesbaden, 104-199

EULER, D. 1987b. "Auf der Suche nach didaktischer Qualität: Eine Analyse neuerer US-amerikanischer Literatur zu computerunterstütztem Lernen." *Kölner Zeitschrift für "Wirtschaft und Pädagogik"*, Heft 3, 115-136

EULER, D. and TWARDY, M. 1988. "Whatever the Orientation, Creativity is Demanded", in: Bernold, T. and Finkelstein, J. (eds.). 1988. *Computer Assisted Approaches to Training.* Amsterdam - New York - Oxford - Tokio, 91-104

EULER, D. u.a. 1987. *Computerunterstützer Unterricht, Möglichkeiten und Grenzen.* Braunschweig - Wiesbaden

KULIK, J.; BANGERT, R. and WILLIAMS, G. 1983. "Effects of Computer-Based Teaching On Secondary School Students." *Journal of Educational Psychology* 1, 19-26

KULIK, J.; KULIK, C. and COHEN, P. 1980. "Effectiveness of Computer-based College Teaching: A Meta-analysis of Findings." *Review of Educational Research* 4, 525-544

KULIK, J.; KULIK, C. and COHEN, P. 1982. "Educational Outcomes of tutoring: A Meta-analysis of Findings." *American Educational Research Journal* 2, 237-248

LARSEN, R.E. 1985. "What communication theories can teach the designer of computer-based training." *Educational Technology*, July 1985, 16-19

SALOMON, G. 1979. *Interaction of Media, Cognition and Learning*. San Francisco - Washington - London

SELDEN, P. and SCHULTZ, N. 1982. "What the research says about CAI's potential." *Training* 11, 61-64

TURKLE, S. 1984. *Die Wunschmaschine - Vom Entstehen der Computerkultur*. Reinbek

WEIZENBAUM, J. 1978. *Die Macht der Computer und die Ohnmacht der Vernunft*. Frankfurt

THE COMPUTER AIDED INSTRUCTOR

Eugene Horber
Department of Political Science
University of Geneva, Carouge
Switzerland

1. Introduction

The purpose of this contribution is to explore important aspects of teaching data analysis using computer software. The few existing studies in this field concentrate mainly on external software aspects and the computer-student (or user) relationship. The perspective here is that of the teacher, i.e. the purpose is to study the relationship between teacher, student and a piece of software as a third partner. This paper intends to show what software can do for a teacher, i.e. the software is seen as a didactical partner in the teacher-student relationship.

The title reflects less a concern with the computer as a teacher in a "classical" CAI/CAL setting, than with the role and function of software in a teacher-student-tool relationship. This paper explores selected aspects of a long term reflection on teaching data analysis to social scientists in the computer age. Many of the ideas presented here are (very) tentative and meant for discussion and further exploration. The intention is to stimulate the reflection on didactical and methodological issues and is motivated by underlying preoccupations, namely teaching in the computer age, teaching with the computer as a partner and tool development and design.

2. Didactical Aspects of EDA

The ideas and results presented here stem from several years of teaching data analysis to social science students using the EDA Software (Horber, 1977-88) for practical work.(1) The EDA software environment grew out of teaching and applied research needs in the area of exploratory techniques on the one hand and multivariate analysis on the other. The program has been developed consequently for truly interactive use. Interactivity here means the interactivity of the data analysis process, and not simply a computer terminal or PC used to produce output essentially on paper or for reading and the screen with some interactive facility, but true terminal centered work, i.e. the main analysis "event" occurs on the terminal, and the analysis progresses from a creative interaction between the results obtained from the tools and the user's knowledge (hopefully growing during the research process).

The EDA package, besides being a complete interactive data analysis package(2), incorporates a number of features useful in a teaching context assisting the teacher in many ways. Here is a list of the most important features oriented towards teaching found in the EDA package.

Group profiles: The environment of a user is defined in a profile, which can be defined at the group level, e.g. a seminar. This environment decides on access to data and macro libraries, as well as to textual information. Future versions of the software will permit changes in the user interface (names of commands, default values etc.) for individual users or groups of users.

Adaptation/modification of the user interface: to some extent, the user interface can be changed by adding macro commands (stored in macro-libraries) and adapting the output to fit specific needs.

Online information is available in a variety of flavours: Information on operation of the software, tutorials, documentation on data, additional information linked to commands or groups of commands (e.g. bibliographies), as well as example libraries. Currently, this kind of textual information might be different from group to group or from one user to another, but without any flexibility, i.e. it is permanently defined in the user's profile. Work is underway to adapt these facilities to individual preferences and progress made in learning, i.e. the information displayed might be quite different for a novice or for a more advanced user. Or a user might prefer a maximum number of informations displayed; others might prefer a terse mode.

Teacher-student communication: there is also a primitive mailing facility in one direction teacher to student(s). This facility is usually made much more powerful by interfacing to the system mail facilities, but there are still systems around not offering such services.

Interfaces to other software, e.g. SPSS or SAS. The macro language can also be used to create facilities not available within EDA. For instance, there is no discriminant analysis in EDA; you might want to write a macro taking the data in the current data matrix, submit it to SPSS with a request to produce a discriminant analysis, without forcing the user to learn SPSS at all.

Care has been taken to make sure that these facilities work in most computing environments, i.e. from mainframes to PCs.

3. User Monitoring

Besides these more classical features, EDA includes user monitoring facilities, i.e. user actions are recorded. The user monitoring facility comprises two aspects, data collection and the analysis of the collected data. Tools are under development and partially implemented producing profiles of students and/or student groups during specific time intervals; these profiles show how the software is used, which errors are made etc.

User monitoring is activated by setting an option in the user's profile. Usually these profiles are created and modified by the EDA system administrator or a group administrator (often a teacher). All information the user enters on the keyboard: EDA commands as well as data, text (descriptive documentation) and responses to prompts. Commands and other types of input are distinguished by a special identification in the transcript file. In addition to this the following informations are recorded:

The command termination status.

The command number (internally each command is identified by a number). This information greatly facilitates processing of the transcripts.

The type of command: Commands are grouped in units reflecting a collection of tasks similar (in nature), e.g. univariate commands, input output commands, dimensional analysis and the like.

The time the command was started (time stamp).

Furthermore, the beginning and the end of a session is also recorded (time and date).

These recordings constitute the raw material for the next step, the analysis of the collected data. To make it clear from the beginning, the ultimate goal is not to quantify all aspects of user behaviour, but to get some ideas how a piece of software can contribute to better teaching and learning, i.e. to learn how to teach better in the computer age, by a better understanding of how students learn and behave with respect to these tools.

The purpose of these analyses is threefold:

Monitoring: Provide information to the teacher how the students assimilate the knowledge presented in the classroom. Where are the main difficulties? Did the explanation lead to wrong conclusions? This enables the teacher to introduce additional information in the next lesson.

Behavioural studies: How do students learn to deal with real problems? How is the knowledge taught applied to real data sets? This preoccupation leads to the study of cognitive styles in learning and using data analytical techniques, enabling teachers to understand better the teaching and learning process.

Software design: Problems with the use of the software clearly appear in these studies; therefore, the software can be, in the long run, adapted in order to become a better partner for teachers and students, as well as for research work.

For several years now recordings have been made, mainly in an advanced social science methodology course, where the accent lies on complex problem solving, i.e. students are trained to tackle a priori unstructured problems by teaching them to use many alternative tools. The main accent lies on the conceptual and practical aspects of those tools, enabling them to interpret their own results and results reported in books and journals.

The UM (user monitor) tool found in the EDA toolbox may be used to process the transcript files for easier analysis. The current state of these tools is still tentative and experimental, but hopefully they help to stimulate further discussion an research in that area.

Currently this tool performs the following functions:

Produce profiles of all sessions for a user or a group of users (provides immediate feedback and a basis for long term analysis).

Produce an output file containing only commands, i.e. filtering out all records which are not commands (text, data etc.).

Produce an output file containing only commands in error (helps to detect main error sources, design problems etc.).

Generate data sets for further analysis directly into the EDA work area.

Profiles currently show the following informations per session:

* Number of total records (commands and other input) per session.
* Number of commands in error.
* Number of data/text records (non-command records).
* Number of help requests.
* Time in minutes per session.
* Date of session.
* Count of selected commands.
* Most oftenly used commands.
* Same, but commands in error.

This kind of numerical information only hints at interesting situations and we will have to analyze more closely by looking at the transcripts.

As all commands are recorded as entered, it is possible to do a very detailed analysis by reading through or rerunning the session(s). This of course is time consuming, but very instructive. As the purpose is not really to monitor exactly what the students do but rather to understand how the students use the computer and what problems they have, the best approach is to use a number of automatic tools for preprocessing the data in order to detect interesting patterns and then choose typical students (representing a type of behaviour or cognitive style) for detailed analysis, i.e. of the transcripts for these students.

4. Conclusion

This contribution intends to stimulate a discussion on what the computer can do in order to help to teach better and to design better software, as well as to understand how students and users react to various tools and how they handle problems.

Of course there are many limits to the approach sketched out here, however, it provides useful information through an immediate feedback. This information is evidently only useful to the teacher who devotes time and effort to didactical problems and gathers didactical information through other channels, like discussions with the students, evaluation questionnaires, careful observation in the classroom and analysis of the written reports. In fact, the various numerical summaries become only meaningful when interpreted in the light of these informations.

The most obvious limit is the fact that the data are collected for individuals; if students work together in groups of two or three on a single project, the picture you get from the transcripts might be completely distorted.

In the near future it is planned to continue developing and exploring the various tools sketched out here. The analysis of cognitive styles is very difficult, if you do not have the appropriate tools, therefore tools have to be created for summarizing command sequences from very large collections of data sets.

Another line of development will be to create facilities for each user for the analysis of his/her computing style and problem areas, i.e. stimulate the user to reflect on what he/she is doing. The EDA software should also be able, by analyzing the computing behaviour of a user, to personalize tutorials and hint (automatically - of course only if the user desires so) at problem areas or easier ways of solving a problem.

The preoccupation with didactical problems in the largest possible sense (including software design) in the computer age is a vital issue for all scientific disciplines, otherwise it could easily loose its autonomy to some specialists...or to some badly designed expert system.

NOTES

1. EDA means of course Exploratory Data Analysis, but also Exploration de Données Agrégatives, i.e. Exploration of Aggregate Data, reflecting the strength of this package in the area of observation centered data analysis.
2. The EDA package is specialized in the following areas: Exploration, multidimensional analysis and cluster analysis. Extensive transformation facilities are also available. See Horber (1988) for details.

REFERENCES

HORBER, E. 1977. 1986. 1988. *EDA, User's Manual*. University of Geneva
TUKEY, J.W. 1977. *Exploratory Data Analysis*. Reading (Addison Wesley)

ACQUISITION AND COMMUNICATION OF KNOWLEDGE ABOUT A COMPUTER PROGRAM(1)

Heinz Neber
University of Essen, Gesamthochschule
FRG

There are two basic questions in teaching and learning computer programming. The first refers to the content of learning and the second relates to methods of instruction. Both questions are interrelated and should be studied integratedly. Recent developments in instructional psychology offer solutions for both questions (Neber 1987, 1988).

Contents of Computer Programming Instruction

Contents of programming instruction should help to acquire competences for performing three kinds of tasks (Neber 1985): Comprehension of complete programs, debugging of faulty programs and designing new programs for defined purposes. These tasks can be classified by problem-solving models. A complete problem-solving cycle contains three components: Problem definition, solution method and solution state. Each of these three components can be given in the instructional setting or has to be self-generated by the subject. The three programming tasks differ in regard to the extent of self-generation of these components (Table 1).

Table 1: Problem-Solving Classification of Programming Tasks

Programming Tasks	Problem Components		
	Definition	Method	Solution
Comprehension	given	given	given
Debugging	given	?	given
Design	given	?	?

?: component must be self-generated by the subject

A second assumption about the content of learning derives from models of knowledge-based problem-solving. Such models have been developed in technical domains (Brown & DeKleer 1984; Greeno & Berger 1987) dealing with understanding and designing machines and software. Programs and machines represent goal-oriented devices with a goal hierarchy and a causal structure. In a similar way Pennington (1987) distinguishes multiple levels of programming knowledge: Text structure knowledge represents the control flow of a program with building blocks like sequence, iteration and conditional enabling a causal segmentation of the program. Plan knowledge represents the functions of the program enabling a goal analysis of its performance. These studies suggest a simple model of the structure of programming knowledge consisting in three components: Objects (e.g. GOTO, loop), conditions for the application of objects (e.g. READ needs DATA) and functions of objects (e.g. loop simplifies recursion).

Table 2: Structure of Programming Knowledge

CONDITION	-	OBJECT	-	FUNCTION

Methods in Programming Instruction

Recent developments in programming instruction represent a search for more self-directed and active methods of learning (Neber 1982). Two methodological developments are especially important for learning and teaching programming.

1. Problem-Oriented Learning

These approaches trace back to learning-by-discovery studies (Neber 1981). In all kinds of such learning knowledge must be generated by the learner himself. This is realized in different fields of computer-science education like learning to use word-processors (Carroll & Mack 1983) or learning programming languages (Meyer, Bayman & Dyck 1987). Problem oriented learning can be realized by fault-finding tasks were learners generate and test hypotheses about bugs in faulty programs (Greif & Janikowski 1987).

2. Cooperative Learning

A recent trend is to consider the social organization in learning programming (Brown 1986). This supplements more traditional discovery- or problem-solving methods which favoured individualistic learning. It seems to be that cooperatively structured instruction could enhance positive effects of problem oriented approaches. Trowbridge (1987) found such effects with science students working in a computer environment. Learning in pairs or dyads resulted in activities like restatement of questions in own words, formulation of hypotheses and tutorial assistance of the partner by social and cognitive supportive verbalizations. In programming instruction cooperative learning was studied by Webb. Webb, Ender & Lewis (1986) found positive correlations of several pair-interaction variables and knowledge of BASIC commands. The most effective variable was "actively giving explanations". More detailed analyses of the variables of cooperative learning are necessary for developing cooperatively organized problem-oriented instructional methods in programming instruction.

Experiment

Design and Procedure

A program comprehension task was accomplished by 24 subjects (electricians) of a vocational school. The short BASIC program (33 lines) controlled a working model of an elevator (Fischertechnik). The experiment proceeded in 3 phases.

1. Phase: Individual knowledge acquisition. 2 groups of subjects acquired knowledge about the BASIC program. Group 1 (debugger) got a faulty program and had to find the fault. Group 2 (understander) got the correct program to understand it. The exploration times in both groups were connected in parallel.

2. Phase: Dyadic explanation. Subjects who acquired knowledge in the first phase had to explain the program as speakers to a naive partner as hearer. After finishing the explanation the hearer could pose questions. These verbal interactions were tape recorded.

3. Phase: Test. Written conditional and functional questions in a multiple-choice format had to be answered by speakers and hearers. A conditional question is: "If the elevator is called in the first floor which line of program starts the motor?" A functional question is: "Which is the function of line 430?"

Hypotheses

The hypotheses tested were derived from the studies mentioned above.

1. Debuggers do have higher test performances than understanders.

2. Debuggers generate more elaborated explanations.

3. Exp-lanations of debuggers result in higher test performances of hearers than explanations of understanders.

Results

1. The first hypothesis was verified. Debuggers answered an average of 7.6 questions and understanders only 4.6 ($F=8.8$; $p<.05$). A more detailed analysis showed that debuggers answer more conditional questions ($X=3.5$) than understanders ($X=1.5$; $F=7.0$; $p<.05$) whereas no differences could be found in answering functional questions.

2. The second hypothesis was tested by analyzing the numbers of conditional and functional statements in the explanations. Both groups did not differ in this respect i.e.

3. The third hypothesis was rejected. Hearer performances did not differ between both experimental groups. The quality of explanations and their effects upon hearers seem to be independent of the method of knowledge acquisition by the speaker.

The quality of explanations was further analyzed in comparing hearers with test performances above ("good hearers": X=6.3 correct answers) and below ("bad hearers: X=2.6 correct answers) the median. Explanations given to these two groups of hearers differed in respect to the number of conditional statements. "Good" hearers received X=13,3 and "bad" hearers X=7.0 conditional statements ($F=6.8$; $p<.05$). Therefore, "good" hearers got more information about the causal structure of the program.

The questioning activity of the hearers was very poor (X=1.2 questions) without any differences between experimental groups and performance levels of hearers.

Discussion

Debugging proved to be an efficient method in acquiring knowledge about a BASIC program and resulted in more conditional knowledge than studying and understanding a complete program. Debugging as a kind of problem-oriented learning improved the knowledge about the causal structure of the program.

On the other side, the knowledge-acquisition method did not have any effects upon the generation of explanations. This indicates that the communication of knowledge to others requires additional social or pedagogical skills which are not an automatic consequence of higher levels of knowledge. Instructional settings should explicitly promote skills for knowledge acquisition as well as skills for knowledge communication.

The quality of explanations depends upon the number of conditional statements i.e. upon the completeness of a causal description of the program flow. This must be seen in respect to the subjects of this study who had been novices in BASIC programming. For these novices, conditional descriptions were more important than differences in the extent of functional explanations. This corresponds to assumptions of Brown & DeKleer (1984) that only after having understood the causal structure of technical systems functional information is inferred.

The negligible number of questions generated by hearers and the rather low quality of explanations given by the speakers in the dyads points to the necessity of promoting active skills of communication in the classroom. This should be the case for an efficient implementation of problem-oriented, cooperatively structured instructional methods.

NOTES

1. Supported by Ministerium für Wissenschaft und Forschung; Land Nordrhein-Westfalen.
2. Schule für Elektrotechnik, Essen.

REFERENCES

BROWN, J.S. 1986. "From cognitive to social ergonomics and beyond", in: Norman, D.A. and Draper, S. (eds.). *User centered system design.* Hillsdale: Erlbaum, 31-61

BROWN, J.S and DeKLEER, J. 1984. "Towards a theory of qualitative reasoning about mechanisms and its role in troubleshooting", in: Rasmussen, J. and Rouse W.B. (eds.). *Human detection and diagnosis of system failures.* New York: Plenum, 317-335

CARROLL, J.M and MACK, R.L. 1983. "Actively learning to use a word processor", in: Cooper, W.E. (ed.). *Cognitive aspects of skilled typewriting.* Berlin: Springer, 259-281

GREENO, J.G. and BERGER, D. 1987. "A model of functional knowledge and insight." *Report* No. GK-1. Berkeley: University of California

GREIF, S. and JANIKOWSKI, A. 1987. "Aktives Lernen durch systematische Fehlerexploration oder programmiertes Lernen durch Tutorials?" *Zeitschrift für Arbeits- und Organisationspsychologie* 35, 94-99

MAYER, R.E.; BAYMAN, P. and DYCK, J.L. 1987. "Learning programming languages: Research and applications", in: Berger, D.E.; Pezdek, K. and Banks, W.P. (eds.). *Applications of cognitive psychology: Problem solving, education, and computing.* Hillsdale: Erlbaum, 33-45

NEBER, H. (ed.). 1981. *Entdeckendes Lernen.* Weinheim: Beltz

NEBER, H. 1982. "Selbstgesteuertes Lernen", in: Treiber, B. und Weinert, F.E. (ed.). *Lehr-Lern-Forschung.* München: Urban & Schwarzenberg, 89-112

NEBER, H. 1985. "Psychologische Untersuchungen zum Lernen und Lehren des Computerprogrammierens", in: Mandl, H. und Fischer, P.M. (eds.). *Lernen im Dialog mit dem Computer.* München: Urban & Schwarzenberg, 218-228

NEBER, H. 1987a. "Problemlösen und Instruktion." *Psychologie in Erziehung und Unterricht* 34, 241-246

NEBER, H. 1987b. *Angewandte Problemlösepsychologie.* Münster: Aschendorff

NEBER, H. 1988. "Technisches Problemlösen: Erwerb, Nutzung und Kommunikation von Wissen", in: Schönpflug, W. (ed.). *Bericht über den 36. Kongress der Deutschen Gesellschaft für Psychologie 1988 in Berlin.* Göttingen: Hogrefe, 368-369

PENNINGTON, N. 1987. "Stimulus structures and mental representations in expert comprehension of computer programs." *Cognitive Psychology* 19, 295-341

TROWBRIDGE, D. 1987. "An investigation of groups working at the computer", in: Berger, D.E.; Pezdek, K. and Banks, W.P. (eds.). *Applications of cognitive psychology.* Hillsdale: Erlbaum, 47-58

WEBB, N.M.; ENDER, P. and LEWIS, S. 1986. "Problem-solving strategies and group processes in small groups learning computer programming." *American Educational Research Journal* 23, 243-261

ACADEMIC COMPUTING CENTERS IN AMERICAN UNIVERSITIES

Lawrence J. McCrank
LIS, Ferris State University
R. Dale Hobart
IRC, Ferris State University
USA

Information technology in academe has brought significant changes in American academe, both in organization and method or procedures, as the ubiquitous computer weaves itself into the very fabric of scholarly endeavor, touching every strand and coloring every decision (Masland, 1984b). During the 1970s most applications were for financial and business operations, and subsequently for such standardized record keeping as course registration. The earliest applications in research came in quantitative studies, especially in the Social Sciences with such statistical packages as SPSS. Entry to the classroom came through text processing, first in the electronic preparation of instructional materials for manual, non-interactive use (Coughlin, 1986). The other major area of computing activity was in library operations, supported by the MARC (Machine-Readable Cataloging) standard, and to a lesser extent inventory control for archives and records management. These were mainframe-hosted operations often requiring customized software and technical expertise available only from a computer center.

This centralized model of computing has changed drastically in the 1980s because of the proliferation of software, the transition to midframe computers and enhanced capacities of micro-computers to do what once required the former, increased computer literacy, and the growth of local area networks (Lourde, 1986). In some years the growth in the number of personal computers on campuses has increased at a rate creating 50%/year, with the greatest acceleration at large comprehensive institutions. After 1985 the average number of students per university-owned PCs was 92 (median 44); this is decreasing all the time (Warlick, 1986). Decentralization has been encouraged by the very idea of the 'personal computer'; it was synonymous with diversification. Unexpected by-products of the individualization have been(1) the breakdown of collaborative research promoted in mainframe, centralized environments,(2) the spread of chaos across campuses with myriad incompatible hardware, idiosyncratic software preferences, and(3) a victimization of campus computing by competing companies and marketing strategies aimed at controlling market shares rather than assisting any campus-wide strategic planning for academic computing. The isolation of research projects from one another, the dependency of these on specific kinds of hardware, and the growth of *vademecum* solutions (while creating new software often re-invented the proverbial wheel), were symptoms of the inability in American colleges and universities to introduce computing and automation in a planned, progressive manner. The spread of computer applications on most campuses has been sporadic if not spontaneous, depending on individual personalities rather than organizational goals, with resulting disorganization that has added to the cost and trauma of introducing computing to academe. Despite such growth in numbers and spectacular investments, there are no standard ratios of personal computers per student, consensus about how to calculate 'computing power', or even an ideal concerning accessibility, transportability of software, or agreement about time-sharing and distributing costs to users either by costing-out time used individually, charging laboratory fees, or building equipment costs into higher tuition.

By 1985 nearly half of the 2600 colleges and universities in the United States and Canada had computer centers, 68% of which combined 'academic' and 'administrative' computing. Conversely 32% of American colleges and universities had separate operations for academic and administrative computing (Warlick, 1968). This separate identification of academic computing as distinct from institutional, operational computers for business transactions and large-scale operations such as registration, is still evolving. It represents a coalescence of instruction and research applications, but tends to exclude bibliographic and archival systems which often form a third 'center' on campus for computing activities. Academic computing centers evolved as such first in four-year colleges (38% in 1985) rather than larger universities (27%), where their directors (one 1985 survey indicated that 754 directors were known by 225 different "boss" titles!) largely to specialize in computer- assisted instruction. These 'centers' were often coordinating boards for hitherto decentralized and autonomous laboratories devoted to particular disciplines and operated for specified clientele such as given majors or students in a school; some were class-specific in origin. Whereas centralized administrative computing operated with a top-down management structure, academic computing centers have been built bottom-up by a coalition of users into self-help, shared-interest groups, with a management style that is collegial and whose structure is often rather loose. Such a generalization is deceptive, however, since the average computing center devotes 51% of its staff time to instruction.

The idea of 'academic computing' is relatively new; it does not appear as a common indexable term in the abstracts and indexes to computer and information science literature until after 1976. Despite increased use, there is little consensus about what the term embraces and/or excludes; its usage lacks precision. In most cases academic and administrative computing overlap in purview, interests and activity (Pengoy, 1974). While some see academic computing as a function of a combined computer center within an overall scheme of multiple functions and clientele, those who favor academic computing as separate entities see these service applications and interests as fundamentally different from administrative concerns and business operations (Roberts, 1971). This is often because personnel trained in computer science or more applied, information systems management, lacked subject-area graduate degrees and they were perceived to be machine- rather than project- or content-oriented. Conversely, technically skilled computer programmers may perceive some subject-area clients as technical amateurs; such perceptions have widened the gulf between administrative and academic computing. At times this dichotomy is oversimplified as mainframe vs. personal computer, even though networking, variable capacities of computers and distributed systems make such divisions unworkable. The portion of time spent on academic computing (i.e., instruction [83%] and research [13%]) seems to be the same for separate and combined centers, and all centers like libraries are shifting personnel resources from technical to public services.

The greatest growth potential in computer use within academe lies in instructional support, especially as this diversifies into textbases and imagebases combined with interactive video (Osgood, 1984). Academic computing centers have great potential, therefore, so that administrative computing centers looking for expansion, more interesting work and diversification, and a line into the personal computer world, are now either expanding services to the academic sector and are trying to consolidate operations to absorb semi-autonomous academic computing operations. The latter when they coalesce into centers:(1) serve a coordination role;(2) disseminate information especially by newsletters and hosting reading rooms with popular computer journals;(3) train faculty users and offer continuing education, often in a laboratory setting;(4) provide technical support and 'trouble shooting';(5) advise in a consulting mode, often by shopping for appropriate software and downloading shareware; and sometimes(6) they have contracts with vendors to operate as campus distributors of hardware, providing educational discounts for college and university personnel.

There is seldom anything so unique in these services to warrant the separation of academic from administrative computing. There are plausible arguments for their integration. However, academic computing has other allies in laboratory users as well as media centers as scanning and digitization impact computerization and interactive work with video and laser technology. There is also the possible alliance with libraries which are automated and because they often house personal-use computer laboratories in addition to the online search services OPAC, (Online Public Access Catalog), and CD-ROM-based reference services (i.e. ARCs, or Automated Reference Centers) (Dougherty, 1987). Because of the preponderant instructional use of PCs on campuses and the library's hold on content, this alliance is potentially as strong as with administrative computing. Less attached but of significance for research support are the growing numbers of data archives in research centers that work only indirectly with central computing, and the recent, impressive strides of automation in museums. These alliances, which in turn are exerting great influence on central computing's unilateral focus on business affairs and members, are being strengthened by the move from databases to electronic text- and imagebases, breakthroughs in digitization and compact storage, optical scanning and the transference of data between media, computer-assisted publishing beyond mere text processing, and the advances of expert systems even if the promises of artificial intelligence have been overstated. Electronic mail, bulletin boards, and conferencing allow interconnectivity and flexibility. The selection of shareware and courseware is increasingly wide, making the advisory role of academic computer personnel ever more demanding.

While prospects look good for academic computing because of trends in software availability and growth in personal computers, problems abound. There is a 'turf war' on many campuses and uneasy alliances based on past histories and personalities rather than strategic plans. Reporting lines are often fuzzy and organizational structures are vague as academic computing tries to find a niche for itself. Sometime a small academic computing center can find itself in a tug-of-war between the library, media services, and administrative computing. Most academic computing operations are under funded. While computer facility budgets escalate at a substantial rate (average 6.7%; median 9.6% after 1985), and some rival the older establishment (i.e. the academic library), the centers as conglomerates and coalitions are often vulnerable to internal competitions and external neglect (Warlick, 1986). In the late 1980s overall, campus computer facilities were allocated ca. 2.6% of the parent institution's education and general budgets - only slightly less than libraries, with higher allocations in research universities. Expenditures per student varied from $95 average in junior colleges to $185 in mega-universities. Incompatibility of hardware, non-transference of software, and the slow spread of standards in an industry composed of competing companies, all contribute to problems in academic computing. There are also complications in control, i.e. public access vs. proprietary rights, copyright law, software pirating and data security, system protection from viruses, etc. that complicate the management of computer laboratories and centers.

All of these problems, prospects, and patterns in the evolution of academic computing on American campuses are evident in the case of Ferris State University, a polytechnic university of nearly 12,000 students in western Michigan. Although now a state university, it originated in 1884 as a private enterprise, the Ferris Institute, founded by Woodbridge Ferris, who became governor of the state of Michigan. It suffered hard times during the depression and World War II, plus a devastating fire in 1955, just before its transfer to the state. It was resuscitated in 1960 as Ferris State College and retained its lower division applied program at the associate degree level, almost like a community college within the college. By the 1980s it grew beyond expectations with over 30 degree programs from the associate to doctorate. It is organized into the Schools of Arts & Sciences, Education, Business, Technology, Allied Health, Optometry, and Pharmacy, plus extension programs including four off-campus sites under an Institute for Lifelong Learning. Its academic computing center was begun as a one-man show in the early 1980s without the support of administrative computing, largely in response to classroom needs and a self-help grouping of a few faculty pioneering in computer-assisted instruction. Its personnel came from subject-areas (business law, statistics, and language instruction) rather than computer science or formal information system management backgrounds. It secured housing in the university media center as an autonomous unit reporting to the office of Academic Affairs which patronized it with modest budgets. It was not so much planned, as it just happened! That is not atypical for academic computing (Masland, 1984b).

By 1987 the FSU Academic Computing office established a statement of goals and underlying philosophy, with attendant activities (Hobart & Sytsma, 1987).

1. *Support FSU faculty and staff in efforts using microcomputer in instruction and instructional support activities.*

1.1 Underlying Philosophy

As a polytechnic institution, it is essential that FSU students become computer literate. Computer literacy implies understanding essential elements of computer hardware and software, and their integration; what computer languages are and how software is created; the social and ethical impact that computers are having on society; ability to use simple computer-based productivity tools such as word processors, spreadsheets, and database managers; and, most importantly, understand how computers are used within the student's chosen career.

Given modest personnel and financial resources for Academic Computing, it is impossible to impact students directly. Thus, Academic Computing's function is to support the faculty in its efforts to make the students computer literate. To have a computer-literate student body requires some modest level of computer-literate faculty.

1.2 Resulting Actions

1.2.1 Introductory computer literacy "hands-on" workshops for faculty and staff.

1.2.2 Specialized intermediate and advanced microcomputer workshops, some of which are natural extensions of the initial workshop; others are selected by faculty and staff to meet particular needs.

1.2.3 Video tapes for computer training, both purchased and Ferris-produced for use by faculty and staff. Many of these have been borrowed for use in classes.

1.2.4 Library of computer publications (about 40 different computer magazines) and about 100 books for research and information.

1.2.5 One-on-one teaching of particular computer topics to faculty with specific individual needs.

1.2.6 Assisting faculty in finding and selecting software of particular interest for instructional use.

1.2.7 Reviewing software at the request of faculty for instructional applications.

2. *Assist the university in finding quality software within the financial resources of the institution to be shared with the entire academic community; to provide mechanisms to distribute that software to students, faculty, staff, and the local community at minimal cost; and to acquire training materials for this software to facilitate the learning process.*

2.1 Underlying Philosophy
Financial resources are too scarce for distribution across the entire academic community. Thousands of quality, inexpensive microcomputer programs exist in the public domain and in freeware/shareware collections that can be copied freely without violating copyright laws. Proprietary software cannot be shared in this manner but requires some formal acquisition and service program.

2.2 Resulting Actions

2.2.1 Academic Computing has promoted more stringent security for existing software in all laboratories.

2.2.2 The ADAPSO booklet on software copyright law was shared with members of the Computer Steering Committee.

2.2.3 Procedures were established to run software through 'vaccine' programs to protect FSU from infection by computer viruses.

2.2.4 Academic Computing maintains a collection of more than 18,000 programs for the IBM PC and compatible computers. The ability to locate specific software is facilitated via indexes on a CD-ROM data base system. Once a specific program is located, it can be copied to floppy disk for personal and/or professional use.

2.2.5 Academic Computing maintains a computer bulletin board with more than 3,000 programs available for copying shareware over the telephone. This free service allows users from all over the U.S. to call and download software.

2.2.6 Extensive training materials have been written to teach many of the more popular and useful software distributed by Academic Computing, including PC-Write, ExpressCalc, PC-File+, QMODEM, and PC-Graph.

3. *Provide the Ferris academic community with a quality, inexpensive source of IBM PC compatible hardware and assist persons interested in this hardware to select a system with components which work well together as a system.*

3.1 Underlying Philosophy
Personal use is more habitual than irregular use and computer literacy requires action and hands-on effort with a computer system. Having one's own system is the single best way to promote this effort. More students, faculty, and staff will purchase a system when costs are lower. The more systems that are acquired personally by the academic community, the fewer are required for purchase by the university.

3.2 Resulting Actions

3.2.1 Academic Computing assists students, faculty, and staff in selecting Zenith brand microcomputers and Epson and NEC brand printers for purchase at education discounts. Last year Academic Computing was responsible for purchases by faculty and staff in excess of $500,000. An automated ordering system has been developed to assist in this task.

3.2.2 Academic Computing is the primary liaison to Zenith Data Systems in solving both ordering and technical problems which may develop when the system arrives and must be set up; Administrative Computing serves a similar liaison role with IBM.

4. *Provide the academic community with elementary support for diagnosing microcomputer-related problems; assist with simple hardware-related tasks such as expanding memory, solve interfacing and configuration problems, and installing and formatting hard disk drives.*

4.1 Underlying Philosophy
Microcomputer use creates many situations where relatively simple but unfamiliar tasks must be performed for the computer system to function properly. An office that sees a large variety of problems can effectively meet new problems as they occur and thus provide a 'troubleshooting' advisory service.

4.2 Resulting Actions

4.2.1 Academic Computing provides elementary support in the following areas for both personal and institutional microcomputers:
(a) installing memory;
(b) installing, formatting, and setting up hard-disk drives;
(c) solving simple interfacing problems;
(d) installing software on particular hardware configurations.

4.2.2 Staff assist users in determining whether malfunctions are hardware or software problems.

5. *Provide services that complement rather than compete with those of the Computer Center and the Instrument Repair department to minimize any duplication of services which might occur.*

5.1 Underlying Philosophy
Because the amount of personnel and financial resources allocated to supporting computer users on the Ferris campus is modest, it is essential that needed services are not duplicated by different service areas and persons requiring these services should be supported with minimal confusion in a timely manner.

5.2 Resulting Actions

5.2.1 Referral service: When clients call Academic Computing and the service needed is outside its area of expertise, the person is immediately referred to the appropriate campus unit. If Academic Computing can provide the service in a competent manner, it does so.

6. *Involve Academic Computing in the planning of all major computer systems across the campus to insure that these systems are compatible and supportable.*

6.1 Underlying Philosophy
Academic Computing and the Computer Center approve all purchase orders for computer equipment in a review process. Last year approximately $40,000 of hardware and software purchase proposals were questioned because of:
(a) incorrect pricing/less expensive pricing elsewhere;
(b) obvious problems in component selection and compatibility;
(c) software compatibility with existing hardware;
(d) vendor selection.

6.2 Resulting Actions

6.2.1 Accurate pricing information for several vendors on many frequently-selected hardware and software items for several vendors is maintained with promotional literature.

6.2.2 Review procedures established to correct component selection or compatibility problems as needed and to recommend alternatives.

6.2.3 The office serves as a clearing house and inventory control for current information about what software and hardware is available on campus.

7. *Attempt to remain current in the microcomputer field, including both new hardware and software, and the books, magazines, and trade publications relating to computer applications in general and microcomputer-based educational applications in particular.*

7.1 Underlying Philosophy
To provide competent service, it is essential that Academic Computing staff read, attend conferences, and continue learning to build state-of-the-art expertise, and thus be able to continue to provide leadership to the campus community.

7.2 Resulting Actions

7.2.1 The staff is encouraged to spend a portion of its time learning new developments in computing as they affect instruction and teaching, by scheduling attendance at key conferences and participating in workshops and other forums.

7.2.2 As new information is discovered, it is shared with persons who may find the information useful. Approximately 40 articles are photocopied and sent to faculty each week as part of a current awareness service and a newsletter is published (*Bulldog Bytes*, a title word-play with the FSU mascot symbol: see Octernaud, 1988-).

In 1988 Academic Computing at Ferris State University was amalgamated into a new administrative unit, Library and Instructional Services (LIS) under a newly appointed Dean. During reorganization it became a unit under a coordinating officer, with collegial units of Media Production, Media Distribution, and an Individualized Learning Center, all as part of an LIS department: Learning Resource Center. The former three units serve faculty and administrators, while the latter is a laboratory serving students with a variety of media - audio, visual, computer-based, models, etc. The ILC exists as a semi-autonomous department within LIS; the other three departments constitute the Library: Collection Management and Services; Reference and Instructional Services; and Library Systems and Operations. The umbrella organization spreads office automation throughout, integrates services, and provides a contextual home for Academic Computing that is large enough to provide human and fiscal resources beyond what the office could muster by itself. This mechanism keeps academic and administrative computing separate but collegial and cooperative, each act as a check and balance on the other to steer the university through difficult decisions in applying information technology.

FSU's LIS units are now undertaking a major automation project combining office and bibliographic control functions for a campus-wide information system. The IRC is accommodating a new Timme Center for Teaching Excellence that provides release time and grants to faculty for the development of courseware. Its current focus is on computer-assisted instruction and integrated video in teaching and instructional support. Academic Computing is a critical component of this new amalgamation which should serve the university well in developing a dynamic information and instructional service program.

REFERENCES

CAUSE. 1986. *The Impact of Converging Information Technologies: Proceedings of the CAUSE National Conference.* (Monterey, CA, Dec. 9-12, 1986). Boulder, CO: CAUSE, 586 pp.

COUGHLIN, P.J. 1986. *Computing Strategies in Small Universities and Colleges.* Boulder, CO: CAUSE, 146 pp.

DOUGHERTY, D.M. 1983. "Academic Computing. The State of the Art in Equipment, Organizations, and the Trend to Terminal Use and Networking." *AEDS Journal* 16(2), 69-78

DOUGHERTY, D.M., et al. 1987. "Libraries and Computing Centers. Issues of Mutual Concern ..." *Journal of Academic Librarianship* 13(1), 4 pp. (insert); 13(6), 4 pp. (insert)

DOUGHERTY, R.M. 1987. "Libraries and Computing Centers: A Blueprint for Collaboration." *College and Research Libraries* 48(4), 289-296

HOBART, D. and SYTSMA, S. 1987. *Office of Academic Computing Goals, Philosophy, Actions.* Big Rapids, MI: Ferris State University

LOURDE, P.J. 1986. "Computing Trends and Strategies." *Cause/Effect* 9(3), 23-25

MASLAND, A.T. 1984a. *Academic Computing as Technological Innovation.* University Park, PA: Pennsylvania St. University Center for the Study of Higher Education, 21 pp. ERIC Doc., ED 244588

MASLAND, A.T. 1984b. "Cultural Influences on Academic Computing: Implications for Liberal Education." *Liberal Education* 70(1), 83-90

OCTERNAUD, S. (ed.). 1988-. *Bulldog Bytes.* Big Rapids, MI: Ferris State University, Office of Academic Computing. Act. title: Academic Computing Newsletter, bi-annual

OSGOOD, D. 1984. "A Computer on Every Desk. A Survey of Personal Computers in American Universities." *BYTE* 9(6), 162-184

PENGOY, R.E. 1974. "A Model for Administration of Computing Services and Facilities in a University Environment." *Journal of Computer-based Instruction* 1(2), 59-63

ROBERTS, M.M. 1971. "A Separatists View of University EDP." *Datamation* 17(5), 28-30

WARLICK, C.H. 1986. "Academic Computing Facilities and Services in Higher Education." *EDUCOM Bulletin* 21(3), 2-7

WARLICK, C.H. (ed.). 1988. *Directory of Computing Facilities in Higher Education.* Austin, TX: University of Texas Computational Center.

COMPUTERS AND THE FREEDOM OF LEARNING: COURSES, SOURCES, NUMBERS AND HISTORICAL UNDERSTANDING

Robert John Morris
Department of Economic and Social History
University of Edinburgh
Scotland

This paper arises from two factors, the experience of teaching history in a social science faculty and the belief that the recent development of micro computer technology presents historians with a vital opportunity for the solution of a particular ideological problem which faces the discipline. Our students come with a wide range of skills and backgrounds, from formal economics to the style of historical enquiry acquired with an arts faculty. We share two features with all history teaching in Britain. We have no tradition of methods teaching and we have no well defined and argued system of concepts and logic after the manner of social science economics.

Our ideological problem arises from the distinctive cultural position which historians face in the 1980s. Traditionally (ie. for the last hundred years), trained history graduates have headed in increasing numbers for position in administration and management. The historians skills of context sensitive assessment of evidence and clear not technical presentations of conclusions based upon that evidence have been vital in a wide variety of positions in politics, business and management. As a result of these information handling skills, the historian has been a traditional power broker. Despite this, historians feel that their discipline is increasingly threatened. That it is no longer "relevant". The reason for this lies in the increasing culture of numbers. Few aspects of power broking do not include the ability to deal with numbers. Which of us has not sat in a meeting, been presented with a table of numbers and been told we cannot, as a result of what those numbers mean, do what would otherwise seem very reasonable and desirable? The national newspapers of Europe regularly publish numbers of all kinds upon which the fate of jobs, the welfare of students and pensioners and the cost of housing and credit may all depend. These numbers all come out of some statistical process.(1) Surely they should be assessed and criticised like any other item of evidence with which the historian might deal. Yet we recruit students and often colleagues from a group which for the most part gratefully gave up maths at 15 and believes itself to be innumerate. This is the background to a situation in which Associations for the Defence of History are established and people of wisdom remind us that the study of the classical cultures of Greece and Rome was a dominant and prestigious subject as little as fifty years ago. Will historical studies shrink in the same way? One way out of this dilemma lies in the use of the new generation of powerful, user friendly, interactive, micro computers. The Edinburgh Social science Micro Laboratory Chose the Apple Macintosh SE system because of the attractive Windows, Icon, Mouse (WIMP)system and the active educational software market.(2) The Macintosh system provided a very short learning curve. Our own experience demonstrates that students can start their first hour of workshop tuition by locating the on-off switch and finish the session with a meaningful graphical output. Once this point has been reached the computing can become "fun" rather than a formidable barrier of skills between the student and "doing history". The subsequent development of the macintosh environment has fully justified the basis of the choice. The intuitive nature of learning within this system means than ta student who has mastered one package, say the statistics-graphic package Cricket with which we start our course, already has the bulk of skills needed to master other applications, say a word processing package like Macwrite or a more sophisticated statistical application like Statview 512. That being said, we should note that debates over "which system?" are likely to be increasingly less important as systems seem likely to converge. At present, the relationships of MS-Dos elements, the mainframe operating system and the Mac system are cumbersome and best left to the skills of a lab manager but ultimately should be transparent for student users. A situation in which road users had to take new driving lessons every time they changed the make of car they drove would not be tolerated for long, yet computer users accept such a situation with enthusiasm. Although at one time the Edinburgh plans envisaged the preparation of in-house software, we are now convinced that commercially available applications can provide the bulk of our needs.(3) In-house programming skills would be better used to customise commercially available applications with powerful macro facilities such as the well known spread sheet EXCEL and the french produced data base application 4th Dimension.

Figure 1:

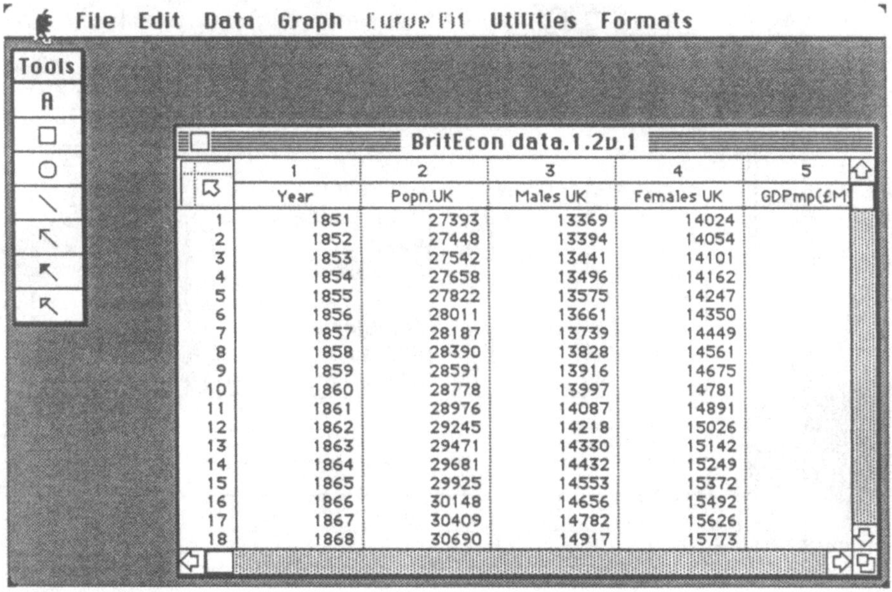

	1	2	3	4	5
	Year	Popn.UK	Males UK	Females UK	GDPmp(£M)
1	1851	27393	13369	14024	
2	1852	27448	13394	14054	
3	1853	27542	13441	14101	
4	1854	27658	13496	14162	
5	1855	27822	13575	14247	
6	1856	28011	13661	14350	
7	1857	28187	13739	14449	
8	1858	28390	13828	14561	
9	1859	28591	13916	14675	
10	1860	28778	13997	14781	
11	1861	28976	14087	14891	
12	1862	29245	14218	15026	
13	1863	29471	14330	15142	
14	1864	29681	14432	15249	
15	1865	29925	14553	15372	
16	1866	30148	14656	15492	
17	1867	30409	14782	15626	
18	1868	30690	14917	15773	

The Edinburgh course which we called "Wealth, consumption and welfare in Britain, 1850-1988" was designed to enable students to trace certain aspects of long run change in Britain over the last 130 years or so. We hope that it enables us, as teachers, to do something which we could not otherwise do without the machine; and that it enables students to tackle the culture of numbers as historians. The machine with its simple easy to learn statistics graphics packages has proved a powerful asset in overcoming the barrier of numbers. In this course we are able to exploit the availability of a vast range of statistical serials in the Unite Kingdom. We have two data rich periods. In the period between 1880 and 1914 *British Parliamentary Papers* published a wide range of topics which were becoming an increasing object of public debate. For example increasing efforts were made to publish data on wages and earnings as the state became interested in labour relations and the link between poverty and low wages.(4) The years between 1950 and the present also present a wide range of information in numerical form. Some are very detailed like the *New Earnings Survey*. Others are part summarized and accompanied by a wide range of explanatory material such as the *Employment Gazette, Regional Trends, Social Trends* and *Economic Trends*. They are also, as it happens the sort of information sources with which students are likely to come into contact in their future places in the labour market.

Figure 2:

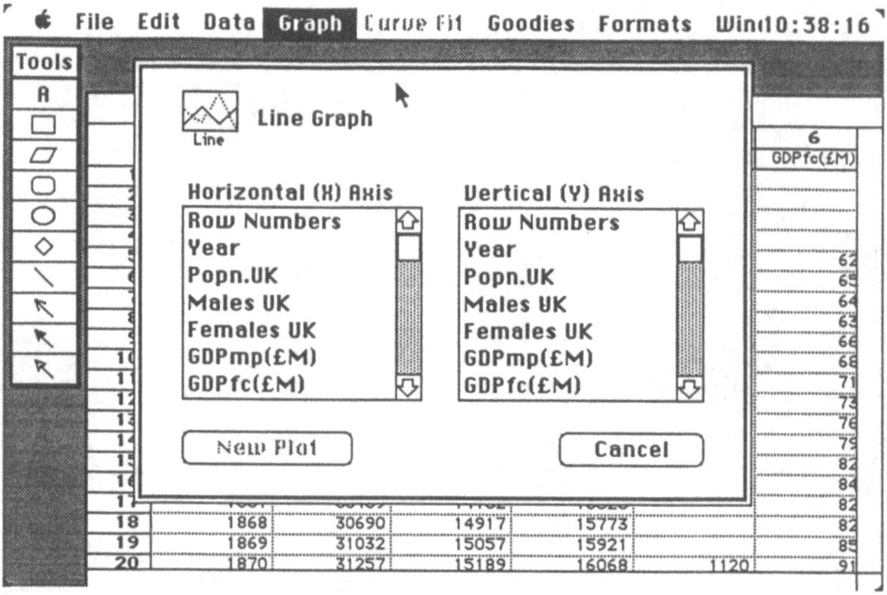

The machine enables us to encourage students to explore and present the numbers they use to describe long run change in a critical way. Let us take an apparently uncontroversial notion like the population of the United Kingdom. If we take a long run series from the standard sources we find the expected steady increase with a levelling off in the 1970s. We find a sharp fall in population in 1914-1917 and a steady and nearly compensating increasing between 1918 and 1920. This was the departure and return of British troops involved in the fighting in France. Here is a lesson in reading "definitions". In the early part of the period, British troops serving overseas were excluded from the United Kingdom population. Later this definitional decision was reversed. But why the sudden loss of four million people in 1922? Students find this difficult to answer because we are brought up on the ideology of this "great island nation" unshaken and unmoved by the great shocks of history. No German historian would find the concept of "the population of Germany between 1850 and 1988" an unproblematic one, yet the British student can easy forget the loss of the Irish Republic in 1922 and imagine that "the United Kingdom" is an uncontroversial and non value laden concept.

Figure 3:

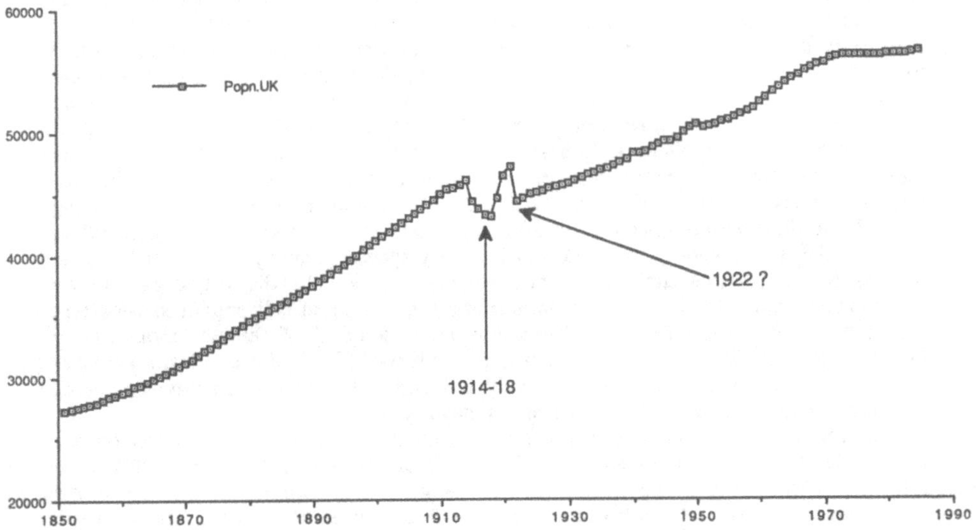

A more complex and fundamental examination of the culture of numbers is involved in the simple requirement to construct and evaluate an unemployment series from 1850 to the present. Generating the percentages is easy enough. The numbers are readily available. Even with, or perhaps especially with recent figures, a student who follows the standard procedure of checking definitions and referring to background material rapidly looses any feeling of security. The background papers in the *Employment Gazette* show clearly that the basis for the calculation has shifted considerably over the past ten years.(5) In Britain, unemployment figures are based upon claimants for unemployment benefit so that in October 1979, when fortnightly attendance at unemployment benefit offices was required, the effect was to add 20,000 to the unemployment total. In November 1981, better rates if supplementary benefit for men over 60 were introduced and an estimated 37,000 reduction in unemployment took place. October 1982, registration at job centres became voluntary and a move from registrations to claimants reduced the count by 190,000. In the 1983 budget, further improved benefits for men over 60 enabled a further 162,000 men to move from the unemployment figures. Other changes in record keeping moved a further 50,000 from the total. Now, unemployment is a percentage. The result of a simple long division sum. This percentage may be reduced by increasing the denominator (the total workforce) as well as reducing the numerator (the number of unemployed). In July 1986, the workforce was increased by adding HM Forces and the self employed to the number of salary and wage earners plus the unemployed who had previously made up the total. This reduced unemployment by 1.4% at a stroke. By comparison the addition of trainees in work related programmes to the labour force in 1988 brought about a mere reduction of 0.1%. Note, that this is not the result of any radical critic of statistics, but simply of the careful analysis of official documents. It may or may not be an accident that the bulk of changes resulted in the reduction of politically difficult numbers, but note that the student may conclude that the reductions were legitimate. For example, why were the self employed and armed forces excluded from the "labour force" for so long? The answer, of course, lies in the nature of the historical process which produced those numbers. "Unemployment" as we know it was invented by Lloyd George in 1911. It was a by product of the provision of certain benefits under National Insurance and associated schemes.(6) Before then the figures come from a limited number of trades unions who provided benefits for members. These figures refer in the main to adult skilled male labour. Whilst asking general questions about typicality, more fundamental issues emerge. "Unemployment" as an idea relates to a concept of work which is very specific, namely work as a full time reasonably homogenous activity for one employer, producing the major part of an individuals income. Studies of casual labour and the income of self employed people in the 19th century, and indeed our increasing under standing of female labour in the present shows that such a notion of work is not universal.(7) Here is one historical basis for understanding the paradox of relatively low rates of female unemployment being associated with high scores for indicators of poverty.

Informed by critical surveys of this sort, students may now gain further independence by literally plunging into the mass of numbers available to seek guidance and information related to a variety of problems of long run changes. For example, was Scotland a low wage economy in the late 19th century and has this changed?(8) With a little guidance and bibliographical backing, a student can begin to assess the available evidence and make choices and selections. Can begin to design an enquiry which will fit into the time budgets of a first degree course. Here, the machine again becomes a crucial weapon. Simple data entry and manipulation skills enable students to explore the shape and meaning of their data. In the illustrations given here, wage data is turned into a data set which is presented graphically ready for critical comment.

Figure 4:

The lesson drawn from this experience is simple. The machine has been used to overcome formidable barriers which many historians feel lie between them and the use of numbers. The demands in terms of mathematical skills have been very limited. Those who have some formal skills in terms of statistics may use them if they wish. The demands in terms of basic historical skills, framing questions, designing a research inquiry, selecting and justifying selections from the data (evidence, sources - which term do you prefer), evaluating that evidence in terms of source criticism and context, summarizing and presenting that evidence are substantial and satisfying. The use of graphics has proved vital here.

The machine then has provided the means of gaining access to the culture of numbers and subjecting that culture to the traditional skills of the historian. The computer has been experienced for what it is, a tool, in this case to learn the discipline of choice, summary and presentation in the wilderness of numbers. It is in this manner that the new generation of micro computers will add a little to the freedom of intellectual enquiry amongst historians and those we train to enter a world dominated by the culture of numbers.

Figure 5:

BUILDING TRADES.

Wages of the Principal Classes of Workpeople employed in the Building Trades (so in January and July of the Year 1891.

England.				Scotland.		Ireland.		United Kingdom.		Period of Year.	Occupation.
Northern Counties.		Total.									
No. on which Average is based.	Average Rate.	No. on which Average is based.	Average Rate.	No. on which Average is based.	Average Rate.	No. on which Average is based.	Average Rate.	No. on which Average is based.	Average Rate.		
	s. d.		s. d.		s. d.		s. d.		s. d.		MEN.
4	46 1	153	46 6	12	37 3	32	42 11	204	45 4	January -	Foremen.
6	43 5	188	48 3	14	38 2	27	42 5	229	47 0	July -	
53	34 6	275	32 3	89	27 6	38	28 7	402	30 10	January -	Masons.
60	36 1	489	34 8	67	32 9	54	35 6	610	34 6	July -	
32	33 5	337	33 2	3	31 11	88	28 6	428	32 3	January -	Bricklayers.
146	36 8	760	38 11	3	37 5	125	36 11	888	36 11	July -	
81	35 2	1,178	33 11	37	28 11	204	33 11	1,419	33 9	January -	Carpenters and Joiners.
62	30 1	1,324	35 6	30	33 6	162	33 11	1,516	35 3	July -	
4	33 0	164	33 4	—	—	9	36 5	173	30 6	January -	Plumbers.
3	32 4	153	34 8	—	—	7	36 7	160	34 9	July -	
2	32 0	416	29 7	53	25 6	—	—	469	29 2	January -	Painters.
5	33 4	688	33 9	110	32 8	15	32 7	813	33 7	July -	
14	33 10	108	32 10	—	—	15	33 11	123	33 0	January -	Plasterers.
26	36 2	140	36 6	—	—	28	33 11	168	36 1	July -	
3	31 0	22	30 10	—	—	—	—	22	30 10	January -	Slaters.
4	33 0	30	34 7	—	—	6	35 3	36	34 8	July -	
—	—	117	33 11	—	—	14	32 7	131	33 9	January -	Other Skilled Men.
—	—	100	36 0	—	—	13	32 4	113	35 7	July -	
10	25 8	64	22 8	—	—	5	20 0	69	22 6	January -	Handy Men.
15	25 7	146	24 1	—	—	9	20 0	155	23 10	July -	
17	22 3	143	22 2	—	—	26	17 3	169	21 5	January -	Carters.
24	22 1	160	23 4	—	—	27	17 3	187	21 7	July -	
64	21 8	1,247	21 5	119	16 7	374	15 4	1,740	19 9	January -	Labourers.
238	23 5	3,352	23 9	127	22 3	366	16 4	2,845	22 9	July -	
10	26 7	43	26 7	11	23 11	—	—	54	26 1	January -	Unclassed Men.
11	26 10	39	28 8	9	25 4	—	—	48	28 0	July -	
											LADS AND BOYS.
29	8 0	382	8 3	30	7 6	78	7 2	511	8 0	January -	Unclassed.
46	9 9	400	8 7	52	7 7	87	7 1	540	8 3	July -	

Figure 6:

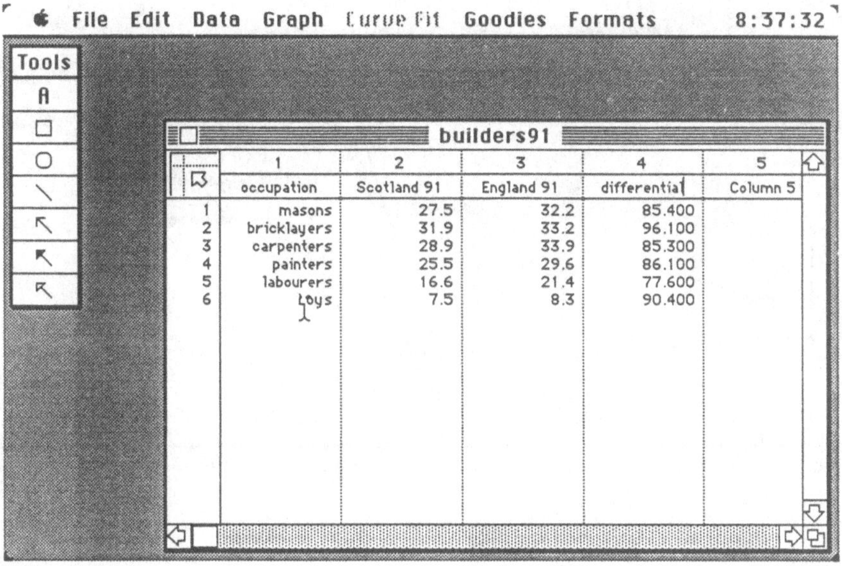

	1	2	3	4	5
	occupation	Scotland 91	England 91	differential	Column 5
1	masons	27.5	32.2	85.400	
2	bricklayers	31.9	33.2	96.100	
3	carpenters	28.9	33.9	85.300	
4	painters	25.5	29.6	86.100	
5	labourers	16.6	21.4	77.600	
6	boys	7.5	8.3	90.400	

Figure 7:

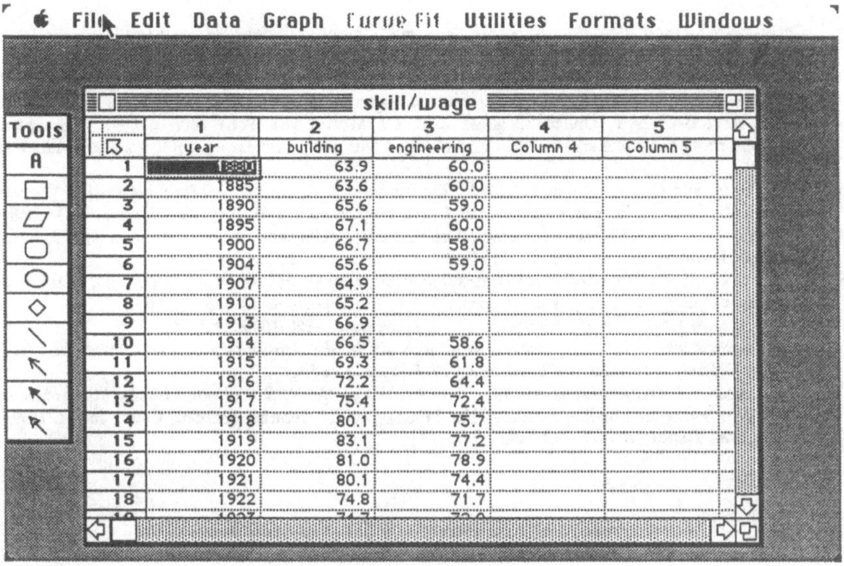

	1	2	3	4	5
	year	building	engineering	Column 4	Column 5
1	1880	63.9	60.0		
2	1885	63.6	60.0		
3	1890	65.6	59.0		
4	1895	67.1	60.0		
5	1900	66.7	58.0		
6	1904	65.6	59.0		
7	1907	64.9			
8	1910	65.2			
9	1913	66.9			
10	1914	66.5	58.6		
11	1915	69.3	61.8		
12	1916	72.2	64.4		
13	1917	75.4	72.4		
14	1918	80.1	75.7		
15	1919	83.1	77.2		
16	1920	81.0	78.9		
17	1921	80.1	74.4		
18	1922	74.8	71.7		

Figure 8:

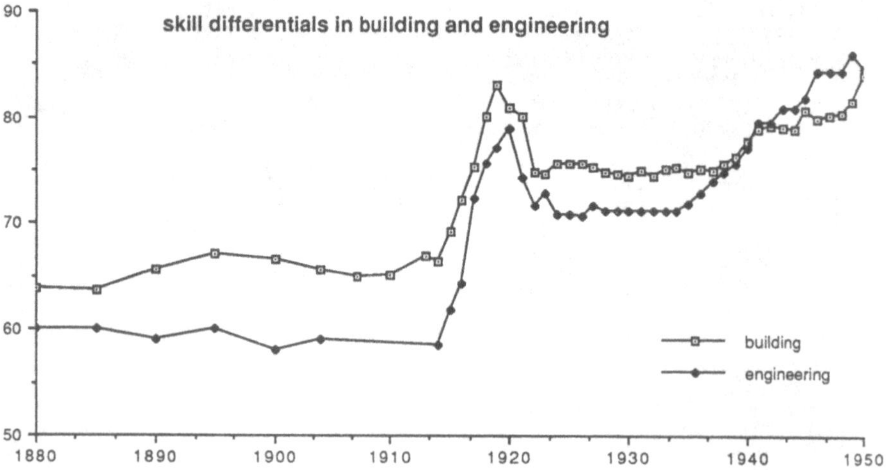

NOTES

1. Christopher Johnson. 1988. *Measuring the Economy. A guide to understanding official statistics*. London; John Irvine, Ian Miles, Jeff Evans et al. (eds.). 1979. *Demystifying Social Statistics*. London
2. see contribution by R.J. Morris to the Computers in Teaching Initiative, Edinburgh University Final Report available from Computers in Teaching Initiative Support Service, University of Bath, Claverton Down, Bath BA2 7AY, United Kingdom; also R.J. Morris with Toby Morris. 1987. "Computers in Teaching: economic and social history at Edinburgh." *University Computing*, vol.9, no.3, September 1987, 177-180
3. R.J. Morris with Charles Anderson. 1987. "The Edinburgh Computers in Teaching Project (Economic and Social History)", in: Peter Denley and Deian Hopkin (eds.). *History and Computing*. Manchester
4. R. Davidson. 1985. "Treasuring Control and Labour Intelligence in late Victorian and Edwardian Britain." Historical Journal, vol. 28, 719-726
5. Measures of Unemployment and characteristics of the unemployed. *Employment Gazette*, October 1986; Changes affecting the unemployment count. *Employment Gazette*, October 1986
6. W.R. Garside. 1980. *The Measurement of Unemployment*. 1850-1979. Oxford
7. G. Stedman Jones. 1971. *Outcaste London. A study in the relationship between classes in Victorian Society*. Oxford; R.E. Pahl. 1984. *Divisions of Labour*. London
8. John Foster and Charles Woolfson. 1986. *The Politics of the UCS Work-in*. London; Richard Rodger. 1986. "The Victorian Building Industry. The Housing of the Scottish Working Class", in: M. Doughty. *Building the Industrial City*. Leicester

CALL - A REASONABLE PERSPECTIVE?

Heike Rautenhaus
University of Oldenburg
FRG

1. Preliminary Remarks

I am not using the acronym CAI (*C*omputer *A*ssisted *I*nstruction) as suggested in the title of this section, but CALL (*C*omputer *A*ssisted *L*anguage *L*earning) in order to stress that I see the *learner* at the center of the process and the computer in a subordinate, serving function.

This paper deals with the question of whether *Call* should be given a chance in our schooling-system or whether we should do our best to keep the computer out of our language classrooms.

2. Analysis of the Interaction Process between Student and Computer

In order to answer the above question, one must find out what students of foreign languages really learn when working with computer-programs by analyzing the language they produce in front of the computer. In order to do this, we (a research group at the university of Oldenburg) made some video-films which were then transcribed word by word.

For example, we had three students work on one of the first programs produced by German schoolbook-publishers: STORY CORNER which has been adapted from the English Wida-software STORYBOARD. It uses a type of exercise that can be realized only on the computer (and by no other means). It is a text-reproduction program in which students read a page of text on the screen. The text then disappears and is replaced by dashes (one for each letter), after which the students have to restore the text word for word from their memory or from their general experience with English texts.

The following protocol is a two-minute segment of a one-hour video. The students are in the middle of discussing whether 'Mike Miller' is to be treated by the user of the program as one word or as two:

No.	Sp.	Speech act	Text
90	B	indicating	This is to send off the information. (meaning the 'enter'-key)
91	A	agreeing	Yes.
92	B	suggesting	But after Mike there must be a hole, and then Miller.
93	R	agreeing	Yes.
94	A	agreeing	Yes, I know.
95		objecting/ suggesting	But I think only Mike is one word, the whole text.

96	B	agreeing	Yes.
97	A	continuing	And Miller is another word, a new
		the suggestion	word...
98	B	agreeing	Yes.
99	A	continuing the suggestion	...and we try once more then.
100		summarizing (what was said so far)	First we take the word Mike and send it out. And then we take the next word Miller and send it out, too.
101	B	agreeing	Ach so! Yes.
102	A	suggesting/ asking	This we send out. (presses the 'enter'-key; screen: Mike)
103	B	agreeing	Yes.
104	A	confirming	Mike.
105		suggesting	And now we can ... write Miller.
106		asking (concerning target)	This one? (types Miller)
107		asking (concerning interaction)	Is it right?
108	B u. R	answering	Yes.
109	A	suggesting/ declaration of intent	Send it out. (screen: Miller)
110		confirming	Miller
111	B	confirming	Mike Miller
112	R	asking	And now?
113	A	asking same question	And now?
114		answering/ requesting	The next one.
115		asking (concerning target)	What was the name of the other?
116	R	answering	He was a milkman.
117	A	agreeing	Yes, milkman.
118		asserting	Milkman is not with capital letters,
119		asking	with little letters?
120	R	answering	Yes.
121	A	repeating	(types and speaks) milkm
122		asking	a?
123	R	answering	a-n
124		commanding	send out (screen: milkman)
125		exclaiming joy	Oh!
126		suggesting/	He *was* a milkman.
127	B	suggesting/ asking	hospital?
128	A	agreeing	hospital, was
129	R	repeating	was

130	A		(types) was (screen: not found)
131		commenting	nix was
132	R	correcting/ suggesting	is, he *is* a milkman.
133	A		(types) is (screen: 3x is)
134	R	reinforcing	yes
135		suggesting	he
136	A	asking	he?
137		suggesting	You want?

What precisely are the students doing here?
Let us read segments of the protocol (you have before you) and analyze them in detail (bit by bit):

1. *Units 90 to 114*: Here, student A explains that the program accepts only one word at a time. The students put forward suggestions, make objections, agree or disagree, ask and answer questions.

2. *Units 115 to 117*: Here, the students are trying to meet the assignment by recollecting the contents of the text from memory. Unit 117 is an abbreviated form which could be expanded into 'Yes, milkman is a good word.' or 'Yes, let's try the word milkman.' Such production of one or two-word sentences is typical for interaction when using the computer: the number of the possible speech acts is limited and, thus, specific speech acts do not need to be explicated since they are obvious from the context.

3. *Units 118-120*: Here, a student asks about a rule of English grammar and receives an answer: small letters are used in nouns. The form of unit 119 is especially interesting: grammatical complexity is replaced by intonation. This is a normal feature of the spoken language, and the student makes use of it because of its simplicity.

4. *Units 121 to 123*: Here, student R helps student A with a spelling-problem. This is important for the assignment because the program would otherwise not accept the word.

5. In *unit 125* something emerges which can be observed throughout the remainder of the video: Student R, who had warned me about his insufficient English, starts feeling at home with the computer and with the program, because his suggestions are accepted. Student A appears to realize this too, and asks student R to take over the typing (*unit 137*).

6. *Units 126 to 130*: These units express different trains of thought of students R and B; student A responds positively to both suggestions by repeating them (*unit 128*, hospital, was), followed by R who, encouraged by his experience, repeats his suggestion (*unit 129*, was). This is the normal way of asserting oneself in communication situations with more than two participants.

7. *Unit 132*: Here, R corrects his own suggestion; he has learned to respect the computer's judgement and he knows the syntactic rules of English well enough to understand that in this case only the tense form of 'to be' can be wrong.

Summary:

The students are involved in intensive discussion. They practice language *use*. They are not focused on producing impressively correct language, however, but on solving a concrete problem - i.e. to restore the text - as economically as possible. To that end they pool their knowledge of the program, the text and the language; they teach each other.

They do not interfere with each other in any way at any point in the entire film. Sometimes it looks as if they are talking at cross-purposes. But a closer look reveals that any time an utterance is not commented on immediately, it is taken up later in the discussion. Nor is there any example of a student entering a message in the computer without first coordinating it with the other participants.

The students are *not* concerned with the correctness of their language in their discussion; this would distract from their focus. The lexical substitutions 'hole' instead of 'space' in *unit 92*, 'little' instead of 'small' in *unit 119*, 'send out' instead of 'enter' in *unit 124* satisfy their communicative functions; the grammatical error in *unit 124* ('send out' instead of 'send it out') seems to go unnoticed. At no point in the whole film do the students correct each other *unless this serves to fulfil their concrete task*. In other words, they do change - later on in the film - 'he know' into 'he knows' and 'much' into 'many' in order to fill gaps that have emerged, but they do *not* correct language that serves as a means of negotiation, like 'You want?' into 'Do you want to/Would you like to type it in?' (*unit 137*).

Spelling errors are corrected constantly, because correct spelling is one of the rules of the game, and the students read from the screen all the time.

Other, more comprehensive, studies have come to the conclusion that in interaction with computer-programs like STORY CORNER, students produce short utterances, replace complicated grammatical structures by means of intonation, and do not observe the rules of correctness (Piper in System, Vol. 14).

But this is quite natural in tasks demanding the most efficient solutions to concrete problems: the speech acts are determined by the situation and the shared goal, only the referent has to be clarified. Focus on the quality of the language used or conscious revision of language competence would be counter-productive.

What then is the value of an exercise as the one shown in the video? I believe it is *basically the extensive, pragmatic use of foreign language. During these 2 minutes, the students conveyed and received more information to and from each other than they would during a whole foreign language lesson in a normal classroom.* During these 2 minutes, the students made suggestions, accepted or rejected them, asked and answered questions, gave explanations to content and - to a smaller extent - to linguistic rules. And they did this although the program was not intended to instigate *discussion* amongst users but to practice vocabulary, grammar and textual knowledge.

So my answer to the question in the title of my paper is *yes* we should give CALL a chance in our schools, *but* we should be on the alert! This becomes clear when we look at the existing software for the foreign language classroom!

3. Some Critical Remarks on the Existing Software

Programs on grammar and vocabulary are rooted in stimulus-response learning, concentrating on form while neglecting content, and suggest to the student that the computer can never fail. Some of the programs cannot be justified for pedagogical reasons (for example: *shooting words*); most of them keep the students and the teachers from developing their own ideas. Only authoring programs make it possible for teachers to develop their own material for class and individual students' use.

Simulation programs are supposed to practice language use by putting the students in realistic situations to develop strategies, make decisions, and take the responsibility for them. Since students need the help of a partner, they work in pairs, thus, practising their speaking ability. But only realistic simulations allow students to identify with assigned roles and tasks and only a careful preparation by the teacher helps them use the target language when working with the program.

The latest technological developments will make it possible to practice listening comprehension and teach foreign culture by interactive videodisk packages using laservision videodisk players. Here we can expect a boom in materials to be scrutinized in terms of content and psychological and pedagogical basis.

4. Conclusion

The programs are manifold, the opportunities and risks, too. The most important question concerning software for the foreign language classroom must be: how can these programs be integrated into the current curriculum as *one* of several media used in foreign language teaching?
Teachers never will be replaced by computers, but teachers *should* be able to evaluate programs and to decide

* if they want to use a program at all, and if so
* when to use it,
* how to get students prepared for it,
* which accompanying materials to give to students, and
* how to make use of the results in follow-up classroom activities.

The readiness of teachers to examine the opportunities, limits and risks of CALL and thus prescribe specific program qualities to software-producers, will decide the future profile of foreign language teaching in our country.

It follows that there is a need for university instructors involved in the training of language teachers to work on this problem as well. We must avoid programs in our schools which are not acceptable for pedagogical, psychological or linguistic reasons. As university instructors we must participate critically and constructively in the development of useful software.

REFERENCES

BADDOCK, Barry. 1988. "Cloze and the Microcomputer." *Praxis des neusprachlichen Unterrichts* 2/1988, 141-146

BALAJTHY, Ernest. 1987. "Computer and Reading/Language Arts: Will We Try to Cure the Problem with Turpentine?" *Computers in the Schools*, vol. 4, No.1, Spring 1987, 67-79

BERGER, Rudolf, u.a. 1985. *Computergestützter Fremdsprachenunterricht - Ein Handbuch*. Langenscheidt

BLAKE, Robert. 1987. "Call and the Language Lab of the Future." *ADFL Bulletin* 18, No. 2, January 1987, 25-29

BURGHARDT, U. und HAUER, M. 1987. "Ein Autorenprogramm für Microcomputer - Der Lehrer bestimmt den Inhalt." *Neusprachliche Mitteilungen* 1/1987, 42-45

DAVIES, Graham (ed.). o.J. *Callboard, News from the World of Computer Assisted Language Learning*, Issue No. 10

DAVIES, Graham. 1988. "Using the Computer to Stimulate Conversation", in: Kühlwein, W. und Spillner, B. (Hrsg.). *Sprache und Individuum*. Gunter Narr, Tübingen, 79-83

DAVIES, G. and HIGGINS, J. 1985. *Using Computers in Language Learning: A Teacher's Guide* (2nd enlarged edition: Information Guide 22). Centre for Information on Language Teaching and Research. Regent's College, Inner Circle, Regent's Park, London NW1 4NS

DICKINSON, Leslie. 1987. *Self-Instruction in Language Learning*. CUP

EAST Heft 2/86 zum Thema 'Computer und Englischunterricht'

EDELHOFF; FUNK; NEUNER. 1981. "Challenges: Theorie und Praxis des Unterrichts im Medienverbund." *EAST* 2/1981, 187-198

FELIX, Sascha W. 1977. "Natürlicher Zweitsprachenerwerb und Fremdsprachenunterricht." *Linguistik und Didaktik* 31, 231-247

GORNY, Peter. 1986. "Computer in der Schule", in: *Zukunft der Schule. Chancen und Risiken*. Universität Oldenburg, 232-255

HIGGINS, J. and JOHNS, T. 1984. *Computers in Language Learning*. Collins

JONES, Christopher. 1983. "Computer assisted language learning: testing or teaching?" *ELT Journal*, vol. 37/3, July 1983, 247-250

JONES, Chr. and FORTESCUE, S. 1987. *Using Computers in the Language Classroom*. Longman

JONES, Glyn. 1987. "Computer and Group Work." *EAST* 3,4/1987, 485-490

KENNING, M.J. and KENNING, M-M. 1984. *An Introduction to Computer Assisted Language Teaching*. OUP

KNAPP-POTTHOFF, Anneliese und KNAPP, Karlfried. 1982. *Fremdsprachenlernen und -lehren*. Kohlhammer

KRASHEN, Stephen D. 1987. *Principles and Practice in Second Language Acquisition*. Prentice-Hall

KRASHEN, Stephen D. and TERRELL, Tracy D. 1988. *The Natural Approach - Language Acquisition in the Classroom*. Prentice-Hall

Landesinstitut für Schule und Weiterbildung: 1986. *Neue Informations- und Kommunikationstechnologien 2*. Soest, Paradieser Weg 64

LEGENHAUSEN, Lienhard and WOLFF, Dieter (eds.). 1987. *Computer Assisted Language Learning and Innovative EFL Methodology*. Universität Augsburg

LEGENHAUSEN, Lienhard und WOLFF, Dieter. 1987. *Computersimulationen im Fremdsprachenunterricht*. Vortrag auf der GAL 1987, Heidelberg

LOVIS, F. and TAGG, E.D. (eds.). 1988. *Computers in Education, Proceedings of the 1st European Conference on Computers in Education - ECCE 88, Lausanne, Switzerland, 24-29 July, 1988*. North-Holland - Amsterdam, New York, Oxford, Tokyo

MYDLARSKI, Donna. o.J. "Cooperative Computer-Assisted Language Learning: Is It Living Up To Its Promise?" *Journal of Educational Techniques and Technologies*, vol. 20, No. 1, 26-29

OLIVIER, Evelyn and William. o.J. "Computer Assisted Language Learning: An Investigation On Some Design And Implementation Issues." *System*, vol. 15, No. 1, 1-17

PIPER, Alison. o.J. "Conversation And The Computer: A Study Of The Conversational Spin-off Generated Among Learners Of English As A Foreign Language Working In Groups." *System*, vol. 14, No. 2, 187-198

PIPER, Alison. 1987. "Helping learners to write: a role for the word processor." *ELT Journal* 41/2, April 1987, 119-125

RÜSCHOFF, Bernd. 1985. "Brauchen wir Computer im Fremdsprachenunterricht?" *EAST* 3/1985, 557-564

RÜSCHOFF, Bernd. 1986. *Fremdsprachenunterricht mit computergestützen Materialien. Didaktische Überlegungen und Beispiele*. Hueber

RÜSCHOFF, Bernd. 1987. "Möglichkeiten der Computernutzung als Unterrichtsmittel im Fremdsprachenunterricht", in: *Perspektiven der angewandten Linguistik*. Gunter Narr

RÜSCHOFF, Bernd. o.J. "The 'Intelligence' of Intelligently Programmed Adaptive Call Materials For Self-Study." *System*, vol. 14, No. 2, 205-210

TRIPPEN, Gaby; LEGENHAUSEN, Lienhard und WOLFF, Dieter. 1988. "Lernerstrategien und Lernerprozesse bei der Bearbeitung von CALL-Software", in: Kühlwein, Spillner. *Sprache und Individuum*. Gunter Narr, 83-86

SCHMID-SCHÖNBEIN, Gisela. 1987. "Computereinsatz als Form der Binnendifferenzierung im Englischunterricht", in: *11. Fremdsprachendidaktiker-Kongreß*. Gunter Narr, 572-578

SCHMID-SCHÖNBEIN, Gisela. 1987. "Der Computer im Fremdsprachenunterricht - ein neuer Nürnberger Trichter für Wortschatzarbeit und Kontextverständnis?" in: *Anglistik & Englischunterricht* Band 32, 123-129

UNDERWOOD, John H. 1984. *Linguistics, Computers, and the Language Teacher. A Communicative Approach*. Rowley, London, Tokyo

WILLIAMS, Gerald T. 1986. "Computer im Fremdsprachen-Unterricht. Warum nicht mehr geschieht." *EAST* 3,4/1986, 640-642

WRAGGE-LANGE, Irmhild. 1980. *Interaktion im Unterricht - Ein Verfahren zur Analyse schulischer Sozialisationsprozesse*. Beltz

ZINNECKER, Jürgen (Hrsg.). 1975. *Der heimliche Lehrplan - Untersuchungen zum Schulunterricht*. Weinheim, Basel

THE INTERACTION OF TEACHING AND RESEARCH IN COMPUTER-BASED HISTORY

Richard Trainor
University of Glasgow
United Kingdom

Teaching is an integral part of historical(1) computing. This proposition does not depend merely on the rising popularity of computer-aided instruction (CAI) which, in higher education as well as in schools, is boosting the appeal of the discipline at a time when its place in the curriculum is often under attack. Nor does the argument depend solely on the increasing attention which meetings such as the Cologne Computer Conference have devoted to teaching. Nor does the argument rest entirely on the utility of computer-based teaching for achieving basic educational objectives (Trainor 1987a). More fundamentally, the centrality of CAI to historical computing is based on the close and mutually beneficial relationship which should, and increasingly does, exist between computerised teaching and computerised research.

The historical computing community must firmly resist the tendency to segregate research from teaching. For too long historical computing has been perceived (by most outside observes and even by many practitioners) as polarised between, on the one hand, high-powered researchers immersed in the complexities of their projects and, on the other hand, instructors adopting intellectually inferior but pedagogically effective tools in order to boost enrolments. This lingering misperception indicates that inadequate attention has been paid to how computerised history can simultaneously further both research and teaching.

Such interaction is facilitated by recent advances in microcomputing, especially the development of simple yet powerful software and the emergence of cheaper and more reliable local area networks. Thus equipped, students can gain quick access to important data, previously inaccessible to them, by querying specially selected teaching datasets downloaded from large mainframe-based research databases.(2)

This advantage is particularly clear in the case of bulky, complex sources such as: manuscript censuses; registers of births, deaths and marriages; pollbooks; and business records. In such cases the computer allows the student to move beyond perusal of facsimiles to active analysis: the computer becomes a tool for active inquiry rather than an all-absorbing end in itself.

These datasets can be exploited through teaching exercises which allow students to link their results both to the wider databases and, more importantly, to the broader historical issues involved. Likewise, in order that the students can analyse the data intelligently and relate their computer-based learning to their more traditional teaching, they must be presented with information about the pitfalls as well as the potential of the raw sources from which the computerised dataset is drawn.

This approach has been adopted in Glasgow's Design and Implementation of Software in History (DISH) Project (Trainor 1987b; Morgan 1987). DISH(3) uses computer-based research in: a new "skills" course ("Computing for Historians"); student dissertations; and "source-based workshops" in a variety of existing introductory and advanced courses.(4) The sources used are varied, including for example medieval English religious records, early modern Baltic trade returns, Victorian Scottish property valuations, 19th-century American electoral data and Soviet prosographic information.

A specific example will illustrate the source-based workshop. It is drawn from a social history course. "Elites in Nineteenth-Century British Society". Available to third and fourth year students(5), the course provides a broad survey of 19th-century British social history, including topics such as industrial relations and social policy as well as the social structures of the aristocracy and the middle class. Half of the sessions are lectures; the remaining half are divided equally between computer workshops and conventional discussion tutorials. Few of the students have extensive prior experience of computing or statistics.

One of the issues explored in the course is the extent to which the various 19th-century British social strata (within the middle class, and across the inexact boundary between the middle and working classes) associated voluntarily with each other. The relevant secondary literature on this subject has frequently used the extent to which partners from the various strata married each other as a surrogate for the degree of association between the groups (Foster 1974; McLeod 1974; Gray 1976; Crossick 1978). Accordingly, the computer workshop for this particular week - in which the lecture also discusses this and related issues - is based on a research database of thousands of marriages compiled by the author from a particular region, the West Midlands, often held to be of pivotal significance for understanding British class structure (Briggs 1952; Tholfsen 1953-54; Behagg 1986). The dataset is a small (less than 1000 cases) subset of the whole, comprising a systematic sample of the marriages for a particular town, West Bromwich, which is arguably typical of the region.

The exercise is distributed a week in advance, and (after discussion on the previous computer workshop) the instructor "talks the students through" it at the start of the workshop itself. The exercise begins with a discussion of the relevant general issues in the course, explaining how marriage patterns can be used to help resolve these questions. There follows a discussion of the marriage registers (aided by a photocopied example) from which the datatest has been compiled. The exercise points out hidden advantages (such as information on marriage age, literacy, residence and social mobility) and disadvantages (notably the systematic under-reporting of brides' occupations, necessitating concentration on the jobs held by their fathers). The students are then given information on the particular town and region from which the data has been drawn, highlighting unusual features which must be taken into account when drawing general implications from results derived from the teaching dataset.

After these preliminaries, the datatest itself is introduced, with an example of a record (see Figure 1), followed by an explanation of the various fields and of the coding procedure. Particular emphasis is put on the categories (industrialists, white collar workers, metal craftsmen, and miners, for example) in which occupations have been grouped, paying special attention to the broader categories (upper middle class, lower middle class, marginal, and working class) into which the occupational groups have in turn been combined.

The problem itself has three parts. First, the students are asked to discover how far marriages occurred within either single occupation or single occupational groups. Second, having been presented with pie charts representing the patterns of groom's father's occupational groups, bride's father's occupational groups, literacy and residence for the dataset as a whole, the students examine prepared subsets, first of marriages occurring entirely within the working class, next of those occurring across

the middle class/working class line, and finally of those occurring within the middle class. They are asked to discover how far each subset differed from the overall patterns of parental occupations, literacy and marriage. Third, the students search for any differences between the pattern of upper middle class and lower middle class marriages. Fourth, there is an opportunity to discover how the patterns of, say, groom's father's occupations may have changed over time (See Figure 2).
Finally, the students are asked to cross-tabulate groom's father's with bride's father's occupation for the dataset as a whole.

Figure 1: An Example of a Record from the Marriages Teaching Datatest in the DISH Project's "Elites" Course

IDENTIFY	: 00062
TOWN	: WEST BROMWICH
PARISH	: CC
DATE	: 1849/12/05
REGNO	: 225
MODE	: LICENCE
GNAME	: OWEN JAMES HIGGINS
GAGE	: 27
GMARCOND	: B
GOCCUP	: ARCHITECT
GGROUP	: PROF
GTRSD	: DUBLIN
GFRNAME	: OWEN JACOB
GFROCCUP	: ARCHITECT
GFRGROUP	: PROF
GFRDEAD	: N
GLITCY	: Y
BNAME	: UNDERHILL ISABELLA
BAGE	: 23
BMARCOND	: S
BOCCUP	: N/A
BGROUP	: N/A
BTRSD	: WEST BROMWICH
BFRNAME	: UNDERHILL THOMAS
BFROCCUP	: SURGEON
BFRGROUP	: PROF
BFRDEAD	: N
BLITCY	: Y
MOREDATA	: N/A
REMARKS	:

The next part of the exercise asks the students to draw implications from their results, keeping in mind the peculiarities of the case study as well as the general characteristics of the source. Finally, the students have a chance to suggest improvements in the workshop.

Does the approach work from the student's point of view? Because the computerised teaching material is drawn from the instructor's own research (or that of a colleague), such teaching can be especially vivid as well as particularly firmly based. Moreover, the students are involved in exploring data actively, and they appear to enjoy this "collaboration" with their instructors, even though the workshops are more time consuming than other classroom formats. Also, they seem to feel that the structured exercises help them to learn about key issues in the course.

Figure 2: An Example of Graphical Analysis of Material from the Marriages Teaching Dataset of the DISH Project's "Elites" Course: A Comparison of the Grooms' Fathers' Occupational Groups, West Bromwich, 1837-41, 1900-02

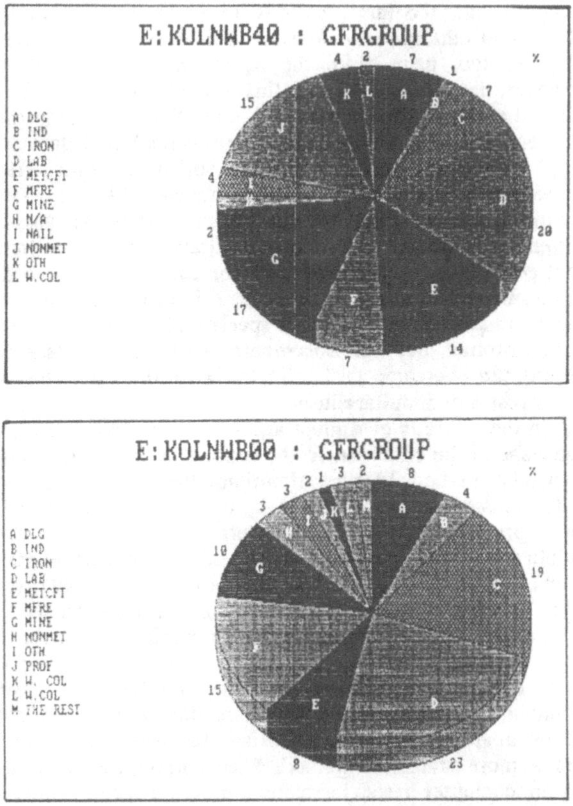

DLG	= Retailers		MINE	= Miners	
IND	= Industrialists		NONMET	= Craftsmen (outside metal trades)	
IRON	= Ironworkers				
LAB	= Labourers		OTH	= Other	
METCFT	= Metal Craftsmen		PROF	= Professional & Commercial	
MFRE	= Employees in Manufacturing		W.COL	= White Collar Workers	

Is the approach too simple for university students? As the example itself suggests, the approach is open-ended rather than "cut and dried". There is no single predetermined set of answers. Moreover, there is no single way of obtaining answers. Although at first exercises must be simple and tightly structured, they can become increasingly challenging and student-directed as the users become more proficient. The marriage exercise described above is about half-way along this spectrum. Later in the course, students are presented, for example, with a dataset drawn from poor law applications, and are simply asked to analyse them to answer general questions such as the categories of applicant most likely to receive relief. By that stage of the course, students are comfortable enough with the computers, the specific software used on them, and the "workshop" method that highly specific questions are no longer necessary. Of course it could be that the approach is all too demanding. However, experience suggests that the large majority of students make at least reasonable progress. Independent educational evaluation has been positive (Trainor 1987c).

The instructor, too, gains from the approach insofar as it is educationally effective. Moreover, the teaching-research link has other significant advantages for the instructor. First, the instruction is especially enjoyable, providing the link between teaching and research that higher education presupposes but seldom achieves. Second, given the need to combine clarity and speculation in computerised instruction, preparing a research database for teaching encourages the instructor to understand better the nature of research data and the questions they can answer. Third, close pedagogical attention to the original sources facilitates research as well as instruction. Fourth, student generation of their own data for course essays and dissertation can, with appropriate safeguards, enhance present and future staff research projects. Even with such student assistance only a highly specialised course be based solely on the research of one historian, but well documented exchanges of datasets between and within institutions can overcome this difficulty. Thus the instructor can improve his teaching and his research simultaneously.

Of course, in the interests of student and instructor alike, the research-based use of the computer should be restricted to those parts of the curriculum where it is an appropriate teaching method. In other situations, the computer can more profitably be employed for illustration purposes, say by using a dataset taken from the tables of a textbook to provide examples for a lecture. Moreover, there will also be parts of the curriculum where no computer usage is suitable, research-based or otherwise. Furthermore, even when the research-based approach to computer-aided teaching is appropriate, the machine's insatiable appetite for the time, funds and patience of academics dictates that they implement the method warily and collaboratively (Trainor 1988).

Although the case for linking teaching and research has been illustrated by means of Glasgow's database workshops, the argument does not rest on them alone. The approach can be adapted to textual materials, for example, or to more complex datasets, or to a more statistical method. Such variety can be found in teaching-research links in computer-based instruction in other British institutions (Trainor 1989). Likewise, the current movement beyond simulations and drill-and-practice in computerised teaching in American universities and colleges also includes a profitable interaction between research and teaching (Burton 1987; Gutmann and Fliess 1986; Miller and Modell 1988; Rohrs 1987). There are also hints of similar interest on the Continent.(6) For the approach does not depend on any particular curriculum or on a high degree of student specialisation either in history or in computing. Indeed, as various projects in British schools have demonstrated the approach is viable even below the university level.

Thus, the interaction between research and teaching, with advantages for students and instructor alike, does much to justify not only the prominent place that computer-aided instruction had in the Cologne Computer Conference but also a heightened general perception of CAI's centrality to historical computing.

NOTES

1. Most of the points made in the paper will apply also to the social sciences.
2. Depending on response times and the "friendliness" of available software, mainframes may also be appropriate.
3. DISH is also developing data entry/editing (DISHData), data analysis (DISHInfo), record linkage (DISHLink), and bibliographical (Strela) software for use beyond as well as within Glasgow (see Candlin and Morgan, 1988).
4. The same approach has characterised: staff training courses; summer schools for academics, school teachers, archivists and librarians; and the planning of the new M. Phil. in History and Computing.
5. The Scottish university curriculum is significantly less specialised than its English counterpart. Students study a range of subjects for two years; they may then specialise in one or two disciplines during their final two years.
6. However, most university-level computer-based history teaching there is mainly in "methods" course, while the use of the computer to help to teach (as in DISH) the general issues of history seems largely restricted to the school sector.

REFERENCES

BEHAGG, C. 1986. "Myths of cohesion: capital and compromise in the historiography of nineteenth-century Birmingham." *Social History* 11, 375-384

BRIGGS, A. 1952. "The Background of the Parliamentary Reform Movement in Three English Cities." *Historical Journal* 10, 293-317

BURTON, V. et al. 1987. "Historical Research Techniques: Teaching with Database Exercises on the Microcomputer." *Social Science History* 11, 433-448

CANDLIN, F. and MORGAN, N.J. 1988. "Messy Data, Clean Software, Beautiful Results." *Cologne Computer Conference 1988*

CROSSICK, G. 1978. *An Artisan Elite in Victorian Society: Kentish London 1840-1880*. London

DENLEY, P. and HOPKIN, D. (eds.). 1987. *History and Computing*. Manchester

FOSTER, J. 1974. *Class Struggle and the Industrial Revolution: Early Industrial Capitalism in Three English Towns*. London

GRAY, R.Q. 1976. *The Labour Aristocracy in Victorian Edinburgh*. Oxford

GUTMANN, M.P. and FLIESS, K.H. 1986. "Reconstructing a Historical Community." *Proceedings of the 1986 Academic Information Systems University AEP Conference*. IBM Academic Information Systems

MEC LEOD, H. 1974. *Class and Religion in the Late Victorian City*. London

MILLER, D.W. and MODELL, J. 1988. "Teaching United States History with the Great American History Machine." *Historical Methods* 21, 121-134

MORGAN, N.J. 1987. "Sources and Resources: the DISH Project at Glasgow", in: Denley, P. and Hopkin, D. (eds.). *History and Computing*. Manchester, 302-308

ROHRS, R.C. 1987. "Sources and Strategies for Computer-Aided Instruction." *Historical Methods* 20, 79-83

THOLFSEN, T.R. 1953-4. "The Artisan and the Culture of Early Victorian Birmingham." *University of Birmingham Historical Journal* 4, 146-166

TRAINOR, R.H. 1987a. "The Role of the Computer in University Teaching: Potential and Problems", in: Rahtz, S. (ed.). *Information Technology in the Humanities: Tools, Techniques and Applications*. Chichester and New York, 31-40

TRAINOR, R.H. 1987b. "An Experiment in Computer-Based Teaching and Research: the DISH Project at Glasgow", in: Denley, P. and Hopkin, D. *History and Computing*. Manchester, 297-302

TRAINOR, R.H. 1987c. "History and Computers: Two Years of Glasgow's DISH Project." *Humanities Communication Newsletter* 9, 39-40

TRAINOR, R.H. 1988. "Implementing Computer-based Teaching and Research: the Need for a Collaborative Approach." *Computers and Education* 12, 37-41

TRAINOR, R.H. 1989. "History, Computing and Higher Education", in: Denley, P.; Fogelvik, S. and Harvey, C. (eds.). *History and Computing 2*. Manchester, 35-42

THE DEMANDS OF THE HISTORICAL DISCIPLINES ON MACHINE READABLE SOURCES - AND THE CONSEQUENCES FOR THEIR STANDARDIZATION

Reinhard Härtel
Forschungsinsitut für Historische Grundwissenschaften
Karl-Franzens-Universität, Graz
Austria

The progress made in standardizing and in the exchange of continuous texts has been rather slow up to now, and it has been rather slow although standardizing of source-oriented input or even a mere text-input seems much easier than standardizing of problem-oriented input. This paper only deals with the treatment of full-text.

First of all, a short analysis of the various requirements, which the historical disciplines can have with respect to historical texts, is presented. So, after seeing the different requirements we have to look for a solution which guarantees at least a certain level of usability of exchanged full-texts by the colleagues of other disciplines. The result will be that a noticeable progress in exchangeability and usability is better gained by standardization of documentation, and not so much by standardization of the texts themselves. In the end, it will be pointed out that there is a glimmer of hope in a way that the standardization of documentation could encourage standardization of text-input itself.

In order to avoid misunderstandings it should be stressed: we discuss fundamental problems of standardizing which lie before the use of the computer and, therefore, beyond all technical details. But of course, all these problems are connected with the computer, and so we always have the computer in view.

Now, first of all as to the analysis of the requirements which the historical disciplines can have. It cannot be avoided to repeat some well-known facts in the beginning.

The demands on a text can only concern four criteria, and it is evident that besides these four criteria there is nothing else to study in a text: firstly its material contents, secondly its structure (both, logical and textual), thirdly the graphic realisation (both, the visual arrangement and the singular graphemes, and here we are especially interested in handwritings) and finally the phonemes behind the graphemes. That given, the specific purposes of the individual researchers are irrelevant. Editors, historians (in the widest sense of the word) and lexicographers cannot study other things in a given text than its contents etc., as has been mentioned above. Because of that it is not necessary to present a long list of individual disciplines; as such, a list will constantly change and will, therefore, be incomplete soon.

As to the content, it is obvious that a well-done summary in whatever language can suffice as a basis for whatever research. But the machine-readable summary offers one of the most difficult problems for standardization, and it is also obvious that this is not part of our topic.

As to the structure, we have to distinguish between logical structure on the one hand and textual structure an the other hand. As to the logical structure, a list of incomes, e.g., can be set up according to people or possessors. As to the textual structure, a chronicle can be written in prose or in verse. Here also belong the grammatical structures. For the purpose of structural research orthographically normalized transcriptions are enough. Such transcriptions can also contain unmarked resolutions of abbreviations and even emendations. This is the well-known model of the historical-diplomatic edition which will also be sufficient for a wide range of historical-diplomatic studies and for history of literature, but only partly for linguistic interests. As far as such historical studies are concerned, which have been mentioned, there will not be any loss of information.

As to the phonemes, linguists are interested in being able to distinguish all phonemes as far as possible and, therefore, they do not agree with any orthographic normalization or other treatment of the text. The results of these principles are the well-known philological editions. For linguistic purposes, there will be no loss of information in such editions.

Regarding the graphemes, the paleographers are almost the only ones who are also interested in distinguishing even between graphemes which obviously do not signify different phonemes, e.g. whether the dots on the *i*-s are there or not, or whether the Latin word *et* is fully spelt by the letters *e* and *t*, or indicated with commercial &, or represented by the Tironian sign which is similar to the figure *7*. Paleographers are also interested in different kinds of characters in a given text, etc. The paleographical transcription which partly meets such demands is obviously the most rigid form of copying a given text. Only a few editions of inscriptions, however, will meet such demands. But we must admit that normally in a paleographical transcription there is not even a possibility to distinguish between medieval and contemporary writers immediately. Even the most precise paleographic transcription means an enormous loss of information with respect to paleographical criteria. We can only hope that in the future a computer-aided classification of scanned graphemes will be able to reduce this loss of information.

Obviously, the philological and paleographical transcriptions can also satisfy the demands of historians in the narrow sense of the word, but a linguist normally needs a philological edition at least, and finally the paleographer has a chance of finding helpful information only in a paleographical transcription.

Now we want to find out which level is recommendable as a standard-level for the exchangeable texts.

As we have seen, the level which could meet all of the demands is the paleographical transcription. But in this respect we are far away from any standard, and perhaps such a standard will never exist: The material is excessively diverging, the terminology far from uniformity, and while the possibilities for computer-aided examination of handwritings will increase and will continuously create new possibilities they will also create new problems. On the other hand, most of the historians (in the narrow sense of the word) and most philologists will not want to do an enormous amount of additional work for a few paleographers. In any way, a common standard of text-input has to be more general, and the paleographers have to find out their own more specialized standards, e.g. for Roman epigraphs, for the inscriptions on medieval coins and seals and so on.

As to the linguists, literal transcription has already been proposed as a standard several times, which means more or less the level of the philological edition. But we run the risk that even such a solution would not work in a satisfactory way. Only recently, great enterprises have been started which follow the historical-diplomatic tradition of normalized edition, and these efforts have been promoted by scientists who are very familiar with the discussion about standardization and also with the suggestions for literal transcription as a desirable standard. Generally, historians do no work for philologists. They would have to transcribe the model firstly according to philological rules and after that to correct the text gained according to their own rules. There are also all the indispensable editions which already exist and which we can make machine-readable only afterwards. They will remain, of course, in their normalized forms, and it will often happen that a substitution for these old editions will not be possible. For that reason, we have to realize that we might declare the literal transcription to be a standard as often as we like, but that our declarations would be useless.

But not even the third level that is the normalized historical edition, is suitable for a standard either. The rules for normalization and treatment of texts not only vary from language to language and from period to period, but also from country to country and even more from edition to edition. It is certainly hopeless to decree a certain rule as a standard, after we have realized that the different results of the different rules of normalization cannot (or can only partly) be converted among themselves.

What is to be done? Neither the paleographical nor any form of the historical-diplomatic transcription can serve as a standard for the whole scientific community. Therefore, we have to define the literal transcription as a desirable standard, but we also have to realize that beyond this standard, the paleographers have to find their own more precisely defined standards, and we have to realize as well that the greatest part of the historians (in a wide sense of the word) do not come up to this standard.

Under those conditions, "standardization" can no longer mean unifying the transcription-rules, but to ensure the comparability of the various transcriptions we have to cope with. This can be done by standardization of documentation.

As to the documentation of machine-readable texts, it is obvious that besides all technical details such a documentation has first of all to meet the same demands as the introduction of a conventional edition as follows: indications concerning the source itself, indications concerning the tradition of the source, bibliography and indications concerning the edition itself, firstly the name of the editor respectively of the reviser. Most of this information in the documentation can hardly be formalized, but a considerable part of it can and should be formalized.

For the treatment of texts before input, the documentation should not only inform the user on the usability of singular details in the machine-readable text, but this part of the documentation should work in a similar way as an algorithm or a lemmatization system. It is most probable that such a standardized documentation is much easier to be put in effect than a standardized text-input itself, especially because there have not yet been established clearly defined rules for the text-treatment itself. We shall have to apply in the field of normalization analogous to the one procedure Mr. Thaller has already roughly developed for the translations of coding-systems and of input-formats. We, however, want to achieve a different effect. The documentation we mentioned should be able to put two things in effect.

A linguist working with different data-bases and trying to investigate orthographic peculiarities must have a simple way to guarantee that normalized forms are ignored (or that they are processed only in clearly defined exceptions). At the same time, the system should provide him with detailed lists, however, showing which texts in a large base of such have actually been processed and which have been excluded for beeing noemalized. In this way the researcher, the linguist e.g., would be able to realize and to evaluate

evaluate right away the wide or narrow basis of his results. These opportunities will be of advantage especially if the given problem requests a checking of a great number of shorter documents which have been transcribed by different researchers or editors. Besides the possibility of generic rules, such a documentation of text-treatment will consist of a sort of list.

Some problems will remain, of course. The system has to learn to distinguish between proper names and other words, between words and Roman figures, and so on. The system also has to learn to find out, if a point in the text is a full stop or an abbreviation symbol, etc. But apart from these problems, such a system could easily be able to disregard e.g. all letters *w* in corresponding normalized documents, even if a researcher wants to study the use of *uu*, *uv*, *vu*, *vv* and *w* in a certain number of data-bases.

It must be admitted that these suggestions make the impression of causing much additional work for researchers and editors. But we can considerably facilitate this workload. We only need such a list for every language or period. These primary lists should contain every orthographic normalization which makes sense. On this basis we could easily create more special lists containing the rules of the large series of editions. We only have to leave out some rules not applied. Normally, in a specific field of research, individual editors or researchers do not create new rules of transcription, but they simply adapt some existing rules. Therefore, some easy adaptations will be enough for obtaining every particular list required.

As to the old editions which only have been made machine-readable afterwards, it can be recommended to use the most complete primary list as long as the principles of the editions have not been examined. In this way, the researcher is best protected from being presented some data as presumed originals whereas these very data might be normalized.

And now we can summarize: an effort in standardization of documentation can - at least partly - close the gap which is unfortunately given in the standardization of text-input itself. We have the chance, firstly, to use all texts as far as possible corresponding to the different demands, and we can manage without doing too much embarrassing additional work. Secondly, we also have the chance to get a list containing the documents used and the documents ignored for the retrieval-work, and this is done without any additional efforts.

But there is also a third prospect, and that is the reason why we have spoken at the beginning about a glimmer of hope that the standardization of documentation could also encourage standardization of text-input itself. The machine-readable documentation could not only serve as documentation, but also as a command-file, and so a literal transcription could be converted into any form of normalized text according to pre-defined rules. The historians who, of course, do not like to transcribe a text twice only for the benefit of linguists, would only have to work out a literal transcription, and the computer would do the normalizing work.

So, the historians would not have to do any extra-work, the linguists could access more machine-readable texts useful to them, and the sacrosanct rules of the various editions (especially historical editions) do not have to be changed. It can be hoped that such a solution will encourage many historians to accept the literal transcription as a standard for text-input. So, in the end we have to ask ourselves: who shall do this work, that is who shall develop this "converting-system"?

It is not because I am a historian that I answer: let the philologists and especially the linguists do this work. I suggest this, because the linguists should be those who are most-interested in it. In any way, I am convinced that a standardisation will not function unless the extra-work has to be done by those researchers who benefit from the efforts. Moreover, it is the linguists who command the necessary knowledge in the first place. Certainly, they will be assisted by interested historians, and I will also join them.

NOTES

Concerning the unsatisfactory progress in standardizing, see the corresponding contributions in HAUSMANN, F. et al. 1987. *Datennetze für die Historischen Wissenschaften/Data Networks for the Historical Disciplines?* Graz, and soon the proceedings of the "Table Ronde: Standardisation et échanges des bases de données historiques", organized by J.-Ph. Genet in Paris 1987, further the corresponding contributions to the Cologne Computer Conference.

Frequently, the discussion on standardization is confined to study description. But also in the case of source-input description technical problems are predominant (coding systems etc.). The full-text treatment *before* the input is far too often neglected. That is also true of the wide-scale "Text Encoding Initiative" as it was presented by N.M. IDE and C.M. SPERBERG-MCQUEEN at the Cologne Computer Conference. Comments on the question of standardized text-treatment *before* the input were rare and rather short: see THALLER, M. 1986. "Vorüberlegungen für einen internationalen Workshop über die Schaffung, Verbindung and Nutzung großer interdisziplinärer Quellenbanken in den historischen Wissenschaften", in: Thaller, M. *Datenbanken und Datenverwaltungssysteme als Werkzeuge historischer Forschung.* (Historisch-sozialwissenschaftliche Forschungen 20), St. Katharinen, 16-17; and especially FOSSIER, L. and PARISSE, M. 1987. "Aufnahme und Verarbeitung mittelalterlicher diplomatischer Texte", p. 81; PARISSE, M. 1987. "Standardisierung and Austausch fortlaufender Texte", p. 195; ZINKO, Ch. 1987. "Aufbereitung hethitischer Keilschrifttexte für eine computerunterstützte Verarbeitung", p. 255 (all in Hausmann et al. 1987). In all cases, the respective authors supported strict authenticity of text - under certain circumstances at least - and this also with special regard to the requirements of other disciplines. The author of this contribution is also prepared to drop input of already treated data, under the condition that an appropriate software spares extra work (see my former ideas in: HÄRTEL, R. and KROPAC, I.H. 1987. "Edition and Auswertung mittelalterlicher Urkunden: Probleme bei Standardisierung und Transfer fortlaufender Texte, p. 106 (in Hausmann et al. 1987).

The reference to Mr. Thaller's "translation program" refers to the paper "A Draft Proposal for a Standard Format Exchange Program". This paper was presented in 1987 in Paris and will also be published in the proceedings of the "Table Ronde".

TOWARDS A STANDARD FOR THE DESCRIPTION OF HISTORICAL DATASETS

Ninette van Hall
Netherlands Historical Data Archive
The Netherlands

1. Introduction

Several countries are planning a data-archive facility for historical datasets. In the archives the data will be extensively documented. A standardized way of describing the machine readable datasets will facilitate the exchange of information. The Standard Study Description Scheme used at the long existing social science data-archives is - in unaltered form - not applicable to historical datasets.

There are many similarities between social scientific datasets and historical datasets. It is useful for historians to use a documentation standard that can be exchanged with the standards in use at social science data-archives. At the same time, the specific demands of the historical datasets should be taken into consideration.

2. Study Description Scheme

2.1 Architecture and contents of the Study Description Scheme

A study description is a detailed account in machine readable form of information on a machine readable dataset. It contains information of different kinds:

* bibliographical:
  the title of the dataset, information on people or institutions that are responsible for the creation of the dataset (primary investigator, the depositor,the funding agency).
* administrative:
  its accessibility, the publications based on the dataset, other datasets and publications that bear a relation to the dataset described
* concerning the contents:
  what the data deal with, what the research topic is, it tells you where the data stem from, it tells you about the relation between the real world and the universe depicted by the dataset
* technical:

how the dataset is organized, the size of it, what can be done with it in terms of the software that can be used in analyzing the data.

2.2 Functions of the Study Description

With the Study Description an instrument is created to get information on machine readable datasets. It is meant to be used by two kinds of people. On one hand the historian, who wants to analyze an existing dataset and on the other hand the archivist who wants to have knowledge about his holdings both, for internal -administrative - uses as well as for optimising his service to the clientele. The way these people can make use of the Study Description is partly overlapping.

To understand its functions the Study Description can be looked upon from several points of view.

On the first ("lowest") level, the description of one dataset, the Study Description, is a necessary prerequisite for doing secondary analysis. It is no use having a tape or a floppy and not knowing what it deals with: what kind of data, what period, what geographical area, what source material is used in creating the dataset, what publications have been based on the dataset. On ground of this information the analyst may decide how to use the dataset concerned, or not to use it at all. The availability of the description in machine readable form will facilitate the retrieval of information.

The usefulness of keeping track of what is in the archive in such a way as described before is even more clear if you step one level higher, the description of all the holdings in the collection of the archive. The potential secondary analyst and the archivist who wants to lend assistance to the researcher can both profit from a well described collection of holdings that gives the opportunity to get a clear view on the whole of the collection.

Besides these, concerning ad hoc uses of the Study Description database, one can also think of a more systematical use. With the Study Description as a basis one can compile a catalogue of the holdings of the archive. In several data-archives data catalogues are more or less automatically produced using data from the Study Description database as input for phototype setting programs.

To take one step further, one level higher, one reaches the what can be called 'intra archival' level. This means dealing with more than one data archive. What is true on the level of one archive becomes even more true on this level: the effectiveness of properly describing datasets multiplies if you - in this way - not only give information on a dataset to the potential users of your own data archive, but to the entire universe of all researchers of all data-archives in the whole world. And, vice versa, if your usergroup can have access to descriptions of datasets stored at other data archives. It is clear that the optimum in exchanging this kind of information will only be reached if the archives will use the same kind of description. The exchange of datasets is only a small step further.

Information on datasets should not only be exchanged among historical data-archives, but also between historical data-archives and social science data archives. One reason for this is the fact that many datasets, interesting to historians, are being stored at social science data-archives; real "historical" datasets as well as "old" social science datasets.

Another reason to consider linking up with the existing data archives, so far as study description is concerned, is the fact that in the past 25 years in those institutions, a lot of experience has been built up in archiving datasets and, hence, in describing the datasets. So it can be taken for granted, supposedly that they have a fair idea on how the description of a dataset should look like, both, from an archiving point of view - what is the best way of describing in order to facilitate intra-archival use, to compile a data catalogue, to advise researchers as well as from a user's point of view - what does a secondary analyst need to know about a dataset.

3. Study Description in the Past

In the social science data archives, cooperation in the field of designing a standardized way of describing datasets has resulted in a widely used Study Description Scheme. It has been a starting point for discussions on the description of historical datafiles. Some of the "traditional" data archives have adapted their Study Description and made room for typical historical items.

In the last couple of years, lots of discussions and publications by European historians regarding the description of historical datasets have taken place. One major event should be included here: The establishment of the 'Centre for Historical Social Research (ZHSF)' in Cologne with roots in the late seventies. Though not in first instance a proper historical data archive, it united data archival roots and thinking with historical training. Both, here in Cologne and elsewhere, where social scientific and historical universes met in the world of computerized research, people started thinking about historical datasets and what should and could be done with it. One of the things that can be done is making them available for secondary use. In order to be able to do something with someone elses datasets, it should be documented properly. Realizing this discussions started on the materialization of this idea.

One major development which is worth focusing upon was started in july 1986 in Göttingen during the International Workshop on the Creation, Linkage an Usage of Large-Scale Interdisciplinary Source Banks in the Historical Disciplines. Here, a working group was formed by Hans Jørgen Marker (Danish Data Archive), Herbert Reinke (ZHSF) and Kevin Schurer (Cambridge Group for the History of Population). Their aim was to draw up standards for describing historical datasets, especially dealing with quantitative data. These three have since then extensively published on the state of the art, on their findings, on what a secondary analyst should know about a dataset before he can start using it. But beside applause for the good job they have done, criticism needs to be added. This is caused mainly by different points of view.

The triumvirate has taken as a starting point that the principal investigator himself makes his data available to other users for secondary analysis. The advantage for the principal investigator is of course that he can control who touches his data. Advantageous for the secondary analyst is the fact that he gets the best possible information on the dataset. The disadvantages, however, are far greater.

* The secondary analyst should have the disposal of the same kind of hardware and very often even of the software, the principal investigator has used.
* If the principal investigator does not take care of maintaining his datasets, the chance exists that within a few years the data can no longer be used. Either because of new releases of the software that should be used, or because the old fashioned floppy no longer fits in the drive, or even because the dataset is simply lost. most of you will be able to sum up at least half a dozen of other reasons.
* One of the biggest disadvantages is that if datasets remain with the one who originally created the dataset, it is hard to get an up-to-date overview of the datasets that are available for secondary use.

When data are stored in a data archive, value may be added to it by upgrading, cleaning, or merging with similar datasets.

All this speaks in favour of archiving datasets centrally and, as a consequence, describing them at the archive according to archival standards. Even if datasets are stored this way the secondary analyst can still get in contact with the principal investigator if the latter wishes so. In the study description, the name of either the principal investigator or the person who should be contacted will be registered. So, if the secondary analyst wants to get in contact, the possibilities are still there.

Putting data at an archive does not necessarily mean that the principal investigator will lose control. If he wishes so he can stipulate that his dataset can only be used after explicit written permission, so he can still decide who may have access to his data.

If a dataset is stored in a data archive, where more datasets are kept and archived, it has its consequences for the way the dataset should be described. If you are not thinking of one dataset, but of a whole bunch of them, it makes sense to draw a distinction between precise and detailed information on the micro level, which could be called data documentation, and more general information that can be put together in machine readable form. If you keep a lot of datasets, and all of them bring about a small drawer full of documentation, it is hard to get a general view of your holdings let alone, then let other people get insight into it.

Now it becomes more and more clear that it is not useful to distribute all the minutely detailed information on a dataset.
It is indispensable for doing secondary analysis, performing the act of analyzing. Then you should precisely know what is what, but if you just want general information, to help you decide whether or not you want to use a specific dataset, then less specific information will suffice.

It is far more sensible to have less information, but still that information that one needs to get an idea about the contents of a dataset, and to have that stored in a way that it can easily be retrieved. Once the secondary analyst has made his choice, he can get the whole of the data documentation, maybe complete with oral explanations by the principal investigator, of the dataset of his preference.

To which extend one can call information essential for general use, and when the line is crossed that makes something a detail that is only of use for those analyzing, is not always easy to say. That the one should be limited and the other can hardly be extensive enough is clear.

In most of the articles on the description of historical datasets, so far no distinction is made between the description of a study as a whole and the documentation on the data level.

Another critical note also stems from a different opinion on where datasets should be stored. So far, no manual has been produced showing how datasets should be described, something like a simple straightforward checklist. In this paper an attempt is made at conceptualizing such a standardized manual.

4. Social Science Versus History in Terms of Dataset Description

The "traditional" Study Description is not applicable to historical usage. Historical data are another kind of data than social scientific data and historians are another kind of people than social scientists, their research questions differ, they stem from another tradition. In brief: their datasets require different descriptions, both seen from the side of the secondary analyst as well as from the side of the archivist.

The "traditional" social science data file is a rectangular file that can be analyzed using software packages like SPSS and SAS. Historical datasets are for the larger part of a relational kind. Hierarchical and network files are included as well. That is why more attention should be paid to this kind of file structure, than currently is being done in the "traditional" Study Description.

Beside these technical differences, there are more differences due to differences in the contents of the datasets. Generalizing, there is only one main difference: the object of research, the source of the data. Historians very often take written sources as a starting point whereas social scientists use survey material. This has its consequences for the description of the studies.

In Study Description for historical datasets more attention should be paid to the sources upon which the dataset is based; the ideas behind the original recording of the source, what was the purpose of the source when it was created. And, very important, what has happened to the source since it has first been recorded. Has any large scale re-arrangement taken place, or have parts of it been lost? What are the results of this in terms of the value of the source?

Something else that also needs attention is, in what way the source is reflected in the dataset. Is the whole, integral, complete, source transformed in machine readable form? How have indistinctnesses been treated. For instance, if a part of the source can no longer be deciphered, what has been done to the missing information. What happens, if the person who composed the source has made a mistake? The actions the primary investigator has taken, the way he has solved this problem in his dataset should be documented. A comparable problem can be found in textfiles in case of misspellings.

If the source is not completely transformed into machine readable format, which parts have been left out and why have they been left out and what are the consequences et cetera? Has some sort of coding taken place or normalization? All these things have to be accounted because everything needs proper documentation.

Beside these actions, taken by the principal investigator in order to create a dataset out of traditional sources, it may occur that the data archivist does some additional cleaning of the dataset. All the changes this results in should also be documented. This, however, is not something new to datasets. The same procedure is also known for social scientific datasets. Although, in the latter more routine, more standard techniques can be applied. A simple check on coding will very often not be fit for use.

5. Summary

The social science data archives have a long history of describing machine readable datasets in a more or less standardized way. As it is very useful for historical data archives to be able to exchange datasets and information on available datasets with these institutes, it is very important to describe historical datasets in a compatible way. It is, however, impossible to copy their Study Descriptions completely because a lot of differences exist between the two kinds.

The differences can be summarized as on the one hand regarding the technical format, the format of the data and the structure of the dataset as a whole and on the other hand regarding the contents of the dataset. Concerning the differences in the contents, the main differences stem from the information historians need on the sources the dataset has been based upon and how these sources have been transformed into machine readable form. And then, of course, from the information what adaptations are made by the archivist.

Although historians are not the same as social scientists and historical datasets differ from social scientific datasets and hence the descriptions of both require different focusing points, a lot of similarities can be seen as well, especially as far as bibliographical and administrative information is concerned.

There is no need for changing the way this information is described in the social scientific Study Description. No doubt, the traditional data archives have enough experience in what needs to be described concerning these topics.

NOTE

A proposed standard for the description of historical datasets - based on the Social Science Study Description Scheme - can be obtained from:

Netherlands Historical Data Archive
PO Box 9515
2300 RA Leiden
The Netherlands

STUDY DESCRIPTION ADJUSTMENTS FOR HISTORICAL RESEARCH

Hans Jørgen Marker
Odense Universitet, Odense
Denmark

In the following I am going to tell you about some of the work which has been undertaken in historical circles with the purpose of making a Study Description (SD)-like instrument for machine readable material produced within historical research.

My own work in this direction is so closely connected with that of Herbert Reinke and Kevin Schurer that it is, in many instances, impossible to distinguish exactly what is generated by whom.

Dating back to the 1970s Herbert Reinke has published quite a lot on problems related to historical archiving.(1) In 1981, Herbert Reinke made nine proposals for enhancements to the Standard Study Description, SSD(2) in order to make it applicable to historical machine readable data.(3)

As I understand it, Herbert Reinke's proposals were actually put forward at the joint IASSIST/IFDO conference in Grenoble in 1981. They were not included in the SSD, though. As the SSD had already been used for several years, one of the reasons may have been that the alterations proposed would lead to redocumentation of a large number of studies.

The Göttingen 1985 Conference

In July 1985 an "International Workshop on the Creation, Linkage and Usage of Large-Scale Interdisciplinary Sourcebanks in the Historical Disciplines" was held in Göttingen at the Max Planck Institut für Geschichte.

Major topics were the exchange of data and the difficulties which have to be overcome in order to accomplish this. A historical data material may be several things. It may be a text made machine readable, but with the original textual structure. It may be a data file formatted to be accessed by specific data base software. It may be a rectangular data file to be used by an SPSS-like statistical software package. It may be a vector representation of a picture. And it may be several other things. This list also presents one of the traditional problems of the science of history. The reality of the past is as complex as reality itself, which means that in order to describe the reality of the past you need all the tools invented for describing reality as such.

One of the outcomes of the discussion in Göttingen was that a working group was formed consisting of Herbert Reinke, Kevin Schurer and myself.

All three members of the working group have a "quantitative history" background. For that reason we immediately decided that we would not claim to present a proposal that would describe all kinds of historical data materials. On the other hand, the scope of our proposal was not limited to describing the traditional rectangular data file type of quantitative data material.

On the basis of the proposal presented, the working group was given a mandate by the Göttingen workshop for proposing standards for the description of machine readable historical data sets.

Current Status of the Proposal for Describing Historical Data

We are currently working on a new edition of the proposal. This version will be presented in an article giving details on how the proposed items should be included in the SSD. Further, the article will give recommendations as to how the standard should be enforced. The version of the proposal that will appear in the forthcoming article will probably be like the following:

Questionnaire to be filled in by the researcher:

A. Description of the source material.
(Section A is supposed to be filled in for each of the sources involved. Some of the information asked for in section A is research questions in itself, but as the primary researcher has worked with the sources he will certainly have a better basis for forming an opinion on the answers to the questions asked. It is thus desirable that the primary researcher states his opinion, even when certain answers are not obtainable.)

A.1 The normative administration of records.
(Information on the regulation under which the source was supposed to have been produced.)
A.1.1 Purpose of the source:
Why was the source established?
A.1.2 Scope of the source:
To whom was the source applicable?
A.1.3 Content of the source:
What was to be recorded?
A.1.4 Time dimension:
When was the information in the source to be recorded?

A.2 The actual administration of records.
(The source may not have been produced in accordance with the regulation governing its creation. Any known differences should be given here.)
A.2.1 Ways of recording:
How did the person(s) producing the source actually do it?
A.2.2 Ways of record keeping:
How was the source material treated at the time when it was originally produced?

A.3 Archival procedures/history.
(Has anything happened to the source material in the time between its creation and its adaptation for this study?)

A.3.1 Rearrangements/transformations:
If the source has been subjected to rearrangements of the archive which it was part of: How did it affect the source?

A.3.2 Intentional partial destruction:
If parts of the source have been scrapped by the archival institution: How do the remaining parts relate to the original entity?

A.3.3 Unintentional partial destruction:
If parts of the source have been destroyed by accidents like for instance fire or flooding:

A.3.3.1 Describe the accident.

A.3.3.2 Which effects did it have on the sources?

A.4 Accessibility of the sources.
(Essential archival and publication reference)

A.4.1 Archival reference:

A.4.1.1 Where is the original of the source found?

A.4.1.2 Under which actual reference?

A.4.1.3 If the source is available in copy: How?

A.4.1.4 If the source has been published: Give the bibliographical reference of the publication.

A.4.2 Bibliographical reference:
Please give a bibliographical reference of the major scientific works concerned with this source.

B. Transformation of the source into machine readable form.

B.1 Time of the transformation.

B.1.1 When was this study commenced?

B.1.2 When was it completed (is it intended to be completed)?

B.2 Software used.
(Give a list of commercially available software packages or a description of custom-produced software applied in the analysis.)

B.3 Physical properties of the data set.

B.3.1 On which media is the data set stored?
(E.g: Disk, data tape, diskette(s))

B.3.2 In which machine is the dataset stored?

B.3.2.1 If mainframe: Give geographical location or preferably EARN/BitNet address.

B.3.2.2 If micro, etc.: Give type (E.g: IBM PC-compatible)

B.3.3 Under which operating system is the data set stored?

B.3.4 Give size and format of the file(s) in which the dataset is stored.

B.4 Logical properties of the data set.

B.4.1 How are the data stored?
(E.g: Flat file, database, running text)

B.4.2 How many units of observation does the dataset consist of?
(E.g: For a flat file give number of variables and number of observations. For a database, give number of files, and for each file the number of records and entries. For a running text, give the word count or line count.)

B.5 Methods applied.
(If standard procedures have been used, a brief listing is sufficient. In other cases, a more detailed description will be appropriate.)

B.5.1 Sampling.
(If sampling has taken place, give a description of the sampling procedures.)

B.5.2 Coding and standardization.
(A list of codings and standardizations carried out should be given.)

B.5.3 Linkage.
(References should be given to the data materials from which the present data material was created.)

B.5.4 Other.
(Specify)

This version is still under consideration and may come out a little different. Some of the information asked for in the questionnaire is already contained in the SSD. My suggestion to accommodate the rest of it to historical data is to make a new block of items, which will only be filled out when the study is classified as a historical study.

Why Have so Many Beautiful Words not Changed Reality?

It may be worthwhile to consider why one proposal develops into a standard and not another. When dealing with historical data materials archived at a data archive, we have currently three important standards involved. The data material is described in an SD abiding by the SSD, it is documented with a codebook, probably a standard OSIRIS codebook, and in the publication based on the data material, the sources and scientific works involved are referred to according to the rules of the source criticism tradition by traditional scientific standards.

The standards referred to are administered a little differently in day-to-day practice at different places. But still the standards are recognised.

Speaking strictly about study descriptions, evidence from the first CESSDA Expert Seminar(4) seems to show that the data archives uses only a fraction of the items actually included in the SSD. It also shows that the responsibility for obtaining the necessary information is usually taken by the data archive which asks the primary investigator for some of the information and provides the rest of it from other sources.

The standards of traditional source criticism work quite differently. Nobody enforces them. Many publishers are quite happy with publishing a work where the "scientific apparatus"(5) is either not existing or is of dubious quality, and very few publishers would actually test and rectify references given in a scientific work. One of the consequences of this is that annotations in scientific publications are of varying quality and that reviews and scholarly discussions in many instances are concerned with the failure of the scientific apparatus at specific places in a given piece of scientific work.

If the data archives find it useful to provide the information asked for in the Trinity proposal to secondary users of historical datasets, the data archives should concern themselves with convenient storage, retrieval and publication methods for that information and they should let the primary investigators provide the information. The data archives should not, I believe, concern themselves with the quality of the answers given from the primary investigators, nor should the data archives try to provide the information contained in the proposal from other sources. But the willingness of the primary investigator to provide the information asked for could serve as a guiding rule for the assessment of the scientific quality of the historical data material in question.

NOTES

1. Reinke, Herbert. 1977. "Quantum extending its services: Building up a dataorganization for historical social research." *Quantum Information* 4, October
   Reinke, Herbert. 1979. "Archiving Machine Readable Historical Data." *Historical Social Research* 12
2. The Standard Study Description was proposed by Per Nielsen, DDA, in: Per Nielsen (ed): Report on Standardization of Study Descriptions and Classification of Indicators. Copenhagen (DDA), 1974
   Nielsen, Per. 1975. *Study Description Guide and Scheme*. Copenhagen (DDA)
   The latter contained the actual scheme which became the international standard.
3. Reinke, Herbert. 1981. "Towards Standard for the Description of Machine-Readable Historical Data." *Historical Social Research* 18
   Reinke, Herbert. 1986. "Datenbeschreibung und Datendokumentation in der historischen Sozialforschung, Problembeschreibung und Empfelungen für die Forschung", in: Manfred Thaller (ed.): *Datenbanken und Datenverwaltungssysteme als Werkzeuge historischer Forschung*. Historisch-Sozialwissenschaftliche Forschungen Bd. 20, St. Katharinen
4. Lauritzen, Astrid Bogh (ed.). 1987. *Workbook of the First CESSDA Expert Seminar. From Localization to Cataloguing of Data Sets*. Odense (DDA), 115-160
5. Videnskabelige apparat: Notes and references, etc.

THE STANDARD STUDY DESCRIPTION AT THE ESRC DATA ARCHIVE

Bridget Winstanley
ESRC Data Archive, Colchester
United Kingdom

Input Procedures

In common with many other social science data archives, the Data Archive describes its holdings in a version of the controlled format of the Standard Study Description as developed at the Danish Data Archives. The use of a structured form which will later be used for both print formatting and retrieval by computer requires that input shall be disciplined to a degree which is more easily attained by validation and checks at the input stage than by manual checking and editing at a later stage, although some of the latter must, of course, still be done.

Each organization needs its own systems, and we have found that within our structure a micro-based interactive system for data input works well. Once the study descriptions are completed on floppies, they are transferred to the mainframe computing environment where they are available for retrieval and printing.

Validation is of two types: format e.g. correct column positions to suit the print programs, and content, by which I mean prompts to the cataloguer to ensure that sensible decisions are made in the fields which need special control because they are fields used to create indexes or are especially important in retrieval or bibliographic control. This latter function will be dealt with in more detail later.

The system is integrated in that only one master copy of the data exists and the system allows for accessioning, study description to two different levels and updating to one single master copy. These processes are carried out by a number of different people in different sections of the Archive, but the integrity of the data is assured. The floppy is passed physically from one section of the Archive to another, with the documentation which is required to complete the study description. Once transferred to the mainframe, new study descriptions remain in a transitional file on the mainframe until used to update the main database. There will be old studies as well as new in the transitional file. Any change to existing studies involves a suite of programs which copy the individual study to be changed to a file, and when changed, it is added to the transitional file. When updating occurs the new version will overwrite the old one. A "manager" system ensures that the same file is not retrieved twice for alteration.

Outputs

We are making greater and greater demands of the Standard Study Description. It has moved from being a surrogate for the dataset itself - a description of a known study in a convenient format for reference in a catalogue or computer printout, with all the attributes which a researcher or archivist could wish to know about it - to being a finely-tuned administrative and bibliographic instrument.

Administrative outputs are concerned with matters such as the number of studies held, their access and data-processing status, their identification by the identification numbers of other institutions, handling charges, the quantity and price of documentation associated with the studies and the identification of past and present users of particular studies.

Bibliographic descriptions should provide for the unique identification of the work being described and the expression of its relationship to all other works. Catalogues, individual study descriptions and searchable bibliographic databases provide descriptions of studies and are accessible through attributes such as titles and names of persons and bodies responsible for the study, as well as by a variety of subject approaches. Unless these key access points are strictly controlled, however, the relationship of the study to others may be lost.

This point may be illustrated by a fictitious example based on some real experiences: Mr. John Taylor-Jones of Jesus College Cambridge deposits a dataset which he calls "VX110.DAT" on the technical data description form, "Northern Ireland employment data" on the licence form and "Study of employment in Northern Ireland, 1976-1986" on his depositor's study description form. Is his name entered under Taylor or Jones? Is his affiliation entered under Jesus College or the University of Cambridge - or indeed, Cambridge University? Which title is the definitive one? It is important that we should know this, because otherwise we may overlook the fact that he has deposited other data in the archive - even perhaps that he has deposited the same study if variant forms of identification are used. Free-text retrieval software will, of course, find variants with a common component, but this is a somewhat hit and miss method and the Archive's responsibility as a supplier of documentation and records as well as data requires that some standardised procedures should be used.

Bibliographic Control of Datasets

The idea of bibliographic control comes to us, of course, from the library world. "Universal bibliographic control" is a term coined in 1971 by F.G. Kaltwasser and adopted by the International Federation of Library Associations (IFLA) as its official policy. This was expressed by Anderson as follows:

The purpose of the [Universal Bibliographic Control] system is to make universally and promptly available, in a form which is internationally acceptable, basic bibliographic data on all publications issued in all countries.

To those working with, creating, or supplying computer-readable data, software, or texts, the idea of bibliographic control of these works is as vital as the control of traditional printed or manuscript bibliographic works and the ESRC Data Archive is very much alive to its responsibilities in this respect.

Standards for Bibliographic Control

The ESRC Data Archive implements two complementary standard systems for its bibliographic control. These are the Standard Study Description, which is a standard format. Other standard formats for bibliographically descriptive records exist, for example the widely used *MARC* (*MA*chine *R*eadable *C*ataloguing) format, or *CCF* (*C*ommon

Communication Format). The second standard being implemented by the Archive is the descriptive standard formulated by the Anglo-American Cataloguing rules. Here, it is important to distinguish between the two types of standard: one is a communication format to facilitate exchange of records and can be visualised as a vessel or container which carries the substantive content, which is covered by the descriptive standard. This may be the Anglo-American Cataloguing Rules, Chapter Nine, or the International Standard Bibliographic Description (Computer Files). Use of a standard which covers substantive content means that records can be output either in any standard format, including the Standard Study Description Format, with good results. However, the use of a standard format without the use of standard descriptive rules leads to non-standard records: imagine the variations which could occur when two or more people describe the example given above, even though the information is entered in the correct fields, if there are no rules governing content.

There is no necessity to adopt rules current in the library world but doing so opens up the possibility of conversion programs which can transform catalogue records held in Standard Study Description format to MARC format records which can appear in library catalogues, thus, extending the possibility of integrated catalogues in established library environments as well as data archival environments.

Upgrading the Quality of Documentation

Like many other data archives, we are both publishers and distributors of data. We actually create new editions of the data and produce our own documentation to accompany it. This carries with it the responsibility ensuring that this documentation, whether internal or external to the file or files being distributed, carries with it a bibliographic identification which corresponds to our own catalogue listings. The obvious way to do this and maintain the integrity of the information is, to produce the bibliographic components of the documentation - title pages, cataloguing in publication and recommended bibliographic citation - from the study description database. The Standard Study Description has a field for the entry of a bibliographic citation, but we are attempting to generate this bibliographic citation from the individual bibliographic items of the Study Description itself. We have recently been testing the possibility of doing this and will shortly begin issuing documentation with this type of information generated from the Study Description.

REFERENCES

ANDERSON, D. 1974. *Universal Bibliographic Control: A Long Term Policy: A Plan for Action.* München: Verlag Dokumentation, 11

Anglo-American Cataloguing Rules. 1978. 2nd edition. London: Library Association

CCF: The Common Communication Format. 1984. Paris: Unesco

Danish Data Archives. 1981 (and subsequent revisions). *Proposed Standard Study Description (DOC0027).* Odense: DDA

International Federation of Library Associations and Institutions. 1987. *ISBD (CF): International Standard Bibliographic Description for Computer Files*. London: IFLA International Office for UBC

KALTWASSER, F.G. 1971. "Universal Bibliographic Control (UBC)." *Unesco Bulletin for Libraries* 25, 252-259

UK MARC Manual. 1980. 2nd edition. London: British Library

DEVELOPMENT OF A STANDARD FOR ENCODING LITERARY AND LINGUISTIC MATERIALS

Nancy M. Ide
Department of Computer Science, Vassar College N.Y.
C.M. Sperberg-McQueen
Computer Center, University of Illinois at Chicago
USA

Researchers involved in computer-assisted work with literary and linguistic materials have long seen the need for a standard or common encoding scheme for machine-readable texts. In 1987 the Association for Computers and the Humanities spearheaded an effort, funded by the American National Endowment for the Humanities, to develop such a common scheme by assembling 31 representatives of the major machine-readable text archives in North America, Europe and Israel as well as representatives of relevant professional societies and North American humanities computing centers. This group developed a set of principles, agreed upon after two very long days of intense discussion, to define the purpose and approach of commonly accepted guidelines for the encoding and interchange of texts in machine-readable form. This paper presents those principles, discusses the issues and questions that gave rise to them, and describes the development effort as it has progressed to date.

The issues of foremost concern to the participants in the meeting on Text Encoding Practices were:

* Is it reasonable to attempt to develop guidelines for encoding literary and linguistic materials at all? If so, which classes of materials should be covered by the guidelines?
* Should the encoding guidelines be prescriptive, indicating both WHAT to encode and HOW to encode it, or only descriptive, providing an account of what textual features previous projects have encoded and the syntax they used, or something in between?
* Should the encoding guidelines address primarily the problems of encoding new materials, or the problems of converting already encoded texts to conform to the new interchange format, or both?
* Should the guidelines specify a "required" minimum of features to be encoded in machine-readable literary and linguistic materials?
* Should the encoding scheme proposed by the guidelines be made compatible with existing schemes? If so, which ones, and to what extent?

To address these questions the group had to consider a number of additional questions concerning the purpose and audience of the guidelines, the status of existing archives, and the degree to which the SGML International Standard answers the encoding needs under consideration.

The principles agreed upon by the group are appended. The effort to develop the guidelines is now underway, under the direction of the Association for Computers and the Humanities, the Association for Computational Linguistics and the Association for Literary and Linguistic Computing. A large number of other organizations form an advisory committee to the project and have agreed to endorse the standard. Working parties, each concerned with one of the four items under (6) in the appended list of principles, and in the case of (6.b) and (6.c), with particular areas of application as well, are being established to develop specific encoding conventions.

Closing Statement of the Vassar Planning Conference

The Preparation of Text Encoding Guidelines
Poughkeepsie, New York, 13 November 1987

1. The guidelines are intended to provide a standard format for data interchange in humanities research.
2. The guidelines are also intended to suggest principles for the encoding of texts in the same format.
3. The guidelines should
   a) define a recommended syntax for the format,
   b) define a metalanguage for the description of text-encoding schemes,
   c) describe the new format and representative existing schemes both in that metalanguage and in prose.
4. The guidelines should propose sets of coding conventions suited for various applications.
5. The guidelines should include a minimal set of conventions for encoding new texts in the format.
6. The guidelines are to be drafted by committees on
   a) text documentation
   b) text representation
   c) text interpretation and analysis
   d) metalanguage definition and description of existing and proposed schemes,
   coordinated by a steering committee of representatives of the principal sponsoringorganizations.
7. Compatibility with existing standards will be maintained as far as possible.
8. A number of large text archives have agreed in principle to support the guidelines in their function as an interchange format. We encourage funding agencies to support development of tools to facilitate this interchange.
9. Conversion of existing machine-readable texts to the new format involves the translation of their conventions into the syntax of the new format. No requirements will be made for the addition of information not already coded in the texts.

LIST OF CONTRIBUTORS

Hans-Jürgen **Andreß**: Fakultät für Soziologie, University of Bielefeld, FRG
René **Arrus**: Centre de Recherche en Informatique Appliqué aux Sciences Sociales, University of Grenoble II, France
Bruno **Aubusson de Cavarlay**: Centre de Recherches Soziologiques sur le Droit et les Institutions Pénales, France

Janet **Bagg**: Computing Laboratory, University of Kent at Canterbury, UK
R. **Bell**: Centrum voor de Geschiedenis van de Materiele Cultuur, UFSAL, University of Brussel, Belgium
Donald **Bender**: Deutsches Jugendinstitut e.V., Munich, FRG
Heinrich **Best**: Zentrum für Historische Sozialforschung (ZHSF) im Zentralarchiv für Empirische Sozialforschung (ZA), Cologne, FRG
Walter **Bien**: Deutsches Jugendinstitut e.V., München, FRG
Jörg **Blasius**: Zentralarchiv für empirische Sozialforschung (ZA), Cologne, FRG
Caroline **Bourlet**: IRHT, CNRS, Institut de Recherche et d'Histoire des Textes, Paris, France
Andrea **Bozzi**: Istituto Linguistica Computazionale Consiglio Nazionale delle Ricerche, CNR, Italy
Philip **Brady**: Department of Sociology and Anthropology, University College of Swansea, UK
Irene **Bragantini**: Istituto Universitario Orientale, Naples, Italy
Gerhard **Budin**: Infoterm, Vienna, Austria

Antonio **Cammelli**: Istituto per la Documentazione Giuridica, CNR, Florence, Italy
Peter **Cannon-Brookes**: Stipple Database Services Ltd. UK
Giuseppe **Cappelli**: Istituto Linguistica Computazionale, CNR, Pisa, Italy
Eddy **van Cauwenberghe**: Centrum voor de Geschiedenis van de Materiele Cultuur, UFSAL, University of Brussel, Belgium
Hélène **Charnassé**: ERATTO/CNRS, Irvy-sur-Seine, France
Kazimierz **Choros**: Department of Information Systems, Technical University of Wroclaw, Poland
Gerhard **Christiansen**: FORSA GmbH, Dortmund, FRG

Antonio Maria **D'Amico**: Facoltà di Giurisprudenza, University of Rome, Italy
José-Gentil **Da Silva**: Laboratoire d'Histoire quantitative, University of Nice, France
Rosa Maria **Di Giorgi**: Istituto per la Documentazione Giuridica del Consiglio Nazionale delle Ricerche, Florence, Italy

Michael **Eisner**: Gesellschaft für Mathematik und Datenverarbeitung, Darmstadt, FRG
Suitbert **Ertel**: Institut für Psychologie, University of Göttingen, FRG
Otto **Esser**: Institut für Afrikanistik, University of Cologne, FRG
Dieter **Euler**: Lehrstuhl für Wirtschafts- und Sozialpädagogik, University of Cologne, FRG

Arlette **Faugères**: Institut d'Histoire Moderne et Contemporaine, Paris, France

Dieter **Geuenich**: Historisches Seminar, University of Freiburg, FRG
Piergiorgio **Gherardini**: Consiglio Nazionale delle Ricerche, Rome, Italy
Johannes **Gordesch**: Institut für Soziologie, Free University of Berlin, FRG
L. **Graca**: Institut für Nachrichtentechnik, Technical University of Braunschweig, FRG
Lorenz **Gräf**: Insitut für Soziologie, University of Cologne, FRG
B. **Gronquist**: Centre de Recherche en Informatique Appliqué aux Sciences Sociales, University of Grenoble II, France
Agnès **Guillaumont**: IRHT, CNRS, Institut de Recherche et d'Histoire des Textes, Paris, France

Reinhard **Härtel**: Forschungsinstitut für Historische Grundwissenschaften, University of Graz, Austria
Ninette **van Hall**: Department of History, University of Leiden, The Netherlands
Hans-Christoph **Hobohm**: Institut für angewandte Sozialforschung (IFAS), University of Cologne, FRG
Jung-Kook **Hong**: IBM Tokyo Research Laboratory, Japan
Eugene **Horber**: Department of Political Science, University of Geneva, Switzerland

Nancy M. **Ide**: Department of Computer Science, Vassar College, New York, USA

Gerhard **Jaritz**: Institut für mittelalterliche Realienkunde, Krems, Austria

Ulrich **Kampffmeyer**: L.A.S. - Laser Archive Service, Wachenheim, FRG
Arno **Kitts**: Skandia Actuarial Research Fellow, Department of Social Statistics, University of Southampton, UK
Wilma **Knoppert**: TNO Institute of Applied Computer Science, Department of Knowledge Based Systems, Delft, The Netherlands
Ingo H. **Kropac**: Forschungsinstitut für Historische Grundwissenschaften, University of Graz, Austria
Steffen **Kühnel**: Zentralarchiv für empirische Sozialforschung (ZA), Cologne, FRG
Ulrich **Küsters**: Wirtschaftswissenschaft, Fachbereich Statistik, University of Wuppertal, FRG
Andreas **Kunz**: Zentralinstitut für Sozialwissenschaftliche Forschung, Free University of Berlin, FRG

Doron **Lamm**: Birkbeck College, University of London, UK
K.-H. **Laudan**: Institut für Nachrichtentechnik, Technical University of Braunschweig, FRG
Dimitri **Lelis**: Centre de Recherche en Informatique Appliqué aux Sciences Sociales, University of Grenoble II, France
Carola **Lipp**: Ludwig-Uhland-Institut für empirische Kulturwissenschaften, University of Tübingen, FRG

Michelle **Magdelaine**: Institut d'Histoire Moderne et Contemporaine, Paris, France, CNRS, Paris, France
Paola **Mariani**: Istituto per la Documentazione Giuridica del Consiglio Nazionale delle Ricerche, Florence, Italy
Hans Jørgen **Marker**: Danish Data Archives, University of Odense, Denmark
Lawrence J. **McCrank**: FSU-LIS Administration Library and Instructional Services, Ferris State University, Big Rapids, Michigan, USA
Ekkehard **Mochmann**: Zentralarchiv für empirische Sozialforschung (ZA), Cologne, FRG
Peter Ph. **Mohler**: Zentrum für Umfragen, Methoden und Analysen, ZUMA e.V., Mannheim, FRG
Robert John **Morris**: Department of Economic and Social History, University of Edinburgh, UK
Barbara **Morris**: Department of Geography, University of Edinburgh, UK
Norbert **Müller**: AG Systemforschung, University of Osnabrück, FRG

Roberta **Nannucci**: Istituto per la Documentazione Giuridica del Consiglio Nazionale delle Ricerche, Florence, Italy
Heinz **Neber**: Gesamthochschule, Fachbereich 2, University of Essen, FRG
Volker **Neuhaus**: Institut für Deutsche Sprache und Literatur, University of Cologne, FRG

Robert L. **Oakman**: Department of Computer Science, University of South Carolina, Columbia, USA
Marc **Ollivier**: Centre de Recherche en Informatique Appliqué aux Sciences Sociales, University of Grenoble II, France
Wilhelm **Ott**: Zentrum für Datenverarbeitung, Abteilung Literarische und Dokumentarische Datenverarbeitung, University of Tübingen, FRG
Kazumasa **Ozawa**: Department of Management Engineering, Osaka Electro-Communication University, Japan

Luigi **Parenti**: Istituto per la Documentazione Giuridica del Consiglio Nazionale delle Ricerche, Florence, Italy
Franca **Parise Badoni**: Istituto Centrale per il Catalogo e la Documentazione Ministero Beni Culturali, Rome, Italy
Werner J. **Patzelt**: Institut für Politische Wissenschaften, University of Passau, FRG
Ralph **Ponemereo**: Zentralarchiv für empirische Sozialforschung (ZA), Cologne, FRG

Franz **Potyka**: Institut für Afrikanistik, University of Cologne, FRG
Hans **Pruyt**: Faculteit der Sociale Wetenschappen, Erasmus University Rotterdam, The Netherlands

Joseph **Raben**: Humanities Computing Consultant, New York, USA
Manette Estelle **Raben**: Department of English, Queens College, New York, USA
Heike **Rautenhaus**: University of Oldenburg, FRG
Paul **Reilly**: Research Fellow Graphics, Archaeology Graphics Applications, IBM UK Scientific Centre, Winchester, Hampshire, UK
Nick **Ryan**: Computer Laboratory, University of Kent at Canterbury, UK

Desireé **Schipper**: Faculteit der Sociale Wetenschappen, Erasmus University Rotterdam, The Netherlands
Sabine **Schmidt**: Völkerkundliches Institut, University of Tübingen, FRG
Hilmar **Schneider**: Institut für Statistik und Mathematik, SFB 3, University of Frankfurt, FRG
Rainer **Schnell**: Institut für angewandte Sozialforschung (IFAS), University of Cologne, FRG
Kevin **Schurer**: Cambridge Group for the History of Population and Social Structure, University of Cambridge, UK
Thomas **Schweizer**: Völkerkundliches Institut, University of Tübingen, FRG
Marion **Selz-Laurière**: Laboratoire d'Anthropologie Sociale, CNRS, Paris, France
Heinrich **Siegmann**: Forschungsprojekt Stabilitätsorientierte Sicherheitspolitik, Max-Planck-Gesellschaft Starnberg, FRG
Fiorenza **Socci**: Istituto per la Documentazione Giuridica, CNR, Florence, Italy
C. Michael **Sperberg-McQueen**: Computer Center, University of Illinois at Chicago, USA
Richard **Startup**: Department of Sociology and Anthropology, University College of Swansea, UK
Cornelius **Steckner**: Archäologisches Institut, University of Cologne, FRG
Ronald **Stenvert**: Institut for Art History, University of Utrecht, The Netherlands
Bernard **Stepien**: ERATTO/CNRS, Irvy-sur-Seine, France
Winfried **Stier**: University of St. Gallen, Switzerland
Sigeharu **Sugita**: National Museum of Ethnology, Osaka, Japan

Giancarlo **Taddei Elmi** Istituto per la Documentazione Giuridica, CNR, Florence, Italy
Zahir **Tari**: Centre de Recherche en Informatique Appliqué aux Sciences Sociales, University of Grenoble II, France
Marcia Freed **Taylor**: ESRC Data Archive, University of Essex, UK
W.-R. **Teegen**: Seminar für Ur- und Frühgeschichte, University of Göttingen, FRG
Michael **Terwey**: Zentralarchiv für empirische Sozialforschung (ZA), Cologne, FRG
Manfred **Thaller**: Max-Planck-Institut für Geschichte, Göttingen, FRG
Bernd **Thober**: AG Systemforschung, University of Osnabrück, FRG
Daniela **Tiscornia**: Istituto per la Documentazione Giuridica, CNR, Florence, Italy

Richard **Trainor**: DISH-Project and Department of Economic History, University of Glasgow, UK

Cheryl M. **Upchurch**: Department of Computer Science, University of South Carolina, Columbia, USA

Dominique **Vignau**: Laboratoire d'Histoire quantitative, University of Nice, France

Andrew **Walter**: Research Fellow Graphics, Archaeology graphics Applications, IBM UK Scientific Centre, Winchester, Hampshire, UK
Charles **Whitaker**: Southampton, UK
Bridget **Winstanley**: ESRC Data Archive, University of Essex, UK

Piero **Zamperoni**: Institut für Nachrichtentechnik, Technical University of Braunschweig, FRG
E. J. **Zimmermann**: Vertriebsgesellschaft für Statistische Programmsysteme, Bonn, FRG
Cornelia **Züll**: Zentrum für Umfragen, Methoden und Analysen, ZUMA e.V., Mannheim, FRG

INDEX

The page numbers are referring to the first page of the related article